Franz Julius Delitzsch

Biblical Commentary on the Psalms

Second Edition. Vol. 3

Franz Julius Delitzsch

Biblical Commentary on the Psalms
Second Edition. Vol. 3

ISBN/EAN: 9783744779708

Printed in Europe, USA, Canada, Australia, Japan

Cover: Foto ©Lupo / pixelio.de

More available books at **www.hansebooks.com**

CLARK'S

FOREIGN

THEOLOGICAL LIBRARY.

FOURTH SERIES.

VOL. XXXI.

Delitzsch's Commentary on the Psalms.

VOL. III.

EDINBURGH:
T. & T. CLARK, 38, GEORGE STREET.
MDCCCLXXXV.

PRINTED BY MORRISON AND GIBB,

FOR

T. & T. CLARK, EDINBURGH.

LONDON, ... HAMILTON, ADAMS, AND CO.
DUBLIN, ... GEORGE HERBERT.
NEW YORK, ... SCRIBNER AND WELFORD.

BIBLICAL COMMENTARY

ON

THE PSALMS.

BY

FRANZ DELITZSCH, D.D.,
PROFESSOR OF OLD AND NEW TESTAMENT EXEGESIS, LEIPSIC.

Translated from the German
(FROM THE SECOND EDITION, REVISED THROUGHOUT)

BY THE

REV. FRANCIS BOLTON, B.A.,
PRIZEMAN IN HEBREW AND NEW TESTAMENT GREEK IN THE UNIVERSITY OF LONDON.

SECOND EDITION.

VOL. III.

EDINBURGH:
T. & T. CLARK, 38, GEORGE STREET.
MDCCCLXXXV.

TABLE OF CONTENTS.

EXPOSITION OF THE PSALTER.

	PAGE
THIRD BOOK OF THE PSALTER, PS. LXXIII.-LXXXIX.—(*continued*)—Psalm lxxxiv. to lxxxix., ...	1–46
FOURTH BOOK OF THE PSALTER, PS. XC.-CVI., .	47–159
FIFTH BOOK OF THE PSALTER, PS. CVII.-CL., .	160–416
The Fifteen Songs of Degrees, Ps. cxx.-cxxxiv., . . .	264–322

EXCURSUS BY J. G. WETZSTEIN.

I. CONCERNING דרור, THE NAME OF A BIRD (On Ps. lxxxiv. 4), .   417

II. CONCERNING THE SIGNIFICATION OF THE WORD מענה IN ITS APPLICATION TO AGRICULTURE (On Ps. cxxix. 3, cf. on Ps. lxv. 11), ...   418

ERRATA.

Vol. III.

Page 15, line 21 from top, *for* One *read* thing.
,, 28, ,, 17 ,, *for* xviii. 15 *read* xviii. 5.
,, 45, ,. 14 ,, *for* referential *read* postliminiar.
,, 110, ,, 2 ,, *for* xxxiv. 15 *read* xxxvi. 5.
,, 124, ,, 4 ,. *for* cv. 7 *read* cxv. 3.
,, 137, note †, line 4 from bottom, *read* פירקא.
,, 169, line 12 from bottom, *for* εἰ; *read* ἐπί.
,, 191, note, line 3 from bottom, *for* cxxxviii. *read* cxxxiii.

These "Errata" and those noted in Vol. II. are, with trifling exception, the result of corrections and suggestions received from Dr. Delitzsch, which reached the printers too late for correction in type. The Scripture references have been carefully verified during the progress of the work, so that the translator trusts the student will, after attention to the above, find no perplexing inaccuracies in this department.

Vol. I.

Page 14, line 18 from top, *delete* comma before "inscribing."
,, 99, first line of note, *read* which show this ancient הכה.
,, 144, line 17 from top, *for* עֲל *read* עַל.
,, 151, in note *, *read* שמם *instead of* שתם.
,, 297, line 11 from bottom, *read* distress.
,, 347, ,, 12 from top, *read* ends.

THIRD BOOK OF THE PSALTER (CONTINUED).

Ps. LXXIII.–LXXXIX.

PSALM LXXXIV.

LONGING FOR THE HOUSE OF GOD, AND FOR THE HAPPINESS OF DWELLING THERE.

2 HOW lovely are Thy dwelling-places, Jahve of Hosts!
3 My soul longeth, yea fainteth, for the courts of Jahve,
My heart and my flesh sing for joy towards the living God.

4 Yea, the sparrow hath found a house,
And the swallow a nest for herself,
Where she hath sheltered her young—
Thine altars, Jahve of Hosts,
My King and my God.

5 Blessed are they who dwell in Thy house,
They shall still praise Thee. (*Sela.*)

6 Blessed is the man whose strength is in Thee—
The pilgrims' ways are in their heart.
7 Passing through the valley of Baca,
They make it a place of springs,
The rain also enshroudeth it in blessings.

8 They go from strength to strength,
There stand they before Elohim in Zion:

9 "Jahve Elohim of Hosts,
Oh hear my prayer,
Give ear, O God of Jacob!" (*Sela.*)

10 Thou our Shield, look into it, Elohim,
And look upon the face of Thine anointed!
11 For better is a day in Thy courts than a thousand;
I had rather lie upon the threshold in the house of my God,
Than dwell in the tents of wickedness.

12 For a sun and shield is Jahve Elohim.
Grace and glory doth Jahve dispense,
He doth not withhold any good thing from those who walk
in uprightness.

13 Jahve of Hosts,
Blessed is the man who trusteth in Thee.

With Ps. lxxxiii. the circle of the Asaphic songs is closed (twelve Psalms, viz. one in the Second Book and eleven in the Third), and with Ps. lxxxiv. begins the other half of the Korahitic circle of songs, opened by the last of the Korahitic Elohim-Psalms. True, Hengstenberg (transl. vol. iii. Appendix, p. xlv) says that no one would, with my *Symbolæ*, p. 22, regard this Ps. lxxxiv. as an Elohimic Psalm; but the marks of the Elohimic style are obvious. Not only that the poet uses *Elohim* twice, and that in ver. 8, where a non-Elohimic Psalm ought to have said *Jahve;* it also delights in compound names of God, which are so heaped up that *Jahve Tsebaoth* occurs three times, and the specifically Elohimic *Jahve Elohim Tsebaoth* once.

The origin of this Psalm has been treated of already in connection with its counterpart, Ps. xlii.–xliii. It is a thoroughly heartfelt and intelligent expression of the love to the sanctuary of Jahve which yearns towards it out of the distance, and calls all those happy who have the like good fortune to have their home there. The prayer takes the form of an intercession for God's anointed; for the poet is among the followers of David, the banished one.* He does not pray, as it were, out of his

---
* Nic. Nonnen takes a different view in his *Dissertatio de Tzippor et*

soul (Hengstenberg, Tholuck, von Gerlach), but for him; for loving Jahve of Hosts, the heavenly King, he also loves His inviolably chosen one. And wherefore should he not do so, since with him a new era for the neglected sanctuary had dawned, and the delightful services of the Lord had taken a new start, and one so rich in song? With him he shares both joy and grief. With his future he indissolubly unites his own.

To the Precentor upon the Gittith, the inscription runs, *by Benê-Korah, a Psalm*. Concerning עַל־הַגִּתִּית, *vid.* on viii. 1. The structure of the Psalm is artistic. It consists of two halves with a distichic *ashrê*-conclusion. The schema is 3. 5. 2 | 5. 5. 5. 3. 2.

Vers. 2–5. How loved and lovely (יְדִידוֹת) is the sacred dwelling-place (*plur.* as in xliii. 3) of the all-commanding, redemptive God, viz. His dwelling-place here below upon Zion! Thither the poet is drawn by the deeply inward yearning of love, which makes him pale (נִכְסְפָה from כָּסַף, to grow pale, xvii. 12) and consumes him (כָּלָה as in Job xix. 27). His heart and flesh joyfully salute the living God dwelling there, who, as a never-failing spring, quenches the thirst of the soul (xlii. 3); the joy that he feels when he throws himself back in spirit into the long-denied delight takes possession even of his bodily nature, the bitter-sweet pain of longing completely fills him (lxiii. 2). The mention of the "courts" (with the exception of the Davidic Psalm lxv. 5, occurring only in the anonymous Psalms) does not preclude the reference of the Psalm to the tent-temple on Zion. The Tabernacle certainly had only one חָצֵר; the arrangement of the Davidic tent-temple, however, is indeed unknown to us, and, according to reliable traces,* it may be well assumed that it was more gorgeous and more spacious than the old Tabernacle which remained in Gibeon. In ver. 4 the preference must be given to that explanation which makes אֶת־מִזְבְּחוֹתֶיךָ dependent upon מָצְאָה, without being obliged to supply an intermediate thought like בַּיִת (with hardening

---

Deror, etc., 1741. He considers one of the Ephraimites who were brought back to the fellowship of the true worship of God in the reign of Jehoshaphat (2 Chron. xix. 4) to be the subject of the Psalm.

* *Vid.* Kuobel on Exodus, S. 253–257, especially S. 255.

Dagesh like בְּ, Gen. xix. 38, *vid.* the rule at lii. 5) and מִן as a more definite statement of the object which the poet has in view. The altars, therefore, or (what this is meant to say without any need for taking אֵת as a preposition) the realm, province of the altars of Jahve—this is the house, this the nest which sparrow and swallow have found for themselves and their young. The poet thereby only indirectly says, that birds have built themselves nests on the Temple-house, without giving any occasion for the discussion whether this has taken place in reality. By the bird that has found a comfortable snug home on the place of the altars of Jahve in the Temple-court and in the Temple-house, he means himself. צִפּוֹר (from צָפַר) is a general name for whistling, twittering birds, like the finch* and the sparrow, just as the LXX. here renders it. דְּרוֹר is not the turtle-dove (LXX., Targum, and Syriac), but the swallow, which is frequently called even in the Talmud צפור דרור (= סְנוּנִית), and appears to take its name from its straightforward darting, as it were, radiating flight (cf. Arabic *jadurru* of the horse: it darts straight forward). Saadia renders *dûrîje*, which is the name of the sparrow in Palestine and Syria (*vid.* Wetzstein's Excursus I. at the end of this volume). After the poet has said that his whole longing goes forth towards the sanctuary, he adds that it could not possibly be otherwise (גַּם standing at the head of the clause and belonging to the whole sentence, as *e.g.* in Isa. xxx. 33; Ewald, § 352, *b*): he, the sparrow, the swallow, has found a house, a nest, viz. the altars of Jahve of Hosts, his King and his God (xliv. 5, xlv. 7), who gloriously and inaccessibly protects him, and to whom he unites himself with most heartfelt and believing love. The addition "where (אֲשֶׁר as in xcv. 9, Num. xx. 13) she layeth her young," is not without its significance. One is here reminded of the fact, that at the time of the second Temple the sons of the priests were called פִּרְחֵי כְהֻנָּה, and the Levite poet means himself together with his family; God's altars secure to them shelter and sustenance. How happy, blessed, therefore, are those who enjoy this good fortune, which he now longs for again with pain in a strange country, viz. to be able to make his home in the house of such an adorable and gracious God! עוֹד here signifies, not

---

* *Vid.* Tobler, *Denkblätter aus Jerusalem*, 1853, S. 117.

"constantly" (Gen. xlvi. 29), for which תָּמִיד would have been used, but "yet," as in xlii. 6. The relation of ver. 5b to 5a is therefore like xli. 2. The present is dark, but it will come to pass even yet that the inmates of God's house (οἰκεῖοι τοῦ Θεοῦ, Eph. ii. 10) will praise Him as their Helper. The music here strikes in, anticipating this praise.

Vers. 6–13. This second half takes up the "blessed" of the distichic epode (ἐπῳδὸς) of the first, and consequently joins member to member chain-like on to it. Many hindrances must be cleared away if the poet is to get back to Zion, his true home; but his longing carries the surety within itself of its fulfilment: blessed, yea in himself blessed, is the man, who has his strength (עוֹז only here *plene*) in God, so that, consequently, the strength of Him to whom all things are possible is mighty in his weakness. What is said in ver. 6b is less adapted to be the object of the being called blessed than the result of that blessed relationship to God. What follows shows that the "high-roads" are not to be understood according to Isa. xl. 3 sq., or any other passage, as an ethical, notional figure (Venema, Hengstenberg, Hitzig, and others), but according to Isa. xxxiii. 8 (cf. Jer. xxxi. 21), with Aben-Ezra, Vatablus, and the majority of expositors, of the roads leading towards Zion; not, however, as referring to the return from the Exile, but to the going up to a festival: the pilgrim-high-roads with their separate halting-places (stations) were constantly present to the mind of such persons. And though they may be driven never so far away from them, they will nevertheless reach the goal of their longing. The most gloomy present becomes bright to them: passing through even a terrible wilderness, they turn it (יְשִׁיתוּהוּ) into a place of springs, their joyous hope and the infinite beauty of the goal, which is worth any amount of toil and trouble, afford them enlivening comfort, refreshing strengthening in the midst of the arid steppe. עֵמֶק הַבָּכָא does not signify the "Valley of weeping," as Hupfeld at last renders it (LXX. κοιλάδα τοῦ κλαυθμῶνος), although Burckhardt found a وَادِي البَكَا (Valley of weeping) in the neighbourhood of Sinai. In Hebrew "weeping" is בְּכִי, בְּכֶה, בָּכוּת, not בְּכָא. Rénan, in the fourth chapter of his *Vie de Jésus*, understands the expression to mean the last station of those who journey from northern

Palestine on this side of the Jordan towards Jerusalem, viz. *Ain el-Haramije*, in a narrow and gloomy valley where a black stream of water flows out of the rocks in which graves are dug, so that consequently עֵמֶק הַבָּכָא signifies Valley of tears or of trickling waters. But such trickling out of the rock is also called בְּכִי, Job xxviii. 11, and not בָּכָא. This latter is the singular to בְּכָאִים in 2 Sam. v. 24 (cf. נְבָאִים, צְבָאִים, ciii. 21), the name of a tree, and, according to the old Jewish lexicographers, of the mulberry-tree (Talmudic תּוּת, توُت); but according to the designation, of a tree from which some kind of fluid flows, and such a tree is the بَكَا, resembling the balsam-tree, which is very common in the arid valley of Mecca, and therefore might also have given its name to some arid valley of the Holy Land (*vid*. Winer's *Realwörterbuch*, s.v. *Bacha*), and, according to 2 Sam. v. 22-25, to one belonging, as it would appear, to the line of valley which leads from the coasts of the Philistines to Jerusalem. What is spoken of in passages like Isa. xxxv. 7, xli. 18, as being wrought by the omnipotence of God, who brings His people home to Zion, appears here as the result of the power of faith in those who, keeping the same end of their journeyings in view, pass through the unfruitful sterile valley. That other side, however, also does not remain unexpressed. Not only does their faith bring forth water out of the sand and rock of the desert, but God also on His part lovingly anticipates their love, and rewardingly anticipates their faithfulness: a gentle rain, like that which refreshes the sown fields in the autumn, descends from above and enwraps it (viz. the Valley of Baca) in a fulness of blessing (יַעְטֶה, *Hiphil* with two accusatives, of which one is to be supplied: cf. on the figure, lxv. 14). The arid steppe becomes resplendent with a flowery festive garment (Isa. xxxv. 1 sq.), not to outward appearance, but to them spiritually, in a manner none the less true and real. And whereas under ordinary circumstances the strength of the traveller diminishes in proportion as he has traversed more and more of his toilsome road, with them it is the very reverse; they go from strength to strength (cf. on the expression, Jer. ix. 2, xii. 2), *i.e.* they receive strength for strength (cf. on the subject-matter, Isa. xl. 31, John i. 16), and that an ever increasing strength, the nearer they come to the desired goal, which also they cannot fail to reach. The pilgrim-band (this is the subject to יִרְאֶה), going on from strength to (אֶל) strength, at last reaches, attains to (אֶל instead of the אֶל־פְּנֵי used in other instances) Elohim in Zion. Having reached this final goal, the pilgrim-band pours forth its heart in the language of prayer such as we have in ver. 9, and the music here strikes up and blends its sympathetic tones with this converse of the church with its God.

The poet, however, who in spirit accompanies them on their pilgrimage, is now all the more painfully conscious of being at the present time far removed from this goal, and in the next strophe prays for relief. He calls God מָגִנֵּנוּ (as in lix. 12), for without His protection David's cause is lost. May He then behold (רָאָה, used just as absolutely as in 2 Chron. xxiv. 22, cf. Lam. iii. 50), and look upon the face of His anointed, which looks up to Him out of the depth of its reproach. The position of the words shows that מָגִנֵּנוּ is not to be regarded as the object to רְאֵה, according to lxxxix. 19 (cf. xlvii. 10) and in opposition to the accentuation, for why should it not then have been אלהים מגננו ראה? The confirmation (ver. 11) puts the fact that we have before us a Psalm belonging to the time of David's persecution by Absalom beyond all doubt. Manifestly, when his king prevails, the poet will at the same time (cf. David's language, 2 Sam. xv. 25) be restored to the sanctuary. A single day of his lfe in the courts of God is accounted by him as better than a thousand other days (מֵאָלֶף with *Olewejored* and preceded by *Rebia parvum*). He would rather lie down on the threshold (concerning the significance of this הִסְתּוֹפֵף in the mouth of a Korahite, *vid. supra*, vol. ii. p. 53) in the house of his God than dwell within in the tents of ungodliness (not "palaces," as one might have expected, if the house of God had at that time been a palace). For how worthless is the pleasure and concealment to be had there, when compared with the salvation and protection which Jahve Elohim affords to His saints! This is the only instance in which God is directly called a sun (שֶׁמֶשׁ) in the sacred writings (cf. Sir. xlii. 16). He is called a shield as protecting those who flee to Him and rendering them inaccessible to their foes, and a sun as the Being who dwells in an unapproachable light, which, going forth from Him in love towards men, is particularized as חֵן and

נכבו, as the gentle and overpowering light of the grace and glory (χάρις and δόξα) of the Father of Lights. The highest good is self-communicative (*communicativum sui*). The God of salvation does not refuse any good thing to those who walk בְּתָמִים (בְּדֶרֶךְ תָּמִים, ci. 6; cf. on xv. 2). Upon all receptive ones, *i.e.* all those who are desirous and capable of receiving His blessings, He freely bestows them out of the abundance of His good things. Strophe and anti-strophe are doubled in this second half of the song. The epode closely resembles that which follows the first half. And this closing *ashrê* is not followed by any *Sela*. The music is hushed. The song dies away with an iambic cadence into a waiting expectant stillness.

PSALM LXXXV.

PETITION OF THE HITHERTO FAVOURED PEOPLE FOR A RESTORATION OF FAVOUR.

2 THOU hast been favourable, Jahve, unto Thy land,
Thou hast turned the captivity of Jacob;
3 Thou hast taken away the iniquity of Thy people,
Thou hast covered all their sin— (*Sela.*)
4 Thou hast drawn in all Thy wrath,
Thou hast turned from the heat of Thine anger.

5 Turn unto us again, O God of our salvation,
And cause Thine indignation against us to cease.
6 Wilt Thou for ever be angry with us,
Wilt Thou draw out Thine anger to all generations?
7 Wilt Thou not quicken us again,
That Thy people may rejoice in Thee?
8 Cause us to see, Jahve, Thy loving-kindness,
And grant us Thy salvation.

9 I will hear what God Jahve will speak — —
Yea, He speaketh peace to His people and to His saints;
Only let them not again fall into folly!
10 Yea, nigh unto those who fear Him is His salvation,
That glory may again dwell in our land.

11 Loving-kindness and truth shall meet together,
Righteousness and peace shall kiss each other.

12 Truth shall spring out of the earth,
And righteousness shall look down from heaven.
13 Jahve shall give every good thing,
And our land shall again yield its increase.
14 Righteousness shall go before Him
And attend unto the way of His steps.

The second part of the Book of Isaiah is written for the Israel of the Exile. It was the incidents of the Exile that first unsealed this great and indivisible prophecy, which in its compass is without any parallel. And after it had been unsealed there sprang up out of it those numerous songs of the Psalm-collection which remind us of their common model, partly by their allegorizing figurative language, partly by their lofty prophetic thoughts of consolation. This first Korahitic Jahve-Psalm (in ver. 13 coming into contact with Ps. lxxxiv., cf. lxxxiv. 12), which more particularly by its allegorizing figurative language points to Isa. ch. xl.–lxvi., belongs to the number of these so-called deutero-Isaianic Psalms.

The reference of Ps. lxxxv. to the period after the Exile and to the restoration of the state, says Dursch, is clearly expressed in the Psalm. On the other hand, Hengstenberg maintains that "the Psalm does not admit of any historical interpretation," and is sure only of this one fact, that vers. 2–4 do not relate to the deliverance out of the Exile. Even this Psalm, however, is not a formulary belonging to no express period, but has a special historical basis; and vers. 2–4 certainly sound as though they came from the lips of a people restored to their fatherland.

Vers. 2–4. The poet first of all looks back into the past, so rich in tokens of favour. The six perfects are a remembrance of former events, since nothing precedes to modify them. Certainly that which has just been experienced might also be intended; but then, as Hitzig supposes, vers. 5–8 would be the petition that preceded it, and ver. 9 would go back to the turning-point of the answering of the request—a retrograde movement which is less probable than that in שְׁבִיתֵנוּ, ver. 5, we have a transition to the petition for a renewal of previously manifested favour. (שְׁבוּת) שֵׁב שְׁבוּת, here said of a cessation of a national judgment, seems to be meant literally, not figuratively (vid. xiv. 7). רָצָה, with the accusative, to have and to show pleasure in any one, as in the likewise Korahitic lamentation-Psalm xliv. 4, cf. cxlvii. 11. In ver. 3a sin is conceived of as a burden of the conscience; in ver. 3b as a blood-stain. The music strikes up in the middle of the strophe in the sense of the "blessed" in xxxii. 1. In ver. 4a God's עֶבְרָה (i.e. unrestrained wrath) appears as an emanation; He draws it back to Himself (אָסַף) as in Joel iv. [iii.] 15, Ps. civ. 29, 1 Sam. xiv. 19) when He ceases to be angry; in ver. 4b, on the other hand, the fierce anger is conceived of as an active manifestation on the part of God which ceases when He turns round (הֵשִׁיב, Hiph. as inwardly transitive as in Ezek. xiv. 6, xxi. 35; cf. the Kal in Ex. xxxii. 12), i.e. gives the opposite turn to His manifestation.

Vers. 5–8. The poet now prays God to manifest anew the loving-kindness He has shown formerly. In the sense of "restore us again," שׁוּבֵנוּ does not form any bond of connection between this and the preceding strophe; but it does if, according to Ges. § 121, 4, it is intended in the sense of (אֵלֵינוּ) שׁוּב לָנוּ, turn again to us. The poet prays that God would manifest Himself anew to His people as He has done in former days. Thus the transition from the retrospective perfects to the petition is, in the presence of the existing extremity, adequately brought about. Assuming the post-exilic origin of the Psalm, we see from this strophe that it was composed at a period in which the distance between the temporal and spiritual condition of Israel and the national restoration, promised together with the termination of the Exile, made itself distinctly felt. On עָמָּנוּ (in relation to and bearing towards us) beside בְּעַסְךָ, cf. Job x. 17, and also on הֵפֵר, lxxxix. 34. In the question in ver. 6 reminding God of His love and of His promise, מָשַׁךְ has the signification of constant endless continuing or pursuing, as in xxxvi. 11. The expression in ver. 7a is like lxxi. 20, cf. lxxx. 19; שׁוּב is here the representative of rursus, Ges. § 142. יָשׁוּב from יָשַׁע, like קָצֶּךָ in xxxviii. 2, has ě (cf. the inflexion of פְּרִי and חֹק) instead of the ĭ in אֱלֹהֵי יִשְׁעֵנוּ. Here at the close of the strophe the prayer turns back inferentially to this attribute of God.

Vers. 9-11. The prayer is followed by attention to the divine answer, and by the answer itself. The poet stirs himself up to give ear to the words of God, like Habakkuk, ch. ii. 1. Beside אִשְׁמְעָה we find the reading אֶשְׁמְעָה, vid. on xxxix. 13. The construction of הָאֵל ה' is appositional, like הַמֶּלֶךְ דָּוִד, Ges. § 113. כִּי neither introduces the divine answer in express words, nor states the ground on which he hearkens, but rather supports the fact that God speaks from that which He has to speak. Peace is the substance of that which He speaks to His people, and that (the particularizing *Waw*) to His saints; but with the addition of an admonition. אַל is dehortative. It is not to be assumed in connection with this ethical notion that the *ah* of לְכִסְלָה is the locative *ah* as in לִשְׁאוֹלָה, ix. 18. כְּסָלָה is related to כְּסֶל like foolery to folly. The present misfortune, as is indicated here, is the merited consequence of foolish behaviour (playing the fool). In vers. 10 sqq. the poet unfolds the promise of peace which he has heard, just as he has heard it. What is meant by יְדַבֵּר is particularized first by the infinitive, and then in perfects of actual fact. The possessions that make a people truly happy and prosperous are mentioned under a charming allegory exactly after Isaiah's manner, ch. xxxii. 16 sq., xlv. 8, lix. 14 sq. The glory that has been far removed again takes up its abode in the land. Mercy or loving-kindness walks along the streets of Jerusalem, and there meets fidelity, like one guardian angel meeting the other. Righteousness and peace or prosperity, these two inseparable brothers, kiss each other there, and fall lovingly into each other's arms.*

Vers. 12-14. The poet pursues this charming picture of the future further. After God's אֱמֶת, i.e. faithfulness to the promises, has descended like dew, אמת, i.e. faithfulness to the covenant, springs up out of the land, the fruit of that fertilizing influence. And צְדָקָה, gracious justice, looks down from heaven,

---

* Concerning St. Bernard's beautiful parable of the reconciliation of the inviolability of divine threatening and of justice with mercy and peace in the work of redemption, which has grown out of this passage of the Psalms, *Misericordia et veritas obviaverunt sibi, justitia et pax osculatæ sunt*, and has been transferred to the painting, poetry, and drama of the middle ages, vid. Piper's *Evangelischer Kalender*, 1859, S. 24-34, and the beautiful miniature representing the ἀσπασμός of δικαιοσύνη and εἰρήνη of a Greek Psalter, 1867, S. 63.

smiling favour and dispensing blessing. גַּם in ver. 13 places these two prospects in reciprocal relation to one another (cf. lxxxiv. 7); it is found once instead of twice. Jahve gives הַטּוֹב, everything that is only and always good and that imparts true happiness, and the land, corresponding to it, yields יְבוּלָהּ, the increase which might be expected from a land so richly blessed (cf. lxvii. 7 and the promise in Lev. xxvi. 4). Jahve Himself is present in the land: righteousness walks before Him majestically as His herald, and righteousness יָשֵׁם לְדֶרֶךְ פְּעָמָיו, sets (viz. its footsteps) upon the way of His footsteps, that is to say, follows Him inseparably. פְּעָמָיו stands once instead of twice; the construct is to a certain extent attractional, as in lxv. 12, Gen. ix. 6. Since the expression is neither דֶרֶךְ (l. 23, Isa. li. 10) nor לְדֶרֶךְ (Isa. xlix. 11), it is natural to interpret the expression thus, and it gives moreover (cf. Isa. lviii. 8, lii. 12) an excellent sense. But if, which we prefer, שִׁים is taken in the sense of שִׁים לֵב (as *e.g.* in Job iv. 20) with the following לְ, to give special heed to anything (Deut. xxxii. 46, Ezek. xl. 4, xliv. 5), to be anxiously concerned about it (1 Sam. ix. 20), then we avoid the supplying in thought of a second פְּעָמָיו, which is always objectionable, and the thought obtained by the other interpretation is brought clearly before the mind: righteousness goes before Jahve, who dwells and walks abroad in Israel, and gives heed to the way of His steps, that is to say, follows carefully in His footsteps.

PSALM LXXXVI.

PRAYER OF A PERSECUTED SAINT.

1 BOW down, Jahve, Thine ear, answer me,
   For I am needy and poor.
2 Preserve my soul, for I am pious;
   Help Thy servant, O Thou my God,
   Who cleaveth confidingly to Thee.
3 Be merciful unto me, Lord,
   For unto Thee do I cry all the day.
4 Rejoice the soul of Thy servant,
   For unto Thee, Lord, do I lift up my soul.

5 For Thou, Lord, art good and ready to forgive,
And plenteous in mercy unto all who call upon Thee.

6 Give ear, Jahve, to my prayer,
And hearken to the cry of my importunate supplications.
7 In the day of my distress do I call unto Thee,
For Thou wilt answer me.
8 There is none like unto Thee among the gods, O Lord,
And Thy works have not their equal.
9 All nations which Thou hast made shall come and worship
    before Thee, Lord,
And give glory to Thy name.
10 For Thou art great and doest wondrous things,
Thou, Thou art God alone.
11 Teach me, Jahve, Thy way,
I desire to walk in Thy truth;
Unite my heart to fear Thy Name.
12 I will give thanks to Thee, O Lord my God, with all my
    heart,
And will glorify Thy Name for ever,
13 That Thy mercy has been great over me,
And Thou hast rescued my soul out of the deep hell.

14 Elohim, the proud are risen against me,
And an assembly of violent men seek my soul,
And have not set Thee before their eyes.
15 But Thou, Lord, art a God compassionate and gracious,
Long-suffering and plenteous in mercy and truth.
16 Turn unto me and be gracious to me,
O give strength unto Thy servant
And save the son of Thy handmaid.
17 Show me a token for good,
That those who hate me may see it and be ashamed,
That Thou, Jahve, hast helped me and comforted me.

A Psalm "by David" which has points of contact with Ps. lxxxv. (cf. lxxxvi. 2, חסיד, with lxxxv. 9; lxxxvi. 15, חסד ואמת, with lxxxv. 11) is here inserted between Korahitic Psalms: it can only be called a Psalm by David as having grown out of Davidic and other model passages. The writer cannot be compared for poetical capability either with David or with the authors of such Psalms as Ps. cxvi. and cxxx. His Psalm is more liturgic than purely poetic, and it is also only entitled תְּפִלָּה, without bearing in itself any sign of musical designation. It possesses this characteristic, that the divine name אדני occurs seven times,* just as it occurs three times in Ps. cxxx., forming the start for a later, Adonajic style in imitation of the Elohimic.

Vers. 1–5. The prayer to be heard runs like lv. 3; and the statement of the ground on which it is based, ver. 1*b*, word for word like xl. 18. It is then particularly expressed as a prayer for preservation (שָׁמְרָה, as in cxix. 167, although imperative, to be read *shăm'rah;* cf. xxx. 4 מְיֹרְדִי, xxxviii. 21 רָדְפִי or רְדָפִי, and what we have already observed on xvi. 1 שָׁמְרֵנִי); for he is not only in need of God's help, but also because חָסִיד (iv. 4, xvi. 10), *i.e.* united to Him in the bond of affection (חֶסֶד, Hos. vi. 4, Jer. ii. 2), not unworthy of it. In ver. 2 we hear the strains of xxv. 20, xxxi. 7; in ver. 3, of lvii. 2 sq.: the confirmation in ver. 4*b* is taken verbally from xxv. 1, cf. also cxxx. 6. Here, what is said in ver. 4 of this shorter Adonajic Psalm, cxxx., is abbreviated in the ἅπαξ γεγραμ. כִּי־ (root כל, של, to allow to hang loose, χαλᾶν, to give up, *remittere*). The Lord is good (טוֹב), *i.e.* altogether love, and for this very reason also ready to forgive, and great and rich in mercy for all who call upon Him as such. The beginning of the following group also accords with Ps. cxxx. in ver. 2.

Vers. 6–13. Here, too, almost everything is an echo of earlier language of the Psalms and of the Law; viz., ver. 7 follows xvii. 6 and other passages; ver. 8*a* is taken from Ex. xv. 11, cf. lxxxix. 9, where, however, אלהים, gods, is avoided; ver. 8*b* follows Deut. iii. 24; ver. 9 follows xxii. 28; ver. 11*a* is taken from xxvii. 11; ver. 11*b* from xxvi. 3; ver. 13, שְׁאוֹל תַּחְתִּיָּה from Deut. xxxii. 22, where instead of this it is תַּחְתִּית, just as in cxxx. 2 תַּחֲנוּנַי (supplicatory prayer) instead of תַּחֲנוּנוֹתַי

---

* For the genuine reading in ver. 4 (where Heidenheim reads יהוה) and in ver. 5 (where Nissel reads יהוה) is also אֲדֹנָי (Bomberg, Hutter, etc.). Both the divine names in vers. 4 and 5 belong to the 134 וְדָאִין. The divine name אֲדֹנָי, which is written and is not merely substituted for יהוה, is called in the language of the Masora וַדָּאִי (the true and real one).

(importunate supplications); and also ver. 10 (cf. lxxii. 18) is a doxological formula that was already in existence. The construction בְּ הִקְשִׁיב is the same as in lxvi. 19. But although for the most part flowing on only in the language of prayer borrowed from earlier periods, this Psalm is, moreover, not without remarkable significance and beauty. With the confession of the incomparableness of the Lord is combined the prospect of the recognition of the incomparable One throughout the nations of the earth. This clear unallegorical prediction of the conversion of the heathen is the principal parallel to Apoc. xv. 4. "All nations, which Thou hast made"—they have their being from Thee; and although they have forgotten it (vid. ix. 18), they will nevertheless at last come to recognise it. כָּל־גּוֹיִם, since the article is wanting, are nations of all tribes (countries and nationalities); cf. Jer. xvi. 16 with Ps. xxii. 18; Tobit xiii. 11, ἔθνη πολλά, with ibid. xiv. 6, πάντα τὰ ἔθνη. And how weightily brief and charming is the petition in ver. 11: *uni cor meum, ut timeat nomen tuum!* Luther has rightly departed from the renderings of the LXX., Syriac, and Vulgate: *lætetur* (יַחְדְּ from חָדָה). The meaning, however, is not so much "keep my heart near to the only One," as "direct all its powers and concentrate them on the one thing." The following group shows us what is the meaning of the deliverance out of the hell beneath (שְׁאוֹל תַּחְתִּיָּה, like אֶרֶץ תַּחְתִּית, the earth beneath, the inner parts of the earth, Ezek. xxxi. 14 sqq.), for which the poet promises beforehand to manifest his thankfulness (כִּי, ver. 13, as in lvi. 14).

Vers. 14–17. The situation is like that in the Psalms of the time of Saul. The writer is a persecuted one, and in constant peril of his life. He has taken ver. 14*ab* out of the Elohimic Ps. liv. ver. 5, and retained the *Elohim* as a proper name of God (cf. on the other hand vers. 8, 10); he has, however, altered זָרִים to זֵדִים, which here, as in Isa. xiii. 11 (cf., however, *ibid*. xxv. 5), is the alternating word to עָרִיצִים. In ver. 15 he supports his petition that follows by Jahve's testimony concerning Himself in Ex. xxxiv. 6. The appellation given to himself by the poet in ver. 16 recurs in cxvi. 16 (cf. Wisd. ix. 5). The poet calls himself "the son of Thy handmaid" as having been born into the relation to Him of servant; it is a relationship that has come to him by birth. How beautifully does the *Adonaj* come in here for the seventh time! He is even from his mother's womb the servant of the sovereign Lord, from whose omnipotence he can therefore also look for a miraculous interposition on his behalf. A "token for good" is a special dispensation, from which it becomes evident to him that God is kindly disposed towards him. לְטוֹבָה as in the mouth of Nehemiah, ch. v. 19, xiii. 31; of Ezra, ch. viii. 22; and also even in Jeremiah and earlier. וְיֵבשׁ is just as parenthetical as in Isa. xxvi. 11.

PSALM LXXXVII.

THE CITY OF THE NEW BIRTH OF THE NATIONS.

1 HIS founded [city] upon the holy mountains—
2 Jahve loveth the gates of Zion
  More than all the dwellings of Jacob.
3 Glorious things are spoken of thee, thou city of God!
  (*Sela.*)
4 "I will proclaim Rahab and Babylon as My intimates;
  Behold Philistia and Tyre, together with Æthiopia—
  That one is born there."

5 And to Zion it shall one day be said:
  Each and every one is born in her,
  And He, the Highest, doth establish her.
6 Jahve shall reckon in the list of the nations:
  That one is born there. (*Sela.*)
7 And singing as well as dancing (they say):
  All my fountains are in thee!

The mission thought in lxxxvi. 9 becomes the ruling thought in this Korahitic Psalm. It is a prophetic Psalm in the style, boldly and expressively concise even to obscurity (Eusebius, σφόδρα αἰνιγματώδης καὶ σκοτεινῶς εἰρημένος), in which the first three oracles of the tetralogy Isa. xxi.-xxii. 14, and the passage Isa. xxx. 6, 7—a passage designed to be as it were a memorial exhibition—are also written. It also resembles these oracles in this respect, that ver. 1*b* opens the whole arsis-like by a solemn statement of its subject, like the emblematical inscriptions there. As to the rest, Isa. xliv. 5 is the key to its meaning. The threefold לְךָ here corresponds to the threefold זֶה in that passage.

Since Rahab and Babylon as the foremost worldly powers are mentioned first among the peoples who come into the congregation of Jahve, and since the prospect of the poet has moulded itself according to a present rich in promise and carrying such a future in its bosom, it is natural (with Tholuck, Hengstenberg, Vaihinger, Keil, and others) to suppose that the Psalm was composed when, in consequence of the destruction of the Assyrian army before Jerusalem, offerings and presents were brought from many quarters for Jahve and the king of Judah (2 Chron. xxxii. 23), and the admiration of Hezekiah, the favoured one of God, had spread as far as Babylon. Just as Micah (ch. iv. 10) mentions Babylon as the place of the chastisement and of the redemption of his nation, and as Isaiah, about the fourteenth year of Hezekiah's reign, predicts to the king a carrying away of his treasures and his posterity to Babylon, so here Egypt and Babylon, the inheritress of Assyria, stand most prominent among the worldly powers that shall be obliged one day to bow themselves to the God of Israel. In a similar connection Isaiah (ch. xix.) does not as yet mention Babylon side by side with Egypt, but Assyria.

Vers. 1-4. The poet is absorbed in the contemplation of the glory of a matter which he begins to celebrate, without naming it. Whether we render it: His founded, or (since מִיסָּד and מוּסָּד are both used elsewhere as *part. pass.*): His foundation (after the form מְלוּכָה, poetically for יְסוֹד, a founding, then that which is set fast = a foundation), the meaning remains the same; but the more definite statement of the object with שַׁעֲרֵי צִיּוֹן is more easily connected with what precedes by regarding it as a participle. The suffix refers to Jahve, and it is Zion, whose praise is a favourite theme of the Korahitic songs, that is intended. We cannot tell by looking to the accents whether the clause is to be taken as a substantival clause (His founded [city] is upon the holy mountains) or not. Since, however, the expression is not יְסוּדָתוֹ הִיא בְּהַרְרֵי־קֹדֶשׁ, יְסוּדָתוֹ בְּהַרְרֵי קֹדֶשׁ is an object placed first in advance (which the antithesis to the other dwellings of Jacob would admit of), and in ver. 2a a new synonymous object is subordinated to אהב by a similar turn of the discourse to Jer. xiii. 27, vi. 2 (Hitzig). By altering the division of the verses as Hupfeld and Hofmann do (His foundation or founded [city] upon the holy mountains doth Jahve love), ver. 2 is decapitated. Even now the God-founded city (surrounded on three sides by deep valleys), whose firm and visible foundation is the outward manifestation of its imperishable inner nature, rises aloft above all the other dwelling-places of Israel. Jahve stands in a lasting, faithful, loving relationship (אֹהֵב, not 3 *præt.* אָהֵב) to the gates of Zion. These gates are named as a periphrasis for Zion, because they bound the circuit of the city, and any one who loves a city delights to go frequently through its gates; and they are perhaps mentioned in prospect of the fulness of the heathen that shall enter into them. In ver. 3 the LXX. correctly, and at the same time in harmony with the syntax, renders: Δεδοξασμένα ἐλαλήθη περὶ σοῦ. The construction of a plural subject with a singular predicate is a syntax common in other instances also, whether the subject is conceived of as a unity in the form of the plural (*e.g.* lxvi. 3, cxix. 137, Isa. xvi. 8), or is individualized in the pursuance of the thought (as is the case most likely in Gen. xxvii. 29, cf. xii. 3); here the glorious things are conceived of as the sum-total of such. The operation of the construction of the active (Ew. § 295, *b*) is not probable here in connection with the participle. בְּ beside דִּבֶּר may signify the place or the instrument, substance and object of the speech (*e.g.* cxix. 46), but also the person against whom the words are spoken (*e.g.* l. 20), or concerning whom they are uttered (as the words of the suitor to the father or the relatives of the maiden, 1 Sam. xxv. 39, Cant. viii. 8; cf. on the construction, 1 Sam. xix. 3). The poet, without doubt, here refers to the words of promise concerning the eternal continuance and future glory of Jerusalem: Glorious things are spoken, *i.e.* exist as spoken, in reference to thee, O thou city of God, city of His choice and of His love.

The glorious contents of the promise are now unfolded, and that with the most vivid directness: Jahve Himself takes up the discourse, and declares the gracious, glorious, world-wide mission of His chosen and beloved city: it shall become the birth-place of all nations. *Rahab* is Egypt, as in lxxxix. 11, Isa. xxx. 7, li. 9, the southern worldly power, and *Babylon* the northern. הַזְכִּיר, as frequently, of loud (Jer. iv. 16) and honourable public mention or commemoration, xlv. 18. It does not signify " to record or register in writing;" for the official name מַזְכִּיר, which is cited in support of this meaning, designates the historian of the empire as one who keeps in remembrance the memorable events of the history of his time It is therefore impossible, with Hofmann, to render: I will add Rahab and Babylon to those who know me. In general לְ is not used to point out to whom the addition is made as belonging to them, but for what purpose, or as what (cf. 2 Sam. v. 3, Isa. iv. 3), these kingdoms, hitherto hostile towards God and His people, shall be declared: Jahve completes what He Himself has brought about, inasmuch as He publicly and solemnly declares them to be those who know Him, *i.e.* those who experimentally (*vid.* xxxvi. 11) know Him as their God. Accordingly, it is clear that זֶה יֻלַּד־שָׁם is also meant to refer to the conversion of the other three nations to whom the finger of God points with הִנֵּה, viz. the war-loving Philistia, the rich and proud Tyre, and the adventurous and powerful Ethiopia (Isa. ch. xviii.). זֶה does not refer to the individuals, nor to the sum-total of these nations, but to nation after nation (cf. זֶה ...ךְזֶה, Isa. xxiii. 13), by fixing the eye upon each one separately. And שָׁם refers to Zion. The words of Jahve, which come in without any intermediary preparation, stand in the closest connection with the language of the poet and seer. Zion appears elsewhere as the mother who brings forth Israel again as a numerous people (Isa. lxvi. 7, liv. 1–3): it is the children of the dispersion (*diaspora*) which Zion regains in Isa. lx. 4 sq.; here, however, it is the nations which are born in Zion. The poet does not combine with it the idea of being born again in the depth of its New Testament meaning; he means, however, that the nations will attain a right of citizenship in Zion (πολιτεία τοῦ Ἰσραήλ, Eph. ii. 12) as in their second mother-city, that they will therefore at any rate experience a spiritual change which, regarded from the New Testament point of view, is the new birth out of water and the Spirit.

Vers. 5–7. Inasmuch now as the nations come thus into the church (or congregation) of the children of God and of the children of Abraham, Zion becomes by degrees a church immeasurably great. To Zion, however, or of Zion (לְ of reference to), shall it be said אִישׁ וְאִישׁ יֻלַּד־בָּהּ. Zion, the one city, stands in contrast to all the countries, the one city of God in contrast to the kingdoms of the world, and אִישׁ וְאִישׁ in contrast to זֶה. This contrast, upon the correct apprehension of which depends the understanding of the whole Psalm, is missed when it is said, "whilst in relation to other countries it is always only the whole nation that comes under consideration, Zion is not reckoned up as a nation, but by persons" (Hofmann). With this rendering the יֻלַּד retires into the background; in that case this giving of prominence to the value of the individual exceeds the ancient range of conception, and it is also an inadmissible appraisement that in Zion each individual is as important as a nation as a whole. Elsewhere אִישׁ אִישׁ, Lev. xvii. 10, 13, or אִישׁ וְאִישׁ, Esth. i. 8, signifies each and every one; accordingly here אִישׁ וְאִישׁ (individual and, or after, individual) affirms a *progressus in infinitum*, where one is ever added to another. Of an immeasurable multitude, and of each individual in this multitude in particular, it is said that he was born in Zion. Now, too, וְהוּא יְכוֹנְנֶהָ עֶלְיוֹן has a significant connection with what precedes. Whilst from among foreign peoples more and more are continually acquiring the right of natives in Zion, and thus are entering into a new national alliance, so that a breach of their original national friendships is taking place, He Himself (cf. 1 Sam. xx. 9), the Most High, will uphold Zion (xlviii. 9), so that under His protection and blessing it shall become ever greater and more glorious. Ver. 6 tells us what will be the result of such a progressive incorporation in the church of Zion of those who have hitherto been far removed, viz. Jahve will reckon when He writeth down (כְּתֹב as in Josh. xviii. 8) the nations; or better,—since this would more readily be expressed by בְּכָתְבוֹ, and the book of the living (Isa. iv. 3) is one already existing from time immemorial,—He will reckon in the list (כָּתוֹב) after the form חֲלוֹם, חֲלִיל, פְּקוֹד = כְּתָב, Ezek. xiii. 9) of the nations, *i.e.* when He goes over the nations that are written down there and chosen for the coming salvation, "this one was born there;" He will therefore acknowledge them one after another as those born in Zion. The end of all history is that Zion shall become the metropolis of all nations. When the fulness of the Gentiles is thus come in, then shall all and each one as well singing as dancing say (supply אָמְרוּ) : All my fountains are in thee. Among the old translators the rendering of Aquila is the best: καὶ ᾄδοντες ὡς χοροί· πᾶσαι πηγαὶ ἐν σοί, which Jerome follows, *et cantores quasi in choris : omnes fontes mei in te.* One would rather render חֹלְלִים, "flute-players" (LXX. ὡς ἐν αὐλοῖς) : but to pipe or play the flute is חִלֵּל (a denominative from חָלִיל), 1 Kings i. 40, whereas to dance is חֹלֵל (*Pilel* of הוּל); it is therefore = מְחֹלְלִים, like לְצִצָּים, Hos. vii. 5. But it must not moreover be rendered, "And singers as well as dancers (will say);" for "singers" is כְּשֹׁרְרִים, not שָׁרִים, which signifies *cantantes*, not *cantores*. Singing as dancing, *i.e.* making known their festive joy as well by the one as by the other, shall the men of all nations incorporated in Zion say : All my fountains, *i.e.* fountains of salvation (after Isa. xii. 3), are in thee (O city of God). It has also been interpreted: my looks (*i.e.* the object on which my eye is fixed, or the delight of my eyes), or : my thoughts (after the modern Hebrew עִין of spiritual meditation); but both are incongruous. The conjecture, too, of Böttcher, and even before him of Schnurrer (*Dissertationes*, p. 150), כָּל־מְעִינַי, all who take up their abode (instead of which Hupfeld conjectures מְעִינַי, all my near-dwellers, *i.e.* those who dwell with me under the same roof*), is not Hebrew, and deprives us of the thought which corresponds to the aim of the whole, that Jerusalem shall be universally regarded as the place where the water of life springs for the whole of mankind, and shall be universally praised as this place of fountains.

PSALM LXXXVIII.

PLAINTIVE PRAYER OF A PATIENT SUFFERER LIKE JOB.

2 JAHVE, God of my salvation,
  In the time when I cry in the night before Thee,

---

* Hupfeld cites Rashi as having thus explained it; but his gloss is to be rendered: my whole inmost part (after the Aramaic = כְּמִי) is with thee, *i.e.* thy salvation.

3 Let my prayer come before Thy face,
 Incline Thine ear to my crying.
4 For satiated with sufferings is my soul,
 And my life is come nigh unto Hades.
5 I am accounted as those who go down to the pit,
 I am become as a man that hath no strength—

6 A freed one among the dead,
 Like the slain, those buried in the grave,
 Whom Thou rememberest no more,
 And they are cut off from Thy hand.
7 Thou hast laid me in the pit of the abysses,
 In darknesses, in the depths of the sea.
8 Upon me Thy fierce anger lieth hard,
 And all Thy waves dost Thou bend down. (*Sela.*)

9 Thou hast removed my familiar friends from me,
 Thou hast made me an abomination to them,
 Who am shut up and cannot come forth.
10 Mine eye languisheth by reason of affliction,
 I call upon Thee, Jahve, every day,
 I stretch out my hands unto Thee.

11 Wilt Thou do wonders unto the dead,
 Or shall the shades arise to give thanks unto Thee? (*Sela.*)
12 Shall Thy loving-kindness be declared in the grave,
 Thy faithfulness in the place of destruction?
13 Shall Thy wonder-working power be made known in the darkness,
 And Thy righteousness in the land of forgetfulness?

14 And as for me—to Thee, Jahve, do I cry,
 Even in the morning my prayer cometh to meet Thee.
15 Wherefore, Jahve, dost Thou cast off my soul,
 Dost Thou hide Thy face from me?
16 Needy am I and ready to die from my youth up,
 I bear Thy terrors, I am utterly helpless.

17 Over me Thy fierce anger hath passed,
 Thy terrors have destroyed me.

18 They have surrounded me like waters all the day,
They compassed me about altogether.
19 Thou hast removed far from me lover and friend,
My familiar friends are darkness.

Ps. lxxxviii. is as gloomy as Ps. lxxxvii. is cheerful; they stand near one another as contrasts. Not Ps. lxxvii., as the old expositors answer to the question *quænam ode omnium tristissima*, but this Ps. lxxxviii. is the darkest, gloomiest, of all the plaintive Psalms; for it is true the name "God of my salvation," with which the praying one calls upon God, and his praying itself, show that the spark of faith within him is not utterly extinguished; but as to the rest, it is all one pouring forth of deep lament in the midst of the severest conflict of temptation in the presence of death, the gloom of melancholy does not brighten up to become a hope, the Psalm dies away in Job-like lamentation. Herein we discern echoes of the Korahitic Ps. xlii. and of Davidic Psalms: compare ver. 3 with xviii. 7; ver. 5 with xxviii. 1; ver. 6 with xxxi. 23; ver. 18 with xxii. 17; ver. 19 (although differently applied) with xxxi. 12; and more particularly the questions in vers. 11–13 with vi. 6, of which they are as it were only the amplification. But these Psalm-echoes are outweighed by the still more striking points of contact with the Book of Job, both as regards linguistic usage (לְאֵין, ver. 10, Job xli. 44; רְפָאִים, ver. 11, Job xxvi. 5; אֲבַדּוֹן, ver. 12, Job xxvi. 6, xxviii. 22; עֲנִי, ver. 16a, Job xxxiii. 25, xxxvi. 14; אֵמִים, ver. 16b, Job xx. 25; עֲתִים, ver. 17, Job vi. 4) and single thoughts (cf. ver. 5 with Job xiv. 10; ver. 9 with Job xxx. 10; ver. 19 with Job xvii. 9, xix. 14), and also the suffering condition of the poet and the whole manner in which this finds expression. For the poet finds himself in the midst of the same temptation as Job not merely so far as his mind and spirit are concerned; but his outward affliction is, according to the tenor of his complaints, the same, viz. the leprosy (ver. 9), which, the disposition to which being born with him, has been his inheritance from his youth up (ver. 16). Now, since the Book of Job is a Chokma-work of the Salomonic age, and the two Ezrahites belonged to the wise men of the first rank at the court of Solomon (1 Kings v. 11 [iv. 31]), it is natural to suppose that the Book of Job has sprung out of this very Chokma-company, and that perhaps this very Heman the Ezrahite who is the author of Ps. lxxxviii. has made a passage of his own life, suffering, and conflict of soul, a subject of dramatic treatment.

The inscription of the Psalm runs: *A Psalm-song by the Korahites; to the Precentor, to be recited* (lit. *to be pressed down*, not after Isa. xxvii. 2 : *to be sung*, which expresses nothing, nor: *to be sung alternatingly*, which is contrary to the character of the Psalm) *after a sad manner* (cf. liii. 1) *with muffled voice, a meditation by Heman the Ezrahite.* This is a double inscription, the two halves of which are contradictory. The bare להימן side by side with לבני־קרח would be perfectly in order, since the precentor Heman is a Korahite according to 1 Chron. vi. 18–23 [33–38]; but הימן האזרחי is the name of one of the four great Israelitish sages in 1 Kings v. 11 [iv. 31], who, according to 1 Chron. ii. 6, is a direct descendant of Zerah, and therefore is not of the tribe of Levi, but of Judah. The suppositions that Heman the Korahite had been adopted into the family of Zerah, or that Heman the Ezrahite had been admitted among the Levites, are miserable attempts to get over the difficulty. At the head of the Psalm there stand two different statements respecting its origin side by side, which are irreconcilable. The assumption that the title of the Psalm originally was either merely שיר מזמור לבני־קרח, or merely למנצח וגו׳, is warranted by the fact that only in this one Psalm למנצח does not occupy the first place in the inscription. But which of the two statements is the more reliable one? Most assuredly the latter; for שיר מזמור לבני־קרח is only a recurrent repetition of the inscription of Ps. lxxxvii. The second statement, on the other hand, by its precise designation of the melody, and by the designation of the author, which corresponds to the Psalm that follows, gives evidence of its antiquity and its historical character.

Vers. 2–8. The poet finds himself in the midst of circumstances gloomy in the extreme, but he does not despair; he still turns towards Jahve with his complaints, and calls Him the God of his salvation. This *actus directus* of fleeing in prayer to the God of salvation, which urges its way through all tha is dark and gloomy, is the fundamental characteristic of all true faith. Ver. 2a is not to be rendered, as a clause of itself: "by day I cry unto Thee, in the night before Thee" (LXX. and Targum), which ought to have been יוֹמָם, but (as it is also pointed, especially in Baer's text) : by day, *i.e.* in the time (lvi. 4, lxxviii. 42, cf. xviii. 1), when I cry before Thee in the night, let my prayer come . . . (Hitzig). In ver. 3b he calls his piercing lamentation, his wailing supplication, רִנָּתִי, as in xvii. 1, lxi. 2. הִטֵּה as in lxxxvi. 1, for which we find הַט in xvii. 6. The *Beth* of בְּרָעוֹת, as in lxv. 5, Lam. iii. 15, 30, denotes that of which his soul has already had abundantly sufficient. On ver. 4b, cf. as to the syntax xxxi. 11. אֱיָל (ἅπαξ λεγομ. like אֱיָלוּת, xxii. 20) signifies succinctness, compactness, vigorousness (ἁδρότης) : he is like a man from whom all vital freshness and vigour is gone, therefore now only like the shadow of a man, in fact like one already dead. חָפְשִׁי, in ver. 6a, the LXX. renders ἐν νεκροῖς ἐλεύθερος (Symmachus, ἀφεὶς ἐλεύθερος) ; and in like manner the Targum, and the Talmud which follows it in formulating the proposition that a deceased person is חפשי מן המצות, free from the fulfilling of the precepts of the Law (cf. Rom. vi. 7). Hitzig, Ewald, Köster, and Böttcher, on the contrary, explain it according to Ezek. xxvii. 20 (where חֹפֶשׁ signifies *stragulum*) : among the dead is my couch (הפשי = יצועי, Job xvii. 13). But in respect of Job iii. 19 the adjectival rendering is the more probable; "one set free among the dead" (LXX.) is equivalent to one released from the bond of life (Job xxxix. 5), somewhat as in Latin a dead person is called *defunctus*. God does not remember the dead, *i.e.* practically, inasmuch as, devoid of any progressive history, their condition remains always the same; they are in fact cut away (נִגְזָרוּ as in xxxi. 23, Lam. iii. 54, Isa. liii. 8) from the hand, viz. from the guiding and helping hand, of God. Their dwelling-place is the pit of the places lying deep beneath (cf. on תַּחְתִּיּוֹת, lxiii. 10, lxxxvi. 13, Ezek. xxvi. 20, and more particularly Lam. iii. 55), the dark regions (מַחֲשַׁכִּים as in cxliii. 3, Lam. iii. 6), the submarine depths (בִּמְצֹלוֹת ; LXX., Symmachus, the Syriac, etc.: ἐν σκιᾷ θανάτου = בצלמות, according to Job x. 21 and frequently, but contrary to Lam. iii. 54), whose open abyss is the grave for each one. On ver. 8b cf. xlii. 8. The *Mugrash* by כָּל־מִשְׁבָּרֶיךָ stamps it as an adverbial accusative (Targum), or more correctly, since the expression is not עָנִיתָ,

as the object placed in advance. Only those who are not conversant with the subject (as Hupfeld in this instance) imagine that the accentuation marks עָנִיתָ as a relative clause (cf. on the contrary viii. 7b, xxi. 3b, etc.). עָנָה, to bow down, press down; here used of the turning or directing downwards (LXX. ἐπήγαγες) of the waves, which burst like a cataract over the afflicted one.

Vers. 9–13. The octastichs are now followed by hexastichs which belong together in pairs. The complaint concerning the alienation of his nearest relations sounds like Job xix. 13 sqq., but the same strain is also frequently heard in the earlier Psalms written in times of suffering, e.g. xxxi. 9. He is forsaken by all his familiar friends (not: acquaintances, for מְיֻדָּעַי signifies more than that), he is alone in the dungeon of wretchedness, where no one comes near him, and whence he cannot make his escape. This sounds, according to Lev. ch. xiii., very much like the complaint of a leper. The Book of Leviticus there passes over from the uncleanness attending the beginning of human life to the uncleanness of the most terrible disease. Disease is the middle stage between birth and death, and, according to the Eastern notion, leprosy is the worst of all diseases, it is death itself clinging to the still living man (Num. xii. 12), and more than all other evils a stroke of the chastening hand of God (נֶגַע), a scourge of God (צָרַעַת). The man suspected of having leprosy was to be subjected to a seven days' quarantine until the determination of the priest's diagnosis; and if the leprosy was confirmed, he was to dwell apart outside the camp (Lev. xiii. 46), where, though not imprisoned, he was nevertheless separated from his dwelling and his family (cf. Job, i. 347), and if a man of position, would feel himself condemned to a state of involuntary retirement. It is natural to refer the כָּלֶא, which is closely connected with שִׁתַּנִי, to this separation. עֵינִי, ver. 10, instead of עֵינִי, as in vi. 8, xxxi. 10: his eye has languished, vanished away (דָּאַב of the same root as *tabescere*, cognate with the root of הָיוּנ, lxviii. 3), in consequence of (his) affliction. He calls and calls upon Jahve, stretches out (שִׁטַּח, *expandere*, according to the Arabic, more especially after the manner of a roof) his hands (*palmas*) towards Him, in order to shield himself from His wrath and to lead Him compassionately to give ear to him. In vers. 11–13 he bases his cry for help upon a twofold wish, viz. to become an object of the miraculous help of God, and to be able to praise Him for it. Neither of these wishes would be realized if he were to die; for that which lies beyond this life is uniform darkness, devoid of any progressive history. With מֵתִים alternates רְפָאִים (sing. רָפָא), the relaxed ones, i.e. shades (σκιαί) of the nether world. With reference to יוֹרְדֵי instead of לְהוֹרִדוֹת, vid. Ewald, § 337, b. Beside חֹשֶׁךְ (Job x. 21 sq.) stands אֶרֶץ נְשִׁיָּה, the land of forgetfulness (λήθη), where there is an end of all thinking, feeling, and acting (Eccles. ix. 5, 6, 10), and where the monotony of death, devoid of thought and recollection, reigns. Such is the representation given in the Old Testament of the state beyond the present, even in Ecclesiastes, and in the Apocrypha (Sir. xvii. 27 sq. after Isa. xxxviii. 18 sq.; Baruch ii. 17 sq.); and it was obliged to be thus represented, for in the New Testament not merely the conception of the state after death, but this state itself, is become a different one.

Vers. 14–19. He who complains thus without knowing any comfort, and yet without despairing, gathers himself up afresh for prayer. With וַאֲנִי he contrasts himself with the dead who are separated from God's manifestation of love. Being still in life, although under wrath that apparently has no end, he strains every nerve to struggle through in prayer until he shall reach God's love. His complaints are petitions, for they are complaints that are poured forth before God. The destiny under which for a long time he has been more like one dying than living, reaches back even into his youth. כְּנֹעַר (since נֹעַר is everywhere undeclined) is equivalent to מִנְּעָרַי. The ἐξηπορήθην of the LXX. is the right indicator for the understanding of the ἅπαξ λεγ. אָפוּנָה. Aben-Ezra and Kimchi derive it from פֶּן, like עָלָה from עַל,* and assign to it the signification of *dubitare*. But it may be more safely explained after the Arabic words اَفِنْ, اَفَنْ, مَأْفُون (root اَفن, to urge forwards, push), in which the fundamental notion of driving back, nar-

---

* The derivation is not contrary to the genius of the language; the supplementing productive force of the language displayed in the liturgical poetry of the synagogue, also changes particles into verbs: vid. Zunz, *Die synagogale Poesie des Mittelalters*, S. 421.

rowing and exhausting, is transferred to a weakening or weakness of the intellect. We might also compare בָּקָה, أَفَلَ, " to disappear, vanish, pass away;" but the ἐξηπορήθην of the LXX. favours the kinship with that أَفِلَ, *infirma mente et consilii inops fuit*,* which has been already compared by Castell. The aorist of the LXX., however, is just as erroneous in this instance as in xlii. 5, lv. 3, lvii. 5. In all these instances the cohortative denotes the inward result following from an outward compulsion, as they say in Hebrew: I lay hold of trembling (Isa. xiii. 8, Job xviii. 20, xxi. 6) or joy (Isa. xxxv. 10, li. 11), when the force of circumstances drives one into such states of mind. Labouring under the burden of divine dispensations of a terrifying character, he finds himself in a state of mental weakness and exhaustion, or of insensible (senseless) fright; over him as their destined goal before many others go God's burnings of wrath (*plur.* only in this instance), His terrible decrees (*vid.* concerning בְּעֵת on xviii. 15) have almost annihilated him. צִמְּתֻתֻנִי is not an impossible form (Olshausen, § 251, *a*), but an intensive form of צִמְּתוּ, the last part of the already inflected verb being repeated, as in אָהֲבוּ הֵבוּ, Hos. iv. 18 (cf. in the department of the noun, פִּיפִיּוֹת, edge-edges = many edges, cxlix. 6), perhaps under the influence of the derivative.† The corrections צִמְּתֻתְנִי (from צִמְּתַת) or צִמְּתוּנִי (from צָמַת) are simple enough; but it is more prudent to let tradition judge of that which is possible in the usage of the language. In ver. 18 the burnings become floods; the wrath of God can be compared to every destroying and overthrowing element. The billows threaten to swallow him up, without any helping hand being stretched out to him on the part of any of his lovers and friends. Is ver. 19*a* to be now explained according to Job xvii. 14, viz. My familiar friends are gloomy darkness;

---

* Abulwalid also explains אֱמוּנָה after the Arabic, but in a way that cannot be accepted, viz. " for a long time onwards," from the Arabic *iffān* (*ibbān, iff, ufuf, ifāf, taiffah*), time, period—time conceived of in the onward rush, the constant succession of its moments.

† Heidenheim interprets: Thy terrors are become to me as צְמִתַת (Lev. xxv. 23), *i.e.* inalienably my own.

i.e. instead of those who were hitherto my familiars (Job xix. 14), darkness is become my familiar friend? One would have thought that it ought then to have been מְיֻדָּעַי (Schnurrer), or, according to Prov. vii. 4, מוֹדָע, and that, in connection with this sense of the noun, מַחְשָׁךְ ought as subject to have the precedence, that consequently מְיֻדָּעַי is subject and מַחְשָׁךְ predicate: my familiar friends have lost themselves in darkness, are become absolutely invisible (Hitzig at last). But the regular position of the words is kept to if it is interpreted: my familiar friends are reduced to gloomy darkness as my familiar friend, and the plural is justified by Job xix. 14: *Mother and sister* (do I call) *the worm*. With this complaint the harp falls from the poet's hands. He is silent, and waits on God, that He may solve this riddle of affliction. From the Book of Job we might infer that He also actually appeared to him. He is more faithful than men. No soul that in the midst of wrath lays hold upon His love, whether with a firm or with a trembling hand, is suffered to be lost.

PSALM LXXXIX.

PRAYER FOR A RENEWAL OF THE MERCIES OF DAVID.

2 OF the loving-kindnesses of Jahve for ever will I sing,
  To remote generations will I make known Thy faithfulness with my mouth.
3 For I say: For ever is mercy being built up,
  In the heavens—there dost Thou establish Thy faithfulness.

4 "I have made a covenant with My chosen,
  I have sworn unto David My servant:
5 For ever will I establish thy seed,
  And build up thy throne to remote generations." (*Sela.*)

6 And the heavens praise Thy wondrousness, Jahve,
  Thy faithfulness also in the assembly of the holy ones.
7 For who in the sky can be compared to Jahve,
  Who among the sons of the gods is like unto Jahve?

8 A God terrible in the great council of the holy ones,
  And fearful above all those who are round about Him.

9 Jahve, God of hosts, who is as Thou?!
A mighty One, Jāh, and Thy faithfulness is round about Thee.

10 Thou art He who restraineth the pride of the sea;
When its waves arise, Thou stillest them.
11 Thou hast crushed Rahab as one that is slain,
By the arm of Thy might hast Thou scattered Thy foes.

12 Thine are the heavens, Thine also is the earth;
The earth and that which filleth it hast Thou founded.
13 North and south, Thou hast created them;
Tabor and Hermon shout for joy at Thy name.

14 Thine is an arm with heroic strength,
Strong is Thy hand, exalted is Thy right hand.
15 Righteousness and right is the foundation of Thy throne,
Mercy and truth stand waiting before Thee.

16 Blessed are the people who know the joyful sound,
Who walk, O Jahve, in the light of Thy countenance!
17 In Thy name do they rejoice continually,
And through Thy righteousness are they exalted.

18 For the glory of their mightiness art Thou,
And through Thy favour is our horn exalted.
19 For to Jahve belongeth our shield,
And to the Holy One of Israel our king.

20 Once Thou spakest in vision to Thy familiar one, and saidst:
"I have granted help to a mighty one,
I have raised a stripling out of the people.
21 I have found David My servant,
With My holy oil have I anointed him;

22 With whom My hand shall be stedfast,
My arm also shall strengthen him.
23 An enemy shall not ensnare him,
And the son of wantonness shall not oppress him.

24 I will break in pieces his oppressors before him,
And I will smite those who hate him.
25 And My faithfulness and My mercy are with him,
And in My Name shall his horn be exalted.
26 I will set his hand upon the sea,
And his right hand upon the rivers.

27 He shall cry unto Me : My Father art Thou,
My God, and the Rock of my salvation !
28 In return I will make him My first-born,
The highest with respect to the kings of the earth.

29 For ever will I preserve to him My mercy,
And My covenant shall be inviolable with him.
30 I will make his seed to endure for ever,
And his throne like the days of heaven.

31 If his children shall forsake My law
And walk not in My judgments ;
32 If they profane My statutes
And keep not My commandments :

33 Then will I visit their transgression with the rod,
And their iniquity with stripes ;
34 Nevertheless My loving-kindness will I not break off from him,
And will not belie My faithfulness—

35 I will not profane My covenant
Nor alter the vow of My lips.
36 One thing have I sworn by My holiness ;
Verily I will not deceive David :

37 His seed shall endure to eternity,
And his throne as the sun before Me.
38 As the moon shall it continue for ever—
And the witness in the sky is faithful !" (*Sela.*)

39 And Thou Thyself hast rejected and despised,
Thou hast been wroth with Thine anointed ;

40 Thou hast shaken off from Thee the covenant of Thy servant,
   Thou hast profaned his diadem to the earth.

41 Thou hast broken down all his hedges,
   Thou hast laid his strongholds in ruins.
42 All who pass by the way spoil him,
   He is become a reproach to his neighbours.

43 Thou hast exalted the right hand of his oppressors,
   Thou hast made all his enemies to rejoice.
44 Thou didst also turn back the edge of his sword,
   And didst not hold him erect in the battle.

45 Thou hast caused him to lose his splendour,
   And hast cast his throne down to the ground.
46 Thou hast shortened the days of his youth,
   Thou hast covered him round with shame. (*Sela.*)

47 How long, Jahve, wilt Thou hide Thyself for ever,
   Shall Thy wrath burn like fire?
48 Remember: I— how utterly perishable!
   For what vanity hast Thou created all the children of men!
49 Who is the man that should live and not see death,
   That should be able to secure his soul against the nether world? (*Sela.*)

50 Where are Thy former loving-kindnesses, Lord,
   Which Thou hast sworn to David in Thy faithfulness?
51 Remember, Lord, the reproach of Thy servants,
   That I carry in my bosom the reproach of many peoples,
52 Which reproach—Thine enemies, Jahve!—
   Which reproach the footsteps of Thine anointed.

53   BLESSED BE JAHVE FOR EVERMORE!
              AMEN, AND AMEN.

After having recognised the fact that the double inscription of Ps. lxxxviii. places two irreconcilable statements concerning the origin of that Psalm side by side, we renounce the artifices by which Ethan (אֵיתָן*) the Ezrahite, of the tribe of Judah (1 Kings v. 11 [iv. 31], 1 Chron. ii. 6), is made to be one and the same person with Ethan (Jeduthun) the son of Kushaiah the Merarite, of the tribe of Levi (1 Chron. xv. 17, vi. 29–32 [44–47]), the master of the music together with Asaph and Heman, and the chief of the six classes of musicians over whom his six sons were placed as sub-directors (1 Chron. ch. xxv.).

The collector has placed the Psalms of the two Ezrahites together. Without this relationship of the authors the juxta-position would also be justified by the reciprocal relation in which the two Psalms stand to one another by their common, striking coincidences with the Book of Job. As to the rest, however, Ps. lxxxviii. is a purely individual, and Ps. lxxxix. a thoroughly national Psalm. Both the poetical character and the situation of the two Psalms are distinct.

The circumstances in which the writer of Ps. lxxxix. finds himself are in most striking contradiction to the promises given to the house of David. He revels in the contents of these promises, and in the majesty and faithfulness of God, and then he pours forth his intense feeling of the great distance between these and the present circumstances in complaints over the afflicted lot of the anointed of God, and prays God to be mindful of His promises, and on the other hand, of the reproach by which at this time His anointed and His people are over-whelmed. The anointed one is not the nation itself (Hitzig), but he who at that time wears the crown. The crown of the king is defiled to the ground; his throne is cast down to the earth; he is become grey-headed before his time, for all the fences of his land are broken through, his fortresses fallen and his enemies have driven him out of the field, so that reproach and scorn follow him at every step.

There was no occasion for such complaints in the reign of Solomon; but surely in the time of Rehoboam, into the first decade of whose reign Ethan the Ezrahite may have survived king Solomon, who died at the age of sixty. In the fifth year of Rehoboam, Shishak (שִׁישַׁק = $\Sigma\acute{\epsilon}\sigma o\gamma\chi\iota s$ = *Sheshonk I.*), the

---

* This name אֵיתָן is also Phœnician in the form יתן, *Itan*, Ιτανί; יתנבל, *litan*, is Phœnician, and equivalent to בעל.

first Pharaoh of the twenty-second (Bubastic) dynasty, marched against Jerusalem with a large army gathered together out of many nations, conquered the fortified cities of Judah, and spoiled the Temple and Palace, even carrying away with him the golden shields of Solomon—a circumstance which the history bewails in a very especial manner. At that time Shemaiah preached repentance, in the time of the greatest calamity of war; king and princes humbled themselves; and in the midst of judgment Jerusalem accordingly experienced the gracious forbearance of God, and was spared. God did not complete his destruction, and there also again went forth דברים טובים, *i.e.* (cf. Josh. xxiii. 14, Zech. i. 13) kindly comforting words from God, in Judah. Such is the narrative in the Book of Kings (1 Kings xiv. 25-28) and as supplemented by the chronicler (2 Chron. xii. 1-12).

During this very period Ps. lxxxix. took its rise. The young Davidic king, whom loss and disgrace make prematurely old, is Rehoboam, that man of Jewish appearance whom Pharaoh Sheshonk is bringing among other captives before the god Amun in the monumental picture of Karnak, and who bears before him in his embattled ring the words *Judhmelek* (King of Judah)—one of the finest and most reliable discoveries of Champollion, and one of the greatest triumphs of his system of hieroglyphics.*

Ps. lxxxix. stands in kindred relationship not only to Ps. lxxiv., but besides Ps. lxxix., also to Ps. lxxvii., lxxviii., all of which glance back to the earliest times in the history of Israel. They are all Asaphic Psalms, partly old Asaphic (lxxvii., lxxviii.), partly later ones (lxxiv., lxxix.). From this fact we see that the Psalms of Asaph were the favourite models in that school of the four wise men to which the two Ezrahites belong.

Vers. 2-5. The poet, who, as one soon observes, is a הכם (for the very beginning of the Psalm is remarkable and ingenious), begins with the confession of the inviolability of the mercies promised to the house of David, *i.e.* of the חַסְדֵי דָוִד

---

* Vid. Blau, *Sisaqs Zug gegen Juda*, illustrated from the monument in Karnak, *Deutsche Morgenländ. Zeitschr.* xv. 233-250.

הַחֲסָדִים, Isa. lv. 3.* God's faithful love towards the house of David, a love faithful to His promises, will he sing without ceasing, and make it known with his mouth, i.e. audibly and publicly (cf. Job xix. 16), to the distant posterity. Instead of הַסְדֵי, we find here, and also in Lam. iii. 22, הַסְדֵּי with a not merely slightly closed syllable. The *Lamed* of לְדֹר וָדֹר is, according to ciii. 7, cxlv. 12, the dativ al *Lamed*. With כִּי־אָמַרְתִּי (LXX., Jerome, contrary to ver. 3*b*, ὅτι εἶπας) the poet bases his resolve upon his conviction. נִבְנָה means not so much to be upheld in building, as to be in the course of continuous building (*e.g.* Job xxii. 23, Mal. iii. 15, of an increasingly prosperous condition). Loving-kindness is for ever (accusative of duration) in the course of continuous building, viz. upon the unshakeable foundation of the promise of grace, inasmuch as it is fulfilled in accordance therewith. It is a building with a most solid foundation, which will not only not fall into ruins, but, adding one stone of fulfilment upon another, will rise ever higher and higher. שָׁמַיִם then stands first as *casus absol.*, and בָּהֶם is, as in xix. 5, a pronoun having a backward reference to it. In the heavens, which are exalted above the rise and fall of things here below, God establishes His faithfulness, so that it stands fast as the sun above the earth, although the condition of things here below seems sometimes to contradict it (cf. cxix. 89). Now follow in vers. 4, 5 the direct words of God, the sum of the promises given to David and to his seed in 2 Sam. ch. vii., at which the poet arrives more naturally in vers. 20 sqq. Here they are strikingly devoid of connection. It is the special substance of the promises that is associated in thought with the "loving-kindness" and "truth" of ver. 3, which is expanded as it were appositionally therein. Hence also אָכִין and תָּכִין, וּבָנִיתִי and יִבְנֶה correspond to one another. David's seed, by virtue of divine faithfulness, has an eternally sure existence; Jahve builds up David's throne "into generation and generation," inasmuch as He causes it to rise ever fresh and vigorous, never as that which is growing old and feeble.

Vers. 6–9. At the close of the promises in vers. 4, 5 the

---

* The Vulgate renders: *Misericordias Domini in æternum cantabo.* The second Sunday after Easter takes its name from this rendering.

music is to become *forte*. And וְיוֹדוּ attaches itself to this jubilant *Sela*. In vers. 6-19 there follows a hymnic description of the exalted majesty of God, more especially of His omnipotence and faithfulness, because the value of the promise is measured by the character of the person who promises. The God of the promise is He who is praised by the heavens and the holy ones above. His way of acting is פֶּלֶא, of a transcendent, paradoxical, wondrous order, and as such the heavens praise it; it is praised (יוֹדוּ, according to Ges. § 137, 3) in the assembly of the holy ones, *i.e.* of the spirits in the other world, the angels (as in Job v. 1, xv. 15, cf. Deut. xxxiii. 2), for He is peerlessly exalted above the heavens and the angels. שַׁחַק, poetic singular instead of שְׁחָקִים (*vid. supra* on lxxvii. 18), which is in itself already poetical; and עָרַךְ, not, as *e.g.* in Isa. xl. 18, in the signification to co-ordinate, but in the medial sense : to rank with, be equal to. Concerning בְּנֵי אֵלִים, *vid.* on xxix. 1. In the great council (concerning סוֹד, of both genders, perhaps like בּוֹס, *vid.* on xxv. 14) of the holy ones also, Jahve is terrible; He towers above all who are about Him (1 Kings xxii. 19, cf. Dan. vii. 10) in terrible majesty. רַבָּה might, according to lxii. 3, lxxviii. 15, be an adverb, but according to the order of the words it may more appropriately be regarded as an adjective; cf. Job xxxi. 34, כִּי אֶעֱרוֹץ הָמוֹן רַבָּה, "when I feared the great multitude." In ver. 9 He is apostrophized with אֱלֹהֵי צְבָאוֹת as being the One exalted above the heavens and the angels. The question "Who is as Thou?" takes its origin from Ex. xv. 11. חֲסִין is not the construct form, but the principal form, like גְּבִיר, יָדִיד, עָוִיל, and is a Syriasm; for the verbal stem ܚܣܢ is native to the Aramaic, in which ܚܣܝܢ = יָדַי. In יָהּ, what God is is reduced to the briefest possible expression (*vid.* lxviii. 19). In the words, "Thy faithfulness compasseth Thee round about," the primary thought of the poet again breaks through. Such a God it is who has the faithfulness with which He fulfils all His promises, and the promises given to the house of David also, as His constant surrounding. His glory would only strike one with terror; but the faithfulness which encompasses Him softens the sunlike brilliancy of His glory, and awakens trust in so majestic a Ruler.

Vers. 10-15. At the time of the poet the nation of the

house of David was threatened with assault from violent foes; and this fact gives occasion for this picture of God's power in the kingdom of nature. He who rules the raging of the sea, also rules the raging of the sea of the peoples, lxv. 8. גֵאוּת, a proud rising, here of the sea, like גֵאוּת in xlvi. 4. Instead of בְּשׂוֹא, Hitzig pleasantly enough reads בְּשִׂיא = בְּשִׂיאוֹ from שָׂאָה; but שׂוֹא is also possible so far as language is concerned, either as an infinitive = נְשׂוֹא, xxviii. 2, Isa. i. 14 (instead of שְׂאֵת), or as an infinitival noun, like שִׂיא, loftiness, Job xx. 6, with a likewise rejected *Nun*. The formation of the clause favours our taking it as a verb: when its waves rise, Thou stillest them. From the natural sea the poet comes to the sea of the peoples; and in the doings of God at the Red Sea a miraculous subjugation of both seas took place at one and the same time. It is clear from lxxiv. 13-17, Isa. li. 9, that Egypt is to be understood by *Rahab* in this passage as in lxxxvii. 4. The word signifies first of all impetuosity, violence, then a monster, like " the wild beast of the reed," lxviii. 31, *i.e.* the leviathan or the dragon. דִּכִּאתָ is conjugated after the manner of the *Lamed He* verbs, as in xliv. 20. בֶּחָלָל is to be understood as describing the event or issue (*vid.* xviii. 43): so that in its fall the proudly defiant kingdom is like one fatally smitten. Thereupon in vers. 12-15 again follows in the same co-ordination first the praise of God drawn from nature, then from history. Jahve's are the heavens and the earth. He is the Creator, and for that very reason the absolute owner, of both. The north and the right hand, *i.e.* the south, represent the earth in its entire compass from one region of the heavens to the other. Tabor on this side of the Jordan represents the west (cf. Hos. v. 1), and Hermon opposite the east of the Holy Land. Both exult by reason of the name of God; by their fresh, cheerful look they give the impression of joy at the glorious revelation of the divine creative might manifest in themselves. In ver. 14 the praise again enters upon the province of history. " An arm with (עִם) heroic strength," says the poet, inasmuch as he distinguishes between the attribute inherent in God and the medium of its manifestation in history. His throne has as its מָכוֹן, *i.e.* its immovable foundation (Prov. xvi. 12, xxv. 5), righteousness of action and right, by which all action is regulated, and which is unceasingly realized by means of the action

And mercy and truth wait upon Him. קִדֵּם פָּנֶיךָ is not: to go before any one (הִלֵּךְ לִפְנֵי, lxxxv. 14), but anticipatingly to present one's self to any one, lxxxviii. 14, xcv. 2, Mic. vi. 6. Mercy and truth, these two genii of sacred history (xliii. 3), stand before His face like waiting servants watching upon His nod.

Vers. 16–19. The poet has now described what kind of God He is upon whose promise the royal house in Israel depends. Blessed, then, is the people that walks in the light of His countenance. הָלַךְ of a self-assured, stately walk. The words יֹדְעֵי תְרוּעָה are the statement of the ground of the blessing interwoven into the blessing itself: such a people has abundant cause and matter for exultation (cf. lxxxiv. 5). תְּרוּעָה is the festive sound of joy of the mouth (Num. xxiii. 21), and of trumpets or sackbuts (xxvii. 6). This confirmation of the blessing is expanded in vers. 17–19. Jahve's שֵׁם, i.e. revelation or manifestation, becomes to them a ground and object of unceasing joy; by His צְדָקָה, i.e. the rigour with which He binds Himself to the relationship He has entered upon with His people and maintains it, they are exalted above abjectness and insecurity. He is תִּפְאֶרֶת עֻזָּמוֹ, the ornament of their strength, i.e. their strength which really becomes an ornament to them. In ver. 18*b* the poet declares Israel to be this happy people. Pinsker's conjecture, קַרְנָם (following the Targum), destroys the transition to ver. 19, which is formed by ver. 18*b*. The plural reading of Kimchi and of older editions (*e.g.* Bomberg's), קַרְנֵינוּ, is incompatible with the figure; but it is immaterial whether we read תָּרִים with the *Chethîb* (Targum, Jerome), or with the *Kerî* (LXX., Syriac) תָּרוּם.* כִּי מָגִנֵּנוּ and מַלְכֵּנוּ in ver. 19 are parallel designations of the human king of Israel; כִּי as in xlvii. 10, but not in lxxxiv. 10. For we are not compelled, with a total disregard of the limits to the possibilities of style (Ew. § 310, *a*), to render ver. 19*b*: and the Holy One

---

* *Zur Geschichte des Karaismus*, pp. קפא and קפב, according to which, reversely, in Josh. v. 1 עֲבָרֵנוּ is to be read instead of עָבְרָם, and Isa. xxxiii. 2 וּרְעֵנוּ instead of וּזְרֹעָם, Ps. xii. 8 תִּשְׁמְרֶנּוּ instead of תִּשְׁמְרֵם, Mic. vii. 19 חֲטָאתֵנוּ instead of חַטֹּאתָם, Job xxxii. 8 תְּבִינֶנּוּ instead of תְּבִינֵם, Prov. xxv. 27 כְּבוֹדֵנוּ instead of כְּבוֹדָם (the limiting of our honour brings honour,—an unlikely interpretation of the חקר).

of Israel, (as to Him, He) is our King (Hitzig), since we do not bring down the Psalm beyond the time of the kings. Israel's shield, Israel's king, the poet says in the holy defiant confidence of faith, is Jahve's, belongs to the Holy One of Israel, *i.e.* he stands as His own possession under the protection of Jahve, the Holy One, who has taken Israel to Himself for a possession; it is therefore impossible that the Davidic throne should become a prey to any worldly power.

Vers. 20–23. Having thus again come to refer to the king of Israel, the poet now still further unfolds the promise given to the house of David. The present circumstances are a contradiction to it. The prayer to Jahve, for which the way is thus prepared, is for the removal of this contradiction. A long line, extending beyond the measure of the preceding lines, introduces the promises given to David. With אָז the respective period of the past is distinctly defined. The intimate friend of Jahve (חָסִיד) is Nathan (1 Chron. xvii. 15) or David, according as we translate בְּחָזוֹן "in a vision" or "by means of a vision." But side by side with the לַחֲסִידְךָ we also find the preferable reading לַחֲסִידֶיךָ, which is followed in the renderings of the LXX., Syriac, Vulgate, Targum, Aquila, Symmachus, and the Quarta, and is adopted by Rashi, Aben-Ezra, and others, and taken up by Heidenheim and Baer. The plural refers to Samuel and Nathan, for the statement brings together what was revealed to these two prophets concerning David. עֵזֶר is assistance as a gift, and that, as the designation of the person succoured by it (עַל שָׁוָה as in xxi. 6) with גִּבּוֹר shows, aid in battle. בָּחוּר (from בָּנַר = בָּחַר in the Mishna: to ripen, to be manly or of marriageable age, distinct from בָּחִיר in ver. 4) is a young man, *adolescens*: while yet a young man David was raised out of his humble lowly condition (lxxviii. 71) high above the people. When he received the promise (2 Sam. ch. vii.) he had been anointed and had attained to the lordship over all Israel. Hence the preterites in vers. 20, 21, which are followed by promissory futures from ver. 22 onwards. יִכּוֹן is *fut. Niph.*, to be established, to prove one's self to be firm, unchangeable (lxxviii. 37), a stronger expression than תִּהְיֶה, 1 Sam. xviii. 12, 14, 2 Sam. iii. 10. The *Hiph.* הִשִּׁיא, derived from נָשָׁא = נָשָׁה, to credit (*vid.* on Isa. xxiv. 2; Gesenius, Hengstenberg), does not give any suitable sense; it therefore signifies here as elsewhere, "to impose upon, surprise," with בְּ, as in lv. 16 with עַל. Ver. 23b is the echo of 2 Sam. vii. 10.

Vers. 24–30. What is promised in ver. 26 is world-wide dominion, not merely dominion within the compass promised in the primeval times (Gen. xv. 18, 2 Chron. ix. 26), in which case it ought to have been said וּבַנָּהָר (of the Euphrates). Nor does the promise, however, sound so definite and boundless here as in lxxii. 8, but it is indefinite and universal, without any need for our asking what rivers are intended by נְהָרוֹת. נָתַן בְּיָד, like שָׁלַח in Isa. xi. 14, of a giving and taking possession. With אַף־אָנִי (with retreated tone, as in cxix. 63, 125) God tells with what He will answer David's filial love. Him who is the latest-born among the sons of Jesse, God makes the first-born (בְּכוֹר from בָּכַר, to be early, opp. לָקֵשׁ, to be late, vid. Job, ii. 21), and therefore the most favoured of the "sons of the Most High," lxxxii. 6. And as, according to Deut. xxviii. 1, Israel is to be high (עֶלְיוֹן) above all nations of the earth, so David, Israel's king, in whom Israel's national glory realizes itself, is made as the high one (עֶלְיוֹן) with respect to the kings, i.e. above the kings, of the earth. In the person of David his seed is included; and it is that position of honour which, after having been only prelusively realized in David and Solomon, must go on being fulfilled in his seed exactly as the promise runs. The covenant with David is, according to ver. 29, one that shall stand for ever. David is therefore, as ver. 30 affirms, eternal in his seed; God will make David's seed and throne לְעַד, into eternal, i.e. into such as will abide for ever, like the days of heaven, everlasting. This description of eternal duration is, as also in Sir. xlv. 15, Bar. i. 11, taken from Deut. xi. 21; the whole of ver. 30 is a poetic reproduction of 2 Sam. vii. 16.

Vers. 31–38. Now follows the paraphrase of 2 Sam. vii. 14, that the faithlessness of David's line in relation to the covenant shall not interfere with (annul) the faithfulness of God—a thought with which one might very naturally console one's self in the reign of Rehoboam. Because God has placed the house of David in a filial relationship to Himself, He will chastise the apostate members as a father chastises his son; cf. Prov. xxiii. 13 sq. In 1 Chron. xvii. 13 the chronicler omits the words of 2 Sam. vii. 14 which there provide against perverted action (הַעֲוֹוֹת) on the part of the seed of David; our

Psalm proves their originality. But even if, as history shows, this means of chastisement should be ineffectual in the case of individuals, the house of David as such will nevertheless remain ever in a state of favour with Him. In ver. 34 וְחַסְדִּי לֹא־אָפִיר מֵעִמּוֹ corresponds to וְחַסְדִּי לֹא־יָסוּר מִמֶּנּוּ in 2 Sam. vii. 15 (LXX., Targum): the *fut. Hiph.* of פרר is otherwise always אָפֵר; the conjecture אָסִיר is therefore natural, yet even the LXX. translators (οὐ μὴ διασκεδάσω) had אפיר before them. בְּקֶר יְ as in xliv. 18. The covenant with David is sacred with God: He will not profane it (חִלֵּל, to loose the bonds of sanctity). He will fulfil what has gone forth from His lips, *i.e.* His vow, according to Deut. xxiii. 24 [23], cf. Num. xxx. 3 [2]. One thing hath He sworn to David; not: once = once for all (LXX.), for what is introduced by ver. 36 (cf. xxvii. 4) and follows in vers. 37, 38, is in reality one thing (as in lxii. 12, two). He hath sworn it *per sanctitatem suam*. Thus, and not *in sanctuario meo*, בְּקָדְשִׁי in this passage and Amos iv. 2 (cf. on lx. 8) is to be rendered, for elsewhere the expression is בִּ֠, Gen. xxii. 16, Isa. xlv. 23, or בְּנַפְשׁוֹ, Amos vi. 8, Jer. li. 14, or בִּשְׁמִי, Jer xliv. 26, or בִּימִינוֹ, Isa. lxii. 8. It is true we do not read any set form of oath in 2 Sam. ch. vii., 1 Chron. ch. xvii., but just as Isaiah, ch. liv. 9, takes the divine promise in Gen. viii. 21 as an oath, so the promise so earnestly and most solemnly pledged to David may be accounted by Psalm-poesy (here and in cxxxii. 11), which reproduces the historical matter of fact, as a promise attested with an oath. With אִם in ver. 36*b* God asserts that He will not disappoint David in reference to this one thing, viz. the perpetuity of his throne. This shall stand for ever as the sun and moon; for these, though they may one day undergo a change (cii. 27), shall nevertheless never be destroyed. In the presence of 2 Sam. vii. 16 it looks as if ver. 38*b* ought to be rendered: and as the witness in the clouds shall it (David's throne) be faithful (perpetual). By the witness in the clouds one would then have to understand the rainbow as the celestial memorial and sign of an everlasting covenant. Thus Luther, Geier, Schmid, and others. But neither this rendering, nor the more natural one, " and as the perpetual, faithful witness in the clouds," is admissible in connection with the absence of the כְּ of comparison. Accordingly Hengstenberg, following the example of Jewish expositors, renders: "and the witness in the clouds is perpetual," viz. the moon, so that the continuance of the Davidic line would be associated with the moon, just as the continuance of the condemned earth is with the rainbow. But in what sense would the moon have the name, without example elsewhere, of witness? Just as the Book of Job was the key to the conclusion of Ps. lxxxviii., so it is the key to this ambiguous verse of the Psalm before us. It has to be explained according to Job xvi. 19, where Job says: "*Behold in heaven is my witness, and my surety in the heights.*" Jahve, the אֵל נֶאֱמָן (Deut. vii. 9), seals His sworn promise with the words, "and the witness in the sky (ethereal heights) is faithful" (cf. concerning this *Waw* in connection with asseverations, Ew. § 340, c). Hengstenberg's objection, that Jahve cannot be called His own witness, is disposed of by the fact that עֵד frequently signifies the person who testifies anything concerning himself; in this sense, in fact, the whole Tôra is called עֵדוּת ה' (the testimony of Jahve).

Vers. 39–46. Now after the poet has turned his thoughts towards the beginnings of the house of David which were so rich in promise, in order that he might find comfort under the sorrowful present, the contrast of the two periods is become all the more sensible to him. With וְאַתָּה in ver. 39 (And Thou — the same who hast promised and affirmed this with an oath) his Psalm takes a new turn, for which reason it might even have been וְעַתָּה. זָנַח is used just as absolutely here as in xliv. 24, lxxiv. 1, lxxvii. 8, so that it does not require any object to be supplied out of ver. 39b. נֵאַרְתָּה in ver. 40 the LXX. renders κατέστρεψας; it is better rendered in Lam. ii. 7 ἀπετίναξε; for נאר is synonymous with נער, to shake off, push away, cf. Arabic *el-menáʿir*, the thrusters (with the lance). עַבְדֶּךָ is a vocational name of the king as such. His crown is sacred as being the insignia of a God-bestowed office. God has therefore made the sacred thing vile by casting it to the ground (הִלֵּל לָאָרֶץ, as in lxxiv. 17, to cast profaningly to the ground). The primary passage to vers. 41, 42 is lxxx. 13. "His hedges" are all the boundary and protecting fences which the land of the king has; and מִבְצָרָיו "the fortresses" of his land (in both instances without כל, because matters have not yet come to such a pass).* In שֵׁפְהוּ the notions of the king and of the land blend together. עֹבְרֵי־דָרֶךְ are the hordes of the peoples passing through the land. שְׁכֵנָיו are the neighbouring peoples that are otherwise liable to pay tribute to the house of David, who sought to take every possible advantage of that weakening of the Davidic kingdom. In ver. 44 we are neither to translate "rock of his sword" (Hengstenberg), nor "O rock" (Olshausen). צוּר does not merely signify *rupes*, but also from another root (צוּר, صار, originally of the grating or shrill noise produced by pressing and squeezing, then more particularly to cut or cut off with pressure, with a sharply set knife or the like) a knife or a blade (cf. English knife, and German *kneifen*, to nip): God has decreed it that the edge or blade of the sword of the king has been turned back by the enemy, that he has not been able to maintain his ground in battle (הֲקֵמֹתוֹ with *ē* instead of *î*, as also when the tone is not moved forward, Mic. v. 4). In ver. 45 the *Mem* of מִטְּהֲרוֹ, after the analogy of Ezek. xvi. 41, xxxiv. 10, and other passages, is a preposition: *cessare fecisti eum a splendore suo*. A noun מִטְהָר = מְטָהָר with *Dag. dirimens*,† like מִקְדָּשׁ Ex. xv. 17, מִזָּר Nah. iii. 17 (Abulwalîd, Aben-Ezra, Parchon, Kimchi, and others), in itself improbable in the signification required here, is not found either in post-biblical or in biblical Hebrew. טֹהַר, like צֹהַר, signifies first of all not purity, but brilliancy. Still the form טֹהַר does not lie at the basis of it in this instance; for the reading found here just happens not to be טָהֳרוֹ, but מִטָּהֳרוֹ; and the reading adopted by Norzi, Heidenheim, and Baer, as also by Nissel and others, so far as form is concerned is not distinct from it, viz. מִטָּהֳרוֹ (*mittŏharo*), the character of the *Shebâ* being determined by the

---

* In the list of the nations and cities conquered by King Sheshonk I. are found even cities of the tribe of Issachar, *e.g. Shen-ma-an*, Sunem; *vid.* Brugsch, *Reiseberichte*, S. 141-145, und Blau as referred to above.

† The view of Pinsker (*Einleitung*, S. 69), that this *Dag.* is not a sign of the doubling of the letter, but a diacritic point (that preceded the invention of the system of vowel-points), which indicated that the respective letter was to be pronounced with a *Chateph* vowel (*e.g. mitŏhar*), is incorrect. The doubling *Dag.* renders the *Shebâ* audible, and having once become audible it readily receives this or that colouring according to the nature of its consonant and of the neighbouring vowel.

analogy of the å following (cf. בְּעֶרָה, 2 Kings ii. 1), which presupposes the principal form טָהָר (Böttcher, § 386, cf. supra, ii. 31, note). The personal tenor of ver. 46a requires that it should be referred to the then reigning Davidic king, but not as dying before his time (Olshausen), but as becoming prematurely old by reason of the sorrowful experiences of his reign. The larger half of the kingdom has been wrested from him; Egypt and the neighbouring nations also threaten the half that remains to him; and instead of the kingly robe, shame completely covers him.

Vers. 47–52. After this statement of the present condition of things the psalmist begins to pray for the removal of all that is thus contradictory to the promise. The plaintive question, ver. 47, with the exception of one word, is *verbatim* the same as lxxix. 5. The wrath to which *quousque* refers, makes itself to be felt, as the intensifying (*vid.* xiii. 2) לִבְצֹח implies, in the intensity and duration of everlasting wrath. חֶלֶד is this temporal life which glides past secretly and unnoticed (xvii. 14); and זְכָר־אֲנִי is not equivalent to זְכָרֵנִי (instead of which by way of emphasis only זְכָרֵנִי אֲנִי can be said), but אֲנִי מֶה־חֶלֶד stands for מֶה־חֶלֶד אֲנִי—according to the sense equivalent to מֶה־חָדֵל אֲנִי, xxxix. 5, cf. 6. The conjecture of Houbigant and modern expositors, זְכֹר אֲדֹנָי (cf. ver. 51), is not needed, since the inverted position of the words is just the same as in xxxix. 5. In ver. 48b it is not pointed עַל־מַה שָּׁוְא, "wherefore (Job x. 2, xiii. 14) hast Thou in vain (cxxvii. 1) created?" (Hengstenberg), but עַל־מַה־שָּׁוְא, on account of or for what a nothing (מַה־שָּׁוְא belonging together as adjective and substantive, as in xxx. 10, Job xxvi. 14) hast Thou created all the children of men? (De Wette, Hupfeld, and Hitzig.) עַל, of the ground of a matter and direct motive, which is better suited to the question in ver. 49 than the other way of taking it: the life of all men passes on into death and Hades; why then might not God, within this brief space of time, this handbreadth, manifest Himself to His creatures as the merciful and kind, and not as the always angry God? The music strikes in here, and how can it do so otherwise than in elegiac *mesto?* If God's justice tarries and fails in this present world, then the Old Testament faith becomes sorely tempted and tried, because it is not able to find consolation in the life beyond. Thus it is with the faith of the poet in the present juncture of affairs, the outward appearance of which is in such perplexing contradiction to the loving-kindness sworn to David and also hitherto vouchsafed. חֲסָדִים has not the sense in this passage of promises of favour, as in 2 Chron. vi. 42, but proofs of favour; הָרִאשֹׁנִים glances back at the long period of the reigns of David and of Solomon.* The Asaph Psalm lxxvii. and the Tephilla Isa. ch. lxiii. contain similar complaints, just as in connection with ver. 51a one is reminded of the Asaph Psalm lxxix. 2, 10, and in connection with ver. 52 of lxxix. 12. The phrase נָשָׂא בְחֵיקוֹ is used in other instances of loving nurture, Num. xi. 12, Isa. xl. 11. In this passage it must have a sense akin to חֶרְפַּת עֲבָדֶיךָ. It is impossible on syntactic grounds to regard כָּל־רַבִּים עַמִּים as still dependent upon חֶרְפַּת (Ewald) or, as Hupfeld is fond of calling it, as a "referential" genitive. Can it be that the כֹּל is perhaps a mutilation of כְּלִמַּת, after Ezek. xxxvi. 15, as Böttcher suggests? We do not need this conjecture. For (1) to carry any one in one's bosom, if he is an enemy, may signify: to be obliged to cherish him with the vexation proceeding from him (Jer. xv. 15), without being able to get rid of him; (2) there is no doubt that רַבִּים can, after the manner of numerals, be placed before the substantive to which it belongs, xxxii. 10, Prov. xxxi. 29, 1 Chron. xxviii. 5, Neh. ix. 28; cf. the other position, e.g., in Jer. xvi. 16; (3) consequently כָּל־רַבִּים עַמִּים may signify the "totality of many peoples" just as well as כֹּל גּוֹיִם רַבִּים in Ezek. xxxi. 6. The poet complains as a member of the nation, as a citizen of the empire, that he is obliged to foster many nations in his bosom, inasmuch as the land of Israel was overwhelmed by the Egyptians and their allies, the Libyans, Troglodytes, and Ethiopians. The אֲשֶׁר which follows in ver. 52 cannot now be referred back over ver. 51b to חֶרְפַּת (quâ calumniâ), and yet the relative sense, not the confirmatory (because, quoniam), is at issue. We therefore refer it to עַמִּים, and take אֹיְבֶיךָ as an apposition, as in cxxxix. 20: who reproach Thee, (as) Thine

---

* The *Pasek* between הראשנים and אדני is not designed merely to remove the limited predicate from the Lord, who is indeed the First and the Last, but also to secure its pronunciation to the guttural *Aleph*, which might be easily passed over after *Mem;* cf. Gen. i. 27, xxi. 17, xxx 20, xlii. 21, and frequently.

enemies, Jahve, who reproach the footsteps (עִקְּבוֹת as in lxxvii. 20 with *Dag. dirimens*, which gives it an emotional turn) of Thine anointed, *i.e.* they follow him everywhere, wheresoever he may go, and whatsoever he may do. With these significant words, עִקְּבוֹת מְשִׁיחֶךָ, the Third Book of the Psalms dies away.

Ver. 53. The closing doxology of the Third Book.

FOURTH BOOK OF THE PSALTER.

Ps. XC.–CVI.

PSALM XC.

TAKING REFUGE IN THE LOVING-KINDNESS OF THE ETERNAL
ONE UNDER THE WRATHFUL JUDGMENT OF DEATH.

1 O LORD, Thou hast been a place of refuge for us in all generations!
2 Before the mountains were brought forth,
And Thou gavest birth to the earth and the world,
And from æon to æon Thou art God!
3 Thou turnest mortal man to dust,
And sayest: Return, ye children of men.
4 For a thousand years in Thine eyes
Are as yesterday when it passeth,
And a watch in the night.

5 Thou carriest them away as with a flood, they become a sleep,
In the morning they are as grass springing up again.
6 In the morning it flourisheth and springeth up again,
In the evening it is cut down and it drieth up.
7 For we are consumed by Thine anger,
And by Thy fierce anger are we scared away.
8 Thou hast set our iniquities before Thee,
Our most secret matter in the light of Thy countenance.

9 For all our days are passed away in Thy wrath;
We have spent our years as a whisper.

10 The days of our years—their sum is seventy years,
   And, if very many, eighty years;
   And their pride is labour and vanity,
   For it passed swiftly and we fled away.
11 Who knoweth the power of Thine anger
   And the fear of Thee according to Thy wrath?
12 Teach us rightly to number our days,
   That we may gain a wise heart!

13 Turn, Jahve—how long?!—
   And have compassion upon Thy servants.
14 Satisfy us at morning-dawn with Thy mercy,
   Then will we joy and rejoice all our days.
15 Make us glad according to the days in which Thou hast humbled us,
   The years wherein we have seen evil.
16 Let Thy work appear unto Thy servants,
   And Thy glory upon their children.
17 And let the graciousness of the Lord our God be upon us,
   And the work of our hands do Thou establish upon us,
   Yea, the work of our hands establish Thou it!

The Fourth Book of the Psalms, corresponding to the ספר במדבר of the Pentateuch, begins with a *Prayer of Moses the man of God*, which comes out of the midst of the dying off of the older generation during the march through the wilderness. To the name, which could not be allowed to remain so bald, because next to Abraham he is the greatest man known to the Old Testament history of redemption, is added the title of honour אִישׁ הָאֱלֹהִים (as in Deut. xxxiii. 1, Josh. xiv. 6), an ancient name of the prophets which expresses the close relationship of fellowship with God, just as "servant of Jahve" expresses the relationship of service, in accordance with the special office and in relation to the history of redemption, into which Jahve has taken the man and into which he himself has entered. There is scarcely any written memorial of antiquity which so brilliantly justifies the testimony of tradition concerning its origin as does this Psalm, which may have been preserved in some one or other of the older works, perhaps the "Book of Jashar" (Josh. x. 13, 2 Sam. i. 18), until the time of the final redaction of the Psalter. Not alone with respect to its contents, but also with reference to the form of its language, it is perfectly suitable to Moses. Even Hitzig can bring nothing of importance against this view, for the objection that the author in ver. 1 glances back upon past generations, whilst Israel was only born in the time of Moses, is removed by the consideration that the existence of Israel reaches back into the patriarchal times; and there is as little truth in the assertion that the *Piel* שַׂבְּעֵנוּ in ver. 14 instead of the *Hiphil* brings the Psalm down into very late times, as in the idea that the *Hiph.* וְהַאֲבַדְתָּ in cxliii. 12 instead of the *Piel* carries this Ps. cxliii. back into very early times. These trifling points dwindle down to nothing in comparison with the fact that Ps. xc. bears within itself distinct traces of the same origin as the song הַאֲזִינוּ (Deut. ch. xxxii.), the blessing of Moses (Deut. ch. xxxiii.), the discourses in Deuteronomy, and in general the directly Mosaic portions of the Pentateuch. The Book of the Covenant, together with the Decalogue (Ex. ch. xix.-xxiv.) and Deuteronomy (with the exception of its supplement), are regarded by us, on very good grounds, as the largest originally Mosaic constituent parts of the Pentateuch. The Book of Deuteronomy is תּוֹרַת מֹשֶׁה in a pre-eminent sense.

Vers. 1–4. The poet begins with the confession that the Lord has proved Himself to His own, in all periods of human history, as that which He was before the world was and will be for evermore. God is designedly appealed to by the name אֲדֹנָי, which frequently occurs in the mouth of Moses in the middle books of the Pentateuch, and also in the Song at the Sea, Ex. xv. 17 and in Deut. iii. 24. He is so named here as the Lord ruling over human history with an exaltation ever the same. Human history runs on in דֹּר וָדֹר, so that one period (περίοδος) with the men living cotemporaneous with it goes and another comes; the expression is Deuteronomic (Deut. xxxii. 7). Such a course of generations lies behind the poet; and in them all the Lord has been מָעוֹן to His church, out of the heart of which the poet discourses. This expression too is Deuteronomic (Deut. xxxiii. 27). מָעוֹן signifies a habitation, dwelling-place (*vid.* on xxvi. 8), more especially God's heavenly and earthly dwelling-place, then the dwelling-place which God

Himself is to His saints, inasmuch as He takes up to Himself, conceals and protects, those who flee to Him from the wicked one and from evil, and turn in to Him (lxxi. 3, xci. 9). In order to express *fuisti* הָיִיתָ was indispensable; but just as *fuisti* comes from *fuo*, φύω, הָיָה (הָוָה) signifies not a closed, shut up being, but a being that discloses itself, consequently it is *fuisti* in the sense of *te exhibuisti*. This historical self-manifestation of God is based upon the fact that He is אֵל, i.e. might absolutely, or the absolutely Mighty One; and He was this, as ver. 2 says, even before the beginning of the history of the present world, and will be in the distant ages of the future as of the past. The foundation of this world's history is the creation. The combination אֶרֶץ וְתֵבֵל shows that this is intended to be taken as the object. וַתְּחוֹלֵל (with *Metheg* beside the ê of the final syllable, which is deprived of its accent, *vid.* on xviii. 20) is the language of address (Rashi): that which is created is in a certain sense born from God (יָלִד), and He brings it forth out of Himself; and this is here expressed by חוֹלֵל (as in Deut. xxxii. 18, cf. Isa. li. 2), creation being compared to travail which takes place amidst pains (*Psychology*, S. 114; tr. p. 137). If, after the example of the LXX. and Targum, one reads as passive וַתְּחוֹלָל (Böttcher, Olshausen, Hitzig) from the *Pulal* חוֹלָל, Prov. viii. 24,—and this commends itself, since the pre-existence of God can be better dated back beyond facts than beyond the acts of God Himself,—then the conception remains essentially the same, since the Eternal and Absolute One is still to be thought of as מְחוֹלֵל. The fact that the mountains are mentioned first of all, harmonizes with Deut. xxxiii. 15. The *modus consecutivus* is intended to say: before the mountains were brought forth and Thou wast in labour therewith . . . The forming of the mountains consequently coincides with the creation of the earth, which is here as a body or mass called אֶרֶץ, and as a continent with the relief of mountains and lowlands is called תֵּבֵל (cf. אֶרֶץ תֵּבֵל, Prov. viii. 31, Job xxxvii. 12). To the double clause with טֶרֶם *seq. præt.* (cf. on the other hand *seq. fut.* Deut. xxxi. 21) is appended וּמֵעוֹלָם as a second definition of time: before the creation of the world, and from eternity to eternity. The Lord was God before the world was—that is the first assertion of ver. 2; His divine existence reaches out of the unlimited past into the unlimited future—this is the second. אַל is not vocative, which it sometimes, though rarely, is in the Psalms; it is a predicate, as *e.g.* in Deut. iii. 24.

This is also to be seen from vers. 3, 4, when ver. 3 now more definitely affirms the omnipotence of God, and ver. 4 the supra-temporality of God or the omnipresence of God in time. The LXX. misses the meaning when it brings over אַל from ver. 2, and reads אַל־תָּשֵׁב. The shorter future form תָּשֵׁב for תָּשִׁיב stands poetically instead of the longer, as *e.g.* in xi. 6, xxv. 9; cf. the same thing in the *inf. constr.* in Deut. xxvi. 12, and both instances together in Deut. xxxii. 8. The poet intentionally calls the generation that is dying away אֱנוֹשׁ, which denotes m̲a̲n̲ from the side of his frailty or perishableness; and the new generation בְּנֵי־אָדָם, with which is combined the idea of entrance upon life. It is clear that תָּשֵׁב עַד־דַּכָּא is intended to be understood according to Gen. iii. 19; but it is a question whether דַּכָּא is conceived of as an adjective (with mutable *ā*), as in xxxiv. 19, Isa. lvii. 15: Thou puttest men back into the condition of crushed ones (cf. on the construction Num. xxiv. 24), or whether as a neutral feminine from דַּךְ (=דַּכָּה): Thou changest them into that which is crushed = dust, or whether as an abstract substantive like דַּכָּה, or according to another reading (cf. cxxvii. 2) דַּכָּא, in Deut. xxiii. 2: to cr̲u̲shing. This last is the simplest way of taking it, but it comes to one and the same thing with the second, since דַּכָּא signifies crushing in the neuter sense. A *fut. consec.* follows. The fact that God causes one generation to die off has as its consequence that He calls another into being (cf. the Arabic epithet of God *el-muʻid* = הַמֵּשִׁיב, the Resuscitator). Hofmann and Hitzig take תָּשֵׁב as imperfect on account of the following וַתֹּאמֶר: Thou didst decree mortality for men; but the *fut. consec.* frequently only expresses the sequence of the thoughts or the connection of the matter, *e.g.* after a future that refers to that which is constantly taking place, Job xiv. 10. God causes men to die without letting them die out; for—so it continues in ver. 4—a thousand years is to Him a very short period, not to be at all taken into account. What now is the connection between that which confirms and that which is confirmed here? It is not so much ver. 3 that is confirmed as ver. 2, to which the former serves for explanation, viz. this, that God as the Almighty (אֵל), in the midst of this change of generations, which is His work, remains Himself eternally the same. This ever the same, absolute existence has its ground herein, that time, although God fills it up with His working, is no limitation to Him. A thousand years, which would make any man who might live through them weary of life, are to Him like a vanishing point. The proposition, as 2 Pet. iii. 8 shows, is also true when reversed: "One day is with the Lord as a thousand years." He is however exalted above all time, inasmuch as the longest period appears to Him very short, and in the shortest period the greatest work can be executed by Him. The standpoint of the first comparison, "*as yesterday*," is taken towards the end of the thousand of years. A whole millennium appears to God, when He glances over it, just as the yesterday does to us when (כִּי) it is passing by (יַעֲבֹר), and we, standing on the border of the opening day, look back upon the day that is gone. The second comparison is an advance upon the first, and an advance also in form, from the fact that the *Caph similitudinis* is wanting: a thousand years are to God a watch in the night. אַשְׁמוּרָה is a night-watch, of which the Israelites reckoned three, viz. the first, the middle, and the morning watch (*vid.* Winer's *Realwörterbuch* s. v. *Nachtwache*). It is certainly not without design that the poet says אַשְׁמוּרָה בַלַּיְלָה instead of אַשְׁמֹרֶת הַלַּיְלָה. The night-time is the time for sleep; a watch in the night is one that is slept away, or at any rate passed in a sort of half-sleep. A day that is past, as we stand on the end of it, still produces upon us the impression of a course of time by reason of the events which we can recall; but a night passed in sleep, and now even a fragment of the night, is devoid of all trace to us, and is therefore as it were timeless. Thus is it to God with a thousand years: they do not last long to Him; they do not affect Him; at the close of them, as at the beginning, He is the Absolute One (אֵל). Time is as nothing to Him, the Eternal One. The changes of time are to Him no barrier restraining the realization of His counsel —a truth which has a terrible and a consolatory side. The poet dwells upon the fear which it produces.

Vers. 5–8. Vers. 5, 6 tell us how great is the distance between men and this eternal selfsameness of God. The suffix of זְרַמְתָּם, referred to the thousand years, produces a synallage (since שָׁנָה is feminine), which is to be avoided whenever it is possible to do so; the reference to בְּנֵי־אָדָם, as being the principal object pointed to in what has gone before, is the more natural, to say the very least. In connection with both ways of applying it, זְרַם does not signify: to cause to rattle down like sudden heavy showers of rain; for the figure that God makes years, or that He makes men (Hitzig: the germs of their coming into being), to rain down from above, is fanciful and strange. זְרַם may also mean to sweep or wash away as with heavy rains, *abripere instar nimbi*, as the old expositors take it. So too Luther at one time: *Du reyssest sie dahyn* (Thou carriest them away), for which he substituted later: *Du lessest sie dahin faren wie einen Strom* (Thou causest them to pass away as a river); but זְרַם always signifies rain pouring down from above. As a sudden and heavy shower of rain, becoming a flood, washes everything away, so God's omnipotence sweeps men away. There is now no transition to another alien figure when the poet continues: שֵׁנָה יִהְיוּ. What is meant is the sleep of death, lxxvi. 6, שְׁנַת עוֹלָם, Jer. li. 39, 57, cf. יָשֵׁן xiii. 4. He whom a flood carries away is actually brought into a state of unconsciousness, he goes entirely to sleep, *i.e.* he dies.

From this point the poet certainly does pass on to another figure. The one generation is carried away as by a flood in the night season, and in the morning another grows up. Men are the subject of יַחֲלֹף, as of יִהְיוּ. The collective singular alternates with the plural, just as in ver. 3 the collective אֱנוֹשׁ alternates with בְּנֵי־אָדָם. The two members of ver. 5 stand in contrast. The poet describes the succession of the generations. One generation perishes as it were in a flood, and another grows up, and this also passes on to the same fate. The meaning in both verses of the חלף, which has been for the most part, after the LXX., Vulgate, and Luther, erroneously taken to be *praeterire = interire*, is determined in accordance with this idea. The general signification of this verb, which corresponds to the Arabic خلف, is "to follow or move after, to go into the place of another, and in general, of passing over from one place or state into another." Accordingly the *Hiphil* signifies to put into a new condition, cii. 27, to set a new thing on the place of an old one, Isa. ix. 9 [10], to gain new strength, to take fresh courage, Isa. xl. 31, xli. 1 ; and of plants : to send forth new shoots, Job xiv. 7; consequently the *Kal*, which frequently furnishes the perfect for the future *Hiphil* (Ew. § 127, *b*, and Hitzig on this passage), of plants signifies : to gain new shoots, not : to sprout (Targum, Syriac), but to sprout again or afresh, *regerminare*; cf. خَلَفَ, an after-growth, new wood. Perishing humanity renews its youth in ever new generations. Ver. 6*a* again takes up this thought : in the morning it grows up and shoots afresh, viz. the grass to which men are likened (a figure appropriated by Isa. ch. xl.), in the evening it is cut down and it dries up. Others translate מוֹלֵל to wither (root מלל, properly to be long and lax, to allow to hang down long, cf. אָמֵל, אֻמְלַל with أَمِلَ, to hope, *i.e.* to look forth into the distance) ; but (1) this *Pilel* of מול or *Poël* of מלל is not favourable to this intransitive way of taking it ; (2) the reflexive in lviii. 8 proves that מוֹלֵל signifies to cut off in the front or above, after which perhaps even xxxvii. 2, Job xiv. 2, xviii. 16, by comparison with Job xxiv. 24, are to be explained. In the last passage it runs: *as the top of the stalk they are cut off* (*fut. Niph.* of מלל). Such a cut or plucked ear of corn is called in Deut. xxiii. 26 מְלִילָה, a Deuteronomic hapaxlegomenon which favours our way of taking the יְמוֹלֵל (with a most general subject = יְמוֹלֵל). Thus, too, וְיָבֵשׁ is better attached to what precedes : the cut grass becomes parched hay. Just such an alternation of morning springing forth and evening drying up is the alternation of the generations of men.

The poet substantiates this in vers. 7 sq. from the experience of those amongst whom he comprehended himself in the לָנוּ of ver. 1. Hengstenberg takes ver. 7 to be a statement of the cause of the transitoriness set forth : its cause is the wrath of God ; but the poet does not begin כי באפך but כי כלינו. The chief emphasis therefore lies upon the perishing, and כי is not argumentative but explicative. If the subject of כלינו were men in general (Olshausen), then it would be elucidating *idem per idem*. But, according to ver. 1, those who speak here are those whose refuge the Eternal One is. The poet therefore speaks in the name of the church, and confirms the lot of men from that which his people have experienced even down to the present time. Israel is able out of its own experience to corroborate what all men pass through; it has to pass through the very same experience as a special decree of God's wrath on account of its sins. Therefore in vers. 7, 8 we stand altogether upon historical ground. The testimony of the inscription is here verified in the contents of the Psalm. The older generation that came out of Egypt fell a prey to the sentence of punishment, that they should gradually die off during the forty years' journey through the desert; and even Moses and Aaron, Joshua and Caleb only excepted, were included in this punishment on special grounds, Num. xiv. 26 sqq., Deut. i. 34–39. This it is over which Moses here laments. God's wrath is here called אַף and חֵמָה; just as the Book of Deuteronomy (in distinction from the other books of the Pentateuch) is fond of combining these two synonyms (Deut. ix. 19, xxix. 22, 27, cf. Gen. xxvii. 44 sq.). The breaking forth of the infinitely great opposition of the holy nature of God against sin has swept away the church in the person of its members, even down to the present moment; נִבְהַל as in civ. 29, cf. בֶּהָלָה, Lev. xxvi. 16. It is the consequence of their sins. עָוֹן signifies sin as the perversion of the right standing and conduct; עָלֻם, that which is veiled in distinction from manifest sins, is the sum-total of hidden moral, and that sinful, conduct. There is no necessity to regard עֲלֻמֵנוּ as a defective plural; עֲלָמִים signifies youth (from a radically distinct word, עָלַם); secret sins would therefore be called עֲלֻמוֹת according to xix. 13. God sets transgressions before Him when, because the measure is full and forgiveness is inadmissible, He makes them an object of punishment. שָׁתָּ (Kerî, as in viii. 7: שַׁתָּה, cf. vi. 4 וְאַתָּ, lxxiv. 6 וְעַתָּ) has the accent upon the *ultima* before an initial guttural. The parallel to לִמְאוֹר is לְנֶגְדְּךָ פָּנֶיךָ. אוֹר is light, and מָאוֹר is either a body of light, as the sun and moon, or, as in this passage, the circle of light which the light forms. The countenance of God (פְּנֵי ה׳) is God's nature in its inclination towards the world, and מְאוֹר פְּנֵי ה׳ is the doxa of His nature that is turned towards the world, which penetrates everything that is conformed to God as a gracious light (Num. vi. 25), and makes manifest to the bottom everything that is opposed to God and consumes it as a wrathful fire.

Vers. 9–12. After the transitoriness of men has now been confirmed in vers. 6 sq. out of the special experience of Israel, the fact that this particular experience has its ground in a divine decree of wrath is more definitely confirmed from the facts of this experience, which, as vers. 11 sq. complain, unfortunately have done so little to urge them on to the fear of God, which is the condition and the beginning of wisdom. In ver. 9 we distinctly hear the Israel of the desert speaking. That was a generation that fell a prey to the wrath of God (דּוֹר עֶבְרָתוֹ, Jer. vii. 29). עֶבְרָה is wrath that passes over, breaks through the bounds of subjectivity. All their days (cf. ciii. 15) are passed away (פָּנָה, to turn one's self, to turn, e.g. Deut. i. 24) in such wrath, i.e. thoroughly pervaded by it. They have spent their years like a sound (כְמוֹ־הֶגֶה), which has hardly gone forth before it has passed away, leaving no trace behind it ; the noun signifies a gentle dull sound, whether a murmur (Job xxxvii. 2) or a groan (Ezek. ii. 10). With בָּהֶם in ver. 10 the sum is stated : there are comprehended therein seventy years ; they include, run up to so many. Hitzig renders : the days wherein (בהם) our years consist are seventy years ; but שְׁנוֹתֵינוּ side by side with יְמֵי must be regarded as its more minute genitival definition, and the accentuation cannot be objected to. Beside the plural שָׁנִים the poetic plural שְׁנוֹת appears here, and it also occurs in Deut. xxxii. 7 (and nowhere else in the Pentateuch). That of which the sum is to be stated stands first of all as a *casus absol.* Luther's rendering : *Siebenzig Jar, wens hoch kompt so sinds achtzig* (seventy years, or at the furthest eighty years), as Symmachus also meant by his ἐν παραδόξῳ (in Chrysostom), is confirmed by the Talmudic הגיע לגבורה, " to attain to extreme old age" (*B. Moëd katan* 28a), and rightly approved of by Hitzig and Olshausen. גְּבוּרֹת signifies in lxxi. 16 full strength, here full measure. Seventy, or at most eighty years, were the average sum of the extreme term of life to which the generation dying out in the wilderness attained. וְרָהְבָּם the LXX. renders τὸ πλεῖον αὐτῶν, but רָהְבָּם is not equivalent to רֻבָּם. The verb רָהַב signifies to behave violently, e.g. of importunate entreaty, Prov. vi. 3, of insolent treatment, Isa. iii. 5, whence רַהַב (here רֹהַב), violence, impetuosity, and more especially a boastful vaunting appearance or coming forward, Job ix. 13, Isa. xxx. 7. The poet means to say that everything of which our life is proud (riches, outward appearance, luxury, beauty, etc.), when regarded in the right light, is after all only עָמָל, inasmuch as it causes us trouble and toil, and אָוֶן, because without any true intrinsic merit and worth. To this second predicate is appended the confirmatory clause. חִישׁ is *infin. adverb.* from חוּשׁ, חִישׁ, Deut. xxxii. 35: speedily, swiftly (Symmachus, the Quinta, and Jerome). The verb גּז signifies *transire* in all the Semitic dialects; and following this signification, which is applied transitively in Num. xi. 31, the Jewish expositors and Schultens correctly render: *nam transit velocissime.* Following upon the perfect גָּז, the *modus consecutivus* וַנָּעֻפָה maintains its retrospective signification. The strengthening of this mood by means of the intentional *ah* is more usual with the 1*st pers. sing.*, *e.g.* Gen. xxxii. 6, than with the 1*st pers. plur.*, as here and in Gen. xli. 11; Ew. § 232, *g*. The poet glances back from the end of life to the course of life. And life, with all of which it had been proud, appears as an empty burden; for it passed swiftly by and we fled away, we were borne away with rapid flight upon the wings of the past.

Such experience as this ought to urge one on to the fear of God; but how rarely does this happen! and yet the fear of God is the condition (stipulation) and the beginning of wisdom. The verb יָדַע in ver. 11*a*, just as it in general denotes not merely notional but practically living and efficient knowledge, is here used of a knowledge which makes that which is known conduce to salvation. The meaning of וְיִרְאָתְךָ is determined in accordance with this. The suffix is here either *gen. subj.*: according to Thy fearfulness (יִרְאָה as in Ezek. i. 18), or *gen. obj.*: according to the fear that is due to Thee, which in itself is at once (cf. v. 8, Ex. xx. 20, Deut. ii. 25) more natural, and here designates the knowledge which is so rarely found, as that which is determined by the fear of God, as a truly religious knowledge. Such knowledge Moses supplicates for himself and for Israel: to number our days teach us rightly to understand. 1 Sam. xxiii. 17, where יֹדֵעַ כֵּן signifies "he does not know it to be otherwise, he is well aware of it," shows how כֵּן is meant. Hitzig, contrary to the accentuation, draws it to לִמְנוֹת יָמֵינוּ; but "to number our days" is in itself equivalent to "hourly to contemplate the fleeting character and brevity of our lifetime;" and כִּי הוֹדַע prays for a true qualification for this, and one that accords with experience. The future that follows is well adapted to the call, as frequently aim and result. But הָבִיא is not to be taken, with Ewald and Hitzig, in the signification of bringing as an offering, a meaning this verb cannot have of itself alone (why should it not have been וְנִקְרִיב?). Böttcher also erroneously renders it after the analogy of Prov. ii. 10: "that we may bring wisdom into the heart," which ought to be בְּלֵב. הָבִיא, deriving its meaning from agriculture, signifies "to carry off, obtain, gain, prop. to bring in," viz. into the barn, 2 Sam. ix. 10, Hagg. i. 6; the produce of the field, and in a general way gain or profit, is hence called תְּבוּאָה. A wise heart is the fruit which one reaps or garners in from such numbering of the days, the gain which one carries off from so constantly reminding one's self of the end. לְבַב חָכְמָה is a poetically intensified expression for לֵב חָכָם, just as לֵב מַרְפֵּא in Prov. xiv. 30 signifies a calm easy heart.

Vers. 13–17. The prayer for a salutary knowledge, or discernment, of the appointment of divine wrath is now followed by the prayer for the return of favour, and the wish that God would carry out His work of salvation and bless Israel's undertakings to that end. We here recognise the well-known language of prayer of Moses in Ex. xxxii. 12, according to which שׁוּבָה is not intended as a prayer for God's return to Israel, but for the turning away of His anger; and the sigh עַד־מָתַי that is blended with it asks how long this being angry, which threatens to blot Israel out, is still to last. וְהִנָּחֵם is explained according to this same parallel passage: May God feel remorse or sorrow (which in this case coincide) concerning His servants, *i.e.* concerning the affliction appointed to them. The naming of the church by עֲבָדֶיךָ (as in Deut. ix. 27, cf. Ex. xxxii. 13 of the patriarchs) reminds one of Deut. xxxii. 36: *concerning His servants He shall feel compassion* (*Hithpa.* instead of the *Niphal*). The prayer for the turning of wrath is followed in ver. 14 by the prayer for the turning towards them of favour. In בַּבֹּקֶר there lies the thought that it has been night hitherto in Israel. "Morning" is therefore the beginning of a new season of favour. In שַׂבְּעֵנוּ (to which חַסְדֶּךָ is a second accusative of the object) is implied the thought that Israel whilst under wrath has been hungering after favour;

cf. the adjective עָנִי in the same tropical signification in Deut. xxxiii. 23. The supplicatory imperatives are followed by two moods expressive of intention: then will we, or: in order that we may rejoice and be glad; for futures like these set forth the intention of attaining something as a result or aim of what has been expressed just before: Ew. § 325, a. בְּכָל־יָמֵינוּ is not governed by the verbs of rejoicing (cxviii. 24), in which case it would have been בְּחַיֵּינוּ, but is an adverbial definition of time (cxlv. 2, Jer. xxxv. 8): within the term of life allotted to us. We see from ver. 15 that the season of affliction has already lasted for a long time. The duration of the forty years of wrath, which in the midst of their course seemed to them as an eternity, is made the measure of the reviving again that is earnestly sought. The plural יְמוֹת instead of יְמֵי is common only to our Psalm and Deut. xxxii. 7; it is not known elsewhere to Biblical Hebrew. And the poetical שְׁנוֹת instead of שְׁנֵי, which also occurs elsewhere, appears for the first time in Deut. xxxii. 7. The meaning of עִנִּיתָנוּ, in which יְמוֹת is specialized after the manner of a genitive, is explained from Deut. viii. 2 sqq., according to which the forty years' wandering in the wilderness was designed to humble (עַנּוֹת) and to prove Israel through suffering. At the close of these forty years Israel stands on the threshold of the Promised Land. To Israel all final hopes were closely united with the taking possession of this land. We learn from Gen. ch. xlix. that it is the horizon of Jacob's prophetic benediction. This Psalm too, in vers. 16, 17, terminates in the prayer for the attainment of this goal. The psalmist has begun in ver. 1 his adoration with the majestic divine name אֲדֹנָי; in ver. 13 he began his prayer with the gracious divine name יְהוָה; and now, where he mentions God for the third time, he gives to Him the twofold name, so full of faith, אֲדֹנָי אֱלֹהֵינוּ. אֶל used once alternates with the thrice repeated עַל: salvation is not Israel's own work, but the work of Jahve; it therefore comes from above, it comes and meets Israel. It is worthy of remark that the noun פֹּעַל occurs only in Deuteronomy in the whole Tôra, and that here also of the gracious rule of Jahve, ch. xxxii. 4, cf. xxxiii. 11. The church calls the work of the Lord מַעֲשֵׂה יָדֵינוּ in so far as He executes it through them. This expression מַעֲשֵׂה יָדַיִם as a designation of human undertakings runs through the whole of the Book of

Deuteronomy: ch. ii. 7, iv. 28, xi. 7, xiv. 29, xvi. 15, xxiv. 19, xxvii. 15, xxviii. 12, xxx. 9. In the work of the Lord the bright side of His glory unveils itself, hence it is called הָדָר; this too is a word not alien at least to the language of Deuteronomy, ch. xxxiii. 17. Therein is made manifest נֹעַם ה׳, His graciousness and condescension—an expression which David has borrowed from Moses in Ps. xxvii. 4. יִרְאֶה and יְהִי are optatives. בְּנֵנָה is an urgent request, *imperat. obsecrantis* as the old expositors say. With *Waw* the same thought is expressed over again (cf. Isa. lv. 1, וּלְכוּ, yea come)—a simple, childlike anadiplosis which vividly reminds us of the Book of Deuteronomy, which revolves in thoughts that are ever the same, and by that very means speaks deeply to the heart. Thus the Deuteronomic impression of this Psalm accompanies us from beginning to end, from מָעוֹן to מַעֲשֵׂה יָדַיִם. Nor will it now be merely accidental that the fondness for comparisons, which is a peculiarity of the Book of Deuteronomy (ch. i. 31, 44, viii. 5, xxviii. 29, 49, cf. xxviii. 13, 44, xxix. 17, 18), is found again in this Psalm.

PSALM XCI.

TALISMANIC SONG IN TIME OF WAR AND PESTILENCE.

First Voice:

1 HE who sitteth in the protection of the Most High,
 Who abideth in the shadow of the Almighty—

Second Voice:

2 I say to Jahve: My refuge and my fortress,
 My God in whom I trust.

First Voice:

3 For HE shall deliver thee from the snare of the fowler,
 from the destroying pestilence.
4 With His feathers shall He defend thee,
 And under His wings art thou hidden;
 A shield and buckler is His truth.
5 Thou shalt not be afraid for any nightly terror,
 For the arrow that flieth by day,

6 For the pestilence that walketh in the darkness,
    For the sickness that wasteth at noon-day.
7 A thousand may fall at thy side and ten thousand at thy right hand,
    It shall not come nigh thee—
8 Nay, with thine own eyes shalt thou look on
    And see the recompense of the wicked.

Second Voice:

9 For Thou, O Jahve, art my refuge!

First Voice:

   The Most High hast thou made thy habitation.
10 The range of misfortune toucheth thee not,
    And the plague doth not come nigh thy tent.
11 For His angels hath He given charge over thee,
    To keep thee in all thy ways.
12 On their hands shall they bear thee up,
    That thou dost not dash thy foot against a stone.
13 Over lions and adders shalt thou walk,
    Thou shalt trample lions and dragons under thy feet.

Third (divine) Voice:

14 For he loveth Me, therefore will I deliver him,
    I will set him on high, for he knoweth My Name.
15 If he shall call upon Me, I will answer him,
    I will be with him in trouble;
    I will rescue him and bring him to honour.
16 With length of life will I satisfy him,
    And cause him to delight himself in My salvation.

The primeval song is followed by an anonymous song (inscribed by the LXX. without any warrant τῷ Δαυίδ), the time of whose composition cannot be determined; and it is only placed in this order because the last verse accords with the last verse but one of Ps. xc. There the revelation of Jahve's work is prayed for, and here Jahve promises: *I will grant him to see My salvation;* the "work of Jahve" is His realized "salvation." The two Psalms also have other points of contact, e.g. in the מָעוֹן referred to God (*vid. Symbolæ,* p. 60).

PSALM XCI.

In this Psalm, the Invocavit Psalm of the church, which praises the protecting and rescuing grace which he who believingly takes refuge in God experiences in all times of danger and distress,* the relation of ver. 2 to ver. 1 meets us at the very beginning as a perplexing riddle. If we take ver. 1 as a clause complete in itself, then it is tautological. If we take אֹמֵר in ver. 2 as a participle (Jerome, *dicens*) instead of אֹמַר, ending with *Pathach* because a construct form (cf. xciv. 9, cxxxvi. 6), then the participial subject would have a participial predicate: "He who sitteth is saying," which is inelegant and also improbable, since אֹמַר in other instances is always the 1st pers. fut. If we take אֹמַר as 1st pers. fut. and ver. 1 as an apposition of the subject expressed in advance: as such an one who sitteth ... I say, then we stumble against יְתְלוֹנָן; this transition of the participle to the finite verb, especially without the copula (וּבְצֵל), is confusing. If, however, we go on and read further into the Psalm, we find that the same difficulty as to the change of person recurs several times later on, just as in the opening. Olshausen, Hupfeld, and Hitzig get rid of this difficulty by all sorts of conjectures. But a reason for this abrupt change of the person is that dramatic arrangement recognised even in the Targum, although awkwardly indicated, which, however, was first of all clearly discerned by J. D. Michaelis and Maurer. There are, to wit, two voices that speak (as in Ps. cxxi.), and at last the voice of Jahve comes in as a third. His closing utterance, rich in promise, forms, perhaps not unaccidentally, a seven-line strophe. Whether the Psalm came also to be executed in liturgical use thus with several voices, perhaps by three choirs, we cannot tell; but the poet certainly laid it out dramatically, as the translation represents it. In spite of the many echoes of earlier models, it is one of the freshest and most beautiful Psalms, resembling the second part of Isaiah in its light-winged, richly coloured, and transparent diction.

---

* Hence in *J. Shabbath* 8, *col.* 2, and *Midrash Shocher tob* on xci. 1 and elsewhere, it is called, together with Ps. iii., (פגעים) שיר פגעים, a song of occurrences, *i.e.* a protective (or talismanic) song in times of dangers that may befall one, just as Sebald Heyden's Psalm-song, "He who is in the protection of the Most High and resigns himself to God," is inscribed "Preservative against the pestilence."

Vers. 1, 2. As the concealing One, God is called עֶלְיוֹן, the inaccessibly high One; and as the shadowing One שַׁדַּי, the invincibly almighty One. Faith, however, calls Him by His covenant name (*Heilsname*) יהוה and, with the suffix of appropriation, אֱלֹהַי (*my* God). In connection with ver. 1 we are reminded of the expressions of the Book of Job, ch. xxxix. 28, concerning the eagle's building its nest in its eyrie. According to the accentuation, ver. 2a ought to be rendered with Geier, "*Dicit: in Domino meo* (or *Domini*) *latibulum*, etc." But the combination אֹמַר לה׳ is more natural, since the language of address follows in both halves of the verse.

Vers. 3-9a. יָקוּשׁ, as in Prov. vi. 5, Jer. v. 26, is the dullest toned form for יָקֹשׁ or יוֹקֵשׁ, cxxiv. 7. What is meant is death, or "he who has the power of death," Heb. ii. 14, cf. 2 Tim. ii. 26. "The snare of the fowler" is a figure for the peril of one's life, Eccles. ix. 12. In connection with ver. 4 we have to call to mind Deut. xxxii. 11: God protects His own as an eagle with its large strong wing. אֶבְרָה is *nom. unitatis*, a pinion, to אֵבֶר, Isa. xl. 31; and the *Hiph.* הֵסֵךְ, from סָכַךְ, with the dative of the object, like the *Kal* in cxl. 8, signifies to afford covering, protection. The ἅπαξ λεγ. סֹחֵרָה, according to its stem-word, is that which encompasses anything round about, and here beside צִנָּה, a weapon of defence surrounding the body on all sides; therefore not corresponding to the Syriac ܣܚܪܬܐ, a stronghold (מִסְגֶּרֶת, סֹהַר), but to ܣܟܪܐ, a shield. The Targum translates צִנָּה with תְּרִיסָא, θυρεός, and סֹחֵרָה with עֲגִילָא, which points to the round *parma*. אֲמִתּוֹ is the truth of the divine promises. This is an impregnable defence (*a*) in war-times, ver. 5, against nightly surprises, and in the battle by day; (*b*) in times of pestilence, ver. 6, when the destroying angel, who passes through and destroys the people (Ex. xi. 4), can do no harm to him who has taken refuge in God, either in the midnight or the noontide hours. The future יַהֲלֹךְ is a more rhythmical and, in the signification to rage (as of disease) and to vanish away, a more usual form instead of יֵלֵךְ. The LXX., Aquila, and Symmachus erroneously associate the demon name שֵׁד with יָשׁוּד. It is a metaplastic (as if formed from שׁוּד) future for שָׁדַד, cf. Prov. xxix. 6, יָרֻן, and Isa. xlii. 4, יָרוּץ, *frangetur*.

Ver. 7a a hypothetical protasis: *si cadant;* the preterite would signify *ceciderint*, Ew. § 357, *b*. With פֶּן that which will solely and exclusively take place is introduced. Burk correctly renders: *nullam cum peste rem habebis, nisi ut videas*. Only a spectator shalt thou be, and that with thine own eyes, being thyself inaccessible and left to survive, conscious that thou thyself art a living one in contrast with those who are dying. And thou shalt behold, like Israel on the night of the Passover, the just retribution to which the evil-doers fall a prey. שִׁלֻּמָה, recompense, retribution, is a hapaxlegomenon, cf. שִׁלֻּמִים, Isa. xxxiv. 8. Ascribing the glory to God, the second voice confirms or ratifies these promises.

Vers. 9*b*–16. The first voice continues this ratification, and goes on weaving these promises still further: thou hast made the Most High thy dwelling-place (מְעוֹנֶי); there shall not touch thee ... The promises rise ever higher and higher, and sound more glorious. The *Pual* אֻנָּה, prop. to be turned towards, is equivalent to "to befall one," as in Prov. xii. 21; Aquila well renders: οὐ μεταχθήσεται πρὸς σὲ κακία. לֹא־יְקָרְב reminds one of Isa. liv. 14, where אֶל follows; here it is בְּ, as in Judg. xix. 13. The angel guardianship which is apportioned to him who trusts in God appears in vers. 11, 12 as a universal fact, not as a solitary fact and occurring only in extraordinary instances. *Hæc est vera miraculorum ratio*, observes Brentius on this passage, *quod semel aut iterum manifeste revelent ea quæ Deus semper abscondite operatur*. In יִשָּׂאוּנְךָ the suffix has been combined with the full form of the future. The LXX. correctly renders ver. 12*b*: μήποτε προσκόψῃς πρὸς λίθον τὸν πόδα σου, for נָגַף everywhere else, and therefore surely here too and in Prov. iii. 23, has a transitive signification, not an intransitive (Aquila, Jerome, Symmachus), cf. Jer. xiii. 16. Ver. 13 tells what he who trusts in God has power to do by virtue of this divine succour through the medium of angels. The promise calls to mind Mark xvi. 18, ὄφεις ἀροῦσι, they shall take up serpents, but still more Luke x. 19: Behold, I give you power to tread ἐπάνω ὄφεων καὶ σκορπίων καὶ ἐπὶ πᾶσαν τὴν δύναμιν τοῦ ἐχθροῦ. They are all kinds of destructive powers belonging to nature, and particularly to the spirit-world, that are meant. They are called lions and fierce lions from the side of their open power, which threatens destruction, and adders and dragons from the side of their venomous secret malice. In ver. 13a it is promised that the man who trusts in God shall walk on over these monsters, these malignant foes, proud in God and unharmed; in ver. 13b, that he shall tread them to the ground (cf. Rom. xvi. 20). That which the divine voice of promise now says at the close of the Psalm is, so far as the form is concerned, an echo taken from Ps. l. Vers. 15 and 23 of that Psalm sound almost word for word the same. Gen. xlvi. 4, and more especially Isa. lxiii. 9, are to be compared on ver. 15b. In *B. Taanith* 16a it is inferred from this passage that God compassionates the suffering ones whom He is compelled by reason of His holiness to chasten and prove. The "salvation of Jahve," as in l. 23, is the full reality of the divine purpose (or counsel) of mercy. To live to see the final glory was the rapturous thought of the Old Testament hope, and in the apostolic age, of the New Testament hope also.

PSALM XCII.

SABBATH THOUGHTS.

2 IT is good to give thanks unto Jahve,
 And to harp unto Thy Name, O Most High—
3 To show forth in the morning Thy loving-kindness,
 And Thy faithfulness in the nights,
4 Upon a ten-stringed instrument and upon the nabla,
 In skilful playing with the cithern.

5 For Thou makest me glad, Jahve, through Thy rule,
 Because of the works of Thy hands can I exult.
6 How great are Thy works, Jahve!
 Very deep are Thy thoughts.
7 A brutish man remains unconscious,
 And a fool doth not discern this.

8 When the ungodly sprang up as the green herb
 And all the workers of evil flourished,
 It came to pass that they were absolutely destroyed.
9 And Thou art exaltation for ever, Jahve!

10 For lo Thine enemies, Jahve—
For lo Thine enemies shall perish,
All the workers of evil shall melt away.

11 And Thou exaltest, as an antelope, my horn,
I am anointed with refreshing oil.
12 And mine eye feasteth upon those that lie in wait for me,
Mine ears see their desire upon those who maliciously rose
up against me.
13 The righteous shall sprout forth as the palm,
As a cedar on Lebanon shall he grow up.

14 Planted in the house of Jahve,
They shall blossom in the courts of our God.
15 They shall be still vigorous in old age,
Full of sap and green shall they remain,
16 To make known that Jahve is upright,
My rock, and there is no unrighteousness in Him.

This *Song-Psalm for the Sabbath-day* was the Sabbath-Psalm among the week's Psalms of the post-exilic service (cf. vol. i. pp. 32, 334); and was sung in the morning at the drink-offering of the first Tamîd lamb, just as at the accompanying Sabbath-musaph-offering (Num. xxviii. 9 sq.) a part of the song Deut. ch. xxxii. (divided into six parts) was sung, and at the service connected with the Mincha or evening sacrifice one of the three pieces, Ex. xv. 1-10, 11-19, Num. xxi. 17-20 (*B. Rosh ha-Shana* 31a). 1 Macc. ix. 23 is a reminiscence from Ps. xcii. deviating but little from the LXX. version, just as 1 Macc. vii. 17 is a quotation taken from Ps. lxxix. With respect to the sabbatical character of the Psalm, it is a disputed question even in the Talmud whether it relates to the Sabbath of the Creation (R. Nehemiah, as it is taken by the Targum) or to the final Sabbath of the world's history (R. Akiba: the day that is altogether Sabbath; cf. Athanasius: αἰνεῖ ἐκείνην τὴν γενησομένην ἀνάπαυσιν). The latter is relatively more correct. It praises God, the Creator of the world, as the Ruler of the world, whose rule is pure loving-kindness and faithfulness, and calms itself, in the face of the flourishing condition of the evil-doers, with the prospect of the final issue, which will brilliantly vindicate the righteousness of God, that was at that time imperceptible to superficial observation, and will change the congregation of the righteous into a flourishing grove of palms and cedars upon holy ground. In this prospect Ps. xcii. 12 and Ps. xci. 8 coincide, just as God is also called "the Most High" at the beginning of these two Psalms. But that the *tetragrammaton* occurs seven times in both Psalms, as Hengstenberg says, does not turn out to be correct. Only the Sabbath-Psalm (and not Ps. xci.) repeats the most sacred Name seven times. And certainly the unmistakeable strophe-schema too, 6. 6. 7. 6. 6, is not without significance. The middle of the Psalm bears the stamp of the sabbatic number. It is also worthy of remark that the poet gains the number seven by means of an anadiplosis in ver. 10. Such an emphatic climax by means of repetition is common to our Psalm with xciii. 3, xciv. 3, xcvi. 13.

Vers. 2-4. The Sabbath is the day that God has hallowed, and that is to be consecrated to God by our turning away from the business pursuits of the working days (Isa. lviii. 13 sq.) and applying ourselves to the praise and adoration of God, which is the most proper, blessed Sabbath employment. It is good, *i.e.* not merely good in the eyes of God, but also good for man, beneficial to the heart, pleasant and blessed. Lovingkindness is designedly connected with the dawn of the morning, for it is morning light itself, which breaks through the night (xxx. 6, lix. 17), and faithfulness with the nights, for in the perils of the loneliness of the night it is the best companion, and nights of affliction are the "foil of its verification." עֲשׂוֹר beside נֵבֶל (נָבֶל) is equivalent to נֵבֶל עָשׂוֹר in xxxiii. 2, cxliv. 9 : the ten-stringed harp or lyre. הִגָּיוֹן is the music of stringed instruments (*vid.* on ix. 17), and that, since הגה in itself is not a suitable word for the rustling (*strepitus*) of the strings, the impromptu or phantasia playing (in Amos vi. 5, scornfully, פָּרַט), which suits both ix. 17 (where it is appended to the *forte* of the interlude) and the construction with *Beth instrumenti.*

Vers. 5-7. Statement of the ground of this commendation of the praise of God. Whilst פֹּעַל is the usual word for God's historical rule (xliv. 2, lxiv. 10, xc. 16, etc.), כְּמַעֲשֵׂי יָדֶיךָ

denotes the works of the Creator of the world, although not
to the exclusion of those of the Ruler of the world (cxliii. 5).
To be able to rejoice over the revelation of God in creation
and the revelation of God in general is a gift from above,
which the poet thankfully confesses that he has received. The
Vulgate begins ver. 5 *Quia delectasti me*, and Dante in his
Purgatorio, xxviii. 80, accordingly calls the Psalm *il Salmo
Delectasti;* a smiling female form, which represents the life of
Paradise, says, as she gathers flowers, she is so happy because,
with the Psalm *Delectasti*, she takes a delight in the glory of
God's works. The works of God are transcendently great;
very deep are His thoughts, which mould human history and
themselves gain form in it (cf. xl. 6, cxxxix. 17 sq., where
infinite fulness is ascribed to them, and Isa. lv. 8 sq., where
infinite height is ascribed to them). Man can neither measure
the greatness of the divine works nor fathom the depth of the
divine thoughts; he who is enlightened, however, perceives the
immeasurableness of the one and the unfathomableness of the
other, whilst a איש־בער, a man of animal nature, *homo brutus*
(*vid.* lxxiii. 22), does not come to the knowledge (לא ידע, used
absolutely as in xiv. 4), and כסיל, a blockhead, or one dull in
mind, whose carnal nature outweighs his intellectual and spiritual nature, does not discern את־זאת (cf. 2 Sam. xiii. 17), *id
ipsum*, viz. how unsearchable are God's judgments and un-
trackable His ways (Rom. xi. 33).

Vers. 8–10. Upon closer examination the prosperity of the
ungodly is only a semblance that lasts for a time. The infinitive construction in ver. 8 is continued in the historic tense,
and it may also be rendered as historical. זאת היתה (Saadia:
ذلك) is to be supplied in thought before להשמדם, as in Job
xxvii. 14. What is spoken of is an historical occurrence
which, in its beginning, course, and end, has been frequently
repeated even down to the present day, and ever confirmed
afresh. And thus, too, in time to come and once finally shall
the ungodly succumb to a peremptory, decisive (עדי־עד) judgment of destruction. Jahve is מרום לעלם, by His nature and
by His rule He is " a height for ever;" *i.e.* in relation to the
creature and all that goes on here below He has a nature
beyond and above all this (*Jenseitigkeit*), ever the same and

absolute; He is absolutely inaccessible to the God-opposed one here below who vaunts himself in stupid pride and rebelliously exalts himself as a titan, and only suffers it to last until the term of his barren blossoming is run out. Thus the present course of history will and must in fact end in a final victory of good over evil: for lo Thine enemies, Jahve—for lo Thine enemies . . . הִנֵּה points as it were with the finger to the inevitable end; and the emotional anadiplosis breathes forth a zealous love for the cause of God as if it were his own. God's enemies shall perish, all the workers of evil shall be disjointed, scattered, יִתְפָּרְדוּ (cf. Job iv. 11). Now they form a compact mass, which shall however fall to pieces, when one day the intermingling of good and evil has an end.

Vers. 11–13. The hitherto oppressed church then stands forth vindicated and glorious. The *futt. consec.*, as preterites of the ideal past, pass over further on into the pure expression of future time. The LXX. renders: καὶ ὑψωθήσεται (וַתָּרֶם) ὡς μονοκέρωτος τὸ κέρας μου. By רֵאִים (incorrect for רְאֵם, primary form רְאֵם), μονόκερως, is surely to be understood the *oryx*, one-horned according to Aristotle and the Talmud (*vid.* on xxix. 6, Job xxxix. 9–12). This animal is called in Talmudic קְרָשׁ (perhaps abbreviated from μονόκερως); the Talmud also makes use of אֲרוֹילָא (the gazelle) as synonymous with רְאֵם (Aramaic definitive or emphatic state רֵימָא).* The primary passages for figures taken from animal life are Num. xxiii. 22, Deut. xxxiii. 17. The horn is an emblem of defensive power and at the same time of stately grace; and the fresh, green oil an emblem of the pleasant feeling and enthusiasm, joyous in the prospect of victory, by which the church is then pervaded (Acts iii. 19). The LXX. erroneously takes בַּלֹּתִי as *injin. Piel*, τὸ γῆράς μου, my being grown old, a signification which the *Piel* cannot have. It is 1st *præt. Kal* from בָּלַל, *perfusus sum* (cf. Arabic *balla*, to be moist, *ballah* and *bullah*, moistness, good health, the freshness of youth), and the *ultima*-accentuation, which also occurs in this form of double *Ajin* verbs without *Waw convers.* (*vid.* on Job xix. 17), ought not to mislead. In the expression שֶׁמֶן רַעֲנָן, the adjective used in other instances only of the olive-tree itself is transferred to the oil,

---

* *Vid.* Lewysohn, *Zoologie des Talmud*, §§ 146 and 174.

which contains the strength of its succulent verdure as an essence. The *ecclesia pressa* is then *triumphans*. The eye, which was wont to look timidly and tearfully upon the persecutors, the ears, upon which even their name and the tidings of their approach were wont to produce terror, now see their desire upon them as they are blotted out. שָׁמַע בְּ (found only here) follows the sense of רָאָה בְּ, cf. نظر فى, to lose one's self in the contemplation of anything. שׁוּרַי is either a substantive after the form בּוּר, גּוּר, or a participle in the signification "those who regarded me with hostility, those who lay in wait for me," like נוּס, fled, Num. xxxv. 32, סוּר, having removed themselves to a distance, Jer. xvii. 13, שׁוּב, turned back, Mic. ii. 8; for this participial form has not only a passive signification (like מוּל, circumcised), but sometimes, too, a deponent perfect signification; and חוּשׁ in Num. xxxii. 17, if it belongs here, may signify hurried = in haste. In שׁוּרַי, however, no such passive colouring of the meaning is conceivable; it is therefore: *insidiati* (Luzatto, *Grammatica*, § 518: *coloro che mi guatavano*). There is no need for regarding the word, with Böttcher and Olshausen, as distorted from שֹׁרְרַי (the apocopated participle *Pilel* of the same verb); one might more readily regard it as a softening of that word as to the sound (Ewald, Hitzig). In ver. 12*b* it is not to be rendered: upon the wicked doers (villains) who rise up against me. The placing of the adjective thus before its substantive must (with the exception of רַב when used after the manner of a numeral) be accounted impossible in Hebrew, even in the face of the passages brought forward by Hitzig, viz. 1 Chron. xxvii. 5, 1 Sam. xxxi. 3;* it is therefore: upon those who as villains rise up against. The circumstance that the poet now in ver. 13 passes from himself to speak of the righteous, is brought about by the fact that it is the congregation of the righteous in general, *i.e.* of those who regulate their life according to the divine order of salvation, into whose future he here takes a glance. When the prosperity [lit. the blossoming] of the un-

---

* In the former passage כֹּהֵן רֹאשׁ is taken as one notion (chief priest), and in the latter אֲנָשִׁים בְּקֶשֶׁת (men with the bow) is, with Keil, to be regarded as an apposition.

godly comes to an end, the springing up and growth of the righteous only then rightly has its beginning. The richness of the inflorescence of the date-palm (תִּמָר) is clear from the fact, that when it has attained its full size, it bears from three to four, and in some instances even as many as six, hundred pounds of fruit. And there is no more charming and majestic sight than the palm of the oasis, this prince among the trees of the plain, with its proudly raised diadem of leaves, its attitude peering forth into the distance and gazing full into the face of the sun, its perennial verdure, and its vital force, which constantly renews itself from the root—a picture of life in the midst of the world of death. The likening of the righteous to the palm, to the " blessed tree," to this " sister of man," as the Arabs call it, offers points of comparison in abundance. Side by side with the palm is the cedar, the prince of the trees of the mountain, and in particular of Mount Lebanon. The most natural point of comparison, as יִשְׂגֶּה (cf. Job viii. 11) states, is its graceful lofty growth, then in general τὸ δασὺ καὶ θερμὸν καὶ θρέψιμον (Theodoret), i.e. the intensity of its vegetative strength, but also the perpetual verdure of its foliage and the perfume (Hos. xiv. 7) which it exhales.

Vers. 14–16. The soil in which the righteous are planted or (if it is not rendered with the LXX. πεφυτευμένοι, but with the other Greek versions μεταφυτευθέντες) into which they are transplanted, and where they take root, a planting of the Lord, for His praise, is His holy Temple, the centre of a family fellowship with God that is brought about from that point as its starting-point and is unlimited by time and space. There they stand as in sacred ground and air, which impart to them ever new powers of life; they put forth buds (הִפְרִיחַ as in Job xiv. 9) and preserve a verdant freshness and marrowy vitality (like the olive, lii. 10, Judg. ix. 9) even into their old age (נוב of a productive force for putting out shoots; vid. with reference to the root נוב, Genesis, S. 635 sq.), cf. Isa. lxv. 22: *like the duration of the trees is the duration of my people;* they live long in unbroken strength, in order, in looking back upon a life rich in experiences of divine acts of righteousness and loving-kindness, to confirm the confession which Moses, in Deut. xxxii. 4, places at the head of his great song. There the expression is אֵין עָוֶל, here it is אֵין עֲלָתָה בּוֹ. This *'ôlâtha,* softened from 'awlātha—so the Kerî—with a transition from the aw, au into ô, is also found in Job v. 16 (cf. עֹלָה = עַוְלָה Ps. lviii. 3, lxiv. 7, Isa. lxi. 8), and is certainly original in this Psalm, which also has many other points of coincidence with the Book of Job (like Ps. cvii., which, however, in ver. 42 transposes עֹלָתָה into עַוְלָה).

PSALM XCIII.

THE ROYAL THRONE ABOVE THE SEA OF THE PEOPLES.

1 JAHVE now is King, He hath clothed Himself with majesty;
Jahve hath clothed Himself, He hath girded Himself with might:
Therefore the world standeth fast without tottering.

2 Thy throne standeth fast from of old,
From everlasting art THOU.

3 The floods have lifted up, Jahve,
The floods have lifted up their roaring,
The floods lift up their noise.

4 More than the rumblings of great waters,
Of the glorious, of the breakers of the sea,
Is Jahve glorious in the height.

5 Thy testimonies are inviolable,
Holiness becometh Thy house,
Jahve, unto length of days.

Side by side with those Psalms which behold in anticipation the Messianic future, whether it be prophetically or only typically, or typically and prophetically at the same time, as the kingship of Jahve's Anointed which overcomes and blesses the world, there are others in which the perfected theocracy as such is beheld beforehand, not, however, as an appearing (*parusia*) of a human king, but as the appearing of Jahve

Himself, as the kingdom of God manifest in all its glory. These theocratic Psalms form, together with the christocratic, two series of prophecy referring to the last time which run parallel with one another. The one has for its goal the Anointed of Jahve, who rules out of Zion over all peoples; the other, Jahve sitting above the cherubim, to whom the whole world does homage. The two series, it is true, converge in the Old Testament, but do not meet; it is the history that fulfils these types and prophecies which first of all makes clear that which flashes forth in the Old Testament only in certain climaxes of prophecy and of lyric too (vid. on xlv. 1), viz. that the parusia of the Anointed One and the parusia of Jahve is one and the same.

Theocracy is an expression coined by Josephus. In contrast with the monarchical, oligarchical, and democratic form of government of other nations, he calls the Mosaic form θεοκρατία, but he does so somewhat timidly, ὡς ἄν τις εἴποι βιασάμενος τὸν λόγον [c. Apion. ii. 17]. The coining of the expression is thankworthy; only one has to free one's self from the false conception that the theocracy is a particular constitution. The alternating forms of government were only various modes of its adjustment. The theocracy itself is a reciprocal relationship between God and men, exalted above these intermediary forms, which had its first manifest beginning when Jahve became Israel's King (Deut. xxxiii. 5, cf. Ex. xv. 18), and which will be finally perfected by its breaking through this national self-limitation when the King of Israel becomes King of the whole world, that is overcome both outwardly and spiritually. Hence the theocracy is an object of prediction and of hope. And the word מָלַךְ is used with reference to Jahve not merely of the first beginning of His imperial dominion, and of the manifestation of the same in facts in the most prominent points of the redemptive history, but also of the commencement of the imperial dominion in its perfected glory. We find the word used in this lofty sense, and in relation to the last time, e.g. in Isa. xxiv. 23, lii. 7, and most unmistakeably in Apoc. xi. 17, xix. 6. And in this sense יְהוָה מָלָךְ is the watchword of the theocratic Psalms. Thus it is used even in Ps. xlvii. 9; but the first of the Psalms beginning with this watchword is Ps. xciii. They are all post-exilic. The prominent point from which this eschatological perspective opens out is the time of the new-born freedom and of the newly restored state.

Hitzig pertinently says: "This Psalm is already contained *in nuce* in ver. 9 of the preceding Psalm, which surely comes from the same author. This is at once manifest from the jerking start of the discourse in ver. 3 (cf. xcii. 10), which resolves the thought into two members, of which the first subsides into the vocative יהוה." The LXX. (*Codd. Vat.* and *Sin.*) inscribes it: Εἰς τὴν ἡμέρην τοῦ προσαββάτου, ὅτε κατῴκισται ἡ γῆ, αἶνος ᾠδῆς τῷ Δαυίδ. The third part of this inscription is worthless. The first part (for which *Cod. Alex.* erroneously has: τοῦ σαββάτου) is corroborated by the Talmudic tradition. Ps. xciii. was really the Friday Psalm, and that, as is said in *Rosh ha-shana* 31a, על שם שגמר מלאכתו (בשישי) ומלך עליהן, because God then (on the sixth day) had completed His creative work and began to reign over them (His creatures); and that ὅτε κατῴκισται (*al.* κατῴκιστο) is to be explained in accordance therewith: when the earth had been peopled (with creatures, and more especially with men).

Vers. 1, 2. The sense of מָלָךְ (with *ā* beside *Zinnor* or *Sarka* as in xcvii. 1, xcix. 1 beside *Dechî**) is historical, and it stands in the middle between the present ה' מֶלֶךְ and the future ה' יִמְלֹךְ: Jahve has entered upon the kingship and now reigns. Jahve's rule heretofore, since He has given up the use of His omnipotence, has been self-abasement and self-renunciation: now, however, He shows Himself in all His majesty, which rises aloft above everything; He has put this on like a garment; He is King, and now too shows Himself to the world in the royal robe. The first לָבֵשׁ has *Olewejored*; then the accentuation

---

* It is well known that this pausal form of the 3d *masc. prœt.* occurs in connection with *Zakeph*; but it is also found with *Rebia* in cxii. 10 (the reading וְכָעָס), Lev. v. 23 (גָּזָל), Josh. x. 13 (עָמָד), Lam. ii. 17 (זָמָם ; but not in Deut. xix. 19, Zech. i. 6, which passages Kimchi counts up with them in his grammar *Michlol*); with *Tarcha* in Isa. xiv. 27 (יָעָץ), Hos. vi. 1 (טָרָף), Amos iii. 8 (שָׁאָג); with *Tebir* in Lev. v. 18 (שָׁגָג); and even with *Munach* in 1 Sam. vii. 17 (שָׁפָט), and according to Abulwalid with *Mercha* in 1 Kings xi. 2 (דָּבַק).

takes 'ה לָבֵשׁ together by means of *Dechî*, and עֹז הִתְאַזָּר together by means of *Athnach*. עֹז, as in Ps. xxix., points to the enemies; what is so named is God's invincibly triumphant omnipotence. This He has put on (Isa. li. 9), with this He has girded Himself—a military word (Isa. viii. 9): Jahve makes war against everything in antagonism to Himself, and casts it to the ground with the weapons of His wrathful judgments. We find a further and fuller description of this עֹז ההאזר in Isa. lix. 17, lxiii. 1 sq., cf. Dan. vii. 9.* That which cannot fail to take place in connection with the coming of this accession of Jahve to the kingdom is introduced with אַף. The world, as being the place of the kingdom of Jahve, shall stand without tottering in opposition to all hostile powers (xcvi. 10). Hitherto hostility towards God and its principal bulwark, the kingdom of the world, have disturbed the equilibrium and threatened all God-appointed relationships with dissolution; Jahve's interposition, however, when He finally brings into effect all the abundant might of His royal government, will secure immoveableness to the shaken earth (cf. lxxv. 4). His throne stands, exalted above all commotion, מֵאָז; it reaches back into the most distant past. Jahve is מֵעוֹלָם; His being loses itself in the immemorial and the immeasurable. The throne and nature of Jahve are not incipient in time, and therefore too are not perishable; but as without beginning, so also they are endless, infinite in duration.

Vers. 3-5. All the raging of the world, therefore, will not be able to hinder the progress of the kingdom of God and its final breaking through to the glory of victory. The sea with its mighty mass of waters, with the constant unrest of its waves, with its ceaseless pressing against the solid land and foaming against the rocks, is an emblem of the Gentile world alienated from and at enmity with God; and the rivers (floods) are emblems of worldly kingdoms, as the Nile of the Egyptian (Jer. xlvi. 7 sq.), the Euphrates of the Assyrian (Isa. viii. 7 sq.), or more exactly, the Tigris, swift as an arrow, of the Assyrian, and the

---

* These passages, together with Ps. xciii. 1, civ. 1, are cited in *Cant. Rabba* 26b (cf. *Debarim Rabba* 291d), where it is said that the Holy One calls Israel כלה (bride) ten times in the Scriptures, and that Israel on the other hand ten times assigns kingly judicial robes to Him.

tortuous Euphrates of the Babylonian empire (Isa. xxvii. 1). These rivers, as the poet says whilst he raises a plaintive but comforted look upwards to Jahve, have lifted up, have lifted up their murmur, the rivers lift up their roaring. The thought is unfolded in a so-called "parallelism with reservation." The perfects affirm what has taken place, the future that which even now as yet is taking place. The ἅπαξ λεγ. 'דְּכִי signifies a striking against (*collisio*), and a noise, a din. One now in ver. 4 looks for the thought that Jahve is exalted above this roaring of the waves. מִן will therefore be the *min* of comparison, not of the cause: "by reason of the roar of great waters are the breakers of the sea glorious" (Starck, Geier),—which, to say nothing more, is a tautological sentence. But if מִן is comparative, then it is impossible to get on with the accentuation of אדירים, whether it be with *Mercha* (Ben-Asher) or *Dechî* (Ben-Naphtali). For to render: More than the roar of great waters are the breakers of the sea glorious (Mendelssohn), is impracticable, since מים רבים are nothing less than ים (Isa. xvii. 12 sq.), and we are prohibited from taking אדירים משברים as a parenthesis (Köster) by the fact that it is just this clause that is exceeded by אדיר במרום ה'. Consequently אדירים has to be looked upon as a second attributive to מים brought in afterwards, and מִשְׁבְּרֵי־יָם (the waves of the sea breaking upon the rocks, or even only breaking upon one another) as a more minute designation of these great and magnificent waters (אדירים, according to Ex. xv. 10 *), and it should have been accented: מִקֹּלוֹת ׀ מַיִם רַבִּים אַדִּירִים מִשְׁבְּרֵי־יָם. Jahve's celestial majesty towers far above all the noisy majesties here below, whose waves, though lashed never so high, can still never reach His throne. He is King of His people, Lord of His church, which preserves His revelation and worships in His temple. This revelation, by virtue of His unapproachable, all-overpowering kingship, is inviolable; His testimonies, which minister to

---

* A Talmudic enigmatical utterance of R. Azaria runs: יבא אדיר ויפרע לאדירים מאדירים באדירים, Let the glorious One (Jahve, Ps. xciii. 4, cf. Isa. x. 34, xxxiii. 21) come and maintain the right of the glorious ones (Israel, Ps. xvi. 3) against the glorious ones (the Egyptians, Ex. xv. 10 according to the construction of the Talmud) in the glorious ones (the waves of the sea, Ps. xciii. 4).

the establishment of His kingdom and promise its future manifestation in glory, are λόγοι πιστοὶ καὶ ἀληθινοί, Apoc. xix. 9, xxii. 6. And holiness becometh His temple (נַאֲוָה־קֹדֶשׁ, 3d præt. *Pilel*, or according to the better attested reading of Heidenheim and Baer, נָאוָה;* therefore the feminine of the adjective with a more loosened syllable next to the tone, like יְחֲשָׁב־לִי in xl. 18), that is to say, it is inviolable (sacrosanct), and when it is profaned, shall ever be vindicated again in its holiness. This clause, formulated after the manner of a prayer, is at the same time a petition that Jahve in all time to come would be pleased to thoroughly secure the place where His honour dwells here below against profanation.

PSALM XCIV.

THE CONSOLATION OF PRAYER UNDER THE OPPRESSION OF TYRANTS.

1 O GOD of vengeance, Jahve,
 O God of vengeance, shine forth!
2 Lift up Thyself, Judge of earth,
 Render recompense unto the haughty!
3 How long shall evil-doers, Jahve,
 How long shall evil-doers triumph?

4 They gush over, they speak arrogant things,
 They boast themselves, all the workers of evil.
5 Thy people, Jahve, they break in pieces,
 And they oppress Thine inheritance.
6 The widow and stranger they slay,
 And they murder the fatherless;
7 And say as they do it: "Jāh seeth not,
 And the God of Jacob hath no knowledge."

---

* The Masora on Ps. cxlvii. reckons four נָאוָה, one וְנָאוָה, and one נָאוֶה, and therefore our נָאוָה is one of the כל חד לית וכל אלף דמפקין כלין יׄ מפק (cf. Frensdorf's *Ochla we-Ochla*, p. 123), *i.e.* one of the seventeen words whose *Aleph* is audible, whilst it is otherwise always quiescent; *e.g.* בְּמַאֲצוּת, otherwise מַצוּאת.

8 Be sensible, ye senseless among the people!
  And ye fools, when will ye become wise?
9 He who hath planted the ear, ought He not to hear?
  Or He who formed the eye, ought He not to see?
10 He who chastiseth the nations, ought He not to reprove,
   He who teacheth men knowledge?
11 Jahve knoweth the thoughts of men
   That they are vanity.

12 Blessed is the man whom Thou chastenest, Jāh,
   And teachest out of Thy Law;
13 To give him rest from the days of adversity,
   Until the pit be digged for the evil-doer.
14 For Jahve doth not thrust away His people,
   And He doth not forsake His inheritance.
15 But right must turn unto righteousness,
   And all the upright in heart shall follow it.

16 Who would rise up for me against the evil-doers?
   Who would stand up for me against the workers of
17 If Jahve had not been my help,   [iniquity?
   My soul would quickly have dwelt in the silence of death.
18 If I say: My foot tottereth,
   Then, Jahve, thy loving-kindness upholdeth me.
19 In the multitude of my cares within me
   Thy comforts delight my soul.

20 Hath the judgment-seat of corruption fellowship with Thee,
   Which frameth trouble by decree?
21 They press in upon the soul of the righteous,
   And condemn innocent blood.
22 But Jahve is a fortress for me,
   And my God is the high rock of my refuge.
23 He turneth back upon them their iniquity,
   And for their wickedness He will destroy them,
   Jahve our God will destroy them.

This Psalm, akin to Ps. xcii. and xciii. by the community of the anadiplosis, bears the inscription Ψαλμὸς ᾠδῆς τῷ Δαυίδ, τετράδι σαββάτου in the LXX. It is also a Talmudic tradition* that it was the Wednesday song in the Temple liturgy (τετράδι σαββάτου = בשבת ברביעי). Athanasius explains it by a reference to the fourth month (Jer. xxxix. 2). The τῷ Δαυίδ, however, is worthless. It is a post-Davidic Psalm; for, although it comes out of one mould, we still meet throughout with reminiscences of older Davidic and Asaphic models. The enemies against whom it supplicates the appearing of the God of righteous retribution are, as follows from a comparison of vers. 5, 8, 10, 12, non-Israelites, who despise the God of Israel and fear not His vengeance, ver. 7; whose barbarous doings, however, call forth, even among the oppressed people themselves, foolish doubts concerning Jahve's omniscient beholding and judicial interposition. Accordingly the Psalm is one of the latest, but not necessarily a Maccabæan Psalm. The later Persian age, in which the Book of Ecclesiastes was written, could also exhibit circumstances and moods such as these.

Vers. 1–3. The first strophe prays that God would at length put a judicial restraint upon the arrogance of ungodliness. Instead of הוֹפִיעַ (a less frequent form of the imperative for הוֹפַע, Ges. § 53, rem. 3) it was perhaps originally written הוֹפִיעָה (lxxx. 2), the *He* of which has been lost owing to the *He* that follows. The plural נְקָמוֹת signifies not merely single instances of taking vengeance (Ezek. xxv. 17, cf. *supra* xviii. 48), but also intensively complete revenge or recompense (Judg. xi. 36, 2 Sam. iv. 8). The designation of God is similar to אֵל גְּמֻלוֹת in Jer. li. 56, and the anadiplosis is like vers. 3, 23, xciii. 1, 3. הִנָּשֵׂא, lift Thyself up, arise, viz. in judicial majesty, calls to mind vii. 7. הָשֵׁיב גְּמוּל is construed with עַל (cf. לְ, xxviii. 4, Isa. lix. 18) as in Joel iv. 4. With גֵּאִים accidentally accord ἀγαυός and κύδεϊ γαίων in the epic poets.

---

* According to *B. Erachin* 11a, at the time of the Chaldæan destruction of Jerusalem the Levites on their pulpits were singing this 94th Psalm, and as they came to the words "and He turneth back upon them their iniquity" (ver. 23), the enemies pressed into the Temple, so that they were not able to sing the closing words, "Jahve, our God, will destroy them." To the scruple that Ps. xciv. is a Wednesday, not a Sunday, Psalm (that fatal day, however, was a Sunday, מוצאי שבת), it is replied, it may have been a lamentation song that had just been put into their mouths by the circumstances of that time (אליא בעלמא דנפל להו בפומייהו).

Vers. 4–7. The second strophe describes those over whom the first prays that the judgment of God may come. יַבִּיעַ (cf. הִטִּיף) is a tropical phrase used of that kind of speech that results from strong inward impulse and flows forth in rich abundance. The poet himself explains how it is here (cf. lix. 8) intended: they speak עָתָק, that which is unrestrained, unbridled, insolent (vid. xxxi. 19). The *Hithpa.* הִתְאַמֵּר Schultens interprets *ut Emiri* (أمير, a commander) *se gerunt;* but אָמִיר signifies in Hebrew the top of a tree (vid. on Isa. xvii. 9); and from the primary signification to tower aloft, whence too אָמַר, to speak, prop. *efferre* = *effari*, הִתְאַמֵּר, like הִתְיַמֵּר in Isa. lxi. 6, directly signifies to exalt one's self, to carry one's self high, to strut. On יְדַכְּאוּ cf. Prov. xxii. 22, Isa. iii. 15; and on their atheistical principle which וַיֹּאמְרוּ places in closest connection with their mode of action, cf. x. 11, lix. 8 *extrem.* The *Dagesh* in יָהּ, distinct from the *Dag.* in the same word in ver. 12, cxviii. 5, 18, is the *Dag. forte conjunct.* according to the rule of the so-called דחיק (vol. ii. p. 354, note).

Vers. 8–11. The third strophe now turns from those bloodthirsty, blasphemous oppressors of the people of God whose conduct calls forth the vengeance of Jahve, to those among the people themselves, who have been puzzled about the omniscience and indirectly about the righteousness of God by the fact that this vengeance is delayed. They are called בֹּעֲרִים and כְּסִילִים in the sense of lxxiii. 21 sq. Those hitherto described against whom God's vengeance is supplicated are this also; but this appellation would be too one-sided for them, and בָּעָם refers the address expressly to a class of men among the people whom those oppress and slay. It is absurd that God, the planter of the ear (הֲנֹטַע, like שֹׁסַע in Lev. xi. 7, with an accented *ultima*, because the *præt. Kal* does not follow the rule for the drawing back of the accent called נסוג אחור) and the former of the eye (cf. xl. 7, Ex. iv. 11), should not be able to hear and to see; everything that is excellent in the creature, God must indeed possess in original, absolute perfection.* The

---

* The questions are not: ought He to have no ear, etc.; as Jerome pertinently observes in opposition to the anthropomorphites, *membra tulit, efficientias dedit.*

poet then points to the extra-Israelitish world and calls God יֹסֵר גּוֹיִם, which cannot be made to refer to a warning by means of the voice of conscience; יֹסֵר used thus without any closer definition does not signify "warning," but "chastening" (Prov. ix. 7). Taking his stand upon facts like those in Job xii. 23, the poet assumes the punitive judicial rule of God among the heathen to be an undeniable fact, and presents for consideration the question, whether He who chasteneth nations cannot and will not also punish the oppressors of His church (cf. Gen. xviii. 25), He who teacheth men knowledge, i.e. He who nevertheless must be the omnipotent One, since all knowledge comes originally from Him? Jahve,—thus does the course of argument close in ver. 11,—sees through (יֹדֵעַ of penetrative perceiving or knowing that goes to the very root of a matter) the thoughts of men that they are vanity. Thus it is to be interpreted, and not: for they (men) are vanity; for this ought to have been כִּי הֶבֶל הֵמָּה, whereas in the dependent clause, when the predicate is not intended to be rendered especially prominent, as in ix. 21, the pronominal subject may precede, Isa. lxi. 9, Jer. xlvi. 5 (Hitzig). The rendering of the LXX. (1 Cor. iii. 20), ὅτι εἰσὶ μάταιοι (Jerome, *quoniam vanæ sunt*), is therefore correct; הֵמָּה, with the customary want of exactness, stands for הֵנָּה. It is true men themselves are הֶבֶל; it is not, however, on this account that He who sees through all things sees through their thoughts, but He sees through them in their sinful vanity.

Vers. 12–15. The fourth strophe praises the pious sufferer, whose good cause God will at length aid in obtaining its right. The "blessed" reminds one of xxxiv. 9, xl. 5, and more especially of Job v. 17, cf. Prov. iii. 11 sq. Here what are meant are sufferings like those bewailed in vers. 5 sq., which are however, after all, the well-meant dispensations of God. Concerning the aim and fruit of purifying and testing afflictions God teaches the sufferer out of His Law (cf. *e.g.* Deut. viii. 5 sq.), in order to procure him rest, viz. inward rest (cf. Jer. xlix. 23 with Isa. xxx. 15), *i.e.* not to suffer him to be disheartened and tempted by days of wickedness, *i.e.* wicked, calamitous days (Ew. § 287, *b*), until (and it will inevitably come to pass) the pit is finished being dug into which the ungodly falls headlong (cf. cxii. 7 sq.). יִכָּרֶה has the emphatic *Dagesh*, which properly does not double, and still less unite, but requires an emphatic pronunciation of the letter, which might easily become inaudible. The initial *Jod* of the divine name might easily lose its consonantal value here in connection with the preceding toneless *û*,* and the *Dag.* guards against this: cf. cxviii. 5, 18. The certainty of the issue that is set in prospect by עַד is then confirmed with כִּי. It is impossible that God can desert His church—He cannot do this, because in general right must finally come to His right, or, as it is here expressed, מִשְׁפָּט must turn to צֶדֶק, i.e. the right that is now subdued must at length be again strictly maintained and justly administered, and "after it then all who are upright in heart," i.e. all such will side with it, joyously greeting that which has been long missed and yearned after. מִשְׁפָּט is fundamental right, which is at all times consistent with itself and raised above the casual circumstances of the time, and צֶדֶק, like אֱמֶת in Isa. xlii. 3, is righteousness (justice), which converts this right into a practical truth and reality.

Vers. 16–19. In the fifth strophe the poet celebrates the praise of the Lord as his sole, but also trusty and most consolatory help. The meaning of the question in ver. 16 is, that there is no man who would rise and succour him in the conflict with the evil-doers; לְ as in Ex. xiv. 25, Judg. vi. 31, and עִם (without נִלְחָם or the like) in the sense of *contra*, as in lv. 19, cf. 2 Chron. xx. 6. God alone is his help. He alone has rescued him from death. הָיָה is to be supplied to לוּלֵי: if He had not been, or: if He were not; and the apodosis is: then very little would have been wanting, then it would soon have come to this, that his soul would have taken up its abode, etc.; cf. on the construction cxix. 92, cxxiv. 1–5, Isa. i. 9, and

---

* If it is correct that, as Aben-Ezra and Parchon testify, the ו, as being compounded of *o* (*u*) + *i*, was pronounced *ü* [like the *u* in the French word *pur*] by the inhabitants of Palestine, then this *Dagesh*, in accordance with its orthophonic function, is the more intelligible in cases like תִּיסְרֶנּוּ יה and קְרָאתִי יה, cf. Pinsker, *Einleitung*, S. 153, and Geiger, *Urschrift*, S. 277. In צָאוּ קוּמוּ, Gen. xix. 14, Ex. xii. 31, קוּמוּ סְעוּ, Deut. ii. 24, *Tsade* and *Samech* have this *Dagesh* for the same reason as the *Sin* in שְׁאוֹר תַּשְׁבִּיתוּ, Ex. xii. 15 (vid. Heidenheim on that passage), viz. because there is a danger in all these cases of slurring over the sharp sibilant. Even Chajug' (vid. Ewald and Dukes' *Beiträge*, iii. 23) confuses this *Dag. orthophonicum* with the *Dag. forte conjunctivum*.

on בְּעָם with the *præt.* lxxiii. 2, cxix. 87, Gen. xxvi. 10 (on the other hand with the *fut.* lxxxi. 15). דּוּמָה is, as in cxv. 17, the silence of the grave and of Hades; here it is the object to שְׁכִינָה, as in xxxvii. 3, Prov. viii. 12, and frequently. When he appears to himself already as one that has fallen, God's mercy holds him up. And when thoughts, viz. sad and fearful thoughts, are multiplied within him, God's comforts delight him, viz. the encouragement of His word and the inward utterances of His Spirit. שַׂרְעַפִּים, as in cxxxix. 23, is equivalent to שְׂעִפִּים, from סָעַף, שָׂעַף, شعب, to split, branch off (*Psychology*, S. 181; tr. p. 214). The plural form יְשַׁעַשְׁעוּ, like the plural of the imperative in Isa. xxix. 9, has two *Pathachs*, the second of which is the "independentification" of the *Chateph* of יְשַׁעֲשַׁע.

Vers. 20–23. In the sixth strophe the poet confidently expects the inevitable divine retribution for which he has earnestly prayed in the introduction. יְחָבְרְךָ is erroneously accounted by many (and by Gesenius too) as *fut. Pual* = יְחֻבַּרְךָ = יְחֻבַּר עִמָּךְ, a vocal contraction together with a giving up of the reduplication in favour of which no example can be advanced. It is *fut. Kal* = יֶחְבָּרְךָ, from יֶחְבָּר = יַחְבֹּר, with the same regression of the modification of the vowel* as in יָחָנְךָ = יָחָנְךָ in Gen. xliii. 29, Isa. xxx. 19 (Hupfeld), but as in verbs *primæ gutturalis*, so also in בְּהָבְם, בְּהַבְם, inflected from כָּתַב, Ew. § 251, *d*. It might be more readily regarded as *Poel* than as *Pual* (like הֶאָכְלֵהוּ, Job xx. 26), but the *Kal* too already signifies to enter into fellowship (Gen. xiv. 3, Hos. iv. 17), therefore (similarly to יִגְרְךָ, v. 5) it is: *num consociabitur tecum*. כִּסֵּא is here the judgment-seat, just as the Arabic *cursi* directly denotes the tribunal of God (in distinction from العَرْش, the throne of His majesty). With reference to הַוּוֹת *vid.* on v. 10. Assuming that חֹק is a divine statute, we obtain this meaning for עֲלֵי־חֹק: which frameth (*i.e.* plots and executes) trouble, by making

---

* By means of a similar transposition of the vowel as is to be assumed in תְּאָהֲבוּ, Prov. i. 22, it also appears that כִּיסָבִין = כִּיסֻבִּין (lying upon the table, ἀνακείμενοι) of the Pesach-Haggada has to be explained, which Joseph Kimchi finds so inexplicable that he regards it as a clerical error that has become traditional.

the written divine right into a rightful title for unrighteous conduct, by means of which the innocent are plunged into misfortune. Hitzig renders: contrary to order, after Prov. xvii. 26, where, however, עַל־יֹשֶׁר is intended like ἕνεκεν δικαιοσύνης, Matt. v. 10. Olshausen proposes to read יְנוּרוּ (lvi. 7, lix. 4) instead of יָגוּדוּ, just as conversely Aben-Ezra in lvi. 7 reads יָגוּדוּ. But גָּדַר, גּוּד, has the secured signification of *scindere, incidere* (cf. جَدَّ, but also خَدَّ, *supra*, i. 399), from which the signification *invadere* can be easily derived (whence גְּדוּד, a breaking in, invasion, an invading host). With reference to דָּם נָקִי *vid. Psychology*, S. 243 (tr. p. 286): because the blood is the soul, that is said of the blood which applies properly to the person. The subject to יָגוּדוּ are the seat of corruption (by which a high council consisting of many may be meant, just as much as a princely throne) and its accomplices. Prophetic certainty is expressed in וַיְהִי and וַיֵּשֶׁב. The figure of God as מִשְׂגָּב is Davidic and Korahitic. צוּר מַחְסִי is explained from xviii. 2. Since הֵשִׁיב designates the retribution as a return of guilt incurred in the form of actual punishment, it might be rendered "requite" just as well as "cause to return;" עֲלֵיהֶם, however, instead of לָהֶם (liv. 7) makes the idea expressed in vii. 17 more natural. On בְּרָעָתָם Hitzig correctly compares 2 Sam. xiv. 7, iii. 27. The Psalm closes with an anadiplosis, just as it began with one; and אֱלֹהֵינוּ affirms that the destruction of the persecutor will follow as surely as the church is able to call Jahve its God.

PSALM XCV.

CALL TO THE WORSHIP OF GOD AND TO OBEDIENCE TO HIS WORD.

1 COME, let us exult unto Jahve,
  Let us make a joyful noise to the Rock of our salvation!
2 Let us come before His face with thanksgiving,
  Let us make a joyful noise unto Him in songs!

3 For a great God is Jahve,
  And a great King above all gods;

4 He, in whose hand are the deep places of the earth,
And to whom belong the tops of the mountains;
5 To whom belongeth the sea, and He hath made it,
And His hands have formed the dry land.
6 Come, let us worship and bow down,
Let us kneel before Jahve our Maker!
7 For He is our God,
And we are the people of His pasture and the flock of His hand.

To-day if ye will but hearken to His voice!
8 Harden not your hearts as at Meribah,
As on the day of Massah in the wilderness,
9 When your fathers tempted Me,
Proved me, although they saw My work.
10 Forty years was I vexed with a generation,
And said: "They are a people that do err in their heart."
But they knew not My ways,
11 So that I sware in My wrath:
"Verily they shall not enter into My rest!"

This Psalm is related to the preceding by the celebration of Jahve as a "Rock." If it has any definite occasion, it is at any rate not manifest what that occasion is. It consists of a four-line introduction and two groups of ten lines.

Vers. 1, 2. Jahve is called the Rock of our salvation (as in lxxxix. 27, cf. xciv. 22) as being its firm and sure ground. Visiting the house of God, one comes before God's face; קדּם פּני, præoccupare faciem, is equivalent to visere (visitare). תּודה is not confessio peccati, but laudis. The Beth before תודה is the Beth of accompaniment, as in Mic. vi. 6; that before זמרות (according to 2 Sam. xxiii. 1 a name for psalms, whilst כּמור can only be used as a technical expression) is the Beth of the medium.

Vers. 3-7b. The adorableness of God receives a threefold confirmation: He is exalted above all gods as King, above all things as Creator, and above His people as Shepherd and Leader. אלהים (gods) here, as in xcvi. 4 sq., xcvii. 7, 9, and frequently, are the powers of the natural world and of the world of men, which the Gentiles deify and call kings (as Moloch (Molech), the deified fire), which, however, all stand under the lordship of Jahve, who is infinitely exalted above everything that is otherwise called god (xcvi. 4, xcvii. 9). The supposition that תּוֹעֲפוֹת הָרִים denotes the pit-works (μέταλλα) of the mountains (Böttcher), is at once improbable, because to all appearance it is intended to be the antithesis to מֶחְקְרֵי־אָרֶץ, the shafts of the earth. The derivation from יָעַף (יָעֵף), κάμνειν, κοπιᾶν, also does not suit תוֹעֲפוֹת in Num. xxiii. 22, xxiv. 8, for "fatigues" and "indefatigableness" are notions that lie very wide apart. The כֶּסֶף תּוֹעֲפוֹת of Job xxii. 25 might more readily be explained according to this "silver of fatigues," *i.e.* silver that the fatiguing labour of mining brings to light, and תועפות הרים in the passage before us, with Gussetius, Geier, and Hengstenberg: *cacumina montium quia defatigantur qui eo ascendunt*, prop. ascendings = summits of the mountains, after which כסף תועפות, Job xxii. 25, might also signify "silver of the mountain-heights." But the LXX., which renders δόξα in the passages in Numbers and τὰ ὕψη τῶν ὀρέων in the passage before us, leads one to a more correct track. The verb יָעַף (וַיַּעַף), transposed from יפע (ופע), goes back to the root יף, וף, to stand forth, tower above, to be high, according to which תועפות = תופעות signifies *eminentiæ*, *i.e.* towerings = summits, or prominences = high (the highest) perfection (*vid.* on Job xxii. 25). In the passage before us it is a synonym of the Arabic

مَيِفَى, مِيفَاةٌ, *pars terræ eminens* (from وفى = יפע, prop. instrumentally: a means of rising above, viz. by climbing), and of the names of eminences derived from يَفَ (after which Hitzig renders: the teeth of the mountains). By reason of the fact that Jahve is the Owner (cf. 1 Sam. ii. 8), because the Creator of all things, the call to worship, which concerns no one so nearly as it does Israel, the people, which before other peoples is Jahve's creation, viz. the creation of His miraculously mighty grace, is repeated. In the call or invitation, הִשְׁתַּחֲוָה signifies to stretch one's self out full length upon the ground, the proper attitude of adoration; כָּרַע, to curtsey, to totter; and בָּרַךְ, Arabic *baraka*, starting from the radical signification *flectere*, to kneel down, *in genua* (πρόχνυ, *pronum = procnum*) *procumbere*, 2 Chron. vi. 13 (cf. Hölemann, *Bibelstudien*, i.

135 f.). Beside עַם מַרְעִיתוֹ, people of His pasture, צֹאן יָדוֹ is not the flock formed by His creating hand (Augustine: *ipse gratiâ suâ nos oves fecit*), but, after Gen. xxx. 35, the flock under His protection, the flock led and defended by His skilful, powerful hand. Böttcher renders: flock of His charge; but יָד in this sense (Jer. vi. 3) signifies only a place, and "flock of His place" would be poetry and prose in one figure.

Vers. 7c–11. The second decastich begins in the midst of the Masoretic ver. 7. Up to this point the church stirs itself up to a worshipping appearing before its God; now the voice of God (Heb. iv. 7), earnestly admonishing, meets it, resounding from out of the sanctuary. Since שָׁמַע בְּ signifies not merely to hear, but to hear obediently, ver. 7c cannot be a conditioning protasis to what follows. Hengstenberg wishes to supply the apodosis: "then will He bless you, His people;" but אִם in other instances too (lxxxi. 9, cxxxix. 19, Prov. xxiv. 11), like לוּ, has an optative signification, which it certainly has gained by a suppression of a promissory apodosis, but yet without the genius of the language having any such in mind in every instance. The word הַיּוֹם placed first gives prominence to the present, in which this call to obedience goes forth, as a decisive turning-point. The divine voice warningly calls to mind the self-hardening of Israel, which came to light at Meribah, on the day of Massah. What is referred to, as also in lxxxi. 8, is the tempting of God in the second year of the Exodus on account of the failing of water in the neighbourhood of Horeb, at the place which is for this reason called *Massah u-Meribah* (Ex. xvii. 1–7); from which is to be distinguished the tempting of God in the fortieth year of the Exodus at *Meribah*, viz. at the waters of contention near Kadesh (written fully *Mê-Meribath Kadesh*, or more briefly *Mê-Meribah*), Num. xx. 2–13 (cf. on lxxviii. 20). Strictly כִּמְרִיבָה signifies nothing but *instar Meribæ*, as in lxxxiii. 10 *instar Midianitarum;* but according to the sense, בְּ is equivalent to כְּ, cvi. 32, just as כְּיוֹם is equivalent to בְּיוֹם. On אֲשֶׁר, *quum*, cf. Deut. xi. 6. The meaning of גַּם־רָאוּ פָעֳלִי is not they also (גַּם as in lii. 7) saw His work; for the reference to the giving of water out of the rock would give a thought that is devoid of purpose here, and the assertion is too indefinite for it to be understood of the judgment upon those who tempted

God (Hupfeld and Hitzig). It is therefore rather to be rendered: notwithstanding (ὅμως, Ew. § 354, a) they had (=although they had, cf. גַּם in Isa. xlix. 15) seen His work (His wondrous guiding and governing), and might therefore be sure that He would not suffer them to be destroyed. The verb קוּט coincides with κοτέω, κότος. בְּדוֹר, for which the LXX. has τῇ γενεᾷ ἐκείνῃ, is anarthrous in order that the notion may be conceived of more qualitatively than relatively: with a (whole) generation. With וָאֹמַר Jahve calls to mind the repeated declarations of His vexation concerning their heart, which was always inclined towards error which leads to destruction—declarations, however, which bore no fruit. Just this ineffectiveness of His indignation had as its result that (אֲשֶׁר, not ὅτι but ὥστε, as in Gen. xiii. 16, Deut. xxviii. 27, 51, 2 Kings ix. 37, and frequently) He sware, etc. (אִם=verily not, Ges. § 155, 2, f, with the emphatic future form in ûn which follows). It is the oath in Num. xiv. 27 sqq. that is meant. The older generation died in the desert, and therefore lost the entering into the rest of God, by reason of their disobedience. If now, many centuries after Moses, they are invited in the Davidic Psalter to submissive adoration of Jahve, with the significant call: "To-day if ye will hearken to His voice!" and with a reference to the warning example of the fathers, the obedience of faith, now as formerly, has therefore to look forward to the gracious reward of entering into God's rest, which the disobedient at that time lost; and the taking possession of Canaan was, therefore, not as yet the final מְנוּחָה (Deut. xii. 9). This is the connection of the wider train of thought which to the writer of the Epistle to the Hebrews, ch. iii., iv., follows from this text of the Psalm.

PSALM XCVI.

A GREETING OF THE COMING KINGDOM OF GOD.

1 SING unto Jahve a new song,
   Sing unto Jahve, all lands.
2 Sing unto Jahve, bless His Name,
   Cheerfully proclaim His salvation from day to day.

3 Declare His glory among the heathen,
His wonders among all peoples.

4 For great is Jahve and worthy to be praised exceedingly,
Terrible is He above all gods.
5 For all the gods of the peoples are idols,
But Jahve hath made the heavens.
6 Brightness and splendour are before Him,
Might and beauty are in His sanctuary.

7 Give unto Jahve, O ye races of the peoples,
Give unto Jahve glory and might.
8 Give unto Jahve the honour of His Name,
Take offerings and come into His courts.
9 Worship Jahve in holy attire,
Tremble before Him, all lands.

10 Say among the heathen: "Jahve is now King,
Therefore the world will stand without tottering,
He will govern the peoples in uprightness."
11 The heavens shall rejoice
And the earth be glad,
The sea shall roar and its fulness.

12 The field shall exult and all that is therein,
Then shall all the trees of the wood shout for joy—
13 Before Jahve, for He cometh,
For He cometh to judge the earth—
He shall judge the world in righteousness
And the peoples in His faithfulness.

What Ps. xcv. 3 says: "*A great God is Jahve, and a great King above all gods*," is repeated in Ps. xcvi. The LXX. inscribes it (1) ᾠδὴ τῷ Δαυίδ, and the chronicler has really taken it up almost entire in the song which was sung on the day when the Ark was brought in (1 Chron. xvi. 23–33); but, as the coarse seams between vers. 22 and 23, 33 and 34 show, he there strings together familiar reminiscences of the Psalms (*vid.* on Ps. cv.) as a sort of mosaic, in order approximately to express the festive mood and festive strains of that day. And

(2) ὅτε ὁ οἶκος ᾠκοδομεῖτο (Cod. Vat. ᾠκοδόμηται) μετὰ τὴν αἰχμαλωσίαν. By this the LXX. correctly interprets the Psalm as a post-exilic song: and the Psalm corresponds throughout to the advance which the mind of Israel has experienced in the Exile concerning its mission in the world. The fact that the religion of Jahve is destined for mankind at large, here receives the most triumphantly joyous, lyrical expression. And so far as this is concerned, the key-note of the Psalm is even deutero-Isaianic. For it is one chief aim of Isa. ch. xl.–lxvi. to declare the pinnacle of glory of the Messianic apostolic mission on to which Israel is being raised through the depth of affliction of the Exile. All these post-exilic songs come much nearer to the spirit of the New Testament than the pre-exilic; for the New Testament, which is the intrinsic character of the Old Testament freed from its barriers and limitations, is in process of coming into being (*im Werden begriffen*) throughout the Old Testament, and the Exile was one of the most important crises in this progressive process.

Ps. xcvi.–xcviii. are more Messianic than many in the strict sense of the word Messianic; for the central (gravitating) point of the Old Testament gospel (*Heilsverkündigung*) lies not in the Messiah, but in the appearing (parusia) of Jahve—a fact which is explained by the circumstance that the mystery of the incarnation still lies beyond the Old Testament knowledge or perception of salvation. All human intervention in the matter of salvation accordingly appears as purely human, and still more, it preserves a national and therefore outward and natural impress by virtue of the national limit within which the revelation of salvation has entered. If the ideal Davidic king who is expected even does anything superhuman, he is nevertheless only a man—a man of God, it is true, without his equal, but not the God-man. The mystery of the incarnation does, it is true, the nearer it comes to actual revelation, cast rays of its dawning upon prophecy, but the sun itself remains below the horizon: redemption is looked for as Jahve's own act, and "Jahve cometh" is also still the watchword of the last prophet (Mal. iii. 1).

The five six-line strophes of the Psalm before us are not to be mistaken. The chronicler has done away with five lines, and thereby disorganized the strophic structure; and one line (ver. 10a) he has removed from its position. The originality of the Psalm in the Psalter, too, is revealed thereby, and the non-independence of the chronicler, who treats the Psalm as an historian.

Vers. 1-3. Call to the nation of Jahve to sing praise to its God and to evangelize the heathen. שִׁירוּ is repeated three times. The new song assumes a new form of things, and the call thereto, a present which appeared to be a beginning that furnished a guarantee of this new state of things, a beginning viz. of the recognition of Jahve throughout the whole world of nations, and of His accession to the lordship over the whole earth. The new song is an echo of the approaching revelation of salvation and of glory, and this is also the inexhaustible material of the joyful tidings that go forth from day to day (מִיּוֹם לְיוֹם as in Esth. iii. 7, whereas in the Chronicles it is מִיּוֹם אֶל־יוֹם as in Num. xxx. 15). We read ver. 1a verbally the same in Isa. xlii. 10; ver. 2 calls to mind Isa. lii. 7, lx. 6; and ver. 3a, Isa. lxvi. 19.

Vers. 4-6. Confirmation of the call from the glory of Jahve that is now become manifest. The clause ver. 4a, as also cxlv. 3, is taken out of xlviii. 2. כֹּל־אֱלֹהִים is the plural of כָּל־אֱלוֹהַּ, every god, 2 Chron. xxxii. 15; the article may stand here or be omitted (xcv. 3, cf. cxiii. 4). All the elohim, i.e. gods, of the peoples are אֱלִילִים (from the negative אַל), nothings and good-for-nothings, unreal and useless. The LXX. renders δαιμόνια, as though the expression were שֵׁדִים (cf. 1 Cor. x. 20), more correctly εἴδωλα in Apoc. ix. 20. What ver. 5 says is wrought out in Isa. ch. xl., xliv., and elsewhere; אֱלִילִים is a name of idols that occurs nowhere more frequently than in Isaiah. The sanctuary (ver. 6) is here the earthly sanctuary. From Jerusalem, over which the light arises first of all (Isa. ch. lx.), Jahve's superterrestrial doxa now reveals itself in the world. הוֹד וְהָדָר is the usual pair of words for royal glory. The chronicler reads ver. 6b עֹז וְחֶדְוָה בִּמְקֹמוֹ, might and joy are in His place (חֶדְוָה a late word, like אַחֲוָה, brotherhood, brotherly affection, from an old root, Ex. xviii. 9). With the place of God one might associate the thought of the celestial place of God transcending space; the chronicler may, however, have altered במקדשו into במקמו because when the Ark was brought in, the Temple (בית המקדש) was not yet built.

Vers. 7–9. Call to the families of the peoples to worship God, the One, living, and glorious God. הָבוּ is repeated three times here as Ps. xxix., of which the whole strophe is an echo. Isaiah (ch. lx.) sees them coming in with the gifts which they are admonished to bring with them into the courts of Jahve (in Chron. only: לְפָנָיו). Instead of בְּהַדְרַת קֹדֶשׁ here and in the chronicler, the LXX. brings the courts (חצרת) in once more; but the dependence of the strophe upon Ps. xxix. furnishes a guarantee for the "holy attire," similar to the wedding garment in the New Testament parable. Instead of מִפָּנָיו, ver. 9b, the chronicler has מִלְּפָנָיו, just as he also alternates with both forms, 2 Chron. xxxii. 7, cf. 1 Chron. xix. 18.

Vers. 10, 11. That which is to be said among the peoples is the joyous evangel of the kingdom of heaven which is now come and realized. The watchword is "Jahve is King," as in Isa. lii. 7. The LXX. correctly renders: ὁ κύριος ἐβασίλευσε,* for מָלָךְ is intended historically (Apoc. xi. 17). אַף, as in xciii. 1, introduces that which results from this fact, and therefore to a certain extent goes beyond it. The world below, hitherto shaken by war and anarchy, now stands upon foundations that cannot be shaken in time to come, under Jahve's righteous and gentle sway. This is the joyful tidings of the new era which the poet predicts from out of his own times, when he depicts the joy that will then pervade the whole creation; in connection with which it is hardly intentional that ver. 11a and 11b acrostically contain the divine names יהוה and יהי. This joining of all creatures in the joy at Jahve's appearing is a characteristic feature of Isa. ch. xl.–lxii. These cords are already struck in Isa. xxxv. 1 sq. "The sea and its fulness" as in Isa. xlii. 10. In the chronicler ver. 10a (ויאמרו instead of אמרו) stands between ver. 11b and 11c,—according to Hitzig, who uses all his ingenuity here in favour of that other recension of the text, by an oversight of the copyist.

---

* In the *Psalterium Veronense* with the addition *apo xylu*, Cod. 156, Latinizing ἀπὸ τῷ ξύλῳ; in the Latin Psalters (the Vulgate excepted) *a ligno*, undoubtedly an addition by an early Christian hand, upon which, however, great value is set by Justin and all the early Latin Fathers.

Vers. 12, 13. The chronicler changes שְׂדַי into the prosaic הַשָּׂדֶה, and כָּל־עֲצֵי־יַעַר with the omission of the כֹּל into עֲצֵי הַיַּעַר. The psalmist on his part follows the model of Isaiah, who makes the trees of the wood exult and clap their hands, ch. lv. 12, xliv. 23. The אָז, which points into this festive time of all creatures which begins with Jahve's coming, is as in Isa. xxxv. 5 sq. Instead of לִפְנֵי, "before," the chronicler has the מִלִּפְנֵי so familiar to him, by which the joy is denoted as being occasioned by Jahve's appearing. The lines ver. 13*bc* sound very much like ix. 9. The chronicler has abridged ver. 13, by hurrying on to the mosaic-work portion taken from Ps. cv. The poet at the close glances from the ideal past into the future. The twofold בָּא is a participle, Ew. § 200. Being come to judgment, after He has judged and sifted, executing punishment, Jahve will govern in the righteousness of mercy and in faithfulness to the promises.

PSALM XCVII.

THE BREAKING THROUGH OF THE KINGDOM OF GOD, THE JUDGE AND SAVIOUR.

1 JAHVE is now King, the earth shouteth for joy,
   Many islands rejoice.
2 Clouds and darkness are round about Him,
   Righteousness and judgment are the pillars of His throne.
3 Fire goeth before Him
   And burneth up His enemies round about.

4 His lightnings lighten the world;
   The earth seeth it, and trembleth because of it.
5 Mountains melt like wax before Jahve,
   Before the Lord of the whole earth.
6 The heavens declare His righteousness,
   And all the peoples see His glory.

7 Confounded are all those who serve graven images,
   Who boast themselves of idols;
   All the gods cast themselves down to Him.
8 Zion heareth it and rejoiceth thereat,

And the daughters of Judah shout for joy—
Because of Thy judgments, Jahve!

9 For Thou, Jahve, art the Most High over all the earth,
Thou art highly exalted above all gods.

10 Ye who love Jahve, hate evil:
He who guardeth the souls of His saints,
Out of the hand of the evil-doer will He rescue them.
11 Light is sown for the righteous,
And for the upright-minded joy.
12 Rejoice, ye righteous, in Jahve,
And sing praise unto His holy Name.

This Psalm, too, has the coming of Jahve, who enters upon His kingdom through judgment, as its theme, and the watchword "Jahve is King" as its key-note. The LXX. inscribes it: τῷ Δαυίδ, ὅτε ἡ γῆ αὐτοῦ καθίσταται (καθίστατο); Jerome: *quando terra ejus restituta est*. The τῷ Δαυίδ is worthless; the time of restoration, from which it takes its rise, is the post-exilic, for it is composed, as mosaic-work, out of the earlier original passages of Davidic and Asaphic Psalms and of the prophets, more especially of Isaiah, and is entirely an expression of the religious consciousness which resulted from the Exile.

Vers. 1–3. We have here nothing but echoes of the older literature: ver. 1, cf. Isa. xlii. 10–12, li. 5; ver. 2a, cf. xviii. 10, 12; ver. 2b = lxxxix. 15; ver. 3a, cf. l. 3, xviii. 9; ver. 3b, cf. Isa. xlii. 25. Beginning with the visible coming of the kingdom of God in the present, with ה מָלָךְ the poet takes his stand upon the standpoint of the kingdom which is come. With it also comes rich material for universal joy. תָּגֵל is indicative, as in xcvi. 11 and frequently. רַבִּים are all, for all of them are in fact many (cf. Isa. liii. 15). The description of the theophany, for which the way is preparing in ver. 2, also reminds one of Hab. ch. iii. God's enshrouding Himself in darkness bears witness to His judicial earnestness. Because He comes as Judge, the basis of His royal throne and of His judgment-seat is also called to mind. His harbinger is fire, which consumes His adversaries on every side, as that which broke forth out of the pillar of cloud once consumed the Egyptians.

Vers. 4–6. Again we have nothing but echoes of the older literature: ver. 4a = lxxvii. 19; ver. 4b, cf. lxxvii. 17; ver. 5a, cf. Mic. i. 4; ver. 5b, cf. Mic. iv. 13; ver. 6a = l. 6; ver. 6b, cf. Isa. xxxv. 2, xl. 5, lii. 10, lxvi. 18. The poet goes on to describe that which is future with historical certainty. That which lxxvii. 19 says of the manifestation of God in the earlier times he transfers to the revelation of God in the last time. The earth sees it, and begins to tremble in consequence of it. The reading וַתָּחֵל, according to Hitzig (cf. Ew. § 232, b) traditional, is, however, only an error of pointing that has been propagated; the correct reading is the reading of Heidenheim and Baer, restored according to MSS., וַתֵּחַל (cf. 1 Sam. xxxi. 3), like וַיָּבֵן, וַתֵּקַע, וַתֵּרֶם, and וַתָּשֶׂם. The figure of the wax is found even in lxviii. 3; and Jahve is also called "Lord of the whole earth" in Zech. iv. 14, vi. 5. The proclamation of the heavens is an expression of joy, xcvi. 11. They proclaim the judicial strictness with which Jahve, in accordance with His promises, carries out His plan of salvation, the realization of which has reached its goal in the fact that all men see the glory of God.

Vers. 7, 8. When the glory of Jahve becomes manifest, everything that is opposed to it will be punished and consumed by its light. Those who serve idols will become conscious of their delusion with shame and terror, Isa. xlii. 17, Jer. x. 14. The superhuman powers (LXX. ἄγγελοι), deified by the heathen, then bow down to Him who alone is *Elohim* in absolute personality. הִשְׁתַּחֲווּ is not imperative (LXX., Syriac), for as a command this clause would be abrupt and inconsequential, but the perfect of that which actually takes place. The quotation in Heb. i. 6 is taken from Deut. xxxii. 43, LXX. In ver. 8 (after xlviii. 12) the survey of the poet again comes back to his own nation. When Zion hears that Jahve has appeared, and all the world and all the powers bow down to Him, she rejoices: for it is in fact her God whose kingship has come to be acknowledged. And all the daughter-churches of the Jewish land exult together with the mother-church over the salvation which dawns through judgments.

Ver. 9. This distichic epiphonema (ver. 9a = lxxxiii. 19;

ver. 9b, cf. xlvii. 3, 10) might close the Psalm; there follows still, however, a hortatory strophe (which was perhaps not added till later on).

Vers. 10–12. It is true ver. 12a is = xxxii. 11, ver. 12b = xxx. 5, and the promise in ver. 10 is the same as in xxxvii. 28, xxxiv. 21; but as to the rest, particularly ver. 11, this strophe is original. It is an encouraging admonition to fidelity in an age in which an effeminate spirit of looking longingly towards [lit. ogling] heathenism was rife, and stedfast adherence to Jahve was threatened with loss of life. Those who are faithful in their confession, as in the Maccabæan age ('Ασιδαῖοι), are called חֲסִידָיו. The beautiful figure in ver. 11 is misapprehended by the ancient versions, inasmuch as they read זרח (cxii. 4) instead of זרע. זרע does not here signify sown = strewn into the earth, but strewn along his life's way, so that he, the righteous one, advances step by step in the light. Hitzig rightly compares κίδναται, σκίδναται, used of the dawn and of the sun. Of the former Virgil also says, *Et jam prima novo spargebat lumine terras.*

PSALM XCVIII.

GREETING TO HIM WHO IS BECOME KNOWN IN RIGHTEOUSNESS AND SALVATION.

1 SING unto Jahve a new song,
  For He hath done marvellous things,
  His right hand and His holy arm helped Him.
2 Jahve hath made known His salvation,
  He hath revealed His righteousness before the eyes of the nations.
3 He remembered His loving-kindness and His faithfulness to the house of Israel,
  All the ends of the earth saw the salvation of our God.

4 Make a joyful noise unto Jahve, all ye lands,
  Break forth into rejoicing and play—
5 Play unto Jahve with the cithern,
  With the cithern and the voice of song.

6 With trumpets and the sound of the horn,
Make a joyful noise before the King Jahve!

7 Let the sea roar, and that which filleth it,
The world, and those who dwell therein.
8 Let the rivers clap their hands,
Together let the mountains rejoice
9 Before Jahve, for He cometh to judge the earth—
He shall judge the world with righteousness,
And the peoples with uprightness.

This is the only Psalm which is inscribed מִזְמוֹר without further addition, whence it is called in *B. Aboda Zara*, 24*b*, מִזְמוֹרָא יְתוֹמָא (the orphan Psalm). The Peshîto Syriac inscribes it *De redemtione populi ex Ægypto*; the "new song," however, is not the song of Moses, but the counterpart of this, cf. Apoc. xv. 3. There "the Lord reigneth" resounded for the first time, at the sea; here the completion of the beginning there commenced is sung, viz. the final glory of the divine kingdom, which through judgment breaks through to its full reality. The beginning and end are taken from Ps. xcvi. Almost all that lies between is taken from the second part of Isaiah. This book of consolation for the exiles is become as it were a Castalian spring for the religious lyric.

Vers. 1–3. Ver. 1*ab* we have already read in xcvi. 1. What follows in ver. 1*c*–3 is taken from Isa. lii. 10, lxiii. 5, cf. 7, lix. 16, cf. xl. 10. The primary passage, Isa. lii. 10, shows that the *Athnach* of ver. 2 is correctly placed. לְעֵינֵי is the opposite of hearsay (cf. اللعين, from one's own observation, עין. الخبر, from the narrative of another person). The dative לְבֵית יִשְׂרָאֵל depends upon וַיִּזְכֹּר, according to cvi. 45, cf. Luke i. 54 sq.

Vers. 4–6. The call in ver. 4 demands some joyful manifestation of the mouth, which can be done in many ways; in ver. 5 the union of song and the music of stringed instruments, as of the Levites; and in ver. 6 the sound of wind instruments, as of the priests. On ver. 4 cf. Isa. xliv. 23, xlix.

13, lii. 9, together with xiv. 7 (inasmuch as פִּצְהוּ וְרַנְּנוּ is equivalent to פִּצְהוּ רִנָּה). קוֹל זִמְרָה is found also in Isa. li. 3.

Vers. 7–9. Here, too, it is all an echo of the earlier language of Psalms and prophets: ver. 7a = xcvi. 11; ver. 7b like xxiv. 1; ver. 8 after Isa. lv. 12 (where we find כְיחָא כַף instead of the otherwise customary הָקַע כַּף, xlvii. 2; or הִכָּה כַף, 2 Kings xi. 12, is said of the trees of the field); ver. 9 = xcvi. 13, cf. 10. In the bringing in of nature to participate in the joy of mankind, the clapping rivers (נְהָרוֹת) are original to this Psalm: the rivers cast up high waves, which flow into one another like clapping hands;* cf. Hab. iii. 10, where the abyss of the sea lifts up its hands on high, *i.e.* causes its waves to run mountain-high.

PSALM XCIX.

SONG OF PRAISE IN HONOUR OF THE THRICE HOLY ONE.

1 JAHVE reigneth, the peoples tremble;
  He sitteth upon the cherubim, the earth tottereth.
2 Jahve in Zion is great,
  And HE is exalted above all the peoples.
3 They shall praise Thy great and fearful name—
  Holy is HE.

4 And the might of a king who loveth the right
  Hast THOU established in righteousness;
  Right and righteousness hast THOU executed in Jacob.
5 Exalt ye Jahve our God,
  And prostrate yourselves at His footstool—
  Holy is HE.

6 Moses and Aaron among His priests,
  And Samuel among those who call upon His name—
  They called unto Jahve and HE answered them;

---

* Luther renders: "the water-floods exult" (*frohlocken*); and Eychman's *Vocabularius predicantium* explains *plaudere* by " to exult (*frohlocken*) for joy, to smite the hands together *præ gaudio*;" cf. Luther's version of Ezek. xxi. 17.

7 In a pillar of cloud He spoke to them ;
   They kept His testimonies,
   And the law which He gave them.
8 Jahve our God, Thou hast answered them ;
   A forgiving God wast Thou unto them,
   And one taking vengeance of their deeds.
9 Exalt ye Jahve our God,
   And prostrate yourselves at His holy mountain,
   For holy is Jahve our God.

This is the third of the Psalms (xciii., xcvii., xcix.) which begin with the watchword ה' מָלָךְ. It falls into three parts, of which the first (vers. 1–3) closes with קדוש הוא, the second (vers. 4, 5) with קדוש הוא, and the third, more full-toned, with קדוש ה' אֱלֹהֵינוּ—an earthly echo of the trisagion of the seraphim. The first two Sanctuses are two hexastichs; and two hexastichs form the third, according to the very same law by which the third and the sixth days of creation each consists of two creative works. This artistic form bears witness against Olshausen in favour of the integrity of the text; but the clare-obscure of the language and expression makes no small demands upon the reader.

Bengel has seen deepest into the internal character of this Psalm. He says, " The 99th Psalm has three parts, in which the Lord is celebrated as He who is to come, as He who is, and as He who was, and each part is closed with the ascription of praise: He is holy." The Psalm is laid out accordingly by Oettinger, Burk, and C. H. Rieger.

Vers. 1–3. The three futures express facts of the time to come, which are the inevitable result of Jahve's kingly dominion bearing sway from heaven, and here below from Zion, over the world; they therefore declare what must and will happen. The participle *insidens cherubis* (lxxx. 2, cf. xviii. 11) is a definition of the manner (Olshausen): He reigns, sitting enthroned above the cherubim. נוּט, like نوع, is a further formation of the root נא, νυ, to bend, nod. What is meant is not a trembling that is the absolute opposite of joy, but a trembling that leads on to salvation. The *Breviarium in Psal-*

terium, which bears the name of Jerome, observes: *Terra quamdiu immota fuerit, sanari non potest; quando vero mota fuerit et intremuerit, tunc recipiet sanitatem.* In ver. 3a declaration passes over into invocation. One can feel how the hope that the " great and fearful Name" (Deut. x. 17) will be universally acknowledged, and therefore that the religion of Israel will become the religion of the world, moves and elates the poet. The fact that the expression notwithstanding is not קָדוֹשׁ אָתָּה, but קָדוֹשׁ הוּא, is explained from the close connection with the seraphic trisagion in Isa. vi. 3. הוּא refers to Jahve; He and His Name are notions that easily glide over into one another.

Vers. 4, 5. The second *Sanctus* celebrates Jahve with respect to His continuous righteous rule in Israel. The majority of expositors construe it: " And (they shall praise) the might of the king, who loves right ;" but this joining of the clause on to יוֹדוּ over the refrain that stands in the way is hazardous. Neither can וְעֹז מֶלֶךְ מִשְׁפָּט אָהֵב, however, be an independent clause, since אָהֵב cannot be said of עֹז, but only of its possessor. And the dividing of the verse at אהב, adopted by the LXX., will therefore not hold good. משפט אהב is an attributive clause to מלך in the same position as in xi. 7 ; and עֹז, with what appertains to it, is the object to כּוֹנַנְתָּ placed first, which has the king's throne as its object elsewhere (ix. 8, 2 Sam. vii. 13, 1 Chron. xvii. 12), just as it here has the might of the king, which, however, here at the same time in מֵישָׁרִים takes another and permutative object (cf. the permutative subject in lxxii. 17), as Hitzig observes; or rather, since מֵישָׁרִים is most generally used as an adverbial notion, this מֵישָׁרִים (lviii. 2, lxxv. 3, ix. 9, and frequently), usually as a definition of the mode of the judging and reigning, is subordinated : and the might of a king who loves the right, *i.e.* of one who governs not according to dynastic caprice but moral precepts, hast Thou established in spirit and aim (directed to righteousness and equity). What is meant is the theocratic kingship, and ver. 4c says what Jahve has constantly accomplished by means of this kingship: He has thus maintained right and righteousness (cf. *e.g.* 2 Sam. viii. 15, 1 Chron. xviii. 14, 1 Kings x. 9, Isa. xvi. 5) among His people. Out of this manifestation of God's righteousness, which is more conspicuous, and can be better estimated, within the nation of the history of redemption than elsewhere, grows the call to highly exalt Jahve the God of Israel, and to bow one's self very low at His footstool. לַהֲדֹם רַגְלָיו, as in cxxxii. 7, is not a statement of the object (for Isa. xlv. 14 is of another kind), but (like אֶל in other instances) of the place in which, or of the direction (cf. vii. 14) in which the προσκύνησις is to take place. The temple is called Jahve's footstool (1 Chron. xxviii. 2, cf. Lam. ii. 1, Isa. lx. 13) with reference to the ark, the *capporeth* of which corresponds to the transparent sapphire (Ex. xxiv. 10) and to the crystal-like firmament of the *mercaba* (Ezek. i. 22, cf. 1 Chron. xxviii. 18).

Vers. 6–9. The vision of the third *Sanctus* looks into the history of the olden time prior to the kings. In support of the statement that Jahve is a living God, and a God who proves Himself in mercy and in judgment, the poet appeals to three heroes of the olden time, and the events recorded of them. The expression certainly sounds as though it had reference to something belonging to the present time ; and Hitzig therefore believes that it must be explained of the three as heavenly intercessors, after the manner of Onias and Jeremiah in the vision 2 Macc. xv. 12–14. But apart from this presupposing an active manifestation of life on the part of those who have fallen happily asleep, which is at variance with the ideas of the latest as well as of the earliest Psalms concerning the other world, this interpretation founders upon ver. 7*a*, according to which a celestial discourse of God with the three " in the pillar of cloud" ought also to be supposed. The substantival clauses ver. 6*ab* bear sufficient evidence in themselves of being a retrospect, by which the futures that follow are stamped as being the expression of the cotemporaneous past. The distribution of the predicates to the three is well conceived. Moses was also a mighty man in prayer, for with his hands uplifted for prayer he obtained the victory for his people over Amalek (Ex. xvii. 11 sq.), and on another occasion placed himself in the breach, and rescued them from the wrath of God and from destruction (cvi. 23, Ex. xxxii. 30–32 ; cf. also Num. xii. 13) ; and Samuel, it is true, is only a Levite by descent, but by office in a time of urgent need a priest (*cohen*), for he sacrifices independently in places where, by reason of the absence of the holy tabernacle with the ark of the covenant, it was not lawful, according to the letter of the law, to offer sacrifices, he builds an altar in Ramah, his residence as judge, and has, in connection with the divine services on the high place (*Bama*) there, a more than high-priestly position, inasmuch as the people do not begin the sacrificial repasts before he has blessed the sacrifice (1 Sam. ix. 13). But the character of a mighty man in prayer is outweighed in the case of Moses by the character of the priest; for he is, so to speak, the protopriest of Israel, inasmuch as he twice performed priestly acts which laid as it were a foundation for all times to come, viz. the sprinkling of the blood at the ratification of the covenant under Sinai (Ex. ch. xxiv.), and the whole ritual which was a model for the consecrated priesthood, at the consecration of the priests (Lev. ch. viii.). It was he, too, who performed the service in the sanctuary prior to the consecration of the priests: he set the shew-bread in order, prepared the candlestick, and burnt incense upon the golden altar (Ex. xl. 22–27). In the case of Samuel, on the other hand, the character of the mediator in the religious services is outweighed by that of the man mighty in prayer: by prayer he obtained Israel the victory of Ebenezer over the Philistines (1 Sam. vii. 8 sq.), and confirmed his words of warning with the miraculous sign, that at his calling upon God it would thunder and rain in the midst of a cloudless season (1 Sam. xii. 16, cf. Sir. xlvi. 16 sq.).

The poet designedly says: Moses and Aaron were among His priests, and Samuel among His praying ones. This third twelve-line strophe holds good, not only of the three in particular, but of the twelve-tribe nation of priests and praying ones to which they belong. For ver. 7a cannot be meant of the three, since, with the exception of a single instance (Num. xii. 5), it is always Moses only, not Aaron, much less Samuel, with whom God negotiates in such a manner. אֲלֵיהֶם refers to the whole people, which is proved by their interest in the divine revelation given by the hand of Moses out of the cloudy pillar (Ex. xxxiii. 7 sq.). Nor can ver. 6c therefore be understood of the three exclusively, since there is nothing to indicate the transition from them to the people: crying (קֹרְאִים, syncopated like חֹטְאִים, 1 Sam. xiv. 33) to Jahve, *i.e.* as often as they (these priests and praying ones, to whom a Moses, Aaron, and Samuel belong) cried unto Jahve, He answered them—He revealed Himself to this people who had such leaders (*choragi*), in the cloudy pillar, to those who kept His testimonies and the law which He gave them. A glance at ver. 8 shows that in Israel itself the good and the bad, good and evil, are distinguished. God answered those who could pray to Him with a claim to be answered. Ver. 7*bc* is, virtually at least, a relative clause, declaring the prerequisite of a prayer that may be granted. In ver. 8 is added the thought that the history of Israel, in the time of its redemption out of Egypt, is not less a mirror of the righteousness of God than of the pardoning grace of God. If vers. 7, 8 are referred entirely to the three, then עֲלִילוֹת and נְקָם, referred to their sins of infirmity, appear to be too strong expressions. But to take the suffix of עֲלִילוֹתָם objectively (*ea quæ in eos sunt moliti Core et socii ejus*), with Symmachus (καὶ ἔκδικος ἐπὶ ταῖς ἐπηρείαις αὐτῶν) and Kimchi, as the *ulciscens in omnes adinventiones eorum* of the Vulgate is interpreted,* is to do violence to it. The reference to the people explains it all without any constraint, and even the flight of prayer that comes in here (cf. Mic. vii. 18). The calling to mind of the generation of the desert, which fell short of the promise, is an earnest admonition for the generation of the present time. The God of Israel is holy in love and in wrath, as He Himself unfolds His Name in Ex. xxxiv. 6, 7. Hence the poet calls upon his fellow-countrymen to exalt this God, whom they may with pride call their own, *i.e.* to acknowledge and confess His majesty, and to fall down and worship at (לְ cf. אֶל, v. 8) the mountain of His holiness, the place of His choice and of His presence.

PSALM C.

CALL OF ALL THE WORLD TO THE SERVICE OF THE TRUE GOD.

1 MAKE a joyful noise unto Jahve, all ye lands!
2 Serve Jahve with gladness,
  Come before Him with rejoicing.

---

* *Vid.* Raemdonck in his *David propheta cet.* 1800 : *in omnes injurias ipsis illatas, uti patuit in Core cet*

3 Know ye that Jahve is God:
He hath made us, and His we are,
His people, and the flock of His pasture.

4 Come into His gates with thanksgiving,
Into His courts with praise.
Give thanks unto Him, bless His name.
5 For Jahve is good,
His mercy is everlasting,
And to generation and generation His faithfulness.

This Psalm closes the series of deutero-Isaianic Psalms, which began with Ps. xci. There is common to all of them that mild sublimity, sunny cheerfulness, unsorrowful spiritual character, and New Testament expandedness, which we wonder at in the second part of the Book of Isaiah; and besides all this, they are also linked together by the figure anadiplosis, and manifold consonances and accords.

The arrangement, too, at least from Ps. xciii. onwards, is Isaianic: it is parallel with the relation of Isa. ch. xxiv.-xxvii. to ch. xiii.-xxiii. Just as the former cycle of prophecies closes that concerning the nations, after the manner of a musical finale, so the Psalms celebrating the dominion of God, from Ps. xciii. onwards, which vividly portray the unfolded glory of the kingship of Jahve, have *Jubilate* and *Cantate* Psalms in succession.

From the fact that this last Jubilate is entirely the echo of the first, viz. of the first half of Ps. xcv., we see how ingenious the arrangement is. There we find all the thoughts which recur here. There it is said in ver. 7, *He is our God, and we are the people of His pasture and the flock of His hand*. And in ver. 2, *Let us come before His face with thanksgiving* (בְּתוֹדָה), *let us make a joyful noise unto Him in songs!*

This תודה is found here in the title of the Psalm, מִזְמוֹר לְתוֹדָה. Taken in the sense of a "Psalm for thanksgiving," it would say but little. We may take לתודה in a liturgical sense (with the Targum, Mendelssohn, Ewald, and Hitzig), like ליום הִשַּׁבַּת, xcii. 1, in this series, and like להזכיר in xxxviii. 1, lxx. 1. What is intended is not merely the *tôda* of the heart, but the *shelamîm-tôda*, זֶבַח תּוֹדָה, cvii. 22, cxvi. 17, which is also called absolutely תודה in lvi. 13, 2 Chron. xxix. 31. That kind of *shelamim* is thus called which is presented עַל־הּוֹרָה, *i.e.* as thankful praise for divine benefits received, more particularly marvellous protection and deliverance (*vid.* Ps. cvii.).

Vers. 1–3. The call in ver. 1 sounds like xcviii. 4, lxvi. 1. כָּל־הָאָרֶץ are all lands, or rather all men belonging to the earth's population. The first verse, without any parallelism and in so far monostichic, is like the signal for a blowing of the trumpets. Instead of "serve Jahve with gladness (בְּשִׂמְחָה)," it is expressed in ii. 11, "serve Jahve with fear (בְּיִרְאָה)." Fear and joy do not exclude one another. Fear becomes the exalted Lord, and the holy gravity of His requirements; joy becomes the gracious Lord, and His blessed service. The summons to manifest this joy in a religious, festive manner springs up out of an all-hopeful, world-embracing love, and this love is the spontaneous result of living faith in the promise that all tribes of the earth shall be blessed in the seed of Abraham, and in the prophecies in which this promise is unfolded. דְעוּ (as in iv. 4) Theodoret well interprets δι' αὐτῶν μάθετε τῶν πραγμάτων. They are to know from facts of outward and inward experience that Jahve is God: *He hath made us, and not we ourselves.* Thus runs the *Chethîb*, which the LXX. follows, αὐτὸς ἐποίησεν ἡμᾶς καὶ οὐχ ἡμεῖς (as also the Syriac and Vulgate); but Symmachus (like Rashi), contrary to all possibilities of language, renders αὐτὸς ἐποίησεν ἡμᾶς οὐκ ὄντας. Even the Midrash (*Bereshith Rabba*, ch. c. *init.*) finds in this confession the reverse of the arrogant words in the mouth of Pharaoh: "I myself have made myself" (Ezek. xxix. 3). The *Kerî*, on the other hand, reads לוֹ,* which the Targum, Jerome, and Saadia follow and render: *et ipsius nos sumus.* Hengstenberg calls this *Kerî* quite unsuitable and bad; and Hupfeld, on the other hand, calls the *Chethîb* an "unspeakable insipidity." But in reality both readings accord with the context, and it is clear that they are both in harmony

---

* According to the reckoning of the Masora, there are fifteen passages in the Old Testament in which לֹא is written and לוֹ is read, viz. Ex. xxi. 8, Lev. xi. 21, xxv. 30, 1 Sam. ii. 3, 2 Sam. xvi. 18, 2 Kings viii. 10, Isa. ix. 2, lxiii. 9, Ps. c. 3, cxxxix. 16, Job xiii. 15 [cf. the note there], xli. 4, Prov. xix. 7, xxvi. 2, Ezra iv. 2. Because doubtful, Isa. xlix. 5, 1 Chron. xi. 20 are not reckoned with these.

with Scripture. Many a one has drawn balsamic consolation from the words *ipse fecit nos et non ipsi nos;* e.g. Melancthon when disconsolately sorrowful over the body of his son in Dresden on the 12th July 1559. But in *ipse fecit nos et ipsius nos sumus* there is also a rich mine of comfort and of admonition, for the Creator is also the Owner, His heart clings to His creature, and the creature owes itself entirely to Him, without whom it would not have had a being, and would not continue in being. Since, however, the parallel passage, xcv. 7, favours ולו rather than ולא; since, further, ולא is the easier reading, inasmuch as הוא leads one to expect that an antithesis will follow (Hitzig); and since the "His people and the sheep of His pasture" that follows is a more natural continuation of a preceding ולו אנחנו than that it should be attached as a predicative object to עשׂנו over a parenthetical ולא אנחנו: the *Kerî* decidedly maintains the preference. In connection with both readings, עשׂה has a sense related to the history of redemption, as in 1 Sam. xii. 6. Israel is Jahve's work (מעשׂה), Isa. xxix. 23, lx. 21, cf. Deut. xxxii. 6, 15, not merely as a people, but as the people of God, who were kept in view even in the calling of Abram.

Vers. 4, 5. Therefore shall the men of all nations enter with thanksgiving into the gates of His Temple and into the courts of His Temple with praise (xcvi. 8), in order to join themselves in worship to His church, which—a creation of Jahve for the good of the whole earth—is congregated about this Temple and has it as the place of its worship. The pilgrimage of all peoples to the holy mountain is an Old Testament dress of the hope for the conversion of all peoples to the God of revelation, and the close union of all with the people of this God. His Temple is open to them all. They may enter, and when they enter they have to look for great things. For the God of revelation (lii. 11, liv. 8) is "good" (xxv. 8, xxxiv. 9), and His loving-kindness and faithfulness endure for ever —the thought that recurs frequently in the later Hallelujah and Hodu Psalms and is become a liturgical formula (Jer. xxxiii. 11). The mercy or loving-kindness of God is the generosity, and His faithfulness the constancy, of His love.

PSALM CI.

THE VOWS OF A KING.

1 OF mercy and right will I sing,
   To Thee, Jahve, will I harp,
2 I will give heed to the way of uprightness—
   When wilt Thou come unto me?!
   I will walk in the innocence of my heart
      within my house,
3 I will not set before mine eyes
      a worthless action;
   The commission of excesses I hate,
      nothing shall cleave to me.
4 A false heart shall keep far from me,
   I will not cherish an evil thing.
5 Whoso secretly slandereth his neighbour,
      him will I destroy;
   Whoso hath a high look and puffed-up heart,
      him will I not suffer.
6 Mine eyes are upon the faithful of the land,
      that they may be round about me;
   Whoso walketh in the way of uprightness,
      he shall serve me.
7 He shall not sit within my house
      who practiseth deceit;
   He who speaketh lies shall not continue
      before mine eyes.
8 Every morning will I destroy
      all the wicked of the earth,
   That I may root out of Jahve's city
      all workers of iniquity.

This is the "prince's Psalm,"* or as it is inscribed in

---

* Eyring, in his *Vita* of Ernest the Pious [Duke of Saxe-Gotha, b. 1601, d. 1675], relates that he sent an unfaithful minister a copy of the 101st Psalm, and that it became a proverb in the country, when an official had done anything wrong: He will certainly soon receive the prince's Psalm to read.

Luther's version, "David's mirror of a monarch." Can there be any more appropriate motto for it than what is said of Jahve's government in xcix. 4? In respect of this passage of Ps. xcix., to which Ps. c. is the finale, Ps. ci. seems to be appended as an echo out of the heart of David. The appropriateness of the words לְדָוִד מִזְמוֹר (the position of the words is as in Ps. xxiv., xl., cix., cx., cxxxix.) is corroborated by the form and contents. Probably the great historical work from which the chronicler has taken excerpts furnished the post-exilic collector with a further gleaning of Davidic songs, or at least songs that were ascribed to David. The Psalm before us belongs to the time during which the Ark was in the house of Obed-Edom, where David had left it behind through terror at the misfortune of Uzzah. David said at that time: "*How shall the Ark of Jahve come to me* (the unholy one)?" 2 Sam. vi. 8. He did not venture to bring the Ark of the Fearful and Holy One within the range of his own house. In our Psalm, however, he gives utterance to his determination as king to give earnest heed to the sanctity of his walk, of his rule, and of his house; and this resolve he brings before Jahve as a vow, to whom, in regard to the rich blessing which the Ark of God diffuses around it (2 Sam. vi. 11 sq.), he longingly sighs: "*When wilt Thou come to me?!*" This cotemporaneous reference has been recognised by Hammond and Venema. From the fact that Jahve comes to David, Jerusalem becomes "the city of Jahve," ver. 8; and to defend the holiness of this the city of His habitation in all faithfulness, and with all his might, is the thing to which David here pledges himself.

The contents of the first verse refer not merely to the Psalm that follows as an announcement of its theme, but to David's whole life: graciousness and right, the self-manifestations united ideally and, for the king who governs His people, typically in Jahve, shall be the subject of his song. Jahve, the primal source of graciousness and of right, it shall be, to whom he consecrates his poetic talent, as also his playing upon the harp. חֶסֶד is condescension which flows from the principle of free love, and מִשְׁפָּט legality which binds itself impartially and uncapriciously to the rule (norm) of that which is right and good. They are two modes of conduct, mutually tempering each other, which God requires of every man (Mic. vi. 8, cf. Matt. xxiii. 23: τὴν κρίσιν καὶ τὸν ἔλεον), and more especially of a king. Further, he has resolved to give heed, thoughtfully and with an endeavour to pursue it (בְּ הִשְׂכִּיל as in Dan. ix. 13), unto the way of that which is perfect, *i.e.* blameless. What is further said might now be rendered as a relative clause: when Thou comest to me. But not until then?! Hitzig renders it differently: I will take up the lot of the just when it comes to me, *i.e.* as often as it is brought to my knowledge. But if this had been the meaning, בְּדָבָר would have been said instead of בְּדֶרֶךְ (Ex. xviii. 16, 19, 2 Sam. xix. 12 [11]); for, according to both its parts, the expression דרך תמים is an ethical notion, and is therefore not used in a different sense from that in ver. 6. Moreover, the relative use of the interrogative מָתַי in Hebrew cannot be supported, with the exception, perhaps, of Prov. xxiii. 35. Athanasius correctly interprets: ποθῶ σου τὴν παρουσίαν, ὦ δέσποτα, ἱμείρομαί σου τῆς ἐπιφανείας, ἀλλὰ δὸς τὸ ποθούμενον. It is a question of strong yearning: when wilt Thou come to me? is the time near at hand when Thou wilt erect Thy throne near to me? If his longing should be fulfilled, David is resolved to, and will then, behave himself as he further sets forth in the vows he makes. He pledges himself to walk within his house, *i.e.* his palace, in the innocence or simplicity of his heart (lxxviii. 72, Prov. xx. 7), without allowing himself to be led away from this frame of mind which has become his through grace. He will not set before his eyes, viz. as a proposition or purpose (Deut. xv. 9, Ex. x. 10, 1 Sam. xxix. 10, LXX.), any morally worthless or vile matter whatsoever (xli. 9, cf. concerning בְּלִיַּעַל, xviii. 5). The commission of excesses he hates: עֲשֹׂה is *infin. constr.* instead of עֲשׂוֹת as in Gen. xxxi. 28, 1. 20, Prov. xxi. 3, cf. רָאֹה Gen. xlviii. 11, שָׁתֹה Prov. xxxi. 4. כֵּתִים (like שֵׂטִים in Hos. v. 2), as the object of עשׂה, has not a personal (Kimchi, Ewald) signification (cf. on the other hand xl. 5), but material signification: (*facta*) *declinantia* (like זֵדִים, xix. 11, *insolentia;* חֲבָלִים, Zech. xi. 7, *vincientia*); all temptations and incitements of this sort he shakes off from himself, so that nothing of the kind cleaves to him. The confessions in ver. 4 refer to his own inward nature: לֵב עִקֵּשׁ (not עִקְּשִׁי־לֵב, Prov. xvii. 20), a false heart that is not faithful in its intentions either to God or to men, shall remain far from him; wickedness (רָע as in xxxiv. 15) he does not wish to know, *i.e.* does not wish to foster and nurture within him. Whoso secretly slanders his neighbour, him will he destroy; it will therefore be so little possible for any to curry favour with him by uncharitable perfidious tale-bearing, of the wiliness of which David himself had had abundant experience in his relation to Saul, that it will rather call forth his anger upon him (Prov. xxx. 10). Instead of the regularly pointed מְלָשְׁנִי the *Kerî* reads מְלָשְׁנִי, *m'lŏshnî*, a *Poel* (לְשֵׁן *linguâ petere*, like עֵין *oculo petere*, elsewhere הֵלְשִׁין, Prov. xxx. 10) with ŏ instead of ō (*vid.* on cix. 10, lxii. 4) and with *Chirek compaginis* (*vid.* on Ps. cxiii.). The "lofty of eyes," *i.e.* supercilious, haughty, and the "broad of heart," *i.e.* boastful, puffed up, self-conceited (Prov. xxviii. 25, cf. xxi. 4), him he cannot endure (אוּכָל, properly *fut. Hoph.*, I am incapable of, viz. לְשֵׂאת, which is to be supplied as in Isa. i. 13, after Prov. xxx. 21, Jer. xliv. 22).* On the other hand, his eyes rest upon the faithful of the land, with the view, viz., of drawing them into his vicinity. Whoso walks in the way of uprightness, he shall serve him (שָׁרֵת, θεραπεύειν, akin to עָבַד, δουλεύειν). He who practises deceit shall not stay within his house; he who speaks lies shall have no continuance (יִכּוֹן is more than equivalent to נָכוֹן) before (under) his eyes. Every morning (לִבְּקָרִים as in lxxiii. 14, Isa. xxxiii. 2, Lam. iii. 23, and לִבְקָרִים, Job vii. 18), when Jahve shall have taken up His abode in Jerusalem, will he destroy all evil-doers (רִשְׁעֵי as in cxix. 119), *i.e.* incorrigibly wicked ones, wherever he may meet them upon the earth, in order that all workers of evil may be rooted out of the royal city, which is now become the city of Jahve.

---

* In both instances the Masora writes אוֹתוֹ (*plene*), but the Talmud, B. *Erachin* 15*b*, had אִתּוֹ before it when it says: "Of the slanderer God says: I and he cannot dwell together in the world, I cannot bear it any longer with him (אִתּוֹ)."

PSALM CII.

PRAYER OF A PATIENT SUFFERER FOR HIMSELF AND FOR THE JERUSALEM THAT LIES IN RUINS.

2 O JAHVE, hear my prayer,
   And let my cry come unto Thee.
3 Hide not Thy face from me in the day that I am in trouble,
   Incline Thine ear unto me,
   In the day that I call answer me speedily.

4 For my days are vanished in smoke,
   And my bones are heated through as a hearth.
5 Smitten like a green herb and dried up is my heart,
   For I have forgotten to eat my bread,
6 Because of my loud crying my bones cleave to my flesh.

7 I am like a pelican of the wilderness,
   I am become as an owl of the ruins.
8 Keeping watch I am as a lonely bird on the house-top.
9 All the day mine enemies reproach me;
   Those who are mad against me swear by me.

10 For I have eaten ashes like bread,
   And mingled my drink with weeping,
11 Because of Thine indignation and Thy raging,
   That Thou hast lifted me up and cast me down.
12 My days are like a lengthened shadow,
   And I myself am dried up like the green herb.

13 But THOU, Jahve, sittest enthroned for ever,
   And Thy remembrance endureth into all generations.
14 THOU wilt arise, have mercy upon Zion,
   For it is time to favour her, yea the time is come—
15 For Thy servants cling lovingly to her stones,
   And they cry sore over her dust.

16 And the heathen shall fear the Name of Jahve,
   And all the kings of the earth Thy glory,

17 Because Jahve hath rebuilt Zion,
   He hath appeared in His glory,
18 He hath turned to the prayer of the destitute,
   And not despised their prayer.

19 It shall be written for the generation to come,
   And a people yet to be created shall praise Jāh,
20 That He hath looked down from His holy height,
   From heaven unto earth hath Jahve looked,
21 To hear the sighing of the prisoner,
   To set at liberty those who are appointed to death,
22 That they may declare in Zion the Name of Jahve,
   And His praise in Jerusalem,
23 When the peoples are gathered together,
   And the kingdoms, to serve Jahve.

24 He hath bowed down my strength in the way,
   He hath shortened my days.
25 I said, My God, take me not away in the midst of my days—
   Into all generations Thy years endure.
26 Of old hast Thou founded the earth,
   And the heavens are the work of Thy hands.
27 Those shall perish, but Thou remainest,
   They all shall wax old like a garment,
   As a vesture dost Thou change them and they change—
28 But Thou art the same and Thy years have no end!
29 The children of Thy servants shall dwell,
   And their seed shall continue before Thee.

Ps. ci. utters the sigh: *When wilt Thou come to me?* and Ps. cii. with the inscription: *Prayer for an afflicted one when he pineth away and poureth forth his complaint before Jahve,* prays, *Let my prayer come unto Thee.* It is to be taken, too, just as personally as it sounds, and the person is not to be construed into a nation. The song of the עני is, however, certainly a national song; the poet is a servant of Jahve, who shares the calamity that has befallen Jerusalem and its homeless people, both in outward circumstances and in the very depth of his soul. עטף signifies to pine away, languish, as in lxi. 3,

Isa. lvii. 16; and שְׁפָךְ שִׂיחוֹ to pour out one's thoughts and complaints, one's anxious care, as in cxlii. 3, cf. 1 Sam. i. 15 sq.

As is the case already with many of the preceding Psalms, the deutero-Isaianic impression accompanies us in connection with this Psalm also, even to the end; and the further we get in it the more marked does the echo of its prophetical proto-type become. The poet also allies himself with earlier Psalms, such as xxii., lxix., and lxxix., although himself capable of lofty poetic flight, in return for which he makes us feel the absence of any safely progressive unfolding of the thoughts.

Vers. 2, 3. The Psalm opens with familiar expressions of prayer, such as rise in the heart and mouth of the praying one without his feeling that they are of foreign origin; cf. more especially xxxix. 13, xviii. 7, lxxxviii. 3; and on ver. 3: xxvii. 9 (*Hide not Thy face from me*); lix. 17 (בְּיוֹם צַר לִי); xxxi. 3 and frequently (*Incline Thine ear unto me*); lvi. 10 (בְּיוֹם אֶקְרָא); lxix. 18, cxliii. 7 (מַהֵר עֲנֵנִי).

Vers. 4–6. From this point onward the Psalm becomes original. Concerning the *Beth* in בְעָשָׁן, *vid.* on xxxvii. 20. The reading בְּמוֹ קֵד (in the Karaite Ben-Jerucham) enriches the lexicon in the same sense with a word which has scarcely had any existence. מוֹקֵד (Arabic *maukid*) signifies here, as in other instances, a hearth. נִחָרוּ is, as in lxix. 4, *Niphal*: my bones are heated through with a fever-heat, as a hearth with the smouldering fire that is on it. הוּכָּה (cf. יָגוֹרִי, xciv. 21) is used exactly as in Hos. ix. 16, cf. Ps. cxxi. 6. The heart is said to dry up when the life's blood, of which it is the reservoir, fails. The verb שָׁכַח is followed by מִן of dislike. On the cleaving of the bones to the flesh from being baked, *i.e.* to the skin (Arabic بَشَر, in accordance with the radical signification, the surface of the body = the skin, from בשׂר, to brush along, rub, scrape, scratch on the surface), cf. Job xix. 20, Lam. iv. 8. לְ (אֶל) with דָּבַק is used just like בְּ. It is unnecessary, with Böttcher, to draw מִקּוֹל אֲנָחָתִי to ver. 5. Continuous straining of the voice, especially in connection with persevering prayer arising from inward conflict, does really make the body waste away.

Vers. 7–9. קָאַת (construct of קָאַת or קָאָת from קָאָה, *vid.*

Isaiah, ii. 73), according to the LXX., is the pelican, and כּוֹס is the night-raven or the little horned-owl.* דָּמָה obtains the signification to be like, equal (*æqualem esse*), from the radical signification to be flat, even, and to spread out flat (as the Dutch have already recognised). They are both unclean creatures, which are fond of the loneliness of the desert and ruined places. To such a wilderness, that of the exile, is the poet unwillingly transported. He passes the nights without sleep (שָׁקַד, to watch during the time for sleep), and is therefore like a bird sitting lonesome (בּוֹדֵד, Syriac erroneously נוֹדֵד) upon the roof whilst all in the house beneath are sleeping. The *Athnach* in ver. 8 separates that which is come to be from the ground of the "becoming" and the "becoming" itself. His grief is that his enemies reproach him as one forsaken of God. מְהוֹלָל, *part. Poal*, is one made or become mad, Eccles. ii. 2: my mad ones = those who are mad against me. These swear by him, inasmuch as they say when they want to curse: "God do unto thee as unto this man," which is to be explained according to Isa. lxv. 15, Jer. xxix. 22.

Vers. 10—12. Ashes are his bread (cf. Lam. iii. 16), inasmuch as he, a mourner, sits in ashes, and has thrown ashes all over himself, Job ii. 8, Ezek. xxvii. 30. The inflected שִׁקּוּי

---

* The LXX. renders it: I am like a pelican of the desert, I am become as a night-raven upon a ruined place (οἰκοπέδῳ). In harmony with the LXX., Saadia (as also the Arabic version edited by Erpenius, the Samaritan Arabic, and Abulwalid) renders קָאַת by توت (here and in Lev. xi. 18, Deut. xiv. 17, Isa. xxxiv. 17), and כּוֹס by بوم ; the latter (*bum*) is an onomatopoetic name of the owl, and the former (*ḳuḳ*) does not even signify the owl or horned-owl (although the small horned-owl is called *um kućik* in Egypt, and in Africa *abu kućik*; vid. the dictionaries of Boethor and Marcel s.v. *chouette*), but the pelican, the "long-necked water-bird" (Damiri after the lexicon *el-'Obâb* of Hasan ben-Mohammed el-Saghani). The Græco-Veneta also renders קָאַת with πελεκάν,—the Peshito, however, with ܩܳܐܳܐ. What Ephrem on Deut. xiv. 17 and the *Physiologus Syrus* (ed. Tychsen, p. 13, cf. pp. 110 sq.) say of ܩܳܐܳܐ, viz. that it is a marsh-bird, is very fond of its young ones, dwells in desolate places, and is incessantly noisy, likewise points to the pelican, although the Syrian lexicographers vary. Cf. also Oedmann, *Vermischte Sammlungen*, Heft 3, Cap. 6. (Fleischer after a communication from Rödiger.)

has שְׂעִי = שִׂפְעוֹ for its principal form, instead of which it is שְׂעִי in Hos. ii. 7. "That Thou hast lifted me up and cast me down" is to be understood according to Job xxx. 22. First of all God has taken away the firm ground from under his feet, then from aloft He has cast him to the ground—an emblem of the lot of Israel, which is removed from its fatherland and cast into exile, *i.e.* into a strange land. In that passage the days of his life are כְּצֵל נָטוּי, like a lengthened shadow, which grows longer and longer until it is entirely lost in darkness, cix. 23. Another figure follows: he there becomes like an (uprooted) plant which dries up.

Vers. 13-15. When the church in its individual members dies off on a foreign soil, still its God, the unchangeable One, remains, and therein the promise has the guarantee of its fulfilment. Faith lays hold upon this guarantee as in Ps. xc. It becomes clear from ix. 8 and Lam. v. 19 how תֵּשֵׁב is to be understood. The Name which Jahve makes Himself by self-attestation never falls a prey to the dead past, it is His ever-living memorial (זֵכֶר, Ex. iii. 15). Thus, too, will He restore Jerusalem; the limit, or appointed time, to which the promise points is, as his longing tells the poet, now come. מוֹעֵד, according to lxxv. 3, Hab. ii. 3, is the juncture, when the redemption by means of the judgment on the enemies of Israel shall dawn. לְחֶנְנָהּ, from the infinitive חֵן, has *ĕ*, flattened from *ă*, in an entirely closed syllable. רָצָה *seq. acc.* signifies to have pleasure in anything, to cling to it with delight; and חָנַן, according to Prov. xiv. 21, affirms a compassionate, tender love of the object. The servants of God do not feel at home in Babylon, but their loving yearning lingers over the ruins, the stones and the heaps of the rubbish (Neh. iii. 34 [iv. 2]), of Jerusalem.

Vers. 16-18. With וְיִירְאוּ we are told what will take place when that which is expected in ver. 14 comes to pass, and at the same time the fulfilment of that which is longed for is thereby urged home upon God: Jahve's own honour depends upon it, since the restoration of Jerusalem will become the means of the conversion of the world—a fundamental thought of Isa. ch. xl.-lxvi. (cf. more particularly ch. lix. 19, lx. 2), which is also called to mind in the expression of this strophe. This prophetic prospect (Isa. xl. 1-5) that the restoration of Jerusalem will take place simultaneously with the glorious parusia of Jahve re-echoes here in a lyric form. כִּי, ver. 17, states the ground of the reverence, just as ver. 20 the ground of the praise. The people of the Exile are called in ver. 18 הָעַרְעָר, from עָרַר, to be naked: homeless, powerless, honourless, and in the eyes of men, prospectless. The LXX. renders this word in Jer. xvii. 6 ἀγριομυρίκη, and its plural, formed by an internal change of vowel, עֲרוֹעֵר, in Jer. xlviii. 6 ὄνος ἄγριος, which are only particularizations of the primary notion of that which is stark naked, neglected, wild. Ver. 18b is an echo of Ps. xxii. 25. In the mirror of this and of other Psalms written in times of affliction the Israel of the Exile saw itself reflected.

Vers. 19–23. The poet goes on advancing motives to Jahve for the fulfilment of his desire, by holding up to Him what will take place when He shall have restored Zion. The evangel of God's redemptive deed will be written down for succeeding generations, and a new, created people, *i.e.* a people coming into existence, the church of the future, shall praise God the Redeemer for it. דּוֹר אַחֲרוֹן as in xlviii. 14, lxxviii. 4. עַם נוֹלָד like עַם נִבְרָא xxii. 32, perhaps with reference to deutero-Isaianic passages like Isa. xliii. 7. On ver. 20, cf. Isa. lxiii. 15; in ver. 21 (cf. Isa. xlii. 7, lxi. 1) the deutero-Isaianic colouring is very evident. And ver. 21 rests still more verbally upon lxxix. 11. The people of the Exile are as it were in prison and chains (אָסִיר), and are advancing towards their destruction (בְּנֵי תְמוּתָה), if God does not interpose. Those who have returned home are the subject to לְסַפֵּר. בְּ in ver. 23 introduces that which takes place simultaneously: with the release of Israel from servitude is united the conversion of the world. נֻקְבְּצוּ occurs in the same connection as in Isa. lx. 4. After having thus revelled in the glory of the time of redemption the poet comes back to himself and gives form to his prayer on his own behalf.

Vers. 24–29. On the way (בְּ as in cx. 7)—not "by means of the way" (בְּ as in cv. 18), in connection with which one would expect to find some attributive minuter definition of the way—God hath bowed down his strength (cf. Deut. viii. 2); it was therefore a troublous, toilsome way which he has been led, together with his people. He has shortened his days, so that he only drags on wearily, and has only a short distance still before him before he is entirely overcome. The *Chethîb* כחו

(LXX. ἰσχύος αὐτοῦ) may be understood of God's irresistible might, as in Job xxiii. 6, xxx. 18, but in connection with it the designation of the object is felt to be wanting. The introductory אֹמַר (cf. Job x. 2), which announces a definite moulding of the utterance, serves to give prominence to the petition that follows. In the expression אַל־תַּעֲלֵנִי life is conceived of as a line the length of which accords with nature; to die before one's time is a being taken up out of this course, so that the second half of the line is not lived through (lv. 24, Isa. xxxviii. 10). The prayer not to sweep him away before his time, the poet supports not by the eternity of God in itself, but by the work of the rejuvenation of the world and of the restoration of Israel that is to be looked for, which He can and will bring to an accomplishment, because He is the ever-living One. The longing to see this new time is the final ground of the poet's prayer for the prolonging of his life. The confession of God the Creator in ver. 26 reminds one in its form of Isa. xlviii. 13, cf. xliv. 24. הֵמָּה in ver. 27 refers to the two great divisions of the universe. The fact that God will create heaven and earth anew is a revelation that is indicated even in Isa. xxxiv. 4, but is first of all expressed more fully and in many ways in the second part of the Book of Isaiah, viz. li. 6, 16, lxv. 17, lxvi. 22. It is clear from the agreement in the figure of the garment (Isa. li. 6, cf. l. 9) and in the expression (עָמַד, *perstare*, as in Isa. lxvi. 22) that the poet has gained this knowledge from the prophet. The expressive אַתָּה הוּא, Thou art He, *i.e.* unalterably the same One, is also taken from the mouth of the prophet, Isa. xli. 4, xliii. 10, xlvi. 4, xlviii. 12; הוּא is a predicate, and denotes the identity (sameness) of Jahve (Hofmann, *Schriftbeweis*, i. 63). In ver. 29 also, in which the prayer for a lengthening of life tapers off to a point, we hear Isa. lxv. 9, lxvi. 22 re-echoed. And from the fact that in the mind of the poet as of the prophet the post-exilic Jerusalem and the final new Jerusalem upon the new earth under a new heaven blend together, it is evident that not merely in the time of Hezekiah or of Manasseh (assuming that Isa. ch. xl.-lxvi. are by the old Isaiah), but also even in the second half of the Exile, such a perspectively foreshortened view was possible. When, moreover, the writer of the Epistle to the Hebrews at once refers vers. 26-28 to Christ, this is justified by the fact that the God whom the poet confesses as the unchangeable One is Jahve who is to come.

PSALM CIII.

HYMN IN HONOUR OF GOD THE ALL-COMPASSIONATE ONE.

1 BLESS, O my soul, Jahve,
  And all that is within me, His holy Name.
2 Bless, O my soul, Jahve,
  And forget not all His benefits—
3 Who forgiveth all thine iniquity,
  Who healeth all thine infirmities,
4 Who redeemeth thy life from the pit,
  Who crowneth thee with loving-kindness and tender
5 Who satisfieth thy mouth with good,   [mercies,
  So that thy youth renews itself like the eagle.

6 Deeds of righteousness doth Jahve perform,
  And judgments on behalf of all that are oppressed.
7 He made known His ways unto Moses,
  To the children of Israel His mighty acts.
8 Merciful and gracious is Jahve,
  Slow to anger and plenteous in mercy.
9 Not always doth He contend,
  And not for ever doth He keep anger.
10 He doth not deal with us after our sins,
  Nor recompense us after our iniquities.

11 For as the heaven is high above the earth,
  So mighty is His mercy upon those who fear Him.
12 As far as the east is from the west,
  So far doth He remove our transgressions from us.
13 Like as a father pitieth his children,
  So Jahve pitieth those who fear Him.
14 For He knoweth our nature,
  He is mindful, that we are dust.

15 A mortal man—his days are as grass,
  As a flower of the field, so he flourisheth.

16 If the wind passeth over him, he is not,
   And his place knoweth him no more.
17 But the mercy of Jahve is from everlasting to everlasting
      upon those who fear Him,
   And His righteousness is manifested to children's children,
18 To those who keep His covenant
   And are mindful of His statutes to do them.

19 Jahve hath established His throne in the heavens,
   And His kingdom ruleth over all.
20 Bless Jahve, ye His angels,
   Ye strong heroes doing His word,
   Hearkening to the call of His word.
21 Bless Jahve, all ye His hosts,
   His servants doing His pleasure.
22 Bless Jahve, all ye His works,
   In all places of His dominion.
   Bless, O my soul, Jahve!

To the "*Thou wilt have compassion upon Zion*" of cii. 14 is appended Ps. ciii., which has this as its substance throughout; but in other respects the two Psalms stand in contrast to one another. The inscription לדוד is also found thus by itself without any further addition even before Psalms of the First Book (xxvi.-xxviii., xxxv., xxxvii.). It undoubtedly does not rest merely on conjecture, but upon tradition. For no internal grounds which might have given rise to the annotation לדוד can be traced. The form of the language does not favour it. This pensive song, so powerful in its tone, has an Aramaic colouring like Ps. cxvi., cxxiv., cxxix. In the heaping up of Aramaizing suffix-forms it has its equal only in the story of Elisha, 2 Kings iv. 1–7, where, moreover, the *Kerî* throughout substitutes the usual forms, whilst here, where these suffix-forms are intentional ornaments of the expression, the *Chethîb* rightly remains unaltered. The forms are 2d *sing. fem. ēchi* for *ēch*, and 2d *sing. plur. ājchi* for *ajich*. The *i* without the tone which is added here is just the one with which originally the pronunciation was אתּי instead of אתּ and לכּי for לךְ. Out of the Psalter (here and cxvi. 7, 19) these suffix-forms *echi* and *ajchi* occur only in

Jer. xi. 15, and in the North-Palestinian history of the prophet in the Book of Kings.

The groups or strophes into which the Psalm falls are vers. 1–5, 6–10, 11–14, 15–18, 19–22. If we count their lines we obtain the schema 10. 10. 8. 8. 10. The Coptic version accordingly reckons 46 CTYXOC, *i.e.* στίχοι.

Vers. 1–5. In the strophe vers. 1–5 the poet calls upon his soul to arise to praiseful gratitude for God's justifying, redeeming, and renewing grace. In such soliloquies it is the Ego that speaks, gathering itself up with the spirit, the stronger, more manly part of man (*Psychology*, S. 104 sq.; tr. p. 126), or even, because the soul as the spiritual medium of the spirit and of the body represents the whole person of man (*Psychology*, S. 203; tr. p. 240), the Ego rendering objective in the soul the whole of its own personality. So here in vers. 3–5 the soul, which is addressed, represents the whole man. The קְרָבִים which occurs here is a more choice expression for מֵעִים (מֵעַיִם): the heart, which is called קֶרֶב κατ' ἐξοχήν, the reins, the liver, etc.; for according to the scriptural conception (*Psychology*, S. 266; tr. p. 313) these organs of the cavities of the breast and abdomen serve not merely for the bodily life, but also the psycho-spiritual life. The summoning בָּרֲכִי is repeated *per anaphoram*. There is nothing the soul of man is so prone to forget as to render thanks that are due, and more especially thanks that are due to God. It therefore needs to be expressly aroused in order that it may not leave the blessing with which God blesses it unacknowledged, and may not forget all His acts performed (גָּמַר = גָּמַל) on it (גְּמוּל, ῥῆμα μέσον, *e.g.* in cxxxvii. 8), which are purely deeds of loving-kindness (benefits). Now follow attributive participles, which attach themselves to אֶת־הּ. Most prominent stands mercy (loving-kindness), which is the primal condition and the foundation of all the others, viz. sin-pardoning mercy. The verbs סָלַח and רָפָא with a dative of the object denote the bestowment of that which is expressed by the verbal notion. תַּחֲלֻאִים (taken from Deut. xxix. 21, cf. 1 Chron. xxi. 19, from חָלָא = חָלָה, root חל, *solutum, laxum esse*) are not merely bodily diseases, but all kinds of inward and outward sufferings. מִשַּׁחַת the LXX. renders ἐκ φθορᾶς (from שַׁחַת, as in Job xvii. 14); but in this antithesis to life it is more natural to render the "pit" (from שׁוּחָה) as a name of Hades, as in xvi. 10. Just as the soul owes its deliverance from guilt and distress and death to God, so also does it owe to God that with which it is endowed out of the riches of divine love. The verb עָטַר, without any such addition as in v. 13, is "to crown," cf. viii. 6. As is usually the case, it is construed with a double accusative; the crown is as it were woven out of lovingkindness and compassion. The *Beth* of בְּטוּב in ver. 5 instead of the accusative (civ. 28) denotes the means of satisfaction, which is at the same time that which satisfies. עֶדְיֵךְ the Targum renders: *dies senectutis tuæ*, whereas in xxxii. 9 it has *ornatus ejus;* the Peshito renders: *corpus tuum*, and in xxxii. 9 inversely, *juventus eorum*. These significations, "old age" or "youth," are pure inventions. And since the words are addressed to the soul, עֶדְיֵךְ cannot also, like כָּבוֹד in other instances, be a name of the soul itself (Aben-Ezra, Mendelssohn, Philippsohn, Hengstenberg, and others). We, therefore, with Hitzig, fall back upon the sense of the word in xxxii. 9, where the LXX. renders τὰς σιαγόνας αὐτῶν, but here more freely, apparently starting from the primary notion of עֲדִי = Arabic *chadd*, the cheek: τὸν ἐμπιπλῶντα ἐν ἀγαθοῖς τὴν ἐπιθυμίαν σου (whereas Saadia's *victum tuum* is based upon a comparison of the Arabic غذا, to nourish). The poet tells the soul (*i.e.* his own person, himself) that God satisfies it with good, so that it as it were gets its cheeks full of it (cf. lxxxi. 11). The comparison בַּנֶּשֶׁר is, as in Mic. i. 16 (cf. Isa. xl. 31), to be referred to the annual moulting of the eagle. Its renewing of its plumage is an emblem of the renovation of his youth by grace. The predicate to נְעוּרָיְכִי (plural of extension in relation to time) stands first regularly in the *sing. fem.*

Vers. 6–10. His range of vision being widened from himself, the poet now in vers. 6–18 describes God's gracious and fatherly conduct towards sinful and perishing men, and that as it shines forth from the history of Israel and is known and recognised in the light of revelation. What ver. 6 says is a common-place drawn from the history of Israel. כְּמִשְׁפָּטִים is an accusative governed by the עֹשֶׂה that is to be borrowed out of עֹשֵׂה (so Baer after the Masora). And because ver. 6 is the result of an historical retrospect and survey, יוֹדִיעַ in ver. 7 can affirm that which happened in the past (cf. xcix. 6 sq.); for the supposition of Hengstenberg and Hitzig, that *Moses* here represents Israel like *Jacob, Isaac,* and *Joseph* in other instances, is without example in the whole Israelitish literature. It becomes clear from ver. 8 in what sense the making of His ways known is meant. The poet has in his mind Moses' prayer: "make known to me now Thy way" (Ex. xxxiii. 13), which Jahve fulfilled by passing by him as he stood in the cleft of the rock and making Himself visible to him as he looked after Him, amidst the proclamation of His attributes. The ways of Jahve are therefore in this passage not those in which men are to walk in accordance with His precepts (xxv. 4), but those which He Himself follows in the course of His redemptive history (lxvii. 3). The confession drawn from Ex. xxxiv. 6 sq. is become a formula of the Israelitish faith (lxxxvi. 15, cxlv. 8, Joel ii. 13, Neh. ix. 17, and frequently). In vers. 9 sqq. the fourth attribute (וְרַב־חֶסֶד) is made the object of further praise. He is not only long (אֶרֶךְ from אָרֵךְ, like כְּבֵד from כָּבֵד) in anger, *i.e.* waiting a long time before He lets His anger loose, but when He contends, *i.e.* interposes judicially, this too is not carried to the full extent (lxxviii. 38), He is not angry for ever (נָטַר, to keep, viz. anger, Amos i. 11; cf. the parallels both as to matter and words, Jer. iii. 5, Isa. lvii. 16). The procedure of His righteousness is regulated not according to our sins, but according to His purpose of mercy. The perfects in ver. 10 state that which God has constantly not done, and the futures in ver. 9 what He continually will not do.

Vers. 11–14. The ingenious figures in vers. 11 sq. (cf. xxxvi. 6, lvii. 11) illustrate the infinite power and complete unreservedness of mercy (loving-kindness). הַרְחִיק has *Gaja* (as have also הִשְׁחִיתוּ and הִתְעִיבוּ, xiv. 1, liii. 2, in exact texts), in order to render possible the distinct pronunciation of the guttural in the combination רח. Ver. 13 sounds just as much like the spirit of the New Testament as vers. 11, 12. The relationship to Jahve in which those stand who fear Him is a filial relationship based upon free reciprocity (Mal. iii. 11). His Fatherly compassion is (ver. 14) based upon the frailty and perishableness of man, which are known to God, much the same as God's promise after the Flood not to decree a like judgment again (Gen. viii. 21). According to this passage and Deut. xxxi. 21, יְצָרֵנוּ appears to be intended of the moral nature; but according to ver. 14b, one is obliged to think rather of the natural form which man possesses from God the Creator (וַיִּיצֶר, Gen. ii. 7) than of the form of heart which he has by his own choice and, so far as its groundwork is concerned, by inheritance (li. 7). In זָכוּר, mindful, the passive, according to Böttcher's correct apprehension of it, expresses a passive state after an action that is completed by the person himself, as in בְּטֻחָה, יָדוּעַ, and the like. In its form ver. 14a reminds one of the Book of Job ch. xi. 11, xxviii. 23, and ver. 14b as to subject-matter recalls Job vii. 7, and other passages (cf. Ps. lxxviii. 39, lxxxix. 48); but the following figurative representation of human frailty, with which the poet contrasts the eternal nature of the divine mercy as the sure stay of all God-fearing ones in the midst of the rise and decay of things here below, still more strongly recalls that book.

Vers. 15–18. The figure of the grass recalls xc. 5 sq., cf. Isa. xl. 6–8, li. 12; that of the flower, Job xiv. 2. אֱנוֹשׁ is man as a mortal being; his life's duration is likened to that of a blade of grass, and his beauty and glory to a flower of the field, whose fullest bloom is also the beginning of its fading. In ver. 16 בּוֹ (the same as in Isa. xl. 7 sq.) refers to man, who is compared to grass and flowers. כִּי is ἐάν with a hypothetical perfect; and the wind that scorches up the plants, referred to man, is an emblem of every form of peril that threatens life: often enough it is really a breath of wind which snaps off a man's life. The bold designation of vanishing away without leaving any trace, " and his place knoweth him no more," is taken from Job vii. 10, cf. ibid. viii. 18, xx. 9. In the midst of this plant-like, frail destiny, there is, however, one strong ground of comfort. There is an everlasting power, which raises all those who link themselves with it above the transitoriness involved in nature's laws, and makes them eternal like itself. This power is the mercy of God, which spans itself above (עַל) all those who fear Him like an eternal heaven. This is God's righteousness, which rewards faithful adherence to His covenant and conscientious fulfilment of His precepts in accordance with the order of redemption, and shows itself even to (לְ) children's children, according to Ex. xx. 6, xxxiv. 7, Deut. vii. 9: on into a thousand generations, i.e. into infinity.

Vers. 19–22. He is able to show Himself thus gracious to His own, for He is the supra-mundane, all-ruling King. With this thought the poet draws on to the close of his song of praise. The heavens in opposition to the earth, as in cv. 7, Eccles. v. 1 [2], is the unchangeable realm above the rise and fall of things here below. On ver. 19*b* cf. 1 Chron. xxix. 12. בַּכֹּל refers to everything created without exception, the universe of created things. In connection with the heavens of glory the poet cannot but call to mind the angels. His call to these to join in the praise of Jahve has its parallel only in Ps. xxix. and cxlviii. It arises from the consciousness of the church on earth that it stands in living like-minded fellowship with the angels of God, and that it possesses a dignity which rises above all created things, even the angels which are appointed to serve it (xci. 11). They are called גִּבֹּרִים as in Joel iv. [iii.] 11, and in fact גִּבֹּרֵי כֹחַ, as the strong to whom belongs strength unequalled. Their life endowed with heroic strength is spent entirely—an example for mortals—in an obedient execution of the word of God. לִשְׁמֹעַ is a definition not of the purpose, but of the manner: *obediendo* (as in Gen. ii. 3 *perficiendo*). Hearing the call of His word, they also forthwith put it into execution. The hosts (צְבָאָיו), as מְשָׁרְתָיו shows, are the celestial spirits gathered around the angels of a higher rank (cf. Luke ii. 13), the innumerable λειτουργικὰ πνεύματα (civ. 4, Dan. vii. 10, Heb. i. 14), for there is a *hierarchia coelestis*. From the archangels the poet comes to the myriads of the heavenly hosts, and from these to all creatures, that they, wheresoever they may be throughout Jahve's wide domain, may join in the song of praise that is to be struck up; and from this point he comes back to his own soul, which he modestly includes among the creatures mentioned in the third passage. A threefold בָּרְכִי נַפְשִׁי now corresponds to the threefold בָּרְכוּ; and inasmuch as the poet thus comes back to his own soul, his Psalm also turns back into itself and assumes the form of a converging circle.

PSALM CIV.

HYMN IN HONOUR OF THE GOD OF THE SEVEN DAYS.

1 BLESS, O my soul, Jahve!
Jahve, my God, Thou art very great,
In splendour and glory hast Thou clothed Thyself;
2 Enwrapping Thyself in light as a garment,
Spreading out the heavens like a tent-cloth,
3 Who layeth the beams of His chambers in the waters,
Who maketh the clouds His chariot,
Who walketh upon the wings of the wind,
4 Making His messengers out of the winds,
His servants out of flaming fire.

5 He hath founded the earth upon its pillars,
That it may not totter for ever and ever.
6 The deep as a garment didst Thou cover over it,
Upon the mountains stood the waters.
7 At Thy rebuke they fled,
At the voice of Thy thunder they hasted away—
8 The mountains rose, the valleys sank—
To the place which Thou hast founded for them.
9 A bound hast Thou set, they may not pass over,
They may not turn back to cover the earth.

10 Who sendeth forth springs in the bottoms of the valleys,
Between the mountains they take their course.
11 They give drink to all the beasts of the field,
The wild asses quench their thirst.
12 Upon them the birds of the heaven have their habitation,
From among the branches they raise their voice.
13 He watereth the mountains out of His chambers—
With the fruit of Thy works is the earth satisfied.
14 He causeth grass to grow for the cattle,
And herb for the service of man—

To bring forth bread out of the earth,
15 And that wine may make glad the heart of mortal man,
To make his face shining from oil,
And that bread may support the heart of mortal man.
16 The trees of Jahve are satisfied,
The cedars of Lebanon, which He hath planted;
17 Where the birds make their nests,
The stork which hath its house upon the cypresses.
18 Mountains, the high ones, are for the wild goats,
The rocks are a refuge for the rock-badgers.

19 He hath made the moon for a measuring of the times,
The sun knoweth its going down.
20 Thou makest darkness, and it is night,
Wherein all the beasts of the forest do move.
21 The young lions roar after their prey,
And seek from God their food.
22 The sun ariseth, they retreat
And lay themselves down in their dens.
23 Man goeth forth to his work,
And to his labour, until the evening.

24 How manifold are Thy works, Jahve,
With wisdom hast Thou executed them altogether,
The earth is full of Thy creatures!
25 Yonder sea, great and far extended—
There it teems with life, innumerable,
Small beasts together with great.
26 There the ships move along,
The leviathan which Thou hast formed to sport therein.
27 They all wait upon Thee,
That Thou mayest give them their food in its season.
28 Thou givest it to them, they gather it up;
Thou openest Thy hand, they are satisfied with good.
29 Thou hidest Thy face, they are troubled;
Thou takest back their breath, they expire,
And return to their dust.
30 Thou sendest forth Thy breath, they are created,
And Thou renewest the face of the ground.

31 Let the glory of Jahve endure for ever,
   Let Jahve rejoice in His works ;
32 He, who looketh on the earth and it trembleth,
   He toucheth the mountains and they smoke.
33 I will sing unto Jahve as long as I live,
   I will harp unto my God as long as I have my being.
34 May my meditation be acceptable to Him,
   I, even I will rejoice in Jahve.
35 Let the sinful disappear from the earth,
   And evil-doers be no more—
   Bless, O my soul, Jahve,
       Hallelujah.

With *Bless, O my soul, Jahve*, as Ps. ciii., begins this anonymous Ps. civ. also, in which God's rule in the kingdom of nature, as there in the kingdom of grace, is the theme of praise, and as there the angels are associated with it. The poet sings the God-ordained present condition of the world with respect to the creative beginnings recorded in Gen. i. 1–ii. 3 ; and closes with the wish that evil may be expelled from this good creation, which so thoroughly and fully reveals God's power, and wisdom, and goodness. It is a Psalm of nature, but such as no poet among the Gentiles could have written. The Israelitish poet stands free and unfettered in the presence of nature as his object, and all things appear to him as brought forth and sustained by the creative might of the one God, brought into being and preserved in existence on purpose that He, the self-sufficient One, may impart Himself in free condescending love —as the creatures and orders of the Holy One, in themselves good and pure, but spotted and disorganized only by the self-corruption of man in sin and wickedness, which self-corruption must be turned out in order that the joy of God in His works and the joy of these works in their Creator may be perfected. The Psalm is altogether an echo of the heptahemeron (or history of the seven days of creation) in Gen. i. 1–ii. 3. Corresponding to the seven days it falls into seven groups, in which the מאד הנה־טוב of Gen. i. 31 is expanded. It is not, however, so worked out that each single group celebrates the work of a day of creation ; the Psalm has the commingling whole of the finished creation as its standpoint, and is therefore not so conformed to any plan. Nevertheless it begins with the light and closes with an allusion to the divine Sabbath. When it is considered that ver. 8a is only with violence accommodated to the context, that ver. 18 is forced in without any connection and contrary to any plan, and that ver. 32 can only be made intelligible in that position by means of an artificial combination of the thoughts, then the supposition of Hitzig, ingeniously wrought out by him in his own way, is forced upon one, viz. that this glorious hymn has decoyed some later poet-hand into enlarging upon it.

Vers. 1–4. The first decastich begins the celebration with work of the first and second days. הוֹד וְהָדָר here is not the doxa belonging to God πρὸ παντὸς τοῦ αἰῶνος (Jude, ver. 25), but the doxa which He has put on (Job xl. 10) since He created the world, over against which He stands in kingly glory, or rather in which He is immanent, and which reflects this kingly glory in various gradations, yea, to a certain extent is this glory itself. For inasmuch as God began the work of creation with the creation of light, He has covered Himself with this created light itself as with a garment. That which once happened in connection with the creation may, as in Amos iv. 13, Isa. xliv. 24, xlv. 7, Jer. x. 12, and frequently, be expressed by participles of the present, because the original setting is continued in the preservation of the world; and determinate participles alternate with participles without the article, as in Isa. xliv. 24–28, with no other difference than that the former are more predicative and the latter more attributive. With ver. 2b the poet comes upon the work of the second day: the creation of the expanse (רקיע) which divides between the waters. God has spread this out (cf. Isa. xl. 22) like a tent-cloth (Isa. liv. 2), of such light and of such fine transparent work; נוֹטֶה here rhymes with עֹטֶה. In those waters which the "expanse" holds aloft over the earth God lays the beams of His upper chambers (עֲלִיּוֹתָיו, instead of which we find מַעֲלוֹתָיו in Amos ix. 6, from עֲלִיָּה, ascent, elevation, then an upper story, an upper chamber, which would be more accurately עִלִּיָּה after the Aramaic and Arabic); but not as though the waters were the material for them, they are only the place for them, that is exalted above the earth, and are able to be this because to the

Immaterial One even that which is fluid is solid, and that which is dense is transparent. The reservoirs of the upper waters, the clouds, God makes, as the lightning, thunder, and rain indicate, into His chariot (רְכוּב), upon which He rides along in order to make His power felt below upon the earth judicially (Isa. xix. 1), or in rescuing and blessing men. רְכוּב (only here) accords in sound with בָּרוּב, xviii. 11. For ver. 3c also recalls this primary passage, where the wings of the wind take the place of the cloud-chariot. In ver. 4 the LXX. (Heb. i. 7) makes the first substantive into an accusative of the object, and the second into an accusative of the predicate: Ὁ ποιῶν τοὺς ἀγγέλους αὐτοῦ πνεύματα καὶ τοὺς λειτουργοὺς αὐτοῦ πυρὸς φλόγα. It is usually translated the reverse way: making the winds into His angels, etc. This rendering is possible so far as the language is concerned (cf. c. 3 Chethib, and on the position of the words, Amos iv. 13 with v. 8), and the plural מְשָׁרְתָיו is explicable in connection with this rendering from the force of the parallelism, and the singular אֵשׁ from the fact that this word has no plural. Since, however, עָשָׂה with two accusatives usually signifies to produce something out of something, so that the second accusative (viz. the accusative of the predicate, which is logically the second, but according to the position of the words may just as well be the first, Ex. xxv. 39, xxx. 25, as the second, Ex. xxxvii. 23, xxxviii. 3, Gen. ii. 7, 2 Chron. iv. 18-22) denotes the *materia ex qua*, it may with equal right at least be interpreted: Who makes His messengers out of the winds, His servants out of flaming or consuming (*vid.* on lvii. 5) fire (אֵשׁ, as in Jer. xlviii. 45, *masc.*). And this may affirm either that God makes use of wind and fire for special missions (cf. cxlviii. 8), or (cf. Hofmann, *Schriftbeweis*, i. 325 f.) that He gives wind and fire to His angels for the purpose of His operations in the world which are effected through their agency, as the materials of their outward manifestation, and as it were of their self-embodiment,* as then in xviii. 11 wind and cherub are both to be associated

---

* It is a Talmudic view that God really makes the angels out of fire, B. *Chagiga*, 14a (cf. *Koran*, xxxviii. 77): Day by day are the angels of the service created out of the stream of fire (נְהַר דִּינוּר), and sing their song of praise and perish.

together in thought as the vehicle of the divine activity in the world, and in xxxv. 5 the angel of Jahve represents the energy of the wind.

Vers. 5-9. In a second decastich the poet speaks of the restraining of the lower waters and the establishing of the land standing out of the water. The suffix, referring back to אֶרֶץ, is intended to say that the earth hanging free in space (Job xxvi. 7) has its internal supports. Its eternal stability is preserved even amidst the judgment predicted in Isa. xxiv. 16 sq., since it comes forth out of it, unremoved from its former station, as a transformed, glorified earth. The deep (תְּהוֹם) with which God covers it is that primordial mass of water in which it lay first of all as it were in embryo, for it came into being ἐξ ὕδατος καὶ δι' ὕδατος (2 Pet. iii. 5). כִּסִּיתוֹ does not refer to תהום (*masc.* as in Job xxviii. 14), because then עָלָיו would be required, but to אֶרֶץ, and the masculine is to be explained either by attraction (according to the model of 1 Sam. ii. 4a), or by a reversion to the masculine ground-form as the discourse proceeds (cf. the same thing with עִיר 2 Sam. xvii. 13, צְעָקָה Ex. xi. 6, יָד Ezek. ii. 9). According to ver. 6b, the earth thus overflowed with water was already mountainous; the primal formation of the mountains is therefore just as old as the תהום mentioned in direct succession to the תהו ובהו. After this, vers. 7-9 describe the subduing of the primordial waters by raising up the dry land and the confining of these waters in basins surrounded by banks. Terrified by the despotic command of God, they started asunder, and mountains rose aloft, the dry land with its heights and its low grounds appeared. The rendering that the waters, thrown into wild excitement, rose up the mountains and descended again (Hengstenberg), does not harmonize with the fact that they are represented in ver. 6 as standing above the mountains. Accordingly, too, it is not to be interpreted after cvii. 26: they (the waters) rose mountain-high, they sunk down like valleys. The reference of the description to the coming forth of the dry land on the third day of creation requires that הָרִים should be taken as subject to יַעֲלוּ. But then, too, the בְּקָעוֹת are the subject to יֵרְדוּ, as Hilary of Poictiers renders it in his *Genesis*, v. 97, etc.: *subsidunt valles*, and not the waters as subsiding into the valleys. Hupfeld is correct; ver. 8a is a parenthesis which affirms that, inasmuch as the waters retreating laid the solid land bare, mountains and valleys as such came forth visibly ; cf. Ovid, *Metam.* i. 344:

Flumina subsidunt, montes exire videntur.

Ver. 8 continues with the words אֶל־מְקוֹם (cf. Gen. i. 9, אֶל־מָקוֹם אֶחָד) : the waters retreat to the place which (זֶה, cf. ver. 26, for אֲשֶׁר, Gen. xxxix. 20) God has assigned to them as that which should contain them. He hath set a bound (גְּבוּל, synon. חֹק, Prov. viii. 29, Jer. v. 22) for them beyond which they may not flow forth again to cover the earth, as the primordial waters of chaos have done.

Vers. 10–14b. The third decastich, passing on to the third day of creation, sings the benefit which the shore-surrounded waters are to the animal creation and the growth of the plants out of the earth, which is irrigated from below and moistened from above. God, the blessed One, being the principal subject of the Psalm, the poet (in ver. 10 and further on) is able to go on in attributive and predicative participles : Who sendeth springs בַּנְּחָלִים, into the wadis (not : בִּנְחָלִים, as brooks). נַחַל, as ver. 10b shows, is here a synonym of בִּקְעָה, and there is no need for saying that, flowing on in the plains, they grow into rivers. The LXX. has ἐν φάραγξιν. חַיְתוֹ שָׂדָי is doubly poetic for חַיַּת הַשָּׂדֶה. God has also provided for all the beasts that roam far from men ; and the wild ass, swift as an arrow, difficult to be hunted, and living in troops (פֶּרֶא, Arabic *ferâ*, root פר, فر, to move quickly, to whiz, to flee; the wild ass, the *onager*, Arabic *ḥimâr el-wahs*, whose home is on the steppes), is made prominent by way of example. The phrase " to break the thirst " occurs only here. עֲלֵיהֶם, ver. 12a, refers to the כְּעָיָנִים, which are also still the subject in ver. 11a. The pointing עֳפָאיִם needlessly creates a hybrid form in addition to עֳפָאִים (like לְבָאִים) and עֳפָיִים. From the tangled branches by the springs the poet insensibly reaches the second half of the third day. The vegetable kingdom at the same time reminds him of the rain which, descending out of the upper chambers of the heavens, waters the waterless mountain-tops. Like the Talmud (*B. Tu'anith*, 10a), by the "fruit of Thy work" (כְּמַעֲשֶׂיךָ as singular) Hitzig understands the rain ; but rain is rather that which fertilizes ; and why might not the fruit be meant which God's works (מַעֲשֶׂיךָ, plural) here below (ver. 24), viz. the vegetable creations, bear, and from which the earth, *i.e.* its population, is satisfied, inasmuch as vegetable food springs up as much for the beasts as for man? In connection with עֵשֶׂב the poet is thinking of cultivated plants, more especially wheat; לַעֲבֹדַת, however, does not signify: *for cultivation by man*, since, according to Hitzig's correct remonstrance, they do not say עבד העשׂב, and להוציא has not man, but rather God, as its subject, but as in 1 Chron. xxvi. 30, *for the service* (use) *of man*.

Vers. 14c–18. In the fourth decastich the poet goes further among the creatures of the field and of the forest. The subject to לְהוֹצִיא is מצמיח. The clause expressing the purpose, which twice begins with an infinitive, is continued in both instances, as in Isa. xiii. 9, but with a change of subject (cf. *e.g.* Amos i. 11, ii. 4), in the finite verb. On what is said of wine we may compare Eccles. x. 19, Sir. xl. 20, and more especially Isaiah, who frequently mentions wine as a representative of all the natural sources of joy. The assertion that מִשֶּׁמֶן signifies "before oil = brighter than oil," is an error that is rightly combated by Böttcher in his *Proben* and two of his "Gleanings,"* which imputes to the poet a mention of oil that is contrary to his purpose in this connection and inappropriate. Corn, wine, and oil are mentioned as the three chief products of the vegetable kingdom (Luther, Calvin, Grotius, Dathe, and Hupfeld), and are assumed under עֵשֶׂב in ver. 14b, as is also the case in other instances where distinction would be superfluous, *e.g.* in Ex. ix. 22. With oil God makes the countenance shining, or bright and cheerful, not by means of anointing,— since it was not the face but the head that was anointed (Matt. vi. 17),—but by the fact of its increasing the savouriness and nutritiveness of the food. לְהַצְהִיל is chosen with reference to יִצְהָר. In ver. 15c לְבַב־אֱנוֹשׁ does not stand after, as in ver. 15a (where it is לְבַב with *Gaja* on account of the distinctive), but before the verb, because לבב as that which is inward stands in antithesis to פנים as that which is outside. Since the fertilization of the earth by the rain is the chief subject of the predi-

---

* *Proben, i.e. Specimens* of Old Testament interpretation, Leipzig 1833, and *Achrenlese* (Gleanings), referred to in the preface of these volumes. —Tr.

cation in vers. 13-15, ver. 16 is naturally attached to what precedes without arousing critical suspicion. That which satisfies is here the rain itself, and not, as in ver. 13b, that which the rain matures. The "trees of Jahve" are those which before all others proclaim the greatness of their Creator. אֲשֶׁר־שָׁם refers to these trees, of which the cedars and then the cypresses (בְּרוֹשִׁים, root בר, to cut) are mentioned. They are places where small and large birds build their nests and lodge, more particularly the stork, which is called the חֲסִידָה as being πτηνῶν εὐσεβέστατον ζώων (Babrius, Fab. xiii.), as avis pia (pietaticultrix in Petronius, lv. 6), i.e. on account of its love of family life, on account of which it is also regarded as bringing good fortune to a house.* The care of God for the lodging of His creatures leads the poet from the trees to the heights of the mountains and the hiding-places of the rocks, in a manner that is certainly abrupt and that disturbs the sketch taken from the account of the creation. הַגְּבֹהִים is an apposition. יָעֵל (Arabic wa'il) is the steinboc, wild-goat, as being an inhabitant of יָעֵל (wa'l, wa'la), i.e. the high places of the rocks, as יָעֵן, Lam. iv. 3, according to Wetzstein, is the ostrich as being an inhabitant of the wa'na, i.e. the sterile desert; and שָׁפָן is the rock-badger, which dwells in the clefts of the rocks (Prov. xxx. 26), and resembles the marmot—South Arabic ثُفُن, Hyrax Syriacus (distinct from the African). By שָׁפָן the Jewish tradition understands the coney, after which the Peshito here renders it חָנָם (לְהנְסָא, cuniculus). Both animals, the coney and the rock-badger, may be meant in Lev. xi. 5, Deut. xiv. 7; for the sign of the cloven hoof (פַּרְסָה שְׁסוּעָה) is wanting in both. The coney has four toes, and the hyrax has a peculiar formation of hoof, not cloven, but divided into several parts.

Vers. 19-23. The fifth decastich, in which the poet passes over from the third to the fourth day, shows that he has the

---

* In the Merg' district, where the stork is not called lcklck as it is elsewhere, but charnuk on account of its bill like a long horn (خرن) standing out in front, the women and children call it بُو العَس, "bringer of good luck." Like the חסידה, the long-legged carrion-vulture (Vultur percnopterus) or mountain-stork, ὀρειπελαργός, is called רָחָם (خرم) on account of its στοργή.

order of the days of creation before his mind. The moon is mentioned first of all, because the poet wishes to make the picture of the day follow that of the night. He describes it in ver. 19 as the calendarial principal star. מוֹעֲדִים are points and divisions of time (epochs), and the principal measurer of these for civil and ecclesiastical life is the moon (cf. Sir. xliii. 7, ἀπὸ σελήνης σημεῖον ἑορτῆς), just as the sun, knowing when he is to set, is the infallible measurer of the day. In ver. 20 the description, which throughout is drawn in the presence of God in His honour, passes over into direct address: jussives (תָּשֵׁת, וִיהִי) stand in the hypothetical protasis and in its apodosis (Ew. § 357, b). It depends upon God's willing only, and it is night, and the wakeful life of the wild beasts begins to be astir. The young lions then roar after their prey, and *flagitaturi sunt a Deo cibum suum*. The infinitive with *Lamed* is an elliptical expression of a *conjugatio periphrastica* (*vid.* on Hab. i. 17), and becomes a varying expression of the future in general in the later language in approximation to the Aramaic. The roar of the lions and their going forth in quest of prey is an asking of God which He Himself has implanted in their nature. With the rising of the sun the aspect of things becomes very different. שֶׁמֶשׁ is feminine here, where the poet drops the personification (cf. Ps. xix.). The day which dawns with sunrise is the time for man. Both as to matter and style, vers. 21–23 call to mind Job xxiv. 5, xxxvii. 8, xxxviii. 40.

Vers. 24–30. Fixing his eye upon the sea with its small and great creatures, and the care of God for all self-living beings, the poet passes over to the fifth and sixth days of creation. The rich contents of this sixth group flow over and exceed the decastich. With מָה־רַבּוּ (not מַה־גָּדְלוּ, xcii. 6) the poet expresses his wonder at the great number of God's works, each one at the same time having its adjustment in accordance with its design, and all, mutually serving one another, co-operating one with another. קִנְיָן, which signifies both bringing forth and acquiring, has the former meaning here according to the predicate: full of creatures, which bear in themselves the traces of the Name of their Creator (קָנָה). Beside קִנְיָנֶיךָ, however, we also find the reading קִנְיָנֶךָ, which is adopted by Norzi, Heidenheim, and Baer, represented by the versions (LXX., Vulgate, and Jerome), by expositors (Rashi: שֶׁלְּךָ קִנְיָן), by the majority of the MSS. (according to Norzi) and old printed copies, which would signify τῆς κτίσεώς σου, or according to the Latin versions κτήσεώς σου (*possessione tua*, Luther "thy possessions"), but is inferior to the plural κτισμάτων σου, as an accusative of the object to מָלְאָה. The sea more particularly is a world of moving creatures innumerable (lxix. 35). זֶה הַיָּם does not properly signify this sea, but that sea, yonder sea (cf. lxviii. 9, Isa. xxiii. 13, Josh. ix. 13). The attributes follow in an appositional relation, the looseness of which admits of the non-determination (cf. lxviii. 28, Jer. ii. 21, Gen. xliii. 14, and the reverse case above in ver. 18a). אֳנִיָּה in relation to אֳנִי is a *nomen unitatis* (the single ship). It is an old word, which is also Egyptian in the form *hani* and *ana*.* *Leviathan*, in the Book of Job, the crocodile, is in this passage the name of the whale (*vid*. Lewysohn, *Zoologie des Talmuds*, §§ 178-180, 505). Ewald and Hitzig, with the Jewish tradition, understand בּוֹ in ver. 26 according to Job xl. 29 [xli. 5] : in order to play with him, which, however, gives no idea that is worthy of God. It may be taken as an alternative word for שָׁם (cf. בּוֹ in ver. 20, Job xl. 20) : to play therein, viz. in the sea (Saadia). In כֻּלָּם, ver. 27, the range of vision is widened from the creatures of the sea to all the living things of the earth; cf. the borrowed passages cxlv. 15 sq., cxlvii. 9. כֻּלָּם, by an obliteration of the suffix, signifies directly "altogether," and בְּעִתּוֹ (cf. Job xxxviii. 32) : when it is time for it. With reference to the change of the subject in the principal and in the infinitival clause, *vid*. Ew. § 338, *a*. The existence, passing away, and origin of all beings is conditioned by God. His hand provides everything; the turning of His countenance towards them upholds everything; and His breath, the creative breath, animates and renews all things. The spirit of life of every creature is the disposing of the divine Spirit, which hovered over the primordial waters and transformed the chaos into the cosmos. תֹּסֵף in ver. 29 is equivalent to תֶּאֱסֹף, as in 1 Sam. xv. 6, and frequently. The full future forms accented

---

* *Vide* Chabas, *Le papyrus magique Harris*, p. 246, No. 826: HANI (אֳנִי), *vaisseau, navire*, and the *Book of the Dead* i. 10, where *hani* occurs with the determinative picture of a ship. As to the form *ana*, *vid*. Chabas *loc. cit.* p. 33.

on the *ultima*, from ver. 27 onwards, give emphasis to the statements. Job xxxiv. 14 sq. may be compared with ver. 29.

Vers. 31–35. The poet has now come to an end with the review of the wonders of the creation, and closes in this seventh group, which is again substantially decastichic, with a sabbatic meditation, inasmuch as he wishes that the glory of God, which He has put upon His creatures, and which is reflected and echoed back by them to Him, may continue for ever, and that His works may ever be so constituted that He who was satisfied at the completion of His six days' work may be able to rejoice in them. For if they cease to give Him pleasure, He can indeed blot them out as He did at the time of the Flood, since He is always able by a look to put the earth in a tremble, and by a touch to set the mountains on fire (וְתִרְעָד) of the result of the looking, as in Amos v. 8, ix. 6, and וְיֶעֱשָׁנוּ of that which takes place simultaneously with the touching, as in cxliv. 5, Zech. ix. 5, cf. on Hab. iii. 10). The poet, however, on his part, will not suffer there to be any lack of the glorifying of Jahve, inasmuch as he makes it his life's work to praise his God with music and song (בְּחַיָּי as in lxiii. 5, cf. Bar. iv. 20, ἐν ταῖς ἡμέραις μου). Oh that this his quiet and his audible meditation upon the honour of God may be pleasing to Him (עָרֵב עַל synonymous with טוֹב עַל, but also שָׁפַר עַל, xvi. 6)! Oh that Jahve may be able to rejoice in him, as he himself will rejoice in his God! Between "I will rejoice," ver. 34, and "He shall rejoice," ver. 31, there exists a reciprocal relation, as between the Sabbath of the creature in God and the Sabbath of God in the creature. When the Psalmist wishes that God may have joy in His works of creation, and seeks on his part to please God and to have his joy in God, he is also warranted in wishing that those who take pleasure in wickedness, and instead of giving God joy excite His wrath, may be removed from the earth (יִתַּמּוּ, cf. Num. xiv. 35); for they are contrary to the purpose of the good creation of God, they imperil its continuance, and mar the joy of His creatures. The expression is not: may sins (חֲטָאִים, as it is meant to be read in *B. Berachoth*, 10a, and as some editions, *e.g.* Bomberg's of 1521, actually have it), but: may sinners, be no more, for there is no other existence of sin than the personal one.

With the words *Bless, O my soul, Jahve*, the Psalm recurs

to its introduction, and to this call upon himself is appended the *Hallelujah* which summons all creatures to the praise of God — a call of devotion which occurs nowhere out of the Psalter, and within the Psalter is found here for the first time, and consequently was only coined in the later age. In modern printed copies it is sometimes written הַלְלוּ־יָהּ, sometimes הַלְלוּ יָהּ, but in the earlier copies (*e.g.* Venice 1521, Wittenberg 1566) mostly as one word הַלְלוּיָהּ.* In the majority of MSS. it is also found thus as one word,† and that always with ה, except the first הַלְלוּיָהּ which occurs here at the end of Ps. civ., which has ה *raphe* in good MSS. and old printed copies. This mode of writing is that attested by the Masora (*vid.* Baer's *Psalterium*, p. 132). The Talmud and Midrash observe this first Hallelujah is connected in a significant manner with the prospect of the final overthrow of the wicked. Ben-Pazzi (*B. Berachoth* 10a) counts 103 פרשיות up to this Hallelujah, reckoning Ps. i. and ii. as one פרשתא.

* More accurately הַלְלוּיָהּ with *Chateph*, as Jekuthiël ha-Nakdan expressly demands. Moreover the mode of writing it as one word is the rule, since the Masora notes the הַלְלוּ־יָהּ, occurring only once, in cxxxv. 3, with לִיחַ בטעם as being the only instance of the kind.

† Yet even in the Talmud (*J. Megilla* i. 9, *Sofrim* v. 10) it is a matter of controversy concerning the mode of writing this word, whether it is to be separate or combined; and in *B. Pesachim* 117a Rab appeals to a Psalter of the school of Chabibi (תילי דבי חביבי) that he has seen, in which הללו stood in one line and יה in the other. In the same place Rab Chasda appeals to a תילי דבי רב חנין that he has seen, in which the *Hallelujah* standing between two Psalms, which might be regarded as the close of the Psalm preceding it or as the beginning of the Psalm following it, was written in the middle between the two (באמצע פרקיא). In the הללויה written as one word, יה is not regarded as strictly the divine name, only as an addition strengthening the notion of the הללו, as in במרהביה cxviii. 5; with reference to this, *vide* Geiger, *Urschrift*, S. 275.

PSALM CV.

THANKSGIVING HYMN IN HONOUR OF GOD WHO IS ATTESTED IN THE EARLIEST HISTORY OF ISRAEL.

1 GIVE thanks unto Jahve, publish His Name,
 Make known among the peoples His deeds.
2 Sing unto Him, harp unto Him,
 Speak of all His wondrous works.
3 Glory ye in His holy Name,
 Let the heart of those rejoice who seek Jahve.
4 Follow after Jahve and His strength,
 Seek ye His face evermore.
5 Remember His wondrous works which He hath done,
 His rare deeds and the decisions of His mouth,
6 O seed of Abraham His servant,
 Ye sons of Jacob, His chosen ones.

7 He, Jahve, is our God,
 His judgments go forth over all lands.
8 He remembereth for ever His covenant,
 The word which He hath established to a thousand generations,
9 Which He made with Abraham,
 And His oath unto Isaac.
10 And He hath established it for Jacob as a statute,
 For Israel as an everlasting covenant,
11 Saying: "Unto thee do I give the land of Canaan
 As the line of your inheritance."

12 When they were a countable people,
 Very small, and sojourning therein,
13 And went to and fro from nation to nation,
 From one kingdom to another people:
14 He suffered no man to oppress them,
 And He reproved kings for their sakes:
15 "Touch not Mine anointed ones,
 And to My prophets do no harm!"

16 Then He called up a famine over the land,
   Every staff of bread He brake.
17 He sent before them a man,
   As a slave was Joseph sold.
18 They hurt his feet with fetters,
   Iron came upon his soul,
19 Until the time that his word came,
   The word of Jahve had proved him.
20 The king sent and loosed him,
   The ruler of the peoples, and let him go free;
21 He made him lord of his house,
   And ruler over all his possession,
22 To bind his princes at his will,
   And to make his elders wiser.
23 Thus Israel came to Egypt,
   And Jacob sojourned in the land of Ham.
24 And He made His people fruitful exceedingly,
   And made them more powerful than their enemies.

25 He turned their heart to hate His people,
   To practise cunning on His servants;
26 He sent Moses His servant,
   Aaron, whom He had chosen.
27 They performed upon them facts of His signs,
   And strange things in the land of Ham.
28 He sent darkness and made it dark,
   And they rebelled not against His words;
29 He turned their waters into blood,
   And thus killed their fish.
30 Their land swarmed forth frogs
   In the chambers of their kings.
31 He spake, and the gad-fly came,
   Gnats in all their border.
32 He gave them as rain hail,
   Flaming fire in their land,
33 And He smote down their vines and fig-trees,
   And brake the trees of their border.
34 He spake, and the locusts came,
   And the grasshopper without number,

35 And devoured all the green herb in their land,
   And devoured the fruit of their ground.
36 Then He smote all the first-born in their land,
   The firstlings of all their strength,
37 And led them forth with silver and gold,
   And there was no stumbling one among His tribes.
38 Egypt rejoiced at their departure,
   For dread of them had fallen upon them.

39 He spread a cloud for a covering,
   And fire to lighten the night;
40 They desired, and He brought quails,
   And satisfied them with the bread of heaven;
41 He opened a rock, and waters gushed out,
   They flowed through the steppes as a river.
42 For He remembered His holy word,
   Abraham His servant;
43 And He led forth His people with gladness,
   And with exulting His chosen ones;
44 And He gave them the lands of the heathen,
   And that gained by the labour of the nations they inherited;
45 That they might observe His laws
   And keep His instructions.
       Hallelujah!

We have here another Psalm closing with *Hallelujah*, which opens the series of the *Hodu*-Psalms. Such is the name we give only to Psalms which begin with הודו (cv., cvii., cxviii., cxxxvi.), just as we call those which begin with הללויה (cvi., cxi.–cxiii., cxvii., cxxxv., cxlvi.–cl.) *Hallelujah*-Psalms (*alleluiatici*.) The expression להלל ולהודות, which frequently occurs in the books of Chronicles, Ezra, and Nehemiah, points to these two kinds of Psalms, or at least to their key-notes.

The festival song which David, according to 1 Chron. xvi. 7, handed over to Asaph and his brethren for musical execution at the setting down of the Ark and the opening of divine service on Zion, is, so far as its first part is concerned (1 Chron. xvi. 8–22), taken from our Psalm (vers. 1–15), which is then followed by Ps. xcvi. as a second part, and is closed with Ps.

cvi. 1, 47, 48. Hitzig regards the festival song in the chronicler as the original, and the respective parallels in the Psalms as "layers or shoots." "The chronicler," says he, "there produces with labour, and therefore himself seeking foreign aid, a song for a past that is dead." But the transition from ver. 22 to ver. 23 and from ver. 33 to ver. 34, so devoid of connection, the taking over of the verse out of Ps. cvi. referring to the Babylonian exile into ver. 35, and even of the doxology of the Fourth Book, regarded as an integral part of the Psalm, into ver. 36, refute that perversion of the right relation, which has been attempted in the interest of the Maccabæan Psalms. That festival song in the chronicler, as has been shown again very recently by Riehm and Köhler, is a compilation of parts of songs already at hand, arranged for a definite purpose. Starting on the assumption that the Psalms as a whole are Davidic (just as all the Proverbs are Salomonic), because David called the poetry of the Psalms used in religious worship into existence, the attempt is made in that festival song to represent the opening of the worship on Zion at that time in strains belonging to the Davidic Psalms.

So far as the subject-matter is concerned, Ps. cv. attaches itself to the Asaph Psalm lxxviii., which recapitulates the history of Israel. The recapitulation here, however, is made not with any didactic purpose, but with the purpose of forming a hymn, and does not come down beyond the time of Moses and Joshua. Its source is likewise the Tôra as it now lies before us. The poet epitomizes what the Tôra narrates, and clothes it in a poetic garb.

Vers. 1-6. Invitation to the praise—praise that resounds far and wide among the peoples—of the God who has become manifest wondrously in the deeds and words connected with the history of the founding of Israel. הוֹדָה לֹה׳, as in xxxiii. 2, lxxv. 2, of a praising and thankful confession offered to God ; קרא בְּשֵׁם ה׳, to call with the name of Jahve, i.e. to call upon it, of an audible, solemn attestation of God in prayer and in discourse (Symmachus, κηρύσσετε). The joy of heart *

---

* The *Mugrash* of יִשְׂמַח with the following *Legarme* seems here to be of equal value with *Zakeph*, 1 Chron. xvi. 10.

that is desired is the condition of a joyous opening of the mouth and Israel's own stedfast turning towards Jahve, the condition of all salutary result; for it is only His " strength" that breaks through all dangers, and His " face" that lightens up all darkness. מִשְׁפְּטֵי־פִיו, as ver. 7 teaches, are God's judicial utterances, which have been executed without any hindrance, more particularly in the case of the Egyptians, their Pharaoh, and their gods. The chronicler has פִיהוּ and זֶרַע יִשְׂרָאֵל, which is so far unsuitable as one does not know whether עבדו is to be referred to "Israel" the patriarch, or to the "seed of Israel," the nation; the latter reference would be deutero-Isaianic. In both texts the LXX. reads עֲבָדָיו (ye His servants).

Vers. 7–11. The poet now begins himself to do that to which he encourages Israel. Jahve is Israel's God: His righteous rule extends over the whole earth, whilst His people experience His inviolable faithfulness to His covenant. יהוה in ver. 7a is in apposition to הוּא, for the God who bears this name is as a matter of course the object of the song of praise. זָכַר is the perfect of practically pledged certainty (cf. cxi. 5, where we find instead the future of confident prospect). The chronicler has זִכְרוּ instead (LXX. again something different: μνημονεύωμεν); but the object is not the demanding but the promissory side of the covenant, so that consequently it is not Israel's remembering but God's that is spoken of. He remembers His covenant in all time to come, so that exile and want of independence as a state are only temporary, exceptional conditions. צִוָּה has its radical signification here, to establish, institute, cxi. 9. לְאֶלֶף דּוֹר (in which expression דּוֹר is a specifying accusative) is taken from Deut. vii. 9. And since דָּבָר is the covenant word of promise, it can be continued אֲשֶׁר כָּרַת; and Hagg. ii. 5 (vid. Köhler thereon) shows that אשר is not joined to בריתו over ver. 8b. וּשְׁבוּעָתוֹ, however, is a second object to זָכַר (since דָּבָר with what belongs to it as an apposition is out of the question). It is the oath on Moriah (Gen. xxii. 16) that is meant, which applied to Abraham and his seed. לְיִשְׂחָק (chronicler לְיִצְחָק), as in Amos vii. 9, Jer. xxxiii. 26. To זָכַר is appended וַיַּעֲמִידֶהָ; the suffix, intended as neuter, points to what follows, viz. this, that Canaan shall be Israel's hereditary land. From Abraham and Isaac we come to Jacob-Israel, who as being the father of the twelve is the twelve-tribe nation itself that is coming into existence; hence the plural can alternate with the singular in ver. 11. אֶֽה־אֶ֫רֶץ כְּנָ֥עַן (chronicler, without the את) is an accusative of the object, and חֶ֥בֶל נַחֲלַתְכֶֽם accusative of the predicate: the land of Canaan as the province of your own hereditary possession measured out with a measuring line (lxxviii. 55).

Vers. 12-15. The poet now celebrates the divine preservation which had sway over the small beginnings of Israel, when it made the patriarchs proof against harm on their wanderings. "Men of number" are such as can be easily counted, vid. the confessions in Gen. xxxiv. 30, Deut. xxvi. 5; וַיִּתְהַלְּכוּ places the claim upon the hospitality at one time of this people and at another time of that people in the connection with it of cause and effect. כִּמְעַט, as a small number, only such a small number, signifies, as being virtually an adjective: inconsiderable, insignificant, worthless (Prov. x. 20). בָּהּ refers to Canaan. In ver. 13 the way in which the words גּוֹי and עַם alternate is instructive: the former signifies the nation, bound together by a common origin, language, country, and descent; the latter the people, bound together by unity of government.* The apodosis does not begin until ver. 14. It is different in connection with בִּהְיֽוֹתְכֶם in the text of the chronicler, and in this passage in the Psalter of the Syriac version, according to which ver. 12 ought to be joined to the preceding group. The variation וּמִמַּמְלָכָה instead of מִמַּמְלָכָה is of no consequence; but לְאִישׁ (to any one whomsoever) instead of אָדָם, in connection with הִנִּיחַ, restores the current mode of expression (Eccles. v. 11, 2 Sam. xvi. 11, Hos. iv. 17) instead of one which is without support elsewhere, but which follows the model of נָתַן, שִׂים, Gen. xxxi. 28 (cf. supra i. 274); whilst on the other hand וּבִנְבִיאַי instead of וְלִנְבִיאַי substitutes an expression that cannot be supported for the current one (Gen. xix. 9, Ruth i. 21). In ver. 14 the poet has the three histories of the preservation of

---

* For this reason a king says עַמִּי, not גּוֹיִי; and גּוֹי only occurs twice with a suffix, which refers to Jahve (cvi. 5, Zeph. ii. 9); for this reason גּוֹי, frequently side by side with עַם, is the nobler word, *e.g.* in Deut. xxxii. 21, Jer. ii. 11; for this reason עַם is frequently added to גּוֹי as a dignitative predicate, Ex. xxxiii. 13, Deut. iv. 6; and for this reason גּוֹיִם and עַם ה׳ are used antithetically.

the wives of the patriarchs in his mind, viz. of Sarah in Egypt (Gen. ch. xii.), and of Sarah and of Rebekah both in Philistia (ch. xx., xxvi., cf. especially xxvi. 11). In the second instance God declares the patriarch to be a "prophet" (ch. xx. 7). The one mention has reference to this and the other to Gen. ch. xvii., where Abram is set apart to be the father of peoples and kings, and Sarai to be a princess. They are called מְשִׁיחִים (a passive form) as being God-chosen princes, and נְבִיאִים (an intensive active form, from נָבָא, root נב, to divulge), not as being inspired ones (Hupfeld), but as being God's spokesmen (cf. Ex. vii. 1 sq. with iv. 15 sq.), therefore as being the recipients and mediators of a divine revelation.

Vers. 16–24. "To call up a famine" is also a prose expression in 2 Kings viii. 1. *To break the staff of bread* (i.e. the staff which bread is to man) is a very old metaphor, Lev. xxvi. 26. That the selling of Joseph was, providentially regarded, a "sending before," he himself says in Gen. xlv. 5. Ps. cii. 24 throws light upon the meaning of עֻנָּה בְ. The *Keri* רַגְלוֹ is just as much without any occasion to justify it as עֵינוֹ in Eccles. iv. 8 (for עֵינָיו). The statement that iron came upon his soul is intended to say that he had to endure in iron fetters sufferings that threatened his life. Most expositors take בַּרְזֶל as equivalent to בְּבַרְזֶל, but Hitzig rightly takes נפשׁו as an object, following the Targum; for ברזל as a name of an iron fetter* can change its gender, as do, e.g., צפון as a name of the north wind, and כבוד as a name of the soul. The imprisonment (so harsh at the commencement) lasted over ten years, until at last Joseph's word came to pass, viz. the word concerning his exaltation which had been revealed to him in dreams (Gen. xlii. 9). According to cvii. 20, דְּבָרוֹ appears to be the word of Jahve, but then one would expect from ver. 19*b* a more parallel turn of expression. What is meant is Joseph's open-hearted word

---

* Also in ancient Arabic فِرْزِل (after the Aramaic פרזלא) directly signifies an iron fetter (and the large smith's shears for cutting the iron), whence the *verb. denom.* فَرْزَلَ *c. acc. pers.*, to put any one into iron chains. Iron is called בַּרְזֶל from בָּרַז, to pierce, like the Arabic حَدِيد, as being the material of which pointed tools are made.

concerning his visions, and 'ה אִמְרַת is the revelation of God conveying His promises, which came to him in the same form, which had to try, to prove, and to purify him (צְרָף as in xvii. 3, and frequently), inasmuch as he was not to be raised to honour without having in a state of deep abasement proved a faithfulness that wavered not, and a confidence that knew no despair. The divine " word" is conceived of as a living effectual power, as in cxix. 50. The representation of the exaltation begins, according to Gen. xli. 14, with שָׁלַח־מֶלֶךְ,* and follows Gen. xli. 39–41, 44, very closely as to the rest, according to which בְּנַפְשׁוֹ is a collateral definition to לְאָסֹר (with an orthophonic *Dag.*) in the sense of בִּרְצוֹנוֹ : by his soul, *i.e.* by virtue of his will (*vid. Psychology*, S. 202 ; tr. p. 239). In consequence of this exaltation of Joseph, Jacob-Israel came then into Egypt, and sojourned there as in a protecting house of shelter (concerning גּוּר, *vid. supra*, ii. 203). Egypt is called (vers. 23, 27) the land of *Châm*, as in lxxviii. 51 ; according to Plutarch, in the vernacular the black land, from the dark ashy grey colouring which the deposited mud of the Nile gives to the ground. There Israel became a powerful, numerous people (Ex. i. 7, Deut. xxvi. 5), greater than their oppressors.

Vers. 25–38. Narration of the exodus out of Egypt after the plagues that went forth over that land. Ver. 25 tells how the Egyptians became their " oppressors." It was indirectly God's work, inasmuch as He gave increasing might to His people, which excited their jealousy. The craft reached its highest pitch in the weakening of the Israelites that was aimed at by killing all the male children that were born. דִּבְרֵי signifies facts, instances, as in lxv. 4, cxlv. 5. Here, too, as in Ps. lxxviii., the miraculous judgments of the ten plagues do not stand in exactly historical order. The poet begins with the ninth, which was the most distinct self-representation of divine wrath, viz. the darkness (Ex. x. 21–29) : *shá'lach chŏ́-shech.* The former word (שָׁלַח) has an orthophonic *Gaja* by

---

* Here שְׁלַח is united by *Makkeph* with the following word, to which it hurries on, whereas in ver. 28 it has its own accent, a circumstance to which the Masora has directed attention in the apophthegm : שלוחי דמלכא זריזין שלוחי דחשובא מתינין (the emissaries of the king are in haste, those of darkness are tardy) ; *vid.* Baer, *Thorath Emeth*, p. 22.

the final syllable, which warns the reader audibly to utter the guttural of the toneless final syllable, which might here be easily slurred over. The *Hiph.* הֶחְשִׁיךְ has its causative signification here, as also in Jer. xiii. 16; the contracted mode of writing with *i* instead of *î* may be occasioned by the *Waw convers*. Ver. 28*b* cannot be referred to the Egyptians; for the expression would be a mistaken one for the final compliance, which was wrung from them, and the interrogative way of taking it: *nonne rebellarunt*, is forced: the cancelling of the לֹא, however (LXX. and Syriac), makes the thought halting. Hitzig proposes וְלֹא שָׁמְרוּ: they observed not His words; but this, too, sounds flat and awkward when said of the Egyptians. The subject will therefore be the same as the subject of שָׂמוּ; and of Moses and Aaron, in contrast to the behaviour at *Mê-Merîbah* (Num. xx. 24, xxvii. 14; cf. 1 Kings xiii. 21, 26), it is said that this time they rebelled not against the words (*Kerî*, without any ground: the word) of God, but executed the terrible commands accurately and willingly. From the ninth plague the poet in ver. 29 passes over to the first (Ex. vii. 14-25), viz. the red blood is appended to the black darkness. The second plague follows, viz. the frogs (Ex. vii. 26 [viii. 1]–viii. 11 [15]); ver. 30*b* looks as though it were stunted, but neither has the LXX. read any וַיָּבֹאוּ (וַיַּעֲלוּ), Ex. vii. 28. In ver. 31 he next briefly touches upon the fourth plague, viz. the gad-fly, עָרֹב, LXX. κυνόμυια (Ex. viii. 16-28 [20-32], *vid.* on lxxviii. 45), and the third (Ex. viii. 12-15 [16-19]), viz. the gnats, which are passed over in Ps. lxxviii. From the third plague the poet in vers. 32, 33 takes a leap over to the seventh, viz. the hail (Ex. ix. 13-35). In ver. 32 he has Ex. ix. 24 before his mind, according to which masses of fire descended with the hail; and in ver. 33 (as in lxxviii. 47) he fills in the details of Ex. ix. 25. The seventh plague is followed by the eighth in vers. 34, 35, viz. the locust (Ex. x. 1-20), to which יֶלֶק (the grasshopper) is the parallel word here, just as חָסִיל (the cricket) is in lxxviii. 46. The expression of innumerableness is the same as in civ. 25. The fifth plague, viz. the pestilence, murrain (Ex. ix. 1-7), and the sixth, viz. שְׁחִין, boils (Ex. ix. 8-12), are left unmentioned; and the tenth plague closes, viz. the smiting of the first-born (Ex. xi. 1 sqq.), which ver. 36 expresses in the Asaphic language of lxxviii. 51. Without any mention of the institution of the Passover, the tenth plague is followed by the departure with the vessels of silver and gold asked for from the Egyptians (Ex. xii. 35, xi. 2, iii. 22). The Egyptians were glad to get rid of the people whose detention threatened them with total destruction (Ex. xii. 33). The poet here draws from Isa. v. 27, xiv. 31, lxiii. 13, and Ex. xv. 16. The suffix of שְׁבָטָיו refers to the chief subject of the assertion, viz. to God, according to cxxii. 4, although manifestly enough the reference to Israel is also possible (Num. xxiv. 2).

Vers. 39–45. Now follows the miraculous guidance through the desert to the taking possession of Canaan. The fact that the cloud (עָנָן, root ען, to meet, to present itself to view, whence the Arabic *'anân*, the visible outward side of the vault of heaven) by day, and becoming like fire by night, was their guide (Ex. xiii. 21), is left out of consideration in ver. 39a. With לְמָסָךְ we are not to associate the idea of a covering against foes, Ex. xiv. 19 sq., but of a covering from the smiting sun, for פָּרַשׂ (Ex. xl. 19), as in Isa. iv. 5 sq., points to the idea of a canopy. In connection with the sending of the quails the tempting character of the desire is only momentarily dwelt upon, the greater emphasis is laid on the omnipotence of the divine goodness which responded to it. שָׂאֲלוּ is to be read instead of שָׁאַל, the ו before ו having been overlooked; and the *Kerî* writes and points שְׂאָלָיו (like כְּתִיו, עֵצָיו) in order to secure the correct pronunciation, after the analogy of the plural termination ־יו. The bread of heaven (lxxviii. 24 sq.) is the manna. In ver. 41 the giving of water out of the rock at Rephidim and at Kadesh are brought together; the expression corresponds better to the former instance (Ex. xvii. 6, cf. Num. xx. 11). הָלְכוּ refers to the waters, and נָהָר for כְּנַהֲרוֹת, lxxviii. 16, is, as in xxii. 14, an equation instead of a comparison. In this miraculous escort the patriarchal promise moves on towards its fulfilment; the holy word of promise, and the stedfast, proved faith of Abraham—these were the two motives. The second את is, like the first, a sign of the object, not a preposition (LXX., Targum), in connection with which ver. 42*b* would be a continuation of ver. 42*a*, dragging on without any parallelism. Joy and exulting are mentioned as the mood of the redeemed ones with reference to the festive joy displayed at the Red Sea and at Sinai. By ver. 43 one is reminded of the same descriptions of the antitype in Isaiah, ch. xxxv. 10, li. 11, lv. 12, just as ver. 41 recalls Isa. xlviii. 21. "The lands of the heathen" are the territories of the tribes of Canaan. עֹמָל is equivalent to יְגִיעַ in Isa. xlv. 14 : the cultivated ground, the habitable cities, and the accumulated treasures. Israel entered upon the inheritance of these peoples in every direction. As an independent people upon ground that is theirs by inheritance, keeping the revealed law of their God, was Israel to exhibit the pattern of a holy nation moulded after the divine will; and, as the beginning of the Psalm shows, to unite the peoples to themselves and their God, the God of redemption, by the proclamation of the redemption which has fallen to their own lot.

PSALM CVI.

ISRAEL'S UNFAITHFULNESS FROM EGYPT ONWARDS, AND GOD'S FAITHFULNESS DOWN TO THE PRESENT TIME.

HALLELUJAH!
1 GIVE thanks unto Jahve, for He is good,
  For His graciousness endureth for ever.
2 Who can utter the mighty acts of Jahve,
  [Who] make all His praise to be heard?
3 Blessed are they who keep the right,
  He who doeth righteousness at all times.
4 Remember me, Jahve, at the favouring of Thy people,
  Visit me with Thy help,
5 That I too may see the prosperity of Thy chosen ones,
  That I too may be glad at the gladness of Thy people,
  That I too may glory with Thine inheritance.

6 We have sinned like unto our fathers,
  We have committed iniquity, we have done wickedly.
7 Our fathers in Egypt heeded not Thy wonders,
  They remembered not the abundance of Thy loving-kindnesses,
  And were rebellious at the sea, at the Red Sea.

8 Yet He saved them for His Name's sake,
   To make His strength known.
9 He rebuked the Red Sea, and it dried up,
   And led them through the floods as upon a plain;
10 And He saved them out of the hand of the hater,
   And redeemed them out of the hand of the enemy.
11 The waters covered their oppressors,
   Not one of them was left—
12 Then they believed His words,
   They sang His praise.

13 They quickly forgat His works,
   They waited not for His counsel.
14 They lusted greedily in the desert,
   And tempted God in the wilderness.
15 Then He gave them their desire,
   And sent consumption into their soul.
16 They manifested envy against Moses in the camp,
   Against Aaron, the holy one of Jahve—
17 The earth opened and swallowed up Dathan,
   And covered the band of Abiram;
18 And fire seized upon their band,
   A flame consumed the evil-doers.
19 They made a calf in Horeb,
   Then they worshipped the molten image,
20 And they bartered their glory
   For the likeness of an ox that eateth grass.
21 They had forgotten God their Saviour,
   Who did great deeds in Egypt,
22 Wondrous works in the land of Ham,
   Terrible deeds at the Red Sea.
23 Then He thought to exterminate them,
   Had not Moses His chosen one
   Stepped into the breach before Him
   To calm His wrath, that He should not destroy.

24 They despised the pleasant land,
   They believed not His word.
25 They murmured in their tents,
   They hearkened not to the voice of Jahve.

26 Then He lifted up His hand against them
   To cast them down in the desert,
27 And to disperse their seed among the heathen,
   And to scatter them in the lands.
28 They joined themselves unto Baal-Peôr,
   And ate the sacrifices for the dead,
29 And excited provocation by their doings;
   And the plague brake in among them.
30 Then stood up Phinehas and arranged,
   And the plague was stayed.
31 And it was counted unto him for righteousness
   Unto all generations for ever.
32 Then they excited displeasure at the waters of strife,
   And it went ill with Moses for their sakes.
33 For they rebelled against God's Spirit,
   And he erred with his lips.

34 They did not exterminate the peoples
   Which Jahve had said to them;
35 But mixed themselves among the heathen,
   And learned their works.
36 They served their idols,
   And they became to them a snare.
37 They sacrificed their sons and their daughters to demons,
38 And shed innocent blood,
   The blood of their sons and their daughters,
   Whom they sacrificed to the idols of Canaan,
   So that the land was polluted by blood-guiltiness.
39 They became impure by their works,
   And became fornicators by their doings.
40 Then was the wrath of Jahve kindled against His people,
   And He abhorred His own inheritance.
41 He gave them over into the hand of the heathen,
   And their haters became their oppressors.
42 Their enemies oppressed them,
   And they were obliged to bow down under their hand.
43 Many times did He rescue them,
   Yet they rebelled in their self-will—
   Then they perished in their iniquity.

44 But He saw how hard it went with them,
When He heard their cry of grief.
45 He remembered for them His covenant,
And had compassion according to the abundance of His mercies.
46 And He caused them to be compassionated
In the presence of all who carried them into captivity.
47 Save us, Jahve our God,
And bring us together out of the heathen,
To give thanks unto Thy holy Name,
And to glory in Thy praise.
48 BLESSED BE JAHVE THE GOD OF ISRAEL FROM EVERLASTING TO EVERLASTING,
AND LET ALL PEOPLE SAY AMEN!
HALLELUJAH!!

With this anonymous Psalm begins the series of the strictly Hallelujah-Psalms, *i.e.* of those Psalms which have הללויה for their arsis-like beginning and for their inscription (cvi., cxi.-cxiii., cxvii., cxxxv., cxlvi.-cl.). The chronicler in his cento, 1 Chron. xvi. 8 sqq., and in fact in ch. xvi. 34–36, puts the first and last verses of this Psalm (vers. 1, 47), together with the *Beracha* (ver. 48) which closes the Fourth Book of the Psalms, into the mouth of David, from which it is to be inferred that this Psalm is no more Maccabæan than Ps. xcvi. and cv. (which see), and that the Psalter was divided into five books which were marked off by the doxologies even in the time of the chronicler. The Beracha, ver. 48, appears even at that period to have been read as an integral part of the Psalm, according to liturgical usage. The Hallelujah Ps. cvi., like the Hodu Ps. cv. and the Asaph Ps. lxxviii., recapitulates the history of the olden times of the Israelitish nation. But the purpose and mode of the recapitulation differ in each of these three Psalms. In Ps. lxxviii. it is didactic; in Ps. cv. hymnic; and here in Ps. cvi. penitential. It is a penitential Psalm, or Psalm of confession, a וִדּוּי (from הִתְוַדָּה to confess, Lev. xvi. 21). The oldest types of such liturgical prayers are the two formularies at the offering of the first-fruits, Deut. ch. xxvi., and Solomon's prayer at the dedication of the Temple, 1 Kings ch. viii. And to this kind of *tephilla*, the *Vidduj*, belong, beyond the range of the Psalter, the prayer of Daniel, ch. ix. (*vid.* the way in which it is introduced in ver. 4), and the prayer (Neh. ix. 5–x. 1 [ix. 38]) which eight Levites uttered in the name of the people at the celebration of the fast-day on the twenty-fourth of Tishri. It is true Ps. cvi. is distinguished from these prayers of confession in the prose style as being a Psalm; but it has three points in common with them and with the liturgical tephilla in general, viz. (1) the fondness for inflexional rhyming, *i.e.* for rhyming terminations of the same suffixes; (2) the heaping up of synonyms; and (3) the unfolding of the thoughts in a continuous line. These three peculiarities are found not only in the liturgical border, vers. 1–6, 47, but also in the middle historical portion, which forms the bulk of the Psalm. The law of parallelism is, it is true, still observed; but apart from these distichic wave-like ridges of the thoughts, it is all one direct, straight-line flow without technical division.

Vers. 1–5. The Psalm begins with the liturgical call, which was not coined for the first time in the Maccabæan age (1 Macc. iv. 24), but was already in use in Jeremiah's time (ch. xxxiii. 11). The LXX. appropriately renders טוֹב by χρηστός, for God is called " good" not so much in respect of His nature as of the revelation of His nature. The fulness of this revelation, says ver. 2 (like xl. 6), is inexhaustible. גְּבוּרוֹת are the manifestations of His all-conquering power which makes everything subservient to His redemptive purposes (xx. 7); and תְּהִלָּה is the glory (praise or celebration) of His self-attestation in history. The proclaiming of these on the part of man can never be an exhaustive echo of them. In ver. 3 the poet tells what is the character of those who experience such manifestations of God; and to the assertion of the blessedness of these men he appends the petition in ver. 4, that God would grant him a share in the experiences of the whole nation which is the object of these manifestations. עַמֶּךָ beside בִּרְצוֹן is a genitive of the object: with the pleasure which Thou turnest towards Thy people, *i.e.* when Thou again (cf. ver. 47) showest Thyself gracious unto them. On פְּקָד cf. viii. 5, lxxx. 15, and on רָאָה בְּ, Jer. xxix. 32; a similar *Beth* is that beside לִשְׂמֹחַ (at, on account of, not: in connection with), xxi. 2, cxxii.

1. God's "inheritance" is His people; the name for them is varied four times, and thereby גּוֹי is also exceptionally brought into use, as in Zeph. ii. 9.

Vers. 6–12. The key-note of the *vidduj*, which is a settled expression since 1 Kings viii. 47 (Dan. ix. 5, cf. Bar. ii. 12), makes itself heard here in ver. 6; Israel is bearing at this time the punishment of its sins, by which it has made itself like its forefathers. In this needy and helpless condition the poet, who all along speaks as a member of the assembly, takes the way of the confession of sin, which leads to the forgiveness of sin and to the removal of the punishment of sin. רָשַׁע, 1 Kings viii. 47, signifies to be, and the *Hiph.* to prove one's self to be, a רָשָׁע. עִם in ver. 6 is equivalent to *æque ac*, as in Eccles. ii. 16, Job ix. 26. With ver. 7 the retrospect begins. The fathers contended with Moses and Aaron in Egypt (Ex. v. 21), and gave no heed to the prospect of redemption (Ex. vi. 9). The miraculous judgments which Moses executed (Ex. iii. 20) had no more effect in bringing them to a right state of mind, and the abundant tokens of loving-kindness (Isa. lxiii. 7) amidst which God redeemed them made so little impression on their memories that they began to despair and to murmur even at the Red Sea (Ex. xiv. 11 sq.). With עַל, ver. 7b, alternates בְּ (as in Ezek. x. 15, בְּנָהָר); cf. the alternation of prepositions in Joel iv. 8b. When they behaved thus, Jahve might have left their redemption unaccomplished, but out of unmerited mercy He nevertheless redeemed them. Vers. 8–11 are closely dependent upon Ex. ch. xiv. Ver. 11b is a transposition (cf. xxxiv. 21, Isa. xxxiv. 16) from Ex. xiv. 28. On the other hand, ver. 9b is taken out of Isa. lxiii. 13 (cf. Wisd. xix. 9); Isa. lxiii. 7–lxiv. is a prayer for redemption which has a similar ground-colouring. The sea through which they passed is called, as in the Tôra, יַם־סוּף, which seems, according to Ex. ii. 3, Isa. xix. 3, to signify the sea of reed or sedge, although the sedge does not grow in the Red Sea itself, but only on the marshy places of the coast; but it can also signify the sea of sea-weed, *mare algosum*, after the Egyptian *sippe*, wool and sea-weed (just as صوف also signifies both these). The word is certainly Egyptian, whether it is to be referred back to the Egyptian word *sippe* (sea-weed) or *sêbe* (sedge), and is therefore used after the manner of a proper name; so that the inference drawn by Knobel on Ex. xiii. 18 from the absence of the article, that סוּף is the name of a town on the northern point of the gulf, is groundless. The miracle at the sea of sedge or sea-weed—as ver. 12 says—also was not without effect. Ex. xiv. 31 tells us that they believed on Jahve and Moses His servant, and the song which they sang follows in Ex. ch. xv. But they then only too quickly added sins of ingratitude.

Vers. 13–23. The first of the principal sins on the other side of the Red Sea was the unthankful, impatient, unbelieving murmuring about their meat and drink, vers. 13–15. For what ver. 13 places foremost was the root of the whole evil, that, falling away from faith in God's promise, they forgot the works of God which had been wrought in confirmation of it, and did not wait for the carrying out of His counsel. The poet has before his eye the murmuring for water on the third day after the miraculous deliverance (Ex. xv. 22–24) and in Rephidim (Ex. xvii. 2). Then the murmuring for flesh in the first and second years of the exodus which was followed by the sending of the quails (Ex. ch. xvi. and Num. ch. xi.), together with the wrathful judgment by which the murmuring for the second time was punished (*Kibrôth ha-Ta'avah*, Num. xi. 33–35). This dispensation of wrath the poet calls רָזוֹן (LXX., Vulgate, and Syriac erroneously πλησμονήν, perhaps מָזוֹן, nourishment), inasmuch as he interprets Num. xi. 33–35 of a wasting disease, which swept away the people in consequence of eating inordinately of the flesh, and in the expression (cf. lxxviii. 31) he closely follows Isa. x. 16. The "counsel" of God for which they would not wait, is His plan with respect to the time and manner of the help. חִכָּה, root حكّ, a weaker power of حتّ, whence also حكل, i. 180, حكم, i. 84 note, signifies prop. to make firm, *e.g.* a knot (cf. on xxxiii. 20), and starting from this (without the intervention of the metaphor *moras nectere*, as Schultens thinks) is transferred to a firm bent of mind, and the tension of long expectation. The epigrammatic expression וַיִּתְאַוּוּ תַאֲוָה (plural of יִתְאָו, xlv. 12, for which codices, as also in Prov. xxiii. 3, 6, xxiv. 1, the Complutensian, Venetian 1521, Elias Levita, and Baer have וַיִּתְאוּ without the tonic lengthening) is taken from Num. xi. 4.

The second principal sin was the insurrection against their superiors, vers. 16-18. The poet has Num. ch. xvi. xvii. in his eye. The rebellious ones were swallowed up by the earth, and their two hundred and fifty noble, non-Levite partisans consumed by fire. The fact that the poet does not mention Korah among those who were swallowed up is in perfect harmony with Num. xvi. 25 sqq., Deut. xi. 6; cf. however Num. xxvi. 10. The elliptical תִּפְתַּח in ver. 17 is explained from Num. xvi. 32, xxvi. 10.

The third principal sin was the worship of the calf, vers. 19-23. The poet here glances back at Ex. ch. xxxii., but not without at the same time having Deut. ix. 8-12 in his mind; for the expression " in Horeb" is Deuteronomic, e.g. Deut. iv. 15, v. 2, and frequently. Ver. 20 is also based upon the Book of Deuteronomy: they exchanged their glory, i.e. the God who was their distinction before all peoples according to Deut. iv. 6-8, x. 21 (cf. also Jer. ii. 11), for the likeness (תַּבְנִית) of a plough-ox (for this is pre-eminently called שׁוֹר, in the dialects תּוֹר), contrary to the prohibition in Deut. iv. 17. On ver. 21a cf. the warning in Deut. vi. 12. " Land of Cham " = Egypt, as in lxxviii. 51, cv. 23, 27. With ויאמר in ver. 23 the expression becomes again Deuteronomic: Deut. ix. 25, cf. Ex. xxxii. 10. God made and also expressed the resolve to destroy Israel. Then Moses stepped into the gap (before the gap), i.e. as it were covered the breach, inasmuch as he placed himself in it and exposed his own life; cf. on the fact, besides Ex. ch. xxxii., also Deut. ix. 18 sq., x. 10, and on the expression, Ezek. xxii. 30 and also Jer. xviii. 20.

Vers. 24-33. The fact to which the poet refers in ver. 24, viz. the rebellion in consequence of the report of the spies, which he brings forward as the fourth principal sin, is narrated in Num. ch. xiii., xiv. The appellation אֶרֶץ חֶמְדָּה is also found in Jer. iii. 19, Zech. vii. 14. As to the rest, the expression is altogether Pentateuchal. " They despised the land," after Num. xiv. 31; " they murmured in their tents," after Deut. i. 27; " to lift up the hand " = to swear, after Ex. vi. 8, Deut. xxxii. 40; the threat לְהַפִּיל, to make them fall down, fall away, after Num. xiv. 29, 32. The threat of exile is founded upon the two great threatening chapters, Lev. xxvi., Deut. xxviii.; cf. more particularly Lev. xxvi. 33 (together with the echoes in

Ezek. v. 12, xii. 14, etc.), Deut. xxviii. 64 (together with the echoes in Jer. ix. 15, Ezek. xxii. 15, etc.). Ezek. xx. 23 stands in a not accidental relationship to ver. 26 sq.; and according to that passage, וּלְהָפִיל is an error of the copyist for וּלְהָפִיץ (Hitzig).

Now follows in ver. 28–31 the fifth of the principal sins, viz. the taking part in the Moabitish worship of Baal. The verb נִצְמַד (to be bound or chained), taken from Num. xxv. 3, 5, points to the prostitution with which Baal Peôr, this Moabitish Priapus, was worshipped. The sacrificial feastings in which, according to Num. xxv. 2, they took part, are called eating the sacrifices of the dead, because the idols are dead beings (νεκροί, Wisd. xiii. 10–18) as opposed to God, the living One. The catena on Apoc. ii. 14 correctly interprets: τὰ τοῖς εἰδώλοις τελεσθέντα κρέα.* The object of "they made angry" is omitted; the author is fond of this, cf. vers. 7 and 32. The expression in ver. 29b is like Ex. xix. 24. The verb עָמַד is chosen with reference to Num. xvii. 13 [xvi. 48]. The result is expressed in ver. 30b after Num. xxv. 8, 18 sq., xvii. 13 [xvi. 48]. With פִּלֵּל, to adjust, to judge adjustingly (LXX., Vulgate, correctly according to the sense, ἐξιλάσατο), the poet associates the thought of the satisfaction due to divine right, which Phinehas executed with the javelin. This act of zeal for Jahve, which compensated for Israel's unfaithfulness, was accounted unto him for righteousness, by his being rewarded for it with the priesthood unto everlasting ages, Num. xxv. 10–13. This accounting of a work for righteousness is only apparently contradictory to Gen. xv. 5 sq.: it was indeed an act which sprang from a constancy in faith, and one which obtained for him the acceptation of a righteous man for the sake of this upon which it was based, by proving him to be such.

---

* In the second section of *Abuda zara*, on the words of the Mishna: "The flesh which is intended to be offered first of all to idols is allowed, but that which comes out of the temple is forbidden, because it is like sacrifices of the dead," it is observed, fol. 32b: "Whence, said R. Jehuda ben Bethêra, do I know that that which is offered to idols (תקרובת לעבודה זרה) pollutes like a dead body? From Ps. cvi. 28. As the dead body pollutes everything that is under the same roof with it, so also does everything that is offered to idols." The Apostle Paul declares the objectivity of this pollution to be vain, cf. more particularly 1 Cor. x. 28 sq.

In vers. 32, 33 follows the sixth of the principal sins, viz. the insurrection against Moses and Aaron at the waters of strife in the fortieth year, in connection with which Moses forfeited the entrance with them into the Land of Promise (Num. xx. 11 sq., Deut. i. 37, xxxii. 51), since he suffered himself to be carried away by the persevering obstinacy of the people against the Spirit of God (הַמְרָה mostly providing the future for מָרָה, as in vers. 7, 43, lxxviii. 17, 40, 56, of obstinacy against God; on אֶת־רוּחוֹ cf. Isa. lxiii. 10) into uttering the words addressed to the people, Num. xx. 10, in which, as the smiting of the rock which was twice repeated shows, is expressed impatience together with a tinge of unbelief. The poet distinguishes, as does the narrative in Num. ch. xx., between the obstinacy of the people and the transgression of Moses, which is there designated, according to that which lay at the root of it, as unbelief. The retrospective reference to Num. xxvii. 14 needs adjustment accordingly.

Vers. 34-43. The sins in Canaan : the failing to exterminate the idolatrous peoples and sharing in their idolatry. In ver. 34 the poet appeals to the command, frequently enjoined upon them from Ex. xxiii. 32 sq. onwards, to extirpate the inhabitants of Canaan. Since they did not execute this command (vid. Judg. ch. i.-iii. 6), that which it was intended to prevent came to pass : the heathen became to them a snare (מוֹקֵשׁ), Ex. xxiii. 33, xxxiv. 12, Deut. vii. 16. They intermarried with them, and fell into the Canaanitish custom in which the abominations of heathenism culminate, viz. the human sacrifice, which Jahve abhorreth (Deut. xii. 31), and only the demons (שֵׁדִים, Deut. xxxii. 17) delight in. Thus then the land was defiled by blood-guiltiness (חָנֵף, Num. xxv. 33, cf. Isa. xxiv. 5, xxvi. 21), and they themselves became unclean (Ezek. xx. 43) by the whoredom of idolatry. In vers. 40-43 the poet (as in Neh. ix. 26 sqq.) sketches the alternation of apostasy, captivity, redemption, and relapse which followed upon the possession of Canaan, and more especially that which characterized the period of the judges. God's "counsel" was to make Israel free and glorious, but they leaned upon themselves, following their own intentions (בַּעֲצָתָם); wherefore they perished in their sins. The poet uses כָּבַךְ (to sink down, fall away) instead of the נָמַק (to moulder, rot) of the primary passage, Lev. xxvi. 39, retained in Ezek. xxiv. 23, xxxiii. 10, which is no blunder (Hitzig), but a deliberate change.

Vers. 44–46. The poet's range of vision here widens from the time of the judges to the history of the whole of the succeeding age down to the present; for the whole history of Israel has essentially the same fundamental character, viz. that Israel's unfaithfulness does not annul God's faithfulness. That verifies itself even now. That which Solomon in 1 Kings viii. 50 prays for on behalf of his people when they may be betrayed into the hands of the enemy, has been fulfilled in the case of the dispersion of Israel in all countries (cvii. 3), Babylonia, Egypt, etc.: God has turned the hearts of their oppressors towards them. On רָאָה בְּ, to regard compassionately, cf. Gen. xxix. 32, 1 Sam. i. 11. בַּצַּר לָהֶם belong together, as in cvii. 6, and frequently. רִנָּה is a cry of lamentation, as in 1 Kings viii. 28 in Solomon's prayer at the dedication of the Temple. From this source comes ver. 6, and also from this source ver. 46, cf. 1 Kings viii. 50 together with Neh. i. 11. In וַיִּנָּחֶם the drawing back of the tone does not take place, as in Gen. xxiv. 67. חסדו beside כְּרֹב is not pointed by the *Kerî* חֲסָדָיו, as in v. 8, lxix. 14, but as in Lam. iii. 32, according to ver. 7, Isa. lxiii. 7, חֲסָדוֹ: in accordance with the fulness (riches) of His manifold mercy or loving-kindness. The expression in ver. 46 is like Gen. xliii. 14. Although the condition of the poet's fellow-countrymen in the dispersion may have been tolerable in itself, yet this involuntary scattering of the members of the nation is always a state of punishment. The poet prays in ver. 47 that God may be pleased to put an end to this.

Ver. 47. He has now reached the goal, to which his whole Psalm struggles forth, by the way of self-accusation and the praise of the faithfulness of God. הִשְׁתַּבֵּחַ (found only here) is the reflexive of the *Piel*, to account happy, Eccles. iv. 2, therefore: in order that we may esteem ourselves happy to be able to praise Thee. In this reflexive (and also passive) sense השׁתבח is customary in Aramaic and post-biblical Hebrew.

Ver. 48. The closing doxology of the Fourth Book. The chronicler has וְאָמְרוּ before ver. 47 (which with him differs only very slightly), an indispensable rivet, so to speak, in the fitting together of cvi. 1 (cvii. 1) and cvi. 47. The means this historian, who joins passages together like mosaic-work, calls to his aid are palpable enough. He has also taken over ver. 48 by transforming *and let all the people say Amen, Hallelujah!* in accordance with his style (cf. 1 Chron. xxv. 3, 2 Chron. v. 13, and frequently, Ezra iii. 11), into an historical clause: וַיֹּאמְרוּ כָל־הָעָם אָמֵן וְהַלֵּל לַיהוָה. Hitzig, by regarding the echoes of the Psalms in the chronicler as the originals of the corresponding Psalms in the Psalter, and consequently 1 Chron. xvi. 36 as the original of the *Beracha* placed after our Psalm, reverses the true relation; *vid.* with reference to this point, Riehm in the *Theolog. Literat. Blatt*, 1866, No. 30, and Köhler in the *Luther. Zeitschrift*, 1867, S. 297 ff. The priority of Ps. cvi. is clear from the fact that ver. 1 gives a liturgical key-note that was in use even in Jeremiah's time (ch. xxxiii. 11), and that ver. 47 reverts to the tephilla-style of the introit, vers. 4 sq. And the priority of ver. 48 as a concluding formula of the Fourth Book is clear from the fact that it has been fashioned, like that of the Second Book (lxxii. 18 sq.), under the influence of the foregoing Psalm. The *Hallelujah* is an echo of the Hallelujah-Psalm, just as there the *Jahve Elohim* is an echo of the Elohim-Psalm. And "let all the people say Amen" is the same closing thought as in ver. 6 of Ps. cl., which is made into the closing doxology of the whole Psalter. Ἀμὴν ἀλληλούϊα together (Apoc. xix. 4) is a laudatory confirmation.

FIFTH BOOK OF THE PSALTER.
Ps. CVII.-CL.

PSALM CVII.
AN ADMONITION TO FELLOW-COUNTRYMEN TO RENDER THANKS ON ACCOUNT OF HAVING GOT THE BETTER OF CALAMITIES.

1 "GIVE thanks unto Jahve, for He is good,
 For His loving-kindness endureth for ever,"
2 Let the redeemed of Jahve say,
 Whom He hath redeemed out of the hand of oppression
3 And gathered out of the lands,
 From the east and from the west, from the north and from the sea.

4 They wandered in the desert in a waste of a way,
 They found not a city of habitation.
5 Under hunger and thirst
 Their soul fainted in them.
6 *Then they cried unto Jahve in their trouble—*
 Out of their distresses He delivered them,
7 And led them by a right way
 To arrive at a city of habitation.—
8 *Let them praise to Jahve His loving-kindness,*
 And His wonders to the children of men,
9 That He hath satisfied the thirsty soul,
 And filled the hungry soul with good.

10 Those who dwelt in darkness and the shadow of death,
 Being bound in torture and iron,
11 Because they rebelled against the words of God
 And derided the counsel of the Most High,

12 And He humbled their heart by labour,
   They fell down, and there was none to help.
13 *Then they cried unto Jahve in their trouble—*
   Out of their distresses He saved them;
14 He led them forth out of darkness and the shadow of death,
   And burst their bonds asunder.
15 *Let them praise to Jahve His goodness,*
   And His wonders to the children of men,
16 That He hath broken in pieces the brazen doors
   And smitten down the iron bars.

17 The foolish, on account of the way of their transgression,
   And on account of their iniquity, had to suffer.
18 All food their soul abhorred,
   And they drew near to the gates of death.
19 *Then they cried unto Jahve in their trouble—*
   Out of their distresses He saved them.
20 He sent His word and healed them,
   And caused them to escape out of their pit-falls.
21 *Let them praise to Jahve His goodness,*
   And His wonders to the children of men,
22 And let them sacrifice sacrifices of thanksgiving
   And declare His works with a shout of joy.

23 Those who go down to the sea in ships,
   Who do business in great waters—
24 These have seen the works of Jahve,
   And His wonders in the deep.
25 He spake and raised a stormy wind,
   Which forced up its waves on high.
26 They went up towards heaven, they went down into the
   Their soul was melted in trouble.   [depths,
27 They whirled and staggered like a drunken man,
   And all their wisdom came of itself to nought.
28 *Then they cried unto Jahve in their trouble,*
   And out of their distresses He brought them forth.
29 He changed the storm into a gentle breeze,
   And their waves were still.
30 Then were they glad that they were abated,
   And He led them to the haven of their desire.

VOL. III.   11

31 *Let them praise to Jahve His goodness,*
   And His wonders to the children of men,
32 And let them exalt Him in the congregation of the people,
   And praise Him in the council of the elders.

33 He changed rivers into a desert
   And water-springs into drought,
34 A fruitful land into a salt-plain,
   Because of the wickedness of those who dwelt therein.
35 He changed the desert into a pool of water,
   And the dry land into water-springs;
36 And made the hungry to dwell there,
   And they built a city of habitation.
37 They sowed fields and planted vineyards,
   And obtained profitable fruit.
38 He blessed them and they multiplied greatly,
   And their cattle He made into not a few.

39 Then they became few and were reduced
   By the pressure of misfortune and sorrow—
40 He who poureth contempt on princes
   And causeth them to wander in the pathless waste:
41 He removed the needy out of the way of affliction,
   And made the families like a flock.
42 The upright see it and rejoice,
   And all knavery stoppeth its mouth.
   * * *
43 Whoso is wise let him observe these things,
   And let them consider the loving-kindnesses of Jahve!

With this Psalm begins the Fifth Book, the Book אלה הדברים of the Psalter. With Ps. cvi. closed the Fourth Book, or the Book במדבר, the first Psalm of which, Ps. xc., bewailed the manifestation of God's wrath in the case of the generation of the desert, and in the presence of the prevailing death took refuge in God the eternal and unchangeable One. Ps. cvi., which closes the book, has בַּמִּדְבָּר (vers. 14, 26) as its favourite word, and makes confession of the sins of Israel on the way to Canaan. Now, just as at the beginning of the Book of Deuteronomy Israel stands on the threshold of the Land of

Promise, after the two tribes and a half have already established themselves on the other side of the Jordan, so at the beginning of this Fifth Book of the Psalter we see Israel restored to the soil of its fatherland. There it is the Israel redeemed out of Egypt, here it is the Israel redeemed out of the lands of the Exile. There the lawgiver once more admonishes Israel to yield the obedience of love to the Law of Jahve, here the psalmist calls upon Israel to show gratitude towards Him, who has redeemed it from exile and distress and death.

We must not therefore be surprised if Ps. cvi. and cvii. are closely connected, in spite of the fact that the boundary of the two Books lies between them. " Ps. cvii. stands in close relationship to Ps. cvi. The similarity of the beginning at once points back to this Psalm. Thanks are here given in ver. 3 for what was there desired in ver. 47. The praise of the Lord which was promised in Ps. cvi. 47 in the case of redemption being vouchsafed, is here presented to Him after redemption vouchsafed." This observation of Hengstenberg is fully confirmed. The Psalms civ.–cvii. really to a certain extent form a tetralogy. Ps. civ. derives its material from the history of the creation, Ps. cv. from the preparatory and early history of Israel, Ps. cvi. from the history of Israel in Egypt, in the desert, and in the Land of Promise down to the Exile, and Ps. cvii. from the time of the restoration.

Nevertheless the connection of Ps. civ. with cv.–cvii. is by far not so close as that of these three Psalms among themselves. These three anonymous Psalms form a trilogy in the strictest sense; they are a tripartite whole from the hand of one author. The observation is an old one. The *Harpffe Davids mit Teutschen Saiten bespannet* (Harp of David strung with German Strings), a translation of the Psalms which appeared in Augsburg in the year 1659, begins Ps. cvi. with the words: " For the third time already am I now come, and I make bold to spread abroad, with grateful acknowledgment, Thy great kindnesses." God's wondrous deeds of loving-kindness and compassion towards Israel from the time of their forefathers down to the redemption out of Egypt according to the promise, and giving them possession of Canaan, are the theme of Ps. cv. The theme of Ps. cvi. is the sinful conduct of Israel from Egypt onwards during the journey through the desert, and then in the

Land of Promise, by which they brought about the fulfilment of the threat of exile (ver. 27); but even there God's mercy was not suffered to go unattested (ver. 46). The theme of Ps. cvii., finally, is the sacrifice of praise that is due to Him who redeemed them out of exile and all kinds of destruction. We may compare cv. 44, *He gave them the lands* (אַרְצוֹת) *of the heathen;* cvi. 27, (*He threatened*) *to cast forth their seed among the heathen and to scatter them in the lands* (בָּאֲרָצוֹת); and cvii. 3, *out of the lands* (מֵאֲרָצוֹת) *hath He brought them together, out of east and west, out of north and south.* The designed similarity of the expression, the internal connection, and the progression in accordance with a definite plan, are not to be mistaken here. In other respects, too, these three Psalms are intimately interwoven. In them Egypt is called "the land of Ham" (cv. 23, 27, cvi. 22), and Israel "the chosen ones of Jahve" (cv. 6, 43, cvi. 5, cf. 23). They are fond of the interrogative form of exclamation (cvi. 2, cvii. 43). There is an approach in them to the hypostatic conception of the Word (דָּבָר, cv. 19. cvi. 20). Compare also יְשִׂימוֹן cvi. 14, cvii. 4; and the *Hithpa.* הִתְהַלֵּל cv. 3, cvi. 5, הִשְׁתַּבֵּחַ cvi. 47, הִתְבַּלֵּעַ cvii. 27. In all three the poet shows himself to be especially familiar with Isa. ch. xl.–lxvi., and also with the Book of Job. Ps. cvii. is the fullest in reminiscences taken from both these Books, and in this Psalm the movement of the poet is more free without recapitulating history that has been committed to writing. Everything therefore favours the assertion that Ps. cv., cvi., and cvii. are a "trefoil" (*trifolium*),—two Hodu-Psalms, and a Hallelujah-Psalm in the middle.

Ps. cvii. consists of six groups with an introit, vers. 1–3, and an epiphonem, ver. 43. The poet unrolls before the dispersion of Israel that has again attained to the possession of its native land the pictures of divine deliverances in which human history, and more especially the history of the exiles, is so rich. The epiphonem at the same time stamps the hymn as a consolatory Psalm; for those who were gathered again out of the lands of the heathen nevertheless still looked for the final redemption under the now milder, now more despotic sceptre of the secular power.

Vers. 1–3. The introit, with the call upon them to grateful

praise, is addressed to the returned exiles. The Psalm carries the marks of its deutero-Isaianic character on the very front of it, viz.: "the redeemed of Jahve," taken from Isa. lxii. 12, cf. lxiii. 4, xxxv. 9 sq.; קִבֵּץ as in Isa. lvi. 8, and frequently; "from the north and from the sea," as in Isa. xlix. 12: "the sea" (יָם) here (as perhaps there also), side by side with east, west, and north, is the south, or rather (since יָם is an established *usus loquendi* for the west) the south-west, viz. the southern portion of the Mediterranean washing the shores of Egypt. With this the poet associates the thought of the exiles of Egypt, as with וּמִיָּם the exiles of the islands, *i.e.* of Asia Minor and Europe; he is therefore writing at a period in which the Jewish state newly founded by the release of the Babylonian exiles had induced the scattered fellow-countrymen in all countries to return home. Calling upon the redeemed ones to give thanks to God the Redeemer in order that the work of the restoration of Israel may be gloriously perfected amidst the thanksgiving of the redeemed ones, he forthwith formulates the thanksgiving by putting the language of thanksgiving of the ancient liturgy (Jer. xxxiii. 11) into their mouth. The nation, now again established upon the soil of the fatherland, has, until it had acquired this again, seen destruction in every form in a strange land, and can tell of the most manifold divine deliverances. The call to sacrifice the sacrifices of thanksgiving is expanded accordingly into several pictures portraying the dangers of the strange land, which are not so much allegorical, personifying the Exile, as rather exemplificative.

Vers. 4-9. It has actually come to pass, the first strophe tells us, that they wandered in a strange land through deserts and wastes, and seemed likely to have to succumb to death from hunger. According to ver. 40 and Isa. xliii. 19, it appears that ver. 4*a* ought to be read לֹא־דָרֶךְ (Olshausen, Baur, and Thenius); but the line is thereby lengthened inelegantly. The two words, joined by *Munach*, stand in the construct state, like פֶּרֶא אָדָם, Gen. xvi. 12: a waste of a way = ἔρημος ὁδός, Acts viii. 26 (Ewald, Hitzig), which is better suited to the poetical style than that דֶּרֶךְ, as in מִשְׁעֶנָה־כָּסֶף, and the like, should be an accusative of nearer definition (Hengstenberg). In connection with עִיר מוֹשָׁב the poet, who is fond of this combination (vers. 7, 36, cf. בֵּית־מוֹשָׁב, Lev. xxv. 29), means any city whatever which might afford the homeless ones a habitable, hospitable reception. With the perfects, which describe what has been experienced, alternates in ver. 5b the imperfect, which shifts to the way in which anything comes about: their soul in them enveloped itself (vid. lxi. 3), i.e. was nigh upon extinction. With the *fut. consec.* then follows in ver. 6 the fact which gave the turn to the change in their misfortune. Their cry for help, as the imperfect וַיִּצְעֲקוּ implies, was accompanied by their deliverance, the fact of which is expressed by the following *fut. consec.* וַיַּצִּילֵם. Those who have experienced such things are to confess to the Lord, with thanksgiving, His loving-kindness and His wonderful works to the children of men. It is not to be rendered: His wonders (supply אֲשֶׁר עָשָׂה) *towards* the children of men (Luther, Olshausen, and others). The two לְ coincide: their thankful confession of the divine loving-kindness and wondrous acts is not to be addressed alone to Jahve Himself, but also to men, in order that out of what they have experienced a wholesome fruit may spring forth for the multitude. נֶפֶשׁ שֹׁקֵקָה (*part. Polel*, the ē of which is retained as a pre-tonic vowel in pause, cf. lxviii. 26 and on Job xx. 27, Ew. § 188, *b*) is, as in Isa. xxix. 9, the thirsting soul (from שָׁקַק, ساق, to urge forward, of the impulse and drawing of the emotions, in Hebrew to desire ardently). The preterites are here an expression of that which has been experienced, and therefore of that which has become a fact of experience. In superabundant measure does God uphold the languishing soul that is in imminent danger of languishing away.

Vers. 10–16. Others suffered imprisonment and bonds; but through Him who had decreed this as punishment for them, they also again reached the light of freedom. Just as in the first strophe, here too, as far as וְיוֹדוּ in ver. 15, is all a compound subject; and in view of this the poet begins with participles. "Darkness and the shadow of death" (*vid.* xxiii. 4) is an Isaianic expression, Isa. ix. 1 (where יֹשְׁבֵי is construed with בְּ), xlii. 7 (where יֹשְׁבֵי is construed as here, cf. Gen. iv. 20, Zech. ii. 11), just as "bound in torture and iron" takes its rise from Job xxxvi. 8. The old expositors call it a hendiadys for "torturing iron" (after cv. 18); but it is more correct to take the one as the general term and the other as the particular:

bound in all sorts of affliction from which they could not break away, and more particularly in iron bonds (בַרְזֶל, like the Arabic *firzil*, an iron fetter, vid. on cv. 18). In ver. 11, which calls to mind Isa. v. 19, and with respect to ver. 12, Isa. iii. 8, the double play upon the sound of the words is unmistakeable. By עֵצָה is meant the plan in accordance with which God governs, more particularly His final purpose, which lies at the basis of His leadings of Israel. Not only had they nullified this purpose of mercy by defiant resistance (הִמְרָה) against God's commandments (אִמְרֵי, Arabic *awâmir*, *âmireh*) on their part, but they had even blasphemed it; נִאֵץ, Deut. xxxii. 19, and frequently, or נִאֵץ (prop. to pierce, then to treat roughly), is an old Mosaic designation of blasphemy, Deut. xxxi. 20, Num. xiv. 11, 23, xvi. 30. Therefore God thoroughly humbled them by afflictive labour, and caused them to stumble (כָּשַׁל). But when they were driven to it, and prayed importunately to Him, He helped them out of their straits. The refrain varies according to recognised custom. Twice the expression is וַיִּזְעֲקוּ, twice וַיִּצְעֲקוּ; once יַצִּילֵם, then twice יוֹשִׁיעֵם, and last of all יֹצִיאֵם, which follows here in ver. 14 as an alliteration. The summary condensation of the deliverance experienced (ver. 16) is moulded after Isa. xlv. 2. The Exile, too, may be regarded as such like a large jail (vid. e.g. Isa. xlii. 7, 22); but the descriptions of the poet are not pictures, but examples.

Vers. 17–22. Others were brought to the brink of the grave by severe sickness; but when they draw nigh in earnest prayer to Him who appointed that they should suffer thus on account of their sins, He became their Saviour. אֱוִיל (cf. e.g. Job v. 3), like נָבָל (vid. xiv. 1), is also an ethical notion, and not confined to the idea of defective intellect merely. It is one who insanely lives only for the passing hour, and ruins health, calling, family, and in short himself and everything belonging to him. Those who were thus minded, the poet begins by saying, were obliged to suffer by reason of (in consequence of) their wicked course of life. The cause of their days of pain and sorrow is placed first by way of emphasis; and because it has a meaning that is related to the past יִתְעַנּוּ thereby comes all the more easily to express that which took place simultaneously in the past. The *Hithpa.* in 1 Kings ii. 26 signifies to suffer willingly or intentionally; here: to be obliged to submit to suffering against one's will. Hengstenberg, for example, construes it differently: "Fools because of their walk in transgression (more than 'because of their transgression'), and those who because of their iniquities were afflicted—all food," etc. But מִ beside יִתְעַנּוּ has the assumption in its favour of being an affirmation of the cause of the affliction. In ver. 18 the poet has the Book of Job (ch. xxxiii. 20, 22) before his eye. And in connection with ver. 20, ἀπέστειλεν τὸν λόγον αὐτοῦ καὶ ἰάσατο αὐτούς (LXX.), no passage of the Old Testament is more vividly recalled to one's mind than cv. 19, even more than cxlvii. 18; because here, as in cv. 19, it treats of the intervention of divine acts within the sphere of human history, and not of the intervention of divine operations within the sphere of the natural world. In the natural world and in history the word (דָּבָר) is God's messenger (cv. 19, cf. Isa. lv. 10 sq.), and appears here as a mediator of the divine healing. Here, as in Job xxxiii. 23 sq., the fundamental fact of the New Testament is announced, which Theodoret on this passage expresses in the words: Ὁ Θεὸς Λόγος ἐνανθρωπήσας καὶ ἀποσταλεὶς ὡς ἄνθρωπος τὰ παντοδαπὰ τῶν ψυχῶν ἰάσατο τραύματα καὶ τοὺς διαφθαρέντας ἀνέρρωσε λογισμούς. The LXX. goes on to render it: καὶ ἐρρύσατο αὐτοὺς ἐκ τῶν διαφθορῶν αὐτῶν, inasmuch as the translators derive שְׁחִיתוֹתָם from שְׁחִיתָה (Dan. vi. 5), and this, as שָׁחַת elsewhere (vid. xvi. 10), from שָׁחַת, διαφθείρειν, which is approved by Hitzig. But Lam. iv. 20 is against this. From שָׁחָה is formed a noun שְׁחוּת (שִׁחַת) in the signification a hollow place (Prov. xxviii. 10), the collateral form of which, שָׁחִית (שְׁחִית), is inflected like חֲנִית, plur. חֲנִיתוֹת with a retention of the substantival termination. The "pits" are the deep afflictions into which they were plunged, and out of which God caused them to escape. The suffix of וירפאם avails also for יַמְלִט, as in Gen. xxvii. 5, xxx. 31, Ps. cxxxix. 1, Isa. xlvi. 5.

Vers. 23-32. Others have returned to tell of the perils of the sea. Without any allegory (Hengstenberg) it speaks of those who by reason of their calling traverse (which is expressed by יָרַד because the surface of the sea lies below the dry land which slopes off towards the coast) the sea in ships (read bo͝onijoth without the article), and that not as fishermen, but (as Luther has correctly understood the choice of the word) in commercial enterprises. These have seen the works and wonders of God in the eddying deep, i.e. they have seen with their own eyes what God can do when in His anger He calls up the powers of nature, and on the other hand when He compassionately orders them back into their bounds. God's mandate (וַיֹּאמֶר as in cv. 31, 34) brought it to pass that a stormy wind arose (cf. עָמַד, xxxiii. 9), and it drove its (the sea's) waves on high, so that the seafarers at one time were tossed up to the sky and then hurled down again into deep abysses, and their soul melted בְּרָעָה, in an evil, anxious mood, i.e. lost all its firmness. They turned about in a circle (יָחוֹגּוּ from חָגַג = חוּג) and reeled after the manner of a drunken man; all their wisdom swallowed itself up, i.e. consumed itself within itself, came of itself to nought, just as Ovid, *Trist.* i. 2, says in connection with a similar description of a storm at sea: *ambiguis ars stupet ipsa malis*. The poet here writes under the influence of Isa. xix. 3, cf. 14. But at their importunate supplication God led them forth out of their distresses (xxv. 17). He turned the raging storm into a gentle blowing (= יָקֵם סְעָרָה לִדְמָמָה, 1 Kings xix. 12). הֵקִים construed with לְ here has the sense of transporting (carrying over) into another condition or state, as Apollinaris renders: αὐτίκα δ' εἰς αὔρην προτέρην μετέθηκε θύελλαν. The suffix of גַּלֵּיהֶם cannot refer to the מַיִם רַבִּים in ver. 23, which is so far removed; "their waves" are those with which they had to battle. These to their joy became calm (חָשָׁה) and were still (שָׁתַק as in Jonah i. 11), and God guided them εἰς λιμένα θελήματος αὐτῶν (LXX.). מָחוֹז, a hapax-legomenon, from حاز (حوز), to shut in on all sides and to draw to one's self (root حز, *gyravit, in gyrum egit*), signifies a place enclosed round, therefore a haven, and first of all perhaps a creek, to use a northern word, a fiord. The verb שָׁתַק in relation to חָשָׁה is the stronger word, like יָבֵשׁ in relation to חָרַב in the history of the Flood. Those who have been thus marvellously rescued are then called upon thankfully to praise God their Deliverer in the place where the national church assembles, and where the chiefs of the nation sit in council; therefore, as it seems, in the Temple and in the Forum.*

---

* In exact editions like Norzi, Heidenheim, and Baer's, before vers. 23,

Now follow two more groups without the two beautiful and impressive refrains with which the four preceding groups are interspersed. The structure is less artistic, and the transitions here and there abrupt and awkward. One might say that these two groups are inferior to the rest, much as the speeches of Elihu are inferior to the rest of the Book of Job. That they are, however, nevertheless from the hand of the very same poet is at once seen from the continued dependence upon the Book of Job and Isaiah. Hengstenberg sees in vers. 33-42 "the song with which they exalt the Lord in the assembly of the people and upon the seat of the elders." But the *materia laudis* is altogether different from that which is to be expected according to the preceding calls to praise. Nor is it any the more clear to us that vers. 33 sq. refer to the overthrow of Babylon, and vers. 35 sqq. to the happy turn of affairs that took place simultaneously for Israel; ver. 35 does not suit Canaan, and the expressions in vers. 36 sq. would be understood in too low a sense. No, the poet goes on further to illustrate the helpful government of God the just and gracious One, inasmuch as he has experiences in his mind in connection therewith, of which the dispersion of Israel in all places can sing and speak.

Vers. 33-38. Since in ver. 36 the historical narration is still continued, a meaning relating to the cotemporaneous past is also retrospectively given to the two correlative שָׂם. It now goes on to tell what those who have now returned have observed and experienced in their own case. Ver. 33a sounds like Isa. l. 2b; ver. 33b like Isa. xxxv. 7a; and ver. 35 takes its rise from Isa. xli. 18b. The juxtaposition of מוֹצָאֵי and צִמָּאוֹן, since Deut. viii. 15, belongs to the favourite antithetical alliterations, *e.g.* Isa. lxi. 3. מְלֵחָה, that which is salty (LXX. cf. Sir. xxxix. 23 : ἅλμη), is, as in Job xxxix. 6, the name for the uncultivated, barren steppe. A land that has been laid waste for the punishment of its inhabitants has very often been changed into flourishing fruitful fields under the hands of a poor and grateful generation; and very often a land that has hitherto lain uncultivated and to all appearance absolutely unprofitable has

---

24, 25, 26, 27, 28, and 40 there stand reversed *Nuns* (נונין הפוכין, in the language of the Masora נונין מנוזרות), as before Num. x. 35 and between x. 36 and xi. 1 (nine in all). Their signification is unknown.

developed an unexpected fertility. The exiles to whom Jeremiah writes, ch. xxix. 5 : *Build ye houses and settle down, and plant gardens and eat their fruit*, may frequently have experienced this divine blessing. Their industry and their knowledge also did their part, but looked at in a right light, it was not their own work but God's work that their settlement prospered, and that they continually spread themselves wider and possessed a not small, *i.e.* (cf. 2 Kings iv. 3) a very large, stock of cattle.

Vers. 39–43. But it also came to pass that it went ill with them, inasmuch as their flourishing prosperous condition drew down upon them the envy of the powerful and tyrannical; nevertheless God put an end to tyranny, and always brought His people again to honour and strength. Hitzig is of opinion that ver. 39 goes back into the time when things were different with those who, according to vers. 36–38, had thriven. The *modus consecutivus* is sometimes used thus retrospectively (*vid.* Isa. xxxvii. 5); here, however, the symmetry of the continuation from vers. 36-38, and the change which is expressed in ver. 39a in comparison with ver. 38b, require an actual consecution in that which is narrated. They became few and came down, were reduced (וַיָּשֹׁחוּ, cf. Prov. xiv. 19 : to come to ruin, or to be overthrown), *a coarctatione malitiæ et mœroris*. עֹצֶר is the restraint of despotic rule, רָעָה the evil they had to suffer under such restraint, and יָגוֹן sorrow, which consumed their life. מֵעֹצֶר has *Tarcha* and רָעָה *Munach* (instead of *Mercha* and *Mugrash, vid. Accentuationssystem,* xviii. 2). There is no reason for departing from this interpunction and rendering: " through tyranny, evil, and sorrow." What is stiff and awkward in the progress of the description arises from the fact that ver. 40 is borrowed from Job xii. 21, 24, and that the poet is not willing to make any change in these sublime words. The version shows how we think the relation of the clauses is to be apprehended. Whilst He pours out His wrath upon tyrants in the contempt of men that comes upon them, and makes them fugitives who lose themselves in the terrible waste, He raises the needy and those hitherto despised and ill-treated on high out of the depth of their affliction, and makes families like a flock, *i.e.* makes their families so increase, that they come to have the appearance of a merrily gamboling and numerous flock. Just as this figure points back to Job xxi. 11, so ver. 42 is made up out of Job xxii. 19, v. 16. The sight of this act of recognition on the part of God of those who have been wrongfully oppressed gives joy to the upright, and all roguery (עֹלָה, vid. xcii. 16) has its mouth closed, i.e. its boastful insolence is once for all put to silence. In ver. 43 the poet makes the strains of his Psalm die away after the example of Hosea, ch. xiv. 10 [9], in the nota bene expressed after the manner of a question: Who is wise—he will or let him keep this, i.e. bear it well in mind. The transition to the jussive together with a change of number is rendered natural by the fact that מִי חָכָם, as in Hos. loc. cit. (cf. Jer. ix. 11, Esth. v. 6, and without *Waw apod.* Judg. vii. 3, Prov. ix. 4, 16), is equivalent to *quisquis sapiens est.* חַסְדֵי ה׳ (חֲסָדַי) are the manifestations of mercy or loving-kindness in which God's ever-enduring mercy unfolds itself in history. He who is wise has a good memory for and a clear understanding of this.

PSALM CVIII.

TWO ELOHIMIC FRAGMENTS BROUGHT TOGETHER.

2 CONFIDENT is my heart, Elohim,
I will sing and play upon the harp,
Yea, this shall my glory do.
3 Awake up, O harp and cithern,
I will awake the morning dawn!

4 I will praise Thee among the peoples, Jahve,
And praise Thee upon the harp among the nations.
5 For great beyond the heavens is Thy mercy, Elohim,
And unto the clouds Thy truth.
6 Oh show Thyself exalted above the heavens, Elohim,
And above the whole earth Thy glory!

7 In order that Thy beloved may be delivered—
Save now with Thy right hand and answer me!

8 Elohim hath promised in His holiness:

I shall rejoice, I shall portion out Shechem,
And measure out the valley of Succoth.
9 Mine is Gilead, mine Manasseh,
And Ephraim is the helm of my head,
Judah is my sceptre,
10 Moab is my wash-pot,
Upon Edom I cast my shoe,
Over Philistia I shout for joy.

11 Who will conduct me to the fortified city,
Who will bring me to Edom?!
12 Hast not Thou, Elohim, cast us off,
And goest not forth, Elohim, with our armies?—
13 Grant us deliverance from the oppressor,
Yea, vain is the help of man.
14 In Elohim shall we obtain the victory,
And HE will tread down our oppressors.

The אָזוּר in ver. 4 and the whole contents of this Psalm is the echo to the יהוה of the preceding Psalm. It is inscribed a *Psalm-song by David*, but only because it is compiled out of ancient Davidic materials. The fact of the absence of the למנצח makes it natural to suppose that it is of later origin. Two Davidic Psalm-pieces in the Elohimic style are here, with trifling variations, just put together, not soldered together, and taken out of their original historical connection. That a poet like David would thus compile a third out of two of his own songs (Hengstenberg) is not conceivable.

Vers. 2-6. This first half is taken from Ps. lvii. 8-12. The repetition of *confident is my heart* in Ps. lvii. is here omitted; and in place of it the " my glory" of the exclamation, *awake my glory*, is taken up to "I will sing and will harp" as a more minute definition of the subject (*vid.* on iii. 5): He will do it, yea, his soul with all its godlike powers shall do it. *Jahve* in ver. 4 is transformed out of the *Adonaj*; and *Waw copul.* is inserted both before ver. 4*b* and ver. 6*b*, contrary to Ps. lvii. מֵעַל, ver. 5*a* (as in Esth. iii. 1), would be a pleasing change for עַד if ver. 5*a* followed 5*b* and the definition of magnitude did not retrograde instead of heightening. Moreover xxxvi. 6, Jer. li. 9 (cf. עַל in cxiii. 4, cxlviii. 13) favour עִי in opposition to מַעַל.

Vers. 7–14. Ps. lx. 7–14 forms this second half. The clause expressing the purpose with לְמַעַן, as in its original, has the following הוֹשִׁיעָה for its principal clause upon which it depends. Instead of וַעֲנֵנוּ, which one might have expected, the expression used here is וַעֲנֵנִי without any interchange of the mode of writing and of reading it; many printed copies have וַעֲנֵנוּ here also; Baer, following Norzi, correctly has וַעֲנֵנִי. Instead of לִי . . . וְלִי, lx. 9, we here read לִי . . . לִי, which is less soaring. And instead of *Cry aloud concerning me, O Philistia* (the plaintive cry of the vanquished), it here is, *Over Philistia do I shout for joy* (the triumphant cry of the victor); in accordance with which Hupfeld wishes to take הִתְרוֹעָעִי in the former as infinitive: "over (עֲלֵי instead of עָלַי) Philistia is my shouting for joy" (הִתְרוֹעֲעִי instead of הִתְרוֹעָעִי), since the infinitive does not admit of this pausal form of the imperative). For עִיר מָצוֹר we have here the more usual form of expression עִיר מִבְצָר. Ver. 12a is weakened by the omission of the אַתָּה (הֲלֹא).

PSALM CIX.

IMPRECATION UPON THE CURSER WHO PREFERS THE CURSE TO THE BLESSING.

1 GOD of my praise, be not silent!
2 For a wicked mouth and a deceitful mouth have they
      opened against me,
   They have spoken against me with a lying tongue,
3 And with animosities have they surrounded me
   And fought against me without cause.
4 For my love they make themselves hostile to me,
   Whilst I am all prayer;
5 And have requited me with evil for good,
   And with hatred for my love.

6 Set Thou a wicked man over him,
   And let Satan stand at his right hand:

7 If he is judged, let him come off as a wicked man,
 And let his prayer become sin.
8 Let his days be few,
 His office let another take.
9 Let his children become orphans,
 And his wife a widow,
10 And let his children wander to and fro begging,
 And let them entreat far from their ruins.

11 Let the creditor surround with snares all that he hath,
 And let strangers spoil what his labour hath gained.
12 Let there be no one to continue kindness to him,
 And let no one bestow [anything] upon his orphans.
13 Let his posterity be rooted out,
 In the next generation let their name be blotted out.
14 Let the guilt of his fathers be remembered with Jahve,
 And let the sin of his mother not be blotted out,
15 Let them be always before Jahve,
 And may He cut off their memory from the earth.

16 Because he hath not remembered to show kindness,
 And hath persecuted a man wretched and poor,
 And terrified of heart, to put him to death.
17 He hath loved the curse, and it hath come upon him;
 And he delighted not in blessing, and it remained far from him.
18 He clothed himself in cursing as his garment,
 And it pressed like water into his bowels,
 And like oil into his bones.
19 So let it become unto him as a coat in which he covereth himself,
 And as a girdle which he continually putteth on.
20 This is the reward of mine adversaries from Jahve,
 And of those who speak evil concerning my soul.

21 But do Thou, Jahve Lord, act for me for Thy Name's sake;
 Because Thy loving-kindness is good, deliver Thou me!
22 For I am wretched and poor,
 And my heart is pierced within me.

23 As a shadow, when it lengtheneth, am I gone,
   I am scared away as a locust.
24 My knees knock together through fasting,
   And my flesh is fallen away from fatness.
25 And I am become a reproach to them,
   They see me, they shake their head.

26 Succour me, Jahve my God,
   Help me according to Thy loving-kindness,
27 That they may know that this is Thy hand,
   Thou, Jahve, hast done it.
28 *They* curse, but THOU blessest;
   They arise and are ashamed, and Thy servant is glad.
29 Mine adversaries shall clothe themselves with reproach,
   And envelope themselves as with a mantle with their own shame.
30 I will give thanks greatly unto Jahve with my mouth,
   And in the midst of many will I praise Him,
31 That He placeth Himself at the right hand of the poor,
   To help him against the judges of his soul.

The אוֹדֶה, corresponding like an echo to the הוֹדוּ of Ps. cvii., is also found here in ver. 30. But Ps. cix. is most closely related to Ps. lxix. Anger concerning the ungodly who requite love with ingratitude, who persecute innocence and desire the curse instead of the blessing, has here reached its utmost bound. The imprecations are not, however, directed against a multitude as in Ps. lxix., but their whole current is turned against one person. Is this Doeg the Edomite, or Cush the Benjamite? We do not know. The marks of Jeremiah's hand, which raised a doubt about the לְדָוִד of Ps. lxix., are wanting here; and if the development of the thoughts appears too diffuse and overloaded to be suited to David, and also many expressions (as the inflected מְעַט in ver. 8, the נְבָאָה, which is explained by the Syriac, in ver. 16, and the half-passive הָלַל in ver. 22) look as though they belong to the later period of the language, yet we feel on the other hand the absence of any certain echoes of older models. For in the parallels ver. 6, cf. Zech. iii. 1, and vers. 18, 29*b*, cf. Isa. lix. 17, it is surely not the mutual relationship but the priority that is doubtful; ver. 22, however, in relation to lv. 5 (cf. ver. 4 with lv. 5) is a variation such as is also allowable in one and the same poet (*e.g.* in the refrains). The anathemas that are here poured forth more extensively than anywhere else speak in favour of David, or at least of his situation. They are explained by the depth of David's consciousness that he is the anointed of Jahve, and by his contemplation of himself in Christ. The persecution of David was a sin not only against David himself, but also against the Christ in him; and because Christ is in David, the outbursts of the Old Testament wrathful spirit take the prophetic form, so that this Psalm also, like Ps. xxii. and lxix., is a typically prophetic Psalm, inasmuch as the utterance of the type concerning himself is carried by the Spirit of prophecy beyond himself, and thus the ἀρὰ is raised to the προφητεία ἐν εἴδει ἀρᾶς (Chrysostom). These imprecations are not, however, appropriate in the mouth of the suffering Saviour. It is not the spirit of Zion but of Sinai which here speaks out of the mouth of David; the spirit of Elias, which, according to Luke ix. 55, is not the spirit of the New Testament. This wrathful spirit is overpowered in the New Testament by the spirit of love. But these anathemas are still not on this account so many beatings of the air. There is in them a divine energy, as in the blessing and cursing of every man who is united to God, and more especially of a man whose temper of mind is such as David's. They possess the same power as the prophetical threatenings, and in this sense they are regarded in the New Testament as fulfilled in the son of perdition (John xvii. 12). To the generation of the time of Jesus they were a deterrent warning not to offend against the Holy One of God, and this *Psalmus Ischarioticus* (Acts i. 20) will ever be such a mirror of warning to the enemies and persecutors of Christ and His Church.

Vers. 1–5. A sigh for help and complaints of ungrateful persecutors form the beginning of the Psalm. "God of my praise" is equivalent to God, who art my praise, Jer. xvii. 14, cf. Deut. x. 21. The God whom the Psalmist has hitherto had reason to praise will also now show Himself to him as worthy to be praised. Upon this faith he bases the prayer: be not silent (xxviii. 1, xxxv. 22)! A mouth such as belongs to the "wicked," a mouth out of which comes "deceit," have they opened against him; they have spoken with him a tongue (accusative, vid. on lxiv. 6), i.e. a language, of falsehood. דִּבְרֵי of things and utterances as in xxxv. 20. It would be capricious to take the suffix of אַהֲבָתִי in ver. 4 as *genit. object.* (love which they owe me), and in ver. 5 as *genit. subject.;* from xxxviii. 21 it may be seen that the love which he has shown to them is also meant in ver. 4. The assertion that he is "prayer" is intended to say that he, repudiating all revenge of himself, takes refuge in God in prayer and commits his cause into His hands. They have loaded him with evil for good, and hatred for the love he has shown to them. Twice he lays emphasis on the fact that it is love which they have requited to him with its opposite. Perfects alternate with aorists: it is no enmity of yesterday; the imprecations that follow presuppose an inflexible obduracy on the side of the enemies.

Vers. 6–10. The writer now turns to one among the many, and in the angry zealous fervour of despised love calls down God's judgment upon him. To call down a higher power, more particularly for punishment, upon any one is expressed by פָּקַד (הִפְקִיד) עַל, Jer. xv. 3, Lev. xxvi. 16. The tormentor of innocence shall find a superior executor who will bring him before the tribunal (which is expressed in Latin by *legis actio per manus injectionem*). The judgment scene in vers. 6b, 7a shows that this is what is intended in ver. 6a: At the right hand is the place of the accuser, who in this instance will not rest before the *damnatus es* has been pronounced. He is called שָׂטָן, which is not to be understood here after 1 Sam. xxix. 4, 2 Sam. xix. 23 [22], but after Zech. iii. 1, 1 Chron. xxi. 1, if not directly of Satan, still of a superhuman (cf. Num. xxii. 22) being which opposes him, by appearing before God as his κατήγωρ; for according to ver. 7a the שָׂטָן is to be thought of as accuser, and according to 7b God as Judge. רָשָׁע has the sense of *reus*, and יָצָא refers to the publication of the sentence. Ver. 7b wishes that his prayer, viz. that by which he would wish to avert the divine sentence of condemnation, may become לַחֲטָאָה, not: a missing of the mark, *i.e.* ineffectual (Thenius), but, according to the usual signification of the word: a sin, viz. because it proceeds from despair, not from true penitence. In ver. 8 the incorrigible one is wished an untimely death (מְעַטִּים as in one other instance only, Eccles. v. 1) and the loss of his office. The LXX. renders: τὴν ἐπισκοπὴν αὐτοῦ λάβοι ἕτερος. פְּקֻדָּה really signifies the office of overseer, oversight, office, and the one individual must have held a prominent position among the enemies of the psalmist. Having died off from this position before his time, he shall leave behind him a family deeply reduced in circumstances, whose former dwelling-place—he was therefore wealthy—becomes "ruins." His children wander up and down far from these ruins (מֵם as *e.g.* in Judg. v. 11, Job xxviii. 4) and beg (וְדָרְשׁוּ, like προσαιτεῖν, ἐπαιτεῖν, Sir. xl. 28 = לֶחֶם בִּקֵּשׁ, xxxvii. 25). Instead of וִירוֹשׁוּ the reading וְדֹרְשׁוּ is also found. A *Poel* is now and then formed from the strong verbs also,* in the inflexion of which the *Cholem* is sometimes shortened to *Kametz chatuph*; *vid.* the forms of לְשֵׁן, to slander, in ci. 5, תֹּאַר, to sketch, mark out in outline, Isa. xliv. 13, cf. also Job xx. 26 (תֹּאכְלֵהוּ) and Isa. lxii. 9 (according to the reading מְאָסְפָיו). To read the *Kametz* in these instances as *â*, and to regard these forms as resolved *Piels*, is, in connection with the absence of the *Metheg*, contrary to the meaning of the pointing; on purpose to guard against this way of reading it, correct codices have וְדָרְשׁוּ (cf. lxix. 19), which Baer has adopted.

Vers. 11-15. The *Piel* נִקֵּשׁ properly signifies to catch in snares; here, like the Arabic نقش, II., IV., corresponding to the Latin *obligare* (as referring to the creditor's right of claim); נֹשֶׁה is the name for the creditor as he who gives time for payment, gives credit (*vid.* Isa. xxiv. 2). In ver. 12 מָשַׁךְ חֶסֶד, to draw out mercy, is equivalent to causing it to continue and last, xxxvi. 11, cf. Jer. xxxi. 3. אַחֲרִיתוֹ, ver. 13*a*, does not signify his future, but as ver. 13*b* (cf. xxxvii. 38) shows: his posterity. יְהִי לְהַכְרִית is not merely *exscindatur*, but *exscindenda sit* (Ezek. xxx. 16, cf. Josh. ii. 6), just as in other instances הָיָה לְ corresponds to the active *fut. periphrasticum, e.g.* Gen. xv. 12, Isa. xxxvii. 26. With reference to יִמַּח instead of יִמַּח (contracted from יִמָּחֶה), *vid.* Ges. § 75, rem. 8. A Jewish acrostic

---

* In connection with the strong verb it frequently represents the *Piel* which does not occur, as with דָּרַשׁ, לָשַׁן, יָפַט, or even represents the *Piel* which, as in the case of שֵׁרַשׁ, is already made use of in another signification (*Piel*, to root out; *Poel*, to take root).

interpretation of the name יְשִׁי runs: יִמַּח שְׁמוֹ וְחֶבְרוֹ. This curse shall overtake the family of the υἱὸς τῆς ἀπωλείας. All the sins of his parents and ancestors shall remain indelible above before God the Judge, and here below the race, equally guilty, shall be rooted out even to its memory, i.e. to the last trace of it.

Vers. 16–20. He whom he persecuted with a thirst for blood, was, apart from this, a great sufferer, bowed down and poor and נִכְאֵה לֵבָב, of terrified, confounded heart. LXX. κατανενυγμένον (Jerome, *compunctum*); but the stem-word is not נכא (נכה), root נך (vol. i. 425), but בָּאָה, Syriac ܢܟܐ, cogn. בָּהָה, to cause to come near, to meet. The verb, and more especially in *Niph.*, is proved to be Hebrew by Dan. xi. 30. Such an one who without anything else is of a terrified heart, inasmuch as he has been made to feel the wrath of God most keenly, this man has persecuted with a deadly hatred. He had experienced kindness (חֶסֶד) in a high degree, but he blotted out of his memory that which he had experienced, not for an instant imagining that he too on his part had to exercise חֶסֶד. The *Poel* מוֹתֵת instead of הֵמִית points to the agonizing death (Isa. liii. 9, cf. Ezek. xxviii. 10 מוֹתֵי) to which he exposes God's anointed. The fate of the shedder of blood is not expressed after the manner of a wish in vers. 16–18, but in the historical form, as being the result that followed of inward necessity from the matter of fact of the course which he had himself determined upon. The verb בּוֹא *seq. acc.* signifies to surprise, suddenly attack any one, as in Isa. xli. 25. The three figures in ver. 18 are climactic: he has clothed himself in cursing, he has drunk it in like water (Job xv. 16, xxxiv. 7), it has penetrated even to the marrow of his bones, like the oily preparations which are rubbed in and penetrate to the bones. In ver. 19 the emphasis rests upon יַעְטֶה and upon תָּמִיד. The summarizing ver. 20 is the close of a strophe. פְּעֻלָּה, an earned reward, here punishment incurred, is especially frequent in Isa. ch. xl.–lxvi., *e.g.* xlix. 4, xl. 10; it also occurs once even in the Tôra, Lev. xix. 13. Those who answer the loving acts of the righteous with such malevolence in word and in deed commit a satanic sin for which there is no forgiveness. The curse is the fruit of their own choice and deed. Arnobius: *Nota ex arbitrio evenisse ut nollet, propter hæresim, quæ dicit Deum alios præ-destinasse ad benedictionem, alios ad maledictionem.*

Vers. 21–25. The thunder and lightning are now as it were followed by a shower of tears of deep sorrowful complaint. Ps. cix. here just as strikingly accords with Ps. lxix., as Ps. lxix. does with Ps. xxii. in the last strophe but one. The twofold name *Jahve Adonaj* (*vid.* Symbolæ, p. 16) corresponds to the deep-breathed complaint. עֲשֵׂה אִתִּי, deal with me, *i.e.* succouring me, does not greatly differ from לְ in 1 Sam. xiv. 6. The confirmation, ver. 21*b*, runs like lxix. 17: Thy loving-kindness is טוֹב, absolutely good, the ground of everything that is good and the end of all evil. Hitzig conjectures, as in lxix. 17, כְּטוֹב חסדך, "according to the goodness of Thy loving-kindness;" but this formula is without example: "for Thy loving-kindness is good" is a statement of the motive placed first and corresponding to the "for Thy Name's sake." In ver. 22 (a variation of lv. 5) חָלַל, not חָלָל, is traditional; this חָלַל, as being *verb. denom.* from חָלָל, signifies to be pierced, and is therefore equivalent to הוּחַל (cf. Luke ii. 35). The metaphor of the shadow in ver. 23 is as in cii. 12. When the day declines, the shadow lengthens, it becomes longer and longer (Virgil, *majoresque cadunt altis de montibus umbræ*), till it vanishes in the universal darkness. Thus does the life of the sufferer pass away. The poet intentionally uses the *Niph.* נֶהֱלָכְתִּי (another reading is הִתְהַלָּכְתִּי); it is a power rushing upon him from without that drives him away thus after the manner of a shadow into the night. The locust or grasshopper (apart from the plague of the locusts) is proverbial as being a defence-less, inoffensive little creature that is soon driven away, Job xxxix. 20. נִנְעַר, to be shaken out or off (cf. Arabic *na'ûra*, a water-wheel that fills its clay-vessels in the river and empties them out above, and הַנֹּעֵר, Zech. xi. 16, where Hitzig wishes to read הַנַּעַר, *dispulsio = dispulsi*). The fasting in ver. 24 is the result of the loathing of all food which sets in with deep grief. כָּחַשׁ מִשֶּׁמֶן signifies to waste away so that there is no more fat left.* In ver. 25 אֲנִי is designedly rendered prominent: in this

---

* The verbal group כחש, בחר, &ﺐَﺞ, ﻛَﺬَﺐ, etc. has the primary signi-fication of withdrawal and taking away or decrease; to deny is the same as to withdraw from agreement, and he becomes thin from whom the fat

the form of his affliction he is the butt of their reproaching, and they shake their heads doubtfully, looking upon him as one who is punished of God beyond all hope, and giving him up for lost. It is to be interpreted thus after lxix. 11 sq.

Vers. 26–31. The cry for help is renewed in the closing strophe, and the Psalm draws to a close very similarly to Ps. lxix. and xxii., with a joyful prospect of the end of the affliction. In ver. 27 the hand of God stands in contrast to accident, the work of men, and his own efforts. All and each one will undeniably perceive, when God at length interposes, that it is His hand which here does that which was impossible in the eyes of men, and that it is His work which has been accomplished in this affliction and in the issue of it. He blesses him whom men curse: they arise without attaining their object, whereas His servant can rejoice in the end of his affliction. The futures in ver. 29 are not now again imprecations, but an expression of believingly confident hope. In correct texts בְּמָעִיל has *Mem raphatum*. The "many" are the "congregation" (*vid*. xxii. 23). In the case of the marvellous deliverance of this sufferer the congregation or church has the pledge of its own deliverance, and a bright mirror of the loving-kindness of its God. The sum of the praise and thanksgiving follows in ver. 31, where כִּי signifies *quod*, and is therefore allied to the ὅτι *recitativum* (cf. xxii. 25). The three Good Friday Psalms all sum up the comfort that springs from David's affliction for all suffering ones in just such a pithy sentence (xxii. 25, lxix. 34). Jahve comes forward at the right hand of the poor, contending for him (cf. cx. 5), to save (him) from those who judge (xxxvii. 33), *i.e.* condemn, his soul. The contrast beween this closing thought and vers. 6 sq. is unmistakeable. At the right hand of the tormentor stands Satan as an accuser, at the right hand of the tormented one stands God as his vindicator; he who delivered him over to human judges is condemned, and he who was delivered up is "taken away out of distress and from judgment" (Isa. liii. 8) by the Judge of the judges, in order that, as we now hear in the following

---

withdraws, goes away. Saadia compares on this passage (פרה) בהמה בְּחִישָׁה, a lean cow, *Berachoth* 32a. In like manner Targum II. renders Gen. xli. 27 תּוֹרְתָא בְּחִישָׁתָא, the lean kine.

Psalm, he may sit at the right hand of the heavenly King. Ἐδικαιώθη ἐν πνεύματι ... ἀνελήμφθη ἐν δόξῃ! (1 Tim. iii. 16.)

PSALM CX.

TO THE PRIEST-KING AT THE RIGHT HAND OF GOD.

1 THE oracle of Jahve unto my Lord :
"Sit thou at My right hand,
Until I make thine enemies
The stool of thy feet."

2 The sceptre of thy might
Will Jahve stretch forth out of Zion :
"Rule thou in the midst of thine enemies!"

3 Thy people are most willing on thy field-day ;
In holy festive garments,
Out of the womb of the morning's dawn
Cometh the dew of thy young men.

4 Jahve hath sworn and will not repent :
"Thou shalt be a priest for ever
After the manner of Melchizedek."

5 The Lord at thy right hand
Dasheth kings in pieces in the day of His wrath,
6 He shall judge among the nations,
It becometh full of corpses.

He dasheth in pieces a head upon a broad country ;
7 Of the brook in the way shall he drink,
Therefore shall he lift up the head on high.

While the Pharisees were gathered together, Jesus asked them : What think ye of Christ? Whose Son is He? They say unto Him : David's. He saith unto them : How then doth David in the spirit call Him Lord, saying : " The LORD hath said unto my Lord: Sit Thou on My right hand until I make Thine enemies the stool of Thy feet?" If David then calls Him Lord, how is He his Son? And no man was able to answer Him a word, neither durst any one from that day forth question Him further.

So we read in Matt. xxii. 41–46, Mark xii. 35–37, Luke xx. 41–44. The inference which it is left for the Pharisees to draw rests upon the two premises, which are granted, that Ps. cx. is Davidic, and that it is prophetico-Messianic, *i.e.* that in it the future Messiah stands objectively before the mind of David. For if those who were interrogated had been able to reply that David does not there speak of the future Messiah, but puts into the mouth of the people words concerning himself, or, as Hofmann has now modified the view he formerly held (*Schriftbeweis*, ii. 1, 496–500), concerning the Davidic king in a general way,* then the question would lack the background of cogency as an argument. Since, however, the pro-

---

* *Vid.* the refutation of this modified view in Kurtz, *Zur Theologie der Psalmen*, in the *Dorpater Zeitschrift* for the year 1861, S. 516.

Supplementary Note.—Von Hofmann now interprets Ps. cx. as prophetico-Messianic. We are glad to be able to give it in his own words. "As the utterance of a prophet who speaks the word of God to the person addressed, the Psalm begins, and this is it then all through, even where it does not, as in ver. 4, expressly make known to the person addressed what God swears to him. God intends to finally subdue his foes to him. Until then, until his day of victory is come, he shall have a dominion in the midst of them, the sceptre of which shall be mighty through the succour of God. His final triumph is, however, pledged to him by the word of God, which appoints him, as another Melchizedek, to an eternal priesthood, that excludes the priesthood of Aaron, and by the victory which God has already given him in the day of His wrath.

"This is a picture of a king on Zion who still looks forward to that which in Ps. lxxii. 8 sqq. has already taken place,—of a victorious, mighty king, who however is still ruling in the midst of foes,—therefore of a king such as Jesus now is, to whom God has given the victory over heathen Rome, and to whom He will subdue all his enemies when he shall again reveal himself in the world; meanwhile he is the kingly priest and the priestly king of the people of God. The prophet who utters this is David. He whom he addresses as Lord is the king who is appointed to become that which Ps. lxxii. describes him; it is therefore he of whom God has spoken according to 2 Sam. xxiii. 3. David beholds him in a moment of his ruling to which the moment in his own ruling in which we find him in 2 Sam. xi. 1 is typically parallel."

phetico-Messianic character of the Psalm was acknowledged at that time (even as the later synagogue, in spite of the dilemma into which this Psalm brought it in opposition to the church, has never been able entirely to avoid this confession), the conclusion to be drawn from this Psalm must have been felt by the Pharisees themselves, that the Messiah, because the Son of David and Lord at the same time, was of human and at the same time of superhuman nature; that it was therefore in accordance with Scripture if this Jesus, who represented Himself to be the predicted Christ, should as such profess to be the Son of God and of divine nature.

The New Testament also assumes elsewhere that David in this Psalm speaks not of himself, but directly of Him, in whom the Davidic kingship should finally and for ever fulfil that of which the promise speaks. For ver. 1 is regarded elsewhere too as a prophecy of the exaltation of Christ at the right hand of the Father, and of His final victory over all His enemies: Acts ii. 34 sq., 1 Cor. xv. 25, Heb. i. 13, x. 13; and the Epistle to the Hebrews (ch. v. 6, vii. 17, 21) bases its demonstration of the abrogation of the Levitical priesthood by the Melchizedek priesthood of Jesus Christ upon ver. 4. But if even David, who raised the Levitical priesthood to the pinnacle of splendour that had never existed before, was a priest after the manner of Melchizedek, it is not intelligible how the priesthood of Jesus Christ after the manner of Melchizedek is meant to be a proof in favour of the termination of the Levitical priesthood, and to absolutely preclude its continuance.

We will not therefore deceive ourselves concerning the apprehension of the Psalm which is presented to us in the New Testament Scriptures. According to the New Testament Scriptures, David speaks in Ps. cx. not merely of Christ in so far as the Spirit of God has directed him to speak of the Anointed of Jahve in a typical form, but directly and objectively in a prophetical representation of the Future One. And would this be impossible? Certainly there is no other Psalm in which David distinguishes between himself and the Messiah, and has the latter before him: the other Messianic Psalms of David are reflections of his radical, ideal contemplation of himself, reflected images of his own typical history; they contain prophetic elements, because David there too speaks ἐν πνεύματι, but elements that are not solved by the person of David. Nevertheless the last words of David in 2 Sam. xxiii. 1-7 prove to us that we need not be surprised to find even a directly Messianic Psalm coming from his lips. After the splendour of all that pertained to David individually had almost entirely expired in his own eyes and in the eyes of those about him, he must have been still more strongly conscious of the distance between what had been realized in himself and the idea of the Anointed of God, as he lay on his death-bed, as his sun was going down. Since, however, all the glory with which God has favoured him comes up once more before his soul, he feels himself, to the glory of God, to be "the man raised up on high, the anointed of the God of Jacob, the sweet singer of Israel," and the instrument of the Spirit of Jahve. This he has been, and he, who as such contemplated himself as the immortal one, must now die: then in dying he seizes the pillars of the divine promise, he lets go the ground of his own present, and looks as a prophet into the future of his seed: *The God of Israel hath said, to me hath the Rock of Israel spoken:* "*A ruler of men, a just one, a ruler in the fear of God; and as the light of the morning, when the sun riseth, a cloudless morning, when after sunshine, after rain it becomes green out of the earth.*" *For not little* (לֹא־כֵן to be explained according to Job ix. 35, cf. Num. xiii. 33, Isa. li. 6) *is my house with God, but an everlasting covenant hath He made with me, one ordered in all things and sure, for all my salvation and all my favour—ought He not to cause it to sprout?* The idea of the Messiah shall notwithstanding be realized, in accordance with the promise, within his own house. The vision of the future which passes before his soul is none other than the picture of the Messiah detached from its subjectivity. And if so there, why may it not also have been so even in Ps. cx.?

The fact that Ps. cx. has points of connection with cotemporaneous history is notwithstanding the less to be denied, as its position in the Fifth Book leads one to suppose that it is taken out of its cotemporary annalistic connection. The first of these connecting links is the bringing of the Ark home to Zion. Girded with the linen ephod of the priest, David had accompanied the Ark up to Zion with signs of rejoicing. There upon Zion Jahve, whose earthly throne is the Ark, now took

His place at the side of David; but, spiritually considered, the matter stood properly thus, that Jahve, when He established Himself upon Zion, granted to David to sit henceforth enthroned at His side. The second connecting link is the victorious termination of the Syro-Ammonitish war, and also of the Edomitish war that came in between. The war with the Ammonites and their allies, the greatest, longest, and most glorious of David's wars, ended in the second year, when David himself joined the army, with the conquest of Rabbah. These two cotemporary connecting links are to be recognised, but they only furnish the Psalm with the typical ground-colour for its prophetical contents.

In this Psalm David looks forth from the height upon which Jahve has raised him by the victory over Ammon into the future of his seed, and there He who carries forward the work begun by him to the highest pitch is his Lord. Over against this King of the future, David is not king, but subject. He calls him, as one out of the people, "my Lord." This is the situation of the prophetico-kingly poet. He has received new revelations concerning the future of his seed. He has come down from his throne and the height of his power, and looks up to the Future One. He too sits enthroned on Zion. He too is victorious from thence. But His fellowship with God is the most intimate imaginable, and the last enemy is also laid at His feet. And He is not merely king, who as a priest provides for the salvation of His people, He is an eternal Priest by virtue of a sworn promise. The Psalm therefore relates to the history of the future upon a typical ground-work. It is also explicable why the triumph in the case of Ammon and the Messianic image have been thus to David's mind disconnected from himself. In the midst of that war comes the sin of David, which cast a shadow of sorrow over the whole of his future life and reduced its typical glory to ashes. Out of these ashes the phœnix of Messianic prophecy here arises. The type, come back to the conscious of himself, here lays down his crown at the feet of the Antitype.

Ps. cx. consists of three sevens, a tetrastich together with a tristich following three times upon one another. The *Rebia magnum* in ver. 2 is a security for this stichic division, and in like manner the *Olewejored* by חֵילְךָ in ver. 3, and in general the interpunction required by the sense. And vers. 1 and 2 show decisively that it is to be thus divided into 4 + 3 lines; for ver. 1 with its rhyming inflexions makes itself known as a tetrastich, and to take it together with ver. 2 as a heptastich is opposed by the new turn which the Psalm takes in ver. 2. It is also just the same with ver. 4 in relation to ver. 3: these seven stichs stand in just the same organic relation to the second divine utterance as the preceding seven to the first utterance. And since vers. 1–4 give twice 4 + 3 lines, vers. 5–7 also will be organized accordingly. There are really seven lines, of which the fifth, contrary to the Masoretic division of the verse, forms with ver. 7 the final tristich.

The Psalm therefore bears the threefold impress of the number seven, which is the number of an oath and of a covenant. Its impress, then, is thoroughly prophetic. Two divine utterances are introduced, and that not such as are familiar to us from the history of David and only reproduced here in a poetic form, as with Ps. lxxxix. and cxxxii., but utterances of which nothing is known from the history of David, and such as we hear for the first time here. The divine name *Jahve* occurs three times. God is designedly called *Adonaj* the fourth time. The Psalm is consequently prophetic; and in order to bring the inviolable and mysterious nature even of its contents into comparison with the contemplation of its outward character, it has been organized as a threefold septiad, which is sealed with the thrice recurring tetragramma.

Vers. 1, 2. In Ps. xx. and xxi. we see at once in the openings that what we have before us is the language of the people concerning their king. Here לַאדֹנִי in ver. 1 does not favour this, and נְאֻם is decidedly against it. The former does not favour it, for it is indeed correct that the subject calls his king " my lord," *e.g.* 1 Sam. xxii. 12, although the more exact form of address is " my lord the king," *e.g.* 1 Sam. xxiv. 9 [8]; but if the people are speaking here, what is the object of the title of honour being expressed as if coming from the mouth of an individual, and why not rather, as in Ps. xx., xxi., לְמַלְכֵּנוּ or לִמְשִׁיחוֹ ? נְאֻם is, however, decisive against the supposition that it is an Israelite who here expresses himself concerning the relation of his king to Jahve. For it is absurd to suppose that an Israelite speaking in the name of the people would begin in the manner of the prophets with נְאֻם, more particularly since this נְאֻם ה׳ placed thus at the head of the discourse is without any perfectly analogous example (1 Sam. ii. 30, Isa. i. 24 are only similar) elsewhere, and is therefore extremely important. In general this opening position of נְאֻם, even in cases where other genitives than יהוה follow, is very rare; נְאֻם is found besides, so placed, only in the mouth of Balaam in Num. xxiv. 3 sq., 15 sq., of David in 2 Sam. xxiii. 1, of Agur in Prov. xxx. 1, and always (even in Ps. xxxvi. 2) in an oracular signification. Moreover, if one from among the people were speaking, the declaration ought to be a retrospective glance at a past utterance of God. But, first, the history knows nothing of any such divine utterance; and secondly, נְאֻם ה׳ always introduces God as actually speaking, to which even the passage cited by Hofmann to the contrary, Num. xiv. 28, forms no exception. Thus it will consequently not be a past utterance of God to which the poet glances back here, but one which David has just now heard ἐν πνεύματι (Matt. xxii. 43), and is therefore not a declaration of the people concerning David, but of David concerning Christ. The unique character of the declaration confirms this. Of the king of Israel it is said that he sits on the throne of Jahve (1 Chron. xxix. 23), viz. as visible representative of the invisible King (1 Chron. xxviii. 5); Jahve, however, commands the person here addressed to take his place at His right hand. The right hand of a king is the highest place of honour, 1 Kings ii. 19.* Here the sitting at the right hand signifies not merely an idle honour, but reception into the fellowship of God as regards dignity and dominion, exaltation to a participation in God's reigning (βασιλεύειν, 1 Cor. xv. 25). Just as Jahve sits enthroned in the heavens and laughs at the rebels here below, so shall he who is exalted henceforth share this blessed calm with Him, until He subdues all enemies to him, and therefore makes him the unlimited, universally acknowledged ruler. עַד as in Hos. x. 12, for עַד־כִּי or עַד־אֲשֶׁר, does not exclude the time that lies beyond,

---

* Cf. the custom of the old Arabian kings to have their viceroy (*ridf*) sitting at their right hand, *Monumenta antiquiss. hist. Arabum*, ed. *Eichhorn*, p. 220.

but as in cxii. 8, Gen. xlix. 10, includes it, and in fact so that it at any rate marks the final subjugation of the enemies as a turning-point with which something else comes about (vid. Acts iii. 21, 1 Cor. xv. 28). הֲדֹם is an accusative of the predicate. The enemies shall come to lie under his feet (1 Kings v. 17 [3]), his feet tread upon the necks of the vanquished (Josh. x. 24), so that the resistance that is overcome becomes as it were the dark ground upon which the glory of his victorious rule arises. For the history of time ends with the triumph of good over evil,—not, however, with the annihilation of evil, but with its subjugation. This is the issue, inasmuch as absolute omnipotence is effectual on behalf of and through the exalted Christ. In ver. 2, springing from the utterance of Jahve, follow words expressing a prophetic prospect. Zion is the imperial abode of the great future King (ii. 6). מַטֵּה עֻזְּךָ (cf. Jer. xlviii. 17, Ezek. xix. 11–14) signifies " the sceptre (as insignia and the medium of exercise) of the authority delegated to thee" (1 Sam. ii. 10, Mic. v. 3 [4]). Jahve will stretch this sceptre far forth from Zion : no goal is mentioned up to which it shall extend, but passages like Zech. ix. 10 show how the prophets understand such Psalms. In ver. 2b follow the words with which Jahve accompanies this extension of the dominion of the exalted One. Jahve will lay all his enemies at his feet, but not in such a manner that he himself remains idle in the matter. Thus, then, having come into the midst of the sphere (בְּקֶרֶב) of his enemies, shall he reign, forcing them to submission and holding them down. We read this רְדֵה in a Messianic connection in lxxii. 8. So even in the prophecy of Balaam (Num. xxiv. 19), where the sceptre (ch. xxiv. 17) is an emblem of the Messiah Himself.

Vers. 3, 4. In order that he may rule thus victoriously, it is necessary that there should be a people and an army. In accordance with this union of the thoughts which ver. 3a anticipates, בְּיוֹם חֵילֶךָ signifies in the day of thy arriere ban, i.e. when thou callest up thy "power of an army" (2 Chron. xxvi. 13) to muster and go forth to battle. In this day are the people of the king willingnesses (נְדָבֹת), i.e. entirely cheerful readiness; ready for any sacrifices, they bring themselves with all that they are and have to meet him. There is no need of any compulsory, lengthy proclamation calling them out: it is no army of mercenaries, but willingly and quickly they present themselves from inward impulse (מִתְנַדֵּב, Judg. v. 2, 9). The punctuation, which makes the principal caesura at חֵילְךָ with *Olewejored*, makes the parallelism of חילך and יַלְדֻתֶךָ distinctly prominent. Just as the former does not signify *roboris tui*, so now too the latter does not, according to Eccles. xi. 9, signify παιδιότητός σου (Aquila), and not, as Hofmann interprets, the dew-like freshness of youthful vigour, which the morning of the great day sheds over the king. Just as גָּלוּת signifies both exile and the exiled ones, so יַלְדוּת, like νεότης, *juventus*, *juventa*, signifies both the time and age of youth, youthfulness, and youthful, young men (the youth). Moreover one does not, after ver. 3*a*, look for any further declaration concerning the nature of the king, but of his people who place themselves at his service. The young men are likened to dew which gently descends upon the king out of the womb (*uterus*) of the morning-red.* מִשְׁחָר is related to שַׁחַר just as מֶחְשָׁךְ is to חֹשֶׁךְ; the notion of שׁחר and חׁשֶׁךְ appears to be more sharply defined, and as it were apprehended more massively, in מִשְׁחָר and מַחְשָׁךְ. The host of young men is likened to the dew both on account of its vigorousness and its multitude, which are like the freshness of the mountain dew and the immense number of its drops, 2 Sam. xvii. 12 (cf. Num. xxiii. 10), and on account of the silent concealment out of which it wondrously and suddenly comes to light, Mic. v. 6 [7]. After not having understood "thy youth" of the youthfulness of the king, we shall now also not, with Hofmann, refer בְּהַדְרֵי־קֹדֶשׁ to the king, the holy attire of his armour. הַדְרַת קֹדֶשׁ is the vestment of the priest

---

* The LXX. renders it: ἐν ταῖς λαμπρότησι τῶν ἁγίων σου (belonging to the preceding clause), ἐκ γαστρὸς πρὸ ἑωσφόρου ἐγέννησά σε (Psalt. Veron. *exegennesa se*; Bamberg. *gegennica se*). The Vulgate, following the Italic closely: *in splendoribus sanctorum; ex utero ante luciferum genui te.* The Fathers in some cases interpret it of the birth of the Lord at Christmas, but most of them of His antemundane birth, and accordingly Apollinaris paraphrases: γαστρὸς καρπὸς ἐμῆς πρὸ ἑωσφόρου αὐτὸς ἐτύχθης. In his own independent translation Jerome reads בהררי (as in lxxxvii. 1), *in montibus sanctis quasi de vulva orietur tibi ros adolescentiæ tuæ*, as Symmachus ἐν ὄρεσιν ἁγίοις,—elsewhere, however, ἐν δόξῃ ἁγίων. The substitution is not unmeaning, since the ideas of dew and of mountains (cxxxviii. 3) are easily united; but it was more important to give prominence to the holiness of the equipment than to that of the place of meeting.

for performing divine service: the Levite singers went forth before the army in "holy attire" in 2 Chron. xx. 21; here, however, the people without distinction wear holy festive garments. Thus they surround the divine king as dew that is born out of the womb of the morning-red. It is a priestly people which he leads forth to holy battle, just as in Apoc. xix. 14 heavenly armies follow the Logos of God upon white horses, ἐνδεδυμένοι βύσσινον λευκὸν καθαρόν—a new generation, wonderful as if born out of heavenly light, numerous, fresh, and vigorous like the dew-drops, the offspring of the dawn. The thought that it is a priestly people leads over to ver. 4. The king who leads this priestly people is, as we hear in ver. 4, himself a priest (*cohen*). As has been shown by Hupfeld and Fleischer, the priest is so called as one who stands (from כֹּהֵן = כֹּהן in an intransitive signification), viz. before God (Deut. x. 8, cf. Ps. cxxxiv. 1, Heb. x. 11), like נָבִיא the spokesman, viz. of God.* To stand before God is the same as to serve Him, viz. as priest. The ruler whom the Psalm celebrates is a priest who intervenes in the reciprocal dealings between God and His people within the province of divine worship; the priestly character of the people who suffer themselves to be led forth to battle and victory by him, stands in causal connection with the priestly character of this their king. He is a priest by virtue of the promise of God confirmed by an oath. The oath is not merely a pledge of the fulfilment of the promise, but also a seal of the high significance of its purport. God the absolutely truthful One (Num. xiii. 19) swears—this is the highest enhancement of the נְאֻם ה׳ of which prophecy is capable (Amos vi. 8).

He appoints the person addressed as a priest for ever "after the manner of Melchizedek" in this most solemn manner. The *i* of דִּבְרָתִי is the same ancient connecting vowel as in the מַלְכִּי of the name Melchizedek; and it has the tone, which it loses when, as in Lam. i. 1, a tone-syllable follows. The wide-

---

* The Arabic lexicographers explain كَاهِن by مَن يَقُوم بِأَمْرِ الرِّجَال, وَيَسْعَى فِى حَاجَتِه "he who stands and does any one's business and manages his affair." That קוּם, תָּם, and מָשַׁל, מִשֵּׁל, side by side with עָמַד are synonyms of כֹּהֵן in this sense of standing ready for service and in an official capacity.

meaning עַל־דִּבְרַת, "in respect to, on account of," Eccles. iii. 18, vii. 14, viii. 2, is here specialized to the signification "after the manner, measure of," LXX. κατὰ τὴν τάξιν. The priesthood is to be united with the kingship in him who rules out of Zion, just as it was in Melchizedek, king of Salem, and that for ever. According to De Wette, Ewald, and Hofmann, it is not any special priesthood that is meant here, but that which was bestowed directly with the kingship, consisting in the fact that the king of Israel, by reason of his office, commended his people in prayer to God and blessed them in the name of God, and also had the ordering of Jahve's sanctuary and service. Now it is true all Israel is a "kingdom of priests" (Ex. xix. 6, cf. Num. xvi. 3, Isa. lxi. 6), and the kingly vocation in Israel must therefore also be regarded as in its way a priestly vocation. But this spiritual priesthood, and, if one will, this princely oversight of sacred things, needed not to come to David first of all by solemn promise; and that of Melchizedek, after which the relationship is here defined, is incongruous to him; for the king of Salem was, according to Canaanitish custom, which admitted of the union of the kingship and priesthood, really a high priest, and therefore, regarded from an Israelitish point of view, united in his own person the offices of David and of Aaron. How could David be called a priest after the manner of Melchizedek, he who had no claim upon the tithes of the priests like Melchizedek, and to whom was denied the authority to offer sacrifice* inseparable from the idea of the priesthood in the Old Testament? (cf. 2 Chron. xxvi. 20.) If David were the person addressed, the declaration would stand in antagonism with the right of Melchizedek as priest recorded in Gen. ch. xiv., which, according to the indisputable representation of the Epistle to the Hebrews, was equal in compass to the Levitico-Aaronic right, and, since "after the manner of" requires a coincident reciprocal relation, in antagonism to itself also.†

One might get on more easily with ver. 4 by referring the

---

* G. Enjedin the Socinian (died 1597) accordingly, in referring this Psalm to David, started from the assumption that priestly functions have been granted exceptionally by God to this king as to no other; vid. the literature of the controversy to which this gave rise in Serpilius, Personalia Davidis, S. 268-274.

† Just so Kurtz, Zur Theologie der Psalmen, loc. cit. S. 523.

Psalm to one of the Maccabæan priest-princes (Hitzig, von Lengerke, and Olshausen); and we should then prefer to the reference to Jonathan who put on the holy *stola*, 1 Macc. x. 21 (so Hitzig formerly), or Alexander Jannæus who actually bore the title of king (so Hitzig now), the reference to Simon, whom the people appointed to "be their governor and high priest for ever, until there should arise a faithful prophet" (1 Macc. xiv. 41), after the death of Jonathan his brother—a union of the two offices which, although an irregularity, was not one, however, that was absolutely illegal. But the priesthood, which the Maccabæans, however, possessed originally as being priests born, is promised to the person addressed here in ver. 4; and even supposing that in ver. 4 the emphasis lay not on a union of the priesthood with the kingship, but of the kingship with the priesthood, then the retrospective reference to it in Zechariah forbids our removing the Psalm to a so much later period. Why should we not rather be guided in our understanding of this divine utterance, which is unique in the Old Testament, by this prophet, whose prophecy in ch. vi. 12 sq. is the key to it? Zechariah removes the fulfilment of the Psalm out of the Old Testament present, with its blunt separation between the monarchical and hierarchical dignity, into the domain of the future, and refers it to Jahve's Branch (צֶמַח) that is to come. He, who will build the true temple of God, satisfactorily unites in his one person the priestly with the kingly office, which were at that time assigned to Joshua the high priest and Zerubbabel the prince. Thus this Psalm was understood by the later prophecy; and in what other sense could the post-Davidic church have appropriated it as a prayer and hymn, than in the eschatological Messianic sense? But this sense is also verified as the original. David here hears that the king of the future exalted at the right hand of God, and whom he calls his Lord, is at the same time an eternal priest. And because he is both these his battle itself is a priestly royal work, and just on this account his people fighting with him also wear priestly garments.

Vers. 5–7. Just as in ver. 2 after ver. 1, so now here too after the divine utterance, the poet continues in a reflective strain. The Lord, says ver. 5, dashes in pieces kings at the right hand of this priest-king, in the day when His wrath is kindled (ii. 12, cf. xxi. 10). אֲדֹנָי is rightly accented as subject. The fact that the victorious work of the person addressed is not his own work, but the work of Jahve on his behalf and through him, harmonizes with ver. 1b. The sitting of the exalted one at the right hand of Jahve denotes his uniform participation in His high dignity and dominion. But in the fact that the Lord, standing at his right hand (cf. the counterpart in cix. 6), helps him to victory, that unchangeable relationship is shown in its historical working. The right hand of the exalted one is at the same time not inactive (see Num. xxiv. 17, cf. ver. 8), and the Lord does not fail him when he is obliged to use his arm against his foes. The subject to יָדִין and to the two מָחַץ is the Lord as acting through him. "He shall judge among the peoples" is an eschatological hope, vii. 9, ix. 9, xcvi. 10, cf. 1 Sam. ii. 10. What the result of this judgment of the peoples is, is stated by the neutrally used verb מָלֵא with its accusative גְוִיוֹת (cf. on the construction lxv. 10, Deut. xxxiv. 9): it there becomes full of corpses, there is there a multitude of corpses covering everything. This is the same thought as in Isa. lxvi. 24, and wrought out in closely related connection in Apoc. xix. 17, xviii. 21. Like the first מָחַץ, the second (ver. 6c) is also a perfect of the ideal past. Accordingly אֶרֶץ רַבָּה seems to signify the earth or a country (cf. אֶרֶץ רְחָבָה, Ex. iii. 8, Neh. ix. 35) broad and wide, like תְּהוֹם רַבָּה the great far-stretching deep. But it might also be understood the "land of Rabbah," as they say the "land of Jazer" (Num. xxxii. 1), the "country of Goshen" (Josh. x. 41), and the like; therefore the land of the Ammonites, whose chief city is Rabbah. It is also questionable whether רֹאשׁ עַל־אֶרֶץ רַבָּה is to be taken like κεφαλὴν ὑπὲρ πάντα, Eph. i. 22 (Hofmann), or whether עַל־אֶרֶץ רַבָּה belongs to מָחַץ as a designation of the battle-field. The parallels as to the word and the thing itself, lxviii. 22, Hab. iii. 13 sq., speak for רֹאשׁ signifying not the chief, but the head; not, however, in a collective sense (LXX., Targum), but the head of the רָשָׁע κατ' ἐξοχήν (vid. Isa. xi. 4). If this is the case, and the construction רֹאשׁ עַל is accordingly to be given up, neither is it now to be rendered: He breaks in pieces a head upon the land of Rabbah, but upon a great (broad) land; in connection with which, however, this designation of the place of battle takes its rise from the fact that the head of the ruler over this great territory is intended, and the choice of the word may have been determined by an allusion to David's Ammonitish war. The subject of ver. 7 is now not that arch-fiend, as he who in the course of history renews his youth, that shall rise up again (as we explained it formerly), but he whom the Psalm, which is thus rounded off with unity of plan, celebrates. Ver. 7a expresses the toil of his battle, and ver. 7b the reward of undertaking the toil. עַל־כֵּן is therefore equivalent to ἀντὶ τούτου. בַּדֶּרֶךְ, however, although it might belong to מִנַּחַל (of the brook by the wayside, lxxxiii. 10, cvi. 7), is correctly drawn to יִשְׁתֶּה by the accentuation: he shall on his arduous way, the way of his mission (cf. cii. 24), be satisfied with a drink from the brook. He will stand still only for a short time to refresh himself, and in order then to fight afresh; he will unceasingly pursue his work of victory without giving himself any time for rest and sojourn, and therefore (as the reward for it) it shall come to pass that he may lift his head on high as victor; and this, understood in a christological sense, harmonizes essentially with Phil. ii. 8 sq., Heb. xii. 2, Apoc. v. 9 sq.

PSALM CXI.
ALPHABETICAL SONG IN PRAISE OF GOD.

HALLELUJAH.

1 א I WILL give thanks unto Jahve with the whole heart,
 ב In the council of the upright and the congregation.
2 ג Great are the deeds of Jahve,
 ד Worthy of being sought after in all their purposes.
3 ה Glory and splendour is His work,
 ו And His righteousness endureth for ever.
4 ז A memorial of His wonderful works hath He founded,
 ח Gracious and compassionate is Jahve.
5 ט Meat hath He given to those who fear Him,
 י He remembereth His covenant for ever. [works,
6 כ He hath made known to His people the power of His
 ל Giving to them the heritage of the heathen.
7 מ The works of His hands are truth and right,
 נ Faithful are all His statutes,
8 ס Firm for ever and ever,
 ע Established according to truth, and upright.

9 ס He hath sent redemption unto His people,
ע He hath pledged His covenant for ever—
פ Holy and reverend is His Name.
10 ר The beginning of wisdom is the fear of Jahve,
ש A good understanding have all dutiful ones;
ת He shall have eternal praise.

With Ps. cxi. begins a trilogy of Hallelujah-Psalms. It may be appended to Ps. cx., because it places the "for ever" of cx. 4 in broader light in relation to the history of redemption, by stringing praise upon praise of the deeds of Jahve and of His appointments. It stands in the closest relationship to Ps. cxii. Whilst Ps. cxi., as Hitzig correctly says, celebrates the glory, might, and loving-kindness of Jahve in the circle of the "upright," Ps. cxii. celebrates the glory flowing therefrom and the happiness of the "upright" themselves, of those who fear Jahve. The two Psalms are twin in form as in contents. They are a mixture of materials taken from older Psalms and gnomical utterances; both are sententious, and both alphabetical. Each consists of twenty-two lines with the twenty-two letters of the alphabet at the beginning,* and every line for the most part consists of three words. Both songs are only chains of acrostic lines without any strophic grouping, and therefore cannot be divided out. The analogous accentuation shows how strong is the impression of the close relationship of this twin pair; and both Psalms also close, in vers. 9 and 10, with two verses of three members, being up to this point divided into verses of two members.

That which the poet purposes doing in ver. 1, he puts into execution from ver. 2 onwards. וְעֵדָה, according to lxiv. 7, cxviii. 14, is equivalent to וְעֵדָתָם. According to ver. 10b, חֶפְצֵיהֶם in ver. 2b apparently signifies those who find pleasure in them (the works of God); but חֶפְצֵי = חֲפֵצֵי (like יִשְׂמְחֵי, Isa. xxiv. 7 = יִשְׂמְחֵי) is less natural than that it should be the construct form of the plural of חֵפֶץ, that occurs in three instances,

---

* Böttcher transposes the verses in Ps. cxi., and in cxii. 5 corrects יִכַלְכֵּל into וִכַלְכֵּל; in the warmth of his critical zeal he runs against the boundary-posts of the letters marking the order, without observing it.

and there was no need for saying that those who make the works of God the object of their research are such as interest themselves in them. We are led to the right meaning by לְכָל־חֶפְצֵיהֶם in 1 Kings ix. 11 in comparison with Isa. xliv. 28, xlvi. 10, cf. liii. 10, where חֵפֶץ signifies God's purpose in accordance with His counsel: constantly searched into, and therefore a worthy object of research (דרשׁ, root דר, to seek to know by rubbing, and in general experimentally, cf. دری of knowledge empirically acquired) according to all their aims, i.e. in all phases of that which they have in view. In ver. 4 זֵכֶר points to the festival which propagates the remembrance of the deeds of God in the Mosaic age; טֶרֶף, ver. 5, therefore points to the food provided for the Exodus, and to the Passover meal, together with the feast of unleavened bread, this memorial (זִכָּרוֹן, Ex. xii. 14) of the exemption in faithfulness to the covenant which was experienced in Egypt. This Psalm, says Luther, looks to me as though it had been composed for the festival of Easter. Even from the time of Theodoret and Augustine the thought of the Eucharist has been connected with ver. 5 in the New Testament mind; and it is not without good reason that Ps. cxi. has become the Psalm of the church at the celebration of the Lord's Supper. In connection with הִגִּיד one is reminded of the Pesach-Haggada. The deed of redemption which it relates has a power that continues in operation; for to the church of Jahve is assigned the victory not only over the peoples of Canaan, but over the whole world. The power of Jahve's deeds, which He has made known to His people, and which they tell over again among themselves, aims at giving them the inheritance of the peoples. The works of His hands are truth and right, for they are the realization of that which is true and which lasts and verifies itself, and of that which is right, that triumphantly maintains its ground. His ordinances are נֶאֱמָנִים (occasionally pointed נֶאֱמָנִים), established, attested, in themselves and in their results authorizing a firm confidence in their salutariness (cf. xix. 8). סְמוּכִים, supported, stayed, viz. not outwardly, but in themselves, therefore imperturbable (cf. סָמוּךְ used of the state of mind, cxii. 8, Isa. xxvi. 3). עֲשׂוּיִם, moulded, arranged, viz. on the part of God, "in truth, and upright;" יָשָׁר is accusative of the predicate (cf. cxix. 37), but without its being clear why it is not pointed וְיֵּרָ. If we have understood vers. 4-6 correctly, then פְּדוּת glances back at the deliverance out of Egypt. Upon this followed the ratification of the covenant on Sinai, which still remains inviolable down to the present time of the poet, and has the holiness and terribleness of the divine Name for a guarantee of its inviolability. The fear of Jahve, this holy and terrible God, is the beginning of wisdom—the motto of the *Chokma* in Job (ch. xxviii. 28) and Proverbs (ch. i. 7, ix. 10), the Books of the *Chokma*. Ver. 10*b* goes on in this Proverbs-like strain: the fear of God, which manifests itself in obedience, is to those who practise them (the divine precepts, פקורים) שֵׂכֶל טוֹב (Prov. xiii. 15, iii. 4, cf. 2 Chron. xxx. 22), a fine sagacity, praiseworthy discernment—such a (dutiful) one partakes of everlasting praise. It is true, in glancing back to ver. 3*b*, תְּהִלָּתוֹ seems to refer to God, but a glance forward to cxii. 3*b* shows that the praise of him who fears God is meant. The old observation therefore holds good: *ubi hæc ode desinit, sequens incipit* (Bakius).

PSALM CXII.

ALPHABETICAL SONG IN PRAISE OF THOSE WHO FEAR GOD.

HALLELUJAH.
1 א BLESSED is the man who feareth Jahve,
   ב Who delighteth greatly in His commandments!
2 ג His seed shall become mighty upon earth,
   ד The generation of the upright is blessed.
3 ה Wealth and riches are in his house,
   ו And his righteousness standeth for ever.
4 ז There ariseth in darkness for the upright a light,
   ח Gracious and compassionate and righteous.
5 ט Blessed is he who giveth and lendeth,
   י In the judgment doth he maintain his cause.
6 כ He tottereth not for ever,
   ל The righteous is had in everlasting remembrance.
7 מ By evil tidings he is not affrighted,
   נ His heart is stedfast, confident in Jahve.

PSALM CXII.

אּ כ His heart is firm, it doth not fear;
   ע Until he see his desire upon his adversaries.
9 פ Freely doth he give to the needy,
   צ His righteousness standeth for ever.
   ק His horn groweth up into honour,
10 ר The wicked seeth it, and is vexed,
   ש Gnashing his teeth and melting away—
   ת The desire of the wicked shall perish.

The alphabetical Hallelujah Ps. cxi., which celebrated the government of God, is now followed by another coinciding with it in structure ($CTYXOC\ \overline{KB}$, i.e. 22 στίχοι, as the Coptic version correctly counts), which celebrates the men whose conduct is ordered after the divine pattern.

As in the preceding Psalm, ver. 1 here also sets forth the theme of that which follows. What is there said in ver. 3 concerning the righteousness of God, ver. 3 here says of the righteousness of him who fears God: this also standeth fast for ever, it is indeed the copy of the divine, it is the work and gift of God (xxiv. 5), inasmuch as God's salutary action and behaviour, laid hold of in faith, works a like form of action and behaviour to it in man, which, as ver. 9 says, is, according to its nature, love. The promise in ver. 4 sounds like Isa. lx. 2. Hengstenberg renders: "There ariseth in the darkness light to the upright who is gracious and compassionate and just." But this is impossible as a matter of style. The three adjectives (as in cxi. 4, pointing back to Ex. xxxiv. 6, cf. cxlv. 8, cxvi. 5) are a mention of God according to His attributes. חַנּוּן and רַחוּם never take the article in Biblical Hebrew, and צַדִּיק follows their example here (cf. on the contrary, Ex. ix. 27). God Himself is the light which arises in darkness for those who are sincere in their dealings with Him; He is the Sun of righteousness with wings of rays dispensing "grace" and "tender mercies," Mal. iii. 20 [iv. 2]. The fact that He arises for those who are compassionate as He is compassionate, is evident from ver. 5. טוֹב being, as in Isa. iii. 10, Jer. xliv. 17, intended of well-being, prosperity, טוֹב אִישׁ is here equivalent to אַשְׁרֵי אִישׁ, which is rendered טוּבֵיהּ דְּגַבְרָא in Targumic phrase. חוֹנֵן signifies, as in xxxvii. 26, 21, one who charitably dispenses his gifts around. Ver. 5b is not an extension of the picture of virtue, but, as in cxxvii. 5c, a promissory prospect: he will uphold in integrity (בְּמִשְׁפָּט, lxxii. 2, Isa. ix. 6 [7], and frequently), or rather (=בְּמִשְׁפָּט) in the cause (cxliii. 2, Prov. xxiv. 23, and frequently), the things which depend upon him, or with which he has to do; for כִּלְכֵּל, sustinere, signifies to sustain, i.e. to nourish, to sustain, i.e. endure, and also to support, maintain, i.e. carry through. This is explanatorily confirmed in ver. 6: he stands, as a general thing, imperturbably fast. And when he dies he becomes the object of everlasting remembrance, his name is still blessed (Prov. x. 7). Because he has a cheerful conscience, his heart too is not disconcerted by any evil tidings (Jer. xlix. 23): it remains נָכוֹן, erect, straight and firm, without suffering itself to bend or warp; בָּטֻחַ בּה׳, full of confidence (passive, "in the sense of a passive state after a completed action of the person himself," like זָכוּר, ciii. 14); סָמוּךְ, stayed in itself and established. The last two designations are taken from Isa. xxvi. 3, where it is the church of the last times that is spoken of. Ps. xci. 8 gives us information with reference to the meaning of רָאָה בְצָרָיו; עַד, as in xciv. 13, of the inevitable goal, on this side of which he remains undismayed. 2 Cor. ix. 9, where Paul makes use of ver. 9 of the Psalm before us as an encouragement to Christian beneficence, shows how little the assertion "his righteousness standeth for ever" is opposed to the New Testament consciousness. פִּוַּר of giving away liberally and in manifold ways, as in Prov. xi. 24. רוּם, ver. 9c, stands in opposition to the egoistical הָרִים in lxxv. 5 as a vegetative sprouting up (cxxxii. 17). The evil-doer must see this and, confounded, vex himself over it; he gnashes his teeth with the rage of envy and chagrin, and melts away, i.e. loses consistency, becomes unhinged, dies off (נָמֵס, 3d præt. Niph. as in Ex. xvi. 21, pausal form of נָמֵס=נָמָס). How often has he desired the ruin of him whom he must now see in honour! The tables are turned; this and his ungodly desire in general come to nought, inasmuch as the opposite is realized. On יִרְאֶה, with its self-evident object, cf. Mic. vii. 10. Concerning the pausal form וְכָעָס, vid. xciii. 1. Hupfeld wishes to read תִּקְוַת after ix. 19, Prov. x. 28. In defence of the traditional reading, Hitzig rightly points to Prov. x. 24 together with ver. 28.

PSALM CXIII.

HALLELUJAH TO HIM WHO RAISETH OUT OF LOW ESTATE.

HALLELUJAH.
1 PRAISE, ye servants of Jahve,
  Praise the Name of Jahve!
2 Blessed be the Name of Jahve
  From this time forth and for evermore!
3 From the rising of the sun unto its going down
  Is the Name of Jahve to be praised.

4 Exalted above all peoples is Jahve,
  Above the heavens His glory.
5 Who is like Jahve our God,
  He who sitteth enthroned on high,
6 He who looketh far below
  In heaven and upon earth?

7 Who raiseth up the lowly out of the dust,
  Who lifteth the poor from the heap of ashes,
8 To set him with nobles,
  With the nobles of His people.
9 Who maketh the barren woman to keep house,
  As a joyful mother of the sons,
        Hallelujah.

With this Psalm begins the *Hallel*, which is recited at the three great feasts, at the feast of the Dedication (*Chanucca*) and at the new moons, and not on New Year's day and the day of Atonement, because a cheerful song of praise does not harmonize with the mournful solemnity of these days. And they are recited only in fragments during the last days of the Passover, for " my creatures, saith the Holy One, blessed be He, were drowned in the sea, and ought ye to break out into songs of rejoicing?" In the family celebration of the Passover night it is divided into two parts, the one half, Ps. cxiii., cxiv., being sung before the repast, before the emptying of the second festal cup, and the other half, Ps. cxv.–cxviii., after the repast, after the filling of the fourth cup, to which the ὑμνήσαντες (Matt. xxvi. 30, Mark xiv. 26) after the institution of the Lord's Supper, which was connected with the fourth festal cup, may refer. Paulus Burgensis styles Ps. cxiii.–cxviii. *Alleluja Judæorum magnum*. This designation is also frequently found elsewhere. But according to the prevailing custom, Ps. cxiii.–cxviii., and more particularly Ps. cxv.–cxviii., are called only *Hallel*, and Ps. cxxxvi., with its " for His mercy endureth for ever" repeated twenty-six times, bears the name of " *the Great Hallel*" (הַלֵּל הַגָּדוֹל).*

A heaping up, without example elsewhere, of the so-called *Chirek compaginis* is peculiar to Ps. cxiii. Gesenius and others call the connecting vowels *i* and *o* (in proper names also *u*) the remains of old case terminations; with the former the Arabic genitive termination is compared, and with the latter the Arabic nominative termination. But in opposition to this it has been rightly observed, that this *i* and *o* are not attached to the dependent word (the genitive), but to the governing word. According to the more probable view of Ewald, § 211, *i* and *o* are equivalent connecting vowels which mark the relation of the genitive case, and are to be explained from the original oneness of the Semitic and Indo-Germanic languages.

The *i* is found most frequently appended to the first member of the *stat. constr.*, and both to the *masc.*, viz. in Deut. xxxiii. 16, Zech. xi. 17 (perhaps twice, *vid.* Köhler *in loc.*), and to the *femin.*, viz. in Gen. xxxi. 39, Ps. cx. 4, Isa. i. 21. Lev. xxvi. 42, Ps. cxvi. 1 hardly belong here. Then this *i* is also fre-

---

* *Vid.* the tractate *Sofrim*, xviii. § 2. Apart from the new moons, a which the recitation of the *Hallel* κατ' ἐξοχήν, i.e. Ps. cxiii.–cxviii., is only according to custom (מִנְהָג), not according to the law, the *Hallel* was recited eighteen times a year during the continuance of the Temple (and in Palestine even in the present day), viz. once at the Passover, once at Shabuoth, eight times at Succoth, eight times at Chanucca (the feast of the Dedication); and now in the Exile twenty-one times, because the Passover and Succoth have received two feast-days and Shabuoth one as an addition, viz. twice at the Passover, twice at Shabuoth, nine times at Succoth. Instead of *Hallel* absolutely we also find the appellation " the Egyptian Hallel" (הַלֵּל הַמִּצְרִי) for Ps. cxiii.–cxviii. The ancient ritual only makes a distinction between this (Egyptian) Hallel and the Great Hallel, Ps. cxxxvi. (see there).

quently found when the second member of the *stat. constr.* has a preposition, and this preposition is consequently in process of being resolved: Gen. xlix. 11, Ex. xv. 6, Obad. ver. 3 (Jer. xlix. 16), Hos. x. 11, Lam. i. 1, Ps. cxxiii. 1, and perhaps Cant. i. 9. Also in the *Chethîb*, Jer. xxii. 23, li. 13, Ezek. xxvii. 3. Thirdly, where a word stands between the two notions that belong together according to the genitival relation, and the *stat. construct.* is consequently really resolved: Ps. ci. 5, Isa. xxii. 16, Mic. vii. 14. It is the same *i* which is found in a great many proper names, both Israelitish, *e.g. Gamaliel* (benefit of God), and Phœnician, *e.g. Melchizedek*, *Hannibaʿal* (the favour of Baal), and is also added to many Hebrew prepositions, like בְּלִתִי (where the *i* however can, according to the context, also be a pronominal suffix), זוּלָתִי (where *i* can likewise be a suffix), מִנִּי (poetical). In אֶפְסִי, on the other hand, the *i* is always a suffix. The tone of the *i* only retreats in accordance with rhythmical rule (*vid.* cx. 4), otherwise *i* is always accented. Ver. 8 shows how our Ps. cxiii. in particular delights in this ancient *i*, where it is even affixed to the infinitive as an ornament, a thing which occurs nowhere else, so that לְהוֹשִׁיבִי excites the suspicion of being written in error for לְהוֹשִׁיבוֹ.

Among those things which make God worthy to be praised the Psalm gives prominence to the condescension of the infinitely exalted One towards the lowly one. It is the lowliness of God lowering itself for the exaltation of the lowly which performs its utmost in the work of redemption. Thus it becomes explicable that Mary in her *Magnificat* breaks forth into the same strain with the song of Hannah (1 Sam. ch. ii.) and this Psalm.

Vers. 1–3. The call, not limited by any addition as in cxxxiv. 1, or even, after the manner of ciii. 20 sq., extended over the earth, is given to the whole of the true Israel that corresponds to its election by grace and is faithful to its mission; and its designation by " servants of Jahve " (lxix. 37, cf. xxxiv. 23), or even " servant of Jahve " (cxxxvi. 22), has come into vogue more especially through the second part of Isaiah. This Israel is called upon to praise Jahve; for the praise and celebration of His Name, *i.e.* of His nature, which is disclosed by means of its manifestation, is a principal element, yea, the proper ground and aim, of the service, and shall finally become that which fills all time and all space. כִּיהֵל, *laudatum* (*est*), is equivalent to αἰνετόν, *laudabile* (LXX., Vulgate), and this does not differ greatly from *laudetur*. The predictive interpretation *laudabitur* is opposed to the context (cf. moreover Köhler on Mal. i. 11).

Vers. 4-6. This praiseworthiness is now confirmed. The opening reminds one of xcix. 2. *Pasek* stands between גוים and יהוה in order to keep them apart. The totality of the nations is great, but Jahve is raised above it; the heavens are glorious, but Jahve's glory is exalted above them. It is not to be explained according to cxlviii. 13; but according to lvii. 6, 12, רם belongs to ver. 4*b* too as predicate. He is the incomparable One who has set up His throne in the height, but at the same time directs His gaze deep downwards (expression according to Ges. § 142, rem. 1) in the heavens and upon earth, *i.e.* nothing in all the realm of the creatures that are beneath Him escapes His sight, and nothing is so low that it remains unnoticed by Him; on the contrary, it is just that which is lowly, as the following strophe presents to us in a series of portraits so to speak, that is the special object of His regard. The structure of vers. 5, 6 militates against the construction of " in the heavens and upon the earth" with the interrogatory "who is like unto Jahve our God?" after Deut. iii. 24.

Vers. 7-9. The thoughts of vers. 7*a* and 8*a* are transplanted from the song of Hannah. עָפָר, according to 1 Kings xvi. 2, cf. xiv. 7, is an emblem of lowly estate (Hitzig), and אַשְׁפֹּת (from שָׁפַת) an emblem of the deepest poverty and desertion; for in Syria and Palestine the man who is shut out from society lies upon the *mezbele* (the dunghill or heap of ashes), by day calling upon the passers-by for alms, and by night hiding himself in the ashes that have been warmed by the sun (*Job*, ii. 152). The movement of the thoughts in ver. 8, as in ver. 1, follows the model of the epizeuxis. Together with the song of Hannah the poet has before his eye Hannah's exaltation out of sorrow and reproach. He does not, however, repeat the words of her song which have reference to this (1 Sam. ii. 5), but clothes his generalization of her experience in his own language. If he intended that עֲקֶרֶת should be understood out of the genitival relation after the form עֲטֶרֶת, why did he not write מוֹשִׁיבִי הַבַּיִת עֲקָרָה? הַבַּיִת would then be equivalent to בַּיְתָה, lxviii. 7. עֲקֶרֶת הַבַּיִת is the expression for a woman who is a wife, and therefore housewife, נְוַת (בְּעֻלַת) הַבַּיִת, but yet not a mother. Such an one has no settled position in the house of the husband, the firm bond is wanting in her relationship to her husband. If God gives her children, He thereby makes her then thoroughly at home and rooted-in in her position. In the predicate notion אֵם הַבָּנִים שְׂמֵחָה the definiteness attaches to the second member of the string of words, as in Gen. xlviii. 19, 2 Sam. xii. 30 (cf. the reverse instance in Jer. xxiii. 26, נִבְּאֵי הַשָּׁקֶר, those prophesying that which is false), therefore: a mother of the children. The poet brings the matter so vividly before him, that he points as it were with his finger to the children with which God blesses her.

PSALM CXIV.

COMMOTION OF NATURE BEFORE GOD THE REDEEMER OUT OF EGYPT.

1 WHEN Israel went forth out of Egypt,
The house of Jacob out of a people of strange language,
2 Then Judah became His sanctuary,
Israel His dominion.

3 The sea saw it, and fled,
Jordan turned backwards,
4 The mountains skipped like rams,
The hills like young sheep.

5 What aileth thee, O sea, that thou fleest?
O Jordan, that thou turnest backwards?
6 Ye mountains, that ye skip like rams?
Ye hills, like young sheep?—

7 Before the face of the Lord tremble, O earth,
Before the face of the God of Jacob,

8 Who changeth the rock into a pool of water,
The flinty rock into water-springs!

To the side of the general Hallelujah Ps. cxiii. comes an historical one, which is likewise adorned in ver. 8 with the *Chirek compaginis,* and still further with *Cholem compaginis,* and is the festival Psalm of the eighth Passover day in the Jewish ritual. The deeds of God at the time of the Exodus are here brought together to form a picture in miniature which is as majestic as it is charming. There are four tetrastichs, which pass by with the swiftness of a bird as it were with four flappings of its wings. The church sings this Psalm in a *tonus peregrinus* distinct from the eight Psalm-tones.

Vers. 1–4. Egypt is called עַם לֹעֵז (from לָעַז, cogn. לָעַג, לָעָה), because the people spoke a language unintelligible to Israel (lxxxi. 6), and as it were a stammering language. The LXX., and just so the Targum, renders ἐκ λαοῦ βαρβάρου (from the Sanscrit *barbaras,* just as onomatopoetic as *balbus,* cf. Fleischer in Levy's *Chaldäisches Wörterbuch,* i. 420). The redeemed nation is called *Judah,* inasmuch as God made it His sanctuary (קֹדֶשׁ) by setting up His sanctuary (מִקְדָּשׁ, Ex. xv. 17) in the midst of it, for Jerusalem (*el-kuds*) was Benjamitish Judæan, and from the time of David was accounted directly as Judæan. In so far, however, as He made this people His kingdom (מַמְשְׁלוֹתָיו, an amplificative plural with *Mem pathachatum*), by placing Himself in the relation of King (Deut. xxxiii. 5) to the people of possession which by a revealed law He established characteristically as His own, it is called *Israel.* The predicate takes the form הָיְתָה, for peoples together with country and city are represented as feminine (cf. Jer. viii. 5). The foundation of that new beginning in connection with the history of redemption was laid amidst majestic wonders, inasmuch as nature was brought into service, co-operating and sympathizing in the work (cf. lxxvii. 15 sqq.). The dividing of the sea opens, and the dividing of the Jordan closes, the journey through the desert to Canaan. The sea stood aside, Jordan halted and was dammed up on the north in order that the redeemed people might pass through. And in the middle, between these great wonders of the exodus from Egypt and the entrance into Canaan, arises the not less mighty wonder of the giving of the Law: the skipping of the mountains like rams, of the hills like בְּנֵי־צֹאן, *i.e.* lambs (Wisd. xix. 9), depicts the quaking of Sinai and its environs (Ex. xix. 18, cf. *supra* lxviii. 9, and on the figure xxix. 6).

Vers. 5–8. The poet, when he asks, "What aileth thee, O sea, that thou fleest . . . ?" lives and moves in this olden time as a cotemporary, or the present and the olden time as it were flow together to his mind; hence the answer he himself gives to the question propounded takes the form of a triumphant mandate. The Lord, the God of Jacob, thus mighty in wondrous works, it is before whom the earth must tremble. אָדוֹן does not take the article because it finds its completion in the following יַעֲקֹב (אֱלוֹהַ); it is the same *epizeuxis* as in cxiii. 8, xciv. 3, xcvi. 7, 13. הַהֹפְכִי has the constructive *î* out of the genitival relation; and in לְמַעְיְנוֹ in this relation we have the constructive *ô*, which as a rule occurs only in the genitival combination, with the exception of this passage and בְּנוֹ בְעֹר, Num. xxiv. 3, 15 (not, however, in Prov. xiii. 4, "his, the sluggard's, soul"), found only in the name for wild animals חַיְתוֹ־אָרֶץ, which occurs frequently, and first of all in Gen. i. 24. The expression calls to mind cvii. 35. הַצּוּר is taken from Ex. xvii. 6; and חַלָּמִישׁ (LXX. τὴν ἀκρότομον, that which is rugged, abrupt) * stands, according to Deut. viii. 15, poetically for סֶלַע, Num. xx. 11, for it is these two histories of the giving of water

---

* One usually compares خلنبوس, *chalnabûs* [the Karaite lexicographer Abraham ben David writes חלמבוס]; but this obsolete word, as a compound from خلس, to be black-grey, and خنبس, to be hard, may originally signify a hard black-grey stone, whereas חלמיש looks like a mingling of the verbal stems حمس, to be hard, and حلس, to be black-brown (as جلمود, a detached block of rock, is of the verbal stems جلد, to be hard, and جمد, to be massive). In Hauran the doors of the houses and the window-shutters are called حلسة when they consist of a massive slab of dolerite, probably from their blackish hue. Perhaps חלמיש is the ancient name for basalt; and in connection with the hardness of this form of rock, which resembles a mass of cast metal, the breaking through of springs is a great miracle.—WETZSTEIN. For other views *vid.* on Isa. xlix. 21, l. 7.

to which the poet points back. But why to these in particular? The causing of water to gush forth out of the flinty rock is a practical proof of unlimited omnipotence and of the grace which converts death into life. Let the earth then tremble before the Lord, the God of Jacob. It has already trembled before Him, and before Him let it tremble. For that which He has been He still ever is; and as He came once, He will come again.

PSALM CXV.

CALL TO THE GOD OF ISRAEL, THE LIVING GOD, TO RESCUE THE HONOUR OF HIS NAME.

1 NOT unto us, Jahve, not unto us,
But unto Thy Name give glory,
Because of Thy loving-kindness, because of Thy truth.
2 Wherefore shall the heathen say:
" Where is now their God?"

3 And our God is in the heavens,
Whatsoever He willeth He carrieth out.
4 Their gods, however, are silver and gold,
The work of men's hands.
5 They have a mouth and speak not,
They have eyes and see not,
6 They have ears and hear not,
They have a nose and smell not.
7 Their hands, with which they handle not,
Their feet, with which they walk not,
They speak not with their throat.
8 Like unto them do those who make them become,
Every one who trusteth in them.

9 Israel, trust thou in Jahve,
Their help and their shield is He.
10 O house of Aaron, trust ye in Jahve,
Their help and their shield is He.
11 Ye who fear Jahve, trust in Jahve,
Their help and their shield is He.

12 Jahve hath been mindful of us, He will bless—
   He will bless the house of Israel,
   He will bless the house of Aaron,
13 He will bless those who fear Jahve,
   The small together with the great.
14 Jahve will add to you,
   To you and your children.

15 Blessed be ye of Jahve,
   The Creator of heaven and earth.
16 The heavens are heavens for Jahve,
   And the earth hath He given to the children of men.
17 The dead praise not Jāh,
   Nor all those who go down into the silence of death;
18 We, however, we will bless Jāh
   From henceforth and for evermore,
          Hallelujah.

This Psalm, which has scarcely anything in common with the preceding Psalm except that the expression "house of Jacob," cxiv. 1, is here broken up into its several members in vers. 12 sq., is found joined with it, making one Psalm, in the LXX., Syriac, Arabic, and Æthiopic versions, just as on the other hand Ps. cxvi. is split up into two. This arbitrary arrangement condemns itself. Nevertheless Kimchi favours it, and it has found admission into not a few Hebrew manuscripts.

It is a prayer of Israel for God's aid, probably in the presence of an expedition against heathen enemies. The two middle strophes of the four are of the same compass. Ewald's conjecture, that whilst the Psalm was being sung the sacrifice was proceeded with, and that in ver. 12 the voice of a priest proclaims the gracious acceptance of the sacrifice, is pleasing. But the change of voices begins even with ver. 9, as Olshausen also supposes.

Vers. 1, 2. It has to do not so much with the honour of Israel, which is not worthy of the honour (Ezek. xxxvi. 22 sq.) and has to recognise in its reproach a well-merited chastisement, as with the honour of Him who cannot suffer the reproaching of His holy name to continue long. He willeth that His name should be sanctified. In the consciousness of his oneness with this will, the poet bases his petition, in so far as it is at the same time a petition on behalf of Israel, upon God's χάρις and ἀλήθεια as upon two columns. The second עַל, according to an express note of the Masora, has no *Waw* before it, although the LXX. and Targum insert one. The thought in ver. 2 is moulded after lxxix. 10, or after Joel ii. 17, cf. Ps. xlii. 4, Mic. vii. 10. אַיֵּה־נָא is the same style as נְגְדָה־נָּא in cxvi. 18, cf. in the older language אֶל־נָא, אִם־נָא, and the like.

Vers. 3–8. The poet, with "And our God," in the name of Israel opposes the scornful question of the heathen by the believingly joyous confession of the exaltation of Jahve above the false gods. Israel's God is in the heavens, and is therefore supramundane in nature and life, and the absolutely unlimited One, who is able to do all things with a freedom that is conditioned only by Himself: *quod vult, valet* (ver. 3*b* = cxxxv. 6, Wisd. xii. 18, and frequently). The carved gods (עָצָב, from עָצַב, cogn. חָצַב, קָצַב) of the heathen, on the contrary, are dead images, which are devoid of all life, even of the sensuous life the outward organs of which are imaged upon them. It cannot be proved with Eccles. v. 16 that יְדֵיהֶם and רַגְלֵיהֶם are equivalent to רגלים להם, ידים להם. They are either subjects which the *Waw apodosis* (cf. Gen. xxii. 24, Prov. xxiii. 24, Hab. ii. 5) renders prominent, or *casus absoluti* (Ges. § 145, 2), since both verbs have the idols themselves as their subjects less on account of their gender (יד and רגל are feminine, but the Hebrew usage of genders is very free and not carried out uniformly) as in respect of ver. 7*c*: with reference to their hands, etc. יֶהְגּוּ is the energetic future form, which goes over from יָהְגּיוּ into מִגּוּ, for יֶהְגּוּ. It is said once again in ver. 7*c* that speech is wanting to them; for the other negations only deny life to them, this at the same time denies all personality. The author might know from his own experience how little was the distinction made by the heathen worship between the symbol and the thing symbolized. Accordingly the worship of idols seems to him, as to the later prophets, to be the extreme of self-stupefaction and of the destruction of human consciousness; and the final destiny of the worshippers of false gods, as he says in ver. 8, is, that they become like to their idols, that is to say, being deprived of their consciousness, life, and existence, they come to nothing, like those their nothingnesses (Isa. xliv. 9). This whole section of the Psalm is repeated in Ps. cxxxv. (vers. 6, 15-18).

Vers. 9-14. After this confession of Israel there now arises a voice that addresses itself to Israel. The threefold division into Israel, the house of Aaron, and those who fear Jahve is the same as in cxviii. 2-4. In Ps. cxxxv. the "house of Levi" is further added to the house of Aaron. Those who fear Jahve, who also stand in the last passage, are probably the proselytes (in the Acts of the Apostles σεβόμενοι τὸν Θεόν, or merely σεβόμενοι*); at any rate these are included even if Israel in ver. 9 is meant to signify the laity, for the notion of "those who fear Jahve" extends beyond Israel. The fact that the threefold refrain of the summons does not run, as in xxxiii. 20, *our help and shield is He*, is to be explained from its being an antiphonal song. In so far, however, as the Psalm supplicates God's protection and help in a campaign the declaration of confident hope, *their help and shield is He*, may, with Hitzig, be referred to the army that is gone or is going forth. It is the same voice which bids Israel to be of good courage and announces to the people the well-pleased acceptance of the sacrifice with the words "Jahve hath been mindful of us" (זְכָרָנוּ ה', cf. עַתָּה יָדַעְתִּי, xx. 7), perhaps simultaneously with the presentation of the memorial portion (אזכרה) of the meat-offering (xxxviii. 1). The יְבָרֵךְ placed at the head is particularized threefold, corresponding to the threefold summons. The special promise of blessing which is added in ver. 14 is an echo of Deut. i. 11, as in 2 Sam. xxiv. 3. The contracted future יֹסֵף we take in a consolatory sense; for as an optative it would be too isolated here. In spite of all oppression on the part of the heathen, God will make His people ever more numerous, more capable of offering resistance, and more awe-inspiring.

Vers. 15-18. The voice of consolation is continued in ver. 15, but it becomes the voice of hope by being blended with

---

* The appellation φοβούμενοι does not however occur, if we do not bring Acts x. 2 in here; but in Latin inscriptions in Orelli-Hentzen No. 2523, and in Auer in the *Zeitschrift für katholische Theologie* 1852, S. 80, the proselyte (*religionis Judaicæ*) is called *metuens*.

the newly strengthened believing tone of the congregation. Jahve is here called the Creator of heaven and earth because the worth and magnitude of His blessing are measured thereby. He has reserved the heavens to Himself, but given the earth to men. This separation of heaven and earth is a fundamental characteristic of the post-diluvian history. The throne of God is in the heavens, and the promise, which is given to the patriarchs on behalf of all mankind, does not refer to heaven, but to the possession of the earth (xxxvii. 22). The promise is as yet limited to this present world, whereas in the New Testament this limitation is removed and the κληρονομία embraces heaven and earth. This Old Testament limitedness finds further expression in ver. 17, where דוּמָה, as in xciv. 17, signifies the silent land of Hades. The Old Testament knows nothing of a heavenly *ecclesia* that praises God without intermission, consisting not merely of angels, but also of the spirits of all men who die in the faith. Nevertheless there are not wanting hints that point upwards which were even better understood by the post-exilic than by the pre-exilic church. The New Testament morn began to dawn even upon the post-exilic church. We must not therefore be astonished to find the tone of vi. 6, xxx. 10, lxxxviii. 11–13, struck up here, although the echo of those earlier Psalms here is only the dark foil of the confession which the church makes in ver. 18 concerning its immortality. The church of Jahve as such does not die. That it also does not remain among the dead, in whatever degree it may die off in its existing members, the psalmist might know from Isa. xxvi. 19, xxv. 8. But the close of the Psalm shows that such predictions which light up the life beyond only gradually became elements of the church's consciousness, and, so to speak, dogmas.

PSALM CXVI.

THANKSGIVING SONG OF ONE WHO HAS ESCAPED FROM DEATH.

1 I LOVE, for Jahve heareth
   My cry, my heartfelt supplication.
2 For He hath inclined His ear unto me,
   Therefore will I call as long as I live.

3 The cords of death compassed me,
  And the straitnesses of Hades came upon me,
  Distress and sorrow did I experience.
4 Then upon the name of Jahve did I call:
  O Jahve, deliver my soul.

5 Gracious is Jahve and righteous,
  And our God a compassionate One.
6 A Guardian of the simple is Jahve;
  I was brought low, and He helped me.
7 Turn in, my soul, unto thy rest,
  For Jahve dealeth bountifully with thee.
8 Yea, Thou hast delivered my soul from death,
  Mine eyes from tears,
  My feet from falling.
9 I will walk before Jahve
  In the lands of the living.

10 I believe now, when I must speak:
   "I, I am afflicted very greatly."
11 I have said to myself in my despair:
   "All men are liars."
12 How can I repay Jahve
   All His benefits toward me?
13 The cup of salvation will I raise,
   And proclaim the Name of Jahve.
14 My vows will I pay unto Jahve,
   I will do it in the presence of all His people.

15 Precious in the eyes of Jahve
   Is the death of His saints.
16 Yea, O Jahve, for I am Thy servant,
   I am Thy servant, the son of Thy handmaid,
   Thou hast loosed my bonds.
17 Unto Thee will I sacrifice a sacrifice of thanksgiving
   And proclaim the Name of Jahve.
18 My vows will I pay unto Jahve,
   I will do it in the presence of all His people,
19 In the courts of Jahve's house,
   In the midst of thee, O Jerusalem!
         Hallelujah.

We have here another anonymous Psalm closing with *Hallelujah*. It is not a supplicatory song with a hopeful prospect before it like Ps. cxv., but a thanksgiving song with a fresh recollection of some deadly peril that has just been got the better of; and is not, like Ps. cxv., from the mouth of the church, but from the lips of an individual who distinguishes himself from the church. It is an individual that has been delivered who here praises the loving-kindness he has experienced in the language of the tenderest affection. The LXX. has divided this deeply fervent song into two parts, cxvi. 1–9, 10–19, and made two Hallelujah-Psalms out of it; whereas it unites Ps. cxiv. and cxv. into one. The four sections or strophes, the beginnings of which correspond to one another (vers. 1 and 10, 5 and 15), are distinctly separate. The words וּבְשֵׁם ה' אֶקְרָא are repeated three times. In the first instance they are retrospective, but then swell into an always more full-toned vow of thanksgiving. The late period of its composition makes itself known not only in the strong Aramaic colouring of the form of the language, which adopts all kinds of embellishments, but also in many passages borrowed from the pre-exilic Psalms. The very opening, and still more so the progress, of the first strophe reminds one of Ps. xviii., and becomes an important hint for the exposition of the Psalm.

Vers. 1–4. Not only is כִּי אָהַבְתִּי, "I love (like, am well pleased) that," like ἀγαπῶ ὅτι, Thucydides vi. 36, contrary to the usage of the language, but the thought, "I love that Jahve answereth me," is also tame and flat, and inappropriate to the continuation in ver. 2. Since vers. 3, 4 have come from xviii. 5–17, אָהַבְתִּי is to be understood according to אֶרְחָמְךָ in xviii. 2, so that it has the following יהוה as its object, not it is true grammatically, but logically. The poet is fond of this pregnant use of the verb without an expressed object, cf. אֶקְרָא in ver. 2, and הֶאֱמַנְתִּי in ver. 10. The *Pasek* after יִשְׁמַע is intended to guard against the blending of the final *a* with the initial '*a* of אֲדֹנָי (cf. lxvi. 18, v. 2, in Baer). In ver. 1*b* the accentuation prevents the rendering *vocem orationis meæ* (Vulgate, LXX.) by means of *Mugrash*. The *i* of קוֹלִי will therefore no more be the archaic connecting vowel (Ew. § 211, *b*) than in Lev. xxvi. 42; the poet has varied the genitival construction of xxviii.

6 to the permutative. The second כי, following close upon the first, makes the continuation of the confirmation retrospective. "In my days" is, as in Isa. xxxix. 8, Bar. iv. 20, cf. בְּחַיַּי in lxiii. 5, and frequently, equivalent to "so long as I live." We even here hear the tone of Ps. xviii. (ver. 2), which is continued in vers. 3, 4 as a freely borrowed passage. Instead of the " bands" (of Hades) there, the expression here is מְצָרֵי, *angustiæ*, plural of מֵצַר, after the form מֵסַב in cxviii. 5, Lam. i. 3 (Böttcher, *De inferis*, § 423); the straitnesses of Hades are deadly perils which can scarcely be escaped. The futures אֶמְצָא and אֶקְרָא, by virtue of the connection, refer to the cotemporaneous past. אָנָּה (viz. בלישן בקשה, *i.e.* in a suppliant sense) is written with *He* instead of *Aleph* here and in five other instances, as the Masora observes. It has its fixed *Metheg* in the first syllable, in accordance with which it is to be pronounced *ânna* (like בָּתִּים, *battim*), and has an accented *ultima* not merely on account of the following אֲדֹנָי = יהוה (*vid.* on iii. 8), but in every instance; for even where (the *Metheg* having been changed into a conjunctive) it is supplied with two different accents, as in Gen. l. 17, Ex. xxxii. 31, the second indicates the tone-syllable.* Instead now of repeating "and Jahve answered me," the poet indulges in a laudatory confession of general truths which have been brought vividly to his mind by the answering of his prayer that he has experienced.

Vers. 5–9. With "gracious" and "compassionate" is here associated, as in cxii. 4, the term "righteous," which comprehends within itself everything that Jahve asserts concerning Himself in Ex. xxxiv. 6 sq. from the words "and abundant in goodness and truth" onwards. His love is turned especially toward the simple (LXX. τὰ νήπια, cf. Matt. xi. 25),

---

* Kimchi, mistaking the vocation of the *Metheg*, regards אָנָּא (אָנָּה) as *Milel*. But the Palestinian and the Babylonian systems of pointing coincide in this, that the beseeching אָנָּא (אָנָּה) is *Milra*, and the interrogatory אָנָא *Milel* (with only two exceptions in our text, which is fixed according to the Palestinian Masora, viz. cxxxix. 7, Deut. i. 28, where the following word begins with *Aleph*), and these modes of accenting accord with the origin of the two particles. Pinsker (*Einleitung*, S. xiii.) insinuates against the Palestinian system, that in the cases where אָנָא has two accents the pointing was not certain of the correct accentuation, only from a deficient knowledge of the bearings of the case.

who stand in need of His protection and give themselves over to it. פְּתָאיִם, as in Prov. ix. 6, is a mode of writing blended out of פְּתָאִים and פְּתָיִים. The poet also has experienced this love in a time of impotent need. דַּלּוֹתִי is accented on the *ultima* here, and not as in cxlii. 7 on the *penult*. The accentuation is regulated by some phonetic or rhythmical law that has not yet been made clear (*vid.* on Job xix. 17).* יְהוֹשִׁיעַ is a resolved *Hiphil* form, the use of which became common in the later period of the language, but is not alien to the earlier period, especially in poetry (xlv. 18, cf. lxxxi. 6, 1 Sam. xvii. 47, Isa. lii. 5). In ver. 7 we hear the form of soliloquy which has become familiar to us from Ps. xlii., xliii., ciii. שׁוּבִי is *Milra* here, as also in two other instances. The plural מְנוּחִים signifies full, complete rest, as it is found only in God; and the suffix in the address to the soul is *ajchi* for *ajich*, as in ciii. 3–5. The perfect גָּמַל states that which is a matter of actual experience, and is corroborated in ver. 8 in retrospective perfects. In vers. 8, 9 we hear lvi. 14 again amplified; and if we add xxvii. 13, then we see as it were to the bottom of the origin of the poet's thoughts. מִן־דִּמְעָה belongs still more decidedly than יְהוֹשִׁיעַ to the resolved forms which multiply in the later period of the language. In ver. 9 the poet declares the result of the divine deliverance. The *Hithpa.* אֶתְהַלֵּךְ denotes a free and contented going to and fro; and instead of "the land of the living," xxvii. 13, the expression here is "the lands (אַרְצוֹת), *i.e.* the broad land, of the living." There he walks forth, with nothing to hinder his feet or limit his view, in the presence of Jahve, *i.e.* having his Deliverer from death ever before his eyes.

Vers. 10–14. Since כִּי אֲדַבֵּר does not introduce anything that could become an object of belief, הֶאֱמִין is absolute here: to have faith, just as in Job xxiv. 22, xxix. 24, with לֹא it signifies "to be without faith, *i.e.* to despair." But how does it now proceed? The LXX. renders ἐπίστευσα, διὸ ἐλάλησα, which the apostle makes use of in 2 Cor. iv. 13, without our being

---

* The national grammarians, so far as we are acquainted with them, furnish no explanation. De Balmis believes that these *Milra* forms דַּלּוֹתִי, בַּלּוֹתִי, and the like, must be regarded as infinitives, but at the same time confirms the difference of views existing on this point.

therefore obliged with Luther to render: *I believe, therefore I speak;* כי does not signify διό. Nevertheless כי might according to the sense be used for לְכֵן, if it had to be rendered with Hengstenberg: "I believed, therefore I spake, but I was very much plagued." But this assertion does not suit this connection, and has, moreover, no support in the syntax. It might more readily be rendered: "I have believed that I should yet speak, *i.e.* that I should once more have a deliverance of God to celebrate;" but the connection of the parallel members, which is then only lax, is opposed to this. Hitzig's attempted interpretation, "I trust, when (כִּי as in Jer. xii. 1) I should speak: I am greatly afflicted," *i.e.* "I have henceforth confidence, so that I shall not suffer myself to be drawn away into the expression of despondency," does not commend itself, since ver. 10*b* is a complaining, but not therefore as yet a desponding assertion of the reality. Assuming that הֶאֱמַנְתִּי and אָמַרְתִּי in ver. 11*a* stand on the same line in point of time, it seems that it must be interpreted *I had faith, for I spake* (was obliged to speak); but אדבר, separated from האמנתי by כי, is opposed to the colouring relating to the cotemporaneous past. Thus ver. 10 will consequently contain the issue of that which has been hitherto experienced: *I have gathered up faith and believe* henceforth, *when I speak* (have to speak, must speak): *I am deeply afflicted* (עָנָה as in cxix. 67, cf. عنى, to be bowed down, more particularly in captivity, whence العُنَاةُ, those who are bowed down). On the other hand, ver. 11 is manifestly a retrospect. He believes now, for he is thoroughly weaned from putting trust in men: *I said in my despair* (taken from xxxi. 23), the result of my deeply bowed down condition: *All men are liars* (πᾶς ἄνθρωπος ψεύστης, Rom. iii. 4). Forsaken by all the men from whom he expected succour and help, he experienced the truth and faithfulness of God. Striding away over this thought, he asks in ver. 12 how he is to give thanks to God for all His benefits. מָה is an adverbial accusative for בַּמָּה, as in Gen. xliv. 16, and the substantive תַּגְמוּל, in itself a later formation, has besides the Chaldaic plural suffix *ôhi*, which is without example elsewhere in Hebrew. The poet says in ver. 13 how alone he can and will give thanks to his Deliverer, by using a figure taken from the Passover (Matt. xxvi. 27), the memorial repast in celebration of the redemption out of Egypt. The cup of salvation is that which is raised aloft and drunk amidst thanksgiving for the manifold and abundant salvation (יְשׁוּעוֹת) experienced. קָרָא בְשֵׁם ה׳ is the usual expression for a solemn and public calling upon and proclamation of the Name of God. In ver. 14 this thanksgiving is more minutely designated as שַׁלְמֵי נֶדֶר, which the poet now discharges. A common and joyous eating and drinking in the presence of God was associated with the *shelamim*. נָא (*vid.* cxv. 2) in the freest application gives a more animated tone to the word with which it stands. Because he is impelled frankly and freely to give thanks before the whole congregation, נָא stands beside נֶגֶד, and נֶגֶד, moreover, has the intentional *ah*.

Vers. 15–19. From what he has experienced the poet infers that the saints of Jahve are under His most especial providence. Instead of הַמָּוֶת the poet, who is fond of such embellishments, chooses the pathetic form הַמָּוְתָה, and consequently, instead of the genitival construct state (מוֹת), the construction with the *Lamed* of "belonging to." It ought properly to be "soul" or "blood," as in the primary passage lxxii. 14. But the observation of Grotius: *quæ pretiosa sunt, non facile largimur*, applies also to the expression "death." The death of His saints is no trifling matter with God; He does not lightly suffer it to come about; He does not suffer His own to be torn away from Him by death.* After this the poet goes on beseechingly: *ánnáh Adonaj*. The prayer itself is not contained in פִּתַּחְתָּ לְמוֹסֵרָי,—for he is already rescued, and the perfect as a precative is limited to such utterances spoken in the tone of an exclamation as we find in Job xxi. 16,—but remains unexpressed; it lies wrapped up as it were in this heartfelt *ánnáh:* Oh remain still so gracious to me as Thou hast already proved Thyself to me. The poet rejoices in and is proud of the fact that he may call himself the servant of God. With אֲמָתֶךָ he is mindful of his pious mother (cf. lxxxvi.

---

* The Apostolic Constitutions (vi. 30) commend the singing of these and other words of the Psalms at the funerals of those who have departed in the faith (cf. Augusti, *Denkwürdigkeiten*, ix. 563). In the reign of the Emperor Decius, Babylas Bishop of Antioch, full of blessed hope, met death singing these words.

16). The Hebrew does not form a feminine, עַבְדָּה; أَمَةٌ signifies a maid, who is not, as such, also عَبْدَةٌ, a slave. The dative of the object, לְמוֹסְרֵי (from מוֹסְרִים for the more usual מוֹסְרוֹת), is used with פתחת instead of the accusative after the Aramaic manner, but it does also occur in the older Hebrew (*e.g.* Job xix. 3, Isa. liii. 11). The purpose of publicly giving thanks to the Gracious One is now more full-toned here at the close. Since such emphasis is laid on the Temple and the congregation, what is meant is literal thank-offerings in payment of vows. In בְּתוֹכֵכִי (as in cxxxv. 9) we have in the suffix the ancient and Aramaic *i* (cf. ver. 7) for the third time. With אָנָּה the poet clings to Jahve, with נֶגְדָּה־נָּא to the congregation, and with בְּתוֹכֵכִי to the holy city. The one thought that fills his whole soul, and in which the song which breathes forth his soul dies away, is *Hallelujah*.

PSALM CXVII.

INVITATION TO THE PEOPLES TO COME INTO THE KINGDOM OF GOD.

1 PRAISE Jahve, all peoples,
   Praise Him, all ye nations!
2 For mighty over us is His loving-kindness,
   And the truth of Jahve endureth for ever,
       Hallelujah!

The thanksgiving Psalm ending in *Hallelujah* is followed by this shortest of all the Psalms, a Hallelujah addressed to the heathen world. In its very brevity it is one of the grandest witnesses of the might with which, in the midst of the Old Testament, the world-wide mission of the religion of revelation struck against or undermined the national limitation. It is stamped by the apostle in Rom. xv. 11 as a *locus classicus* for the fore-ordained (*gnadenrathschlussmässig*) participation of the heathen in the promised salvation of Israel.

Even this shortest Psalm has its peculiarities in point of

language. אֶמִים (Aramaic אֵמְתָא, Arabic أمّ) is otherwise alien to Old Testament Hebrew. The Old Testament Hebrew is acquainted only with אֵמִים as an appellation of Ismaelitish or Midianitish tribes. כָּל־גּוֹיִם are, as in lxxii. 11, 17, all peoples without distinction, and כָּל־הָאֻמִּים all nations without exception. The call is confirmed from the might of the mercy or loving-kindness of Jahve, which proves itself mighty over Israel, *i.e.* by its intensity and fulness superabundantly covering (גָּבַר as in ciii. 11; cf. ὑπερεπερίσσευσε, Rom. v. 20, ὑπερεπλεόνασε, 1 Tim. i. 14) human sin and infirmity; and from His truth, by virtue of which history on into eternity ends in a verifying of His promises. Mercy and truth are the two divine powers which shall one day be perfectly developed and displayed in Israel, and going forth from Israel, shall conquer the world

PSALM CXVIII.

FESTIVAL PSALM AT THE DEDICATION OF THE NEW TEMPLE.

(At the setting out.)

1 GIVE thanks unto Jahve, for He is good,
 Yea, His mercy endureth for ever.
2 Let Israel say:
 " Yea, His mercy endureth for ever."
3 Let the house of Aaron say:
 " Yea, His mercy endureth for ever."
4 Let those who fear Jahve say:
 " Yea, His mercy endureth for ever."

(On the way.)

5 Out of straitness I cried unto Jah,
 Jah answered me upon a broad plain.
6 Jahve is for me—I do not fear,
 What can men do unto me?
7 Jahve is for me as my help,
 Therefore shall I see my desire upon those who hate me.

8 It is better to hide one's self in Jahve
  Than to put confidence in men.
9 It is better to take refuge in Jahve
  Than to put confidence in princes.
10 Let all the heathen compass me about—
  In the name of Jahve will I verily cut them in pieces.
11 Let them compass me about on all sides—
  In the name of Jahve will I verily cut them in pieces.
12 Let them compass me about like bees—
  They are extinguished like a fire of thorns,
  In the name of Jahve will I verily cut them in pieces.
13 Thou gavest me indeed a thrust that I might fall,
  But Jahve hath helped me.
14 My pride and my song is Jah,
  And He became my salvation.
15 The cry of exultation and of salvation resoundeth in the tents of the righteous:
  The right hand of Jahve getteth the victory.
16 The right hand of Jahve is highly exalted,
  The right hand of Jahve getteth the victory.
17 I shall not die, nay I shall live,
  And declare the deeds of Jah.
18 Jah hath chastened me sore,
  But hath not given me over unto death.

(At the going in.)

19 Open to me the gates of righteousness,
  That I may enter into them, that I may give thanks to Jah!

(Those who receive the festal procession.)

20 This is the gate of Jahve,
  The righteous may enter there.
21 I give thanks unto Thee, for Thou hast answered me,
  And art become my salvation.
22 The stone, which the builders despised,
  Is become the corner and head stone.
23 From Jahve is this come to pass,
  It is marvellous in our eyes.
24 This is the day which Jahve hath made,
  Let us exult and rejoice at it!

25 O Jahve, save I beseech Thee,
O Jahve, grant I beseech Thee prosperity!!
26 Blessed be he who cometh in the name of Jahve,
We bless you from the house of Jahve.
27 God is Jahve and hath given us light—
Bind the festive sacrifice with cords
Even up to the horns of the altar!

(*Answer of those who have arrived.*)
28 My God art Thou, therefore will I give Thee thanks,
My Deity, I will exalt Thee.

(*All together.*)
29 Give thanks unto Jahve, for He is good,
Yea, His mercy endureth for ever.

What the close of Ps. cxvii. says of God's truth, viz. that it endureth for ever, the beginning of Ps. cxviii. says of its sister, His mercy or loving-kindness. It is the closing Psalm of the *Hallel*, which begins with Ps. cxiii., and the third *Hodu* (*vid.* on Ps. cv.). It was Luther's favourite Psalm: his beauteous *Confitemini*, which " had helped him out of troubles out of which neither emperor nor king, nor any other man on earth, could have helped him." With the exposition of this his noblest jewel, his defence and his treasure, he occupied himself in the solitude of his Patmos.

It is without any doubt a post-exilic song. Here too Hupfeld sweeps away everything into vague generality; but the history of the period after the Exile, without any necessity for our coming down to the Maccabæan period, as do De Wette and Hitzig, presents three occasions which might have given birth to it; viz. (1) The first celebration of the Feast of Tabernacles in the seventh month of the first year of the Return, when there was only a plain altar as yet erected on the holy place, Ezra iii. 1-4 (to be distinguished from a later celebration of the Feast of Tabernacles on a large scale and in exact accordance with the directions of the Law, Neh. ch. viii.). So Ewald. (2) The laying of the foundation-stone of the Temple in the second month of the second year, Ezra iii. 8 sqq. So Hengstenberg. (3) The dedication of the completed Temple in the twelfth month of the sixth year of Darius, Ezra vi. 15 sqq. So Stier. These references to cotemporary history have all three more or less in their favour. The first is favoured more especially by the fact, that at the time of the second Temple ver. 25 was the festal cry amidst which the altar of burnt-offering was solemnly compassed on the first six days of the Feast of Tabernacles once, and on the seventh day seven times. This seventh day was called the great Hosanna (*Hosanna rabba*), and not only the prayers for the Feast of Tabernacles, but even the branches of willow trees (including the myrtles) which are bound to the palm-branch (*lulab*), were called *Hosannas* (הוֹשַׁעְנוֹת, Aramaic הוֹשַׁעְנֵי).* The second historical reference is favoured by the fact, that the narrative appears to point directly to our Psalm when it says: *And the builders laid the foundation of the Temple of Jahve, and the priests were drawn up there in official robes with trumpets, and the Levites the descendants of Asaph with cymbals, to praise Jahve after the direction of David king of Israel, and they sang* בְּהַלֵּל וּבְהוֹדֹת לַיהוָה כִּי טוֹב כִּי־לְעוֹלָם חַסְדּוֹ עַל־יִשְׂרָאֵל; *and all the people raised a great shout* בְּהַלֵּל לַיהוָה, *because the house of Jahve was founded*. But both of these derivations of the Psalm are opposed by the fact that vers. 19 and 20 assume that the Temple-building is already finished; whereas the unmistakeable allusions to the events that transpired during the building of the Temple, viz. the intrigues of the Samaritans, the hostility of the neighbouring peoples, and the capriciousness of the Persian kings, favour the third. In connection with this reference of the Psalm to the post-exilic dedication of the Temple, vers. 19, 20, too, now present no difficulty. Ver. 22 is better understood as spoken in the presence of the now upreared Temple-building, than as spoken in the presence of the foundation-stone; and the words "unto the horns of the altar" in ver. 27, interpreted in many different ways, come into the light of Ezra vi. 17.

The Psalm falls into two divisions. The first division (vers. 1-19) is sung by the festive procession brought up by the priests and Levites, which is ascending to the Temple with

---

* *Vid.* my Talmudic Studies, vi. (*Der Hosianna-Ruf*), in the *Lutherische Zeitschrift*, 1855, S. 653-656.

the animals for sacrifice. With ver. 19 the procession stands at the entrance. The second part (vers. 20–27) is sung by the body of Levites who receive the festive procession. Then ver. 28 is the answer of those who have arrived, and ver. 29 the concluding song of all of them. This antiphonal arrangement is recognised even by the Talmud (*B. Pesachim* 119*a*) and Midrash. The whole Psalm, too, has moreover a peculiar formation. It resembles the *Mashal* Psalms, for each verse has of itself its completed sense, its own scent and hue; one thought is joined to another as branch to branch and flower to flower.

Vers. 1–18. The Hodu-cry is addressed first to all and every one; then the whole body of the laity of Israel and the priests, and at last (as it appears) the proselytes (*vid.* on cxv. 9–11) who fear the God of revelation, are urgently admonished to echo it back; for " yea, His mercy endureth for ever," is the required hypophon. In ver. 5, Israel too then begins as one man to praise the ever-gracious goodness of God. יָהּ, the *Jod* of which might easily become inaudible after קְרָאתִי, has an emphatic *Dagesh* as in ver. 18*a*, and הַמֵּצַר has the orthophonic stroke beside צַר (the so-called מַקֵּל), which points to the correct tone-syllable of the word that has *Dechî*.* Instead of עֲנֵנִי it is here pointed עָנָנִי, which also occurs in other instances not only with distinctive, but also (though not uniformly) with conjunctive accents.† The construction is a pregnant one (as in xxii. 22, xxviii. 1, lxxiv. 7, 2 Sam. xviii. 19, Ezra ii. 62, 2 Chron. xxxii. 1): He answered me by removing me to a free space

---

* *Vid.* Baer's *Thorath Emeth*, p. 7 note, and p. 21, end of note 1.

† Hitzig on Prov. viii. 22 considers the pointing קָנָנִי to be occasioned by *Dechi*, and in fact עֲנֵנִי in the passage before us has *Tarcha*, and in 1 Sam. xxviii. 15 *Munach;* but in the passage before us, if we read בְּמוּרחָבְיָה as one word according to the Masora, עֲנֵנִי is rather to be accented with *Mugrash;* and in 1 Sam. xxviii. 15 the reading עֲנֵנִי is found side by side with עָנָנִי (*e.g.* in *Bibl. Bomberg.* 1521). Nevertheless צְרַפְתָּנִי xvii. 3, and הַרְנִי Job xxx. 19 (according to Kimchi's *Michlol*, 30*a*), beside *Mercha*, show that the pointing beside conjunctive as beside disjunctive accents wavers between *ă* and *ā*, although *ā* is properly only justified beside disjunctive accents, and צֻוֵּנִי also really only occurs in pause.

(xviii. 20). Both lines end with יָהּ; nevertheless the reading בַּמֶּרְחַבְיָה is attested by the Masora (*vid.* Baer's *Psalterium*, pp. 132 sq.), instead of בַּמֶּרְחָב יָהּ. It has its advocates even in the Talmud (*B. Pesachim* 117*a*), and signifies a boundless extent, יָהּ expressing the highest degree of comparison, like מַאְפֵּלְיָה in Jer. ii. 31, the deepest darkness. Even the LXX. appears to have read מרחביה thus as one word (εἰς πλατυσμόν, Symmachus εἰς εὐρυχωρίαν). The Targum and Jerome, however, render it as we do; it is highly improbable that in one and the same verse the divine name should not be intended to be used in the same force of meaning. Ps. lvi. (vers. 10; 5, 12) echoes in ver. 6; and in ver. 7 Ps. liv. (ver. 6) is in the mind of the later poet. In that passage it is still more clear than in the passage before us that by the *Beth* of בְּעֹזְרַי Jahve is not meant to be designated as *unus e multis*, but as a helper who outweighs the greatest multitude of helpers. The Jewish people had experienced this helpful succour of Jahve in opposition to the persecutions of the Samaritans and the satraps during the building of the Temple; and had at the same time learned what is expressed in vers. 7, 8 (cf. cxlvi. 3), that trust in Jahve (for which חָסָה בְּ is the proper word) proves true, and trust in men, on the contrary, and especially in princes, is deceptive; for under Pseudo-Smerdis the work, begun under Cyrus, and represented as open to suspicion even in the reign of Cambyses, was interdicted. But in the reign of Darius it again became free: Jahve showed that He disposes events and the hearts of men in favour of His people, so that out of this has grown up in the minds of His people the confident expectation of a world-subduing supremacy expressed in ver. 10.

The clauses vers. 10*a*, 11*a*, and 12*a*, expressed in the perfect form, are intended more hypothetically than as describing facts. The perfect is here set out in relief as a hypothetical tense by the following future. כָּל־גּוֹיִם signifies, as in cxvii. 1, the heathen of every kind. דְּבֹרִים (in the Aramaic and Arabic with ז) are both bees and wasps, which make themselves especially troublesome in harvest time. The suffix of אֲמִילַם (from מוּל = מָלַל, to hew down, cut in pieces) is the same as in Ex. xxix. 30, ii. 17, and also beside a conjunctive accent in lxxiv. 8. Yet the reading אֲמִילֵם, like יְחִיתַן Hab. ii. 17, is here the better supported (*vid.* Gesenius, *Lehrgebäude*, S. 177), and it has been adopted by Norzi, Heidenheim, and Baer. The כִּי is that which states the ground or reason, and then becomes directly confirmatory and assuring (cxxviii. 2, 4), which here, after the "in the name of Jahve" that precedes it, is applied and placed just as in the oath in 1 Sam. xiv. 44. And in general, as Redslob has demonstrated, כִּי has not originally a relative, but a positive (determining) signification, כ being just as much a demonstrative sound as ד, ז, שׁ, and ה (cf. ἐκεῖ, ἐκεῖνος, κεῖνος, *ecce*, *hic*, *illic*, with the Doric τηνεί, τῆνος). The notion of compassing round about is heightened in ver. 11a by the juxtaposition of two forms of the same verb (Ges. § 67, rem. 10), as in Hos. iv. 18, Hab. i. 5, Zeph. ii. 1, and frequently. The figure of the bees is taken from Deut. i. 44. The perfect דֹּעֲכוּ (cf. Isa. xliii. 17) describes their destruction, which takes place instantly and unexpectedly. The *Pual* points to the punishing power that comes upon them: they are extinguished (*exstinguuntur*) like a fire of thorns, the crackling flame of which expires as quickly as it has blazed up (lviii. 10). In ver. 13 the language of Israel is addressed to the hostile worldly power, as the antithesis shows. It thrust, yea thrust (*inf. intens.*) Israel, that it might fall (לִנְפֹּל; with reference to the pointing, *vid.* on xl. 15); but Jahve's help would not suffer it to come to that pass. Therefore the song at the Red Sea is revived in the heart and mouth of Israel. Ver. 14 (like Isa. xii. 2) is taken from Ex. xv. 2. עָזִּי (in MSS. also written עֻזִּי) is a collateral form of עֹז (Ew. § 255, *a*), and here signifies the lofty self-consciousness which is united with the possession of power: pride and its expression an exclamation of joy. Concerning זִמְרָת *vid.* on xvi. 6. As at that time, the cry of exultation and of salvation (*i.e.* of deliverance and of victory) is in the tabernacles of the righteous: the right hand of Jahve—they sing עֹשָׂה חָיִל (Num. xxiv. 18), practises valour, proves itself energetic, gains (maintains) the victory. רוֹמֵמָה is *Milra*, and therefore an adjective: *victoriosa* (Ew. § 120, *d*), from רָמַם = רוּם like שׁוֹמֵם from שָׁמֵם. It is not the *part. Pil.* (cf. Hos. xi. 7), since the rejection of the participial *Mem* occurs in connection with *Poal* and *Pual*, but not elsewhere with *Pilel* (רוֹמֵם = מְרוֹמֵם from רוּם). The word yields a simpler sense, too, as *adject. participiale Kal*; *romēmā'h* is only the fuller form for *ramā'h*,

Ex. xiv. 8 (cf. *rā'mah*, Isa. xxvi. 11). It is not its own strength that avails for Israel's exultation of victory, but the energy of the right hand of Jahve. Being come to the brink of the abyss, Israel is become anew sure of its immortality through Him. God has, it is true, most severely chastened it (יִסְּרַנִּי with the suffix *anni* as in Gen. xxx. 6, and יָהּ with the emphatic *Dagesh*, which neither reduplicates nor connects, cf. ver. 5, xciv. 12), but still with moderation (Isa. xxvii. 7 sq.). He has not suffered Israel to fall a prey to death, but reserved it for its high vocation, that it may see the mighty deeds of God and proclaim them to all the world. Amidst such celebration of Jahve the festive procession of the dedication of the Temple has arrived at the enclosure wall of the Temple.

Vers. 19-29. The gates of the Temple are called gates of righteousness because they are the entrance to the place of the mutual intercourse between God and His church in accordance with the order of salvation. First the "gates" are spoken of, and then the one "gate," the principal entrance. Those entering in must be "righteous ones;" only conformity with the divine loving will gives the right to enter. With reference to the formation of the conclusion ver. 19*b*, *vid.* Ew. § 347, *b*. In the Temple-building Israel has before it a reflection of that which, being freed from the punishment it had had to endure, it is become through the mercy of its God. With the exultation of the multitude over the happy beginning of the rebuilding there was mingled, at the laying of the foundation-stone, the loud weeping of many of the grey-headed priests, Levites, and heads of the tribes who had also seen the first Temple (Ezra iii. 12 sq.). It was the troublous character of the present which made them thus sad in spirit; the consideration of the depressing circumstances of the time, the incongruity of which weighed so heavily upon their soul in connection with the remembrance of the former Temple, that memorably glorious monument of the royal power of David and Solomon.* And even further on there towered aloft before Zerubbabel, the leader of the building, a great mountain; gigantic difficulties and hindrances arose between the powerlessness of the present

---

* Kurtz, in combating our interpretation, reduces the number of the weeping ones to "some few," but the narrative says the very opposite.

position of Zerubbabel and the completion of the building of the Temple, which had it is true been begun, but was impeded. This mountain God has made into a plain, and qualified Zerubbabel to bring forth the top and key-stone (הָאֶבֶן הָרֹאשָׁה) out of its past concealment, and thus to complete the building, which is now consecrated amidst a loud outburst of incessant shouts of joy (Zech. iv. 7). Ver. 22 points back to that disheartened disdain of the small troublous beginning, which was at work among the builders (Ezra iii. 10) at the laying of the foundation-stone, and then further at the interruption of the building. That rejected (disdained) corner-stone is nevertheless become רֹאשׁ פִּנָּה, *i.e.* the head-stone of the corner (Job xxxviii. 6), which being laid upon the corner, supports and protects the stately edifice—an emblem of the power and dignity to which Israel has attained in the midst of the peoples out of deep humiliation.

In connection with this only indirect reference of the assertion to Israel we avoid the question,—perplexing in connection with the direct reference to the people despised by the heathen,—how can the heathen be called "the builders?" Kurtz answers: "For the building which the heathen world considers it to be its life's mission and its mission in history to rear, viz. the Babel-tower of worldly power and worldly glory, they have neither been able nor willing to make use of Israel . . ." But this conjunction of ideas is devoid of scriptural support and without historical reality; for the empire of the world has set just as much value, according to political relations, upon the incorporation of Israel as upon that of every other people. Further, if what is meant is Israel's own despising of the small beginning of a new era that is dawning, it is then better explained as in connection with the reference of the declaration to Jesus the Christ in Matt. xxi. 42–44, Mark xii. 10 sq., Acts iv. 11 (ὑφ' ὑμῶν τῶν οἰκοδομούντων), 1 Pet. ii. 7, the builders are the chiefs and members of Israel itself, and not the heathen. From 1 Pet. ii. 6, Rom. ix. 33, we see how this reference to Christ is brought about, viz. by means of Isa. xxviii. 16, where Jahve says: *Behold I am He who hath laid in Zion a stone, a stone of trial, a precious corner-stone of well-founded founding—whoever believeth shall not totter.* In the light of this Messianic prophecy of Isaiah ver. 22 of our Psalm also comes to have a Messianic meaning, which is warranted by the fact, that the history of Israel is recapitulated and culminates in the history of Christ; or, according to John ii. 19-21 (cf. Zech. vi. 12 sq.), still more accurately by the fact, that He who in His state of humiliation is the despised and rejected One is become in His state of glorification the eternal glorious Temple in which dwelleth all the fulness of the Godhead bodily, and is united with humanity which has been once for all atoned for. In the joy of the church at the Temple of the body of Christ which arose after the three days of burial, the joy which is here typically expressed in the words: "From with Jahve, i.e. by the might which dwells with Him, is this come to pass, wonderful is it become (has it been carried out) in our eyes," therefore received its fulfilment. It is not נִפְלָאת but נִפְלָאת, like הָבֵאת in Gen. xxxiii. 11, קָרָאת from קָרָא = קָרָה in Deut. xxxi. 29, Jer. xliv. 23, קָרָאת from קָרָא, to call, Isa. vii. 14. We can hear Isa. xxv. 9 sounding through this passage, as above in vers. 19 sq., Isa. xxvi. 1 sq. The God of Israel has given this turn, so full of glory for His people, to the history.* He is able now to plead for more distant salvation and prosperity with all the more fervent confidence. אָנָּא (six times אָנָּה) is, as in every other instance (vid. on cxvi. 4), Milra. הוֹשִׁיעָה is accented regularly on the penult., and draws the following נָא towards itself by means of Dag. forte conj.; הַצְלִיחָה on the other hand is Milra according to the Masora and other ancient testimonies, and נָא is not dageshed, without Norzi being able to state any reason for this different accentuation. After this watchword of prayer of the thanksgiving feast, in ver. 26 those who receive them bless those who are coming (הַבָּא with Dechî) in the name of Jahve, i.e. bid them welcome in His name. The expression "from the house of Jahve," like "from the fountain of Israel" in lxviii. 27, is equivalent to, ye who belong to His house and to the church congregated around it. In the mouth of the people welcoming Jesus as the Messiah, 'Ωσαννά was a "God save the king" (vid. on xx. 10); they scattered palm branches at the same time, like the lulabs at the joyous cry of the Feast of Tabernacles, and saluted Him

---

* The verse, " This is the day which the Lord hath made," etc., was, according to Chrysostom, an ancient hypophon of the church. It has a glorious history.

with the cry, " Blessed is He who cometh in the name of the Lord," as being the longed-for guest of the Feast (Matt. xxi. 9). According to the Midrash, in ver. 26 it is the people of Jerusalem who thus greet the pilgrims. In the original sense of the Psalm, however, it is the body of Levites and priests above on the Temple-hill who thus receive the congregation that has come up. The many animals for sacrifice which they brought with them are enumerated in Ezra vi. 17. On the ground of the fact that Jahve has proved Himself to be אל, the absolutely mighty One, by having granted light to His people, viz. lovingkindness, liberty, and joy, there then issues forth the ejaculation, " Bind the sacrifice," etc. The LXX. renders συστήσασθε ἑορτὴν ἐν τοῖς πυκάζουσιν, which is reproduced by the *Psalterium Romanum: constituite diem solemnem in confrequentationibus*, as Eusebius, Theodoret, and Chrysostom (although the last waveringly) also interpret it; on the other hand, it is rendered by the *Psalterium Gallicum: in condensis*, as Apollinaris and Jerome (*in frondosis*) also understand it. But much as Luther's version, which follows the latter interpretation, " Adorn the feast with green branches even to the horns of the altar," accords with our German taste, it is still untenable; for אסר cannot signify to encircle with garlands and the like, nor would it be altogether suited to חג in this signification.* Thus then in this instance A. Lobwasser renders it comparatively more correctly, although devoid of taste: " The Lord is great and mighty of strength who lighteneth us all; *fasten your bullocks to the horns beside the altar*." To the horns?! So even Hitzig and others render it. But such a " binding to" is unheard of. And can אסר עד possibly signify to bind on to anything? And what would be the object of binding them to the horns of the altar? In order that they might not run away?! Hengstenberg and von Lengerke at least disconnect the words " unto the horns of the altar" from any relation to this precautionary measure, by interpreting: until it (the animal for the festal

---

* Symmachus has felt this, for instead of συστήσασθε ἑορτὴν ἐν τοῖς πυκάζουσιν (*in condensis*) of the LXX., he renders it, transposing the notions, συνδήσατε ἐν πανηγύρει πυκάσματα. Chrysostom interprets this: στέψανώματα καὶ κλάδους ἀνάψατε τῷ ναῷ, for Montfaucon, who regards this as the version of the *Sexta*, is in error.

sacrifice) is raised upon the horns of the altar and sacrificed. But how much is then imputed to these words! No indeed, חג denotes the animals for the feast-offering, and there was so vast a number of these (according to Ezra loc. cit. seven hundred and twelve) that the whole space of the court of the priests was full of them, and the binding of them consequently had to go on as far as to the horns of the altar. Ainsworth (1627) correctly renders: "unto the hornes, that is, all the Court over, untill you come even to the hornes of the altar, intending hereby many sacrifices or boughs." The meaning of the call is therefore: Bring your hecatombs and make them ready for sacrifice.* The words "unto (as far as) the horns of the altar" have the principal accent. In ver. 28 (cf. Ex. xv. 2) the festal procession replies in accordance with the character of the feast, and then the Psalm closes, in correspondence with its beginning, with a *Hodu* in which all voices join.

PSALM CXIX.

A TWENTY-TWO-FOLD STRING OF APHORISMS BY ONE WHO IS PERSECUTED FOR THE SAKE OF HIS FAITH.

Aleph.

1 BLESSED are those whose ways are blameless,
   Who walk in the law of Jahve!
2 Blessed are those who keep His testimonies,
   Who seek Him with the whole heart,
3 They also do no unrighteousness—
   They walk in His ways.
4 THOU hast enjoined Thy precepts
   To keep them diligently.
5 Oh that my ways were directed
   To keep Thy statutes!
6 Then shall I not be ashamed,
   When I have respect unto all Thy commandments.

---

* In the language of the Jewish ritual *Isru-chag* is become the name of the after-feast day which follows the last day of the feast. Ps. cxviii. is the customary Psalm for the *Isru-chag* of all מועדים.

7 I will give thanks to Thee with an upright heart,
  When I learn the judgments of Thy righteousness.
8 I will keep Thy statutes:
  Forsake me not utterly.

Beth.

9 Wherewithal shall a young man keep his way pure?
  If he taketh heed according to Thy word.
10 With the whole heart have I sought Thee:
   Let me not wander from Thy commandments.
11 In my heart do I treasure up Thy word,
   That I may not sin against Thee.
12 Blessed art Thou, Jahve,
   Teach me Thy statutes.
13 With my lips do I recount
   All the judgments of Thy mouth.
14 In the way of Thy testimonies do I rejoice,
   As in all manner of possession.
15 I will meditate in Thy precepts,
   And have respect unto Thy paths.
16 In Thy statutes do I delight myself,
   I will not forget Thy word.

Gimel.

17 Deal bountifully with Thy servant, that I may live,
   So will I keep Thy word.
18 Open Thou mine eyes, that I may behold
   Wondrous things out of Thy law.
19 I am a stranger in the earth:
   Hide not Thy commandments from me
20 My soul is crushed with longing
   After Thy judgments at all times.
21 Thou hast rebuked the proud;
   Cursed are those who do err from Thy commandments.
22 Remove from me reproach and contempt;
   For I keep Thy testimonies.
23 Though princes sit and deliberate against me,
   Thy servant doth meditate in Thy statutes.
24 Nevertheless Thy testimonies are my delight,
   The men of my counsel.

Daleth.

25 My soul cleaveth unto the dust:
 Quicken Thou me according to Thy word.
26 I declared my ways, and Thou heardest me:
 Teach me Thy statutes.
27 Make me to understand the way of Thy precepts:
 So will I meditate on Thy wondrous works.
28 My soul melteth for heaviness:
 Strengthen Thou me according to Thy word.
29 Remove from me the way of lying,
 And with Thy law be gracious unto me.
30 The way of truth I have chosen:
 Thy judgments have I set before me.
31 I have given myself up to Thy testimonies:
 Jahve, put me not to shame.
32 I run the way of Thy commandments,
 For Thou dost enlarge my heart.

He.

33 Teach me, Jahve, the way of Thy statutes,
 That I may keep it unto the end.
34 Give me understanding, that I may keep Thy instruction,
 And observe it with the whole heart.
35 Make me to walk in the path of Thy commandments;
 For therein do I delight.
36 Incline my heart unto Thy testimonies,
 And not to covetousness.
37 Turn away mine eyes from beholding vanity;
 In Thy way quicken Thou me.
38 Stablish Thy word unto Thy servant,
 As that which makes them fear Thee.
39 Take away my reproach which I fear;
 For Thy judgments are good.
40 Behold, I long after Thy precepts:
 Quicken me in Thy righteousness.

Vav.

41 And let Thy mercies come unto me, Jahve,
 Thy salvation, according to Thy word,

42 And I will answer him who reproacheth me;
  For I trust in Thy word.
43 And take not the word of truth utterly out of my mouth;
  For I hope in Thy judgments.
44 And I will keep Thy law continually,
  For ever and ever,
45 And I will walk at liberty;
  For I seek Thy precepts.
46 And I will speak of Thy testimonies before kings,
  And will not be ashamed.
47 And I will delight myself in Thy commandments,
  Which I love.
48 And my hands will I lift up unto Thy commandments [which I love],
  And I will meditate in Thy statutes.

Zajin.

49 Remember the word unto Thy servant,
  Because Thou hast caused me to hope.
50 This is my comfort in my affliction,
  That Thy word hath quickened me.
51 The proud have had me greatly in derision—
  I have not declined from Thy law.
52 I remembered Thy judgments of old, Jahve,
  And comforted myself.
53 Indignation hath taken hold upon me because of the wicked,
  Who forsake Thy law.
54 Thy statutes are my songs
  In the house of my pilgrimage.
55 I have remembered Thy name, Jahve, in the night,
  And I have kept Thy law.
56 This is appointed to me,
  That I should keep Thy precepts.

Heth.

57 Thou art my portion, Jahve:
  I have said that I would keep Thy words.
58 I entreated Thee with the whole heart:
  Be merciful unto me according to Thy word.

59 I thought on my ways,
   And turned my feet unto Thy testimonies.
60 I make haste, and delay not
   To keep Thy commandments.
61 The cords of the wicked are round about me—
   I do not forget Thy law.
62 At midnight I will rise to give thanks unto Thee
   Because of the judgments of Thy righteousness.
63 I am a companion of all those who fear Thee,
   And of those who keep Thy precepts.
64 The earth, Jahve, is full of Thy mercy:
   Teach me Thy statutes.

Teth.

65 Thou hast dealt well with Thy servant,
   Jahve, according unto Thy word.
66 Teach me good judgment and knowledge,
   For I believe in Thy commandments.
67 Before I was afflicted I went astray,
   And now I keep Thy word.
68 Thou art good, and doest good;
   Teach me Thy statutes.
69 The proud have forged a lie against me—
   I will keep Thy precepts with the whole heart.
70 Their heart is as fat as grease—
   I delight in Thy law.
71 It was good for me that I was afflicted,
   That I might learn Thy statutes.
72 The law of Thy mouth is better unto me
   Than thousands of gold and silver.

Jod.

73 Thy hands have made me and fashioned me:
   Give me understanding, that I may learn Thy command- [ments.
74 Let those who fear Thee be glad when they see me;
   For I hope in Thy word.
75 I know, Jahve, that righteousness are Thy judgments,
   And that Thou in faithfulness hast afflicted me.
76 Let Thy merciful kindness be for my comfort,
   According to Thy promise unto Thy servant.

77 Let Thy tender mercies come unto me, that I may live;
For Thy law is my delight.
78 Let the proud be ashamed that they dealt falsely with me—
But I meditate on Thy precepts.
79 Let those who fear Thee turn unto me,
And those who know Thy testimonies.
80 Let my heart be sound in Thy statutes,
That I be not ashamed.

Kaph.

81 My soul fainteth for Thy salvation:
I hope in Thy word.
82 Mine eyes fail with longing for Thy word,
Saying, When wilt Thou comfort me?—
83 Verily, though I am become like a bottle in the smoke,
Do I not forget Thy statutes.
84 Short indeed are the days of Thy servant,
When wilt Thou execute judgment on those who persecute
85 The proud have digged pits for me,   [me?
They who are not after Thy law.
86 All Thy commandments are faithful:
They persecute me wrongfully; help Thou me!
87 They had almost consumed me in the land;
Yet do I not forsake Thy precepts.
88 Quicken me after Thy loving-kindness,
So will I keep the testimony of Thy mouth.

Lamed.

89 For ever, Jahve,
Thy word is settled in heaven.
90 Thy faithfulness is unto all generations:
Thou hast established the earth, and it abideth.
91 They continue this day according to Thy judgments;
For all beings are Thy servants.
92 Unless Thy law had been my delight,
I should then have perished in mine affliction.
93 I will never forget Thy precepts;
For with them Thou hast quickened me.
94 I am Thine, save me;
For I seek Thy precepts.

95 If the wicked lie in wait for me to destroy me—
I consider Thy testimonies.
96 To all perfection, as I have seen, there is an end,
Yet Thy commandment is without any limits.

Mem.

97 O how love I Thy law!
It is my meditation all the day.
98 Thy commandments make me wiser than mine enemies;
For they are ever my portion.
99 I have more understanding than all my teachers;
For Thy testimonies are my meditation.
100 I understand more than aged men;
For I keep Thy precepts.
101 I refrain my feet from every evil way,
That I may keep Thy word.
102 I have not departed from Thy judgments;
For Thou hast taught me.
103 How sweet are Thy words unto my taste,
Sweeter than honey to my mouth!
104 From Thy precepts I get understanding:
Therefore I hate every false way.

Nun.

105 Thy word is a lamp unto my feet,
And a light unto my path.
106 I have sworn, and I will perform it,
That I will keep Thy righteous judgments.
107 I am afflicted very much—
Quicken me, Jahve, according unto Thy word!
108 Accept the freewill offerings of my mouth, Jahve,
And teach me Thy judgments.
109 My soul is continually in my hand:
Yet do I not forget Thy law.
110 The wicked have laid a snare for me:
Yet do I not err from Thy precepts.
111 Thy testimonies have I taken as a heritage for ever;
For they are the rejoicing of my heart.
112 I have inclined mine heart to perform Thy statutes
For ever, even unto the end.

Samech.

113 I hate the double-minded,
And Thy law do I love.
114 My hiding-place and my shield art Thou:
I hope in Thy word.
115 Depart from me, ye evil-doers—
I will keep the commandments of my God.
116 Uphold me according unto Thy word, and I shall live,
And let me not be ashamed of my hope.
117 Hold Thou me up, and I shall be safe,
And I will have respect unto Thy statutes continually.
118 Thou hast trodden down all them that err from Thy
For their intrigue is falsehood.   [statutes;
119 Thou puttest away all the wicked of the earth like dross:
Therefore I love Thy testimonies.
120 My flesh is rigid for terror of Thee,
And I am afraid of Thy judgments.

Ajin.

121 I have done judgment and righteousness:
Thou wilt not leave me to mine oppressors.
122 Be surety for Thy servant for good:
Let not the proud oppress me.
123 Mine eyes fail for Thy salvation,
And for the word of Thy righteousness.
124 Deal with Thy servant according unto Thy mercy,
And teach me Thy statutes.
125 Thy servant am I, give me understanding,
That I may know Thy testimonies.
126 It is time to interpose for Jahve:
They have made void Thy law.
127 Therefore I love Thy commandments
More than gold, and than fine gold.
128 Therefore I esteem all precepts concerning all things to
I hate every false way.   [be right;

Phe (Pe).

129 Wonderful are Thy testimonies:
Therefore doth my soul keep them.

130 The unfolding of Thy words giveth light;
    Giving understanding unto the simple.
131 I opened my mouth, and panted;
    For I long for Thy commandments.
132 Look Thou upon me, and be merciful unto me,
    As is right towards those who love Thy name.
133 Establish my steps by Thy word,
    And let not any iniquity have dominion over me.
134 Deliver me from the oppression of man,
    And I will keep Thy precepts.
135 Make Thy face to shine upon Thy servant,
    And teach me Thy statutes.
136 Mine eyes run down rivers of waters,
    Because they keep not Thy law.

Tsade.

137 Righteous art Thou, Jahve,
    And upright are Thy judgments.
138 Thou hast commanded Thy testimonies in righteousness,
    And in very faithfulness.
139 My zeal consumeth me,
    For mine adversaries have forgotten Thy words.
140 Thy word is very pure,
    And Thy servant loveth it.
141 I am young and despised:
    Yet do not I forget Thy precepts.
142 Thy righteousness is that which is right for ever,
    And Thy law truth.
143 Trouble and anguish have taken hold on me:
    Yet thy commandments are my delight.
144 Thy testimonies are that which is right for ever:
    Give me understanding that I may live.

Koph.

145 I call with the whole heart—answer me;
    Jahve, Thy statutes will I keep!
146 When I cry unto Thee, save me,
    And I will keep Thy testimonies!
147 Early, even before the dawning of the morning, did I [make supplication:
    I hoped in Thy word.

148 Mine eyes anticipate the night-watches,
    To meditate on Thy word.
149 Hear my voice according unto Thy loving-kindness;
    Jahve, quicken me according to Thy judgments.
150 They draw nigh who follow after mischief,
    Who are far from Thy law:
151 Thou comest all the nearer, O Jahve,
    And all Thy commandments are truth.
152 From Thy testimonies I have known for a long time
    That Thou hast founded them for ever.

Resh.

153 Look upon mine affliction, and deliver me;
    For I do not forget Thy law.
154 Plead my cause and deliver me,
    Quicken me according to Thy word.
155 Salvation is far from the wicked,
    For they seek not Thy statutes.
156 Abundant are Thy tender mercies, Jahve;
    Quicken me according to Thy judgments.
157 Many are my persecutors and mine oppressors;
    I decline not from Thy testimonies.
158 I beheld the transgressors, and was grieved,
    Because they kept not Thy word.
159 Consider that I love Thy precepts:
    Quicken me, Jahve, according to Thy loving-kindness.
160 The sum of Thy word is truth,   [for ever.
    And every one of the judgments of Thy righteousness is

Sin, Shin.

161 Princes have persecuted me without a cause,
    But my heart standeth in awe of Thy words.
162 I rejoice over Thy word,
    As one that findeth great spoil.
163 Pretended faith I hate, and I abhor it:
    Thy law do I love.
164 Seven times a day do I praise Thee
    Because of the judgments of Thy righteousness.
165 Great peace have they who love Thy law,
    And nothing causeth them to stumble.

166 Jahve, I hope for Thy salvation,
   And do Thy commandments.
167 My soul keepeth Thy testimonies,
   And I love them exceedingly.
168 I keep Thy precepts and Thy testimonies,
   For all my ways are before Thee.

Thav (Tav).

169 Let my cry come up before Thee, Jahve;
   Give me understanding according to Thy word.
170 Let my supplication come up before Thee,
   Deliver me according to Thy promise.
171 My lips shall utter praise,
   That Thou dost teach me Thy statutes.
172 My tongue doth speak of Thy word,
   For all Thy commandments are righteousness.
173 Let Thy hand be a help unto me,
   For I have chosen Thy precepts.
174 I have longed for Thy salvation, Jahve,
   And Thy law is my delight.
175 Let my soul live and praise Thee,
   And let Thy judgments help me.
176 If I should go astray—as a lost sheep seek Thy servant,
   For I do not forget Thy commandments.

To the *Hodu* Ps. cxviii., written in gnome-like, wreathed style, is appended the throughout gnomico-didactic Ps. cxix., consisting of one hundred and seventy-six Masoretic verses, or regarded in relation to the strophe, distichs, which according to the twenty-two letters of the alphabet fall into twenty-two groups (called by the old expositors the ὀγδοάδες or *octonarii* of this *Psalmus literatus s. alphabetites*); for each group contains eight verses (distichs), each of which begins with the same consecutive letter (8 × 22 = 176). The Latin Psalters (as the *Psalterium Veronense*, and originally perhaps all the old Greek Psalters) have the name of the letter before each group; the Syriac has the signs of the letters; and in the Complutensian Bible, as also elsewhere, a new line begins with each group. The Talmud, *B. Berachoth*, says of this Psalm: "it consists of eight *Alephs*," etc.; the Masora styles it אלפא ביתא רבא; the Midrash on it is called מדרש אלפא ביתא, and the Pesikta פסיקתא דתמניא אפי. In our German version it has the appropriate inscription, "The Christian's golden A B C of the praise, love, power, and use of the word of God;" for here we have set forth in inexhaustible fulness what the word of God is to a man, and how a man is to behave himself in relation to it. The Masora observes that the Psalm contains only the one verse 122, in which some reference or other to the word of revelation is not found as in all the 175 others*—a many-linked chain of synonyms which runs through the whole Psalm. In connection with this ingenious arrangement, so artfully devised and carried out, it may also not be merely accidental that the address *Jahve* occurs twenty-two times, as Bengel has observed : *bis et vicesies pro numero octonariorum.*

All kinds of erroneous views have, however, been put forth concerning this Psalm. Köster, von Gerlach, Hengstenberg, and Hupfeld renounce all attempts to show that there is any accordance whatever with a set plan, and find here a series of maxims without any internal progression and connection. Ewald begins at once with the error, that we have before us the long prayer of an old experienced teacher. But from vers. 9 sq. it is clear that the poet himself is a " young man," a fact that is also corroborated by vers. 99 and 100. The poet is a young man, who finds himself in a situation which is clearly described: he is derided, oppressed, persecuted, and that by those who despise the divine word (for apostasy encompasses him round about), and more particularly by a government hostile to the true religion, vers. 23, 46, 161. He is lying in bonds (ver. 61, cf. 83), expecting death (ver. 109), and recognises in his affliction, it is true, God's salutary humbling, and in the midst of it God's word is his comfort and his wisdom, but he also yearns for help, and earnestly prays for it.—The whole Psalm is a prayer for stedfastness in the midst of an ungodly, degenerate race, and in the midst of great trouble, which is heightened by the

---

* " In every verse," this is the observation of the Masora on ver. 122, " ver. 122 only excepted, we find one of the ten (pointing to the ten fundamental words or decalogue of the Sinaitic Law) expressions: *word, saying, testimonies, way, judgment, precept, commandment* (צוה), *law, statute, truth*" (according to another reading, *righteousness*).

pain he feels at the prevailing apostasy, and a prayer for ultimate deliverance which rises in group *Kaph* to an urgent *how long!* If this sharply-defined physiognomy of the Psalm is recognised, then the internal progression will not fail to be discerned.

After the poet has praised fidelity to the word of God (*Aleph*), and described it as the virtue of all virtues which is of service to the young man and to which he devotes himself (*Beth*), he prays, in the midst of the scoffing and persecuting persons that surround him, for the grace of enlightenment (*Gimel*), of strengthening (*Daleth*), of preservation (*He*), of suitable and joyful confession (*Vav*); God's word is all his thought and pursuit (*Zajin*), he cleaves to those who fear God (*Heth*), and recognises the salutary element of His humbling (*Teth*), but is in need of comfort (*Jod*) and sighs: how long! (*Kaph*.) Without the eternal, sure, mighty word of God he would despair (*Lamed*); this is his wisdom in difficult circumstances (*Mem*); he has sworn fidelity to it, and maintains his fidelity as being one who is persecuted (*Nun*), and abhors and despises the apostates (*Samech*). He is oppressed, but God will not suffer him to be crushed (*Ajin*); He will not suffer the doings of the ungodly, which wring from him floods of tears, to prevail over him (*Phe*)—over him, the small (still youthful) and despised one whom zeal concerning the prevailing godlessness is consuming away (*Tsade*). Oh that God would hear his crying by day and by night (*Koph*), would revive him speedily with His helpful pity (*Resh*)—him, viz., who being persecuted by princes clings fast to Him (*Shin*), and would seek him the isolated and so sorely imperilled sheep! (*Tav*.) This outline does not exhaust the fundamental thoughts of the separate ogdoades, and they might surely be still more aptly reproduced, but this is sufficient to show that the Psalm is not wanting in coherence and progressive movement, and that it is not an ideal situation and mood, but a situation and mood based upon public relationships, from which this manifold celebration of the divine word, as a fruit of its teaching, has sprung.

It is natural to suppose that the composition of the Psalm falls in those times of the Greek domination in which the government was hostile, and a large party from among the Jews themselves, that was friendly towards the government, persecuted all decided confessors of the Tôra. Hitzig says, "It can be safely maintained that the Psalm was written in the Maccabæan age by a renowned Israelite who was in imprisonment under Gentile authorities." It is at least probable that the plaited work of so long a Psalm, which, in connection with all that is artificial about it, from beginning to end gives us a glimpse of the subdued afflicted mien of a confessor, is the work of one in prison, who whiled away his time with this plaiting together of his complaints and his consolatory thoughts.

Vers. 1–8. The eightfold *Aleph*. Blessed are those who act according to the word of God; the poet wishes to be one of these. The alphabetical Psalm on the largest scale begins appropriately, not merely with a simple (cxii. 1), but with a twofold *ashrê*. It refers principally to those *integri viæ* (*vitæ*). In ver. 3 the description of those who are accounted blessed is carried further. Perfects, as denoting that which is habitual, alternate with futures used as presents. In ver. 4 לִשְׁמֹר expresses the purpose of the enjoining, as in ver. 5 the goal of the directing. אַחֲלַי (whence אַחֲלֵי, 2 Kings v. 3) is compounded of אָח (*vid. supra*, i. 428) and לְ (לִי), and consequently signifies *o si*. On יִכֹּנוּ cf. Prov. iv. 26 (LXX. κατευθυνθείησαν). The retrospective אָז is expanded anew in ver. 6*b*: then, when I namely. "Judgments of Thy righteousness" are the decisions concerning right and wrong which give expression to and put in execution the righteousness of God.* בְּלָמְדִי refers to Scripture in comparison with history.

Vers. 9–16. The eightfold *Beth*. Acting in accordance with the word of God, a young man walks blamelessly; the poet desires this, and supplicates God's gracious assistance in order to it. To purify or cleanse one's way or walk (זָכָה, cf. lxxiii. 13, Prov. xx. 9) signifies to maintain it pure (זַךְ, root זך,

---

* The word "judgments" of our English authorized version is retained in the text as being the most convenient word; it must, however, be borne in mind that in this Psalm it belongs to the "chain of synonyms," and does not mean God's acts of judgment, its more usual meaning in the Old Testament Scriptures, but is used as defined above, and is the equivalent here of the German *Rechte*, not *Gerichte*.—TR.

لَجَّ, to prick, to strike the eye, *nitere;* * *vid.* Fleischer in Levy's *Chaldäisches Wörterbuch,* i. 424) from the spotting of sin, or to free it from it. Ver. 9*b* is the answer to the question in ver. 9*a*; לִשְׁמֹר signifies *custodiendo semetipsum,* for שָׁמַר can also signify " to be on one's guard" without נַפְשׁוֹ (Josh. vi. 18). The old classic (*e.g.* xviii. 31) אִמְרָתֶךָ alternates throughout with דְּבָרְךָ; both are intended collectively. One is said to hide (צָפַן) the word in one's heart when one has it continually present with him, not merely as an outward precept, but as an inward motive power in opposition to selfish action (Job xxiii. 12). In ver. 12 the poet makes his way through adoration to petition. סִפַּרְתִּי in ver. 13 does not mean enumeration, but recounting, as in Deut. vi. 7. עֵדוֹת is the plural to עֵדוּת; עֵדוֹת, on the contrary, in ver. 138 is the plural to עֵדָה: both are used of God's attestation of Himself and of His will in the word of revelation. כְּעַל signifies, according to ver. 162, " as over " (short for בַּאֲשֶׁר עַל), not: as it were more than (Olshausen); the כְּ would only be troublesome in connection with this interpretation. With reference to הוֹן, which has occurred already in xliv. 13, cxii. 3 (from הִן, هون, to be light, *levem*), *aisance,* ease, opulence, and concrete, goods, property, *vid.* Fleischer in Levy's *Chald. Wörterb.* i. 423 sq. אׇרְחֹתֶיךָ, ver. 15, are the paths traced out in the word of God; these he will studiously keep in his eye.

Vers. 17-24. The eightfold *Gimel.* This is his life's aim: he will do it under fear of the curse of apostasy; he will do it also though he suffer persecution on account of it. In ver. 17 the expression is only אֶחְיֶה as cxviii. 19, not וְאֶחְיֶה as in vers. 77, 116, 144: the *apodosis imper.* only begins with וְאֶשְׁמְרָה, whereas אֶחְיֶה is the good itself for the bestowment of which the poet prays. גַּל in ver. 18*a* is *imper. apoc. Piel* for גַּלֵּה, like נַס in Dan. i. 12. נִפְלָאוֹת is the expression for everything supernatural and mysterious which is incomprehensible to the ordinary understanding and is left to the perception of faith. The Tôra beneath the surface of its letter contains an abundance of such " wondrous things," into which only eyes from which

---

* The word receives the meaning of νικᾶν (*vid. supra,* ii. 136), like بلج and شع, from the signification of outshining = overpowering.

God has removed the covering of natural short-sightedness penetrate; hence the prayer in ver. 18. Upon earth we have no abiding resting-place, we sojourn here as in a strange land (ver. 19, xxxix. 13, 1 Chron. xxix. 15). Hence the poet prays in ver. 19 that God would keep His commandments, these rules of conduct for the journey of life, in living consciousness for him. Towards this, according to ver. 20, his longing tends. גָּרַס (*Hiph.* in Lam. iii. 16) signifies to crush in pieces, جرش, and here, like the Aramaic גְּרַס, גְּרַם, to be crushed, broken in pieces. לְתַאֲבָה (from תָּאַב, vers. 40, 174, a secondary form of אָבָה) states the bias of mind in or at which the soul feels itself thus overpowered even to being crushed: it is crushing from longing after God's judgments, viz. after a more and more thorough knowledge of them. In ver. 21 the LXX. has probably caught the meaning of the poet better than the pointing has done, inasmuch as it draws ἐπικατάρατοι to ver. 21*b*, so that ver. 21*a* consists of two words, just like vers. 59*a*, 89*a*; and Kamphausen also follows this in his rendering. For אֲרוּרִים as an attribute is unpoetical, and as an accusative of the predicate far-fetched; whereas it comes in naturally as a predicate before הַשֵּׁגִים מִמִּצְוֺתֶיךָ: cursed (אָרַר = جر, *detestari*), viz. by God. Instead of גַּל, "roll" (from גָּלַל, Josh. v. 9), it is pointed in ver. 22 (מֵעַל) גַּל, "uncover" = גַּלֵּה, as in ver. 18, reproach being conceived of as a covering or veil (as *e.g.* in lxix. 8), cf. Isa. xxii. 8 (perhaps also Lam. ii. 14, iv. 22, if גִּלָּה עַל there signifies "to remove the covering upon anything"). גַּם in ver. 23*a*, as in Jer. xxxvi. 25, has the sense of גַּם־כִּי, *etiamsi*; and גַּם in ver 24*a* the sense of nevertheless, ὅμως, Ew. § 354, *a*. On נִדְבָּר בְּ (reciprocal), cf. Ezek. xxxiii. 30. As in a criminal tribunal, princes sit and deliberate how they may be able to render him harmless.

Vers. 25–32. The eightfold *Daleth*. He is in deep trouble, and prays for consolation and strengthening by means of God's word, to which he resigns himself. His soul is fixed to the dust (xliv. 26) in connection with such non-recognition and proscription, and is incapable of raising itself. In ver. 25*b* he implores new strength and spirits (חָיָה as in lxxi. 20, lxxxv. 7) from God, in conformity with and by reason of His word. He has rehearsed his walk in every detail to God, and has not been left without an answer, which has assured him of His good pleasure: may He then be pleased to advance him ever further and further in the understanding of His word, in order that, though men are against him, he may nevertheless have God on his side, vers. 26, 27. The complaint and request expressed in ver. 25 are renewed in ver. 28. דָּלְפָה refers to the soul, which is as it were melting away in the trickling down of tears; קִיֵּם is a *Piel* of Aramaic formation belonging to the later language. In vers. 29, 30 the way of lies or of treachery, and the way of faithfulness or of perseverance in the truth, stand in opposition to one another. חָנַן is construed with a double accusative, inasmuch as תּוֹרָה has not the rigid notion of a fixed teaching, but of living empirical instruction. שִׁוָּה (short for שִׁוָּה לְנֶגֶד, xvi. 8) signifies to put or set, viz. as a *norma normans* that stands before one's eyes. He cleaves to the testimonies of God; may Jahve not disappoint the hope which to him springs up out of them, according to the promise, ver. 31. He runs, *i.e.* walks vigorously and cheerfully, in the way of God's commandments, for He has widened his heart, by granting and preserving to the persecuted one the joyfulness of confession and the confidence of hope.

Vers. 33–40. The eightfold *He*. He further prays for instruction and guidance that he may escape the by-paths of selfishness and of disavowal. The noun עֵקֶב, used also elsewhere as an *accus. adverb.*, in the signification *ad extremum* (vers. 33 and 112) is peculiar to our poet. אֶצְּרֶנָּה (with a *Shebâ* which takes a colouring in accordance with the principal form) refers back to דֶּרֶךְ. In the petition "give me understanding" (which occurs six times in this Psalm) הָבֵן is causative, as in Job xxxii. 8, and frequently in the post-exilic writings. בֶּצַע (from בָּצַע, *abscindere*, as κέρδος accords in sound with κείρειν) signifies gain and acquisition by means of the damage which one does to his neighbour by depreciating his property, by robbery, deceit, and extortion (1 Sam. viii. 3), and as a name of a vice, covetousness, and in general selfishness. שָׁוְא is that which is without real, *i.e.* without divine, contents or intrinsic worth,—God-opposed teaching and life. בִּדְרָכֶךָ*

---

* Heidenheim and Baer erroneously have בִּדְרָכֶיךָ with *Jod. plural.*, contrary to the Masora.

is a defective plural; cf. חֻקֶּךָ, ver. 41, וּמִשְׁפָּטֶךָ, ver. 43, and frequently. Establishing, in ver. 38, is equivalent to a realizing of the divine word or promise. The relative clause אֲשֶׁר לְיִרְאָתֶךָ is not to be referred to לְעַבְדְּךָ according to ver. 85 (where the expression is different), but to אִמְרָתֶךָ: fulfil to Thy servant Thy word or promise, as that which (*quippe quæ*) aims at men attaining the fear of Thee and increasing therein (cf. cxxx. 4, xl. 4). The reproach which the poet fears in ver. 39 is not the reproach of confessing, but of denying God. Accordingly מִשְׁפָּטֶיךָ are not God's judgments [*i.e.* acts of judgment], but revealed decisions or judgments: these are good, inasmuch as it is well with him who keeps them. He can appeal before God to the fact that he is set upon the knowledge and experience of these with longing of heart; and he bases his request upon the fact that God by virtue of His righteousness, *i.e.* the stringency with which He maintains His order of grace, both as to its promises and its duties, would quicken him, who is at present as it were dead with sorrow and weariness.

Vers. 41–48. The eightfold *Vav.* He prays for the grace of true and fearlessly joyous confession. The LXX. renders ver. 41*a*: καὶ ἔλθοι ἐπ᾽ ἐμὲ τὸ ἔλεός σου; but the Targum and Jerome rightly (cf. ver. 77, Isa. lxiii. 7) have the plural: God's proofs of loving-kindness in accordance with His promises will put him in the position that he will not be obliged to be dumb in the presence of him who reproaches him (חֹרֵף, prop. a plucker, cf. خَرَفَ, a lamb=a plucker of leaves or grass), but will be able to answer him on the ground of his own experience. The verb עָנָה, which in itself has many meanings, acquires the signification "to give an answer" through the word, דָּבָר, that is added (synon. הֵשִׁיב דָּבָר). Ver. 43 also refers to the duty of confessing God. The meaning of the prayer is, that God may not suffer him to come to such a pass that he will be utterly unable to witness for the truth; for language dies away in the mouth of him who is unworthy of it before God. The writer has no fear of this for himself, for his hope is set towards God's judgments (לְמִשְׁפָּטֶךָ, defective plural, as also in ver. 149; in proof of which, compare vers. 156 and 175), his confidence takes its stand upon them. The futures which follow from vers. 44 to 48 declare that what he would willingly do by the grace of God, and strives to do, is to walk בִּרְחָבָה, in a broad space (elsewhere בַּמֶּרְחָב), therefore unstraitened, which in this instance is not equivalent to happily, but courageously and unconstrainedly, without allowing myself to be intimidated, and said of inward freedom which makes itself known outwardly. In ver. 46 the Vulgate renders: *Et loquebar de (in) testimoniis tuis in conspectu regum et non confundebar*—the motto of the Augsburg Confession, to which it was adapted especially in connection with this historical interpretation of the two verbs, which does not correspond to the original text. The lifting up of the hands in ver. 48 is an expression of fervent longing desire, as in connection with prayer, xxviii. 2, lxiii. 5, cxxxiv. 2, cxli. 2, and frequently. The second אֲשֶׁר אָהַבְתִּי is open to the suspicion of being an inadvertent repetition. שִׂיחַ בְּ (synon. הָגָה בְּ) signifies a still or audible meditating that is absorbed in the object.

Vers. 49–56. The eightfold *Zajin*. God's word is his hope and his trust amidst all derision; and when he burns with indignation at the apostates, God's word is his solace. Since in ver. 49 the expression is not דְּבָרְךָ but דָּבָר, it is not to be interpreted according to xcviii. 3, cvi. 45, but: remember the word addressed to Thy servant, because Thou hast made me hope (*Piel causat.* as *e.g.* נִשָּׁה, to cause to forget, Gen. xli. 51), *i.e.* hast comforted me by promising me a blessed issue, and hast directed my expectation thereunto. This is his comfort in his dejected condition, that God's promissory declaration has quickened him and proved its reviving power in his case. In הֱלִיצֻנִי (חָלִיצֻנִי), *ludificantur*, it is implied that the זֵדִים are just לֵצִים, frivolous persons, libertines, free-thinkers (Prov. xxi. 24). מִשְׁפָּטֶיךָ, ver. 52, are the valid, verified decisions (judgments) of God revealed from the veriest olden times. In the remembrance of these, which determine the lot of a man according to the relation he holds towards them, the poet found comfort. It can be rendered: then I comforted myself; or according to a later usage of the *Hithpa.*: I was comforted. Concerning זַלְעָפָה, *æstus*, *vid.* xi. 6, and on the subject-matter, vers. 21, 104. The poet calls his earthly life "the house of his pilgrimage;" for it is true the earth is man's (cxv. 16), but he has no abiding resting-place there (1 Chron. xxix. 15), his בֵּית עוֹלָם (Eccles. xii. 5) is elsewhere (*vid. supra*, ver. 19, xxxix.

13). God's statutes are here his "songs," which give him spiritual refreshing, sweeten the hardships of the pilgrimage, and measure and hasten his steps. The Name of God has been in his mind hitherto, not merely by day, but also by night; and in consequence of this he has kept God's law (וָאֶשְׁמְרָה, as five times besides in this Psalm, cf. iii. 6, and to be distinguished from וְאֶשְׁמְּרָה, ver. 44). Just this, that he keeps (*observat*) God's precepts, has fallen to his lot. To others something else is allotted (iv. 8), to him this one most needful thing.

Vers. 57-64. The eightfold *Heth*. To understand and to keep God's word is his portion, the object of his incessant praying and thanksgiving, the highest grace or favour that can come to him. According to xvi. 5, lxxiii. 26, the words חֶלְקִי ה׳ belong together. Ver. 57b is an inference drawn from it (אָמַר לְ as in Ex. ii. 14, and frequently), and the existing division of the verse is verified. חִלִּיתִי פְנֵי, as in xlv. 13, is an expression of caressing, flattering entreaty; in Latin, *caput mulcere* (*demulcere*). His turning to the word of God the poet describes in ver. 59 as a result of a careful trying of his actions. After that he quickly and cheerfully, ver. 60, determined to keep it without any long deliberation with flesh and blood, although the snares of wicked men surround him. The meaning of חֶבְלֵי is determined according to ver. 110: the pointing does not distinguish so sharply as one might have expected between חֶבְלֵי, ὠδῖνας, and חַבְלֵי, snares, bonds (*vid*. xviii. 5 sq.); but the plural nowhere, according to the usage of the language as we now have it, signifies bands (companies), from the singular in 1 Sam. x. 5 (Böttcher, § 800). Thankfulness urges him to get up at midnight (*acc. temp.* as in Job xxxiv. 20) to prostrate himself before God and to pray. Accordingly he is on friendly terms with, he is closely connected with (Prov. xxviii. 24), all who fear God. Out of the fulness of the loving-kindness of God, which is nowhere unattested upon earth (ver. 64a = xxxiii. 5), he implores for himself the inward teaching concerning His word as the highest and most cherished of mercies.

Vers. 65-72. The eightfold *Teth*. The good word of the gracious God is the fountain of all good; and it is learned in the way of lowliness. He reviews his life, and sees in everything that has befallen him the good and well-meaning appointment of the God of salvation in accordance with the plan and order of salvation of His word. The form עָבְדְּךָ, which is the form out of pause, is retained in ver. 65a beside *Athnach*, although not preceded by *Olewejored* (cf. xxxv. 19, xlviii. 11, Prov. xxx. 21). Clinging believingly to the commandments of God, he is able confidently to pray that He would teach him "good discernment" and "knowledge." טַעַם is ethically the capacity of distinguishing between good and evil, and of discovering the latter as it were by touch; טוּב טַעַם, good discernment, is a coupling of words like טוּב לֵב, a happy disposition, cheerfulness. God has brought him into this relationship to His word by humbling him, and thus setting him right out of his having gone astray. אִמְרָה in ver. 67b, as in ver. 11, is not God's utterance conveying a promise, but imposing a duty. God is called טוֹב as He who is graciously disposed towards man, and מֵטִיב as He who acts out this disposition; this loving and gracious God he implores to become his Teacher. In his fidelity to God's word he does not allow himself to be led astray by any of the lies which the proud try to impose upon him (Böttcher), or better absolutely (cf. Job xiii. 4): to patch together over him, making the true nature unrecognisable as it were by means of false plaster or whitewash (טָפַל, to smear over, bedaub, as the Targumic, Talmudic, and Syriac show). If the heart of these men, who by slander make him into a caricature of himself, is covered as it were with thick fat (a figure of insensibility and obduracy, xvii. 10, lxxiii. 7, Isa. vi. 10, LXX. ἐτυρώθη, Aquila ἐλιπάνθη, Symmachus ἐμυαλώθη) against all the impressions of the word of God, he, on the other hand, has his delight in the law of God (שִׁעֲשֵׁעַ with an accusative of the object, not of that which is delighted, xciv. 19, but of that which delights). How beneficial has the school of affliction through which he has attained to this, been to him! The word proceeding from the mouth of God is now more precious to him than the greatest earthly riches.

Vers. 73–80. The eightfold *Jod*. God humbles, but He also exalts again according to His word; for this the poet prays in order that he may be a consolatory example to the God-fearing, to the confusion of his enemies. It is impossible that God should forsake man, who is His creature, and deny to him that which makes him truly happy, viz. the understanding and knowledge of His word. For this spiritual gift the poet prays in ver. 73 (cf. on 73a, Deut. xxxii. 6, Job x. 8, xxxi. 15); and he wishes in ver. 74 that all who fear God may see in him with joy an example of the way in which trust in the word of God is rewarded (cf. xxxiv. 3, xxxv. 27, lxix. 33, cvii. 42, and other passages). He knows that God's acts of judgment are pure righteousness, *i.e.* are regulated by God's holiness, out of which they spring, and by the salvation of men, at which they aim; and he knows that God has humbled him אֱמוּנָה (*accus. adverb.* for בֶּאֱמוּנָה), being faithful in His intentions towards him; for it is just in the school of affliction that one first learns rightly to estimate the worth of His word, and comes to feel its power. But trouble, though sweetened by an insight into God's salutary design, is nevertheless always bitter; hence the well-justified prayer of ver. 76, that God's mercy may notwithstanding be bestowed upon him for his consolation, in accordance with the promise which is become his (לְ as in ver. 49a), His servant's. עִוֵּת, ver. 78, instead of being construed with the accusative of the right, or of the cause, that is perverted, is construed with the accusative of the person upon whom such perversion of right, such oppression by means of misrepresentation, is inflicted, as in Job xix. 6, Lam. iii. 36. Chajug' reads עִוְּדוּנִי as in ver. 61. The wish expressed in ver. 79 is to be understood according to lxxiii. 10, Jer. xv. 19, cf. Prov. ix. 4, 16. If instead of וְיֹדְעֵי (which is favoured by ver. 63), we read according to the *Chethîb* וְיֵדְעוּ (cf. ver. 125), then what is meant by יָשׁוּבוּ לִי is a turning towards him for the purpose of learning: may their knowledge be enriched from his experience. For himself, however, in ver. 80 he desires unreserved, faultless, unwavering adherence to God's word, for only thus is he secure against being ignominiously undeceived.

Vers. 81–88. The eightfold *Kaph*. This strengthening according to God's promise is his earnest desire (כָּלְתָה) now, when within a very little his enemies have compassed his ruin (כִּלָּה). His soul and eyes languish (כָּלָה as in lxix. 4, lxxxiv. 3, cf. Job xix. 27) for God's salvation, that it may be unto him according to God's word or promise, that this word may be fulfilled. In ver. 83 כִּי is hypothetical, as in xxi. 12 and frequently; here, as perhaps also in xxvii. 10, in the sense of "although" (Ew. § 362, *b*). He does not suffer anything to drive God's word out of his mind, although he is already become like a leathern bottle blackened and shrivelled up in the smoke. The custom of the ancients of placing jars with wine over the smoke in order to make the wine prematurely old, *i.e.* to mellow it (*vid.* Rosenmüller), does not yield anything towards the understanding of this passage: the skin-bottle that is not intended for present use is hung up on high; and the fact that it had to withstand the upward ascending smoke is intelligible, notwithstanding the absence of any mention of the chimney. The point of comparison, in which we agree for the most part with Hitzig, is the removal of him who in his dungeon is continually exposed to the drudgery of his persecutors. כַּמָּה in ver. 84 is equivalent to "how few." Our life here below is short, so also is the period within which the divine righteousness can reveal itself. שִׁיחוֹת (instead of which the LXX. erroneously reads שִׂיחוֹת), pits, is an old word, lvii. 7. The relative clause, ver. 85*b*, describes the "proud" as being a contradiction to the revealed law; for there was no necessity for saying that to dig a pit for others is not in accordance with this law. All God's commandments are an emanation of His faithfulness, and therefore too demand faithfulness; but it is just this faithfulness that makes the poet an object of deadly hatred. They have already almost destroyed him "in the land." It is generally rendered "on earth;" but "in heaven" at the beginning of the following octonary is too far removed to be an antithesis to it, nor does it sound like one (cf. on the other hand ἐν τοῖς οὐρανοῖς, Matt. v. 12). It is therefore: in the land (cf. lviii. 3, lxxiii. 9), where they think they are the only ones who have any right there, they have almost destroyed him, without shaking the constancy of his faith. But he stands in need of fresh grace in order that he may not, however, at last succumb.

Vers. 89–96. The eightfold *Lamed*. Eternal and imperishable in the constant verifying of itself is the vigorous and consolatory word of God, to which the poet will ever cling. It has heaven as its standing-place, and therefore it also has the qualities of heaven, and before all others, heaven-like stability. Ps. lxxxix. (ver. 3) uses similar language in reference to God's faithfulness, of which here ver. 90 says that it endureth into all generations. The earth hath He creatively set up, and it standeth, viz. as a practical proof and as a scene of His infinite, unchangeable faithfulness. Heaven and earth are not the subjects of ver. 91 (Hupfeld), for only the earth is previously mentioned; the reference to the heavens in ver. 89 is of a very different character. Hitzig and others see the subject in לְמִשְׁפָּטֶיךָ: with respect to Thy judgments, they stand fast unto this day; but the עֲבָדֶיךָ which follows requires another meaning to be assigned to עָמְדוּ: either of taking up one's place ready for service, or, since עָמַד לְמִשְׁפָּט is a current phrase in Num. xxxv. 12, Josh. xx. 6, Ezek. xliv. 24, of placing one's self ready to obey (Böttcher). The subject of עָמְדוּ, as the following הַכֹּל shows, is meant to be thought of in the most general sense (cf. Job xxxviii. 14): all beings are God's servants (subjects), and have accordingly to be obedient and humble before His judicial decisions—הַיּוֹם, "even to this day," the poet adds, for these judicial decisions are those which are formulated beforehand in the Tôra. Joy in this ever sure, all-conditioning word has upheld the poet in his affliction, ver. 92. He who has been persecuted and cast down as it were to death, owes his reviving to it, ver. 93. From Him whose possession or property he is in faith and love he also further looks for his salvation, ver. 94. Let evildoers lie in wait for him (קִוָּה in a hostile sense, as in lvi. 7, קָוָה, cf. חָבָה, going back to קָוָה, قَوِيَ, with the broad primary signification, to be tight, firm, strong) to destroy him, he meditates on God's testimonies. He knows from experience that all (earthly) perfection (תִּכְלָה) has an end (inasmuch as, having reached its height, it changes into its opposite); God's commandment (singular as in Deut. xi. 22), on the contrary, is exceeding broad (cf. Job xi. 9), unlimited in its duration and verification.

Vers. 97–104. *The eightfold Mem.* The poet praises the practical wisdom which the word of God, on this very account so sweet to him, teaches. God's precious law, with which he unceasingly occupies himself, makes him superior in wisdom (Deut. iv. 6), intelligence, and judgment to his enemies, his teachers, and the aged (Job xii. 20). There were therefore at that time teachers and elders (πρεσβύτεροι), who (like the Hellenizing Sadducees) were not far from apostasy in their laxness, and hostilely persecuted the young and strenuous zealot for God's law. The construction of ver. 98a is like Joel i. 20,

Isa. lix. 12, and frequently. הִיא refers to the commandments in their unity: he has taken possession of them for ever (cf. ver. 111a). The Mishna (Aboth iv. 1) erroneously interprets: from all my teachers do I acquire understanding. All three כִּי in vers. 98–100 signify præ (LXX. ὑπέρ). In פִּלְאָתִי, ver. 101a, from the mode of writing we see the verb Lamed Aleph passing over into the verb Lamed He. הוֹרְתָנִי is, as in Prov. iv. 11 (cf. Ex. iv. 15), a defective mode of writing for הוֹרֵיתָנִי. נִמְלְצוּ, ver. 103a, is not equivalent to נִמְרְצוּ, Job vi. 25 (vid. Job, i. 118, 279), but signifies, in consequence of the dative of the object לְחִכִּי, that which easily enters, or that which tastes good (LXX. ὡς γλυκέα); therefore surely from מָלַט = מָלַץ, to be smooth: how smooth, entering easily (Prov. xxiii. 31), are Thy words (promises) to my palate or taste! The collective singular אִמְרָתֶךָ is construed with a plural of the predicate (cf. Ex. i. 10). He has no taste for the God-estranged present, but all the stronger taste for God's promised future. From God's laws he acquires the capacity for proving the spirits, therefore he hates every path of falsehood (= ver. 128b), i.e. all the heterodox tendencies which agree with the spirit of the age.

Vers. 105–112. *The eightfold Nun.* The word of God is his constant guide, to which he has entrusted himself for ever. The way here below is a way through darkness, and leads close past abysses: in this danger of falling and of going astray the word of God is a lamp to his feet, i.e. to his course, and a light to his path (Prov. vi. 23); his lamp or torch and his sun That which he has sworn, viz. to keep God's righteous requirements, he has also set up, i.e. brought to fulfilment, but not without being bowed down under heavy afflictions in confessing God; wherefore he prays (as in ver. 25) that God would revive him in accordance with His word, which promises life to those who keep it. The confessions of prayer coming from the inmost impulse of his whole heart, in which he owns his indebtedness and gives himself up entirely to God's mercy, he calls the free-will offerings of his mouth in ver. 108 (cf. l. 14, xix. 15). He bases the prayer for a gracious acceptance of these upon the fact of his being reduced to extremity. "To have one's soul in one's hand" is the same as to be in conscious peril of one's life, just as "to take one's soul into one's hand" (Judg. xii. 3, 1 Sam. xix. 5, xxviii. 21, Job xiii. 14) is the same as to be ready to give one's life for it, to risk one's life.* Although his life is threatened (ver. 87), yet he does not waver and depart from God's word; he has taken and obtained possession of God's testimonies for ever (cf. ver. 98); they are his "heritage," for which he willingly gives up everything else, for they (הֵמָּה inexactly for הֵנָּה) it is which bless and entrance him in his inmost soul. In ver. 112 it is not to be interpreted after xix. 12: eternal is the reward (of the carrying out of Thy precepts), but in ver. 33 עֵקֶב is equivalent to לְעַד, and ver. 44 proves that ver. 112*b* need not be a thought that is complete in itself.

Vers. 113–120. The eightfold *Samech*. His hope rests on God's word, without allowing itself to be led astray by doubters and apostates. סֵעֲפִים (the form of nouns which indicate defects or failings) are those inwardly divided, halting between two opinions (סְעִפִּים), 1 Kings xviii. 21, who do homage partly to the worship of Jahve, partly to heathenism, and therefore are trying to combine faith and naturalism. In contrast to such, the poet's love, faith, and hope are devoted entirely to the God of revelation; and to all those who are desirous of drawing him away he addresses in ver. 115 (cf. vi. 9) an indignant "depart." He, however, stands in need of grace in order to persevere and to conquer. For this he prays in vers. 116, 117. The כִּי in מִשַּׂבְרִי is the same as in בּוֹשׁ מִן. The *ah* of וְאֶשְׁעָה is the intentional *ah* (Ew. § 228, *c*), as in Isa. xli. 23. The statement of the ground of the קָלִיתָ, *vilipendis*, does not mean: unsuccessful is their deceit (Hengstenberg, Olshausen), but falsehood without the consistency of truth is their self-deceptive and seductive tendency. The LXX. and Syriac read תַּרְעִיתָם, "their sentiment;" but this is an Aramaic word that is unintelligible in Hebrew, which the old translators have conjured into the text only on account of an apparent tautology. The reading חִשַּׁבְתָּ or חָשַׁבְתָּ (Aquila, Symmachus, and Jerome; LXX. ἐλογισάμην, therefore חִשַּׁבְתִּי) instead of הִשְׁבַּתָּ might more readily be justified in ver. 119*a*; but the former gives too narrow a meaning, and the reading rests on a mistaking of the construction of הִשְׁבִּית with an accusative of

---

* Cf. *B. Taanith* 8*a*: "The prayer of a man is not answered אִם לֹא כָּן בְּשִׁי נַפְשׁוֹ בְּכַפּוֹ, *i.e.* if he is not ready to sacrifice his life."

the object and of the effect : all the wicked, as many of them as are on the earth, dost Thou put away as dross (סִגִים). Accordingly מִשְׁפָּטֶיךָ in ver. 120 are God's punitive judgments, or rather (cf. ver. 91) God's laws (judgments) according to which He judges. What is meant are sentences of punishment, as in Lev. ch. xxvi., Deut. ch. xxviii. Of these the poet is afraid, for omnipotence can change words into deeds forthwith. In fear of the God who has attested Himself in Ex. xxxiv. 7 and elsewhere, his skin shudders and his hair stands on end.

Vers. 121–128. *The eightfold Ajin.* In the present time of apostasy and persecution he keeps all the more strictly to the direction of the divine word, and commends himself to the protection and teaching of God. In the consciousness of his godly behaviour (elsewhere always צֶדֶק וּמִשְׁפָּט, here in one instance מִשְׁפָּט וָצֶדֶק) the poet hopes that God will surely not (בַּל) leave him to the arbitrary disposal of his oppressors. This hope does not, however, raise him above the necessity and duty of constant prayer that Jahve would place Himself between him and his enemies. עָרַב *seq. acc.* signifies to stand in any one's place as furnishing a guarantee, and in general as a mediator, Job xvii. 3, Isa. xxxviii. 14; לְטוֹב similar to לְטוֹבָה, lxxxvi. 17, Neh. v. 19: in my behalf, for my real advantage. The expression of longing after redemption in ver. 123 sounds like vers. 81 sq. "The word of Thy righteousness" is the promise which proceeds from God's " righteousness," and as surely as He is " righteous" cannot remain unfulfilled. The one chief petition of the poet, however, to which he comes back in vers. 124 sq., has reference to the ever deeper knowledge of the word of God ; for this knowledge is in itself at once life and blessedness, and the present calls most urgently for it. For the great multitude (which is the subject to הֵפֵרוּ) practically and fundamentally break God's law ; it is therefore time to act for Jahve (עָשָׂה לְ as in Gen. xxx. 30, Isa. lxiv. 3 [4], Ezek. xxix. 20), and just in order to this there is need of well-grounded, reliable knowledge. Therefore the poet attaches himself with all his love to God's commandments; to him they are above gold and fine gold (xix. 11), which he might perhaps gain by a disavowal of them. Therefore he is as strict as he possibly can be with God's word, inasmuch as he acknowledges and observes all precepts of all things (כָּל־פִּקּוּדֵי כֹל), *i.e.* all divine precepts, let them have reference to whatsoever they will, as יְשָׁרִים, right (יָשָׁר, to declare both in avowal and deed to be right); and every false (lying) tendency, all pseudo-Judaism, he hates. It is true ver. 126a may be also explained: it is time that Jahve should act, i.e. interpose judicially; but this thought is foreign to the context, and affords no equally close union for עַל־כֵּן; moreover it ought then to have been accented עֵת לַעֲשׂוֹת לַיהוָה. On כֹּל, כָּל־פִּקּוּדֵי, "all commands of every purport," cf. Isa. xxix. 11, and more as to form, Num. viii. 16, Ezek. xliv. 30. The expression is purposely thus heightened; and the correction כָּל־פִּקּוּדֶיךָ (Ewald, Olshausen, and Hupfeld) is also superfluous, because the reference of what is said to the God of revelation is self-evident in this connection.

Vers. 129–136. The eightfold *Phe*. The deeper his depression of spirit concerning those who despise the word of God, the more ardently does he yearn after the light and food of that word. The testimonies of God are פְּלָאוֹת, wonderful and strange (paradoxical) things, exalted above every-day life and the common understanding. In this connection of the thoughts נְצָרָתַם is not intended of careful observance, but of attentive contemplation that is prolonged until a clear penetrating understanding of the matter is attained. The opening, disclosure (פֵּתַח, *apertio*, with *Tsere* in distinction from פֶּתַח, *porta*) of God's word giveth light, inasmuch as it makes the simple (פְּתָיִים as in Prov. xxii. 3) wise or sagacious; in connection with which it is assumed that it is God Himself who unfolds the mysteries of His word to those who are anxious to learn. Such an one, anxious to learn, is the poet: he pants with open mouth, viz. for the heavenly fare of such disclosures (פָּעַר like פָּעַר פֶּה in Job xxix. 23, cf. Ps. lxxxi. 11). יָאַב is a hapaxlegomenon, just as תָּאַב is also exclusively peculiar to the Psalm before us; both are secondary forms of אָבָה. Love to God cannot indeed remain unresponded to. The experience of helping grace is a right belonging to those who love the God of revelation; love in return for love, salvation in return for the longing for salvation, is their prerogative. On the ground of this reciprocal relation the petitions in vers. 133–135 are then put up, coming back at last to the one chief prayer "teach me." אִמְרָה, ver. 133, is not merely a "promise" in this instance, but the declared will of God in general. כָּל־אָוֶן refers pre-eminently to all sin of disavowal (denying God), into which he might fall under outward and inward pressure (עָשֵׁק). For he has round about him those who do not keep God's law. On account of these apostates (עַל לֹא as in Isa. liii. 9, equivalent to עַל־אֲשֶׁר לֹא) his eyes run down rivers of water (יָרַד as in Lam. iii. 48, with an accusative of the object). His mood is not that of unfeeling self-glorying, but of sorrow like that of Jeremiah, because of the contempt of Jahve, and the self-destruction of those who contemn Him.

Vers. 137–144. The eightfold Tsade. God rules righteously and faithfully according to His word, for which the poet is accordingly zealous, although young and despised. The predicate יָשָׁר in ver. 137b precedes its subject מִשְׁפָּטֶיךָ (God's decisions in word and in deed) in the primary form (after the model of the verbal clause cxxiv. 5), just as in German [and English] the predicative adjective remains undeclined. The accusatives צֶדֶק and אֱמוּנָה in ver. 138 are not predicative (Hitzig), to which the former ("as righteousness")—not the latter however—is not suited, but adverbial accusatives (in righteousness, in faithfulness), and מְאֹד according to its position is subordinate to ואמונה as a virtual adjective (cf. Isa. xlvii. 9) : the requirements of the revealed law proceed from a disposition towards and mode of dealing with men which is strictly determined by His holiness (צדק), and beyond measure faithfully and honestly designs the well-being of men (אמונה מאד). To see this good law of God despised by his persecutors stirs the poet up with a zeal, which brings him, from their side, to the brink of extreme destruction (lxix. 10, cf. צִמְּתַת, lxxxviii. 17). God's own utterance is indeed without spot, and therefore not to be carped at; it is pure, fire-proved, noblest metal (xviii. 31, xii. 7), therefore he loves it, and does not, though young (LXX. νεώτερος, Vulgate adolescentulus) and lightly esteemed, care for the remonstrances of his proud opponents who are old and more learned than himself (the organization of ver. 141 is like ver. 95, and frequently). The righteousness (צְדָקָה) of the God of revelation becomes eternal righteousness (צֶדֶק), and His law remains eternal truth (אֱמֶת). צדקה is here the name of the attribute and of the action that is conditioned in accordance with it; צדק the name of the state that thoroughly accords with the idea of that which is right. So too in ver. 144: צדק

are Jahve's testimonies for ever, so that all creatures must give glory to their harmony with that which is absolutely right. To look ever deeper and deeper into this their perfection is the growing life of the spirit. The poet prays for this vivifying insight.

Vers. 145–152. The eightfold *Koph*. Fidelity to God's word, and deliverance according to His promise, is the purport of his unceasing prayer. Even in the morning twilight (נֶשֶׁף) he was awake praying. It is not הַנֶּשֶׁף, I anticipated the twilight; nor is קִדַּמְתִּי, according to lxxxiv. 14, equivalent to קִדַּמְתִּיךָ, but וָאֲשַׁוֵּעַ . . . קִדַּמְתִּי is the resolution of the otherwise customary construction קִדַּמְתִּי לְשַׁוֵּעַ, Jonah iv. 2, inasmuch as קָדַם may signify "to go before" (lxviii. 26), and also "to make haste (with anything):" even early before the morning's dawn I cried. Instead of לדבריך the *Kerî* (Targum, Syriac, Jerome) more appropriately reads לִדְבָרְךָ after vers. 74, 81, 114. But his eyes also anticipated the night-watches, inasmuch as they did not allow themselves to be caught not sleeping by any of them at their beginning (cf. לְרֹאשׁ, Lam. ii. 19). אִמְרָה is here, as in vers. 140, 158, and frequently, the whole word of God, whether in its requirements or its promises. In ver. 149 כְּמִשְׁפָּטֶךָ is a defective plural as in ver. 43 (*vid.* on ver. 37), according to ver. 156, although according to ver. 132 the singular (LXX., Targum, Jerome) would also be admissible: what is meant is God's order of salvation, or His appointments that relate thereto. The correlative relation of vers. 150 and 151 is rendered natural by the position of the words. With קָרְבוּ (cf. קָרֵב) is associated the idea of rushing upon him with hostile purpose, and with קָרוֹב, as in lxix. 19, Isa. lviii. 2, of hastening to his succour. זִמָּה is infamy that is branded by the law: they go forth purposing this, but God's law is altogether self-verifying truth. And the poet has long gained the knowledge from it that it does not aim at merely temporary recompense. The sophisms of the apostates cannot therefore lead him astray. יְסַדְתָּם for יְסַדְתָּן, like הֵמָּה in ver. 111.

Vers. 153–160. The eightfold *Resh*. Because God cannot suffer those who are faithful to His word to succumb, he supplicates His help against his persecutors. רִיבָה is *Milra* before the initial (half-guttural) *Resh*, as in xliii. 1, lxxiv. 22. The *Lamed* of לְאִמְרָתֶךָ is the *Lamed* of reference (with respect to Thine utterance), whether the reference be normative (=כְּאִמְרָתֶךָ, ver. 58), as in Isa. xi. 3, or causal, xxv. 2, Isa. lv. 5, Job xlii. 5. The predicate רָחוֹק, like יָשָׁר in ver. 137, stands first in the primary, as yet indefinite form. Concerning ver. 156b vid. on ver. 149. At the sight of the faithless he felt a profound disgust; וָאֶתְקוֹטָטָה, pausal aorist, supply בָּהֶם, cxxxix. 21. It is all the same in the end whether we render אֲשֶׁר quippe qui or siquidem. רֹאשׁ in ver. 160 signifies the head-number or sum. If he reckons up the word of God in its separate parts and as a whole, truth is the denominator of the whole, truth is the sum-total. This supplicatory חַיֵּנִי is repeated three times in this group. The nearer it draws towards its end the more importunate does the Psalm become.

Vers. 161-168. The eightfold שׁ (both Shin and Sin *). In the midst of persecution God's word was still his fear, his joy, and his love, the object of his thanksgiving, and the ground of his hope. Princes persecute him without adequate cause, but his heart does not fear before them, but before God's words (the Kerî likes the singular, as in ver. 147), to deny which would be to him the greatest possible evil. It is, however, a fear that is associated with heartfelt joy (ver. 111). It is the joy of a conflict that is rewarded by rich spoil (Judg. v. 30, Isa. ix. 2 [3]). Not merely morning and evening, not merely three times a day (lv. 18), but seven times (שֶׁבַע) as in Lev. xxvi. 18, Prov. xxiv. 16), i.e. ever again and again, availing himself of every prayerful impulse, he gives thanks to God for His word, which so righteously decides and so correctly guides, is a source of transcendent peace to all who love it, and beside which one is not exposed to any danger of stumbling (מִכְשׁוֹל, LXX. σκάνδαλον, cf. 1 John ii. 10) without some effectual counter-working. In ver. 166a he speaks like Jacob in Gen. xlix. 18, and can speak thus, inasmuch as he has followed earnestly and untiringly after sanctification. He endeavours to keep God's law most conscientiously, in proof of which he is able to appeal to God, the Omniscient One. שָׁמְרָה is here the 3d præt., where-

---

* Whilst even in the oldest alphabetical *Pijutim* the *Sin* perhaps represents the *Samech* as well, but never the *Shin*, it is the reverse in the Biblical alphabetical pieces. Here *Sin* and *Shin* coincide, and *Samech* is specially represented.

as in lxxxvi. 2 it is *imperat*. The future of אֶהֱרַב is both אֵהַב and אֶהֱרַב, just as of אָהַב both אֹהֵב and אֹאֲהֵב.

Vers. 169–176. The eightfold *Tav.* May God answer this his supplication as He has heard his praise, and interest Himself on behalf of His servant, the sheep that is exposed to great danger. The petitions "give me understanding" and "deliver me" go hand-in-hand, because the poet is one who is persecuted for the sake of his faith, and is just as much in need of the fortifying of his faith as of deliverance from the outward restraint that is put upon him. רִנָּה is a shrill audible prayer; תְּחִנָּה, a fervent and urgent prayer. עָנָה, prop. to answer, signifies in ver. 172 to begin, strike up, attune (as does ἀποκρίνεσθαι also sometimes). According to the rule in l. 23 the poet bases his petition for help upon the purpose of thankful praise of God and of His word. Knowing how to value rightly what he possesses, he is warranted in further supplicating and hoping for the good that he does not as yet possess. The "salvation" for which he longs (תָּאַב as in vers. 40, 20) is redemption from the evil world, in which the life of his own soul is imperilled. May then God's judgments (defective plural, as in vers. 43, 149, which the Syriac only takes as singular) succour him (יַעְזְרֻנִי, not יַעְזְרֵנִי). God's hand, ver. 173, and God's word afford him succour; the two are involved in one another, the word is the medium of His hand. After this relationship of the poet to God's word, which is attested a hundredfold in the Psalm, it may seem strange that he can say of himself תָּעִיתִי כְּשֶׂה אֹבֵד; and perhaps the accentuation is correct when it does not allow itself to be determined by Isa. liii. 6, but interprets: If I have gone astray—seek Thou like a lost sheep Thy servant. שֶׂה אֹבֵד is a sheep that is lost (cf. אֹבְדִים as an appellation of the dispersion, Isa. xxvii. 13) and in imminent danger of total destruction (cf. xxxi. 13 with Lev. xxvi. 38). In connection with that interpretation which is followed by the interpunction, ver. 176*b* is also more easily connected with what precedes: his going astray is no apostasy; his home, to which he longs to return when he has been betrayed into by-ways, is beside the Lord.

THE FIFTEEN SONGS OF DEGREES, OR GRADUAL PSALMS.

Ps. CXX.–CXXXIV.

These songs are all inscribed שִׁיר הַמַּעֲלוֹת. The LXX., according to the most natural signification of the word, renders: ᾠδὴ τῶν ἀναβαθμῶν; the Italic and Vulgate, *canticum graduum* (whence the liturgical term " gradual Psalms "). The meaning at the same time remains obscure. When, however, Theodotion renders ᾆσμα τῶν ἀναβάσεων, Aquila and Symmachus ᾠδὴ εἰς τὰς ἀναβάσεις (as though it were absolutely לַמַּעֲלוֹת, as in cxxi. 1), it looks even like an explanation. The fathers, more particularly Theodoret, and in general the Syrian church, associate with it the idea of ἡ ἀπὸ Βαβυλῶνος ἐπάνοδος. Ewald has long advocated this view. In his Introduction to *Die poetischen Bücher des Alten Bundes* (1839), and elsewhere, he translated it "Songs of the Pilgrim caravans" or "of the homeward marches," and explained these fifteen Psalms as old and new travelling songs of those returning from the Exile. The verb עָלָה certainly is the usual word for journeying to Palestine out of the Babylonian low country, as out of the country of the Egyptian Nile Valley. And the fact that the Return from the Exile is called הַמַּעֲלָה מִבָּבֶל in Ezra vii. 9 is enticing. Some of these Psalms, as cxxi., cxxiii.–cxxv., cxxix., cxxx., cxxxii., cxxxiii., are also suited to this situation, or can at least be adapted to it. But Ps. cxx., if it is to be referred to the Exile, is a song that comes out of the midst of it; Ps. cxxvi. might, so far as its first half is concerned, be a travelling song of those returning, but according to its second half it is a prayer of those who have returned for the restoration of the whole of Israel, based upon thanksgiving; and Ps. cxxii. assumes the existence and frequenting of the Temple and of the holy city, and Ps. cxxxiv. the full exercise of the Temple-service. It is also inconvenient that מַעֲלָה, which in itself only expresses a journey up, not a journey homewards, is without any closer definition; and more particularly since, in connection with this form of the word, the signification of a something (a step, a sun-dial, rising thoughts, Ezek. xi. 5) is at least just as natural as that of an action. שִׁיר הָעֳלִים would have been at once palpable. And what is meant by the plural? The interpretation of the plural of the different caravans or companies in which the exiles returned, assumes a *usus loquendi* with which we are altogether unacquainted.

Relatively more probable is the reference to the pilgrimage-journeyings at the three great feasts,—according to a later Hebrew expression, the שָׁלשׁ רְגָלִים. This going up to Jerusalem required by the Law is also usually called עֲלִיָּה. So Agellius (1606), Herder, Eichhorn, Maurer, Hengstenberg, Keil, and others, and so now even Ewald in the second edition (1866) of the Introduction to *Die Dichter des Alten Bundes*, so Kamphausen, and Reuss in his treatise *Chants de Pèlerinage ou petit Psautier des Pèlerins du second temple* (in the *Nouvelle Revue de Théologie*, i. 273-311), and Liebusch in the Quedlinburg Easter Programm, 1866: "The pilgrim songs in the Fifth Book of the Psalter." But מַעֲלָה in this signification is without precedent; and when Hupfeld says in opposition to this, "the fact that a noun accidentally does not occur in the Old Testament does not matter, since here at any rate it is a question of the interpretation of a later usage of the language," we may reply that neither does the whole range of the post-biblical Hebrew exhibit any trace of this usage. Thenius accordingly tries another way of doing justice to the word. He understands מַעֲלוֹת of the different stations, *i.e.* stages of the journey up, that are to be found in connection with the festive journeys to high-lying Jerusalem. But the right name for "stations" would be מַסָּעוֹת or מַעֲמָדוֹת; and besides, the notion borrowed from the processions to Mount Calvary is without historical support in the religious observances of Israel. Thus, then, the needful ground in language and custom for referring this title of the Psalms to the journeyings up to the feasts is taken from under us; and the consideration that the first three and the last three songs are suited to the hymn-book of a festal pilgrimage, and that they all bear in them, as Liebusch has demonstrated, the characteristic features of the spiritual national song, is not able to decide the doubtful meaning of מַעֲלוֹת.

We will now put the later Jewish interpretation to the proof. According to *Middoth* ii. 5, *Succa* 15*b*, a semi-circular staircase with fifteen steps led out of the court of the Israelitish men (עזרת ישראל) down into the court of the women (עזרת נשים), and upon these fifteen steps, which correspond to the fifteen gradual Psalms, the Levites played musical instruments on the evening of the first day of the Feast of Tabernacles in connection with the joyful celebration of the water-drawing,* and above them in the portal (upon the threshold of the Nicanor-gate or Agrippa-gate†) stood two priests with trumpets. It has been said that this is a Talmudic fable invented on behalf of the inscription שיר המעלות, and that the fifteen steps are got out of Ezek. xl. 26, 31 by reading the two verses together. This aspersion is founded on ignorance. For the Talmud does not say in that passage that the fifteen Psalms have taken their name from the fifteen steps; it does not once say that these Psalms in particular were read aloud upon the fifteen steps, but it only places the fifteen steps on a parallel with the fifteen Psalms; and, moreover, interprets the name שיר המעלות quite differently, viz. from a legend concerning David and Ahithophel, *Succa* 53a, *Maccoth* 11a (differently rendered in the section *Chelek* of the tractate *Sanhedrin* in the Jerusalem Talmud). This legend to which the Targum inscription relates (*vid.* Buxtorf, *Lex. Talmud.* s.v. קםא) is absurd enough, but it has nothing to do with the fifteen steps. It is not until a later period that Jewish expositors say that the fifteen Psalms had their name from the fifteen steps.‡ Even Hippolytus must have heard something similar when he says (p. 190, ed. *Lagarde*): πάλιν τε αὐτοῦ εἰσί τινες τῶν ἀναβαθμῶν ᾠδαί, τὸν ἀριθμὸν πεντεκαίδεκα, ὅσοι καὶ οἱ ἀναβαθμοὶ τοῦ ναοῦ, τάχα δελοῦσαι τὰς ἀναβάσεις περιέχεσθαι ἐν τῷ ἑβδόμῳ καὶ ὀγδόῳ ἀριθμῷ, upon which Hilary relies: *esse autem in templo gradus quindecim historia*

---

* *Vid.* my *Geschichte der jüdischen Poesie*, S. 193 f.

† It was called the Nicanor-gate in the Temple of Zerubbabel, and the Agrippa-gate in the Temple of Herod: in both of them they ascended to its threshold by fifteen steps; *vid.* Unruh, *Das alte Jerusalem und seine Bauwerke* (1861), S. 137, cf. 194.

‡ Lyra in his *Postillæ*, and Jacob Leonitius in his Hebrew *Libellus effigiei templi Salomonis* (Amsterdam 1650, 4to), even say that the Levites sang one of the fifteen songs of degrees on each step. Luther has again generalized this view; for his rendering "a song in the higher choir" is intended to say, *cantores harum odarum stetisse in loco eminentiori* (Bakius).

nobis locuta est; viz. 15 (7 + 8) steps leading out of the court of the priests into the Holy of holies. In this, then, the allegory in which the interpretation of the church delighted for a long time seemed naturally at hand, viz., as Otmar Nachtgal explains, " Song of the steps or ascents, which indicate the spirit of those who ascend from earthly things to God." The Furtmaier Codex in Maihingen accordingly inscribes them " Psalm of the first step" (*Psalm der ersten staffeln*), and so on. If we leave this *sensus anagogicus* to itself, then the title, referred to the fifteen steps, would indeed not be inappropriate in itself (cf. *Graduale* or *Gradale* in the service of the Romish Church), but is of an external character such as we find nowhere else.*

Gesenius has the merit of having first discerned the true meaning of the questioned inscription, inasmuch as first in 1812 (*Hallische Lit. Zeitschrift*, 1812, Nr. 205), and frequently since that time, he has taught that the fifteen songs have their name from their step-like progressive rhythm of the thoughts, and that consequently the name, like the triolet (roundelay) in Western poetry, does not refer to the liturgical usage, but to the technical structure. The correctness of this view has been duly appraised more particularly by De Wette, who adduces this rhythm of steps or degrees, too, among the more artificial rhythms. The songs are called Songs of degrees or Gradual Psalms as being songs that move onward towards a climax, and that by means of πλοκή (ἐπιπλοκή), *i.e.* a taking up again of the immediately preceding word by way of giving intensity to the expression; and they are placed together on account of this common characteristic, just like the *Michtammim*, which bear that name from a similar characteristic. The fact, as Liebusch objects, that there is no trace of מעלות in this figurative signification elsewhere, is of no consequence, since in the inscriptions of the Psalms in general we become acquainted with a technical language which (apart from a few echoes in the Chronicles) is without example elsewhere, in relation to poetical and musical technology. Neither are we refuted by the fact that this as it were climbing movement of the thoughts which plants upon a

---

* Hitzig, in his Commentary (1865), has attempted a new combination of these Psalms, in regard to the number of verses of cxx. and cxxi. (7 + 8) and their total number, with the steps of the Temple.

preceding word, and thus carries itself forward, is not without example even outside the range of these fifteen songs in the Psalter itself (*e.g.* xciii., xcvi.), as also elsewhere (Isa. xvii. 12 sq., xxvi. 5 sq., and more particularly in the song of Deborah, Judg. v. 3, 5, 6, etc.), and that it is not always carried out in the same manner in the fifteen Psalms. It is quite sufficient that the parallelism retires into the background here as nowhere else in fifteen songs that are linked together (even in cxxv., cxxvii., cxxviii., cxxxii.); and the onward course is represented with decided preference as a gradation or advance step by step, that which follows being based upon what goes before, and from that point advancing and ascending still higher.

PSALM CXX.

CRY OF DISTRESS WHEN SURROUNDED BY CONTENTIOUS MEN.

1 TO Jahve in my distress
  Do I cry, and He answereth me.
2 O Jahve, deliver my soul from a lying lip,
  From a crafty tongue!

3 What shall He give to thee, and what shall He further give
  Thou crafty tongue?   [to thee,
4 Arrows of a mighty one, sharpened,
  Together with coals of broom.

5 Woe is me that I sojourn in Meshech,
  That I *dwell* beside the tents of Kedar!
6 Long enough hath my soul *dwelt*
  With those who hate *peace.*
7 I am *peace;* yet when I speak,
  They are for war.

This first song of degrees attaches itself to Ps. cxix. 176. The writer of Ps. cxix., surrounded on all sides by apostasy and persecution, compares himself to a sheep that is easily lost, which the shepherd has to seek and bring home if it is not to perish; and the writer of Ps. cxx. is also "as a sheep in the midst of wolves." The period at which he lived is uncertain, and it is consequently also uncertain whether he had to endure such endless malignant attacks from foreign barbarians or from his own worldly-minded fellow-countrymen. E. Tilling has sought to establish a third possible occasion in his *Disquisitio de ratione inscript. XV Pss. grad.* (1765). He derives this and the following songs of degrees from the time immediately succeeding the Return from the Exile, when the secret and open hostility of the Samaritans and other neighbouring peoples (Neh. ii. 10, 19, iv. 1 [7], vi. 1) sought to keep down the rise of the young colony.

Vers. 1–4. According to the pointing וַיַּעֲנֵנִי, the poet appears to base his present petition, which from ver. 2 onwards is the substance of the whole Psalm, upon the fact of a previous answering of his prayers. For the petition in ver. 2 manifestly arises out of his deplorable situation, which is described in vers. 5 sqq. Nevertheless there are also other instances in which וַיַּעֲנֵנִי might have been expected, where the pointing is וַיַּעֲנֵנִי (iii. 5, Jonah ii. 3), so that consequently וַיַּעֲנֵנִי may, without any prejudice to the pointing, be taken as a believing expression of the result (cf. the future of the consequence in Job ix. 16) of the present cry for help. צָרָתָה, according to the original signification, is a form of the definition of a state or condition, as in iii. 3, xliv. 27, lxiii. 8, Jonah ii. 10, Hos. viii. 7, and בַּצָּרָתָה לּוֹ = בַּצַּר־לִי, xviii. 7, is based upon the customary expression צַר לִי. In ver. 2 follows the petition which the poet sends up to Jahve in the certainty of being answered. רְמִיָּה beside לָשׁוֹן, although there is no masc. רָמִי (cf. however the Aramaic רַמָּי, רַמָּאִי), is taken as an adjective after the form עֲנִיָּה, טְרִיָּה, which it is also perhaps in Mic. vi. 12. The parallelism would make לָשׁוֹן natural, like לְשׁוֹן מִרְמָה in lii. 6; the pointing, which nevertheless disregarded this, will therefore rest upon tradition. The apostrophe in ver. 3 is addressed to the crafty tongue. לָשׁוֹן is certainly feminine as a rule; but whilst the tongue as such is feminine, the לְשׁוֹן רְמִיָּה of the address, as in lii. 6, refers to him who has such a kind of tongue (cf. Hitzig on Prov. xii. 27), and thereby the לְךָ is justified; whereas the rendering, "what does it bring to thee, and what does it profit thee?" or, "of what use to thee and what advancement to thee is the crafty tongue?" is indeed possible so far as concerns the syntax (Ges. § 147, e), but is unlikely as being ambiguous and confusing in expression. It is also to be inferred from the correspondence between מַה־יִּתֵּן לְךָ וּמַה־יֹּסִיף לָךְ and the formula of an oath כֹּה יַעֲשֶׂה־לְּךָ אֱלֹהִים וְכֹה יֹסִיף, 1 Sam. iii. 17, xx. 13, xxv. 22, 2 Sam. iii. 35, Ruth i. 17, that God is to be thought of as the subject of יִתֵּן and יֹסִיף: "what will," or rather, in accordance with the otherwise precative use of the formula and with the petition that here precedes: "what shall He (is He to) give to thee (נָתַן as in Hos. ix. 14), and what shall He add to thee, thou crafty tongue?" The reciprocal relation of ver. 4a to מַה־יִּתֵּן, and of ver. 4b with the superadding עִם to מַה־יֹּסִיף, shows that ver. 4 is not now a characterizing of the tongue that continues the apostrophe to it, as Ewald supposes. Consequently ver. 4 gives the answer to ver. 3 with the twofold punishment which Jahve will cause the false tongue to feel. The question which the poet, sure of the answering of his cry for help, puts to the false tongue is designed to let the person addressed hear by a flight of sarcasm what he has to expect. The evil tongue is a sharp sword (lvii. 5), a pointed arrow (Jer. ix. 7 [8]), and it is like a fire kindled of hell (Jas. iii. 6). The punishment, too, corresponds to this its nature and conduct (lxiv. 4). The "mighty one" (LXX. δυνατός) is God Himself, as it is observed in B. Erachin 15b with a reference to Isa. xlii. 13: "There is none mighty but the Holy One, blessed is He." He requites the evil tongue like with like. Arrows and coals (cxl. 11) appear also in other instances among His means of punishment. It, which shot piercing arrows, is pierced by the sharpened arrows of an irresistibly mighty One; it, which set its neighbour in a fever of anguish, must endure the lasting, sure, and torturingly consuming heat of broomcoals. The LXX. renders it in a general sense, σὺν τοῖς ἄνθραξι τοῖς ἐρημικοῖς; Aquila, following Jewish tradition, ἀρκευθίναις; but רְתָמִים, Arabic رتم, ratem, is the broom-shrub (e.g. uncommonly frequent in the Belká).

Vers. 5-7. Since arrows and broom-fire, with which the evil tongue is requited, even now proceed from the tongue itself, the poet goes on with the deep heaving אֹיָה (only found here). גּוּר with the accusative of that beside which one sojourns, as in v. 5, Isa. xxxiii. 14, Judg. v. 17. The Moschi (מֶשֶׁךְ, the name of which the LXX. takes as an appellative in the signification of long continuance; cf. the reverse instance in Isa. lxvi. 19 LXX.) dwelt between the Black and the Caspian Seas, and it is impossible to dwell among them and the inhabitants of Kedar (vid. lxxxiii. 7) at one and the same time. Accordingly both these names of peoples are to be understood emblematically, with Saadia, Calvin, Amyraldus, and others, of *homines similes ejusmodi barbaris et truculentis nationibus.** Meshech is reckoned to Magog in Ezek. xxxviii. 2, and the Kedarites are possessed by the lust of possession (Gen. xvi. 12) of the *bellum omnium contra omnes*. These rough and quarrelsome characters have surrounded the poet (and his fellow-countrymen, with whom he perhaps comprehends himself) too long already. רַבַּת, abundantly (vid. lxv. 10), appears, more particularly in 2 Chron. xxx. 17 sq., as a later prose word. The לָהּ, which throws the action back upon the subject, gives a pleasant, lively colouring to the declaration, as in cxxii. 3, cxxiii. 4. He on his part is peace (cf. Mic. v. 4 [5], Ps. cix. 4, cx. 3), inasmuch as the love of peace, willingness to be at peace, and a desire for peace fill his soul; but if he only opens his mouth, they are for war, they are abroad intent on war, their mood and their behaviour become forthwith hostile. Ewald (§ 362, *b*) construes it (following Saadia): and I—although I speak peace; but if כִּי (like עַד, cxli. 10) might even have this position in the clause, yet וְכִי cannot. שָׁלוֹם is not on any account to be supplied in thought to אֲדַבֵּר, as Hitzig suggests (after cxxii. 8, xxviii. 3, xxxv. 20). With the shrill dissonance of שָׁלוֹם and מִלְחָמָה the Psalm closes; and the cry for help with which it opens hovers over it, earnestly desiring its removal.

---

* If the Psalm were a Maccabæan Psalm, one might think מֹשֶׁךָ, from מָשַׁךְ, σύρειν, alluded to the Syrians or even to the Jewish apostates with reference to מֹשֵׁךְ עָרְלָה, ἐπισπᾶσθαι τὴν ἀκροβυστίαν (1 Cor. vii. 18).

PSALM CXXI.

THE CONSOLATION OF DIVINE PROTECTION.

1 I LIFT up mine eyes unto the mountains:
Whence shall come *my help?*
2 *My help* cometh from Jahve,
The Creator of heaven and earth.

3 He will not indeed suffer thy foot to totter,
Thy Keeper will not slumber.
4 Behold *slumbereth not* and sleepeth not
The Keeper of Israel.

5 *Jahve* is *thy Keeper*,
Jahve is thy shade upon thy right hand:
6 By day the sun shall not smite thee,
And the moon in the night.

7 *Jahve* shall *keep thee* from all evil,
He *shall keep* thy soul.
8 Jahve *shall keep* thy going out and thy coming in
From this time forth and for evermore.

This song of degrees is the only one that is inscribed שִׁיר לַמַּעֲלוֹת and not שִׁיר הַמַּעֲלוֹת. The LXX., Targum, and Jerome render it as in the other instances; Aquila and Symmachus, on the contrary, ᾠδή (ᾆσμα) εἰς τὰς ἀναβάσεις, as the Midrash *Sifri* also mystically interprets it: Song upon the steps, upon which God leads the righteous up into the other world. Those who explain הַמַּעֲלוֹת of the homeward caravans or of the pilgrimages rightly regard this לַמַּעֲלוֹת, occurring only once, as favouring their explanation. But the *Lamed* is that of the rule or standard. The most prominent distinguishing mark of Ps. cxxi. is the step-like movement of the thoughts: it is formed לַמַּעֲלוֹת, after the manner of steps. The view that we have a pilgrim song before us is opposed by the beginning, which leads one to infer a firmly limited range of vision, and therefore a fixed place of abode and far removed from his native mountains. The tetrastichic arrangement of the Psalm is unmistakeable.

Vers. 1–4. Apollinaris renders as meaninglessly as possible: ὄμματα δενδροκόμων ὀρέων ὑπερεξετάνυσσα—with a reproduction of the misapprehended ἦρα of the LXX. The expression in fact is אֶשָּׂא, and not יִנָּשֵׂאוּ. And the mountains towards which the psalmist raises his eyes are not any mountains whatsoever. In Ezekiel the designation of his native land from the standpoint of the Mesopotamian plain is "the mountains of Israel." His longing gaze is directed towards the district of these mountains, they are his *kibla*, *i.e.* the sight-point of his prayer, as of Daniel's, ch. vi. 11 [10]. To render " from which my help cometh" (Luther) is inadmissible. מֵאַיִן is an interrogative even in Josh. ii. 4, where the question is an indirect one. The poet looks up to the mountains, the mountains of his native land, the holy mountains (cxxxiii. 3, lxxxvii. 1, cxxv. 2), when he longingly asks: whence will my help come? and to this question his longing desire itself returns the answer, that his help comes from no other quarter than from Jahve, the Maker of heaven and earth, from Him who sits enthroned behind and upon these mountains, whose helpful power reaches to the remotest ends and corners of His creation, and with (עִם) whom is help, *i.e.* both the willingness and the power to help, so that therefore help comes from nowhere but from (מִן) Him alone. In ver. 1*b* the poet has propounded a question, and in ver. 2 replies to this question himself. In ver. 3 and further the answering one goes on speaking to the questioner. The poet is himself become objective, and his Ego, calm in God, promises him comfort, by unfolding to him the joyful prospects contained in that hope in Jahve. The subjective אַל expresses a negative in both cases with an emotional rejection of that which is absolutely impossible. The poet says to himself: He will, indeed, surely not abandon thy foot to the tottering (לַמּוֹט, as in lxvi. 9, cf. lv. 23), thy Keeper will surely not slumber; and then confirms the assertion that this shall not come to pass by heightening the expression in accordance with the step-like character of the Psalm : Behold the Keeper of Israel slumbereth not and sleepeth not, *i.e.* He does not fall into slumber from weariness, and His life is not an alternate waking and sleeping. The eyes of His providence are ever open over Israel.

Vers. 5–8. That which holds good of " the Keeper of

Israel" the poet applies believingly to himself, the individual among God's people, in ver. 5 after Gen. xxviii. 15. Jahve is his Keeper, He is his shade upon his right hand (יְמִינֶךָ as in Judg. xx. 16, 2 Sam. xx. 9, and frequently; the construct state instead of an apposition, cf. *e.g.* جانب الغربي, the side of the western = the western side), which protecting him and keeping him fresh and cool, covers him from the sun's burning heat. עַל, as in cix. 6, cx. 5, with the idea of an overshadowing that screens and spreads itself out over anything (cf. Num. xiv. 9). To the figure of the shadow is appended the consolation in ver. 6. הִכָּה of the sun signifies to smite injuriously (Isa. xlix. 10), plants, so that they wither (cii. 5), and the head (Jonah iv. 8), so that symptoms of sun-stroke (2 Kings iv. 19, Judith viii. 2 sq.) appear. The transferring of the word to the moon is not zeugmatic. Even the moon's rays may become insupportable, may affect the eyes injuriously, and (more particularly in the equatorial regions) produce fatal inflammation of the brain.* From the hurtful influences of nature that are round about him the promise extends in vers. 7, 8 in every direction. Jahve, says the poet to himself, will keep (guard) thee against all evil, of whatever kind it may be and whencesoever it may threaten; He will keep thy soul, and therefore thy life both inwardly and outwardly; He will keep (יִשְׁמָר, cf. on the other hand יְשׁוּפֶךָ in ix. 9) thy going out and coming in, *i.e.* all thy business and intercourse of life (Deut. xxviii. 6, and frequently); for, as Chrysostom observes, ἐν τούτοις ὁ βίος ἅπας, ἐν εἰσόδοις καὶ ἐξόδοις, therefore: everywhere and at all times; and that from this time forth even for ever. In connection with this the thought is natural, that the life of him who stands under the so universal and unbounded protection of eternal love can suffer no injury.

---

* Many expositors, nevertheless, understand the destructive influence of the moon meant here of the nightly cold, which is mentioned elsewhere in the same antithesis, Gen. xxxi. 40, Jer. xxxvi. 30. De Sacy observes also: *On dit quelquefois d'un grand froid, comme d'un grand chaud, qu'il est brûlant.* The Arabs also say of snow and of cold as of fire: *jaḥrik*, it burns.

PSALM CXXII.

A WELL-WISHING GLANCE BACK AT THE PILGRIMS' CITY.

1 I REJOICED in those who said to me:
"Let us go into the house of Jahve!"
2 Our feet stood still
Within thy gates, O *Jerusalem*,
3 *Jerusalem*, thou that art built up again
As a city which is compact in itself!

4 Whither *the tribes* went up,
The tribes of Jāh—
A precept for Israel—
To give thanks unto the Name of Jahve.
5 For there were set *thrones* for judgment,
Thrones for the house of David.

6 Wish ye Jerusalem *peace* :
May it be well with those who love thee!
7 *Peace* be within thy walls,
Prosperity within thy palaces!
8 For my brethren and my friends' sakes
Will I speak *peace* concerning thee.
9 For the sake of the house of Jahve, our God,
Will I seek thy good.

If by "the mountains" in cxxi. 1 the mountains of the Holy Land are to be understood, it is also clear for what reason the collector placed this Song of degrees, which begins with the expression of joy at the pilgrimage to the house of Jahve, and therefore to the holy mountain, immediately after the preceding song. By its peace-breathing (שלום) contents it also, however, touches closely upon Ps. cxx. The poet utters aloud his hearty benedictory salutation to the holy city in remembrance of the delightful time during which he sojourned there as a visitor at the feast, and enjoyed its inspiring aspect. If in respect of the לדוד the Psalm were to be regarded as an old Davidic Psalm, it would belong to the series of those Psalms of the time of the persecution by Absalom, which cast a yearning look back towards home, the house of God (xxiii., xxvi., lv. 15, lxi., and more particularly lxiii.). But the לרו is wanting in the LXX., *Codd. Alex.* and *Vat.*; and the *Cod. Sinait.*, which has TΩ ΔΑΔ, puts this before Ps. cxxiv., εἰ μὴ ὅτι κύριος, κ.τ.λ., also, contrary to *Codd. Alex.* and *Vat.* Here it is occasioned by ver. 5, but without any critical discernment. The measures adopted by Jeroboam I. show, moreover, that the pilgrimages to the feasts were customary even in the time of David and Solomon. The images of calves in Dan and Bethel, and the changing of the Feast of Tabernacles to another month, were intended to strengthen the political rupture, by breaking up the religious unity of the people and weaning them from visiting Jerusalem. The poet of the Psalm before us, however, lived much later. He lived, as is to be inferred with Hupfeld from ver. 3, in the time of the post-exilic Jerusalem which rose again out of its ruins. Thither he had been at one of the great feasts, and here, still quite full of the inspiring memory, he looks back towards the holy city; for, in spite of Reuss, Hupfeld, and Hitzig, vers. 1 sq., so far as the style is concerned, are manifestly a retrospect.

Vers. 1–3. The preterite שָׂמַחְתִּי may signify: I rejoice (1 Sam. ii. 1), just as much as: I rejoiced. Here in comparison with ver. 2a it is a retrospect; for הָיָה with the participle has for the most part a retrospective signification, Gen. xxxix. 22, Deut. ix. 22, 24, Judg. i. 7, Job i. 14. True, עֹמְדוֹת הָיוּ might also signify: they have been standing and still stand (as in x. 14, Isa. lix. 2, xxx. 20); but then why was it not more briefly expressed by עָמְדוּ (xxvi. 12)? The LXX. correctly renders: εὐφράνθην and ἑστῶτες ἦσαν. The poet, now again on the journey homewards, or having returned home, calls to mind the joy with which the cry for setting out, "Let us go up to the house of Jahve!" filled him. When he and the other visitors to the feast had reached the goal of their pilgrimage, their feet came to a stand-still, as if spell-bound by the overpowering, glorious sight.* Reviving this memory, he

---

* So also Veith in his, in many points, beautiful Lectures on twelve gradual Psalms (Vienna 1863), S. 72, "They arrested their steps, in order

exclaims: Jerusalem, O thou who art built up again—true, בָּנָה in itself only signifies " to build," but here, where, if there is nothing to the contrary, a closed sense is to be assumed for the line of the verse, and in the midst of songs which reflect the joy and sorrow of the post-exilic restoration period, it obtains the same meaning as in cii. 17, cxlvii. 2, and frequently (Gesenius: *O Hierosolyma restituta*). The parallel member, ver. 3b, does not indeed require this sense, but is at least favourable to it. Luther's earlier rendering, " as a city which is compacted together," was happier than his later rendering, " a city where they shall come together," which requires a *Niph.* or *Hithpa.* instead of the passive. חֻבַּר signifies, as in Ex. xxviii. 7, to be joined together, to be united into a whole; and יַחְדָּו strengthens the idea of that which is harmoniously, perfectly, and snugly closed up (cf. cxxxiii. 1). The *Kaph* of כְּעִיר is the so-called *Kaph veritatis*: Jerusalem has risen again out of its ruined and razed condition, the breaches and gaps are done away with (Isa. lviii. 12), it stands there as a closely compacted city, in which house joins on to house. Thus has the poet seen it, and the recollection fills him with rapture.*

Vers. 4, 5. The imposing character of the impression was still greatly enhanced by the consideration, that this is the city where at all times the twelve tribes of God's nation (which were still distinguished as its elements even after the Exile, Rom. xi. 1, Luke ii. 36, Jas. i. 1) came together at the three great feasts. The use of the שׁ twice as equivalent to אֲשֶׁר is (as in Canticles) appropriate to the ornamental, happy, miniature-like manner of these Songs of degrees. In שָׁשָּׁם the שָׁם is, as in Eccles. i. 7, equivalent to שָׁמָּה, which on the other hand in ver. 5 is no more than an emphatic שָׁם (cf. lxxvi. 4, lxviii. 7). עָלָה affirms a habit (cf. Job i. 4) of the past, which extends into the present. עֵדוּת לְיִשְׂרָאֵל is not an accusative of the definition or destination (Ew. § 300, c), but an apposition to the previous clause, as e.g. in Lev. xxiii. 14, 21, 31 (Hitzig), referring to the appointment in Ex. xxiii. 17, xxxiv. 23, Deut.

---

to give time to the amazement with which the sight of the Temple, the citadel of the king, and the magnificent city filled them."

* In synagogue and church it is become customary to interpret ver. 3 of the parallelism of the heavenly and the earthly Jerusalem.

xvi. 16. The custom, which arose thus, is confirmed in ver. 5 from the fact, that Jerusalem, the city of the one national sanctuary, was at the same time the city of the Davidic kingship. The phrase יָשְׁבוּ לְמִשְׁפָּט is here transferred from the judicial persons (cf. xxix. 10 with ix. 5, Isa. xxviii. 6), who sit in judgment, to the seats (thrones) which are set down and stand there for judgment (cf. cxxv. 1, and θρόνος ἔκειτο, Apoc. iv. 2). The Targum is thinking of seats in the Temple, viz. the raised (in the second Temple resting upon pillars) seat of the king in the court of the Israelitish men near the שַׁעַר הָעֶלְיוֹן, but לְמִשְׁפָּט points to the palace, 1 Kings vii. 7. In the flourishing age of the Davidic kingship this was also the highest court of judgment of the land; the king was the chief judge (2 Sam. xv. 2, 1 Kings iii. 16), and the sons, brothers, or kinsmen of the king were his assessors and advisers. In the time of the poet it is different; but the attractiveness of Jerusalem, not only as the city of Jahve, but also as the city of David, remains the same for all times.

Vers. 6–9. When the poet thus calls up the picture of his country's "city of peace" before his mind, the picture of the glory which it still ever possesses, and of the greater glory which it had formerly, he spreads out his hands over it in the distance, blessing it in the kindling of his love, and calls upon all his fellow-countrymen round about and in all places: *apprecamini salutem Hierosolymis*. So Gesenius correctly (*Thesaurus*, p. 1347); for just as שָׁאַל לוֹ לְשָׁלוֹם signifies to inquire after any one's well-being, and to greet him with the question: הֲשָׁלוֹם לְךָ (Jer. xv. 5), so שָׁאַל שָׁלוֹם signifies to find out any one's prosperity by asking, to gladly know and gladly see that it is well with him, and therefore to be animated by the wish that he may prosper; Syriac, שאל שלמא ד directly: to salute any one; for the interrogatory הֲשָׁלוֹם לְךָ and the well-wishing שָׁלוֹם לְךָ, εἰρήνη σοί (Luke x. 5, John xx. 19 sqq.), have both of them the same source and meaning. The reading אֹהֲלָיִךְ, commended by Ewald, is a recollection of Job xii. 6 that is violently brought in here. The loving ones are comprehended with the beloved one, the children with the mother. שָׁלָה forms an alliteration with שָׁלוֹם; the emphatic form יִשְׁלָיוּ occurs even in other instances out of pause (*e.g.* lvii. 2). In ver. 7 the alliteration of שָׁלוֹם and שַׁלְוָה is again taken up, and both accord with the name of Jerusalem. *Ad elegantiam facit*, as Venema observes, *perpetua vocum ad se invicem et omnium ad nomen Hierosolymae alliteratio*. Both together mark the Song of degrees as such. Happiness, cries out the poet to the holy city from afar, be within thy bulwarks, prosperity within thy palaces, *i.e.* without and within. חֵיל, ramparts, circumvallation (from חוּג, to surround, Arabic حول, round about, equally correct whether written חֵיל or חֵל), and אַרְמְנוֹת as the parallel word, as in xlviii. 14. The twofold motive of such an earnest wish for peace is love for the brethren and love for the house of God. For the sake of the brethren is he cheerfully resolved to speak peace (τὰ πρὸς εἰρήνην αὐτῆς, Luke xix. 42) concerning (דִּבֶּר בְּ, as in lxxxvii. 3, Deut. vi. 7, LXX. περὶ σοῦ; cf. דִּבֶּר שָׁלוֹם with אֶל and לְ, to speak peace to, lxxxv. 9, Esth. x. 3) Jerusalem, for the sake of the house of Jahve will he strive after good (*i.e.* that which tends to her well-being) to her (like בִּקֵּשׁ טוֹבָה לְ in Neh. ii. 10, cf. דָּרַשׁ שָׁלוֹם, Deut. xxiii. 7 [6], Jer. xxix. 7). For although he is now again far from Jerusalem after the visit that is over, he still remains united in love to the holy city as being the goal of his longing, and to those who dwell there as being his brethren and friends. Jerusalem is and will remain the heart of all Israel as surely as Jahve, who has His house there, is the God of all Israel.

PSALM CXXIII.

UPWARD GLANCE TO THE LORD IN TIMES OF CONTEMPT.

1 TO Thee do I lift up mine *eyes*,
   Thou who art enthroned in the heavens!
2 Behold, *as the eyes* of servants
   unto the hand of their master,
 As the eyes of a maid unto the hand
   of her mistress:
 So our *eyes* are unto Jahve our God,
   until He *be gracious* unto us.

3 *Be gracious* unto us, Jahve, *be gracious* unto us,
   for of *contempt* are we *full enough*.

4 *Full enough* is our soul
With the scorn of the haughty,
the *contempt* of despots.

This Psalm is joined to the preceding Psalm by the community of the divine name *Jahve our God*. Alsted (died 1638) gives it the brief, ingenious inscription *oculus sperans*. It is an upward glance of waiting faith to Jahve under tyrannical oppression. The fact that this Psalm appears in a rhyming form, "as scarcely any other piece in the Old Testament" (Reuss), comes only from those inflexional rhymes which creep in of themselves in the tephilla style.

Vers. 1, 2. The destinies of all men, and in particular of the church, are in the hand of the King who sits enthroned in the unapproachable glory of the heavens and rules over all things, and of the Judge who decides all things. Up to Him the poet raises his eyes, and to Him the church, together with which he may call Him "Jahve our God," just as the eyes of servants are directed towards the hand of their lord, the eyes of a maid towards the hand of her mistress; for this hand regulates the whole house, and they wait upon their winks and signs with most eager attention. Those of Israel are Jahve's servants, Israel the church is Jahve's maid. In His hand lies its future. At length He will take compassion on His own. Therefore its longing gaze goes forth towards Him, without being wearied, until He shall graciously turn its distress. With reference to the *i* of הַיֹּשְׁבִי, *vid.* on cxiii., cxiv. אֲדוֹנֵיהֶם is their common lord; for since in the antitype the sovereign Lord is meant, it will be conceived of as *plur. excellentiæ*, just as in general it occurs only rarely (Gen. xix. 2, 18, Jer. xxvii. 4) as an actual plural.

Vers. 3, 4. The second strophe takes up the " be gracious unto us" as it were in echo. It begins with a *Kyrie eleison*, which is confirmed in a *crescendo* manner after the form of steps. The church is already abundantly satiated with ignominy. רַב is an abstract "much," and רַבַּת (cf. lxv. 10, cxx. 6) is concrete, "a great measure," like רַבָּה, lxii. 3, something great (*vid.* Böttcher, *Lehrbuch*, § 624). The subjectivizing, intensive לָהּ accords with cxx. 6—probably an indication of one and the same author. בָּם is strengthened by לְעֵי, like בֹּ in Ezek. xxxvi. 4. The article of הַזֵּד is retrospectively demonstrative: full of such scorn of the haughty (Ew. § 290, d). הַמַּיִם is also retrospectively demonstrative; but since a repetition of the article for the fourth time would have been inelegant, the poet here says לִנְאֵיוֹנִים with the *Lamed*, which serves as a circumlocution of the genitive. The Masora reckons this word among the fifteen " words that are written as one and are to be read as two." The *Kerî* runs viz. לִגְאֵי יוֹנִים, *superbis oppressorum* (יוֹנִים, *part. Kal*, like הַיּוֹנָה Zeph. iii. 1, and frequently). But apart from the consideration that instead of אֵי, from the unknown גֵּאֶה, it might more readily be pointed אֵי, from גֵּאֶה (a form of nouns indicating defects, contracted גֵּא), this genitival construction appears to be far-fetched, and, inasmuch as it makes a distinction among the oppressors, inappropriate. The poet surely meant לִגְאֵיוֹנִים or לַגֵּאֵיוֹנִים. This word גֵּאֶיוֹן (after the form רָעְיוֹן, אֶבְיוֹן, עֶלְיוֹן) is perhaps an intentional new formation of the poet. Saadia interprets it after the Talmudic לִגְיוֹן, *legio;* but how could one expect to find such a Grecized Latin word (λεγεών) in the Psalter! Dunash ben-Labrat (about 960) regards גאיונים as a compound word in the signification of הַגֵּאִים הַיּוֹנִים. In fact the poet may have chosen the otherwise unused adjectival form גֵּאֵיוֹנִים because it reminds one of יוֹנִים, although it is not a compound word like דִּבְיוֹנִים. If the Psalm is a Maccabæan Psalm, it is natural to find in לִגְאֵיוֹנִים an allusion to the despotic domination of the יְוָנִים.

PSALM CXXIV.

THE DELIVERER FROM DEATH IN WATERS AND IN A SNARE.

1 *HAD not Jahve been for us,*
   Let Israel say—
2 *Had not Jahve been for us,*
   When men rose up against us:

3 *Then* had they swallowed us up alive,
   When their anger was kindled against us—
4 *Then* had the *waters* overwhelmed us,
   The stream *had gone over our soul*—

5 *Then had gone over our soul*
   The proudly swelling *waters*.

6 Blessed be Jahve, who hath not abandoned us
   A prey to their teeth!
7 Our soul, like a bird hath it *escaped*
   Out of *the snare* of the fowlers:
   The snare was broken
   And we—we *escaped*.

8 Our help is in the Name of Jahve,
   The Creator of heaven and earth.

The statement "the stream had gone over our soul" of this fifth Song of degrees, coincides with the statement "our soul is full enough" of the fourth; the two Psalms also meet in the synonymous new formations גֵּאִיוֹנִים and זֵידוֹנִים, which also look very much as though they were formed in allusion to cotemporary history. The לְדָוִד is wanting in the LXX., *Codd. Alex.* and *Vat.*, here as in Ps. cxxii., and with the exception of the Targum is wanting in general in the ancient versions, and therefore is not so much as established as a point of textual criticism. It is a Psalm in the manner of the Davidic Psalms, to which it is closely allied in the metaphors of the overwhelming waters, xviii. 5, 17 (cf. cxliv. 7), lxix. 2 sq., and of the little bird; cf. also on לְצִפּוֹר xxvii. 13, on אָדָם used of hostile men lvi. 12, on בָּלַע חַיִּים lv. 16, on בָּרוּךְ ה' xxviii. 6, xxxi. 22. This beautiful song makes its modern origin known by its Aramaizing character, and by the delight, after the manner of the later poetry, in all kinds of embellishments of language. The art of the form consists less in strophic symmetry than in this, that in order to take one step forward it always goes back half a step. Luther's imitation (1524), "Were God not with us at this time" (*Wäre Gott nicht mit uns diese Zeit*), bears the inscription "The true believers' safeguard."

Vers. 1–5. It is commonly rendered, "If it had not been Jahve who was for us." But, notwithstanding the subject that is placed first (cf. Gen. xxiii. 13), the שֶׁ belongs to the לוּלֵי;

since in the Aramaizing Hebrew (cf. on the other hand Gen. xxxi. 42) שֶׁלּוּלֵי (cf. لَوْ أَنَّ) signifies *nisi* (prop. *nisi quod*), as in the Aramaic (דְּ) שֶׁ (לְוַי) לְוַי, *o si* (prop. *o si quod*). The אֲזַי, peculiar to this Psalm in the Old Testament, instead of אָז follows the model of the dialectic אֱדַיִן, וּ֯, הָ֯ס֯מִ֯ (הֵידֵין, הֲרֵין).

In order to begin the apodosis of לוּלֵי (לוּלָא) emphatically the older language makes use of the confirmatory כִּי, Gen. xxxi. 42, xliii. 10; here we have אֲזַי (well rendered by the LXX. ἄρα), as in cxix. 92. The *Lamed* of הָיָה לָנוּ is *raphe* in both instances, according to the rule discussed above, vol. ii. 145. When men (אָדָם) rose up against Israel and their anger was kindled against them, they who were feeble in themselves over against the hostile world would have been swallowed up alive if they had not had Jahve for them, if they had not had Him on their side. This "swallowing up alive" is said elsewhere of Hades, which suddenly and forcibly snatches away its victims, lv. 16, Prov. i. 12; here, however, as ver. 6 shows, it is said of the enemies, who are represented as wild beasts. In ver. 4 the hostile power which rolls over them is likened to an overflowing stream, as in Isa. viii. 7 sq., the Assyrian. נַחְלָה, a stream or river, is *Milel*; it is first of all accusative: towards the stream (Num. xxxiv. 5); then, however, it is also used as a nominative, like הַמּוּתָה, לַיְלָה, and the like (cf. common Greek ἡ νύχθα, ἡ νεότητα); so that ־תָה is related to ־ת (־ה) as ־נָה, ־מוֹ to ־ן and ־ם (Böttcher, § 615). These latest Psalms are fond of such embellishments by means of adorned forms and Aramaic or Aramaizing words. זֵידוֹנִים is a word which is indeed not unhebraic in its formation, but is more indigenous to Chaldee; it is the Targum word for זֵדִים in lxxxvi. 14, cxix. 51, 78 (also in liv. 5 for זָרִים), although according to Levy the MSS. do not present זֵידוֹנִין but זֵידָנִין. In the passage before us the Targum renders: the king who is like to the proud waters (לְמוֹי זֵידוֹנַיָא) of the sea (Antiochus Epiphanes?—A scholium explains οἱ ὑπερήφανοι). With reference to עָבַר before a plural subject, *vid.* Ges. § 147.

Vers. 6-8. After the fact of the divine succour has been expressed, in ver. 6 follows the thanksgiving for it, and in ver. 7 the joyful shout of the rescued one. In ver. 6 the enemies are conceived of as beasts of prey on account of their bloodthirstiness, just as the worldly empires are in the Book of Daniel; in ver. 7 as "fowlers" on account of their cunning. According to the punctuation it is not to be rendered: Our soul is like a bird that is escaped, in which case it would have been accented נַפְשֵׁנוּ כְּצִפּוֹר, but: our soul (subject with *Rebia magnum*) is as a bird (כְּצִפּוֹר as in Hos. xi. 11, Prov. xxiii. 32, Job xiv. 2, instead of the syntactically more usual כַּצִּפּוֹר) escaped out of the snare of him who lays snares (יוֹקְשִׁים, elsewhere יָקוֹשׁ, יָקֻשׁ, a fowler, xci. 3). וְנִשְׁבָּר (with *a* beside *Rebia*) is 3d *præt.*: the snare was burst, and we—we became free. In ver. 8 (cf. cxxi. 2, cxxxiv. 3) the universal, and here pertinent thought, viz. the help of Israel is in the name of Jahve, the Creator of the world, *i.e.* in Him who is manifest as such and is continually verifying Himself, forms the epiphonematic close. Whether the power of the world seeks to make the church of Jahve like to itself or to annihilate it, it is not a disavowal of its God, but a faithful confession, stedfast even to death, that leads to its deliverance.

PSALM CXXV.

ISRAEL'S BULWARK AGAINST TEMPTATION TO APOSTASY.

1 THEY who trust in Jahve are as Mount Zion,
  Which doth not totter, it standeth fast *for ever*.
2 As for Jerusalem—mountains are *round about* her,
  And Jahve is *round about* His people
  From this time and *for evermore*.

3 For the sceptre of wickedness shall not rest
  Upon the lot of *the righteous*,
  Lest *the righteous* stretch out
  Their hands unto iniquity.

4 O show Thyself *good*, Jahve, unto the *good*
  And to those who are upright in their hearts.

5 But those who turn aside their crooked paths—
Jahve cause them to pass away with the workers of iniquity.
Peace be upon Israel!

The favourite word *Israel* furnished the outward occasion for annexing this Psalm to the preceding. The situation is like that in Ps. cxxiii. and cxxiv. The people are under foreign dominion. In this lies the seductive inducement to apostasy. The pious and the apostate ones are already separated. Those who have remained faithful shall not, however, always remain enslaved. Round about Jerusalem are mountains, but more important still: Jahve, of rocks the firmest, Jahve encompasses His people.

That this Psalm is one of the latest, appears from the circumstantial expression "the upright in their hearts," instead of the old one, "the upright of heart," from פֹּעֲלֵי הָאָוֶן instead of the former פֹּעֲלֵי אָוֶן, and also from לְמַעַן לֹא (beside this passage occurring only in cxix. 11, 80, Ezek. xix. 9, xxvi. 20, Zech. xii. 7) instead of לְמַעַן אֲשֶׁר לֹא or פֶּן.

Vers. 1, 2. The stedfastness which those who trust in Jahve prove in the midst of every kind of temptation and assault is likened to Mount Zion, because the God to whom they believingly cling is He who sits enthroned on Zion. The future יֵשֵׁב signifies: He sits and will sit, that is to say, He continues to sit, cf. ix. 8, cxxii. 5. Older expositors are of opinion that the heavenly Zion must be understood on account of the Chaldæan and the Roman catastrophes; but these, in fact, only came upon the buildings on the mountain, not upon the mountain itself, which in itself and according to its appointed destiny (*vid.* Mic. iii. 12, iv. 1) remained unshaken. In ver. 2 also it is none other than the earthly Jerusalem that is meant. The holy city has a natural circumvallation of mountains, and the holy nation that dwells and worships therein has a still infinitely higher defence in Jahve, who encompasses it round (*vid.* on xxxiv. 8), as perhaps a wall of fire (Zech. ii. 9 [5]), or an impassably broad and mighty river (Isa. xxxiii. 21); a statement which is also now confirmed, for, etc. Instead of inferring from the clause ver. 2 that which is to be expected with לָכֵן, the poet confirms it with כִּי by that which is surely to be expected.

Ver. 3. The pressure of the worldly power, which now lies heavily upon the holy land, will not last for ever; the duration of the calamity is exactly proportioned to the power of resistance of the righteous, whom God proves and purifies by calamity, but not without at the same time graciously preserving them. "The rod of wickedness" is the heathen sceptre, and "the righteous" are the Israelites who hold fast to the religion of their fathers. The holy land, whose sole entitled inheritors are these righteous, is called their "lot" (גּוֹרָל, κλῆρος = κληρονομία). נוּחַ signifies to alight or settle down anywhere, and having alighted, to lean upon or rest (cf. Isa. xi. 2 with John i. 32, ἔμεινεν). The LXX. renders οὐκ ἀφήσει, i.e. לֹא יַנִּיחַ (cf. on the other hand יַנִּיחַ, He shall let down, cause to come down, in Isa. xxx. 32). Not for a continuance shall the sceptre of heathen tyranny rest upon the holy land, God will not suffer that: in order that the righteous may not at length, by virtue of the power which pressure and use exercises over men, also participate in the prevailing ungodly doings. שָׁלַח with *Beth*: to seize upon anything wrongfully, or even only (as in Job xxviii. 9) to lay one's hand upon anything (frequently with עַל). As here in the case of עַוְלָתָה, in lxxx. 3 too the form that is the same as the locative is combined with a preposition.

Vers. 4, 5. On the ground of the strong faith in vers. 1 sq. and of the confident hope in ver. 3, the petition now arises that Jahve would speedily bestow the earnestly desired blessing of freedom upon the faithful ones, and on the other hand remove the cowardly [lit. those afraid to confess God] and those who have fellowship with apostasy, together with the declared wicked ones, out of the way. For such is the meaning of vers. 4 sq. טוֹבִים (in Proverbs alternating with the "righteous," ch. ii. 20, the opposite being the "wicked," רְשָׁעִים, ch. xiv. 19) are here those who truly believe and rightly act in accordance with the good will of God,* or, as the parallel

---

* The Midrash here calls to mind a Talmudic riddle: There came a good one (Moses, Ex. ii. 2) and received a good thing (the Tôra, Prov. iv. 2) from the good One (God, Ps. cxlv. 9) for the good ones (Israel, Ps. cxxv. 4).

member of the verse explains (where לְיְשָׁרִים did not require the article on account of the addition), those who in the bottom of their heart are uprightly disposed, as God desires to have it. The poet supplicates good for them, viz. preservation against denying God and deliverance out of slavery; for those, on the contrary, who bend (הִטָּה) their crooked paths, i.e. turn aside their paths in a crooked direction from the right way (עַקַלְקַלּוֹתָם, cf. Judg. v. 6, no less than in Amos ii. 7, Prov. xvii. 23, an accusative of the object, which is more natural than that it is the accusative of the direction, after Num. xxii. 23 *extrem.*, cf. Job xxiii. 11, Isa. xxx. 11)—for these he wishes that Jahve would clear them away (הוֹלִיךְ like اَذْهَلَ, *perire facere* = *perdere*) together with the workers of evil, *i.e.* the open, manifest sinners, to whom these lukewarm and sly, false and equivocal ones are in no way inferior as a source of danger to the church. LXX. correctly: τοὺς δὲ ἐκκλίνοντας εἰς τὰς στραγγαλιὰς (Aquila διαπλοκάς, Symmachus σκολιότητας, Theodotion διεστραμμένα) ἀπάξει κύριος μετὰ, κ.τ.λ. Finally, the poet, stretching out his hand over Israel as if pronouncing the benediction of the priest, gathers up all his hopes, prayers, and wishes into the one prayer: "Peace be upon Israel." He means "the Israel of God," Gal. vi. 16. Upon this Israel he calls down peace from above. Peace is the end of tyranny, hostility, dismemberment, unrest, and terror; peace is freedom and harmony and unity and security and blessedness.

PSALM CXXVI.

THE HARVEST OF JOY AFTER THE SOWING OF TEARS.

1 WHEN Jahve brought back the returning ones of Zion,
   We were as those who dream.
2 *Then* laughter filled our mouth,
        And our tongue a shout of joy.
   Then said they among the heathen:
        "*Great things hath Jahve done for them*"—
3 *Great things hath Jahve done for us*,
        We became glad.

4 Oh lead back, Jahve, our captive ones,
As streams in the south country!
5 Those who sow with tears,
Shall reap with a shout of joy.
6 He goeth to and fro amidst weeping,
Bearing the scattering of the seed—
He cometh along with a shout of joy,
Bearing his sheaves.

It is with this Psalm, which the favourite word *Zion* connects with the preceding Psalm, exactly as with Ps. lxxxv., which also gives thanks for the restoration of the captive ones of Israel on the one hand, and on the other hand has to complain of the wrath that is still not entirely removed, and prays for a national restoration. There are expositors indeed who also transfer the grateful retrospect with which this Song of degrees (vers. 1–3), like that Korahitic Psalm (vers. 2–4), begins, into the future (among the translators Luther is at least more consistent than the earlier ones); but they do this for reasons which are refuted by Ps. lxxxv., and which are at once silenced when brought face to face with the requirements of the syntax.

Vers. 1–3. When passages like Isa. i. 9, Gen. xlvii. 25, or others where ויהי is *perf. consec.*, are appealed to in order to prove that הָיִינוּ כְּחֹלְמִים may signify *erimus quasi somniantes*, they are instances that are different in point of syntax. Any other rendering than that of the LXX. is here impossible, viz.: Ἐν τῷ ἐπιστρέψαι κύριον τὴν αἰχμαλωσίαν Σιὼν ἐγενήθημεν ὡς παρακεκλημένοι (כְּנֶחָמִים?—Jerome correctly, *quasi somniantes*). It is, however, just as erroneous when Jerome goes on to render: *tunc implebitur risu os nostrum;* for it is true the future after אָז has a future signification in passages where the context relates to matters of future history, as in xcvi. 12, Zeph. iii. 9, but it always has the signification of the imperfect after the key-note of the historical past has once been struck, Ex. xv. 1, Josh. viii. 30, x. 12, 1 Kings xi. 7, xvi. 21, 2 Kings xv. 16, Job xxxviii. 21; it is therefore, *tunc implebatur*. It is the exiles at home again upon the soil of their fatherland who here cast back a glance into the happy time when their destiny suddenly took another turn, by the God of Israel disposing the heart of the conqueror of Babylon to set them at liberty, and to send them to their native land in an honourable manner. שִׁיבַת is not equivalent to שְׁבִית, nor is there any necessity to read it thus (Olshausen, Böttcher, and Hupfeld). שִׁיבָה (from שׁוּב, like בִּיאָה, קִימָה) signifies the return, and then those returning; it is, certainly, an innovation of this very late poet. When Jahve brought home the homeward-bound ones of Zion —the poet means to say—we were as dreamers. Does he mean by this that the long seventy years' term of affliction lay behind us like a vanished dream (Joseph Kimchi), or that the redemption that broke upon us so suddenly seemed to us at first not to be a reality but a beautiful dream? The tenor of the language favours the latter: as those not really passing through such circumstances, but only dreaming. Then—the poet goes on to say—our mouth was filled with laughter (Job viii. 21) and our tongue with a shout of joy, inasmuch, namely, as the impression of the good fortune which contrasted so strongly with our trouble hitherto, compelled us to open our mouth wide in order that our joy might break forth in a full stream, and our jubilant mood impelled our tongue to utter shouts of joy, which knew no limit because of the inexhaustible matter of our rejoicing. And how awe-inspiring was Israel's position at that time among the peoples! and what astonishment the marvellous change of Israel's lot produced upon them! Even the heathen confessed that it was Jahve's work, and that He had done great things for them (Joel ii. 20 sq., 1 Sam. xii. 24)—the glorious predictions of Isaiah, as in ch. xlv. 14, lii. 10, and elsewhere, were being fulfilled. The church on its part seals that confession coming from the mouth of the heathen. This it is that made them so joyful, that God had acknowledged them by such a mighty deed.

Vers. 4–6. But still the work so mightily and graciously begun is not completed. Those who up to the present time have returned, out of whose heart this Psalm is, as it were, composed, are only like a small vanguard in relation to the whole nation. Instead of שְׁבוּתֵנוּ the *Kerî* here reads שְׁבִיתֵנוּ, from שְׁבִית, Num. xxi. 29, after the form בְּרִית in Gen. l. 4. As we read elsewhere that Jerusalem yearns after her children, and Jahve solemnly assures her, " thou shalt put them all on as jewels and gird thyself like a bride" (Isa. xlix. 18), so here the poet proceeds from the idea that the holy land yearns after an abundant, reanimating influx of population, as the *Negeb* (*i.e.* the Judæan south country, Gen. xx. 1, and in general the south country lying towards the desert of Sinai) thirsts for the rain-water streams, which disappear in the summer season and regularly return in the winter season. Concerning אֲפִיק, " a water-holding channel," *vid.* on xviii. 16. If we translate *converte captivitatem nostram* (as Jerome does, following the LXX.), we shall not know what to do with the figure, whereas in connection with the rendering *reduc captivos nostros* it is just as beautifully adapted to the object as to the governing verb. If we have rightly referred *negeb* not to the land of the Exile but to the Land of Promise, whose appearance at this time is still so unlike the promise, we shall now also understand by those who sow in tears not the exiles, but those who have already returned home, who are again sowing the old soil of their native land, and that with tears, because the ground is so parched that there is little hope of the seed springing up. But this tearful sowing will be followed by a joyful harvest. One is reminded here of the drought and failure of the crops with which the new colony was visited in the time of Haggai, and of the coming blessing promised by the prophet with a view to the work of the building of the Temple being vigorously carried forward. Here, however, the tearful sowing is only an emblem of the new foundation-laying, which really took place not without many tears (Ezra iii. 12), amidst sorrowful and depressed circumstances; but in its general sense the language of the Psalm coincides with the language of the Preacher on the Mount, Matt. v. 4: Blessed are those who mourn, for they shall be comforted. The subject to ver. 6 is the husbandman, and without a figure, every member of the *ecclesia pressa*. The gerundial construction in ver. 6*a* (as in 2 Sam. iii. 16, Jer. l. 4, cf. the more Indo-Germanic style of expression in 2 Sam. xv. 30) depicts the continual passing along, here the going to and fro of the sorrowfully pensive man; and ver. 6*b* the undoubted coming and sure appearing of him who is highly blessed beyond expectation. The former bears מֶשֶׁךְ הַזָּרַע, the seed-draught, *i.e.* the handful of seed taken from the rest for casting out (for מֹשֵׁךְ הַזֶּרַע in Amos.ix. 13 signifies to cast forth the seed along the furrows); the latter his sheaves, the produce (תְּבוּאָה), such as puts him to the blush, of his, as it appeared to him, forlorn sowing. As by the sowing we are to understand everything that each individual contributes towards the building up of the kingdom of God, so by the sheaves, the wholesome fruit which, by God bestowing His blessing upon it beyond our prayer and comprehension, springs up from it.

PSALM CXXVII.

EVERYTHING DEPENDS UPON THE BLESSING OF GOD.[*]

1 *IF Jahve build not* the house,
  They labour *in vain* thereon who *build* it.
  If Jahve watch not over the city,
  In vain doth he keep awake *who watcheth over it.*

2 *In vain* is it that ye rise up early
  And only sit down late,
  Eating the bread of sorrowful labour
  Even so He giveth to His beloved in sleep.

3 Behold a heritage of Jahve are *sons*,
  A reward is the fruit of the womb.
4 As arrows in the hand of a mighty man,
  So are *sons* of the youth.

5 Blessed is the man
  Who hath his quiver full of them:
  They shall not be ashamed,
  When they speak with enemies in the gate.

The inscribed לִשְׁלֹמֹה is only added to this Song of degrees because there was found in ver. 2 not only an allusion to the name *Jedidiah*, which Solomon received from Nathan (2 Sam. xii. 25), but also to his being endowed with wisdom and riches in the dream at Gibeon (1 Kings iii. 5 sqq.). And to these is

---

[*] *An Gottes Segen ist alles gelegen.*

still to be added the Proverbs-like form of the Psalm; for, like the proverb-song, the extended form of the *Mashal*, it consists of a double string of proverbs, the expression of which reminds one in many ways of the Book of Proverbs (עֲצָבִים in ver. 2, toilsome efforts, as in Prov. v. 10; מְאַחֲרֵי, as in Prov. xxiii. 30; בְּנֵי הַנְּעוּרִים in ver. 4, sons begotten in one's youth, as in Prov. v. 18 אֵשֶׁת נְעוּרִים, a wife married in one's youth; בַּשַּׁעַר in ver. 5, as in Prov. xxii. 22, xxiv. 7), and which together are like the unfolding of the proverb, ch. x. 22: *The blessing of Jahve, it maketh rich, and labour addeth nothing beside it.* Even Theodoret observes, on the natural assumption that ver. 1 points to the building of the Temple, how much better the Psalm suits the time of Zerubbabel and Joshua, when the building of the Temple was imperilled by the hostile neighbouring peoples; and in connection with the relatively small number of those who had returned home out of the Exile, a numerous family, and more especially many sons, must have seemed to be a doubly and threefoldly precious blessing from God.

Vers. 1, 2. The poet proves that everything depends upon the blessing of God from examples taken from the God-ordained life of the family and of the state. The rearing of the house which affords us protection, and the stability of the city in which we securely and peaceably dwell, the acquisition of possessions that maintain and adorn life, the begetting and rearing of sons that may contribute substantial support to the father as he grows old—all these are things which depend upon the blessing of God without natural preliminary conditions being able to guarantee them, well-devised arrangements to ensure them, unwearied labours to obtain them by force, or impatient care and murmuring to get them by defiance. Many a man builds himself a house, but he is not able to carry out the building of it, or he dies before he is able to take possession of it, or the building fails through unforeseen misfortunes, or, if it succeeds, becomes a prey to violent destruction: if God Himself do not build it, they labour thereon (בְּ עָמֵל, Jonah iv. 10, Eccles. ii. 21) in vain who build it. Many a city is well-ordered, and seems to be secured by wise precautions against every misfortune, against fire and sudden attack; but if God Himself do not guard it, it is in vain that those to whom its protection is entrusted give themselves no sleep and perform (עֵרֶךְ, a word that has only come into frequent use since the literature of the Salomonic age) the duties of their office with the utmost devotion. The perfect in the apodosis affirms what has been done on the part of man to be ineffectual if the former is not done on God's part; cf. Num. xxxii. 23. Many rise up early in order to get to their work, and delay the sitting down as long as possible; *i.e.* not: the lying down (Hupfeld), for that is שָׁכַב, not יָשַׁב; but to take a seat in order to rest a little, and, as what follows shows, to eat (Hitzig). קוּם and שֶׁבֶת stand opposed to one another: the latter cannot therefore mean to remain sitting at one's work, in favour of which Isa. v. 11 (where בַּבֹּקֶר and בַּנֶּשֶׁף form an antithesis) cannot be properly compared. 1 Sam. xx. 24 shows that prior to the incursion of the Grecian custom they did not take their meals lying or reclining (ἀνα- or κατακείμενος), but sitting. It is vain for you—the poet exclaims to them—it will not after all bring what you think to be able to acquire; in so doing you eat only the bread of sorrow, *i.e.* bread that is procured with toil and trouble (cf. Gen. iii. 17, בְּעִצָּבוֹן): כֵּן, in like manner, *i.e.* the same as you are able to procure only by toilsome and anxious efforts, God gives to His beloved (lx. 7, Deut. xxxiii. 12) שֵׁנָא (= שֵׁנָה), in sleep (an adverbial accusative like בַּבֹּקֶר, לַיְלָה, עֶרֶב), *i.e.* without restless self-activity, in a state of self-forgetful renunciation, and modest, calm surrender to Him: " God bestows His gifts during the night," says a German proverb, and a Greek proverb even says: εὕδοντι κύρτος αἱρεῖ. Büttcher takes כֵּן in the sense of " so = without anything further ;" and כֵּן certainly has this meaning sometimes (*vid.* introduction to Ps. cx.), but not in this passage, where, as referring back, it stands at the head of the clause, and where what this mimic כֵּן would import lies in the word שֵׁנָא.

Vers. 3–5. With הִנֵּה it goes on to refer to a specially striking example in support of the maxim that everything depends upon God's blessing. פְּרִי הַבֶּטֶן (Gen. xxx. 2, Deut. vii. 13) beside בָּנִים also admits of the including of daughters. It is with שָׂכָר (recalling Gen. xxx. 18) just as with נַחֲלָה. Just as the latter in this passage denotes an inheritance not according to hereditary right, but in accordance with the free-will of the giver, so the former denotes not a reward that is paid out as in duty bound, but a recompense that is bestowed according to one's free judgment, and in fact looked for in accordance with a promise given, but cannot by any means be demanded. Sons are a blessed gift from above. They are—especially when they are the offspring of a youthful marriage (*opp.* בְּנֵי־זְקֻנִים, Gen. xxxvii. 3, xliv. 20), and accordingly themselves strong and hearty (Gen. xlix. 3), and at the time that the father is growing old are in the bloom of their years—like arrows in the hand of a warrior. This is a comparison which the circumstances of his time made natural to the poet, in which the sword was carried side by side with the trowel, and the work of national restoration had to be defended step by step against open enemies, envious neighbours, and false brethren. It was not sufficient then to have arrows in the quiver; one was obliged to have them not merely at hand, but in the hand (בְּיַד), in order to be able to discharge them and defend one's self. What a treasure, in such a time when it was needful to be constantly ready for fighting, defensive or offensive, was that which youthful sons afforded to the elderly father and weaker members of the family! Happy is the man—the poet exclaims—who has his quiver, *i.e.* his house, full of such arrows, in order to be able to deal out to the enemies as many arrows as may be needed. The father and such a host of sons surrounding him (this is the complex notion of the subject) form a phalanx not to be broken through. If they have to speak with enemies in the gate—*i.e.* candidly to upbraid them with their wrong, or to ward off their unjust accusation—they shall not be ashamed, *i.e.* not be overawed, disheartened, or disarmed. Gesenius in his *Thesaurus*, as Ibn-Jachja has already done, takes דִּבֶּר here in the signification "to destroy;" but in Gen. xxxiv. 13 this *Piel* signifies to deal behind one's back (deceitfully), and in 2 Chron. xxii. 10 to get rid of by assassination. This shade of the notion, which proceeds from שׂוּם, *pone esse* (*vid.* xviii. 48, xxviii. 2), does not suit the passage before us, and the expression לֹא־יֵבֹשׁוּ is favourable to the idea of the gate as being the forum, which arises from taking יְדַבְּרוּ in its ordinary signification. Unjust judges, malicious accusers, and false witnesses retire shy and faint-hearted before a family so capable of defending itself. We read the opposite of this in Job v. 4 of sons upon whom the curse of their fathers rests.

PSALM CXXVIII.

THE FAMILY PROSPERITY OF THE GOD-FEARING MAN.

1 *HAPPY* is every one who feareth Jahve,
   Who walketh in His ways.
2 The labour of thy hands shalt thou surely eat,
   Happy art thou, and it is well with thee.

3 Thy wife, like a fruitful vine is she,
   In the inner part of thy house ;
   Thy children are like shoots of olive-trees
   Round about thy table.

4 Behold, surely thus is the man *blessed*
   Who feareth Jahve.
5 Jahve *bless* thee out of Zion,
   And *see thou* the prosperity of Jerusalem
   All the days of thy life,
6 *And see thou* thy children's children—
   Peace be upon Israel!

Just as Ps. cxxvii. is appended to Ps. cxxvi. because the fact that Israel was so surprised by the redemption out of exile that they thought they were dreaming, finds its interpretation in the universal truth that God bestows upon him whom He loves, in sleep, that which others are not able to acquire by toiling and moiling day and night: so Ps. cxxviii. follows Ps. cxxvii. for the same reason as Ps. ii. follows Ps. i. In both instances they are Psalms placed together, of which one begins with *ashrê* and one ends with *ashrê*. In other respects Ps. cxxviii. and cxxvii. supplement one another. They are related to one another much as the New Testament parables of the treasure in the field and the one pearl are related. That which makes man happy is represented in Ps. cxxvii. as a gift coming as a blessing, and in Ps. cxxviii. as a reward coming as a blessing, that which is briefly indicated in the word יְגִיעַ in cxxvii. 3 being here expanded and unfolded. There it appears as a gift of grace in contrast to the God-estranged self-activity of man, here as a fruit of the *ora et labora*. Ewald considers this and the preceding Psalm to be songs to be sung at table. But they are ill-suited for this purpose; for they contain personal mirrorings instead of petitions, and instead of benedictions of those who are about to partake of the food provided.

Vers. 1–3. The כִּי in ver. 2 signifies neither "for" (Aquila, κόπον τῶν ταρσῶν σου ὅτι φάγεσαι), nor "when" (Symmachus, κόπον χειρῶν σου ἐσθίων); it is the directly affirmative כִּי, which is sometimes thus placed after other words in a clause (cxviii. 10–12, Gen. xviii. 20, xli. 32). The proof in favour of this asseverating כִּי is the very usual כִּי עַתָּה in the apodoses of hypothetical protases, or even כִּי־אָז in Job xi. 15, or also only כִּי in Isa. vii. 9, 1 Sam. xiv. 39: "surely then;" the transition from the confirmative to the affirmative signification is evident from ver. 4 of the Psalm before us. To support one's self by one's own labour is a duty which even a Paul did not wish to avoid (Acts xx. 34), and so it is a great good fortune (טוֹב לְךָ as in cxix. 71) to eat the produce of the labour of one's own hands (LXX. τοὺς καρποὺς τῶν πόνων, or according to an original reading, τοὺς πόνους τῶν καρπῶν*); for he who can make himself useful to others and still is also independent of them, he eats the bread of blessing which God gives, which is sweeter than the bread of charity which men give. In close connection with this is the prosperity of a house that is at peace and contented within itself, of an amiable and tranquil and hopeful (rich in hope) family life. "Thy wife (אֶשְׁתְּךָ, found only here, for אִשְׁתְּךָ) is as a fruit-producing vine." פֹּרִיָּה for פָּרָה, from פָּרָה = פָּרִי, with the *Jod* of the root retained, like בּוֹכִיָּה, Lam. i. 16. The figure of the vine is admirably suited to the wife, who is a shoot or sprig of the husband, and stands in need of the man's support as the vine needs a stick or the wall of a house (*pergula*). בְּיַרְכְּתֵי בֵיתֶךָ does not belong to the figure,

---

* The fact that the τῶν καρπῶν of the LXX. here, as in Prov. xxxi. 20, is intended to refer to the hands is noted by Theodoret and also by Didymus (in Rosenmüller): καρποὺς φησι νῦν ὡς ἀπὸ μέρους τὰς χεῖρας (i.e. *per synecdochen partis pro toto*), τουτέστι τῶν πρακτικῶν σου δυνάμεων φάγεσαι τοὺς πόνους.

as Kimchi is of opinion, who thinks of a vine starting out of the room and climbing up in the open air outside. What is meant is the angle, corner, or nook (יַרְכְּתֵי, in relation to things and artificial, equivalent to the natural יַרְכְּי), i.e. the background, the privacy of the house, where the housewife, who is not to be seen much out of doors, leads a quiet life, entirely devoted to the happiness of her husband and her family. The children springing from such a noble vine, planted around the family table, are like olive shoots or cuttings; cf. in Euripides, *Medea*, 1098: τέκνων ἐν οἴκοις γλυκερὸν βλάστημα, and *Herc. Fur.* 839: καλλίπαις στέφανος. Thus fresh as young layered small olive-trees and thus promising are they.

Vers. 4–6. Pointing back to this charming picture of family life, the poet goes on to say: behold, for thus = behold, thus is the man actually blessed who fears Jahve. כִּי confirms the reality of the matter of fact to which the הִנֵּה points. The promissory future in ver. 5a is followed by imperatives which call upon the God-fearing man at once to do that which, in accordance with the promises, stands before him as certain. מִצִּיוֹן as in cxxxiv. 3, xx. 3. בָּנִים לְבָנֶיךָ instead of בְּנֵי בָנֶיךָ gives a designed indefiniteness to the first member of the combination. Every blessing the individual enjoys comes from the God of salvation, who has taken up His abode in Zion, and is perfected in participation in the prosperity of the holy city and of the whole church, of which it is the centre. A New Testament song would here open up the prospect of the heavenly Jerusalem. But the character of limitation to this present world that is stamped upon the Old Testament does not admit of this. The promise refers only to a present participation in the well-being of Jerusalem (Zech. viii. 15) and to long life prolonged in one's children's children; and in this sense calls down intercessorily peace upon Israel in all its members, and in all places and all ages.

PSALM CXXIX.

THE END OF THE OPPRESSORS OF ZION.

1 *ENOUGH have they oppressed me from my youth up,*
    Let Israel say—

2 *Enough have they oppressed me from my youth up,*
Nevertheless they have not prevailed against me.

3 Upon my back the ploughers ploughed,
They made long their furrow-strip.
4 Jahve is righteous:
He hath cut asunder the cords of the wicked.
5 They must be ashamed and turn back,
All who hate Zion.

6 They must become as grass of the house-tops,
Which, ere it shooteth up, withereth—
7 Wherewith the reaper filleth not his hand,
Nor he who bindeth sheaves his bosom,
8 Neither do they who pass by say:
The blessing of Jahve be upon you!
" *We bless you in the name of Jahve!!*"

Just as Ps. cxxiv. with the words " *let Israel say*" was followed by Ps. cxxv. with " *peace be upon Israel,*" so Ps. cxxviii. with " *peace be upon Israel*" is followed by Ps. cxxix. with " *let Israel say.*" This Ps. cxxix. has not only the call " *let Israel say,*" but also the situation of a deliverance that has been experienced (cf. ver. 4 with cxxiv. 6 sq.), from which point it looks gratefully back and confidently forward into the future, and an Aramaic tinge that is noticeable here and there by the side of all other classical character of form, in common with Ps. cxxiv.

Vers. 1, 2. Israel is gratefully to confess that, however much and sorely it was oppressed, it still has not succumbed. רַבַּת, together with רַבָּה, has occurred already in lxv. 10, lxii. 3, and it becomes usual in the post-exilic language, cxx. 6, cxxiii. 4, 2 Chron. xxx. 18; Syriac *rebath.* The expression " from my youth " glances back to the time of the Egyptian bondage; for the time of the sojourn in Egypt was the time of Israel's youth (Hos. ii. 17 [15], xi. 1, Jer. ii. 2, Ezek. xxiii. 3). The protasis ver. 1*a* is repeated in an interlinked, chain-like conjunction in order to complete the thought; for ver. 2*b* is the turning-point, where גַּם, having reference to the whole negative clause, signifies " also" in the sense of " nevertheless," ὅμως (synon. בְּכָל־זֹאת), as in Ezek. xvi. 28, Eccles. vi. 7, cf. above, cxix. 24 : although they oppressed me much and sore, yet have they not overpowered me (the construction is like Num. xiii. 30, and frequently).

Vers. 3-5. Elsewhere it is said that the enemies have driven over Israel (lxvi. 12), or have gone over its back (Isa. li. 23) ; here the customary figurative language אָרַשׁ חָרֵשׁ in Job iv. 8 (cf. Hos. x. 13) is extended to another figure of hostile dealing : without compassion and without consideration they ill-treated the stretched-forth back of the people who were held in subjection, as though it were arable land, and, without restraining their ferocity and setting a limit to their spoiling of the enslaved people and country, they drew their furrow-strip (מַעֲנִיתָם, according to the *Keri* מַעֲנוֹתָם) long. But מַעֲנָה does not signify (as Keil on 1 Sam. xiv. 14 is of opinion, although explaining the passage more correctly than Thenius) the furrow (= תֶּלֶם, גְּדוּד), but, like مَسَاحَة, a strip of arable land which the ploughman takes in hand at one time, at both ends of which consequently the ploughing team (צֶמֶד) always comes to a stand, turns round, and ploughs a new furrow ; from עָנָה, to bend, turn (*vid.* Wetzstein's Excursus II. at the end of this volume). It is therefore : they drew their furrow-turning long (dative of the object instead of the accusative with *Hiph.*, as *e.g.* in Isa. xxix. 2, cf. with *Piel* in xxxiv. 4, cxvi. 16, and *Kal* lxix. 6, after the Aramaic style, although it is not unhebraic). Righteous is Jahve—this is an universal truth, which has been verified in the present circumstances ;—He hath cut asunder the cords of the wicked (עֲבוֹת as in ii. 3 ; here, however, it is suggested by the metaphor in ver. 3, cf. Job xxxix. 10 ; LXX. αὐχένας, *i.e.* עֲנוֹק), with which they held Israel bound. From that which has just been experienced Israel derives the hope that *all* Zion's haters (a newly coined name for the enemies of the religion of Israel) will be obliged to retreat with shame and confusion.

Vers. 6-8. The poet illustrates the fate that overtakes them by means of a picture borrowed from Isaiah and worked up (ch. xxxvii. 27) : they become like " grass of the housetops," etc. שֶׁ is a relative to שֶׁבְּ (*quod exarescit*), and קָדְמַת,

priusquam, is Hebraized after כְּמִקַּדְמַת דְּנָה in Dan. vi. 11, or מִקַּדְמַת דְּנָה in Ezra v. 11. שָׁלַף elsewhere has the signification "to draw forth" of a sword, shoe, or arrow, which is followed by the LXX., Theodotion, and the Quinta: πρὸ τοῦ ἐκσπασθῆναι, before it is plucked. But side by side with the ἐκσπασθῆναι of the LXX. we also find the reading ἐξανθῆσαι; and in this sense Jerome renders (*statim ut*) *viruerit*, Symmachus ἐκκαυλῆσαι (to shoot into a stalk), Aquila ἀνέθαλεν, the Sexta ἐκστερεῶσαι (to attain to full solidity). The Targum paraphrases שלף in both senses: to shoot up and to pluck off. The former signification, after which Venema interprets: *antequam se evaginet vel evaginetur*, i.e. *antequam e vaginulis suis se evolvat et succrescat*, is also advocated by Parchon, Kimchi, and Aben-Ezra. In the same sense von Ortenberg conjectures שָׁחֲלָף. Since the grass of the house-tops or roofs, if one wishes to pull it up, can be pulled up just as well when it is withered as when it is green, and since it is the most natural thing to take חָצִיר as the subject to שלף, we decide in favour of the intransitive signification, "to put itself forth, to develop, shoot forth into ear." The roof-grass withers before it has put forth ears or blossoms, just because it has no deep root, and therefore cannot stand against the heat of the sun.* The poet pursues the figure of the grass of the house-tops still further. The encompassing lap or bosom (κόλπος) is called elsewhere חֵצֶן (Isa. xlix. 22, Neh. v. 13); here it is חֹצֶן, like the Arabic *hidn* (diminutive *hodein*), of the same root with מָחוֹז, a creek, in cvii. 30. The enemies of Israel are as grass upon the house-tops, which is not garnered in; their life closes with sure destruction, the germ of which they (without any need for any rooting out) carry within themselves. The observation of Knapp, that any Western poet would have left off with ver. 6, is based upon the error that vers. 7, 8 are an idle embellishment. The greeting addressed to the reapers in ver. 8 is taken from life; it is not denied even to heathen reapers. Similarly Boaz (Ruth

---

* So, too, Geiger in the *Deutsche Morgenländische Zeitschrift*, xiv. 278 f., according to whom شلف (شلف) occurs in Saadia and Abu-Said in the signification "to be in the first maturity, to blossom,"—a sense שלף may also have here; cf. the Talmudic שַׁלְבּוּצֵי used of unripe dates that are still in blossom.

ii. 4) greets them with "Jahve be with you," and receives the counter-salutation, "Jahve bless thee." Here it is the passers-by who call out to those who are harvesting: *The blessing* (בְּרִכַּת) *of Jahve happen to you* (אֲלֵיכֶם,* as in the Aaronitish blessing), and (since "we bless you in the name of Jahve" would be a purposeless excess of politeness in the mouth of the same speakers) receive in their turn the counter-salutation: *We bless you in the name of Jahve*. As a contrast it follows that there is before the righteous a garnering in of that which they have sown amidst the exchange of joyful benedictory greetings.

PSALM CXXX.

DE PROFUNDIS.

1 OUT of the depths do I call unto Thee, Jahve.
2 Lord, O hearken to my voice,
   Let Thine ears be attentive
   To the voice of my supplication!

3 If Thou keepest iniquities, Jāh—
   Lord, who can stand?!
4 Yet with Thee is the forgiveness,
   That Thou mayest be feared.

5 *I hope* in Jahve, *my soul hopeth,*
   And upon His word do I wait.
6 *My soul waiteth for the Lord,*
   More than the night-watchers for the morning,
   The night-watchers for the morning.

7 Wait, *Israel,* for Jahve,
   For with Jahve is the mercy,
   And abundantly is there with Him *redemption.*
8 And HE will *redeem Israel*
   From all its iniquities.

---

* Here and there עֲלֵיכֶם is found as an error of the copyist. The *Hebrew Psalter*, Basel 1547, 12mo, notes it as a various reading.

Luther, being once asked which were the best Psalms, replied, *Psalmi Paulini;* and when his companions at table pressed him to say which these were, he answered: Ps. xxxii., li., cxxx., and cxliii. In fact in Ps. cxxx. the condemnability of the natural man, the freeness of mercy, and the spiritual nature of redemption are expressed in a manner thoroughly Pauline. It is the sixth among the seven *Psalmi pœnitentiales* (vi., xxxii., xxxviii., li., cii., cxxx., cxliii.).

Even the chronicler had this Psalm before him in the present classification, which puts it near to Ps. cxxxii.; for the independent addition with which he enriches Solomon's prayer at the dedication of the Temple, 2 Chron. vi. 40–42, is compiled out of passages of Ps. cxxx. (ver. 2, cf. the divine response, 2 Chron. vii. 15) and Ps. cxxxii. (vers. 8, 16, 10).

The mutual relation of Ps. cxxx. to Ps. lxxxvi. has been already noticed there. The two Psalms are first attempts at adding a third, Adonajic style to the Jehovic and Elohimic Psalm-style. There *Adonaj* is repeated seven times, and three times in this Psalm. There are also other indications that the writer of Ps. cxxx. was acquainted with that Ps. lxxxvi. (compare ver. 2a, שִׁמְעָה בְקוֹלִי, with lxxxvi. 6, הַקְשִׁיבָה בְּקוֹל; ver. 2b, לְקוֹל תַּחֲנוּנָי, with lxxxvi. 6, בְּקוֹל תַּחֲנוּנוֹתָי; ver. 4, עִמְּךָ הַסְּלִיחָה, with lxxxvi. 5, וְסַלָּח; ver. 8, עִם ה' הַחֶסֶד, with lxxxvi. 5, 15, רַב־חֶסֶד). The fact that קַשּׁוּב (after the form שָׁבוּל) occurs besides only in those dependent passages of the chronicler, and קָשֻׁב only in Neh. i. 6, 11, as סְלִיחָה besides only in Dan. ix. 9, Neh. ix. 17, brings our Psalm down into a later period of the language; and moreover Ps. lxxxvi. is not Davidic.

Vers. 1–4. The depths (מַעֲמַקִּים) are not the depths of the soul, but the deep outward and inward distress in which the poet is sunk as in deep waters (lxix. 3, 15). Out of these depths he cries to the God of salvation, and importunately prays Him who rules all things and can do all things to grant him a compliant hearing (בְּ שָׁמֵעַ, Gen. xxi. 12, xxvii. 13, xxx. 6, and other passages). God hears indeed even in Himself, as being the omniscient One, the softest and most secret as well as the loudest utterance; but, as Hilary observes, *fides officium suum exsequitur, ut Dei auditionem roget, ut qui per naturam suam audit per orantis precem dignetur audire.* In this sense the poet prays that His ears may be turned קַשֻּׁבוֹת (duller collateral form of קַשָּׁב, to be in the condition of *arrectae aures*), with strained attention, to his loud and urgent petition (xxviii. 2). His life hangs upon the thread of the divine compassion. If God preserves iniquities, who can stand before Him?! He preserves them (שָׁמַר) when He puts them down to one (xxxii. 2) and keeps them in remembrance (Gen. xxxvii. 11), or, as it is figuratively expressed in Job xiv. 17, sealed up as it were in custody in order to punish them when the measure is full. The inevitable consequence of this is the destruction of the sinner, for nothing can stand against the punitive justice of God (Nah. i. 6, Mal. iii. 2, Ezra ix. 15). If God should show Himself as Jāh,* no creature would be able to stand before Him, who is *Adonaj*, and can therefore carry out His judicial will or purpose (Isa. li. 16). He does not, however, act thus. He does not proceed according to the legal stringency of recompensative justice. This thought, which fills up the pause after the question, but is not directly expressed, is confirmed by the following כִּי, which therefore, as in Job xxii. 2, xxxi. 18, xxxix. 14, Isa. xxviii. 28 (cf. Eccles. v. 6), introduces the opposite. With the Lord is the willingness to forgive (הַסְּלִיחָה), in order that He may be feared; *i.e.* He forgives, as it is expressed elsewhere (*e.g.* lxxix. 9), for His Name's sake: He seeks therein the glorifying of His Name. He will, as the sole Author of our salvation, who, putting all vain-glorying to shame, causes mercy instead of justice to take its course with us (cf. li. 6), be reverenced; and gives the sinner occasion, ground, and material for reverential thanksgiving and praise by bestowing "forgiveness" upon him in the plenitude of absolutely free grace.

Vers. 5–8. Therefore the sinner need not, therefore too the poet will not, despair. He hopes in Jahve (*acc. obj.* as in xxv. 5, 21, xl. 2), his soul hopes; hoping in and waiting upon God is the mood of his inmost and of his whole being. He waits upon God's word, the word of His salvation (cxix. 81), which, if it penetrates into the soul and cleaves there, calms

---

* Eusebius on Ps. lxviii. (lxvii.) 5 observes that the Logos is called Ἰα as μορφὴν δούλου λαβὼν καὶ τὰς ἀκτῖνας τῆς ἑαυτοῦ θεότητος συστείλας καὶ ὥσπερ καταδὺς ἐν τῷ σώματι. There is a similar passage in Vincentius Ciconia (1567), which we introduced into our larger Commentary on the Psalms (1859-60).

all unrest, and by the appropriated consolation of forgiveness transforms and enlightens for it everything in it and outside of it. His soul is לַאדֹנָי, *i.e.* stedfastly and continually directed towards Him; as Chr. A. Crusius when on his death-bed, with hands and eyes uplifted to heaven, joyfully exclaimed : " My soul is full of the mercy of Jesus Christ. *My whole soul is towards God.*" The meaning of לאדני becomes at once clear in itself from cxliii. 6, and is defined moreover, without supplying שֹׁמְרִת (Hitzig), according to the following לַבֹּקֶר. Towards the Lord he is expectantly turned, like those who in the night-time wait for the morning. The repetition of the expression "those who watch for the morning" (cf. Isa. xxi. 11) gives the impression of protracted, painful waiting. The wrath, in the sphere of which the poet now finds himself, is a nightly darkness, out of which he wishes to be removed into the sunny realm of love (Mal. iii. 20 [iv. 2]); not he alone, however, but at the same time all Israel, whose need is the same, and for whom therefore believing waiting is likewise the way to salvation. With Jahve, and with Him exclusively, with Him, however, also in all its fulness, is הַחֶסֶד (contrary to lxii. 13, without any pausal change in accordance with the varying of the segolates), the mercy, which removes the guilt of sin and its consequences, and puts freedom, peace, and joy into the heart. And plenteous (הַרְבֵּה, an adverbial *infin. absol.*, used here, as in Ezek. xxi. 20, as an adjective) is with Him redemption; *i.e.* He possesses in the richest measure the willingness, the power, and the wisdom, which are needed to procure redemption, which rises up as a wall of partition (Ex. viii. 19) between destruction and those imperilled. To Him, therefore, must the individual, if he will obtain mercy, to Him must His people, look up hopingly; and this hope directed to Him shall not be put to shame: He, in the fulness of the might of His free grace (Isa. xliii. 25), will redeem Israel from all its iniquities, by forgiving them and removing their unhappy inward and outward consequences. With this promise (cf. xxv. 22) the poet comforts himself. He means complete and final redemption, above all, in the genuinely New Testament manner, spiritual redemption.

PSALM CXXXI.
CHILD-LIKE RESIGNATION TO GOD.

1 JAHVE, my heart is not haughty, and mine eyes are not
Neither have I to do with great things   [lofty,
And extraordinary which are beyond me.

2 Verily I have smoothed down and calmed my soul;
Like a child that is weaned beside its mother,
Like the child that is weaned is my soul beside me.

3 Wait, Israel, upon Jahve
From henceforth and for ever.

This little song is inscribed לְדָוִד because it is like an echo of the answer (2 Sam. vi. 21 sq.) with which David repelled the mocking observation of Michal when he danced before the Ark in a linen ephod, and therefore not in kingly attire, but in the common raiment of the priests: *I esteem myself still less than I now show it, and I appear base in mine own eyes.* In general David is the model of the state of mind which the poet expresses here. He did not push himself forward, but suffered himself to be drawn forth out of seclusion. He did not take possession of the throne violently, but after Samuel has anointed him he willingly and patiently traverses the long, thorny, circuitous way of deep abasement, until he receives from God's hand that which God's promise had assured to him. The persecution by Saul lasted about ten years, and his kingship in Hebron, at first only incipient, seven years and a half. He left it entirely to God to remove Saul and Ishbosheth. He let Shimei curse. He left Jerusalem before Absalom. Submission to God's guidance, resignation to His dispensations, contentment with that which was allotted to him, are the distinguishing traits of his noble character, which the poet of this Psalm indirectly holds up to himself and to his cotemporaries as a mirror, viz. to the Israel of the period after the Exile, which, in connection with small beginnings under difficult circumstances, had been taught humbly contented and calm waiting.

With לֹא־גָבַהּ לִבִּי the poet repudiates pride as being the state of his soul; with לֹא־רָמוּ עֵינַי (lo-ramû' as in Prov. xxx. 13, and before Ajin, e.g., also in Gen. xxvi. 10, Isa. xi. 2, in accordance with which the erroneous placing of the accent in Baer's text is to be corrected), pride of countenance and bearing; and with וְלֹא־הִלַּכְתִּי, pride of endeavour and mode of action. Pride has its seat in the heart, in the eyes especially it finds its expression, and great things are its sphere in which it diligently exercises itself. The opposite of "great things" (Jer. xxiii. 3, xlv. 5) is not that which is little, mean, but that which is small; and the opposite of "things too wonderful for me" (Gen. xviii. 14) is not that which is trivial, but that which is attainable.

אִם־לֹא does not open a conditional protasis, for where is the indication of the apodosis to be found? Nor does it signify "but," a meaning it also has not in Gen. xxiv. 38, Ezek. iii. 6. In these passages too, as in the passage before us, it is asseverating, being derived from the usual formula of an oath: verily I have, etc. שִׁוָּה signifies (Isa. xxviii. 25) to level the surface of a field by ploughing it up, and has an ethical sense here, like יָשָׁר with its opposites עָקֹב and עָפֵל. The Poel דּוֹמֵם is to be understood according to דּוּמִיָּה in lxii. 2, and דּוּמָם in Lam. iii. 26. He has levelled or made smooth his soul, so that humility is its entire and uniform state; he has calmed it so that it is silent and at rest, and lets God speak and work in it and for it: it is like an even surface, and like the calm surface of a lake. Ewald and Hupfeld's rendering: "as a weaned child on its mother, so my soul, being weaned, lies on me," is refuted by the consideration that it ought at least to be כִּגְמוּלָה, but more correctly כֵּן גמולה; but it is also besides opposed by the article which is swallowed up in כַּגָּמֻל, according to which it is to be rendered: like one weaned beside its mother (here כִּגְמוּל on account of the determinative collateral definition), like the weaned one (here כַּגָּמוּל because without any collateral definition: cf., with Hitzig, Deut. xxxii. 2, and the like; moreover, also, because referring back to the first גמול, cf. Hab. iii. 8), is my soul beside me (Hitzig, Hengstenberg, and most expositors). As a weaned child—viz. not one that is only just begun to be weaned, but an actually weaned child (גָּמֻל, cognate גָּמַר, to bring to an end, more particularly to bring suckling to an end, to wean)—lies upon its mother without crying impatiently and craving for its mother's breast, but contented with the fact that it has its mother—like such a weaned child is his soul upon him, *i.e.* in relation to his Ego (which is conceived of in עָל as having the soul upon itself, cf. xlii. 7, Jer. viii. 18; *Psychology*, S. 151 f., tr. p. 180): his soul, which is by nature restless and craving, is stilled; it does not long after earthly enjoyment and earthly good that God should give these to it, but it is satisfied in the fellowship of God, it finds full satisfaction in Him, it is satisfied (satiated) in Him.

By the closing strain, ver. 3, the individual language of the Psalm comes to have a reference to the congregation at large. Israel is to renounce all self-boasting and all self-activity, and to wait in lowliness and quietness upon its God from now and for evermore. For He resisteth the proud, but giveth grace unto the humble.

PSALM CXXXII.

PRAYER FOR THE HOUSE OF GOD AND THE HOUSE OF DAVID.

1 REMEMBER, Jahve, to DAVID
   All the trouble endured by him,
2 Him who hath sworn unto Jahve,
   Hath vowed unto *the Mighty One of Jacob:*
3 " I will not enter into the tent of my house,
   I will not go up to the bed of my couch;
4 I will not give sleep to mine eyes,
   Slumber to mine eyelids,
5 Until I find a place for Jahve,
   A dwelling-tent for *the Mighty One of Jacob!*"

6 Behold it was, we heard it, in Ephrâthah,
   We found it in the fields of Ja'ar.
7 So let us go into His dwelling-tent,
   Let us prostrate ourselves before His footstool.
8 Arise, Jahve, to Thy rest,
   Thou and the Ark of Thy majesty!

9 *Let Thy priests clothe themselves with righteousness,*
And Thy saints shout for joy.
10 For the sake of DAVID Thy servant
Turn not back the face of Thine anointed!

11 Jahve hath sworn to DAVID
In truth that which He will not recall:
" Of the fruit of thy body
Do I appoint a possessor of thy throne.
12 If thy children keep My covenant
And My testimony, which I teach them:
Their children also shall for ever
Sit upon thy throne."
13 For Jahve hath chosen Zion,
He hath desired it as an abode for Himself.

14 "This is my rest for ever,
Here will I dwell, *for I have desired it.*"
15 Her provision will I bless abundantly,
Her poor will I satisfy with bread,
16 *And her priests will I clothe with salvation,*
And her saints shall shout aloud for joy.
17 There will I make a horn to shoot forth for DAVID,
I will prepare a lamp for mine anointed.
18 His enemies will I clothe with shame,
And upon himself shall his crown blossom.

Ps. cxxxi. designedly precedes Ps. cxxxii. The former has grown out of the memory of an utterance of David when he brought home the Ark, and the latter begins with the remembrance of David's humbly zealous endeavour to obtain a settled and worthy abode for the God who sits enthroned above the Ark among His people. It is the only Psalm in which the sacred Ark is mentioned. The chronicler put vers. 8–10 into the mouth of Solomon at the dedication of the Temple (2 Chron. vi. 41 sq.). After a passage borrowed from Ps. cxxx. 2 which is attached by עַתָּה to Solomon's Temple-dedication prayer, he appends further borrowed passages out of Ps. cxxxii. with וְעַתָּה. The variations in these verses of the Psalms, which are annexed by him with a free hand and from memory (*Jahve Elohim* for

Jahve, לְנֻחֶךָ for לִמְנוּחָתֶךָ, תְּשׁוּעָה for צֶדֶק, יִשְׂמְחוּ בַטּוֹב for יָרֹנּוּ), just as much prove that he has altered the Psalm, and not reversely (as Hitzig persistently maintains), that the psalmist has borrowed from the Chronicles. It is even still distinctly to be seen how the memory of Isa. lv. 3 has influenced the close of ver. 42 in the chronicler, just as the memory of Isa. lv. 2 has perhaps also influenced the close of ver. 41.

The psalmist supplicates the divine favour for the anointed of Jahve for David's sake. In this connection this anointed one is neither the high priest, nor Israel, which is never so named (*vid.* Hab. iii. 13), nor David himself, who "in all the necessities of his race and people stands before God," as Hengstenberg asserts, in order to be able to assign this Song of degrees, as others, likewise to the post-exilic time of the new colony. Zerubbabel might more readily be understood (Baur), with whom, according to the closing prophecy of the Book of Haggai, a new period of the Davidic dominion is said to begin. But even Zerubbabel, the פַּחַת יְהוּדָה, could not be called מָשִׁיחַ, for this he was not. The chronicler applies the Psalm in accordance with its contents. It is suited to the mouth of Solomon. The view that it was composed by Solomon himself when the Ark of the covenant was removed out of the tent-temple on Zion into the Temple-building (Amyraldus, De Wette, Tholuck, and others), is favoured by the relation of the circumstances, as they are narrated in 2 Chron. v. 5 sqq., to the desires of the Psalm, and a close kinship of the Psalm with Ps. lxxii. in breadth, repetitions of words, and a laboured forward movement which is here and there a somewhat uncertain advance. At all events it belongs to a time in which the Davidic throne was still standing and the sacred Ark was not as yet irrecoverably lost. That which, according to 2 Sam. ch. vi., vii., David did for the glory of Jahve, and on the other hand is promised to him by Jahve, is here made by a post-Davidic poet into the foundation of a hopeful intercessory prayer for the kingship and priesthood of Zion and the church presided over by both.

The Psalm consists of four ten-line strophes. Only in connection with the first could any objection be raised, and the strophe be looked upon as only consisting of nine lines. But the other strophes decide the question of its measure; and the breaking up of the weighty ver. 1 into two lines follows the accentuation, which divides it into two parts and places את by itself as being את (according to *Accentssystem*, xviii. 2, with *Mugrash*). Each strophe is adorned once with the name of *David;* and moreover the step-like progress which comes back to what has been said, and takes up the thread and carries it forward, cannot fail to be recognised.

Vers. 1–5. One is said to remember anything to another when he requites him something that he has done for him, or when he does for him what he has promised him. It is the post-Davidic church which here reminds Jahve of the hereinafter mentioned promises (of the "mercies of David," 2 Chron. vi. 42, cf. Isa. lv. 3) with which He has responded to David's ענות. By this verbal substantive of the *Pual* is meant all the care and trouble which David had in order to procure a worthy abode for the sanctuary of Jahve. ענה ב signifies to trouble or harass one's self about anything, *afflictari* (as frequently in the Book of Ecclesiastes); the *Pual* here denotes the self-imposed trouble, or even that imposed by outward circumstances, such as the tedious wars, of long, unsuccessful, and yet never relaxed endeavours (1 Kings v. 17 [3]). For he had vowed unto God that he would give himself absolutely no rest until he had obtained a fixed abode for Jahve. What he said to Nathan (2 Sam. vii. 2) is an indication of this vowed resolve, which was now in a time of triumphant peace, as it seemed, ready for being carried out, after the first step towards it had already been taken in the removal of the Ark of the covenant to Zion (2 Sam. ch. vi.); for 2 Sam. ch. vii. is appended to 2 Sam. ch. vi. out of its chronological order and only on account of the internal connection. After the bringing home of the Ark, which had been long yearned for (cf. ci. 2), and did not take place without difficulties and terrors, was accomplished, a series of years again passed over, during which David always carried about with him the thought of erecting God a Temple-building. And when he had received the tidings through Nathan that he should not build God a house, but that it should be done by his son and successor, he nevertheless did as much towards the carrying out of the desire of his heart as was possible in connection with this declaration of the will of Jahve. He consecrated the site of the future Temple, he procured the necessary means and materials for the building of it, he made all the necessary arrangements for the future Temple-service, he inspirited the people for the gigantic work of building that was before them, and handed over to his son the model for it, as it is all related to us in detail by the chronicler. The divine name "the mighty One of Jacob" is taken from Gen. xlix. 24, as in Isa. i. 24, xlix. 26, lx. 16. The Philistines with their Dagon had been made to feel this mighty Rock of Jacob when they took the sacred Ark along with them (1 Sam. ch. v.). With אִם David solemnly declares what he is resolved not to do. The meaning of the hyperbolically expressed vow in the form of an oath is that for so long he will not rejoice at his own dwelling-house, nor give himself up to sleep that is free from anxiety; in fine, for so long he will not rest. The genitives after אֹהֶל and עֶרֶשׂ are appositional genitives; Ps. xliv. delights in similar combinations of synonyms. יְצוּעָי (Latin *strata mea*) is a poetical plural, as also is מִשְׁכָּנוֹת. With תְּנוּמָה (which is always said of the eyelids, Gen. xxxi. 40, Prov. vi. 4, Eccles. viii. 16, not of the eyes) alternates שְׁנָת (according to another reading שְׁנַת) for שֵׁנָה. The *ath* is the same as in נַחֲלַת in xvi. 6, cf. lx. 13, Ex. xv. 2, and frequently. This Aramaizing rejection of the syllable before the tone is, however, without example elsewhere. The LXX. adds to ver. 4, καὶ ἀνάπαυσιν τοῖς κροτάφοις μου (וּמְנוּחָה לְרַקּוֹתָי), but this is a disagreeable overloading of the verse.

Vers. 6–10. In ver. 6 begins the language of the church, which in this Psalm reminds Jahve of His promises and comforts itself with them. Olshausen regards this ver. 6 as altogether inexplicable. The interpretation nevertheless has some safe starting-points. (1) Since the subject spoken of is the founding of a fixed sanctuary, and one worthy of Jahve, the suffix of שְׁמַעֲנוּהָ (with *Chateph* as in Hos. viii. 2, Ew. § 60, *a*) and מְצָאנוּהָ refers to the Ark of the covenant, which is *fem.* also in other instances (1 Sam. iv. 17, 2 Chron. viii. 11). (2) The Ark of the covenant, fetched up out of Shiloh by the Israelites to the battle at Ebenezer, fell into the hands of the victors, and remained, having been again given up by them, for twenty years in Kirjath-Jearim (1 Sam. vii. 1 sq.), until David removed it out of this Judæan district to Zion (2 Sam. vi. 2–4; cf.

2 Chron. i. 4). What is then more natural than that שְׂדֵי־יַעַר is a poetical appellation of Kirjath-Jearim (cf. "the field of Zoan" in lxxviii. 12)? Kirjath-Jearim has, as a general thing, very varying names. It is also called *Kirjath-ha-jearim* in Jer. xxvi. 20 (*Kirjath-'arim* in Ezra ii. 25, cf. Josh. xviii. 28), *Kirjath-ba'al* in Josh. xv. 60, *Ba'alah* in Josh. xv. 9, 1 Chron. xiii. 6 (cf. *Har-ha-ba'alah*, Josh. xv. 11, with *Har-Jearim* in Josh. xv. 10), and, as it seems, even *Ba'alê Jehudah* in 2 Sam. vi. 2. Why should it not also have been called *Ja'ar* side by side with *Kirjath-Jearim*, and more especially if the mountainous district, to which the mention of a hill and mountain of *Jearim* points, was, as the name "city of the wood" implies, at the same time a wooded district? We therefore fall in with Kühnöl's (1799) rendering: we found it in the meadows of Jaar, and with his remark: "Jaar is a shortened name of the city of Kirjath-Jearim."

The question now further arises as to what *Ephrathah* is intended to mean. This is an ancient name of Bethlehem; but the Ark of the covenant never was in Bethlehem. Accordingly Hengstenberg interprets, "We knew of it in Bethlehem (where David had spent his youth) only by hearsay, no one had seen it; we found it in Kirjath-Jearim, yonder in the wooded environs of the city, where it was as it were buried in darkness and solitude." So even Anton Hulsius (1650): *Ipse David loquitur, qui dicit illam ipsam arcam, de qua quum adhuc Bethlehemi versaretur inaudivisset, postea a se (vel majoribus suis ipso adhuc minorenni) inventam fuisse in campis Jaar.* But (1) the supposition that David's words are continued here does not harmonize with the way in which they are introduced in ver. 2, according to which they cannot possibly extend beyond the vow that follows. (2) If the church is speaking, one does not see why Bethlehem is mentioned in particular as the place of the hearsay. (3) *We heard it in Ephrathah* cannot well mean anything else than, *per antiptosin* (as in Gen. i. 4, but without כִּי), we heard that it was in Ephrathah. But the Ark was before Kirjath-Jearim in Shiloh. The former lay in the tribe of Judah close to the western borders of Benjamin, the latter in the midst of the tribe of Ephraim. Now since אֶפְרָתִי quite as often means an Ephraimite as it does a Bethlehemite, it may be asked whether *Ephrathah* is not intended of the

Ephraimitish territory (Kühnöl, Gesenius, Maurer, Tholuck, and others). The meaning would then be: we had heard that the sacred Ark was in Shiloh, but we found it not there, but in Kirjath-Jearim. And we can easily understand why the poet has mentioned the two places just in this way. *Ephrâth*, according to its etymon, is fruitful fields, with which are contrasted the fields of the wood—the sacred Ark had fallen from its original, more worthy abode, as it were, into the wilderness. But is it probable, more especially in view of Mic. v. 1, that in a connection in which the memory of David is the ruling idea, *Ephrathah* signifies the land of Ephraim? No, *Ephrathah* is the name of the district in which Kirjath-Jearim lay. Caleb had, for instance, by Ephrath, his third wife, a son named Hûr (Chûr), 1 Chron. ii. 19. This Hûr, the first-born of Ephrathah, is the father of the population of Bethlehem (1 Chron. iv. 4), and Shobal, a son of this Hûr, is father of the population of Kirjath-Jearim (1 Chron. ii. 50). Kirjath-Jearim is therefore, so to speak, the daughter of Bethlehem. This was called Ephrathah in ancient times, and this name of Bethlehem became the name of its district (Mic. v. 1). Kirjath-Jearim belonged to *Caleb-Ephrathah* (1 Chron. ii. 24), as the northern part of this district seems to have been called in distinction from *Negeb-Caleb* (1 Sam. xxx. 14).

But מִשְׁכְּנוֹתָיו in ver. 7 is now neither a designation of the house of Abinadab in Kirjath-Jearim, for the expression would be too grand, and in relation to ver. 5 even confusing, nor a designation of the Salomonic Temple-building, for the expression standing thus by itself is not enough alone to designate it. What is meant will therefore be the tent-temple erected by David for the Ark when removed to Zion (2 Sam. vii. 2, יְרִיעָה). The church arouses itself to enter this, and to prostrate itself in adoration towards (*vid.* xcix. 5) the footstool of Jahve, *i.e.* the Ark; and to what purpose? The Ark of the covenant is now to have a place more worthy of it; the מְנוּחָה, *i.e.* the בֵּית מְנוּחָה, 1 Chron. xxviii. 2, in which David's endeavours have through Solomon reached their goal, is erected: let Jahve and the Ark of His sovereign power, that may not be touched (see the examples of its inviolable character in 1 Sam. ch. v., vi., 2 Sam. vi. 6 sq.), now enter this fixed abode! Let His priests who are to serve Him there clothe themselves in "righteousness," *i.e.* in conduct that is according to His will and pleasure; let His saints, who shall there seek and find mercy, shout for joy! More especially, however, let Jahve for David's sake, His servant, to whose restless longing this place of rest owes its origin, not turn back the face of His anointed one, *i.e.* not reject his face which there turns towards Him in the attitude of prayer (cf. lxxxiv. 10). The chronicler has understood ver. 10 as an intercession on behalf of Solomon, and the situation into which we are introduced by vers. 6–8 seems to require this. It is, however, possible that a more recent poet here, in vers. 7, 8, reproduces words taken from the heart of the church in Solomon's time, and blends petitions of the church of the present with them. The subject all through is the church, which is ever identical although changing in the persons of its members. The Israel that brought the sacred Ark out of Kirjath-Jearim to Zion and accompanied it thence to the Temple-hill, and now worships in the sanctuary raised by David's zeal for the glory of Jahve, is one and the same. The prayer for the priests, for all the saints, and more especially for the reigning king, that then resounded at the dedication of the Temple, is continued so long as the history of Israel lasts, even in a time when Israel has no king, but has all the stronger longing for the fulfilment of the Messianic promise.

Vers. 11–13. The "for the sake of David" is here set forth in detail. אֱמֶת in ver. 11a is not the accusative of the object, but an adverbial accusative. The first member of the verse closes with לְדָוִד, which has the distinctive *Pazer*, which is preceded by *Legarmeh* as a sub-distinctive; then follows at the head of the second member אֱמֶת with *Zinnor*, then לֹא־יָשׁוּב מִמֶּנָּה with *Olewejored* and its conjunctive *Galgal*, which regularly precedes after the sub-distinctive *Zinnor*. The suffix of מִמֶּנָּה refers to that which was affirmed by oath, as in Jer. iv. 28. Lineal descendants of David will Jahve place on the throne (לְכִסֵּא like לְרֵאשִׁי in xxi. 4) to him, *i.e.* so that they shall follow him as possessors of the throne. David's children shall for ever (which has been finally fulfilled in Christ) sit לְכִסֵּא to him (cf. ix. 5, Job xxxvi. 7). Thus has Jahve promised, and expects in return from the sons of David the observance of His Law. Instead of עֵדֹתִי זוּ it is pointed עֵדֹתִי זוֹ. In Hahn's edition עֵדֹתִי has *Mercha* in the *penult.* (cf. the retreat of the tone in אֲדֹנָי זֶה, Dan. x. 17), and in Baer's edition the still better attested reading *Mahpach* instead of the counter-tone *Metheg*, and *Mercha* on the *ultima*. It is not plural with a singular suffix (cf. Deut. xxviii. 59, Ges. § 91, 3), but, as זֹאת = indicates, the singular for עֵדוּתִי, like תְּהִנָּתִי for תְּחִנּוּתִי in 2 Kings vi. 8; and signifies the revelation of God as an attestation of His will. אֲלַמְּדֵם has *Mercha mahpach.*, זוּ *Rebia parvum*, and עֵדֹתִי *Mercha*; and according to the interpunction it would have to be rendered: "and My self-attestation there" (*vid.* on ix. 16), but זוּ is relative: My self-attestation (revelation), which I teach them. The divine words extend to the end of ver. 12. The hypotheses with אִם, as the fulfilment in history shows, were conditions of the continuity of the Davidic succession; not, however,—because human unfaithfulness does not annul the faithfulness of God,—of the endlessness of the Davidic throne. In ver. 13 the poet states the ground of such promissory mercy. It is based on the universal mercy of the election of Jerusalem. אִוָּהּ has *He mappic*. like עֲנָהּ in Deut. xxii. 29, or the stroke of *Raphe* (Ew. § 247, *d*), although the suffix is not absolutely necessary. In the following strophe the purport of the election of Jerusalem is also unfolded in Jahve's own words.

Vers. 14–18. Shiloh has been rejected (lxxviii. 60), for a time only was the sacred Ark in Bethel (Judg. xx. 27) and Mizpah (Judg. xxi. 5), only somewhat over twenty years was it sheltered by the house of Abinadab in Kirjath-Jearim (1 Sam. vii. 2), only three months by the house of Obed-Edom in Perez-Uzzah (2 Sam. vi. 11)—but Zion is Jahve's abiding dwelling-place, His own proper settlement, מְנוּחָה (as in Isa. xi. 10, lxvi. 1, and besides 1 Chron. xxviii. 2). In Zion, His chosen and beloved dwelling-place, Jahve blesses everything that belongs to her temporal need (צֵידָהּ for צֵידָתָהּ, *vid.* on xxvii. 5, note); so that her poor do not suffer want, for divine love loves the poor most especially. His second blessing refers to the priests, for by means of these He will keep up His intercourse with His people. He makes the priesthood of Zion a real institution of salvation: He clothes her priests with salvation, so that they do not merely bring it about instrumentally, but personally possess it, and their whole outward appearance is one which proclaims salvation. And to all her saints He

gives cause and matter for high and lasting joy, by making
Himself known also to the church, in which He has taken
up His abode, in deeds of mercy (loving-kindness or grace).
There (םָשׁ, cxxxiii. 3) in Zion is indeed the kingship of promise, which cannot fail of fulfilment. He will cause a horn
to shoot forth, He will prepare a lamp, for the house of David,
which David here represents as being its ancestor and the
anointed one of God reigning at that time; and all who hostilely
rise up against David in his seed, He will cover with shame as
with a garment (Job viii. 22), and the crown consecrated by
promise, which the seed of David wears, shall blossom like an
unfading wreath. The horn is an emblem of defensive might
and victorious dominion, and the lamp (נֵר, 2 Sam. xxi. 17, cf
נִיר, 2 Chron. xxi. 7, LXX. λύχνον) an emblem of brilliant
dignity and joyfulness. In view of Ezek. xxix. 21, of the
predictions concerning the Branch (*zemach*) in Isa. iv. 2, Jer.
xxiii. 5, xxxiii. 15, Zech. iii. 8, vi. 12 (cf. Heb. vii. 14), and of
the fifteenth Beracha of the *Shemone-Esre* (the daily Jewish
prayer consisting of eighteen benedictions): "make the branch
(*zemach*) of David Thy servant to shoot forth speedily, and let
his horn rise high by virtue of Thy salvation,"—it is hardly to
be doubted that the poet attached a Messianic meaning to this
promise. With reference to our Psalm, Zacharias, the father
of John the Baptist, changes that supplicatory beracha of his
nation (Luke i. 68–70) into a praiseful one, joyfully anticipating the fulfilment that is at hand in Jesus.

PSALM CXXXIII.

PRAISE OF BROTHERLY FELLOWSHIP.

1 BEHOLD how good it is, and how delightful,
   That brethren also dwell together!
2 Like the fine oil upon the head,
   Flowing gently down upon the beard, the beard of Aaron,
   Which flows gently down upon the hem of his garments—
3 Like the dew of Hermon, *which flows gently down* upon the
     mountains of Zion,
   For there hath Jahve commanded the blessing,
   Life, for evermore.

In this Psalm, says Hengstenberg, " David brings to the consciousness of the church the glory of the fellowship of the saints, that had so long been wanting, the restoration of which had begun with the setting up of the Ark in Zion." The Psalm, in fact, does not speak of the termination of the dispersion, but of the uniting of the people of all parts of the land for the purpose of divine worship in the one place of the sanctuary: and, as in the case of Ps. cxxii., its counterpart, occasions can be found in the history of David adapted to the לדוד of the inscription. But the language witnesses against David; for the construction of שׁ with the participle, as שֶׁיָּרֵד, *qui descendit* (cf. cxxxv. 2, שֶׁעֹמְדִים, *qui stant*), is unknown in the usage of the language prior to the Exile. Moreover the inscription לדוד is wanting in the LXX. *Cod. Vat.* and the Targum; and the Psalm may only have been so inscribed because it· entirely breathes David's spirit, and is as though it had sprung out of his love for Jonathan.

With גַּם the assertion passes on from the community of nature and sentiment which the word " brethren" expresses to the outward active manifestation and realization that correspond to it: good and delightful (cxxxv. 3) it is when brethren united by blood and heart also (corresponding to this their brotherly nature) dwell together—a blessed joy which Israel has enjoyed during the three great Feasts, although only for a brief period (*vid.* Ps. cxxii.). Because the high priest, in whom the priestly mediatorial office culminates, is the chief personage in the celebration of the feast, the nature and value of that local reunion is first of all expressed by a metaphor taken from him. שֶׁמֶן הַטּוֹב is the oil for anointing described in Ex. xxx. 22-33, which consisted of a mixture of oil and aromatic spices strictly forbidden to be used in common life. The sons of Aaron were only sprinkled with this anointing oil; but Aaron was expressly anointed with it, inasmuch as Moses poured it upon his head; hence he is called *par excellence* " the anointed priest " (הַכֹּהֵן הַמָּשִׁיחַ), whilst the other priests are only " anointed " (מְשֻׁחִים, Num. iii. 3) in so far as their garments, like Aaron's, were also sprinkled with the oil (together with the blood of the ram of consecration), Lev. viii. 12, 30. In the time of the second Temple, to which the holy oil of anointing was wanting, the installation into the office of high priest took place by his being invested in the pontifical robes. The poet, however, when he calls the high priest as such *Aaron*, has the high-priesthood in all the fulness of its divine consecration (Lev. xxi. 10) before his eyes. Two drops of the holy oil of anointing, says a Haggada, remained for ever hanging on the beard of Aaron like two pearls, as an emblem of atonement and of peace. In the act of the anointing itself the precious oil freely poured out ran gently down upon his beard, which in accordance with Lev. xxi. 5 was unshortened.

In that part of the Tôra which describes the robe of the high priest, שׁוּלֵי is its hems, פִּי רֹאשׁ, or even absolutely פֶּה, the opening for the head, or the collar, by means of which the sleeveless garment was put on, and שָׂפָה the binding, the embroidery, the border of this collar (vid. Ex. xxviii. 32, xxxix. 23; cf. Job xxx. 18, פִּי כֻתָּנְתִּי, the collar of my shirt). פִּי must apparently be understood according to these passages of the Tôra, as also the appellation מִדּוֹת (only here for מַדִּים, מְדִים), beginning with Lev. vi. 3, denotes the whole vestment of the high priest, yet without more exact distinction. But the Targum translates פִּי with אִמְרָא (*ora* = *fimbria*) — a word which is related to אִמְּרָא, *agnus*, like ᾤα to ὄις. This ᾤα is used both of the upper and lower edge of a garment. Accordingly Apollinaris and the Latin versions understand the ἐπὶ τὴν ᾤαν of the LXX. of the hem (*in oram vestimenti*); Theodoret, on the other hand, understands it to mean the upper edging: ᾤαν ἐκάλεσεν ὃ καλοῦμεν περιτραχήλιον, τοῦτο δὲ καὶ ὁ Ἀκύλας στόμα ἐνδυμάτων εἴρηκε. So also De Sacy: *sur le bord de son vêtement, c'est-à-dire, sur le haut de ses habits pontificaux*. The decision of the question depends upon the aim of this and the following figure in ver. 3. If we compare the two figures, we find that the point of the comparison is the uniting power of brotherly feeling, as that which unites in heart and soul those who are most distant from one another locally, and also brings them together in outward circumstance. If this is the point of the comparison, then Aaron's beard and the hem of his garments stand just as diametrically opposed to one another as the dew of Hermon and the mountains of Zion. פִּי is not the collar above, which gives no advance, much less the antithesis of two extremes, but the hem at the bottom (cf. שָׂפָה, Ex. xxvi.

4, of the edge of a curtain). It is also clear that שׁיּרֵד cannot now refer to the beard of Aaron, either as flowing down over the upper border of his robe, or as flowing down upon its hem; it must refer to the oil, for peaceable love that brings the most widely separated together is likened to the oil. This reference is also more appropriate to the style of the onward movement of the gradual Psalms, and is confirmed by ver. 3, where it refers to the dew, which takes the place of the oil in the other metaphor. When brethren united in harmonious love also meet together in one place, as is the case in Israel at the great Feasts, it is as when the holy, precious chrism, breathing forth the blended odour of many spices, upon the head of Aaron trickles down upon his beard, and from thence to the extreme end of his vestment. It becomes thoroughly perceptible, and also outwardly visible, that Israel, far and near, is pervaded by one spirit and bound together in unity of spirit.

This uniting spirit of brotherly love is now symbolized also by the dew of Hermon, which descends in drops upon the mountains of Zion. "What we read in the 133d Psalm of the dew of Hermon descending upon the mountains of Zion," says Van de Velde in his *Travels* (Bd. i. S. 97), "is now become quite clear to me. Here, as I sat at the foot of Hermon, I understood how the water-drops which rose from its forest-mantled heights, and out of the highest ravines, which are filled the whole year round with snow, after the sun's rays have attenuated them and moistened the atmosphere with them, descend at evening-time as a heavy dew upon the lower mountains which lie round about as its spurs. One ought to have seen Hermon with its white-golden crown glistening aloft in the blue sky, in order to be able rightly to understand the figure. Nowhere in the whole country is so heavy a dew perceptible as in the districts near to Hermon." To this dew the poet likens brotherly love. This is as the dew of Hermon : of such pristine freshness and thus refreshing, possessing such pristine power and thus quickening, thus born from above (cx. 3), and in fact like the dew of Hermon which comes down upon the mountains of Zion—a feature in the picture which is taken from the natural reality; for an abundant dew, when warm days have preceded, might very well be diverted to Jerusalem by the operation of the cold current of air sweeping down from the north over Hermon. We know, indeed, from our own experience how far off a cold air coming from the Alps is perceptible and produces its effects. The figure of the poet is therefore as true to nature as it is beautiful. When brethren bound together in love also meet together in one place, and in fact when brethren out of the north unite with brethren in the south in Jerusalem, the city which is the mother of all, at the great Feasts, it is as when the dew of Mount Hermon, which is covered with deep, almost eternal snow,* descends upon the bare, unfruitful—and therefore longing for such quickening—mountains round about Zion. In Jerusalem must love and all that is good meet. For there (שָׁם as in cxxxii. 17) hath Jahve commanded (צִוָּה as in Lev. xxv. 21, cf. Ps. xlii. 9, lxviii. 29) the blessing, *i.e.* there allotted to the blessing its rendezvous and its place of issue. אֶת־הַבְּרָכָה is appositionally explained by חַיִּים: life is the substance and goal of the blessing, the possession of all possessions, the blessing of all blessings. The closing words עַד־הָעוֹלָם (cf. xxviii. 9) belong to צִוָּה: such is God's inviolable, ever-enduring order.

PSALM CXXXIV.

NIGHT-WATCH GREETING AND COUNTER-GREETING.

The Call.

1 BEHOLD, *bless ye Jahve,* all ye servants of Jahve,
Who serve in the house of Jahve by night!
2 Lift up your hands to the sanctuary
And bless ye Jahve!

---

* A Hauranitish poem in Wetzstein's *Lieder-Sammlungen* begins:

البارحة هبّت علينا شرارة | من عالي الثلمِ — —, "Yesterday there blew across to me a spark | from the lofty snow-mountain (the Hermon)," on which the commentator dictated to him the remark, that شرار, the glowing spark, is either the snow-capped summit of the mountain glowing in the morning sun or a burning cold breath of air, for one says in everyday life الصَّقعة يحرق, the frost burns [*vid.* note to cxxi. 6].

The Answer.

3 *Jahve bless thee* out of Zion,
The Creator of heaven and earth!

This Psalm consists of a greeting, vers. 1, 2, and the reply thereto. The greeting is addressed to those priests and Levites who have the night-watch in the Temple; and this antiphon is purposely placed at the end of the collection of Songs of degrees in order to take the place of a final beracha. In this sense Luther styles this Psalm *epiphonema superiorum*. It is also in other respects (*vid. Symbolæ*, p. 66) an appropriate finale.

Vers. 1, 2. The Psalm begins, like its predecessor, with הִנֵּה; there it directs attention to an attractive phenomenon, here to a duty which springs from the office. For that it is not the persons frequenting the Temple who are addressed is at once clear from the fact that the tarrying of these in the Temple through the night, when such a thing did actually occur (Luke ii. 37), was only an exception. And then, however, from the fact that עָמַד is the customary word for the service of the priests and Levites, Deut. x. 8, xviii. 7, 1 Chron. xxiii. 30, 2 Chron. xxix. 11 (cf. on Isa. lxi. 10, and Ps. cx. 4), which is also continued in the night, 1 Chron. ix. 33. Even the Targum refers ver. 1*b* to the Temple-watch. In the second Temple the matter was arranged thus. After midnight the chief over the gate-keepers took the keys of the inner Temple and went with some of the priests through the little wicket of the Fire Gate (שַׁעַר בֵּית הַמּוֹקֵד). In the inner court this patrol divided into two companies, each with a burning torch; one company turned west, the other east, and so they compassed the court to see whether everything was in readiness for the service of the dawning day. At the bakers' chamber, in which the *Mincha* of the high priest was baked (לְשִׁכַּת עֹשֵׂי הֲבִיתִין), they met with the cry: All is well. In the meanwhile the rest of the priests also arose, bathed, and put on their garments. Then they went into the stone chamber (one half of which was the place of session of the Sanhedrim), where, under the superintendence of the chief over the drawing of the lots and of a judge, around whom stood all the priests in their robes of office, the functions of the priests in the service of the coming day were assigned to them by lot (Luke i. 9). Accordingly Tholuck, with Köster, regards vers. 1 sq. and 3 as the antiphon of the Temple-watch going off duty and those coming on. It might also be the call and counter-call with which the watchmen greeted one another when they met. But according to the general keeping of the Psalm, vers. 1 sq. have rather to be regarded as a call to devotion and intercession, which the congregation addresses to the priests and Levites entrusted with the night-service in the Temple. It is an error to suppose that "in the nights" can be equivalent to "early and late." If the Psalter contains Morning Psalms (iii., lxiii.) and Evening Psalms (iv., cxli.), why should it then not contain a vigil Psalm? On this very ground Venema's idea too, that בַּלֵּילוֹת is syncopated from בְּהַלְלִילוֹת, "with *Hallels*, *i.e.* praises," is useless. Nor is there any reason for drawing ἐν ταῖς νυξίν, as the LXX. does, to ver. 2,* or, what would be more natural, to the בָּרְכוּ that opens the Psalm, since it is surely not strange that, so long as the sanctuary was standing, a portion of the servants of God who ministered in it had to remain up at night to guard it, and to see to it that nothing was wanting in the preparations for the early service. That this ministering watching should be combined with devotional praying is the purport of the admonition in ver. 2. Raising suppliant hands (יְדֵכֶם, negligently written for יְדֵיכֶם) towards the Most Holy Place (τὰ ἅγια), they are to bless Jahve. קֹדֶשׁ (according to *B. Sota* 39a, the accusative of definition: in holiness, *i.e.* after washing of hands), in view of xxviii. 2, v. 8, cxxxviii. 2 (cf. רוֹם in Hab. iii. 10), has to be regarded as the accusative of the direction.

Ver. 3. Calling thus up to the Temple-hill, the church receives from above the benedictory counter-greeting: Jahve bless thee out of Zion (as in cxxviii. 5), the Creator of heaven and earth (as in cxv. 15, cxxi. 2, cxxiv. 8). From the time of Num. vi. 24 *jebarêchja* is the ground-form of the priestly benediction. It is addressed to the church as one person, and to each individual in this united, unit-like church.

---

* The LXX. adjusts the shortening of ver. 1*b* arising from this, by reading העמדים בבית ה' בחצרות בית אלהינו after cxxxv. 2.

PSALM CXXXV.

FOUR-VOICED HALLELUJAH TO THE GOD OF ISRAEL, THE GOD OF GODS.

HALLELUJAH.
1 PRAISE ye the Name of Jahve,
    Praise ye, O ye servants of Jahve,
2 Who stand in the house of Jahve,
    In the courts of the house of our God!
3 Praise ye Jāh, for Jahve is good;
    Harp unto His Name, for it is lovely;
4 For Jacob hath Jāh chosen for Himself,
    Israel as His possession.

5 For I know that Jahve is great
    And our Lord above all gods.
6 All that Jahve willeth He carrieth out
    In heaven and upon earth,
    In the seas and in all the depths;
7 Who bringeth the vapours up from the end of the earth,
    He maketh lightnings for the rain,
    Who bringeth forth wind out of His treasuries.

8 Who smote the first-born of Egypt
    From man down to the cattle,
9 Sent signs and wonders
    Into the midst of thee, O Egypt,
    Against Pharaoh and all his servants!

10 Who smote great nations
    And slew mighty kings,
11 Sihon, king of the Amorites,
    And Og, king of Bashan,
    And all the kingdoms of Canaan;
12 And gave over their land as a heritage,
    As a heritage to Israel His people.

13 Jahve, Thy Name endureth for ever,
    Thy memorial, Jahve, unto all generations.

14 For Jahve will render justice to His people,
And repent Himself concerning His servants.

15 The idols of the heathen are silver and gold,
The work of men's hands.
16 A mouth have they and cannot speak,
Eyes have they and cannot see,
17 Ears have they and cannot hear,
Nor is there any breath at all in their mouth.
18 Like unto them must they who made them become,
Every one who trusted in them.

19 O house of Israel, bless ye Jahve!
O house of Aaron, bless ye Jahve!
20 O house of Levi, bless ye Jahve!
Ye who fear Jahve, bless Jahve!—
21 Blessed be Jahve out of Zion,
Who dwelleth in Jerusalem,
Hallelujah!

Ps. cxxxv. is here and there (*vid. Tôsefôth Pesachim* 117*a*) taken together with Ps. cxxxiv. as one Psalm. The combining of Ps. cxv. with cxiv. is a misapprehension caused by the inscriptionless character of Ps. cxv, whereas Ps. cxxxv. and cxxxiv. certainly stand in connection with one another. For the Hallelujah Ps. cxxxv. is, as the mutual relation between the beginning and close of Ps. cxxxiv. shows, a Psalm-song expanded out of this shorter hymn, that is in part drawn from Ps. cxv.

It is a Psalm in the mosaic style. Even the Latin poet Lucilius transfers the figure of mosaic-work to style, when he says: *quam lepide lexeis compostae ut tesserulae omnes* . . . In the case of Ps. cxxxv. it is not the first time that we have met with this kind of style. We have already had a glimpse of it in Ps. xcvii. and xcviii. These Psalms were composed more especially of deutero-Isaianic passages, whereas Ps. cxxxv. takes its *tesserulae* out of the Law, Prophets, and Psalms.

Vers. 1-4. The beginning is taken from cxxxiv. 1; ver. 2*b*

recalls cxvi. 19 (cf. xcii. 14); and ver. 4 is an echo of Deut. vii. 6. The servants of Jahve to whom the summons is addressed, are not, as in cxxxiv. 1 sq., His official servants in particular, but according to ver. 2b, where the courts, in the plural, are allotted to them as their standing-place, and according to vers. 19, 20, those who fear Him as a body. The threefold *Jahve* at the beginning is then repeated in *Jah* (הַלְלוּיָהּ, cf. note * to civ. 35), *Jahve*, and *Jah*. The subject of כִּי נָעִים is by no means Jahve (Hupfeld), whom they did not dare to call נָעִים in the Old Testament, but either the Name, according to liv. 8 (Luther, Hitzig), or, which is favoured by cxlvii. 1 (cf. Prov. xxii. 18), the praising of His Name (Apollinaris: ἐπεὶ τόδε καλὸν ἀείδειν): His Name to praise is a delightful employ, which is incumbent on Israel as the people of His choice and of His possession.

Vers. 5–7. The praise itself now begins. כִּי in ver. 4a set forth the ground of the pleasant duty, and the כִּי that begins this strophe confirms that which warrants the summons out of the riches of the material existing for such a hymn of praise. Worthy is He to be praised, for Israel knows full well that He who hath chosen it is the God of gods. The beginning is taken from cxv. 3, and ver. 7 from Jer. x. 13 (li. 16). Heaven, earth, and water are the three kingdoms of created things, as in Ex. xx. 4. נָשִׂיא signifies that which is lifted up, ascended; here, as in Jeremiah, a cloud. The meaning of בְּרָקִים לַמָּטָר עָשָׂה is not: He makes lightnings into rain, *i.e.* resolves them as it were into rain, which is unnatural; but either according to Zech. x. 1: He produces lightnings in behalf of rain, in order that the rain may pour down in consequence of the thunder and lightning, or poetically: He makes lightnings for the rain, so that the rain is announced (Apollinaris) and accompanied by them. Instead of מוֹצָא (cf. lxxviii. 16, cv. 43), which does not admit of the retreating of the tone, the expression is מוֹצֵא, the ground-form of the *part. Hiph.* for plurals like מְעַזְּרִים, מַחְלְמִים, מַחְצְרִים, perhaps not without being influenced by the וַיּוֹצֵא in Jeremiah, for it is not כּוֹצֵא from כָּצָא that signifies "producing," but מוֹצִיא=מֵפִיק. The metaphor of the treasuries is like Job xxxviii. 22. What is intended is the fulness of divine power, in which lie the grounds of the origin and the impulses of all things in nature.

Vers. 8, 9. Worthy is He to be praised, for He is the Redeemer out of Egypt. בְּתוֹכֵכִי as in cxvi. 19, cf. cv. 27.

Vers. 10–12. Worthy is He to be praised, for He is the Conqueror of the Land of Promise. In connection with ver. 10 one is reminded of Deut. iv. 38, vii. 1, ix. 1, xi. 23, Josh. xxiii. 9. גּוֹיִם רַבִּים are here not many, but great peoples (cf. גְּדֹלִים in cxxxvi. 17), since the parallel word עֲצוּמִים is by no means intended of a powerful number, but of powerful might (cf. Isa. liii. 12). As to the rest also, the poet follows the Book of Deuteronomy: viz. לְכֹל מַמְלְכוֹת as in Deut. iii. 21, and נָתַן נַחֲלָה as in Deut. iv. 38 and other passages. It is all Deuteronomic with the exception of the שׁ, and the לְ in ver. 11 as the *nota accus.* (as in cxxxvi. 19 sq., cf. lxix. 6, cxvi. 16, cxxix. 3); the construction of הָרַג is just as Aramaizing in Job v. 2, 2 Sam. iii. 30 (where vers. 30, 31, like vers. 36, 37, are a later explanatory addition). The הָרַג alternating with הִכָּה is, next to the two kings, also referred to the kingdoms of Canaan, viz. their inhabitants. Og was also an Amoritish king, Deut. iii. 8.

Vers. 13, 14. This God who rules so praiseworthily in the universe and in the history of Israel is the same yesterday, and to-day, and for ever. Just as ver. 13 (cf. cii. 13) is taken from Ex. iii. 15, so ver. 14 is taken from Deut. xxxii. 36, cf. xc. 13, and *vid.* on Heb. x. 30, 31 (vol. ii. 191).

Vers. 15–18. For the good of His proved church He ever proves Himself to be the Living God, whereas idols and idol-worshippers are vain—throughout following cxv. 4–8, but with some abridgments. Here only the אַף used as a particle recalls what is said there of the organ of smell (אַף) of the idols that smells not, just as the רוּחַ which is here (as in Jer. x. 14) denied to the idols recalls the הָרִיחַ denied to them there. It is to be rendered: also there is not a being of breath, *i.e.* there is no breath at all, not a trace thereof, in their mouth. It is different in 1 Sam. xxi. 9, where אִן יֵשׁ (not אַיִן) is meant to be equivalent to the Aramaic אִין אִית, *num (an) est;* אַיִן is North-Palestinian, and equivalent to the interrogatory אִם (after which the Targum renders אִית אִלּוּ).

Vers. 19–21. A call to the praise of Jahve, who is exalted above the gods of the nations, addressed to Israel as a whole, rounds off the Psalm by recurring to its beginning. The threefold call in cxv. 9–11, cxviii. 2–4, is rendered fourfold here by the introduction of the house of the Levites, and the wishing of a blessing in cxxxiv. 3 is turned into an ascription of praise. Zion, whence Jahve's self-attestation, so rich in power and loving-kindness, is spread abroad, is also to be the place whence His glorious attestation by the mouth of men is spread abroad. History has realized this.

PSALM CXXXVI.

O GIVE THANKS UNTO THE LORD, FOR HE IS GOOD.

1 GIVE thanks unto Jahve, for He is good,
  For His goodness endureth for ever.
2 Give thanks unto the God of gods,
  For His goodness endureth for ever.
3 Give thanks unto the Lord of lords—
  For His goodness endureth for ever.

4 To Him who alone doeth great wonders,
  For His goodness endureth for ever.
5 To Him who by wisdom made the heavens,
  For His goodness endureth for ever.
6 To Him who stretched out the earth above the waters—
  For His goodness endureth for ever.

7 To Him who made great lights,
  For His goodness endureth for ever.
8 The sun for dominion by day,
  For His goodness endureth for ever.
9 The moon and stars for dominions by night—
  For His goodness endureth for ever.

10 To Him who smote the Egyptians in their first-born,
  For His goodness endureth for ever.
11 And brought forth Israel out of their midst,
  For His goodness endureth for ever.
12 With a strong hand and a stretched-out arm—
  For His goodness endureth for ever.

13 To Him who divided the Red Sea into parts,
  For His goodness endureth for ever.

14 And made Israel to pass through in the midst of it,
    For His goodness endureth for ever.
15 And overthrew Pharaoh and his host in the Red Sea—
    For His goodness endureth for ever.

16 To Him who led His people in the desert,
    For His goodness endureth for ever.
17 To Him who smote great kings,
    For His goodness endureth for ever.
18 And slew glorious kings—
    For His goodness endureth for ever.

19 Sihon, king of the Amorites,
    For His goodness endureth for ever.
20 And Og, king of Bashan,
    For His goodness endureth for ever.
21 And gave their land as a heritage,
    For His goodness endureth for ever.
22 As a heritage to Israel His servant—
    For His goodness endureth for ever.

23 Who in our low estate remembered us,
    For His goodness endureth for ever.
24 And redeemed us from our adversaries,
    For His goodness endureth for ever.
25 Giving bread to all flesh—
    For His goodness endureth for ever.
26 Give thanks unto the God of heaven,
    For His goodness endureth for ever.

The cry cxxxv. 3, *Praise ye Jāh, for good is Jahve*, is here followed by a *Hodu*, the last of the collection, with " for His goodness endureth for ever" repeated twenty-six times as a *versus intercalaris*. In the liturgical language this Psalm is called *par excellence* the great Hallel, for according to its broadest compass the great Hallel comprehends Ps. cxx. to cxxxvi.,*

---

* There are three opinions in the Talmud and Midrash concerning the compass of the " Great Hallel," viz. (1) Ps. cxxxvi., (2) Ps. cxxxv. 4–cxxxvi., (3) Ps. cxx.–cxxxvi.

whilst the Hallel which is absolutely so called extends from Ps. cxiii. to cxviii. Down to ver. 18 the song and counter-song organize themselves into hexastichic groups or strophes, which, however, from ver. 19 (and therefore from the point where the dependence on Ps. cxxxv., already begun with ver. 17, becomes a borrowing, onwards) pass over into octastichs. In Heidenheim's Psalter the Psalm appears (after Norzi) in two columns (like Deut. ch. xxxii.), which it is true has neither tradition (*vid.* on Ps. xviii.) nor MSS. precedent in its favour, but really corresponds to its structure.

Vers. 1–9. Like the preceding Psalm, this Psalm allies itself to the Book of Deuteronomy. Vers. 2a and 3a (*God of gods and Lord of lords*) are taken from Deut. x. 17; ver. 12a (*with a strong hand and stretched-out arm*) from Deut. iv. 34, v. 15, and frequently (cf. Jer. xxxii. 21); ver. 16a like Deut. viii. 15 (cf. Jer. ii. 6). With reference to the Deuteronomic colouring of vers. 19–22, *vid.* on cxxxv. 10–12; also the expression "Israel His servant" recalls Deut. xxxii. 36 (cf. cxxxv. 14, xc. 13), and still more Isa. xl.–lxvi., where the comprehension of Israel under the unity of this notion has its own proper place. In other respects, too, the Psalm is an echo of earlier model passages. *Who alone doeth great wonders* sounds like lxxii. 18 (lxxxvi. 10); and the adjective "great" that is added to "wonders" shows that the poet found the formula already in existence. In connection with ver. 5a he has Prov. iii. 19 or Jer. x. 12 in his mind; תְּבוּנָה, like חָכְמָה, is the demiurgic wisdom. Ver. 6a calls to mind Isa. xlii. 5, xliv. 24; the expression is "above the waters," as in xxiv. 2 "upon the seas," because the water is partly visible and partly invisible מִתַּחַת לָאָרֶץ (Ex. xx. 4). The plural אוֹרִים, *luces*, instead of מְאֹרוֹת, *lumina* (cf. Ezek. xxxii. 8, מְאוֹרֵי אוֹר), is without precedent. It is a controverted point whether אֹרֹת in Isa. xxvi. 19 signifies lights (cf. אוֹרָה, cxxxix. 12) or herbs (2 Kings iv. 39). The plural כְּמִשְׁלוֹת is also rare (occurring only besides in cxiv. 2): it here denotes the dominion of the moon on the one hand, and (going beyond Gen. i. 16) of the stars on the other. בַּלַּיְלָה, like בַּיּוֹם, is the second member of the *stat. construct.*

Vers. 10–26. Up to this point it is God the absolute in general, the Creator of all things, to the celebration of whose praise they are summoned; and from this point onwards the God of the history of salvation. In ver. 13a וַיְגַן (instead of בָּקַע, lxxviii. 13, Ex. xiv. 21, Neh. ix. 11) of the dividing of the Red Sea is peculiar; גְזָרִים (Gen. xv. 17, side by side with בְּתָרִים) are the pieces or parts of a thing that is cut up into pieces. נָעַר is a favourite word taken from Ex. xiv. 27. With reference to the name of the Egyptian ruler *Pharaoh* (Herodotus also, ii. 111, calls the Pharaoh of the Exodus the son of Sesostris-Rameses Miamun, not Μενόφθας, as he is properly called, but absolutely Φερῶν), vid. on lxxiii. 22. After the God to whom the praise is to be ascribed has been introduced with ל by always fresh attributes, the ל before the names of Sihon and of Og is perplexing. The words are taken over, as are the six lines of vers. 17a–22a in the main, from cxxxv. 10–12, with only a slight alteration in the expression. In ver. 23 the continued influence of the construction ל הוֹדוּ is at an end. The connection by means of שׁ (cf. cxxxv. 8, 10) therefore has reference to the preceding " for His goodness endureth for ever." The language here has the stamp of the latest period. It is true זָכַר with *Lamed* of the object is used even in the earliest Hebrew, but שֶׁפֶל is only authenticated by Eccles. x. 6, and פָּרַק, to break loose = to rescue (the customary Aramaic word for redemption), by Lam. v. 8, just as in the closing verse, which recurs to the beginning, " God of heaven " is a name for God belonging to the latest literature, Neh. i. 4, ii. 4. In ver. 23 the praise changes suddenly to that which has been experienced very recently. The attribute in ver. 25a (cf. cxlvii. 9, cxlv. 15) leads one to look back to a time in which famine befell them together with slavery.

PSALM CXXXVII.

BY THE RIVERS OF BABYLON.

1 BY the rivers of Babylon, there we sat and wept,
  When we remembered Zion.
2 Upon the willows in the midst thereof
  We hung our citherns.

3 For there our oppressors asked of us
  The words of songs,
  And our tormentors joy:
  Sing us a song of Zion!

4 How are we to sing Jahve's songs
  Upon strange soil?!
5 If I forget thee, O Jerusalem,
  Let my right hand become lame!

6 Let my tongue cleave to the roof of my mouth,
  If I do not remember thee,
  If I do not set Jerusalem
  Above all my joys!

7 Remember, Jahve, the children of Edom
  In the day of Jerusalem,
  Who said: Raze, raze it
  Even to the foundation!

8 O daughter of Babylon, thou wasted one, blessed is he who
       giveth thee thy reward,
  Which thou hast merited for us!
9 Blessed is he who taketh and dasheth thy little ones
  Against the rock!

The Hallelujah Ps. cxxxv. and the Hodu Ps. cxxxvi. are followed by a Psalm which glances back into the time of the Exile, when such cheerful songs as they once sang to the accompaniment of the music of the Levites at the worship of God on Mount Zion were obliged to be silent. It is anonymous. The inscription Τῷ Δαυιδ (διὰ) Ἰερεμίου found in codices of the LXX., which is meant to say that it is a Davidic song coming from the heart of Jeremiah,* is all the more erroneous as Jeremiah never was one of the Babylonian exiles.

The ש, which is repeated three times in vers. 8 sq., corre-

---

* Reversely Ellies du Pin (in the preface of his *Bibliothèque des Auteurs Ecclésiastiques*) says: *Le Pseaume 136 porte le nom de David et de Jeremie, ce qu'il faut apparement entendre ainsi: Pseaume de Jeremie fait à l'imitation de David.*

sponds to the time of the composition of the Psalm which is required by its contents. It is just the same with the paragogic *i* in the future in ver. 6. But in other respects the language is classic; and the rhythm, at the beginning softly elegiac, then more and more excited, and abounding in guttural and sibilant sounds, is so expressive that scarcely any Psalm is so easily impressed on the memory as this, which is so pictorial even in sound.

The metre resembles the elegiac as it appears in the so-called cæsura schema of the Lamentations and in the cadence of Isa. xvi. 9, 10, which is like the Sapphic strophe. Every second line corresponds to the pentameter of the elegiac metre.

Vers. 1-6. Beginning with perfects, the Psalm has the appearance of being a Psalm not belonging to the Exile, but written in memory of the Exile. The bank of a river, like the seashore, is a favourite place of sojourn of those whom deep grief drives forth from the bustle of men into solitude. The boundary line of the river gives to solitude a safe back; the monotonous splashing of the waves keeps up the dull, melancholy alternation of thoughts and feelings; and at the same time the sight of the cool, fresh water exercises a soothing influence upon the consuming fever within the heart. The rivers of Babylon are here those of the Babylonian empire: not merely the Euphrates with its canals, and the Tigris, but also the Chaboras (*Chebar*) and Eulæos (*'Ulai*), on whose lonesome banks Ezekiel (ch. i. 3) and Daniel (ch. viii. 2) beheld divine visions. The שָׁם is important: there, in a strange land, as captives under the dominion of the power of the world. And גַּם is purposely chosen instead of וְ: with the sitting down in the solitude of the river's banks weeping immediately came on; when the natural scenery around contrasted so strongly with that of their native land, the remembrance of Zion only forced itself upon them all the more powerfully, and the pain at the isolation from their home would have all the freer course where no hostilely observant eyes were present to suppress it. The willow (צַפְצָפָה) and viburnum, those trees which are associated with flowing water in hot low-lying districts, are indigenous in the richly watered lowlands of Babylonia. עֲרָבָה (עָרָב), if one and the same with غرب, is not the willow, least of all the weeping-willow, which is called *ṣafṣâf mustaḥi* in Arabic, "the bending-down willow," but the viburnum with dentate leaves, described by Wetzstein on Isa. xliv. 4. The Talmud even distinguishes between *tsaph-tsapha* and *'araba*, but without our being able to obtain any sure botanic picture from it. The עֲרָבָה, whose branches belong to the constituents of the *lulab* of the Feast of Tabernacles (Lev. xxiii. 40), is understood of the crack-willow [*Salix fragilis*], and even in the passage before us is surely not distinguished with such botanical precision but that the *gharab* and willow together with the weeping-willow (*Salix Babylonica*) might be comprehended under the word עֲרָבָה. On these trees of the country abounding in streams the exiles hung their citherns. The time to take delight in music was past, for μουσικὰ ἐν πένθει ἄκαιρος διήγησις, Sir. xxii. 6. Joyous songs, as the word שִׁיר designates them, were ill suited to their situation.

In order to understand the כִּי in ver. 3, vers. 3 and 4 must be taken together. They hung up their citherns; for though their lords called upon them to sing in order that they might divert themselves with their national songs, they did not feel themselves in the mind for singing songs as they once resounded at the divine services of their native land. The LXX., Targum, and Syriac take תּוֹלָלֵינוּ as a synonym of שׁוֹבֵינוּ, synonymous with שׁוֹלָלֵינוּ, and so, in fact, that it signifies not, like שׁוֹלָל, the spoiled and captive one, but the spoiler and he who takes others prisoners. But there is no Aramaic תְּלַל = שָׁלַל. It might more readily be referred back to a *Poel* הוֹלֵל (= הֵתֵל), to disappoint, deride (Hitzig); but the usage of the language does not favour this, and a stronger meaning for the word would be welcome. Either תּוֹלֵל = תְּהוֹלֵל, like מְהוֹלָל, cii. 9, signifies the raving one, *i.e.* a bloodthirsty man or a tyrant, or from יָלַל, *ejulare*, one who causes the cry of woe or a tormentor,—a signification which commends itself in view of the words תּוֹשָׁב and תַּלְמִיד, which are likewise formed with the preformative ת. According to the sense the word ranks itself with an *Hiph.* הוֹלִיל, like תּוֹכֵחָה, תּוֹעֵלֶת, with הוֹעִיל and הוֹכִיחַ, in a mainly abstract signification (Dietrich, *Abhandlungen*, S. 160 f.). The דִּבְרֵי beside שִׁיר is used as in xxxv. 20, lxv. 4, cv. 27, cxlv. 5, viz. partitively, dividing up the genitival notion of the species: words of songs as being parts or fragments of the national treasury of song, similar to כְּשִׁיר a little further on, on which Rosenmüller correctly says: *sacrum aliquod carmen ex veteribus illis suis Sionicis.* With the expression "song of Zion" alternates in ver. 4 "song of Jahve," which, as in 2 Chron. xxix. 27, cf. 1 Chron. xxv. 7, denotes sacred or liturgical songs, that is to say, songs belonging to Psalm poesy (including the *Cantica*).

Before ver. 4 we have to imagine that they answered the request of the Babylonians at that time in the language that follows, or thought thus within themselves when they withdrew themselves from them. The meaning of the interrogatory exclamation is not that the singing of sacred songs in a foreign land (חוּצָה לָאָרֶץ) is contrary to the law, for the Psalms continued to be sung even during the Exile, and were also enriched by new ones. But the *shir* had an end during the Exile, in so far as that it was obliged to retire from publicity into the quiet of the family worship and of the houses of prayer, in order that that which is holy might not be profaned; and since it was not, as at home, accompanied by the trumpets of the priests and the music of the Levites, it became more recitative than singing properly so called, and therefore could not afford any idea of the singing of their native land in connection with the worship of God on Zion. From the striking contrast between the present and the former times the people of the Exile had in fact to come to the knowledge of their sins, in order that they might get back by the way of penitence and earnest longing to that which they had lost. Penitence and home-sickness were at that time inseparable; for all those in whom the remembrance of Zion was lost gave themselves over to heathenism and were excluded from the redemption. The poet, translated into the situation of the exiles, and arming himself against the temptation to apostasy and the danger of denying God, therefore says: If I forget thee, O Jerusalem, תִּשְׁכַּח יְמִינִי. תִּשְׁכַּח has been taken as an address to Jahve: *obliviscaris dexteræ meæ* (*e.g.* Wolfgang Dachstein in his song "*An Wasserflüssen Babylon*"), but it is far from natural that Jerusalem and Jahve should be addressed in one clause. Others take יְמִינִי as the subject and תִּשְׁכַּח transitively: *obliviscatur dextera mea, scil. artem psallendi* (Aben-Ezra, Kimchi, Pagninus, Grotius, Hengstenberg, and others); but this ellipsis is arbitrary, and the interpolation of מִפְּנֵי after יְמִינִי (von Ortenberg, following Olshausen) produces an inelegant cadence. Others again assign a passive sense to הִשְׁכַּח: *oblivioni detur* (LXX., Italic, Vulgate, and Luther), or a half-passive sense, *in oblivione sit* (Jerome) ; but the thought : let my right hand be forgotten, is awkward and tame. *Obliviscatur me* (Syriac, Saadia, and the Psalterium Romanum) comes nearer to the true meaning. תִּשְׁכַּח is to be taken reflexively : *obliviscatur sui ipsius*, let it forget itself, or its service (Amyraldus, Schultens, Ewald, and Hitzig), which is equivalent to let it refuse or fail, become lame, become benumbed, much the same as we say of the arms or legs that they " go to sleep," and just as the Arabic نسي signifies both to forget and to become lame (cf. Gesenius, *Thesaurus*, p. 921b). La Harpe correctly renders : *O Jerusalem ! si je t'oublie jamais, que ma main oublie aussi le mouvement !* Thus there is a correspondence between vers. 5 and 6 : My tongue shall cleave to my palate if I do not remember thee, if I do not raise Jerusalem above the sum of my joy. אַזְכְּרֵכִי has the affixed *Chirek*, with which these later Psalms are so fond of adorning themselves. ראֹשׁ is apparently used as in cxix. 160 : *supra summam* (the totality) *lætitiæ meæ*, as Coccejus explains, *h.e. supra omnem lætitiam meam.* But why not then more simply עַל כָּל, above the totality ? ראֹשׁ here signifies not κεφάλαιον, but κεφαλή : if I do not place Jerusalem upon the summit of my joy, *i.e.* my highest joy ; therefore, if I do not cause Jerusalem to be my very highest joy. His spiritual joy over the city of God is to soar above all earthly joys.

Vers. 7–9. The second part of the Psalm supplicates vengeance upon Edom and Babylon. We see from Obadiah's prophecy, which is taken up again by Jeremiah, how shamefully the Edomites, that brother-people related by descent to Israel and yet pre-eminently hostile to it, behaved in connection with the destruction of Jerusalem by the Chaldæans as their malignant, rapacious, and inhuman helpers. The repeated *imper. Piel* עָרוּ, from עָרָה (not *imper. Kal* from עָרַר, which would be עֹרוּ), ought to have been accented on the *ult.;* it is, however, in both cases accented on the first syllable, the pausal עָרוּ (cf. כָּלוּ in xxxvii. 20, and also הָסוּ, Neh. viii. 11) giving rise to the same accentuation of the other (in order that two tone-syllables might not come together). The *Pasek* also stands between the two repeated words in order that they may be duly separated, and secures, moreover, to the guttural initial of the second עָרוּ its distinct pronunciation (cf. Gen. xxvi. 28, Num. xxxv. 16). It is to be construed: lay bare, lay bare (as in Hab. iii. 13, cf. גַּלֵּה in Mic. i. 6) in it (*Beth* of the place), or in respect of it (*Beth* of the object), even to the foundation, *i.e* raze it even to the ground, leave not one stone upon another. From the false brethren the imprecation turns to Babylon, the city of the imperial power of the world. The daughter, *i.e.* the population, of Babylon is addressed as הַשְּׁדוּדָה. It certainly seems the most natural to take this epithet as a designation of its doings which cry for vengeance. But it cannot in any case be translated: thou plunderer (Syriac like the Targum: *bozuzto;* Symmachus ἡ λῃστρίς), for שָׁדַד does not mean to rob and plunder, but to offer violence and to devastate. Therefore: thou devastator; but the word so pointed as we have it before us cannot have this signification: it ought to be הַשָּׁדוֹדָה, like בְּגוֹדָה in Jer. iii. 7, 10, or הַשָּׁדוּדָה (with an unchangeable *ā*), corresponding to the Syriac active intensive form *ālûso*, oppressor, *gōdûfo*, slanderer, and the Arabic likewise active intensive form فَاعُول, *e.g. fâshûs*, a boaster, and also as an adjective: *ǵôz fâshûs*, empty nuts, cf. יָקוֹשׁ = קוֹשׁ, a fowler, like *nâṭûr* (נאטור), a field-watcher. The form as it stands is *partic. pass.*, and signifies προνενομευμένη (Aquila), *vastata* (Jerome). It is possible that this may be said in the sense of *vestanda*, although in this sense of a *part. fut. pass.* the participles of the *Niphal* (*e.g.* xxii. 32, cii. 19) and of the *Pual* (xviii. 4) are more commonly used. It cannot at any rate signify *vastata* in an historical sense, with reference to the destruction of Babylon by Darius Hystaspes (Hengstenberg); for ver. 7 only prays that the retribution may come: it cannot therefore as yet have been executed; but if השדודה signified the already devastated one, it must (at least in the main) have been executed already. It might be more readily understood as a prophetical representation of the executed judgment of devastation; but this prophetic rendering coincides with the imprecative: the imagination of the Semite when he utters a curse sees the future as a realized fact. "Didst thou see the smitten one (*madrûb*)," *i.e.* he whom God must smite? Thus the Arab inquires for a person who is detested. "Pursue him who is seized (*illak el-ma'chûdh*)," *i.e.* him whom God must allow thee to seize! They speak thus inasmuch as the imagination at once anticipates the seizure at the same time with the pursuit. Just as here both *madrûb* and *ma'chûdh* are participles of *Kal*, so therefore הַשְּׁדוּדָה may also have the sense of *vastanda* (which must be laid waste!). That which is then further desired for Babylon is the requital of that which it has done to Israel, Isa. xlvii. 6. It is the same penal destiny, comprehending the children also, which is predicted against it in Isa. xiii. 16–18, as that which was to be executed by the Medes. The young children (with reference to עוֹלֵל, עוֹלָל, *vid.* on viii. 3) are to be dashed to pieces in order that a new generation may not raise up again the world-wide dominion that has been overthrown, Isa. xiv. 21 sq. It is zeal for God that puts such harsh words into the mouth of the poet. "That which is Israel's excellency and special good fortune the believing Israelite desires to have bestowed upon the whole world, but for this very reason he desires to see the hostility of the present world of nations against the church of God broken" (Hofmann). On the other hand, it cannot be denied that the "blessed" of this Psalm is not suited to the mouth of the New Testament church. In the Old Testament the church as yet had the form of a nation, and the longing for the revelation of divine righteousness clothed itself accordingly in a warlike garb.

PSALM CXXXVIII.

THE MEDIATOR AND PERFECTER.

1 I WILL give thanks unto Thee with my whole heart,
    Before the gods will I harp unto Thee.
2 I will worship towards Thy holy Temple,
    And give thanks unto Thy Name because of Thy mercy and
        Thy truth,
    That Thou hast magnified Thy promise above all Thy Name.

3 In the day that I called Thou didst answer me,
    Thou didst inspire me with courage—a lofty feeling pervaded my soul.

4 All the kings of the earth shall give thanks unto Thee, Jahve,
When they have heard the utterances of Thy mouth·
5 And they shall sing of the ways of Jahve,
That great is the glory of Jahve:
6 For exalted is Jahve and He seeth the lowly,
And the proud He knoweth well afar off.

7 If I walk in the midst of trouble, Thou dost revive me,
Over the wrath of mine enemies dost Thou stretch forth
Thy hand,
And Thy right hand saveth me.
8 Jahve will perfect for me;
Jahve, Thy mercy endureth for ever,
The work of Thy hands—Thou wilt not forsake it.

There will come a time when the praise of Jahve, which according to cxxxvii. 3 was obliged to be dumb in the presence of the heathen, will, according to cxxxviii. 5, be sung by the kings of the heathen themselves. In the LXX. Ps. cxxxvii. side by side with τῷ Δαυίδ also has the inscription Ἰερεμίου, and Ps. cxxxviii. has Ἀγγαίου καὶ Ζαχαρίου. Perhaps these statements are meant to refer back the existing recension of the text of the respective Psalms to the prophets named (vid. Köhler, Haggai, S. 33). From the fact that these names of psalmodists added by the LXX. do not come down beyond Malachi, it follows that the Psalm-collection in the mind of the LXX. was made not later than in the time of Nehemiah.

The speaker in Ps. cxxxviii., to follow the lofty expectation expressed in ver. 4, is himself a king, and according to the inscription, David. There is, however, nothing to favour his being the author; the Psalm is, in respect of the Davidic Psalms, composed as it were out of the soul of David—an echo of 2 Sam. ch. vii. (1 Chron. ch. xvii.). The superabundant promise which made the throne of David and of his seed an eternal throne is here gratefully glorified. The Psalm can at any rate be understood, if with Hengstenberg we suppose that it expresses the lofty self-consciousness to which David was raised after victorious battles, when he humbly ascribed the glory to God and resolved to build Him a Temple in place of the tent upon Zion.

Vers. 1, 2 The poet will give thanks to Him, whom he means without mentioning Him by name, for His mercy, i.e. His anticipating, condescending love, and for His truth, i.e. truthfulness and faithfulness, and more definitely for having magnified His promise (אִמְרָה) above all His Name, i.e. that He has given a promise which infinitely surpasses everything by which He has hitherto established a name and memorial for Himself (עַל־כָּל־שְׁמֶךָ, with ō instead of ŏ, an anomaly that is noted by the Masora, vid. Baer's *Psalterium*, p. 133). If the promise by the mouth of Nathan (2 Sam. ch. vii.) is meant, then we may compare 2 Sam. vii. 21. גָּדֹל, גְּדֻלָּה, גָּדַל are repeated in that promise and its echo coming from the heart of David so frequently, that this הִגְדַּלְתָּ seems like a hint pointing to that history, which is one of the most important crises in the history of salvation. The expression נֶגֶד אֱלֹהִים also becomes intelligible from this history. Ewald renders it: "in the presence of God!" which is surely meant to say: in the holy place (De Wette, Olshausen). But "before God will I sing praise to Thee (O God!)"—what a jumble! The LXX. renders ἐναντίον ἀγγέλων, which is in itself admissible and full of meaning,* but without coherence in the context of the Psalm, and also is to be rejected because it is on the whole very questionable whether the Old Testament language uses אֱלֹהִים thus, without anything further to define it, in the sense of "angels." It might be more readily rendered "in the presence of the gods," viz. of the gods of the peoples (Hengstenberg, Hupfeld, and Hitzig); but in order to be understood of gods which are only seemingly such, it would require some addition. Whereas אֱלֹהִים can without any addition denote the magisterial possessors of the dignity that is the type of the divine, as follows from lxxxii. 1 (cf. xlv. 7) in spite of Knobel, Graf, and Hupfeld; and thus, too (cf. נֶגֶד מְלָכִים in cxix. 46), we understand it here, with Rashi, Aben-Ezra, Kimchi, Flaminius, Bucer, Clericus, and others. What is meant are "the great who are in the earth," 2 Sam. vii. 9, with whom David, inasmuch as he became king from being a shepherd, is ranked, and

---

* Bellarmine: *Scio me psallentem tibi ab angelis, qui tibi assistunt, videri et attendi et ideo ita considerate me geram in psallendo, ut qui intelligam, in quo theatro consistam.*

above whom he has been lifted up by the promise of an eternal kingship. Before these earthly "gods" will David praise the God of the promise; they shall hear for their salutary confusion, for their willing rendering of homage, that God hath made him "the highest with respect to the kings of the earth" (lxxxix. 28).

Vers. 3–6. There are two things for which the poet gives thanks to God: He has answered him in the days of trouble connected with his persecution by Saul and in all distresses; and by raising him to the throne, and granting him victory upon victory, and promising him the everlasting possession of the throne, He has filled him with a proud courage, so that lofty feeling has taken up its abode in his soul, which was formerly fearful about help. Just as רהב signifies impetuosity, vehemence, and then also a monster, so הִרְהִיב signifies both to break in upon one violently and overpoweringly (Cant. vi. 5; cf. Syriac *arheb*, Arabic *arhaba*, to terrify), and to make any one courageous, bold, and confident of victory. בְּנַפְשִׁי עֹז forms a corollary to the verb that is marked by *Mugrash* or *Dechî*: so that in my soul there was עֹז, *i.e.* power, viz. a consciousness of power (cf. Judg. v. 21). The thanksgiving, which he, the king of the promise, offers to God on account of this, will be transmitted to all the kings of the earth when they shall hear (שָׁמְעוּ in the sense of a *fut. exactum*) the words of His mouth, *i.e.* the divine אִמְרָה, and they shall sing of (שִׁיר with בְּ, like דִּבֶּר בְּ in lxxxvii. 3, שִׂיחַ בְּ in cv. 2 and frequently, הִלֵּל בְּ in xliv. 9, הִזְכִּיר בְּ in xx. 8, and the like) the ways of the God of the history of salvation, they shall sing that great is the glory of Jahve. Ver. 6 tells us by what means He has so super-gloriously manifested Himself in His leadings of David. He has shown Himself to be the Exalted One who in His all-embracing rule does not leave the lowly (cf. David's confessions in cxxxi. 1, 2 Sam. vi. 22) unnoticed (cxiii. 6), but on the contrary makes him the especial object of His regard; and on the other hand even from afar (cf. cxxxix. 2) He sees through (יֵדָע as in xciv. 11, Jer. xxix. 23) the lofty one who thinks himself unobserved and conducts himself as if he were answerable to no higher being (x. 4). In correct texts וגבה has *Mugrash*, and ממרחק *Mercha*. The form of the *fut. Kal* יֵדָע is formed after the analogy of the *Hiphil* forms יֵילִיל in Isa. xvi. 7, and frequently, and יָשֵׁב in Job xxiv. 21; probably the word is intended to be all the more emphatic, inasmuch as the first radical, which disappears in יֵדַע, is thus in a certain measure restored.*

Vers. 7, 8. Out of these experiences—so important for all mankind—of David, who has been exalted by passing through humiliation, there arise for him confident hopes concerning the future. The beginning of this strophe calls xxiii. 4 to mind. Though his way may lead through the midst of heart-oppressing trouble, Jahve will loose these bands of death and quicken him afresh (חָיָה as in xxx. 4, lxxi. 20, and frequently). Though his enemies may rage, Jahve will stretch forth His hand threateningly and tranquillizingly over their wrath, and His right hand will save him. יְמִינֶךָ is the subject according to cxxxix. 10 and other passages, and not (for why should it be supposed to be this?) *accus. instrumenti* (*vid.* lx. 7). In ver. 8 יִגְמֹר is intended just as in lvii. 3: the work begun He will carry out, ἐπιτελεῖν (Phil. i. 6); and בַּעֲדִי (according to its meaning, properly: covering me) is the same as עָלַי in that passage (cf. xiii. 6, cxlii. 8). The pledge of this completion is Jahve's everlasting mercy, which will not rest until the promise is become perfect truth and reality. Thus, therefore, He will not leave, forsake the works of His hands (*vid.* xc. 16 sq.), *i.e.*, as Hengstenberg correctly explains, everything that He has hitherto accomplished for David, from his deliverance out of the hands of Saul down to the bestowment of the promise— He will not let one of His works stand still, and least of all one that has been so gloriously begun. הִרְפָּה (whence תֶּרֶף) signifies to slacken, to leave slack, *i.e.* leave uncarried out, to leave to

---

* The Greek imperfects with the double (syllabic and temporal) augment, as ἑώρων, ἀνέῳγον, are similar. Chajug' also regards the first *Jod* in these forms as the preformative and the second as the radical, whereas Abulwalîd, *Gramm.* cb. xxvi. p. 170, explains the first as a prosthesis and the second as the preformative. According to the view of others, *e.g.* cf Kimchi, יֵידַע might be *fut. Hiph.* weakened from יְהִידַע (יְהֵידִיעַ), which, apart from the unsuitable meaning, assumes a change of consonants that is all the more inadmissible as יָדַע itself springs from וַדָע. Nor is it to be supposed that יֵידַע is modified from יֵדַע (Luzzatto, § 197), because it is nowhere written יֵדַע.

itself, as in Neh. vi. 3. אַל expresses a negation with a measure of inward excitement.

PSALM CXXXIX.

ADORATION OF THE OMNISCIENT AND OMNIPRESENT ONE.

1 JAHVE, Thou searchest and knowest me!
2 THOU knowest my sitting down and my rising up,
Thou understandest my thought afar off.
3 My path and my lying down Thou searchest,
And with all my ways art Thou familiar.
4 For there is not a word on my tongue—
Lo, Thou, O Jahve, knowest it altogether.
5 Behind and before dost Thou surround me,
And hast laid Thy hand upon me.
6 Incomprehensible to me is such knowledge,
It is too high, I have not grown up to it.
7 Whither could I go from Thy Spirit,
And whither could I flee from Thy presence?!
8 If I should ascend to heaven, there art THOU;
And if I should make Hades my resting-place, here art Thou also.
9 If I should raise the wings of the morning,
If I should settle down at the extremity of the sea—
10 There also Thy hand would guide me,
And Thy right hand lay hold of me.
11 And if I should say: Let nothing but darkness enwrap me,
And let the light round about me become night—
12 Even the darkness would not be too dark for Thee,
And the night would be to Thee bright as the day;
Darkness and light are alike to Thee.

13 For THOU hast brought forth my reins,
Thou didst interweave me in my mother's womb.
14 I give Thee thanks that I am fearfully, wonderfully made;
Wonderful are Thy works,
And my soul knoweth it right well.

15 My bones were not hidden from Thee,
   I who was wrought in secret,
   Curiously wrought in the depths of the earth.
16 When an embryo Thine eyes saw me,
   And in Thy book were they all written:
   Days which were already sketched out,
   And for it one among them.
17 And how precious are Thy thoughts unto me, O God,
   How mighty is their sum!
18 If I would count them, they are more than the sand;
   I awake and I am still with Thee.

19 Oh that Thou wouldest slay the wicked, Eloah;
   And ye men of blood-guiltiness, depart from me!
20 They who mention Thee craftily,
   Speak out deceitfully—Thine adversaries.
21 Should I not hate those who hate Thee, Jahve,
   And be indignant at those who rise up against Thee?!
22 With the utmost hatred do I hate them,
   They are to me as mine own enemies.
23 Search me, O God, and know my heart,
   Prove me and know my thoughts,
24 And see whether there is in me any way of pain,
   And lead me in the everlasting way!

In this Aramaizing Psalm what the preceding Psalm says in ver. 6 comes to be carried into effect, viz.: *for Jahve is exalted and He seeth the lowly, and the proud He knoweth from afar.* This Psalm has manifold points of contact with its predecessor. From a theological point of view it is one of the most instructive of the Psalms, and both as regards its contents and poetic character in every way worthy of David. But it is only inscribed לדוד because it is composed after the Davidic model, and is a counterpart to such Psalms as Ps. xix. and to other Davidic didactic Psalms. For the addition למנצח neither proves its ancient Davidic origin, nor in a general way its origin in the period prior to the Exile, as Ps. lxxiv. for example shows, which was at any rate not composed prior to the time of the Chaldæan catastrophe.

The Psalm falls into three parts: vers. 1*b*-12, 13-18,

19–24; the strophic arrangement is not clear. The first part celebrates the Omniscient and Omnipresent One. The poet knows that he is surrounded on all sides by God's knowledge and His presence; His Spirit is everywhere and cannot be avoided; and His countenance is turned in every direction and inevitably, in wrath or in love. In the second part the poet continues this celebration with reference to the origin of man; and in the third part he turns in profound vexation of spirit towards the enemies of such a God, and supplicates for himself His proving and guidance. In vers. 1 and 4 God is called *Jahve*, in ver. 17 *El*, in ver. 19 *Eloah*, in ver. 21 again *Jahve*, and in ver. 23 again *El*. Strongly as this Psalm is marked by the depth and pristine freshness of its ideas and feeling, the form of its language is still such as is without precedent in the Davidic age. To all appearance it is the Aramæo-Hebrew idiom of the post-exilic period pressed into the service of poetry. The Psalm apparently belongs to those Psalms which, in connection with a thoroughly classical character of form, bear marks of the influence which the Aramaic language of the Babylonian kingdom exerted over the exiles. This influence affected the popular dialect in the first instance, but the written language also did not escape it, as the Books of Daniel and Ezra show; and even the poetry of the Psalms is not without traces of this retrograde movement of the language of Israel towards the language of the patriarchal ancestral house. In the *Cod. Alex.* Ζαχαρίου is added to the τῷ Δαυὶδ ψαλμός, and by a second hand ἐν τῇ διασπορᾷ, which Origen also met with " in some copies."

Vers. 1–7. The Aramaic forms in this strophe are the ἅπαξ λεγομ. רֵעַ (ground-form רְעִי) in vers. 2 and 17, endeavour, desire, thinking, like רְעוּת and רַעְיוֹן in the post-exilic books, from רָעָה (רְעָא), *cupere, cogitare;* and the ἅπ. λεγ. רְבַע in ver. 3, equivalent to רְבֵץ, a lying down, if רִבְעִי be not rather an infinitive like בִּלְעִי in Job vii. 19, since אָרְחִי is undoubtedly not inflected from אֹרַח, but, as being infinitive, like עָבְרִי in Deut. iv. 21, from אָרַח; and the verb אָרַח also, with the exception of this passage, only occurs in the speeches of Elihu (Job xxxiv. 8), which are almost more strongly Aramaizing than the Book of Job itself. Further, as an Aramaizing feature we have the objective relation marked by *Lamed* in the expression בִּנְתָה לְרֵעִי, Thou understandest my thinking, as in cxvi. 16, cxxix. 3, cxxxv. 11, cxxxvi. 19 sq. The monostichic opening is after the Davidic style, *e.g.* xxiii. 1*b*. Among the prophets, Isaiah in particular is fond of such thematic introductions as we have here in ver. 1*b*. On וַתֵּדַע instead of וַתְּדָעֵנִי *vid.* on cvii. 20; the pronominal object stands once beside the first verb, or even beside the second (2 Kings ix. 25), instead of twice (Hitzig). The " me" is then expanded: sitting down, rising up, walking and lying, are the sum of human conditions or states. רֵעִי is the totality or sum of the life of the spirit and soul of man, and דְּרָכַי the sum of human action. The divine knowledge, as וַתֵּדַע says, is the result of the scrutiny of man. The poet, however, in vers. 2 and 3 uses the perfect throughout as a mood of that which is practically existing, because that scrutiny is a scrutiny that is never unexecuted, and the knowledge is consequently an ever-present knowledge. מֵרָחוֹק is meant to say that He sees into not merely the thought that is fully fashioned and matured, but even that which is being evolved. זֵרִיתָ from זָרָה is combined by Luther (with Azulai and others) with זֵר, a *wreath* (from זָרַר, *constringere, cingere*), inasmuch as he renders: whether I walk or lie down, Thou art round about me (*Ich gehe oder lige, so bistu vmb mich*). זָרָה ought to have the same meaning here, if with Wetzstein one were to compare the Arabic, and more particularly Beduin, ذرى, *dherrâ,* to protect; the notion of affording protection does not accord with this train of thought, which has reference to God's omniscience: what ought therefore to be meant is a hedging round which secures its object to the knowledge, or even a protecting that places it in security against any exchanging, which will not suffer the object to escape it.*

---

* This *Verb. tert.* و et ى is old, and the derivative *dherâ*, protection, is an elegant word; with reference to another derivative, *dherwe*, a wall of rock protecting one from the winds, *vid.* Job, ii. 23, note. The II. form (*Piel*) signifies to protect in the widest possible sense, *e.g.* (in *Nshwân,* ii. 343*b*), " ذرى الشاذ, he protected the sheep (against being exchanged) by leaving a lock of wool upon their backs when they were shorn, by which they might be r co_nised among other sheep."

The Arabic ذرى, to know, which is far removed in sound, is by no means to be compared; it is related to ذرا, to push, urge forward, and denotes knowledge that is gained by testing and experimenting. But we also have no need of that ذرى, to protect, since we can remain within the range of the guaranteed Hebrew usage, inasmuch as זָרָה, to winnow, *i.e.* to spread out that which has been threshed and expose it to the current of the wind, in Arabic likewise ذرى (whence מִזְרֶה, *midhrâ*, a winnowing-fork, like רַחַת, *racht*, a winnowing-shovel), gives an appropriate metaphor. Here it is equivalent to: to investigate and search out to the very bottom; LXX., Symmachus, and Theodotion, ἐξιχνίασας, after which the Italic renders *investigasti*, and Jerome *eventilasti*. הִסְכַּנְתָּ with the accusative, as in Job xxii. 21 with עִם: to enter into neighbourly, close, familiar relationship, or to stand in such relationship, with any one; cogn. שָׁכֵן, سكن. God is acquainted with all our ways not only superficially, but closely and thoroughly, as that to which He is accustomed.

In ver. 4 this omniscience of God is illustratively corroborated with כִּי; ver. 4b has the value of a relative clause, which, however, takes the form of an independent clause. מִלָּה (pronounced by Jerome in his letter to Sunnia and Fretela, § 82, *MALA*) is an Aramaic word that has been already incorporated in the poetry of the Davidico-Salomonic age. כֻּלָּהּ signifies both all of it and every one. In ver. 5 Luther has been misled by the LXX. and Vulgate, which take צוּר in the signification *formare* (whence צוּרָה, *forma*); it signifies, as the definition "behind and before" shows, to surround, encompass. God is acquainted with man, for He holds him surrounded on all sides, and man can do nothing, if God, whose confining hand he has lying upon him (Job ix. 23), does not allow him the requisite freedom of motion. Instead of דַּעְתְּךָ (LXX. ἡ γνῶσίς σου) the poet purposely says in ver. 6a merely דַּעַת: a knowledge, so all-penetrating, all-comprehensive as God's knowledge. The *Kerî* reads פְּלִיאָה, but the *Chethîb* פְּלִאיָה is supported by the *Chethîb* פִּלְאִי in Judg. xiii. 18, the *Kerî* of which there is not פִּלְיָא, but פֶּלִי (the pausal form of an adjective פְּלִי,

the feminine of which would be פְּלִיָּה). With מִמֶּנִּי the transcendence, with נִשְׂגְּבָה the unattainableness, and with לֹא־אוּכַל לָהּ the incomprehensibleness of the fact of the omniscience of God is expressed, and with this, to the mind of the poet, coincides God's omnipresence; for true, not merely phenomenal, knowledge is not possible without the immanence of the knowing one in the thing known. God, however, is omnipresent, sustaining the life of all things by His Spirit, and revealing Himself either in love or in wrath,—what the poet styles His countenance. To flee from this omnipresence (מִן, away from), as the sinner and he who is conscious of his guilt would gladly do, is impossible. Concerning the first אָנָה, which is here accented on the *ultima*, vid. on cxvi. 4.

Vers. 8-12. The future form אֶסַּק, customary in the Aramaic, may be derived just as well from סָלַק (סְלֵק), by means of the same mode of assimilation as in יִסֹּב=יִסְבֹּב, as from נָסַק (נְסַק), which latter is certainly only insecurely established by Dan. vi. 24, לְהַנְסָקָה (cf. לְהִנְסָקַת, Ezra iv. 22; הֻנַּק, Dan. v. 2), since the *Nun*, as in לְהִנְעָלָה, Dan. iv. 3, can also be a compensation for the resolved doubling (vid. Bernstein in the *Lexicon Chrestom. Kirschianæ*, and Levy *s.v.* נָסַק). אִם with the simple future is followed by cohortatives (vid. on lxxiii. 16) with the equivalent אֶשָּׂא among them: *et si stratum facerem* (*mihi*) *infernum* (accusative of the object as in Isa. lviii. 5), etc. In other passages the wings of the sun (Mal. iii. 20 [iv. 2]) and of the wind (xviii. 11) are mentioned, here we have the wings of the morning's dawn. *Pennæ auroræ*, Eugubinus observes (1548), *est velocissimus auroræ per omnem mundum decursus*. It is therefore to be rendered: If I should lift wings (נָשָׂא כְנָפַיִם as in Ezek. x. 16, and frequently) such as the dawn of the morning has, *i.e.* could I fly with the swiftness with which the dawn of the morning spreads itself over the eastern sky, towards the extreme west and alight there. Heaven and Hades, as being that which is superterrestrial and subterrestrial, and the east and west are set over against one another. אַחֲרִית יָם is the extreme end of the sea (of the Mediterranean with the "isles of the Gentiles"). In ver. 10 follows the apodosis: nowhere is the hand of God, which governs everything, to be escaped, for *dextera Dei ubique est.* וָאֹמַר (not וָאֵמַר, Ezek. xiii. 15), "therefore I spake," also has the value of a hypothetical protasis: *quodsi dixerim.* אַךְ and חֹשֶׁךְ belong together: *meræ tenebræ* (vid. xxxix. 6 sq.); but יְשׁוּפֵנִי is obscure. The signification secured to it of *conterere, contundere*, in Gen. iii. 15, Job ix. 17, which is followed by the LXX. (Vulgate) καταπατήσει, is inappropriate to darkness. The signification *inhiare*, which may be deduced as possible from שָׁאַף, suits relatively better, yet not thoroughly well (why should it not have been יִבְלָעֵנִי?). The signification *obvelare*, however, which one expects to find, and after which the Targum, Symmachus, Jerome, Saadia, and others render it, seems only to be guessed at from the connection, since שׁוּף has not this signification in any other instance, and in favour of it we cannot appeal either to נָשַׁף—whence נֶשֶׁף, which belongs together with נָשַׁב, נָשַׁם, and נָפַשׁ—or to עוּף, the root of which is עט (עָטָה), or to עָצָה, whence עָצִיף, which does not signify to cover, veil, but according to ضعف, to fold, fold together, to double. We must therefore either assign to יְשׁוּפֵנִי the signification *operiat me* without being able to prove it, or we must put a verb of this signification in its place, viz. יְשׂוּכֵנִי (Ewald) or יְעֻפֵנִי (Böttcher), which latter is the more commendable here, where darkness (חֹשֶׁךְ, synon. עֵיפָה, מָעוּף) is the subject: And if I should say, let nothing but darkness cover me, and as night (the predicate placed first, as in Amos iv. 13) let the light become about me, *i.e.* let the light become night that shall surround and cover me (בַּעֲדֵנִי, poetic for בַּעֲדִי, like תַּחְתֵּנִי in 2 Sam. ch. xxii.)—the darkness would spread abroad no obscurity (cv. 28) that should extend beyond (מִן) Thy piercing eye and remove me from Thee. In the word יָאִיר, too, the *Hiphil* signification is not lost: the night would give out light from itself, as if it were the day; for the distinction of day and night has no conditioning influence upon God, who is above and superior to all created things (*der Uebercreatürliche*), who is light in Himself. The two כ are correlative, as *e.g.* in 1 Kings xxii. 4. חֲשֵׁיכָה (with a superfluous *Jod*) is an old word, but אוֹרָה (cf. Aramaic אוֹרְתָּא) is a later one.

Vers. 13–18. The fact that man is manifest to God even to the very bottom of his nature, and in every place, is now confirmed from the origin of man. The development of the child in the womb was looked upon by the Israelitish Chokma as one of the greatest mysteries, Eccles. xi. 5; and here the poet praises this coming into being as a marvellous work of the omniscient and omnipresent omnipotence of God. קָנָה here signifies *condere*; and כָּבַן not: to cover, protect, as in cxl. 8, Job. xl. 22, prop. to cover with network, to hedge in, but: to plait, interweave, viz. with bones, sinews, and veins, like שָׂבַךְ in Job x. 11. The reins are made specially prominent in order to mark them, the seat of the tenderest, most secret emotions, as the work of Him who trieth the heart and the reins. The προσευχή becomes in ver. 14 the εὐχαριστία: I give thanks unto Thee that I have wonderfully come into being under fearful circumstances, *i.e.* circumstances exciting a shudder, viz. of astonishment (נוֹרָאוֹת as in lxv. 6). נִפְלָה (= נִפְלָא) is the passive to הִפְלָה, iv. 4, xvii. 7. Hitzig regards נִפְלֵיתָה (Thou hast shown Thyself wonderful), after the LXX., Syriac, Vulgate, and Jerome, as the only correct reading; but the thought which is thereby gained comes indeed to be expressed in the following line, ver. 14*b*, which sinks down into tautology in connection with this reading. עֶצֶם (collectively equivalent to עֲצָמִים, Eccles. xi. 5) is the bones, the skeleton, and, starting from that idea, more generally the state of being as a sum-total of elements of being. אֲשֶׁר, without being necessarily a conjunction (Ew. § 333, *a*), attaches itself to the suffix of עָצְמִי. רֻקַּם, "to be worked in different colours, or also embroidered," of the system of veins ramifying the body, and of the variegated colouring of its individual members, more particularly of the inward parts; perhaps, however, more generally with a retrospective conception of the colours of the outline following the undeveloped beginning, and of the forming of the members and of the organism in general.* The mother's womb is here called not merely סֵתֶר (cf. Æschylus' *Eumenides*, 665: ἐν σκότοισι νηδύος τεθραμμένη, and the designation of the place where the foetus is formed as " a threefold darkness" in the Koran, *Sur.* xxxix. 8), the *ē* of which is retained here in pause (*vid.* Böttcher, *Lehrbuch*, § 298), but by a bolder appellation תַּחְתִּיּוֹת אָרֶץ, the lowest parts of the earth, *i.e.* the interior of the earth (*vid.* on lxiii. 10) as being the secret laboratory of the earthly origin, with the same retro-

---

* In the Talmud the egg of a bird or of a reptile is called מְרֻקֶּמֶת, when the outlines of the developed embryo are visible in it; and likewise the mole (*mola*), when traces of human organization can be discerned in it.

spective reference to the first formation of the human body out of the dust of the earth, as when Job says, ch. i. 21 : "naked came I out of my mother's womb, and naked shall I return thither"—שָׁמָּה, viz. εἰς τὴν γῆν τὴν μητέρα πάντων, Sir. xl. 1. The interior of Hades is also called בֶּטֶן שְׁאוֹל in Jonah ii. 3 [2], Sir. li. 5. According to the view of Scripture the mode of Adam's creation is repeated in the formation of every man, Job xxxiii. 6, cf. 4. The earth was the mother's womb of Adam, and the mother's womb out of which the child of Adam comes forth is the earth out of which it is taken.

(Ver. 16.) The embryo folded up in the shape of an egg is here called גֹּלֶם, from גָּלַם, to roll or wrap together (cf. *glomus*, a ball), in the Talmud said of any kind of unshapen mass (LXX. ἀκατέργαστον, Symmachus ἀμόρφωτον) and raw material, *e.g.* of the wood or metal that is to be formed into a vessel (*Chullin* 25a, to which Saadia has already referred).* As to the rest, compare similar retrospective glances into the embryonic state in Job x. 8–12, 2 Macc. vii. 22 sq. (*Psychology*, S. 209 ff., tr. pp. 247 sq.). On the words *in libro tuo* Bellarmine makes the following correct observation: *quia habes apud te exemplaria sive ideas omnium, quomodo pictor vel sculptor scit ex informi materia quid futurum sit, quia videt exemplar.* The signification of the future יִכָּתֵבוּ is regulated by רָאָה, and becomes, as relating to the synchronous past, *scribebantur*. The days יֻצָּרוּ, which were already formed, are the subject. It is usually rendered: "the days which had first to be formed." If יֻצָּרוּ could be equivalent to יֻצָּרוּ, it would be to be preferred; but this rejection of the *præform. fut.* is only allowed in the *fut. Piel* of the verbs *Pe Jod*, and that after a *Waw convertens, e.g.* וַיִּיבַּשׁ = וַיְיַבֵּשׁ, Nah. i. 4 (cf. Caspari on Obad. ver. 11).† Accordingly, assuming the original character of the לֹא in a negative signification, it is to be rendered: The days which were (already) formed, and there was not one among them, *i.e.* when none among them had as yet become a reality. The suffix of בָּהֶם

---

* Epiphanius, *Hær.* xxx. § 31, says the Hebrew γολμη signifies the peeled grains of spelt or wheat before they are mixed up and backed, the still raw (only bruised) flour-grains—a signification that can now no longer be supported by examples.

† But outside the Old Testament it also occurs in the *Pual*, though as a wrong use of the word; *vide* my *Anekdota* (1811), S. 372 f.

points to the succeeding יָמִים, to which יֻצָּרוּ is appended as an attributive clause; וְלֹא אֶחָד בָּהֶם is subordinated to this יֻצָּרוּ : *cum non* or *nondum* (Job xxii. 16) *unus inter eos = unus eorum* (Ex. xiv. 28) *esset*. But the expression (instead of וְעוֹד לֹא הָיָה or טֶרֶם יִהְיֶה) remains doubtful, and it becomes a question whether the *Kerî* וְלוֹ (*vid.* on c. 3), which stands side by side with the *Chethîb* ולא (which the LXX., Aquila, Symmachus, Theodotion, the Targum, Syriac, Jerome, and Saadia follow), is not to be preferred. This וְלוֹ, referred to גלמי, gives the acceptable meaning: and for it (viz. its birth) one among them (these days), without our needing to make any change in the proposed exposition down to יצרו. We decide in favour of this, because this ולו אחד בהם does not, as ולא אחד בהם, make one feel to miss any הָיָה, and because the וְלִי which begins ver. 17 connects itself to it by way of continuation. The accentuation has failed to discern the reference of כֻּלָּם to the following יָמִים, inasmuch as it places *Olewejored* against יכתבו. Hupfeld follows this accentuation, referring כֻּלָּם back to גלמי as a coil of days of one's life; and Hitzig does the same, referring it to the embryos. But the precedence of the relative pronoun occurs in other instances also,* and is devoid of all harshness, especially in connection with כֻּלָּם, which directly signifies altogether (*e.g.* Isa. xliii. 14). It is the confession of the omniscience that is united with the omnipotence of God, which the poet here gives utterance to with reference to himself, just as Jahve says with reference to Jeremiah, Jer. i. 5. Among the days which were preformed in the idea of God (cf. on יצרו, Isa. xxii. 11, xxxvii. 26) there was also one, says the poet, for the embryonic beginning of my life. The divine knowledge embraces the beginning, development, and completion of all things (*Psychology*, S. 37 ff., tr. pp. 46 sqq.). The knowledge of the thoughts of God which are written in the book of creation and revelation is the poet's cherished possession, and to ponder over them is his favourite pursuit: they are precious to him, יָקְרוּ (after xxxvi. 8), not: difficult of comprehension (*schwerbegreiflich*, Maurer, Olshausen), after Dan. ii. 11, which

---

* The Hebrew poet, says Gesenius (*Lehrgebäude*, S. 739 f.), sometimes uses the pronoun before the thing to which it referred has even been spoken of. This phenomenon belongs to the Hebrew style generally, *vid.* my *Anekdota* (1841), S. 382.

would surely have been expressed by עָמְקוּ (xcii. 6), more readily: very weighty (*schwergewichtig*, Hitzig), but better according to the prevailing Hebrew usage: highly valued (*schwergewerthet*), *cara*.* "Their sums" are powerful, prodigious (xl. 6), and cannot be brought to a *summa summarum*. If he desires to count them (*fut. hypothet.* as in xci. 7, Job xx. 24), they prove themselves to be more than the sand with its grains, that is to say, innumerable. He falls asleep over the pondering upon them, wearied out; and when he wakes up, he is still with God, *i.e.* still ever absorbed in the contemplation of the Unsearchable One, which even the sleep of fatigue could not entirely interrupt. Ewald explains it somewhat differently: if I am lost in the stream of thoughts and images, and recover myself from this state of reverie, yet I am still ever with Thee, without coming to an end. But it could only perhaps be interpreted thus if it were הַעִירוֹתִי or הִתְעוֹרַרְתִּי. Hofmann's interpretation is altogether different: I will count them, the more numerous than the sand, when I awake and am continually with Thee, viz. in the other world, after the awaking from the sleep of death. This is at once impossible, because הקיצתי cannot here, according to its position, be a *perf. hypotheticum*. Also in connection with this interpretation עוֹד would be an inappropriate expression for "continually," since the word only has the sense of the continual duration of an action or a state already existing; here of one that has not even been closed and broken off by sleep. He has not done; waking and dreaming and waking up, he is carried away by that endless, and yet also endlessly attractive, pursuit, the most fitting occupation of one who is awake, and the sweetest (cf. Jer. xxxi. 26) of one who is asleep and dreaming.

Vers. 19–21. And this God is by many not only not believed in and loved, but even hated and blasphemed! The poet now turns towards these enemies of God in profound vexation of spirit. The אִם, which is conditional in ver. 8, here is an optative *o si*, as in lxxxi. 9, xcv. 7. The expression תִּקְטֹל אֱלוֹהַּ reminds one of the Book of Job, for, with the exception of our Psalm, this is the only book that uses the verb קָטַל, which

---

* It should be noted that the radical idea of the verb, viz. being heavy (German *schwer*), is retained in all these renderings.—TR.

is more Aramaic than Hebrew, and the divine name *Eloah* occurs more frequently in it than anywhere else. The transition from the optative to the imperative כּוּרוּ is difficult; it would have been less so if the *Waw copul.* had been left out: cf. the easier expression in vi. 9, cxix. 115. But we may not on this account seek to read יְסוּרוּ, as Olshausen does. Everything here is remarkable; the whole Psalm has a characteristic form in respect to the language. מִי is the ground-form of the overloaded מִמֶּנִּי, and is also like the Book of Job, ch. xxi. 16, cf. מֶנְהוּ ch. iv. 12, Ps. lxviii. 24. The mode of writing יֹמְרוּךָ (instead of which, however, the Babylonian texts had יֹאמְרוּךָ) is the same as in 2 Sam. xix. 15, cf. in 2 Sam. xx. 9 the same melting away of the *Aleph* into the preceding vowel in connection with אַחַ, in 2 Sam. xxii. 40 in connection with אָוָר, and in Isa. xiii. 20 with אָהֵל. Construed with the accusative of the person, אָמַר here signifies to declare any one, *profiteri*, a meaning which, we confess, does not occur elsewhere. But לַמִּזְמָּה (cf. לְמִרְמָה, xxiv. 4; the Targum: who swear by Thy name for wantonness) and the parallel member of the verse, which as it runs is moulded after Ex. xx. 7, show that it has not to be read יַמְרוּךָ (Quinta: παρεπίκραναν σε). The form נָשֻׂא, with *Aleph otians*, is also remarkable; it ought at least to have been written נָשְׂאוּ (cf. גֻּרְפְּאוּ, Ezek. xlvii. 8) instead of the customary נָשְׂאוּ; yet the same mode of writing is found in the *Niphal* in Jer. x. 5, יִנָּשׂוּא, it assumes a ground-form נִשׂה (xxxii. 1) = נִשָּׂא, and is to be judged of according to אָבוֹא in Isa. xxviii. 12 [Ges. § 23, 3, rem. 3]. Also one feels the absence of the object to נָשֻׂא לַשָּׁוְא. It is meant to be supplied according to the decalogue, Ex. xx. 7, which certainly makes the alteration יְדֶךָ (Böttcher, Olsh.) or זִכְרְךָ (Hitzig on Isa. xxvi. 13), instead of עָרֶיךָ, natural. But the text as we now have it is also intelligible: the object to נָשֻׂא is derived from יֹמְרוּךָ, and the following עָרֶיךָ is an explanation of the subject intended in נָשֻׂא that is introduced subsequently. Ps. lxxxix. 52 proves the possibility of this structure of a clause. It is correctly rendered by Aquila ἀντί-ζηλοί σου, and Symmachus οἱ ἐναντίοι σου. עָר, an enemy, prop. one who is zealous, a zealot (from עוּר, or rather עִיר, = غار *med.* Je, ζηλοῦν, whence עִיר, غَيْر = קִנְאָה), is a word that is guaranteed by 1 Sam. xxviii. 16, Dan. iv. 16, and as being an Aramaism is appropriate to this Psalm. The form תְּקוֹמֵם for מְתְקוֹמֵם has cast away the preformative *Mem* (cf. שְׁפָתִים and מִשְׁפָּתַיִם, מִקְרֵה in Deut. xxiii. 11 for מִמְּקְרֵה); the suffix is to be understood according to xvii. 7. *Pasek* stands between יהוה and אֶשְׂנָא in order that the two words may not be read together (cf. Job xxvii. 13, and above x. 3). הִתְקוֹטֵט as in the recent Ps. cxix. 158. The emphasis in ver. 22*b* lies on לִי; the poet regards the adversaries of God as enemies of his own. תַּכְלִית takes the place of the adjective: *extremo* (*odio*) *odi eos*. Such is the relation of the poet to the enemies of God, but without indulging any self-glorying.

Vers. 23, 24. He sees in them the danger which threatens himself, and prays God not to give him over to the judgment of self-delusion, but to lay bare the true state of his soul. The fact "Thou hast searched me," which the beginning of the Psalm confesses, is here turned into a petitioning "search me." Instead of רֵעִים in ver. 17, the poet here says שַׂרְעַפִּים, which signifies branches (Ezek. xxxi. 5) and branchings of the act of thinking (thoughts and cares, xciv. 19). The *Resh* is epenthetic, for the first form is שְׂעִפִּים, Job iv. 13, xx. 2. The poet thus sets the very ground and life of his heart, with all its outward manifestations, in the light of the divine omniscience. And in ver. 24 he prays that God would see whether any דֶּרֶךְ־עֹצֶב cleaves to him (בִּי as in 1 Sam. xxv. 24), by which is not meant "a way of idols" (Rosenmüller, Gesenius, and Maurer), after Isa. xlviii. 5, since an inclination towards, or even apostasy to, heathenism cannot be an unknown sin; nor to a man like the writer of this Psalm is heathenism any power of temptation. דרך בֶּצַע (Grätz) might more readily be admissible, but דרך עֹצֶב is a more comprehensive notion, and one more in accordance with this closing petition. The poet gives this name to the way that leads to the pain, torture, viz. of the inward and outward punishments of sin; and, on the other hand, the way along which he wishes to be guided he calls דֶּרֶךְ עוֹלָם, the way of endless continuance (LXX., Vulgate, Luther), not the way of the former times, after Jer. vi. 16 (Maurer, Olshausen), which thus by itself is ambiguous (as becomes evident from Job xxii. 15, Jer. xviii. 15), and also does not furnish any direct antithesis. The "everlasting way" is the way of God (xxvii. 11), the way of the righteous, which stands fast for ever and shall not "perish" (i. 6).

PSALM CXL.

PRAYER FOR PROTECTION AGAINST WICKED, CRAFTY MEN.

2 DELIVER me, Jahve, from wicked men,
From the violent man preserve me,
3 Who plot wickedness in the heart,
Daily do they stir up wars.
4 They sharpen their tongue like a serpent,
Adder's poison is under their lips. (*Sela.*)

5 Keep me, Jahve, from the hands of the wicked,
From the violent man preserve me,
Who purpose to thrust aside my footsteps
6 The proud hide snares for me and cords,
They spread nets close by the path,
They set traps for me. (*Sela.*)

7 I say to Jahve : My God art Thou,
Oh give ear, Jahve, to the cry of my supplication.
8 Jahve the Lord is the stronghold of my salvation,
Thou coverest my head in the day of equipment.
9 Grant not, Jahve, the desires of the wicked ;
Let not his device prosper, that they may not be lifted up.
(*Sela.*)

10 The head of those who compass me about—let the trouble
of their lips cover them !
11 Let burning coals be cast down upon them, let them be
cast into the fire,
Into abysses out of which they may never rise up !
12 Let not the man of the tongue be established on the earth,
The man of violence—let wickedness hunt him in violent
haste !

13 I know that Jahve will carry through the cause of the
afflicted,
The right of the poor.
14 Yea, the righteous shall give thanks unto Thy Name,
The upright shall dwell beside Thy countenance.

The close of the preceding Psalm is the key to David's position and mood in the presence of his enemies which find expression in this Psalm. He complains here of serpent-like, crafty, slanderous adversaries, who are preparing themselves for war against him, and with whom he will at length have to fight in open battle. The Psalm, in its form more bold than beautiful, justifies its לְדָוִד in so far as it is Davidic in thoughts and figures, and may be explained from the circumstances of the rebellion of Absalom, to which as an outbreak of Ephraimitish jealousy the rebellion of Sheba ben Bichri the Benjamite attached itself. Ps. lviii. and lxiv. are very similar. The close of all three Psalms sounds much alike, they agree in the use of rare forms of expression, and their language becomes fearfully obscure in style and sound where they are directed against the enemies.

Vers. 2-4. The assimilation of the *Nun* of the verb נָצַר is given up, as in lxi. 8, lxxviii. 7, and frequently, in order to make the form more full-toned. The relative clause shows that אִישׁ חֲמָסִים (vid. vol. i. 277) is not intended to be understood exclusively of one person. בְּלֵב strengthens the notion of that which is deeply concealed and premeditated. It is doubtful whether יָגוּרוּ signifies to form into troops or to stir up. But from the fact that גּוּר in lvi. 7, lix. 4, Isa. liv. 15, signifies not *congregare* but *se congregare*, it is to be inferred that גּוּר in the passage before us, like גֵּרָה (or הִתְגָּרָה in Deut. ii. 9, 24), in Syriac and Targumic גָּרֵי, signifies *concitare*, to excite (cf. שׂוּר together with שָׂרָה, Hos. xii. 4 sq.). In ver. 4 the Psalm coincides with lxiv. 4, lviii. 5. They sharpen their tongue, so that it inflicts a fatal sting like the tongue of a serpent, and under their lips, shooting out from thence, is the poison of the adder (cf. Cant. iv. 11). עַכְשׁוּב is a ἅπαξ λεγομ. not from כָּשַׁב (*Jesurun*, p. 207), but from עָכַשׁ, عكس and عكش, root علك (vid. Fleischer on Isa. lix. 5, עַכָּבִישׁ), both of which have the significations of bending, turning, and coiling after the manner of a serpent; the *Beth* is an organic addition modifying the meaning of the root.*

---

* According to the original Lexicons عكس signifies to bend one's self, to wriggle, to creep sideways like the roots of the vine, in the V. form to

Vers. 5, 6. The course of this second strophe is exactly parallel with the first. The perfects describe their conduct hitherto, as a comparison of ver. 3b with 3a shows. פְּעָמִים is poetically equivalent to רַגְלַיִם, and signifies both the foot that steps (lvii. 7, lviii. 11) and the step that is made by the foot (lxxxv. 14, cxix. 133), and here the two senses are undistinguishable. They are called גֵּאִים on account of the inordinate ambition that infatuates them. The metaphors taken from the life of the hunter (cxli. 9, cxlii. 4) are here brought together as it were into a body of synonyms. The meaning of לְיַד־מַעְגָּל becomes explicable from cxlii. 4; לְיַד, at hand, is equivalent to "immediately beside" (1 Chron. xviii. 17, Neh. xi. 24). Close by the path along which he has to pass, lie gins ready to spring together and ensnare him when he appears.

Vers. 7-9. Such is the conduct of his enemies; he, however, prays to his God and gets his weapons from beside Him. The day of equipment is the day of the crisis when the battle is fought in full array. The perfect סַכֹּתָה states what will then take place on the part of God: He protects the head of His anointed against the deadly blow. Both ver. 8a and 8b point to the helmet as being מָעוֹז רֹאשׁ, lx. 9; cf. the expression "the helmet of salvation" in Isa. lix. 17. Beside מַאֲוַיֵּי, from the ἅπ. λεγ. מַאֲוָה, there is also the reading מַאֲוַיֵּי, which Abulwalid found in his Jerusalem codex (in Saragossa). The

---

move one's self like an adder (according to the *Ḳamûs*) and to walk like a drunken man (according to *Neshwân*); but عكش signifies to be intertwined, knit or closely united together, said of hairs and of the branches of trees, in the V. form to fight hand to hand and to get in among the crowd. The root is apparently expanded into עֲכֹשׁוּב by an added *Beth* which serves as a notional speciality, as in عرنوب the convex bend of the steep side of a rock, or in the case of the knee of the hind-legs of animals,

and in خرنوب (in the dialect of the country along the coast of Palestine, where the tree is plentiful, in Neshwân *churnûb*), the horn-like curved pod of the carob-tree (*Ceratonia Siliqua*), syncopated خروب, *charrûb* (not *charûb*), from خرن, cogn. قرن a horn, cf. خرنايَة the beak of a bird of prey, خرنوق the stork [*vid.* on civ. 17], خرنين the rhinoceros [*vid.* on xxix. 6], خرنيت the unicorn [*vid. ibid.*].—WETZSTEIN.

regular form would be מְאֹי, and the doubly irregular ma'awajjê follows the example of מְחֻמַּדַי, מְחֻתָּשַׁבַּי, and the like, in a manner that is without example elsewhere. זְמֹמוֹ for מְזִמָּתוֹ is also a hapaxlegomenon; according to Gesenius the principal form is זְמָם, but surely more correctly זְמָם (like קְרָב), which in Aramaic signifies a bridle, and here a plan, device. The *Hiph.* הֵפִיק (root פוק, whence פֵּיק, نفق) signifies *educere* in the sense of *reportare*, Prov. iii. 13, viii. 35, xii. 2, xviii. 22, and of *porrigere*, cxliv. 13, Isa. lviii. 10. A reaching forth of the plan is equivalent to the reaching forth of that which is projected. The choice of the words used in this Psalm coincides here, as already in מַעֲגָל, with Proverbs and Isaiah. The future יָרוּמוּ expresses the consequence (cf. lxi. 8) against which the poet wishes to guard.

Vers. 10-12. The strophic symmetry is now at an end. The longer the poet lingers over the contemplation of the rebels the more lofty and dignified does his language become, the more particular the choice of the expressions, and the more difficult and unmanageable the construction. The *Hiph.* הֵסֵב signifies, causatively, to cause to go round about (Ex. xiii. 18), and to raise round about (2 Chron. xiv. 6); here, after Josh. vi. 11, where with an accusative following it signifies to go round about: to make the circuit of anything, as enemies who surround a city on all sides and seek the most favourable point for assault; מְסִבַּי from the participle מֵסֵב. Even when derived from the substantive מֵסַב (Hupfeld), "my surroundings" is equivalent to אֹיְבַי סְבִיבוֹתַי in xxvii. 6. Hitzig, on the other hand, renders it: the head of my slanderers, from סָבַב, to go round about, Arabic to tell tales of any one, defame; but the Arabic

سَبَّ, *fut. u*, to abuse, the IV. form (*Hiphil*) of which moreover is not used either in the ancient or in the modern language, has nothing to do with the Hebrew סבב, but signifies originally to cut off round about, then to clip (injure) any one's honour and good name.* The fact that the enemies who surround

---

* The lexicographer *Neshwân* says, i. 279b: السَبُّ الشَتْمُ وقيلَ ان
أصل السبِ انقطع ثم صار الشتم, "*sebb* is to abuse; still, the more original signification of cutting off is said to lie at the foundation of this

the psalmist on every side are just such calumniators, is intimated here in the word שְׂפָתֵימוֹ. He wishes that the trouble which the enemies' slanderous lips occasion him may fall back upon their own head. רֹאשׁ is head in the first and literal sense according to vii. 17; and יְכַסֵּימוֹ (with the *Jod* of the groundform כסי, as in Deut. xxxii. 26, 1 Kings xx. 35; *Chethîb* יְכַסּוּמוֹ,* after the attractional schema, 2 Sam. ii. 4, Isa. ii. 11, and frequently; cf. on the masculine form, Prov. v. 2, x. 21) refers back to רֹאשׁ, which is meant of the heads of all persons individually. In ver. 11 יָמִיטוּ (with an indefinite subject of the higher punitive powers, Ges. § 137, note), in the signification to cause to descend, has a support in lv. 4, whereas the *Niph.* יִמּוֹט, fut. יִמֹּט, which is preferred by the *Keri*, in the signification to be made to descend, is contrary to the usage of the language. The ἅπ. λεγ. מַהֲמֹרוֹת has been combined by Parchon and others with the Arabic همر, which, together with other significations (to strike, stamp, cast down, and the like), also has the signification to flow (whence *e.g.* in the Koran, *mâ' munhamir*, flowing water). "Fire" and "water" are emblems of perils that cannot be escaped, lxvi. 12, and the mention of fire is therefore appropriately succeeded by places of flowing water, pits of water. The signification "pits" is attested by the Targum, Symmachus, Jerome, and the quotation in Kimchi: "first of all they buried them in מהמורות; when the flesh was consumed they collected the bones and buried them in coffins." On בַּל־יָקוּמוּ cf. Isa. xxvi. 14. Like vers. 10, 11, ver. 12 is also not to be taken as a general maxim, but as expressing a wish in accordance with the excited tone of this strophe. אִישׁ לָשׁוֹן is not a great talker, *i.e.* boaster, but an idle talker, *i.e.* slanderer (LXX. ἀνὴρ γλωσσώδης, cf. Sir. viii. 4). According to the accents, אִישׁ חָמָס רָע is the parallel; but what would be the object of this designation of violence as worse or more malignant? With Sommer, Olshausen, and others, we take רָע as the subject

---

signification." That قطع is synonymous with it, *e.g.* ليش تنطع فينا, why dost thou cut into us? *i.e.* why dost thou insult our honour?— WETZSTEIN.

* Which is favoured by Ex. xv. 5, *j'chasjûmû* with *mû* instead of *mô*, which is otherwise without example.

to יֶצוּדֶנּוּ: let evil, *i.e.* the punishment which arises out of evil, hunt him; cf. Prov. xiii. 21, חַטָּאִים תְּרַדֵּף רָעָה, and the opposite in xxiii. 6. It would have to be accented, according to this our construction of the words, אִישׁ חָמָס רָע יְצוּדֶנּוּ לְמַדְחֵפֹת. The ἅπ. λεγ. לְמַדְחֵפֹת we do not render, with Hengstenberg, Olshausen, and others: push upon push, with repeated pushes, which, to say nothing more, is not suited to the figure of hunting, but, since דָּחַף always has the signification of precipitate hastening: by hastenings, that is to say, forced marches.

Vers. 13, 14. With ver. 13 the mood and language now again become cheerful, the rage has spent itself; therefore the style and tone are now changed, and the Psalm trips along merrily as it were to the close. With reference to ידעת for ידעתי (as in Job xlii. 2), *vid.* xvi. 2. That which David in ix. 5 confidently expects on his own behalf is here generalized into the certain prospect of the triumph of the good cause in the person of all its representatives at that time oppressed. אַךְ, like יָדַעְתִּי, is an expression of certainty. After seeming abandonment God again makes Himself known to His own, and those whom they wanted to sweep away out of the land of the living have an ever sure dwelling-place with His joyful countenance (xvi. 11).

PSALM CXLI.

EVENING PSALM IN THE TIMES OF ABSALOM.

1 JAHVE, I call upon Thee, Oh haste Thee unto me;
 Oh hearken to my voice, when I call upon Thee!
2 Let my prayer be accounted as incense before Thee,
 The lifting up of my hands as the evening meat-offering.

3 Oh set a watch, Jahve, upon my mouth,
 A protection upon the door of my lips.
4 Incline not my heart to an evil matter,
 To practise knavish things in iniquity
 With the lords who rule wickedly,
 And let me not taste their dainties.

5 Let a righteous man smite me lovingly and rebuke me,

Such oil upon the head let not my head refuse,
For still do I meet their wickedness only with prayer.
6 Hurled down upon the sides of the rock are their judges,
And they hear my words as welcome.
7 As when one furroweth and breaketh up the earth,
Are our bones sowed at the gate of Hades.

8 For unto Thee, Jahve Lord! do mine eyes look,
In Thee do I hide, pour not my soul out!
9 Keep me from the hands of the snare of those who lay snares for me,
And from the traps of those who rule wickedly.
10 Let the wicked fall into their own net,
Whilst *I* altogether escape.

The four Psalms, cxl., cxli., cxlii., and cxliii., are interwoven with one another in many ways (*Symbolæ*, pp. 67 sq.). The following passages are very similar, viz. cxl. 7, cxli. 1, cxlii. 2, and cxliii. 1. Just as the poet complains in cxlii. 4, " when my spirit veils itself within me," so too in cxliii. 4; as he prays in cxlii. 8, " Oh bring my soul out of prison," so in cxliii. 11, " bring my soul out of distress," where צרה takes the place of the metaphorical מסגר. Besides these, compare cxl. 5, 6 with cxli. 9; cxlii. 7 with cxliii. 9; cxl. 3 with cxli. 5, רעות; cxl. 14 with cxlii. 8; cxlii. 4 with cxliii. 8.

The right understanding of the Psalm depends upon the right understanding of the situation. Since it is inscribed לדוד, it is presumably a situation corresponding to the history of David, out of the midst of which the Psalm is composed, either by David himself or by some one else who desired to give expression in Davidic strains to David's mood when in this situation. For the gleaning of Davidic Psalms which we find in the last two Books of the Psalter is for the most part derived from historical works in which these Psalms, in some instances only free reproductions of the feelings of David with respect to old Davidic models, adorned the historic narrative. The Psalm before us adorned the history of the time of the persecution by Absalom. At that time David was driven out of Jerusalem, and consequently cut off from the sacrificial worship of God upon Zion; and our Psalm is an evening hymn of one of those troublous days. The ancient church, even prior to the time of Gregory (*Constitutiones Apostolicæ*, ii. 59), had chosen it for its evening hymn, just as it had chosen Ps. lxiii. for its morning hymn. Just as Ps. lxiii. was called ὁ ὀρθρινός (*ibid.* viii. 37), so this Psalm, as being the Vesper Psalm, was called ὁ ἐπιλύχνιος (*ibid.* viii. 35).

Vers. 1, 2. The very beginning of Ps. cxli. is more after the manner of David than really Davidic; for instead of *haste thee to me*, David always says, *haste thee for my help*, xxii. 20, xxxviii. 23, xl. 14. The לְ that is added to בְּקָרְאִי (as in iv. 2) is to be explained, as in lvii. 3: when I call to Thee, *i.e.* when I call Thee, who art now far from me, to me. The general cry for help is followed in ver. 2 by a petition for the answering of his prayer. Luther has given an excellent rendering: Let my prayer avail to Thee as an offering of incense; the lifting up of my hands, as an evening sacrifice (*Mein Gebet müsse für dir tügen wie ein Reuchopffer, Meine Hende auffheben, wie ein Abendopffer*). תִּכּוֹן is the *fut. Niph.* of כּוּן, and signifies properly to be set up, and to be established, or reflexive: to place and arrange or prepare one's self, Amos iv. 12; then to continue, *e.g.* ci. 7; therefore, either let it place itself, let it appear, *sistat se*, or better: let it stand, continue, *i.e.* let my prayer find acceptance, recognition with Thee קְטֹרֶת, and the lifting up of my hands מִנְחַת־עָרֶב. Expositors say that this in both instances is the *comparatio decurtata*, as in xi. 1 and elsewhere: as an incense-offering, as an evening *mincha*. But the poet purposely omits the כְּ of the comparison. He wishes that God may be pleased to regard his prayer as sweet-smelling smoke or as incense, just as this was added to the *azcara* of the meal-offering, and gave it, in its ascending perfume, the direction upward to God,* and that He may be pleased to regard the

---

* It is not the priestly קְטֹרֶת תָּמִיד, *i.e.* the daily morning and evening incense-offering upon the golden altar of the holy place, Ex. xxx. 8, that is meant (since it is a non-priest who is speaking, according to Hitzig, of course John Hyrcanus), but rather, as also in Isa. i. 13, the incense of the *azcara* of the meal-offering which the priest burnt (הִקְטִיר) upon the altar; the incense (Isa. lxvi. 3) was entirely consumed, and not merely a handful taken from it.

lifting up of his hands (מַשְׂאַה, the construct with the reduplication given up, from מַשְׂאֵת, or even, after the form מִנְחַת, from מִשְׂאָה, here not *oblatio*, but according to the phrase וַיִּשָּׂא כַפָּיִם [יָדָיו], *elevatio*, Judg. xx. 38, 40, cf. Ps. xxviii. 2, and frequently) as an evening *mincha*, just as it was added to the evening *tamid* according to Ex. xxix. 38–42, and concluded the work of the service of the day.*

Vers. 3, 4. The prayer now begins to be particularized, and that in the first instance as a petition for the grace of silence, calling to mind old Davidic passages like xxxix. 2, xxxiv. 14. The situation of David, the betrayed one, requires caution in speaking; and the consciousness of having sinned, not indeed against the rebels, but against God, who would not visit him thus without his deserving it, stood in the way of any outspoken self-vindication. In *pone custodiam ori meo* שָׁמְרָה is ἅπ. λεγ., after the infinitive form עָצְמָה, עָזְבָה, דִּבְקָה. In ver. 3*b* דַּל is ἅπ. λεγ. for דֶּלֶת; cf. "doors of the mouth" in Mic. vii. 5, and πύλαι στόματος in Euripides. נִצְּרָה might be *imper. Kal:* keep I pray, with *Dag. dirimens* as in Prov. iv. 13. But נְצָר־ עַל is not in use; and also as the parallel word to שָׁמְרָה, which likewise has the appearance of being imperative, נִצְּרָה is explicable as regards its pointing by a comparison of יְקְהָה in Gen. xlix. 10, דִּבְּרָה in Deut. xxxiii. 3, and קִרְבָה in lxxiii. 28. The prayer for the grace of silence is followed in ver. 4 by a prayer for the breaking off of all fellowship with the existing rulers. By a flight of irony they are called אִישִׁים, lords, in the sense of בְּנֵי אִישׁ, iv. 3 (cf. the Spanish *hidalgos = hijos d'algo*, sons of somebody). The evil thing (דְּבַר־רָע), with *Pasek* between the two ר, as in Num. vii. 13, Deut. vii. 1 between the two ם, and in 1 Chron. xxii. 3 between the two ל), to which Jahve may be pleased never to incline his heart (תֵּט, *fut. apoc. Hiph.* as in xxvii. 9), is forthwith more particularly designated: *perpetrare faci-*

---

* The reason of it is this, that the evening *mincha* is oftener mentioned than the morning *mincha* (see, however, 2 Kings iii. 20). The whole burnt-offering of the morning and the meat-offering of the evening (2 Kings xvi. 15, 1 Kings xviii. 29, 36) are the beginning and close of the daily principal service; whence, according to the example of the *usus loquendi* in Dan. ix. 21, Ezra ix. 4 sq., later on *mincha* directly signifies the afternoon or evening.

nova maligne cum dominis, etc. עֲלִילוֹת of great achievements in the sense of infamous deeds, also occurs in xiv. 1, xcix. 8. Here, however, we have the *Hithpo.* הִתְעֹלֵל, which, with the accusative of the object עֲלִלוֹת, signifies: wilfully to make such actions the object of one's acting (cf. تَعَلَّلَ بِالشَّيْ, to meddle with any matter, to amuse, entertain one's self with a thing). The expression is made to express disgust as strongly as possible; this poet is fond of glaring colouring in his language. In the dependent passage *neve eorum vescar cupediis*, לְחֹם is used poetically for אָכַל, and בּ is the partitive *Beth*, as in Job xxi. 25. מַנְעַמִּים is another hapaxlegomenon, but as being a designation of dainties (from נָעֵם, to be mild, tender, pleasant), it may not have been an unusual word. It is a well-known thing that usurpers revel in the *cuisine* and cellars of those whom they have driven away.

Vers. 5–7. Thus far the Psalm is comparatively easy of exposition; but now it becomes difficult, yet not hopelessly so. David, thoroughly conscious of his sins against God and of his imperfection as a monarch, says, in opposition to the abuse which he is now suffering, that he would gladly accept any friendly reproof: " let a righteous man smite in kindness and reprove me—head-oil (*i.e.* oil upon the head, to which such reproof is likened) shall my head not refuse." So we render it, following the accents, and not as Hupfeld, Kurtz, and Hitzig do: "if a righteous man smites me, it is love; if he reproves me, an anointing of the head is it unto me;" in connection with which the designation of the subject with הִיא would be twice wanting, which is more than is admissible. צַדִּיק stands here as an abstract substantive: the righteous man, whoever he may be, in antithesis, namely, to the rebels and to the people who have joined them. Amyraldus, Maurer, and Hengstenberg understand it of God; but it only occurs of God as an attribute, and never as a direct appellation. חֶסֶד, as in Jer. xxxi. 3, is equivalent to בְּחֶסֶד, *cum benignitate* = *benigne*. What is meant is, as in Job vi. 14, what Paul (Gal. vi. 1) styles πνεῦμα πραΰτητος. And הָלַם, *tundere*, is used of the strokes of earnest but well-meant reproof, which is called " the blows of a friend" in Prov. xxvii. 6. Such reproof shall be to him as head-oil (xxiii. 5, cxxxiii. 2), which his head does not despise. יָנִי, written defectively for יָנִיא, like יְשׁ in lv. 10, אָבִי, 1 Kings xxi. 29 and frequently; הֵנִיא (root נא, 'ύ, with the nasal *n*, which also expresses the negation in the Indo-Germanic languages) here signifies to deny, as in xxxiii. 10 to bring to nought, to destroy. On the other hand, the LXX. renders μὴ λιπανάτω τὴν κεφαλήν μου, which is also followed by the Syriac and Jerome, perhaps after the Arabic غنى, to become or to be fat, which is, however, altogether foreign to the Aramaic, and is, moreover, only used of fatness of the body, and in fact of camels. The meaning of the figure is this: well-meant reproof shall be acceptable and spiritually useful to him. The confirmation כִּי־עוֹד וגו׳ follows, which is enigmatical both in meaning and expression. This עוֹד is the cipher of a whole clause, and the following ו is related to this עוֹד as the *Waw* that introduces the apodosis, not to כִּי, as in 2 Chron. xxiv. 20, since no progression and connection is discernible if כִּי is taken as a subordinating *quia*. We interpret thus: *for it is still so* (the matter still stands thus), *that my prayer is against their wickednesses;* i.e. that I use no weapon but that of prayer against these, therefore let me always be in that spiritual state of mind which is alive to well-meant reproof. Mendelssohn's rendering is similar: I still pray, whilst they practise infamy. On עוֹד ו cf. Zech. viii. 20 עוֹד אֲשֶׁר (*vid.* Köhler), and Prov. xxiv. 27 אַחַר ו. He who has prayed God in ver. 3 to set a watch upon his mouth is dumb in the presence of those who now have dominion, and seeks to keep himself clear of their sinful doings, whereas he willingly allows himself to be chastened by the righteous; and the more silent he is towards the world (see Amos v. 13), the more constant is he in his intercourse with God. But there will come a time when those who now behave as lords shall fall a prey to the revenge of the people who have been misled by them; and on the other hand, the confession of the salvation, and of the order of the salvation, of God, that has hitherto been put to silence, will again be able to make itself freely heard, and find a ready hearing.

As ver. 6 says, the new rulers fall a prey to the indignation of the people and are thrown down the precipices, whilst the people, having again come to their right mind, obey the words

of David and find them pleasant and beneficial (*vid.* Prov. xv.
26, xvi. 24). וְשִׁמְטוּ is to be explained according to 2 Kings
ix. 33. The casting of persons down from the rock was not an
unusual mode of execution (2 Chron. xxv. 12). יְדֵי־סֶלַע are the
sides (cxl. 6, Judg. xi. 26) of the rock, after which the expression ἐχόμενα πέτρας of the LXX., which has been misunderstood by Jerome, is intended to be understood;* they are therefore
the sides of the rock conceived of as it were as the hands of the
body of rock, if we are not rather with Böttcher to compare the
expressions בְּיְדֵי and עַל־יְדֵי construed with verbs of abandoning
and casting down, Lam. i. 14, Job xvi. 11, and frequently. In
ver. 7 there follows a further statement of the issue on the side
of David and his followers: *instar findentis et secantis terram*
(בֹּקֵעַ with Beth, elsewhere in the hostile signification of *irrumpere*)
dispersa sunt ossa nostra ad ostium (לְפִי as in Prov. viii. 3) *orci;*
Symmachus: ὥσπερ γεωργὸς ὅταν ῥήσσῃ τὴν γῆν, οὕτως ἐσκορ-
πίσθη τὰ ὀστᾶ ἡμῶν εἰς στόμα ᾅδου; Quinta: ὡς καλλιεργῶν
καὶ σκάπτων ἐν τῇ γῇ, κ.τ.λ. Assuming the very extreme, it is
a look of hope into the future: should his bones and the bones
of his followers be even scattered about the mouth of Sheôl (cf.
the Syrian picture of Sheôl: "the dust upon its threshold '*al-
escûfteh*," *Deutsche Morgenländ. Zeitschrift*, xx. 513), their soul
below, their bones above—it would nevertheless be only as
when one in ploughing cleaves the earth; *i.e.* they do not lie
there in order that they may continue lying, but that they may
rise up anew, as the seed that is sown sprouts up out of the up-
turned earth. LXX. *Codd. Vat. et Sinait.* τὰ ὀστᾶ ἡμῶν, beside
which, however, is found the reading αὐτῶν (*Cod. Alex.* by a
second hand, and the Syriac, Arabic, and Æthiopic versions),
as Böttcher also, *pro ineptissimo utcunque*, thinks עצמימו must be
read, understanding this, according to 2 Chron. xxv. 12 *extrem.*,
of the mangled bodies of those cast down from the rock. We
here discern the hope of a resurrection, if not directly, at least
(cf. Oehler in Herzog's *Real-Encyklopädie*, concluding volume,
S. 422) as an emblem of victory in spite of having succumbed.
That which authorizes this interpretation lies in the figure of

---

* Beda Pieringer in his *Psalterium Romana Lyra Redditum* (Ratisbonæ
1859) interprets κατεπόθησαν ἐχόμενα πέτρας; οἱ κοατωιοὶ αὐτῶν, *absorpti*, i.e.
operti sunt loco ad petram pertinente signiferi turpis consilii eorum.

the husbandman, and in the conditional clause (ver. 8), which
leads to the true point of the comparison; for as a complaint
concerning a defeat that had been suffered: "so are our bones
scattered for the mouth of the grave (in order to be swallowed
up by it)," ver. 7, would be alien and isolated with respect to
what precedes and what follows.

Vers. 8–10. If ver. 7 is not merely an expression of the
complaint, but at the same time of hope, we now have no need
to give the כִּי the adversative sense of *imo*, but we may leave it
its most natural confirmatory signification *namque*. From this
point the Psalm gradually dies away in strains comparatively
easy to be understood and in perfect keeping with the situation.
In connection with ver. 8 one is reminded of xxv. 15, xxxi. 2;
with vers. 9 sq., of vii. 16, lxix. 23, and other passages. In
"pour not out (תְּעַר with sharpened vowel instead of תַּעַר, Ges.
§ 75, rem. 8) my soul," עָרָה, *Piel*, is equivalent to the *Hiph.* הֶעֱרָה
in Isa. liii. 12. יְדֵי פַּח are as it were the hands of the seizing
and capturing snare; and יָקְשׁוּ לִי is virtually a genitive: *qui in-
sidias tendunt mihi*, since one cannot say יָקֹשׁ פַּח, *ponere laqueum*.
מַכְמֹרִים, nets, in ver. 10 is another hapaxlegomenon; the *enal-
lage numeri* is as in lxii. 5, Isa. ii. 8, v. 23,—the singular that
slips in refers what is said of the many to each individual in
particular. The plural מֹקְשׁוֹת for מֹקְשִׁים, xviii. 6, lxiv. 6, also
occurs only here. יַחַד is to be explained as in iv. 9: it is intended
to express the coincidence of the overthrow of the enemies and
the going forth free of the persecuted one. With יַחַד אָנֹכִי the
poet gives prominence to his simultaneous, distinct destiny:
simul ego dum (עַד as in Job viii. 21, cf. i. 18) *prætereo h. e.
evado*. The inverted position of the כִּי in cxviii. 10–12 may be
compared; with cxx. 7 and 2 Kings ii. 14, however (where
instead of אַף־הוּא it is with Thenius to be read אֵפוֹא), the case is
different.

PSALM CXLII.

CRY SENT FORTH FROM THE PRISON TO THE
BEST OF FRIENDS.

2 WITH my voice to Jahve do I cry,
With my voice to Jahve do I make supplication,

3 I pour forth before Him my complaint,
  My trouble do I make known before Him.
4 When my spirit veils itself within me,
  Thou indeed art acquainted with my way.

  On the path along which I must go,
      they hide a trap for me.
5 Look to the right and see,
      no friend appeareth for me;
  All refuge hath failed me,
      no one careth for my soul.
6 I cry unto Thee, Jahve,
  I say: Thou art my refuge,
  My portion in the land of the living.

7 Oh hearken to my cry of woe,
      for I am very weak;
  Deliver me from my persecutors,
      for they are too strong for me.
8 Oh lead my soul out of imprisonment,
      to praise Thy Name—
  In me shall the righteous glory:
      that Thou dealest bountifully with me.

This the last of the eight Davidic Psalms, which are derived by their inscriptions from the time of the persecution by Saul (*vid.* on Ps. xxxiv.), is inscribed: *A Meditation by David, when he was in the cave, a Prayer.* Of these eight Psalms, Ps. lii. and liv. also bear the name of *Maskîl* (*vid.* on Ps. xxxii.); and in this instance תְּפִלָּה (which occurs besides as an inscription only in xc. 1, cii. 1, Hab. iii. 1) is further added, which looks like an explanation of the word *maskîl* (not in use out of the range of Psalm-poetry). The article of בַּמְּעָרָה, as in lvii. 1, points to the cave of Adullam (1 Sam. ch. xxii.) or the cave of Engedi (1 Sam. ch. xxiv.), which latter, starting from a narrow concealed entrance, forms such a labyrinthine maze of passages and vaults that the torches and lines of explorers have not to the present time been able to reach the extremities of it.

The Psalm does not contain any sure signs of a post-Davidic age; still it appears throughout to be an imitation of older models, and pre-eminently by means of vers. 2 sq. (cf. lxxvii. 2 sq.) and ver. 4 (cf. lxxvii. 4) it comes into a relation of dependence to Ps. lxxvii., which is also noticeable in Ps. cxliii. (cf. ver. 5 with lxxvii. 12 sq.). The referring back of the two Psalms to David comes under one and the same judgment.

Vers. 2–4a. The emphasis of the first two lines rests upon אֶל־ה׳. Forsaken by all created beings, he confides in Jahve. He turns to Him in pathetic and importunate prayer (זָעַק, the parallel word being הִתְחַנֵּן, as in xxx. 9), and that not merely inwardly (Ex. xiv. 15), but with his voice (vid. on iii. 5)—for audible prayer reacts soothingly, strengtheningly, and sanctifyingly upon the praying one—he pours out before Him his trouble which distracts his thoughts (שָׂפַךְ שִׂיחַ as in cii. 1, cf. lxii. 9, lxiv. 2, 1 Sam. i. 16), he lays open before Him everything that burdens and distresses him. Not as though He did not also know it without all this; on the contrary, when his spirit (רוּחִי as in cxliii. 4, lxxvii. 4, cf. וַיִּתְעַטֵּף Jonah ii. 8 [7], Ps. cvii. 5, לִבִּי lxi. 3) within him (עָלַי, see xlii. 5) is enshrouded and languishes, just this is his consolation, that Jahve is intimately acquainted with his way together with the dangers that threaten him at every step, and therefore also understands how to estimate the title (right) and meaning of his complaints. The *Waw* of וְאַתָּה is the same as in 1 Kings viii. 36, cf. 35. Instead of saying: then I comfort myself with the fact that, etc., he at once declares the fact with which he comforts himself. Supposing this to be the case, there is no need for any alteration of the text in order to get over that which is apparently incongruous in the relation of ver. 4b to 4a.

Vers. 4b–6. The prayer of the poet now becomes deep-breathed and excited, inasmuch as he goes more minutely into the details of his straitened situation. Everywhere, whithersoever he has to go (cf. on cxliii. 8), the snares of craftily calculating foes threaten him. Even God's all-seeing eye will not discover any one who would right faithfully and carefully interest himself in him. הַבֵּיט, look! is a graphic hybrid form of הַבֵּט and הַבִּיט, the usual and the rare imperative form; cf. הָבִיא 1 Sam. xx. 40 (cf. Jer. xvii. 18), and the same modes of writing the *inf. absol.* in Judg. i. 28, Amos ix. 8, and the *fut. conv.* in Ezek. xl. 3. מַכִּיר is, as in Ruth ii. 19, cf. 10, one who looks kindly upon any one, a considerate (cf. the phrase הִבִּיר פָּנִים) well-wisher and friend. Such an one, if he had one, would be עֹמֵר עַל־יְמִינוֹ or יְמִינוֹ (xvi. 8), for an open attack is directed to the arms-bearing right side (cix. 6), and there too the helper in battle (cx. 5) and the defender or advocate (cix. 31) takes his place in order to cover him who is imperilled (cxxi. 5). But then if God looks in that direction, He will find him, who is praying to Him, unprotected. Instead of וְאֵין one would certainly have sooner expected אֲשֶׁר or כִּי as the form of introducing the condition in which he is found; but Hitzig's conjecture, הַבֵּיט יָמִין וְרָאֹה, "looking for days and seeing," gives us in the place of this difficulty a confusing half-Aramaism in יָמִין=יוֹמִין in the sense of יָמִים in Dan. viii. 27, Neh. i. 4. Ewald's rendering is better: "though I look to the right hand and see (וְרָאֹה), yet no friend appears for me;" but this use of the *inf. absol.* with an adversative apodosis is without example. Thus therefore the pointing appears to have lighted upon the correct idea, inasmuch as it recognises here the current formula הַבֵּט וּרְאֵה, *e.g.* Job xxxv. 5, Lam. v. 1. The fact that David, although surrounded by a band of loyal subjects, confesses to having no true friend, is to be understood similarly to the language of Paul when he says in Phil. ii. 20: "I have no man like-minded." All human love, since sin has taken possession of humanity, is more or less selfish, and all fellowship of faith and of love imperfect; and there are circumstances in life in which these dark sides make themselves felt overpoweringly, so that a man seems to himself to be perfectly isolated and turns all the more urgently to God, who alone is able to supply the soul's want of some object to love, whose love is absolutely unselfish, and unchangeable, and unbeclouded, to whom the soul can confide without reserve whatever burdens it, and who not only honestly desires its good, but is able also to compass it in spite of every obstacle. Surrounded by bloodthirsty enemies, and misunderstood, or at least not thoroughly understood, by his friends, David feels himself broken off from all created beings. On this earth every kind of refuge is for him lost (the expression is like Job xi. 20). There is no one there who should ask after or care for his soul, and should right earnestly exert himself for its deliverance. Thus, then, despairing of all visible things, he cries to the Invisible One. He is his "refuge" (xci. 9) and his "portion" (xvi. 5, lxxiii. 26), *i.e.* the share in a possession that satisfies him. To be allowed to call Him his God—this it is which suffices him and outweighs everything. For Jahve is the Living One, and he who possesses Him as his own finds himself thereby " in the land of the living" (xxvii. 13, lii. 7). He cannot die, he cannot perish.

Vers. 7, 8. His request now ascends all the more confident of being answered, and becomes calm, being well-grounded in his feebleness and the superiority of his enemies, and aiming at the glorifying of the divine Name. In ver. 7 רוּחִי calls to mind xvii. 1; the first confirmation, lxxix. 8, and the second, xviii. 18. But this is the only passage in the whole Psalter where the poet designates the "distress" in which he finds himself as a prison (מַסְגֵּר). Ver. 8*b* brings the whole congregation of the righteous in in the praising of the divine Name. The poet therefore does not after all find himself so absolutely alone, as it might seem according to ver. 5. He is far from regarding himself as the only righteous person. He is only a member of a community or church whose destiny is interwoven with his own, and which will glory in his deliverance as its own; for "if one member is honoured, all the members rejoice with it" (1 Cor. xii. 26). We understand the differently interpreted יַכְתִּירוּ after this "rejoicing with" (συγχαίρει). The LXX., Syriac, and Aquila render: the righteous wait for me; but to wait is בָּתַר and not הִכְתִּיר. The modern versions, on the other hand, almost universally, like Luther after Felix Pratensis, render: the righteous shall surround me (flock about me), in connection with which, as Hengstenberg observes, בִּ֯ denotes the tender sympathy they feel with him: crowding closely upon me. But there is no instance of a verb of surrounding (אָפַף, סָבַב, כִּתֵּר, עוּד, עָטַר, הִקִּיף) taking בְּ; the accusative stands with הִכְתִּיר in Hab. i. 4, and כִּתֵּר in xxii. 13, in the signification *cingere*. Symmachus (although erroneously rendering: τὸ ὄνομά σου στεφανώσονται δίκαιοι), Jerome (*in me coronabuntur justi*), Parchon, Aben-Ezra, Coccejus, and others, rightly take יַכְתִּירוּ as a denominative from כֶּתֶר, to put on a crown or to crown (cf. Prov. xiv. 18): on account of me the righteous shall adorn themselves as with crowns, *i.e.* shall triumph, that Thou dealest bountifully with me (an echo of xiii. 6). According to passages like lxiv. 11, xl. 17, one might have expected בּוֹ instead of בִּי. But the close of Ps. xxii. (vers. 23

sqq.), cf. cxl. 12 sq., shows that בְּ is also admissible. The very fact that David contemplates his own destiny and the destiny of his foes in a not merely ideal but foreordainedly causal connection with the general end of the two powers that stand opposed to one another in the world, belongs to the characteristic impress of the Psalms of David that come from the time of Saul's persecution.

PSALM CXLIII.

LONGING AFTER MERCY IN THE MIDST OF DARK IMPRISONMENT.

1 JAHVE, hear my prayer, oh give ear to my supplication;
  In Thy faithfulness answer me, in Thy righteousness.
2 And enter not into judgment with Thy servant,
  For before Thee no man living is righteous.
3 For the enemy hath persecuted my soul,
  He hath crushed my life to the ground,
  He hath made me to lie down in terrible darkness, like
    those for ever dead.

4 And my spirit languisheth within me,
  In my inward part my heart is benumbed.
5 I remember the days of old,
  I meditate upon all Thy doing,
  I muse upon the work of Thy hands.
6 I stretch forth my hands unto Thee,
  My soul is as a thirsty land unto Thee! (*Sela.*)

7 Answer me speedily, Jahve, my spirit yearneth:
  Hide not Thy face from me,
  I should become like those who go down to the pit.
8 Let me hear Thy loving-kindness with the dawn of the
  For I trust in Thee.   [morning,
  Make known to me the way in which I am to go,
  For unto Thee do I lift up my soul.

9 Deliver me from mine enemies, Jahve!
  I have hidden myself with Thee.

10 Teach me to do Thy will,
  For Thou art my God;
  Let Thy good Spirit lead me in an even land.
11 For Thy Name's sake, Jahve, quicken me again,
  In Thy righteousness be pleased to bring my soul out of trouble,
12 And in Thy loving-kindness cut off mine enemies,
  And destroy all the oppressors of my soul,
  For I am Thy servant.

In some codices of the LXX. this Psalm (as Euthymius also bears witness) has no inscription at all; in others, however, it has the inscription: Ψαλμὸς τῷ Δαυεὶδ ὅτε αὐτὸν ἐδίωκεν Ἀβεσσαλώμ ὁ υἱὸς αὐτοῦ (*Cod. Sinait.* οτε αυτον ο υσ κατα‑διωκει). Perhaps by the same poet as Ps. cxlii., with which it accords in vers. 4, 8, 11 (cf. cxlii. 4, 8), it is like this a modern offshoot of the Davidic Psalm-poetry, and is certainly composed as coming out of the situation of him who was persecuted by Absalom. The Psalms of this time of persecution are distinguished from those of the time of the persecution by Saul by the deep melancholy into which the mourning of the dethroned king was turned by blending with the penitential sorrowfulness of one conscious of his own guilt. On account of this fundamental feature the church has chosen Ps. cxliii. for the last of its seven *Psalmi pœnitentiales*. The *Sela* at the close of ver. 6 divides the Psalm into two halves.

Vers. 1–6. The poet pleads two motives for the answering of his prayer which are to be found in God Himself, viz. God's אֱמֶת, truthfulness, with which He verifies the truth of His promises, that is to say, His faithfulness to His promises; and His צְדָקָה, righteousness, not in a recompensative legal sense, but in an evangelical sense, in accordance with His counsel, *i.e.* the strictness and earnestness with which He maintains the order of salvation established by His holy love, both against the ungratefully disobedient and against those who insolently despise Him. Having entered into this order of salvation, and within the sphere of it serving Jahve as his God and Lord, the poet is the servant of Jahve. And because the conduct of the God of salvation, ruled by this order of salvation, or His "righteousness" according to its fundamental manifestation, consists in His justifying the sinful man who has no righteousness that he can show corresponding to the divine holiness, but penitently confesses this disorganized relationship, and, eager for salvation, longs for it to be set right again,—because of all this, the poet prays that He would not also enter into judgment (בּוֹא בְמִשְׁפָּט as in Job ix. 32, xxii. 4, xiv. 3) with him, that He therefore would let mercy instead of justice have its course with him. For, apart from the fact that even the holiness of the good spirits does not coincide with God's absolute holiness, and that this defect must still be very far greater in the case of spirit-corporeal man, who has earthiness as the basis of his origin,—yea, according to li. 7, man is conceived in sin, so that he is sinful from the point at which he begins to live onward,—his life is indissolubly interwoven with sin, no living man possesses a righteousness that avails before God (Job iv. 17, ix. 2, xiv. 3 sq., xv. 14, and frequently).*

With כִּי (ver. 3) the poet introduces the ground of his petition for an answer, and more particularly for the forgiveness of his guilt. He is persecuted by deadly foes and is already nigh unto death, and that not without transgression of his own, so that consequently his deliverance depends upon the forgiveness of his sins, and will coincide with this. "The enemy persecuteth my soul" is a variation of language taken from vii. 6 (חַיָּה for חַיִּים, as in lxxviii. 50, and frequently in the Book of Job, more particularly in the speeches of Elihu). Ver. 3c also recalls vii. 6, but as to the words it sounds like Lam. iii. 6 (cf. lxxxviii. 7). מֵתֵי עוֹלָם (LXX. νεκροὺς αἰῶνος) are either those for ever dead (the Syriac), after שְׁנַת עוֹלָם in Jer. li. 39, cf. בֵּית עוֹלָמוֹ in Eccles. xii. 5, or those dead time out of mind (Jerome), after עַם עוֹלָם in Ezek. xxvi. 20. The genitive construction admits both senses; the former, however, is rendered more natural by the consideration that הוֹשִׁיבַנִי glances back to the beginning that seems to have no end: the poet seems to himself like one who is buried alive for ever. In consequence

---

* Gerson observes on this point (*vid.* Thomasius, *Dogmatik*, iv. 251): I desire the righteousness of pity, which Thou bestowest in the present life, not the judgment of that righteousness which Thou wilt put into operation in the future life—the righteousness which justifies the repentant one.

of this hostility which aims at his destruction, the poet feels his spirit within him, and consequently his inmost life, veil itself (the expression is the same as cxlii. 4, lxxvii. 4); and in his inward part his heart falls into a state of disturbance (בְּתוֹכִי, a *Hithpo.* peculiar to the later language), so that it almost ceases to beat. He calls to mind the former days, in which Jahve was manifestly with him; he reflects upon the great redemptive work of God, with all the deeds of might and mercy in which it has hitherto been unfolded; he meditates upon the doing (בְּמַעֲשֵׂה, Ben-Naphtali בְּמַעֲשֵׂה) of His hands, *i.e.* the hitherto so wondrously moulded history of himself and of his people. They are echoes out of lxxvii. 4–7, 12 sq. The contrast which presents itself to the Psalmist in connection with this comparison of his present circumstances with the past opens his wounds still deeper, and makes his prayer for help all the more urgent. He stretches forth his hands to God that He may protect and assist him (*vid.* Hölemann, *Bibelstudien*, i. 150 f.). Like a parched land is his soul turned towards Him,—language in which we recognise a bending round of the primary passage lxiii. 2. Instead of לְךָ it would be לָךְ, if כְּאֶרֶץ (Targum לְעַלְמִין) were not, as it always is, taken up and included in the sequence of the accents.

Vers. 7–12. In this second half the Psalm seems still more like a reproduction of the thoughts of earlier Psalms. The prayer, "answer me speedily, hide not Thy face from me," sounds like lxix. 18, xxvii. 9, cf. cii. 3. The expression of languishing longing, כָּלְתָה רוּחִי, is like lxxxiv. 3. And the apodosis, "else I should become like those who go down into the pit," agrees word for word with xxviii. 1, cf. lxxxviii. 5. In connection with the words, "cause me to hear Thy loving-kindness in the early morning," one is reminded of the similar prayer of Moses in xc. 14, and with the confirmatory " for in Thee do I trust" of xxv. 2, and frequently. With the prayer that the night of affliction may have an end with the next morning's dawn, and that God's helping loving-kindness may make itself felt by him, is joined the prayer that God would be pleased to grant him to know the way that he has to go in order to escape the destruction into which they are anxious to ensnare him. This last prayer has its type in Ex. xxxiii. 13, and in the Psalter in xxv. 4 (cf. cxlii. 4); and its confirmation:

for to Thee have I lifted up my soul, viz. in a craving after salvation and in the confidence of faith, has its type in xxv. 1, lxxxvi. 4. But the words אֵלֶיךָ כִסִּתִי, which are added to the petition " deliver me from mine enemies" (lix. 2, xxxi. 16), are peculiar, and in their expression without example. The Syriac version leaves them untranslated. The LXX. renders: ὅτι πρὸς σὲ κατέφυγον, by which the defective mode of writing כסתי is indirectly attested, instead of which the translators read נסתי (cf. נוּס עַל in Isa. x. 3); for elsewhere not כָסָה but נוּס is reproduced with καταφυγεῖν. The Targum renders it מֵימְרָךְ מָנֵיתִי לְפָרִיק, Thy Logos do I account as (my) Redeemer (i.e. regard it as such), as if the Hebrew words were to be rendered: upon Thee do I reckon or count, כִסִּתִי = כָסָתִי, Ex. xii. 4. Luther closely follows the LXX.: " to Thee have I fled for refuge." Jerome, however, inasmuch as he renders: *ad te protectus sum*, has pointed כִסִּיתִי (כָסֵיתִי). Hitzig (on the passage before us and Prov. vii. 20) reads כָסָתִי from כְסָא = סְכָא, to look (" towards Thee do I look"). But the Hebrew contains no trace of that verb; the full moon is called כְסֵא (כֶּסֶה), not as being " a sight or vision, *species*," but from its covered orb (vol. ii. 394).

The כִסִּתִי before us only admits of two interpretations : (1) *Ad* (*apud*) *te texi* = to Thee have I secretly confided it (Rashi, Aben-Ezra, Kimchi, Coccejus, J. H. Michaelis, J. D. Michaelis, Rosenmüller, Gesenius, and De Wette). But such a *constructio prægnans*, in connection with which כָסָה would veer round from the signification to veil (cf. כסה מן, Gen. xviii. 17) into its opposite, and the clause have the meaning of כִּי אֵלֶיךָ גִּלִּיתִי, Jer. xi. 20, xx. 12, is hardly conceivable. (2) *Ad* (*apud*) *te abscondidi*, scil. *me* (Saadia, Calvin, Maurer, Ewald, and Hengstenberg), in favour of which we decide; for it is evident from Gen. xxxviii. 14, Deut. xxii. 12, cf. Jonah iii. 6, that כָסָה can express the act of covering as an act that is referred to the person himself who covers, and so can obtain a reflexive meaning. Therefore: towards Thee, with Thee have I made a hiding = hidden myself, which according to the sense is equivalent to הִסִּיתִי (*vid.* vol. i. 99), as Hupfeld (with a few MSS.) wishes to read; but Abulwalîd has already remarked that the same goal is reached with כִסִּתִי. Jahve, with whom he hides himself, is alone able to make known to him what is right and beneficial in the position in which he finds himself, in which he is exposed to temporal and spiritual dangers, and is able to teach him to carry out the recognised will of God (" the will of God, good and well-pleasing and perfect," Rom. xii. 2); and this it is for which he prays to Him in ver. 10 (רְצוֹנְךָ; another reading, רְצוֹנֶךָ). For Jahve is indeed his God, who cannot leave him, who is assailed and tempted without and within, in error; may His good Spirit then (רוּחֲךָ טוֹבָה for הַטּוֹבָה, Neh. ix. 20*) lead him in a level country, for, as it is said in Isaiah, ch. xxvi. 7, in looking up to Jahve, "the path which the righteous man takes is smoothness; Thou makest the course of the righteous smooth." The geographical term אֶרֶץ מִישׁוֹר, Deut. iv. 43, Jer. xlviii. 21, is here applied spiritually. Here, too, reminiscences of Psalms already read meet us everywhere: cf. on "to do Thy will," xl. 9; on "for Thou art my God," xl. 6, and frequently; on "Thy good Spirit," li. 14; on "a level country," and the whole petition, xxvii. 11 (where the expresssion is "a level path"), together with v. 9, xxv. 4 sq., xxxi. 4. And the Psalm also further unrolls itself in such now well-known thoughts of the Psalms: For Thy Name's sake, Jahve (xxv. 11), quicken me again (lxxi. 20, and frequently); by virtue of Thy righteousness be pleased to bring my soul out of distress (cxlii. 8, xxv. 17, and frequently); and by virtue of Thy loving-kindness cut off mine enemies (liv. 7). As in ver. 1 faithfulness and righteousness, here loving-kindness (mercy) and righteousness, are coupled together; and that so that mercy is not named beside תּוֹצִיא, nor righteousness beside תַּצְמִית, but the reverse (vid. on ver. 1). It is impossible that God should suffer him who has hidden himself in Him to die and perish, and should suffer his enemies on the other hand to triumph. Therefore the poet confirms

---

* Properly, "Thy Spirit, a good one," so that טוֹבָה is an adjectival apposition; as we can also say רוּחַ הַטּוֹבָה, a spirit, the good one, although such irregularities may also be a negligent usage of the language, like the Arabic المسجد الجامع, the chief mosque, which many grammarians regard as a construct relationship, others as an ellipsis (inasmuch as they supply الجامع between the words); the former is confirmed from the Hebrew, vid. Ewald, § 287, a.

the prayer for the cutting off (הַצְמִית as in xciv. 23) of his enemies and the destruction (הַאֲבִיד, elsewhere אָבֵד) of the oppressors of his soul (elsewhere צֹרְרֵי) with the words: *for I am Thy servant.*

PSALM CXLIV.

TAKING COURAGE IN GOD BEFORE A DECISIVE COMBAT.

The blessed condition of God's people.

1 BLESSED be Jahve my Rock,
Who traineth my hands for the fight,
My fingers for the war—
2 My loving-kindness and my fortress,
My high tower and my deliverer for me,
My shield and He in whom I hide,
Who subdueth my people under me!

3 Jahve, what is man that Thou takest knowledge of him,
The child of mortal man that Thou heedest him!
4 As for man, he is like a breath,
His days are as a shadow that vanisheth away.

5 Jahve, bow Thy heavens and come down,
Touch the mountains that they smoke.
6 Cast forth lightnings to scatter them;
Send forth Thine arrows to destroy them.
7 Send Thy hands from above,
Rescue me and deliver me out of great waters:
Out of the hand of the sons of the strange land,
8 Whose mouth speaketh vanity,
And whose right hand is a right hand of falsehood.

9 Elohim, a new song will I sing unto Thee,
Upon a ten-stringed nabla will I play unto Thee,
10 Who giveth salvation unto kings,
Who rescueth David His servant from the evil sword,
11 Rescue and deliver me out of the hand of the sons of the strange land,

Whose mouth speaketh vanity,
Whose right hand is a right hand of falsehood.

12 *Because our sons are as high-reared plants in their youthful vigour,
Our daughters as adorned corners after the mode of structure of a palace;*
13 *Our garners full, affording every kind of store;
Our sheep bringing forth by thousands, multiplying by tens of thousands in our pastures;*
14 *Our kine bearing without mishap and without loss,
And no lamentation in our streets.*
15 *Blessed is the people that is in such a case,
Blessed is the people whose God is Jahve!*

Praised be Jahve who teacheth me to fight and conquer (vers. 1, 2), me the feeble mortal, who am strong only in Him, vers. 3, 4. May Jahve then be pleased to grant a victory this time also over the boastful, lying enemies, vers. 5–8; so will I sing new songs of thanksgiving unto Him, the bestower of victory, vers. 9, 10. May He be pleased to deliver me out of the hand of the barbarians who envy us our prosperity, which is the result of our having Jahve as our God, vers. 11–15. A glance at this course of the thought commends the additional inscription of the LXX. (according to Origen only "in a few copies"), πρὸς τὸν Γολιάδ, and the Targumist's reference of the "evil sword" in ver. 10 to the sword of Goliath (after the example of the Midrash). Read 1 Sam. xvii. 47. The Psalm has grown out of this utterance of David. In one of the old histories, just as several of these lie at the foundation of our Books of Samuel as sources of information that are still recognisable, it was intended to express the feelings with which David entered upon the single-handed combat with Goliath and decided the victory of Israel over the Philistines. At that time he had already been anointed by Samuel, as both the narratives which have been worked up together in the First Book of Samuel assume: see 1 Sam. xvi. 13, x. 1. And this victory was for him a gigantic stride to the throne.

If אֲשֶׁר in ver. 12a is taken as *eo quod*, so that envy is brought under consideration as a motive for the causeless (שָׁוְא),

lyingly treacherous rising (יְמִין שָׁקֶר) of the neighbouring peoples, then the passage vers. 12–15 can at any rate be comprehended as a part of the form of the whole. But only thus, and not otherwise; for אֲשֶׁר cannot be intended as a statement of the aim or purpose: in order that they may be . . . (Jerome, De Wette, Hengstenberg, and others), since nothing but illustrative substantival clauses follow; nor do these clauses admit of an optative sense: We, whose sons, may they be . . . (Maurer); and אֲשֶׁר never has an assuring sense (Vaihinger). It is also evident that we cannot, with Saadia, go back to ver. 9 for the interpretation of the אֲשֶׁר (اسمهم على ما). But that junction by means of *eo quod* is hazardous, since envy or ill-will (קִנְאָה) is not previously mentioned, and וִימִינָם יְמִין שָׁקֶר expresses a fact, and not an action. If it is further considered that nothing is wanting in the way of finish to the Psalm if it closes with ver. 11, it becomes all the more doubtful whether vers. 12–15 belonged originally to the Psalm. And yet we cannot discover any Psalm in its immediate neighbourhood to which this piece might be attached. It might the most readily, as Hitzig correctly judges, be inserted between vers. 13 and 14 of Ps. cxlvii. But the rhythm and style differ from this Psalm, and we must therefore rest satisfied with the fact that a fragment of another Psalm is here added to Ps. cxliv., which of necessity may be accounted as an integral part of it; but in spite of the fact that the whole Psalm is built up on a gigantic scale, this was not its original corner-stone, just as one does not indeed look for anything further after the refrain, together with the mention of David in vers. 10 sq., cf. xviii. 51.

Vers. 1, 2. The whole of this first strophe is an imitation of David's great song of thanksgiving, Ps. xviii. Hence the calling of Jahve "my rock," xviii. 3, 47; hence the heaping up of other appellations in ver. 2a, in which xviii. 3 is echoed; but וּמְפַלְטִי־לִי (with Lamed deprived of the *Dagesh*) follows the model of 2 Sam. xxii. 2. The naming of Jahve with חַסְדִּי is a bold abbreviation of אֱלֹהֵי חַסְדִּי in lix. 11, 18, as also in Jonah ii. 9 [8] the God whom the idolatrous ones forsake is called חַסְדָּם. Instead of מִלְחָמָה the Davidic Psalms also poetically say קְרָב, lv. 22, cf. lxxviii. 9. The expression "who traineth my hands for the fight" we have already read in xviii. 35. The last words of the strophe, too, are after xviii. 48; but instead of וַיֶּרֶד this poet says הָרוֹדֵד, from רָדָה=רָדַד (cf. Isa. xlv. 1, xli. 2), perhaps under the influence of וּמֹרִיד in 2 Sam. xxii. 48. In Ps. xviii. 48 we however read עַמִּים, and the Masora has enumerated Ps. cxliv. 2, together with 2 Sam. xxii. 44, Lam. iii. 14, as the three passages in which it is written עַמִּי, whilst one expects עַמִּים (עמים דכבירין נ'), as the Targum, Syriac, and Jerome (yet not the LXX.) in fact render it. But neither from the language of the books nor from the popular dialect can it be reasonably expected that they would say עַמִּי for עַמִּים in such an ambiguous connection. Either, therefore, we have to read עַמִּים,* or we must fall in with the strong expression, and this is possible: there is, indeed, no necessity for the subduing to be intended of the use of despotic power, it can also be intended of God-given power, and of subjugating authority. David, the anointed one, but not having as yet ascended the throne, here gives expression to the hope that Jahve will grant him deeds of victory which will compel Israel to submit to him, whether willingly or reluctantly.

Vers. 3, 4. It is evident that ver. 3 is a variation of viii. 5 with the use of other verbs. יָדַע in the sense of loving intimacy; חָשַׁב, properly to count, compute, here *rationem habere*. Instead of כִּי followed by the future there are consecutive futures here, and בֶּן־אָדָם is aramaizingly (בַּר אֱנָשׁ) metamorphosed into בֶּן־אֱנוֹשׁ. Ver. 4 is just such another imitation, like a miniature of xxxix. 6 sq., 11, cf. lxii. 10. The figure of the shadow is the same as in cii. 12, cf. cix. 23. The connection of the third stanza with the second is still more disrupt than that of the second with the first.

Vers. 5-8. The deeds of God which Ps. xviii. celebrates are here made an object of prayer. We see from xviii. 10 that וְתֵרֵד, ver. 5a, has Jahve and not the heavens as its subject; and from xviii. 15 that the suffix *em* in ver. 6 is meant in both instances to be referred to the enemies. The enemies are called sons of a foreign country, *i.e.* barbarians, as in xviii. 45 sq. The fact that Jahve stretches forth His hand out of

---

* Rashi is acquainted with an otherwise unknown note of the Masora החתיו קרי; but this *Kerî* is imaginary.

the heavens and rescues David out of great waters, is taken
verbatim from xviii. 17; and the poet has added the interpretation to the figure here. On ver. 8a cf. xii. 3, xli. 7. The
combination of words "right hand of falsehood" is the same as
in cix. 2. But our poet, although so great an imitator, has,
however, much also that is peculiar to himself. The verb בָּרַק,
"to send forth lightning;" the verb פָּצָה in the Aramæo-Arabic
signification "to tear out of, rescue," which in David always
only signifies "to tear open, open wide" (one's mouth), xxii. 14,
lxvi. 14; and the combination "the right hand of falsehood"
(like "the tongue of falsehood" in cix. 2), *i.e.* the hand raised
for a false oath, are only found here. The figure of Omnipotence, "He toucheth the mountains and they smoke," is, as in
civ. 32, taken from the mountains that smoked at the giving
of the Law, Ex. xix. 18, xx. 15. The mountains, as in lxviii.
17 (cf. lxxvi. 5), point to the worldly powers. God only needs
to touch these as with the tip of His finger, and the inward fire,
which will consume them, at once makes itself known by the
smoke, which ascends from them. The prayer for victory is
followed by a vow of thanksgiving for that which is to be bestowed.

Vers. 9–11. With the exception of Ps. cviii., which is
composed of two Davidic Elohim-Psalms, the *Elohim* in ver. 9
of this strophe is the only one in the last two Books of the
Psalter, and is therefore a feeble attempt also to reproduce the
Davidic Elohimic style. The "new song" calls to mind xxxiii.
3, xl. 4; and נֵבֶל עָשׂוֹר also recalls xxxiii. 2 (which see). The
fact that David mentions himself by name in his own song
comes about in imitation of xviii. 51. From the eminence of
thanksgiving the song finally descends again to petition, vers.
7c, 8 being repeated as a refrain. The petition develops itself
afresh out of the attributes of the Being invoked (ver. 10), and
these are a pledge of its fulfilment. For how could the God
to whom all victorious kings owe their victory (xxxiii. 16, cf.
2 Kings v. 1, 1 Sam. xvii. 47) possibly suffer His servant David
to succumb to the sword of the enemy! חֶרֶב רָעָה is the sword
that is engaged in the service of evil.

Vers. 12–15. With reference to the relation of this passage
to the preceding, *vid.* the introduction. אֲשֶׁר (it is uncertain
whether this is a word belonging originally to this piece or one

added by the person who appended it as a sort of clasp or rivet) signifies here *quoniam*, as in Judg. ix. 17, Jer. xvi. 13, and frequently. LXX. ὧν οἱ υἱοί (אֲשֶׁר בְּנֵיהֶם); so that the temporal prosperity of the enemies is pictured here, and in ver. 15 the spiritual possession of Israel is contrasted with it. The union becomes satisfactorily close in connection with this reading, but the reference of the description, so designedly set forth, to the enemies is improbable. In vers. 12-14 we hear a language that is altogether peculiar, without any assignable earlier model. Instead of נְטִעִים we read נְטָעִים elsewhere; "in their youth" belongs to "our sons." מְזָוֵינוּ, our garners or treasuries, from a singular מֶזֶו or מָזוּ (apparently from a verb מָזָה, but contracted out of מִזְוֶה), is a hapaxlegomenon; the older language has the words אָסָם, אוֹצָר, מִסְכְּנוּת instead of it. In like manner זַן, *genus* (vid. Ewald, *Lehrbuch*, S. 380), is a later word (found besides only in 2 Chron. xvi. 14, where זִנִים signifies *et varia quidem*, Syriac *z'nonoje*, or directly spices from *species*); the older language has מִין for this word. Instead of אֲלֻפִים, kine, which signifies "princes" in the older language, the older language says אֲלָפִים in viii. 8. The *plena scriptio* צֹאונֵנוּ, in which the *Waw* is even inaccurate, corresponds to the later period; and to this corresponds שֶׁ=אֲשֶׁר in ver. 15, cf. on the other hand xxxiii. 12. Also מְסֻבָּלִים, laden = bearing, like the Latin *forda* from *ferre* (cf. מְעֻבָּר in Job xxi. 10), is not found elsewhere. צֹאן is (contrary to Gen. xxx. 39) treated as a feminine collective, and אַלּוּף (cf. שׁוֹר in Job xxi. 10) as a *nomen epicœnum*. Contrary to the usage of the word, Maurer, Köster, Von Lengerke, and Fürst render it: our princes are set up (after Ezra vi. 3); also, after the mention of animals of the fold upon the meadows out-of-doors, one does not expect the mention of princes, but of horned cattle that are to be found in the stalls. זָוִית elsewhere signifies a corner, and here, according to the prevailing view, the corner-pillars; so that the elegant slender daughters are likened to tastefully sculptured Caryatides—not to sculptured projections (Luther). For (1) זוית does not signify a projection, but a corner, an angle, Arabic زاوية, *záwïa* (in the terminology of the stone-mason the square-stone = אֶבֶן פִּנָּה, in the terminology of the carpenter the square), from زوى, *aldere* (cf. *e.g.* the proverb: *fi 'l zawáji* *chabâjâ*, in the corners are treasures). (2) The upstanding pillar is better adapted to the comparison than the overhanging projection. But that other prevailing interpretation is also doubtful. The architecture of Syria and Palestine—the ancient, so far as it can be known to us from its remains, and the new—exhibits nothing in connection with which one would be led to think of "corner-pillars." Nor is there any trace of that signification to be found in the Semitic זָוִית. On the other hand, the corners of large rooms in the houses of persons of position are ornamented with carved work even in the present day, and since this ornamentation is variegated, it may be asked whether מְחֻטָּבוֹת does here signify "sculptured," and not rather "striped in colours, variegated," which we prefer, since חָטַב (cogn. חָצַב) signifies nothing more than to hew firewood;* and on the other side, the signification of the Arabic خَطَبَ, to be striped, many-coloured (IV. to become green-striped, of the coloquintida), is also secured to the verb חָטַב side by side with that signification by Prov. vii. 16. It is therefore to be rendered: our daughters are as corners adorned in varied colours after the architecture of palaces.† The words הָאֲלֵיף,

---

* In every instance where חטב (cogn. חצב) occurs, frequently side by side with שׁאב מים (to draw water), it signifies to hew wood for kindling; wherefore in Arabic, in which the verb has been lost, خَطَب signifies firewood (in distinction from خَشَب, wood for building, timber), and not merely this, but fuel in the widest sense, *e.g.* in villages where wood is scarce, cow-dung (*vid. Job*, i. 377, note), and the hemp-stalk, or stalk of the maize, in the desert the بَعَر, *i.e.* camel-dung (which blazes up with a blue flame), and the perennial steppe-plant or its root. In relation to خَطَب, اِحْتَطَب signifies lopped, pruned, robbed of its branches (of a tree), and حَرْب حَاطِب a pruning war, which devastates a country, just as the wood-gathering women of a settlement (styled الْحَاطِبَات or الْحَوَاطِب) with their small hatchet (مِحْطَب) lay a district covered with tall plants bare in a few days. In the villages of the *Merg'* the little girls who collect the dry cow-dung upon the pastures are called بَنَات حَاطِبَات, בְּנוֹת חֹטְבוֹת.—WETZSTEIN.

† Corners with variegated carved work are found even in the present

to bring forth by thousands, and מְרֻבָּב (denominative from רְבָבָה), which surpasses it, multiplied by tens of thousands, are freely formed. Concerning חוּצוֹת, meadows, vid. on Job xviii. 17. פֶּרֶץ, in a martial sense a defeat, clades, e.g. in Judg. xxi. 15, is here any violent misfortune whatever, as murrain, which causes a breach, and יוֹצֵאת any head of cattle which goes off by a single misfortune. The lamentation in the streets is intended as in Jer. xiv. 2. שְׁוָחָה is also found in Cant. v. 9; nor does the poet, however, hesitate to blend this שׁ with the tetragrammaton into one word. The Jod is not dageshed (cf. cxxiii. 2), because it is to be read שֶׁאֲדֹנָי, cf. מְיַהְוָה = כַּאדֹנָי in Gen. xviii. 14. Luther takes ver. 15a and 15b as contrasts: Blessed is the people that is in such a case, But blessed is the people whose God is the Lord. There is, however, no antithesis intended, but only an exceeding of the first declaration by the second. For to be allowed to call the God from whom every blessing comes his God, is still infinitely more than the richest abundance of material blessing. The pinnacle of Israel's good fortune consists in being, by the election of grace, the people of the Lord (xxxii. 12).

day in Damascus in every reception-room (the so-called قَاعَة) of respectable houses [cf. Lane, *Manners and Customs of the Modern Egyptians*, Introduction]. An architectural ornament composed with much good taste and laborious art out of wood carvings, and glittering with gold and brilliant colours, covers the upper part of the corners, of which a *ká'a* may have as many as sixteen, since three wings frequently abut upon the *bêt el-baḥára*, i.e. the square with its marble basin. This decoration, which has a most pleasing effect to the eye, is a great advantage to saloons from two to three storeys high, and is evidently designed to get rid of the darker corners above on the ceiling, comes down from the ceiling in the corners of the room for the length of six to nine feet, gradually becoming narrower as it descends. It is the broadest above, so that it there also covers the ends of the horizontal corners formed by the walls and the ceiling. If this crowning of the corners, the technical designation of which, if I remember rightly, is الْقَرْنِيَة, *ḳornía*, might be said to go back into Biblical antiquity, the Psalmist would have used it as a simile to mark the beauty, gorgeous dress, and rich adornment of women. Perhaps, too, because they are not only modest and chaste (cf. Arabic *mesturât*, a veiled woman, in opposition to *memshushât*, one shone on by the sun), but also, like the children of respectable families, hidden from the eyes of strangers; for the Arabic proverb quoted above says, "treasures are hidden in the corners," and the superscription of a letter addressed to a lady of position runs: "May it kiss the hand of the protected lady and of the hidden jewel."—WETZSTEIN.

PSALM CXLV.

HYMN IN PRAISE OF THE ALL-BOUNTIFUL KING.

1 א I will extol Thee, my God O King,
 And I will bless Thy Name for ever and ever.
2 ב Every day will I bless Thee,
 And I will glorify Thy Name for ever and ever.
3 ג Great is Jahve, and greatly worthy to be praised,
 And His greatness is unsearchable.
4 ד One generation to another praiseth Thy works,
 And they declare Thy mighty deeds.
5 ה On the glorious honour of Thy majesty
 And on Thy wondrous works will I meditate.
6 ו And they shall speak forth thy mightily terrible deeds,
 And Thy mighty acts will I declare.
7 ז The praise of Thy great goodness shall they abundantly utter,
 And sing aloud of Thy righteousness.
8 ח Gracious and full of compassion is Jahve,
 Long-suffering and great in goodness.
9 ט Good is Jahve unto all,
 And His tender mercies are over all His works.
10 י All Thy works praise Thee, Jahve,
 And Thy saints do bless Thee.
11 כ They talk of the glory of Thy kingship,
 And confess Thy might—
12 ל To make known to the sons of men His mighty acts,
 And the stately glory of His kingship.
13 מ Thy kingship is a kingship for all ages,
 And Thy dominion endureth into all generations.
14 ס Jahve upholdeth all those who fall,
 And raiseth up all those who are bowed down.
15 ע The eyes of all wait upon Thee,
 And Thou givest them their food in due season;
16 פ Thou openest out Thine abundance,
 And satisfiest every living thing with delight.

17 צ Jahve is righteous in all His ways,
   And gracious in all His works.
18 ק Jahve is nigh unto all those who call upon Him,
   To all who call upon Him in truth;
19 ר He fulfilleth the desire of those who fear Him,
   And He heareth their cry and delivereth them.
20 ש Jahve preserveth all those who love Him,
   And all the wicked doth He destroy.
21 ת Let my mouth then speak the praise of Jahve,
   And let all flesh bless His holy Name for ever and ever!

With Ps. cxliv. the collection draws doxologically towards its close. This Psalm, which begins in the form of the *beracha* (ברוך ה'), is followed by another in which *benedicam* (vers. 1, 2) and *benedicat* (ver. 21) is the favourite word. It is the only Psalm that bears the title תְּהִלָּה, whose plural תְּהִלִּים is become the collective name of the Psalms. In *B. Berachoth* 4b it is distinguished by the apophthegm: "Every one who repeats the תהלה לדוד three times a day may be sure that he is a child of the world to come (בן העולם הבא)." And why? Not merely because this Psalm, as the Gemara says, אתיא באלף בית, *i.e.* follows the course of the alphabet (for Ps. cxix. is in fact also alphabetical, and that in an eightfold degree), and not merely because it celebrates God's care for all creatures (for this the Great Hallel also does, Ps. cxxxvi. 25), but because it unites both these prominent qualities in itself (משום דאית ביה תרתי). In fact, Ps. cxlv. 16 is a celebration of the goodness of God which embraces every living thing, with which only cxxxvi. 25, and not cxi. 5, can be compared. *Valde sententiosus hic Psalmus est*, says Bakius; and do we not find in this Psalm our favourite *Benedicite* and *Oculi omnium* which our children repeat before a meal? It is the ancient church's Psalm for the noon-day repast (*vid.* Armknecht, *Die heilige Psalmodie*, 1855, S. 54); ver. 15 was also used at the holy communion, hence Chrysostom says it contains τὰ ῥήματα ταῦτα, ἅπερ οἱ μεμυημένοι συνεχῶς ὑποψάλλουσι λέγοντες· Οἱ ὀφθαλμοὶ πάντων εἰς σὲ ἐλπίζουσιν καὶ σὺ δίδως τὴν τροφὴν αὐτῶν ἐν εὐκαιρίᾳ.

Κατὰ στοιχεῖον, observes Theodoret, καὶ οὗτος ὁ ὕμνος σύγκειται. The Psalm is distichic, and every first line of the distich has the ordinal letter; but the distich *Nun* is wanting.

The Talmud (*loc. cit.*) is of opinion that it is because the fatal נׇפְלָה (Amos v. 2), which David, going on at once with סוֹמֵךְ ה׳ לְכׇל־הַנֹּפְלִים, skips over, begins with *Nun*. On the other hand, Ewald, Vaihinger, and Sommer, like Grotius, think that the *Nun*-strophe has been lost. The LXX. (but not Aquila, Symmachus, Theodotion, nor Jerome in his translation after the original text) gives such a strophe, perhaps out of a MS. (like the Dublin *Cod. Kennicot*, 142) in which it was supplied: Πιστὸς (נאמן as in cxi. 7) κύριος ἐν (πᾶσι) τοῖς λόγοις αὐτοῦ καὶ ὅσιος ἐν πᾶσι τοῖς ἔργοις αὐτοῦ (according with ver. 17, with the change only of two words of this distich). Hitzig is of opinion that the original *Nun*-strophe has been welded into Ps. cxli.; but only his clairvoyant-like historical discernment is able to amalgamate ver. 6 of this Psalm with our Ps. cxlv. We are contented to see in the omission of the *Nun*-strophe an example of that freedom with which the Old Testament poets are wont to handle this kind of forms. Likewise there is no reason apparent for the fact that Jeremiah has chosen in ch. ii., iii., and iv. of the Lamentations to make the *Ajin*-strophe follow the *Pe*-strophe three times, whilst in ch. i. it precedes it.

Vers. 1-7. The strains with which this hymn opens are familiar Psalm-strains. We are reminded of xxx. 2, and the likewise alphabetical song of praise and thanksgiving xxxiv. 2. The *plena scriptio* אֱלוֹהַי in cxliii. 10 is repeated here. God is called "the King" as in xx. 10, xcviii. 6. The language of address "my God the King," which sounds harsh in comparison with the otherwise usual "my King and my God" (v. 3, lxxxiv. 4), purposely calls God with unrelated generality, that is to say in the most absolute manner, the King. If the poet is himself a king, the occasion for this appellation of God is all the more natural and the signification all the more pertinent. But even in the mouth of any other person it is significant. Whosoever calls God by such a name acknowledges His royal prerogative, and at the same time does homage to Him and binds himself to allegiance; and it is just this confessory act of exalting Him who in Himself is the absolutely lofty One that is here called אֲרוֹמִמְךָ. But how can the poet express the purpose of praising God's Name *for ever*? Because the praise of God is a need of his inmost nature, he has a perfect right to forget his own mortality when engaged upon this devotion to the ever-living King. Clinging adoringly to the Eternal One, he must seem to himself to be eternal; and if there is a practical proof for a life after death, it is just this ardent desire of the soul, wrought of God Himself, after the praise of the God of its life (lit. its origin) which affords it the highest, noblest delight. The idea of the silent Hades, which forces itself forward elsewhere, as in vi. 6, where the mind of the poet is beclouded by sin, is here entirely removed, inasmuch as here the mind of the poet is the undimmed mirror of the divine glory. Therefore ver. 2 also does not concede the possibility of any interruption of the praise: the poet will daily (lxviii. 20) bless God, be they days of prosperity or of sorrow, uninterruptedly in all eternity will he glorify His Name (אֲהַלְלָה as in lxix. 31). There is no worthier and more exhaustless object of praise (ver. 3) : Jahve is great, and greatly to be praised (מְהֻלָּל, taken from xlviii. 2, as in xcvi. 4, cf. xviii. 4), and of His "greatness" (cf. 1 Chron. xxix. 11, where this attribute precedes all others) there is no searching out, *i.e.* it is so abysmally deep that no searching can reach its bottom (as in Isa. xl. 28, Job xi. 7 sq.). It has, however, been revealed, and is being revealed continually, and is for this very reason thus celebrated in ver. 4: one generation propagates to the next the growing praise of the works that He has wrought out (עָשָׂה מַעֲשִׂים), and men are able to relate all manner of proofs of His victorious power which prevails over everything, and makes everything subject to itself (גְּבוּרֹת as in xx. 7, and frequently). This historically manifest and traditional divine doxa and the facts (דִּבְרֵי as in cv. 27) of the divine wonders the poet will devoutly consider. הֲדַר stands in attributive relation to כְּבוֹד, as this on its part does to הוֹדְךָ : Thy brilliantly glorious (kingly) majesty (cf. Jer. xxii. 18, Dan. xi. 21). The poet does not say אַף גַּם, nor may we insert it, either here in ver. 5, or in ver. 6, where the same sequence of thoughts recurs, more briefly expressed. The emphasis lies on the objects. The mightiness (עֱזוּז as in lxxviii. 4, and in Isa. xlii. 25, where it signifies violence) of His terrible acts shall pass from mouth to mouth (אָמַר with a substantival object as in xl. 11), and His mighty acts (גְּדֻלּוֹת, *magnalia*, as in 1 Chron. xvii. 19, 21)—according to the *Kĕri* (which is determined by the suffix of אֲכַבְּרֶנָּה; cf., however, 2 Sam. xxii. 23, 2 Kings iii. 3, x. 26, and frequently): His greatness (גֻּדְלָה)—will he also on his part make the matter of his narrating. It is, however, not alone the awe-inspiring majesty of God which is revealed in history, but also the greatness (רַב used as a substantive as in xxxi. 20, Isa. lxiii. 7, xxi. 7, whereas רַבִּים in xxxii. 10, lxxxix. 51 is an adjective placed before the noun after the manner of a numeral), *i.e.* the abundant measure, of His goodness and His righteousness, *i.e.* His acting in inviolable correspondence with His counsel and order of salvation. The memory of the transcendent goodness of God is the object of universal, overflowing acknowledgment, and the righteousness of God is the object of universal exultation (רִנֵּן with the accusative as in li. 16, lix. 17). After the poet has sung the glorious self-attestation of God according to both its sides, the fiery and the light sides, he lingers by the light side, the front side of the Name of Jahve unfolded in Ex. xxxiv. 6.

Vers. 8—13. This memorable utterance of Jahve concerning Himself the writer of Ps. ciii., which is of kindred import, also interweaves into his celebration of the revelation of divine love in ver. 8. Instead of רַב־חֶסֶד the expression here, however, is וּגְדָל חָסֶד (*Keri*, as in Nah. i. 3, cf. lxxxix. 29, with *Makkeph* וּגְדָל־). The real will of God tends towards favour, which gladly giving stoops to give (חַנּוּן), and towards compassion, which interests itself on behalf of the sinner for his help and comfort (רַחוּם). Wrath is only the background of His nature, which He reluctantly and only after long waiting (אֶרֶךְ אַפַּיִם) lets loose against those who spurn His great mercy. For His goodness embraces, as ver. 9 says, all; His tender mercies are over all His works, they hover over and encompass all His creatures. Therefore, too, all His works praise Him: they are all together loud-speaking witnesses of that sympathetic all-embracing love of His, which excludes no one who does not exclude himself; and His saints, who live in God's love, bless Him (יְבָרְכוּכָה written as in 1 Kings xviii. 44): their mouth overflows with the declaration (יֹאמֵרוּ) of the glory of the kingdom of this loving God, and in speaking (יְדַבֵּרוּ) of the sovereign power with which He maintains and extends this kingdom. This confession they make their employ, in order that the knowledge of the mighty acts of God and the glorious majesty of His kingdom may at length become the general possession of mankind. When the poet in ver. 12 sets forth the purpose of the proclamation, he drops the form of address. God's kingdom is a kingdom of all æons, and His dominion is manifested without exception and continually in all periods or generations (בְּכָל־דּוֹר וָדֹר as in xlv. 18, Esth. ix. 28, a pleonastic strengthening of the expression דֹּר וָדֹר, xc. 1). It is the eternal circumference of the history of time, but at the same time its eternal substance, which more and more unfolds and achieves itself in the succession of the periods that mark its course. For that all things in heaven and on earth shall be gathered up together (ἀνακεφαλαιώσασθαι, Eph. i. 10) in the all-embracing kingdom of God in His Christ, is the goal of all history, and therefore the substance of history which is working itself out. With ver. 13 (cf. Dan. iii. 33 [iv. 3], iv. 31 [34], according to Hitzig the primary passages) another paragraph is brought to a close.

Vers. 14–21. The poet now celebrates in detail the deeds of the gracious King. The words with לְ are pure datives, cf. the accusative expression in cxlvi. 8. He in person is the support which holds fast the falling ones (נֹפְלִים, here not the fallen ones, see xxviii. 1) in the midst of falling (Nicephorus: τοὺς καταπεσεῖν μέλλοντας ἑδραιοῖ, ὥστε μὴ καταπεσεῖν), and the stay by which those who are bowed together raise themselves. He is the Provider for all beings, the Father of the house, to whom in the great house of the world the eyes (עֵינֵי with the second ê toneless, Ew. § 100, b) of all beings, endowed with reason and irrational, are directed with calm confidence (Matt. vi. 26), and who gives them their food in its, i.e. in due season. The language of civ. 27 is very similar, and it proceeds here, too, as there in ver. 28 (cf. Sir. xl. 14).- He opens His hand, which is ever full, much as a man who feeds the doves in his court does, and gives רָצוֹן, pleasure, i.e. that which is good, which is the fulfilling of their desire, in sufficient fulness to all living things (and therefore those in need of support for the body and the life). Thus it is to be interpreted, according to Deut. xxxiii. 23 (after which here in the LXX. the reading varies between εὐδοκίας and εὐλογίας), cf. Acts xiv. 17, ἐμπιπλῶν τροφῆς καὶ εὐφροσύνης τὰς καρδίας ἡμῶν. הִשְׂבִּיעַ is construed with a dative and accusative of the object instead of with two accusatives of the object (Ges. § 139. 1, 2). The usage of the language is unacquainted with רָצוֹן as an adverb in the sense of "willingly" (Hitzig), which would rather be

בִּרְצוֹנְךָ. In all the ways that Jahve takes in His historical rule He is "righteous," *i.e.* He keeps strictly to the rule (norm) of His holy love; and in all His works which He accomplishes in the course of history He is merciful (חָסִיד), *i.e.* He practises mercy (חֶסֶד, see xii. 2); for during the present time of mercy the primary essence of His active manifestation is free preventing mercy, condescending love. True, He remains at a distance from the hypocrites, just as their heart remains far from Him (Isa. xxix. 13); but as for the rest, with impartial equality He is nigh (קָרוֹב as in xxxiv. 19) to all who call upon Him בֶּאֱמֶת, in firmness, certainty, truth, *i.e.* so that the prayer comes from their heart and is holy fervour (cf. Isa. x. 20, xlviii. 1). What is meant is true and real prayer in opposition to the νεκρὸν ἔργον, as is also meant in the main in John iv. 23 sq. To such true praying ones Jahve is present, viz. in mercy (for in respect of His power He is everywhere); He makes the desire of those who fear Him a reality, their will being also His; and He grants them the salvation (σωτηρία) prayed for. Those who are called in ver. 19 those who fear Him, are called in ver. 20 those who love Him. Fear and love of God belong inseparably together; for fear without love is an unfree, servile disposition, and love without fear, boldfaced familiarity: the one dishonours the all-gracious One, and the other the all-exalted One. But all who love and fear Him He preserves, and on the other hand exterminates all wanton sinners. Having reached the *Tav*, the hymn of praise, which has traversed all the elements of the language, is at an end. The poet does not, however, close without saying that praising God shall be his everlasting employment (פִּי יְדַבֶּר־ with *Olewejored*, the *Mahpach* or rather *Jethib* sign of which above represents the *Makkeph*), and without wishing that all flesh, *i.e.* all men, who are σὰρξ καὶ αἷμα, בָּשָׂר וָדָם, may bless God's holy Name to all eternity. The realization of this wish is the final goal of history. It will then have reached ver. 43 of the great song in Deut. ch. xxxii.—Jahve one and His Name one (Zech. xiv. 9), Israel praising God ὑπὲρ ἀληθείας, and the Gentiles ὑπὲρ ἐλέους (Rom. xv. 8 sq.).

PSALM CXLVI.

HALLELUJAH TO GOD THE ONE TRUE HELPER.

HALLELUJAH.
1 PRAISE, O my soul, Jahve!
2 I will praise Jahve as long as I live,
   I will harp unto my God as long as I have any being.
3 Trust not in princes,
   In the son of man, who is not capable of help!
4 If his breath goeth forth, he returneth to his clod—
   In that day his devices perish.

5 Happy is he whose help is the God of Jacob,
   Whose confidence is in Jahve his God,
6 The Creator of heaven and earth,
   Of the sea and all that is therein—
   Who keepeth truth for ever,
7 Obtaining judgment for the oppressed,
   Giving bread to the hungry.

   Jahve looseth those who are bound,
8 Jahve maketh the blind to see,
   Jahve raiseth up those who are bowed down,
   Jahve loveth the righteous,
9 Jahve preserveth the strangers,
   He helpeth up the orphan and widow,
   And the way of the wicked He turneth down.
10 Jahve reigneth as King for ever,
   Thy God, O Zion, unto all generations—
      Hallelujah.

The Psalter now draws to a close with five Hallelujah Psalms. This first closing Hallelujah has many points of coincidence with the foregoing alphabetical hymn (compare אֲהַלְלָה in ver. 2 with cxlv. 2; שַׂבְּרוֹ in ver. 5 with cxlv. 15; "who giveth bread to the hungry" in ver. 7 with cxlv. 15 sq.: "who maketh the blind to see" in ver. 8 with cxlv. 14; "Jahve reigneth, etc.," in ver. 10 with cxlv. 13)—the same range of thought betrays one author. In the LXX. Ps. cxlvi.-cxlviii. (according to its enumeration four Psalms, viz. cxlv.-cxlviii., Ps. cxlvii. being split up into two) have the inscription Ἀλληλούια. Ἀγγαίου καὶ Ζαχαρίου, which is repeated four times. These Psalms appear to have formed a separate Hallel, which is referred back to these prophets, in the old liturgy of the second Temple. Later on they became, together with Ps. cxlix., cl., an integral part of the daily morning prayer, and in fact of the פסוקי דזמרה, i.e. of the mosaic-work of Psalms and other poetical pieces that was incorporated in the morning prayer, and are called even in Shabbath 118b Hallel,* but expressly distinguished from the Hallel to be recited at the Passover and other feasts, which is called "the Egyptian Hallel." In distinction from this, Krochmal calls these five Psalms the Greek Hallel. But there is nothing to oblige us to come down beyond the time of Ezra and Nehemiah. The agreement between 1 Macc. ii. 63 (ἔστρεψεν εἰς τὸν χοῦν αὐτοῦ, καὶ ὁ διαλογισμὸς αὐτοῦ ἀπώλετο) and ver. 4 of our Psalm, which Hitzig has turned to good account, does not decide anything concerning the age of the Psalm, but only shows that it was in existence at the time of the author of the First Book of Maccabees,—a point in favour of which we were not in need of any proof. But there was just as much ground for dissuading against putting confidence in princes in the time of the Persians as in that of the Grecian domination.

Vers. 1-4. Instead of "bless," as in ciii. 1, civ. 1, the poet of this Psalm says "praise." When he attunes his soul to the praise of God, he puts himself personally into this mood of mind, and therefore goes on to say "I will praise." He will, however, not only praise God in the song which he is beginning, but בְּחַיַּי (vid. on lxiii. 5), filling up his life with it, or בְּעוֹדִי (prop. "in my yet-being," with the suffix of the noun, whereas עוֹדֶנִּי with the verbal suffix is "I still am"), so that his continued life is also a constant continued praising, viz. (and this is in the mind of the poet here, even at the commencement of the Psalm) of the God and King who, as being the Almighty, Eternal, and

---

* Rashi, however, understands only Ps. cxlviii. and cl. by בסוקי דזמרה in that passage.

unchangeably Faithful One, is the true ground of confidence. The warning against putting trust in princes calls to mind cxviii. 8 sq. The clause: the son of man, who has no help that he could afford, is to be understood according to lx. 13. The following לְאַדְמָתוֹ shows that the poet by the expression בֶּן־אָדָם combines the thoughts of Gen. ii. 7 and iii. 19. If his breath goes forth, he says, basing the untrustworthiness and feebleness of the son of Adam upon the inevitable final destiny of the son of Adam taken out of the ground, then he returns to his earth, *i.e.* the earth of his first beginning; cf. the more exact expression אֶל־עֲפָרָם, after which the εἰς τὴν γῆν αὐτοῦ of the LXX. is exchanged for εἰς τὸν χοῦν αὐτοῦ in 1 Macc. ii. 63. On the hypothetical relation of the first future clause to the second, cf. cxxxix. 8–10, 18; Ew. § 357, *b*. In that day, the inevitable day of death, the projects or plans of man are at once and for ever at an end. The ἅπ. λεγ. עֶשְׁתֹּנֹת describes these with the collateral notion of subtleness and magnitude.

Vers. 5–7*a*. Man's help is of no avail; blessed is he (this is the last of the twenty-five אַשְׁרֵי of the Psalter), on the contrary, who has the God of Jacob (שֶׁאֵל like שֶׁיְהֹוָה in cxliv. 15) as Him in whom is his succour (בְּעֶזְרוֹ with *Beth essentiæ*, *vid.* on xxxv. 2),—he, whose confidence (שִׂבְרוֹ as in cxix. 116) rests on Jahve, whom he can by faith call his God. Men often are not able to give help although they might be willing to do so: He, however, is the Almighty, the Creator of the heavens, the earth, and the sea, and of all living things that fill these three (cf. Neh. ix. 6). Men easily change their mind and do not keep their word: He, however, is He who keepeth truth or faithfulness, inasmuch as He unchangeably adheres to the fulfilling of His promises. שָׁמַר אֱמֶת is in form equivalent substantially to שָׁמַר חֶסֶד and שָׁמַר הַבְּרִית. And that which He is able to do as being the Almighty, and cannot as being the Truthful One leave undone, is also really His mode of active manifestation made evident in practical proofs: He obtains right for the oppressed, gives bread to the hungry, and consequently proves Himself to be the succour of those who suffer wrong without doing wrong, and as the provider for those who look for their daily bread from His gracious hand. With הַשֹּׁמֵר, the only determinate participle, the faithfulness of God His promises is made especially prominent.

Vers. 7b–10. The five lines beginning with *Jahve* belong together. Each consists of three words, which in the main is also the favourite measure of the lines in the Book of Job. The expression is as brief as possible. הַתִּיר is transferred from the yoke and chains to the person himself who is bound, and פֹּקֵחַ is transferred from the eyes of the blind to the person himself. The five lines celebrate the God of the five-divisioned Tôra, which furnishes abundant examples for these celebrations, and is directed with most considerate tenderness towards the strangers, orphans, and widows in particular. The orphan and the widow, says the sixth line, doth He recover, strengthen (with reference to עוֹדֵד see xx. 9, xxxi. 12). *Valde gratus mihi est hic Psalmus*, Bakius observes, *ob Trifolium illud Dei: Advenas, Pupillos, et Viduas, versu uno luculentissime depictum, id quod in toto Psalterio nullibi fit.* Whilst Jahve, however, makes the manifold sorrows of His saints to have a blessed issue, He bends (יְעַוֵּת) the way of the wicked, so that it leads into error and ends in the abyss (i. 6). This judicial manifestation of Jahve has only one line devoted to it. For He rules in love and in wrath, but delights most of all to rule in love. Jahve is, however, the God of Zion. The eternal duration of His kingdom is also the guarantee for its future glorious completion, for the victory of love. Hallelujah!

PSALM CXLVII.

HALLELUJAH TO THE SUSTAINER OF ALL THINGS, THE
RESTORER OF JERUSALEM

1   HALLELUJAH,
  For it is good to celebrate our God in song,
  For it is lovely, comely is a hymn of praise.
2 The builder up of Jerusalem is Jahve,
  The outcasts of Israel He gathereth together;
3 He healeth the broken in heart,
  And bindeth up their wounds;
4 Telling the number of the stars,
  He calleth them all by names.
5 Great is our Lord and rich in strength,
  To His understanding there is no number.

6 Jahve helpeth up the afflicted,
  He casteth the wicked down to the ground.

7 Sing unto Jahve a thanksgiving song,
  Play unto our God upon the cithern!
8 Who covereth the heaven with clouds,
  Who prepareth rain for the earth,
  Who maketh the mountains shoot forth grass;
9 Giving to the beast its food,
  To the young ravens which call.
10 Not in the strength of the horse doth He delight,
  Not in the legs of a man doth He take pleasure—
11 Jahve hath pleasure in those who fear Him,
  In those who hope in His mercy.

12 Celebrate, O Jerusalem, Jahve,
  Praise Thy God, O Zion!
13 For He hath made the bolts of thy gates fast,
  He hath blessed thy children in the midst of thee—
14 He it is who giveth thy border peace,
  He satisfieth thee with the fat of wheat;
15 Who sendeth forth His commandment to the earth,
  His word runneth very swiftly;
16 Who giveth snow like wool,
  He scattereth hoar-frost like ashes,
17 He casteth down His ice like morsels—
  Before His cold, who can stand?!
18 He sendeth forth His word and causeth everything to melt,
  He causeth His wind to blow, forthwith the waters flow.
19 He made known His word unto Jacob,
  His statutes and His judgments unto Israel.
20 He hath not dealt so with any nation;
  And as for His judgments—they do not know them,
        Hallelujah.

It is the tone of the restoration-period of Ezra and Nehemiah that meets us sounding forth out of this and the two following Psalms, even more distinctly and recognisably than out of the nearly related preceding Psalm (cf. ver. 6 with cxlvi. 9). In Ps. cxlvii. thanksgiving is rendered to God for the restoration of Jerusalem, which is now once more a city with walls and gates; in Ps. cxlviii. for the restoration of the national independence; and in Ps. cxlix. for the restoration of the capacity of joyously and triumphantly defending themselves to the people so long rendered defenceless and so ignominiously enslaved.

In the seventh year of Artachshasta (Artaxerxes I. Longimanus) Ezra the priest entered Jerusalem, after a journey of five months, with about two thousand exiles, mostly out of the families of the Levites (458 B.C.). In the twentieth year of this same clement king, that is to say, thirteen years later (445 B.C.), came Nehemiah, his cup-bearer, in the capacity of a *Tirshâtha* (*vid. Isaiah*, vol. i. 2). Whilst Ezra did everything for introducing the Mosaic Law again into the mind and commonwealth of the nation, Nehemiah furthered the building of the city, and more particularly of the walls and gates. We hear from his own mouth, in ch. ii.–vii. of the Book that is extracted from his memoirs, how indefatigably and cautiously he laboured to accomplish this work. Ch. xii. 27–45 is closely connected with these notes of Nehemiah's own hand. After having been again in the meanwhile in Susa, and there neutralized the slanderous reports that had reached the court of Persia, he appointed, at his second stay in Jerusalem, a feast in dedication of the walls. The Levite musicians, who had settled down for the most part round about Jerusalem, were summoned to appear in Jerusalem. Then the priests and Levites were purified; and they purified the people, the gates, and the walls, the bones of the dead (as we must with Herzfeld picture this to ourselves) being taken out of all the tombs within the city and buried before the city; and then came that sprinkling, according to the Law, with the sacred lye of the red heifer, which is said (*Para* iii. 5) to have been introduced again by Ezra for the first time after the Exile. Next the princes of Judah, the priests, and Levite musicians were placed in the west of the city in two great choirs (תּוֹדֹת*) and processions

---

* The word has been so understood by Menahem, Juda ben Koreish, and Abulwalid; whereas Herzfeld is thinking of hecatombs for a thank-offering, which might have formed the beginning of both festive processions.

(תְּהִלָּה). The one festal choir, which was led by the one half of the princes, and among the priests of which Ezra went on in front, marched round the right half of the city, and the other round the left, whilst the people looked down from the walls and towers. The two processions met on the east side of the city and drew up in the Temple, where the festive sacrifices were offered amidst music and shouts of joy.

The supposition that Ps. cxlvii.-cl. were all sung at this dedication of the walls under Nehemiah (Hengstenberg) cannot be supported; but as regards Ps. cxlvii., the composition of which in the time of Nehemiah is acknowledged by the most diverse parties (Keil, Ewald, Dillmann, Zunz), the reference to the Feast of the Dedication of the walls is very probable. The Psalm falls into two parts, vers. 1-11, 12-20, which exhibit a progression both in respect of the building of the walls (vers. 2, 13), and in respect of the circumstances of the weather, from which the poet takes occasion to sing the praise of God (vers. 8 sq., 16-18). It is a double Psalm, the first part of which seems to have been composed, as Hitzig suggests, on the appearing of the November rain, and the second in the midst of the rainy part of the winter, when the mild spring breezes and a thaw were already in prospect.

Vers. 1-6. The Hallelujah, as in cxxxv. 3, is based upon the fact, that to sing of our God, or to celebrate our God in song (זַמֵּר with an accusative of the object, as in xxx. 13, and frequently), is a discharge of duty that reacts healthfully and beneficially upon ourselves: "comely is a hymn of praise" (taken from xxxiii. 1), both in respect of the worthiness of God to be praised, and of the gratitude that is due to Him. Instead of זַמֵּר or לְזַמֵּר, xcii. 2, the expression is זַמְּרָה, a form of the *infin. Piel*, which at least can still be proved to be possible by לְיִסְרָה in Lev. xxvi. 18. The two כִּי are co-ordinate, and כִּי־נָעִים no more refers to God here than in cxxxv. 3, as Hitzig supposes when he alters ver. 1 so that it reads: "Praise ye Jah because He is good, play unto our God because He is lovely." Ps. xcii. 2 shows that כִּי־טוֹב can refer to God; but נָעִים said of God is contrary to the custom and spirit of the Old Testament, whereas טוֹב and נָעִים are also in cxxxiii. 1 neuter predicates of a subject that is set forth in the infinitive form. In ver. 2 the praise begins, and at the same time the confirmation of the delightful duty. Jahve is the builder up of Jerusalem, He brings together (כִּנֵּס as in Ezekiel, the later word for אָסַף and קִבֵּץ) the outcasts of Israel (as in Isa. xi. 12, lvi. 8); the building of Jerusalem is therefore intended of the rebuilding up, and to the dispersion of Israel corresponds the holy city laid in ruins. Jahve healeth the heart-broken, as He has shown in the case of the exiles, and bindeth up their pains (xvi. 4), *i.e.* smarting wounds; רָפָא, which is here followed by חִבֵּשׁ, also takes to itself a dative object in other instances, both in an active and (Isa. vi. 10) an impersonal application; but for שְׁבוּרֵי לֵב the older language says נִשְׁבְּרֵי לֵב, xxxiv. 19, Isa. lxi. 1. The connection of the thoughts, which the poet now brings to the stars, becomes clear from the primary passage, Isa. xl. 26, cf. 27. To be acquainted with human woe and to relieve it is an easy and small matter to Him who allots a number to the stars, that are to man innumerable (Gen. xv. 5), *i.e.* who has called them into being by His creative power in whatever number He has pleased, and yet a number known to Him (מֹנֶה, the *part. præs.*, which occurs frequently in descriptions of the Creator), and calls to them all names, *i.e.* names them all by names which are the expression of their true nature, which is well known to Him, the Creator. What Isaiah says (ch. xl. 26) with the words, "because of the greatness of might, and as being strong in power," and (ver. 28) "His understanding is unsearchable," is here asserted in ver. 5 (cf. cxlv. 3): great is our Lord, and capable of much (as in Job xxxvii. 23, שַׂגִּיא כֹחַ), and to His understanding there is no number, *i.e.* in its depth and fulness it cannot be defined by any number. What a comfort for the church as it traverses its ways, that are often so labyrinthine and entangled! Its Lord is the Omniscient as well as the Almighty One. Its history, like the universe, is a work of God's infinitely profound and rich understanding. It is a mirror of gracious love and righteous anger. The patient sufferers (עֲנָוִים) He strengthens (מְעוֹדֵד as in cxlvi. 9); malevolent sinners (רְשָׁעִים), on the other hand, He casts down to the earth (עֲדֵי־אָרֶץ, cf. Isa. xxvi. 5), casting deep down to the ground those who exalt themselves to the skies.

Vers. 7-11. With ver. 7 the song takes a new flight. עָנָה לְ signifies to strike up or sing in honour of any one, Num. xxi. 27, Isa. xxvii. 2. The object of the action is conceived of in בְּתוֹדָה as the medium of it (cf. *e.g.* Job xvi. 4). The participles in vers. 8 sq. are attributive clauses that are attached in a free manner to לֵאלֹהֵינוּ. הֵכִין signifies to prepare, procure, as *e.g.* in Job xxxviii. 41—a passage which the psalmist has had in his mind in connection with ver. 9. מַצְמִיחַ, as being the causative of a *verb. crescendi*, is construed with a double accusative: "making mountains (whither human agriculture does not reach) to bring forth grass;" and the advance to the thought that God gives to the cattle the bread that they need is occasioned by the "He causeth grass to grow for the cattle" of the model passage civ. 14, just as the only hinting אֲשֶׁר יִקְרָאוּ, which is said of the young of the raven (which are forsaken and cast off by their mothers very early), is explained from יְלָדָיו אֶל־אֵל יְשַׁוֵּעוּ in Job *loc. cit.* The verb קָרָא, κράζειν (cf. κρώζειν), is still more expressive for the cry of the raven, κόραξ, Sanscrit *kárava*, than that שָׁוַע; κοράττειν and κορακεύεσθαι signify directly to implore incessantly, without taking any refusal. Towards Him, the gracious Sustainer of all beings, are the ravens croaking for their food pointed (cf. Luke xii. 24, "Consider the ravens"), just like the earth that thirsts for rain. He is the all-conditioning One. Man, who is able to know that which the irrational creature unconsciously acknowledges, is in the feeling of his dependence to trust in Him and not in himself. In all those things to which the God-estranged self-confidence of man so readily clings, God has no delight (יֶחְפָּץ, pausal form like יַחְבִּשׁ) and no pleasure, neither in the strength of the horse, whose rider imagines himself invincible, and, if he is obliged to flee, that he cannot be overtaken, nor in the legs of a man, upon which he imagines himself so firm that he cannot be thrown down, and which, when he is pursued, will presumptively carry him far enough away into safety. שׁוֹק, ساق, is the leg from the knee to the foot, from ساق, root سق, to drive, urge forward, more particularly to urge on to a gallop (like *crus*, according to Pott, from the root *car*, to go). What is meant here is, not that the strength of the horse and muscular power are of no avail when God wills to destroy a man (xxxiii. 16 sq., Amos ii. 14

sq.), but only that God has no pleasure in the warrior's horse and in athletic strength. Those who fear Him, *i.e.* with a knowledge of the impotency of all power possessed by the creature in itself, and in humble trust feel themselves dependent upon His omnipotence—these are they in whom He takes pleasure (רָצָה with the accusative), those who, renouncing all carnal defiance and self-confident self-working, hope in His mercy.

Vers. 12-20. In the LXX. this strophe is a Psalm (*Lauda Jerusalem*) of itself. The call goes forth to the church again on the soil of the land of promise assembled round about Jerusalem. The holy city has again risen out of its ruins; it now once more has gates which can stand open in the broad daylight, and can be closed and bolted when the darkness comes on for the security of the municipality that is only just growing into power (Neh. vii. 1-4). The blessing of God again rests upon the children of the sacred metropolis. Its territory, which has experienced all the sufferings of war, and formerly resounded with the tumult of arms and cries of woe and destruction, God has now, from being an arena of conflict, made into peace (the accusative of the effect, and therefore different from Isa. lx. 17); and since the land can now again be cultivated in peace, the ancient promise (lxxxi. 17) is fulfilled, that God would feed His people, if they would only obey Him, with the fat of wheat. The God of Israel is the almighty Governor of nature. It is He who sends His fiat (אִמְרָתוֹ) after the manner of the וַיֹּאמֶר of the history of creation, cf. xxxiii. 9) earthwards (אָרֶץ, the accusative of the direction). The word is His messenger (*vid.* on cvii. 20), עַד־מְהֵרָה, *i.e.* it runs as swiftly as possible, viz. in order to execute the errand on which it is sent. He it is who sends down snow-flakes like flocks of wool, so that the fields are covered with snow as with a white-woollen warming covering.* He scatters hoar-frost (כְּפוֹר from כָּפַר, to cover over) about like ashes, so that trees, roofs, etc., are crusted over with the fine frozen dew or mist as though they were powdered with ashes that the wind had blown about. Another time He casts His

---

* Bochart in his *Hierozoicon* on this passage compares an observation of Eustathius on Dionysius Periegetes: τὴν χιόνα ἐριώδες ὕδωρ ἀστείως οἱ παλαιοὶ ἐκάλουν.

ice * (קְרָחוֹ from קְרַח; or according to another reading, קָרְחוֹ from קֹרַח) down like morsels, fragments, כְפִתִּים, viz. as hail-stones, or as sleet. The question : before His cold—who can stand? is formed as in Nah. i. 6, cf. cxxx. 3. It further comes to pass that God sends forth His word and causes them (snow, hoarfrost, and ice) to melt away : He makes His thawing wind blow, waters flow; *i.e.* as soon as the one comes about, the other also takes place forthwith. This God now, who rules all things by His word and moulds all things according to His will, is the God of the revelation pertaining to the history of salvation, which is come to Israel, and as the bearer of which Israel takes the place of honour among the nations, Deut. iv. 7 sq., 32–34. Since the poet says מַגִּיד and not הִגִּיד, he is thinking not only of the Tôra, but also of prophecy as the continuous self-attestation of God, the Lawgiver. The *Kerî* דְּבָרָיו, occasioned by the plurals of the parallel member of the verse, gives an unlimited indistinct idea. We must keep to דְּבָרוֹ, with the LXX., Aquila, Theodotion, the Quinta, Sexta, and Jerome. The word, which is the medium of God's cosmical rule, is gone forth as a word of salvation to Israel, and, unfolding itself in statutes and judgments, has raised Israel to a legal state founded upon a positive divine law or judgment such as no Gentile nation possesses. The Hallelujah does not exult over the fact that these other nations are not acquainted with any such positive divine law, but (cf. Deut. iv. 7 sq., Baruch iv. 4) over the fact that Israel is put into possession of such a law. It is frequently attested elsewhere that this possession of Israel is only meant to be a means of making salvation a common property of the world at large.

PSALM CXLVIII.

HALLELUJAH OF ALL HEAVENLY AND EARTHLY BEINGS.

HALLELUJAH.

1 PRAISE ye Jahve from the heavens,
  Praise ye Him in the heights.

---

* LXX. (Italic, Vulgate) κρύσταλλον, *i.e.* ice, from the root κευ, to freeze, to congeal (Jerome *glaciem*). *Quid est crystallum?* asks Augustine, and replies : *Nix est glacie durata per multos annos ita ut a sole vel igne non cito dissolvi non possit.*

2 Praise ye Him, all His angels,
  Praise ye Him, all His host.
3 Praise ye Him, sun and moon,
  Praise Him all ye stars of light.
4 Praise Him ye heavens of heavens,
  And ye waters that are above the heavens.
5 Let them praise the Name of Jahve,
  For HE commanded and they were created,
6 And He set them there for ever and ever;
  He gave a law, and not one transgresseth it.

7 Praise ye Jahve from the earth,
  Sea-monsters and all deeps;
8 Fire and hail, snow and vapour,
  Stormy wind fulfilling His word;
9 Ye mountains and all hills,
  Fruit-trees and all cedars;
10 Ye wild beasts and all cattle,
  Creeping things and winged birds;
11 Kings of the earth and all tribes,
  Princes and all judges of the earth;
12 Young men and also maidens,
  Old men together with youths—
13 Let them praise the Name of Jahve,
  For His Name is highly exalted, He alone,
  His glory is above earth and heaven.
14 And He hath raised a horn for His people,
  For a praise for all His saints,
  For the children of Israel, for the people near unto Him
    Hallelujah.

After the Psalmist in the foregoing Hallelujah has made the gracious self-attestation of Jahve in the case of the people of revelation, in connection with the general government of the almighty and all-benevolent One in the world, the theme of his praise, he calls upon all creatures in heaven and on earth, and more especially mankind of all peoples and classes and races and ages, to join in concert in praise of the Name of Jahve, and that on the ground of the might and honour which He has bestowed upon His people, *i.e.* has bestowed upon them once more now when they are gathered together again out of exile and Jerusalem has risen again out of the ruins of its overthrow. The hymn of the three in the fiery furnace, which has been interpolated in ch. iii. of the Book of Daniel in the LXX., is for the most part an imitation of this Psalm. In the language of the liturgy this Psalm has the special name of *Laudes* among the twenty *Psalmi alleluiatici*, and all the three Psalms cxlviii.-cl. which close the Psalter are called αἶνοι, Syriac *shabchûh* (praise ye Him).

In this Psalm the loftiest consciousness of faith is united with the grandest contemplation of the world. The church appears here as the choir-leader of the universe. It knows that its experiences have a central and universal significance for the whole life of creation; that the loving-kindness which has fallen to its lot is worthy to excite joy among all beings in heaven and on earth. And it calls not only upon everything in heaven and on earth that stands in fellowship of thought, of word, and of freedom with it to praise God, but also the sun, moon, and stars, water, earth, fire, and air, mountains, trees, and beasts, yea even such natural phenomena as hail, snow, and mist. How is this to be explained? The easiest way of explaining is to say that it is a figure of speech (Hupfeld); but this explanation explains nothing. Does the invitation in the exuberance of feeling, without any clearness of conception, here overstep the boundary of that which is possible? Or does the poet, when he calls upon these lifeless and unconscious things to praise God, mean that we are to praise God on their behalf—ἀφορᾶν εἰς ταῦτα, as Theodoret says, καὶ τοῦ Θεοῦ τὴν σοφίαν καταμανθάνειν καὶ διὰ πάντων αὐτῷ πλέκειν τὴν ὑμνῳδίαν? Or does the "praise ye" in its reference to these things of nature proceed on the assumption that they praise God when they redound to the praise of God, and find its justification in the fact that the human will enters into this matter of fact which relates to things, and is devoid of any will, and seizes it and drags it into the concert of angels and men? All these explanations are unsatisfactory. The call to praise proceeds rather from the wish that all creatures, by becoming after their own manner an echo and reflection of the divine glory, may participate in the joy at the glory which God has bestowed upon His people after their deep humiliation. This wish, however, after all rests upon the great truth, that the way through suffering to glory which the church is traversing, has not only the glorifying of God in itself, but by means of this glorifying, the glorifying of God in all creatures and by all creatures, too, as its final aim, and that these, finally transformed (glorified) in the likeness of transformed (glorified) humanity, will become the bright mirror of the divine doxa and an embodied hymn of a thousand voices. The calls also in Isa. xliv. 23, xlix. 13, cf. lii. 9, and the descriptions in Isa. xxxv. 1 sq., xli. 19, lv. 12 sq., proceed from the view to which Paul gives clear expression from the stand-point of the New Testament in Rom. viii. 18 sqq.

Vers. 1-6. The call does not rise step by step from below upwards, but begins forthwith from above in the highest and outermost spheres of creation. The place whence, before all others, the praise is to resound is the heavens; it is to resound in the heights, viz. the heights of heaven (Job xvi. 19, xxv. 2, xxxi. 2). The מִן might, it is true, also denote the birth or origin: ye of the heavens, *i.e.* ye celestial beings (cf. lxviii. 27), but the parallel בַּמְּרוֹמִים renders the immediate construction with הַלְלוּ more natural. Vers. 2-4 tell who are to praise Jahve there: first of all, all His angels, the messengers of the Ruler of the world—all His host, *i.e.* angels and stars, for צְבָאוֹ (*Chethîb*) or צְבָאָיו (*Kerî* as in ciii. 21) is the name of the heavenly host armed with light which God Tsebaoth commands (*vid.* on Gen. ii. 1),—a name including both stars (*e.g.* in Deut. iv. 19) and angels (*e.g.* in Josh. v. 14 sq., 1 Kings xxii. 19); angels and stars are also united in the Scriptures in other instances (*e.g.* Job xxxviii. 7). When the psalmist calls upon these beings of light to praise Jahve, he does not merely express his delight in that which they do under any circumstances (Hengstenberg), but comprehends the heavenly world with the earthly, the church above with the church here below (*vid.* on Ps. xxix., ciii.), and gives a special turn to the praise of the former, making it into an echo of the praise of the latter, and blending both harmoniously together. The heavens of heavens are, as in Deut. x. 14, 1 Kings viii. 27, Sir. xvi. 18, and frequently, those which lie beyond the heavens of the earth which were created on the fourth day, therefore they are the outermost and highest spheres The waters which are above the heavens are, according to Hupfeld, "a product of the fancy, like the upper heavens and the whole of the inhabitants of heaven." But if in general the other world is not a notion to which there is no corresponding entity, this notion may also have things for its substance which lie beyond our knowledge of nature. The Scriptures, from the first page to the last, acknowledge the existence of celestial waters, to which the rain-waters stand in the relation as it were of a finger-post pointing upwards (see Gen. i. 7). All these beings belonging to the superterrestrial world are to praise the Name of Jahve, for HE, the God of Israel, it is by whose fiat (צִוָּה, like אָמַר in xxxiii. 9*) the heavens and all their host are created (xxxiii. 6). He has set them, which did not previously exist, up (הֶעֱמִיד as *e.g.* in Neh. vi. 7, the causative to עָמַד in xxxiii. 9, cf. cxix. 91), and that for ever and ever (cxi. 8), *i.e.* in order for ever to maintain the position in the whole of creation which He has assigned to them. He hath given a law (חֹק) by which its distinctive characteristic is stamped upon each of these heavenly beings, and a fixed bound is set to the nature and activity of each in its mutual relation to all, and not one transgresses (the individualizing singular) this law given to it. Thus וְלֹא יַעֲבֹר is to be understood, according to Job xiv. 5, cf. Jer. v. 22, Job xxxviii. 10, Ps. civ. 9. Hitzig makes the Creator Himself the subject; but then the poet would have at least been obliged to say הִקְנִחַן לָמוֹ, and moreover it may be clearly seen from Jer. xxxi. 36, xxxiii. 20, how the thought that God inviolably keeps the orders of nature in check is expressed θεοπρεπῶς. Jer. v. 22, by way of example, shows that the law itself is not, with Ewald, Maurer, and others, following the LXX., Syriac, Italic, Jerome, and Kimchi, to be made the subject: a law hath He given, and it passes not away (an imperishable one). In combination with חֹק, עָבַר always signifies "to pass over, transgress."

Vers. 7–14. The call to the praise of Jahve is now turned, in the second group of verses, to the earth and everything belonging to it in the widest extent. Here too מִן־הָאָרֶץ, like מִן־הַשָּׁמַיִם, ver. 1, is intended of the place whence the praise is to resound, and not according to x. 18 of earthly beings. The call

---

* The interpolated parallel member, αὐτὸς εἶπε καὶ ἐγενήθησαν. here in the LXX. is taken over from that passage.

is addressed in the first instance to the sea-monsters or dragons (lxxiv. 13), *i.e.*, as Pindar (*Nem.* iii. 23 sq.) expresses it, θῆρας ἐν πελάγεϊ ὑπερόχους, and to the surging mass of waters (תְּהֹמוֹת) above and within the earth. Then to four phenomena of nature, coming down from heaven and ascending heavenwards, which are so arranged in ver. 8*a*, after the model of the chiasmus (crosswise position), that fire and smoke (קִיטוֹר), more especially of the mountains (Ex. xix. 18), hail and snow stand in reciprocal relation; and to the storm-wind (רוּחַ סְעָרָה, an appositional construction, as in cvii. 25), which, beside a seeming freeness and untractableness, performs God's word. What is said of this last applies also to the fire, etc.; all these phenomena of nature are messengers and servants of God, civ. 4, cf. ciii. 20. When the poet wishes that they all may join in concert with the rest of the creatures to the praise of God, he excepts the fact that they frequently become destructive powers executing judicial punishment, and only has before his mind their (more especially to the inhabitant of Palestine, to whom the opportunity of seeing hail, snow, and ice was more rare than with us, imposing) grandeur and their relatedness to the whole of creation, which is destined to glorify God and to be itself glorified. He next passes over to the mountains towering towards the skies and to all the heights of earth; to the fruit-trees, and to the cedars, the kings among the trees of the forest; to the wild beasts, which are called הַחַיָּה because they represent the most active and powerful life in the animal world, and to all quadrupeds, which, more particularly the four-footed domestic animals, are called בְּהֵמָה; to the creeping things (רֶמֶשׂ) which cleave to the ground as they move along; and to the birds, which are named with the descriptive epithet winged (צִפּוֹר כָּנָף as in Deut. iv. 17, cf. Gen. vii. 14, Ezek. xxxix. 17, instead of עוֹף כָּנָף, Gen. i. 21). And just as the call in Ps. ciii. finds its centre of gravity, so to speak, at last in the soul of man, so here it is addressed finally to humanity, and that, because mankind lives in nations and is comprehended under the law of a state commonwealth, in the first instance to its heads: the kings of the earth, *i.e.* those who rule over the earth by countries, to the princes and all who have the administration of justice and are possessed of supreme power on the earth, then to men of both sexes and of every age.

All the beings mentioned from ver. 1 onwards are to praise the Name of Jahve; for His Name, He (the God of this Name) alone (Isa. ii. 11, Ps. lxxii. 18) is נִשְׂגָּב, so high that no name reaches up to Him, not even from afar; His glory (His glorious self-attestation) extends over earth and heaven (vid. viii. 2). כִּי, without our being able and obliged to decide which, introduces the matter and the ground of the praise; and the fact that the desire of the poet comprehends in יְהַלְלוּ all the beings mentioned is seen from his saying "earth and heaven," as he glances back from the nearer things mentioned to those mentioned farther off (cf. Gen. ii. 4). In ver. 14 the statement of the object and of the ground of the praise is continued. The motive from which the call to all creatures to Hallelujah proceeds, viz. the new mercy which God has shown towards His people, is also the final ground of the Hallelujah which is to sound forth; for the church of God on earth is the central-point of the universe, the aim of the history of the world, and the glorifying of this church is the turning-point for the transformation of the world. It is not to be rendered: He hath exalted the horn of His people, any more than in cxxxii. 17: I will make the horn of David to shoot forth. The horn in both instances is one such as the person named does not already possess, but which is given him (different from lxxxix. 18, 25, xcii. 11, and frequently). The Israel of the Exile had lost its horn, *i.e.* its comeliness and its defensive and offensive power. God has now given it a horn again, and that a high one, *i.e.* has helped Israel to attain again an independence among the nations that commands respect. In Ps. cxxxii., where the horn is an object of the promise, we might directly understand by it the Branch (*Zemach*). Here, where the poet speaks out of his own present age, this is at least not the meaning which he associates with the words. What now follows is an apposition to וַיָּרֶם קֶרֶן לְעַמּוֹ: He has raised up a horn for His people —praise (we say: to the praise of; cf. the New Testament εἰς ἔπαινον) to all His saints, the children of Israel, the people who stand near Him. Others, as Hengstenberg, take תְּהִלָּה as a second object, but we cannot say הֵרִים תְּהִלָּה. Israel is called עַם קְרֹבוֹ, the people of His near = of His nearness or vicinity (Köster), as Jerusalem is called in Eccles. viii. 10 מְקוֹם קָדוֹשׁ

instead of מְקוֹם קֹדֶשׁ (Ew. § 287, a, b). It might also be said, according to Lev. x. 3, עַם קְרֹבָיו, the nation of those who are near to Him (as the Targum renders it). In both instances עַם is the governing noun, as, too, surely גֶּבֶר is in גֶּבֶר עֲמִיתִי, Zech. xiii. 7, which need not signify, by going back to the abstract primary signification of עָמִית, a man of my near fellowship, but can also signify a man of my neighbour, *i.e.* my nearest man, according to Ew. *loc. cit.* (cf. above on cxliii. 10, lxxviii. 49). As a rule, the principal form of עַם is pointed עָם; and it is all the more unnecessary, with Olshausen and Hupfeld, to take the construction as adjectival for עַם קרוב לוֹ. It might, with Hitzig after Aben-Ezra, be more readily regarded as appositional (to a people, His near, *i.e.* standing near to Him). We have here an example of the genitival subordination, which is very extensive in Hebrew, instead of an appositional co-ordination: *populo propinqui sui*, in connection with which *propinqui* may be referred back to *propinquum = propinquitas*, but also to *propinquus* (literally: a people of the kind of one that is near to Him). Thus is Israel styled in Deut. iv. 7. In the consciousness of the dignity which lies in this name, the nation of the God of the history of salvation comes forward in this Psalm as the leader (*choragus*) of all creatures, and strikes up a Hallelujah that is to be followed by heaven and earth.

PSALM CXLIX.

HALLELUJAH TO THE GOD OF VICTORY OF HIS PEOPLE.

HALLELUJAH.
1 SING unto Jahve a new song,
 His praise in the congregation of the saints.
2 Let Israel rejoice in its Maker,
 Let the children of Zion be joyful in their King
3 Let them praise His Name with dance,
 With timbrel and cithern let them play unto Him
4 For Jahve taketh pleasure in His people,
 He adorneth the humble with salvation.

5 Let the saints exult in glory,
   Let them shout aloud upon their beds.

6 Hymns of God fill their throats,
   And a two-edged sword is in their hand,
7 To execute vengeance among the nations,
   Punishments among the peoples;
8 To bind their kings with chains
   And their nobles with iron fetters,
9 To execute upon them the written judgment—
   It is glory for all His saints,
       Hallelujah.

This Psalm is also explained, as we have already seen on Ps. cxlvii., from the time of the restoration under Ezra and Nehemiah. The new song to which it summons has the supreme power which Israel has attained over the world of nations for its substance. As in cxlviii. 14 the fact that Jahve has raised up a horn for His people is called תְּהִלָּה לְכָל־חֲסִידָיו, so here in cxlix. 9 the fact that Israel takes vengeance upon the nations and their rulers is called הָדָר לְכָל־חֲסִידָיו. The writer of the two Psalms is one and the same. The fathers are of opinion that it is the wars and victories of the Maccabees that are here prophetically spoken of. But the Psalm is sufficiently explicable from the newly strengthened national self-consciousness of the period after Cyrus. The stand-point is somewhere about the stand-point of the Book of Esther. The New Testament spiritual church cannot pray as the Old Testament national church here prays. Under the illusion that it might be used as a prayer without any spiritual transmutation, Ps. cxlix. has become the watchword of the most horrible errors. It was by means of this Psalm that Caspar Scloppius in his *Classicum Belli Sacri*, which, as Bakius says, is written not with ink, but with blood, inflamed the Roman Catholic princes to the Thirty Years' religious War. And in the Protestant Church Thomas Münzer stirred up the War of the Peasants by means of this Psalm. We see that the Christian cannot make such a Psalm directly his own without disavowing the apostolic warning, "the weapons of our warfare are not carnal" (2 Cor. x. 4). The praying Christian must therefore transpose the letter of this Psalm into the spirit of the New Covenant; the Christian expositor, however, has to ascertain the literal meaning of this portion of the Scriptures of the Old Testament in its relation to cotemporary history.

Vers. 1–5. A period, in which the church is renewing its youth and drawing nearer to the form it is finally to assume, also of inward necessity puts forth new songs. Such a new era has now dawned for the church of the saints, the Israel that has remained faithful to its God and the faith of its fathers. The Creator of Israel (עֹשָׂיו, plural, with the plural suffix, like עָשָׂיו in Job xxxv. 10, עֹשַׂיִךְ in Isa. liv. 5, cf. עֹשֵׂיו in Job xl. 19; according to Hupfeld and Hitzig, cf. Ew. § 256, b, Ges. § 93, 9, singular; but *aj, ajich, aw*, are always really plural suffixes) has shown that He is also Israel's Preserver and the King of Zion, that He cannot leave the children of Zion for any length of time under foreign dominion, and has heard the sighing of the exiles (Isa. lxiii. 19, xxvi. 13). Therefore the church newly appropriated by its God and King is to celebrate Him, whose Name shines forth anew out of its history, with festive dance, timbrel, and cithern. For (as the occasion, hitherto only hinted at, is now expressly stated) Jahve takes a pleasure in His people; His wrath in comparison with His mercy is only like a swiftly passing moment (Isa. liv. 7 sq.). The futures that follow state that which is going on at the present time. עֲנָוִים is, as frequently, a designation of the *ecclesia pressa*, which has hitherto, amidst patient endurance of suffering, waited for God's own act of redemption. He now adorns them with יְשׁוּעָה, help against and victory over the hostile world; now the saints, hitherto enslaved and contemned, exult בְּכָבוֹד, in honour, or on account of the honour which vindicates them before the world and is anew bestowed upon them (בְּ of the reason, or, which is more probable in connection with the boldness of the expression, of the state and mood*); they shout for joy upon their beds, upon which they have hitherto poured forth their complaints over the present (cf. Hos. vii. 14), and ardently longed for a better future (Isa

---

* Such, too (with pomp, not "with an army"), is the meaning of μετὰ δόξης in 1 Macc. x. 60, xiv. 4, 5, *vid.* Grimm *in loc.*

xxvi. 8); for the bed is the place of soliloquy (iv. 5), and the tears shed there (vi. 7) are turned into shouts of joy in the case of Israel.

Vers. 6-9. The glance is here directed to the future. The people of the present have again, in their God, attained to a lofty self-consciousness, the consciousness of their destiny, viz. to subjugate the whole world of nations to the God of Israel. In the presence of the re-exaltation which they have experienced their throat is full of words and songs exalting Jahve (רוֹמְמוֹת, plural of רוֹמָם, or, according to another reading, רוֹמֵם, lvi. 17), and as servants of this God, the rightful Lord of all the heathen (lxxxii. 8), they hold in their hand a many-mouthed, *i.e.* many-edged sword (*vid. supra*, p. 28), in order to take the field on behalf of the true religion, as the Maccabees actually did, not long after: ταῖς μὲν χερσὶν ἀγωνιζόμενοι, ταῖς δὲ καρδίαις πρὸς τὸν Θεὸν εὐχόμενοι (2 Macc. xv. 27). The meaning of ver. 9*a* becomes a different one, according as we take this line as co-ordinate or subordinate to what goes before. Subordinated, it would imply the execution of a penal jurisdiction over those whom they carried away, and כָּתוּב would refer to prescriptive facts such as are recorded in Num. xxxi. 8, 1 Sam. xv. 32 sq. (Hitzig). But it would become the religious lyric poet least of all to entertain such an unconditional prospect of the execution of the conquered worldly rulers. There is just as little ground for thinking of the judgment of extermination pronounced upon the nations of Canaan, which was pronounced upon them for an especial reason. If ver. 9*a* is taken as co-ordinate, the "written judgment" (*Recht*) consists in the complete carrying out of the subjugation; and this is commended by the perfectly valid parallel, Isa. xlv. 14. The poet, however, in connection with the expression "written," has neither this nor that passage of Scripture in his mind, but the testimony of the Law and of prophecy in general, that all kingdoms shall become God's and His Christ's. Subjugation (and certainly not without bloodshed) is the scriptural מִשְׁפָּט for the execution of which Jahve makes use of His own nation. Because the God who thus vindicates Himself is Israel's God, this subjugation of the world is הָדָר, splendour and glory, to all who are in love devoted to Him. The glorifying of Jahve is also the glorifying of Israel.

PSALM CL.

THE FINAL HALLELUJAH.

1 HALLELUJAH,
PRAISE YE GOD IN HIS SANCTUARY,
PRAISE HIM IN HIS STRONG FIRMAMENT!
2 PRAISE HIM IN HIS MIGHTY ACTS,
PRAISE HIM ACCORDING TO THE ABUNDANCE OF HIS GREATNESS!
3 PRAISE HIM WITH THE SOUND OF HORNS,
PRAISE HIM WITH HARP AND CITHERN!
4 PRAISE HIM WITH TIMBREL AND DANCE,
PRAISE HIM WITH STRINGS AND SHALM!
5 PRAISE HIM WITH CLEAR CYMBALS,
PRAISE HIM WITH CLASHING CYMBALS!

6 LET EVERYTHING THAT HATH BREATH PRAISE JAH,
HALLELUJAH.

The call to praise Jahve "with dance and with timbrel" in cxlix. 3 is put forth here anew in ver. 4, but with the introduction of all the instruments; and is addressed not merely to Israel, but to every individual soul.

Vers. 1–5. The Synagogue reckons up thirteen divine attributes according to Ex. xxxiv. 6 sq. (שְׁלֹשׁ עֶשְׂרֵה מִדּוֹת), to which, according to an observation of Kimchi, correspond the thirteen הַלֵּל of this Psalm. It is, however, more probable that in the mind of the poet the tenfold הַלְלוּ encompassed by Hallelujahs is significative; for ten is the number of rounding off, completeness, exclusiveness, and of the extreme exhaustibleness. The local definitions in ver. 1 are related attributively to God, and designate that which is heavenly, belonging to the other world, as an object of praise. קָדְשׁוֹ (the possible local meaning of which is proved by the קֹדֶשׁ and קֹדֶשׁ קָדָשִׁים of the Tabernacle and of the Temple) is in this passage the heavenly הֵיכָל; and רְקִיעַ עֻזּוֹ is the firmament spread out by God's omnipotence and testifying of God's omnipotence (lxviii. 35), not according to its front side, which is turned towards the earth, but according to the reverse or inner side, which is turned towards the celestial world, and which marks it off from the earthly world. The third and fourth *hal^elu* give as the object of the praise that which is at the same time the ground of the praise: the tokens of His גְבוּרָה, *i.e.* of His all-subduing strength, and the plenitude of His greatness (גָּדְלוֹ = גֻּדְלוֹ), *i.e.* His absolute, infinite greatness. The fifth and sixth *hal^elu* bring into the concert in praise of God the ram's horn, שׁוֹפָר, the name of which came to be improperly used as the name also of the metallic חֲצֹצְרָה (*vid.* on lxxxi. 4), and the two kinds of stringed instruments (*vid.* xxxiii. 2), viz. the nabla (*i.e.* the harp and lyre) and the kinnor (the cithern), the ψαλτήριον and the κιθάρα (κινύρα). The seventh *hal^elu* invites to the festive dance, of which the chief instrumental accompaniment is the תֹּף (Arabic *duff*, Spanish *adufe*, derived from the Moorish) or tambourine. The eighth *hal^elu* brings on the stringed instruments in their widest compass, מִנִּים (cf. xlv. 9) from מֵן, Syriac *menîn*, and the shepherd's pipe, עֻגָב (with the *Gimel raphe* = עֻנָב); and the ninth and tenth, the two kinds of castanets (צִלְצְלֵי, construct form of צְלְצְלִים, singular צֶלְצָל), viz. the smaller clear-sounding, and the larger deeper-toned, more noisy kinds (cf. κύμβαλον ἀλαλάζον, 1 Cor. xiii. 1), as צִלְצְלֵי שָׁמַע (pausal form of שֶׁמַע = שֵׁמַע, like סֵתֶר in Deut. xxvii. 15, and frequently, from כָּתַר = סֵתֶר) and צִלְצְלֵי תְרוּעָה are, with Schultens, Pfeifer, Burk, Köster, and others, to be distinguished.

Ver. 6. The call to praise has thus far been addressed to persons not mentioned by name, but, as the names of instruments thus heaped up show, to Israel especially. It is now generalized to "the totality of breath," *i.e.* all the beings who are endowed by God with the breath of life (נִשְׁמַת חַיִּים), *i.e.* to all mankind.

With this full-toned Finale the Psalter closes. Having risen as it were by five steps, in this closing Psalm it hovers over the blissful summit of the end, where, as Gregory of Nyssa says, all creatures, after the disunion and disorder caused by sin have been removed, are harmoniously united for one choral dance (εἰς μίαν χοροστασίαν), and the chorus of mankind concerting with the angel chorus are become one cymbal of divine praise, and the final song of victory shall salute God, the triumphant Conqueror (τῷ τροπαιούχῳ), with shouts of joy. There is now no need for any special closing *beracha*. This whole closing Psalm is such. Nor is there any need even of an *Amen* (cvi. 48, cf. 1 Chron. xvi. 36). The *Hallelujah* includes it within itself and exceeds it.

EXCURSUS BY J. G. WETZSTEIN.

I.—CONCERNING דרור, THE NAME OF A BIRD.

On Ps. lxxxiv. 4 (p. 4).

SAADIA GAON explains דְּרוֹר by the Arabic دُورِيَّة, a word the correctness of which has been doubted. It is, however, perfectly correct; for in Syria and Palestine the common sparrow is called دُورِي, dûrî, whence the *nomen unitatis* دُورِيَّة. The word is to be traced back to دُور, the plural of دار, the "farm-yard one," and signifies properly "that which is found or dwells in the farm-yards;" thus the *Kamûs* (s.v. دار) cites the phrase ما بِهِ دُورِيّ (used of a desolated locality), "there is no being that dwells in farm-yards therein," where we should say: "no living soul." In this phrase it is exchanged at pleasure for the synonyms دَارِي, دَيَّار, and دَيُّور, which are likewise denominatives of دار.

The word *dûrî* is a thoroughly characteristic appellation for the sparrow, which inhabits the villages in immense flocks, where the standing corn and the corn lying on the threshing-floors in the open fields feed it for one half of the year, whilst it finds its food during the other half in the courts of the houses. It builds its nest in the walls by digging out the mortar between the air-dried bricks. These holes are stopped up once a year, because they injure the walls; and the birds that are then taken out always furnish an abundant repast, the only one of the kind, moreover, in the year, for no one takes the trouble to make a sport of shooting sparrows.

It is another question, whether the *derôr*, also, really corresponds to the *dûrî*? This would be impossible if the *sippôr*, which is connected with *derôr* in Ps. lxxxiv. 4 and Prov. xxvi. 2, as is supposed, signifies the sparrow. Saadia is consequently obliged to interpret צִפּוֹר differently. But is צִפּוֹר then the sparrow? Is it possible for a word which the Bible uses to designate almost all kinds of birds to be the name of a particular species? Its comparison with the Arabic عُصْفُور, from which it certainly differs only dialectically, does not support that supposition; for this word is a collective name for the whole bulk of the small chirping and singing birds, side by side with which the separate species must also have its special name. The fact that in Syria one rarely sees and hears anything of any other '*osfûr* than the sparrow, arises from the fact that the sparrow has multiplied so excessively there, whilst the land, that has been deprived of its woods and is overrun with birds of prey, is very poor in singing birds of all kinds. But if the *sippôr* corresponds to the '*osfûr* in this sense, then the *derôr* might well be the *dûrî*. The *swallow*, which one usually thinks of, has its own name; and the *wood-pigeon*, which others suppose to be the *derôr*, does not suit Prov. xxvi. 2.

The etymology of the word *derôr* is obscure. If it signifies the sparrow, it will be a so-called primitive; at least it is then more natural to regard the Syro-Arabic *dûrî* as a *derôr* that has been corrupted by a later supposition of a more transparent etymology, than to regard *derôr* as a defectively written and hence erroneously pointed פְּעֲלוֹל form (perhaps like דָּרוֹר) from the root דּוּר.

II.—CONCERNING THE SIGNIFICATION OF THE WORD מַעֲנָה IN ITS APPLICATION TO AGRICULTURE.

On Ps. cxxix. 3 (p. 299), cf. on Ps. lxv. 11 (vol. ii. p. 230).

THE word מַעֲנָה, Arabic مَعْنَاة, signifies a strip of arable land which the ploughman takes in hand at one time, at both ends of which consequently the ploughing-team always comes to a stand, turns round, and begins a new furrow. The length of the *ma'nâh* is of course the same as the length of the furrows. Since the ordinary ox of Palestine is smaller and weaker than ours, and easily becomes tired under the yoke, which presses heavily on the nape of its neck and confines its neck, they are obliged to give it time to recover its strength by frequent resting. This always takes place at the termination of a furrow, when the peasant raises the unwieldy plough out of the earth, and turns it over, when he is obliged to clear off the moist earth with the *jábút* (יאבות, a small iron shovel at the lower end of the oxen-stick or goad) and to hammer the loosened wedges and rings tight again, during which time the team is able to recover itself by resting. Hence, too, they do not make the furrows a great length. If the field is under two hundred feet long, it forms only one *ma'náh*; but when in level districts the long parcels of ground (*sihâm* from the singular שֶׂהֶם) of the separate peasant farmers of a village frequently extend to the distance of a mile and a half, the ploughman is compelled to divide his parcel of ground into several مَعَانِي (כִּעֲנוֹת), each of which is ploughed by itself. The furrows, that is to say, cannot be made breadthwise, because the small plots are mostly far too narrow, and because the fields of his neighbours on either side that might be already tilled would be injured by it; for the boundaries of the fields (*hudûd* from the singular חַד) are not formed, as with us, by rows, *i.e.* by broad strips of green sward, but only by isolated heaps of stones, of which two larger ones lie between every two fields, and are called *amâmí* (from the singular אֶמָּה, "mother ridge, *i.e.* main ridge"), and a number of smaller ones called *ka'ákír* (from the singular קַעְקוּר). Moreover cross-ploughing would be rendered difficult by these boundary stones, and the plough would often be seriously injured. In my collection of Hauranitish peasants' proverbs and maxims the following is to be found: "One ox is as much use to thee as two, and the shortness of the *ma'náh* as much as its length" (يَغْنِيكَ عَنْ ثَوْرَيْنِ ثَوْرٌ وَيَغْنِيكَ عَنْ طُولِ الْمَعَانِي قِصَرُهَا), on which I have recorded the following original interpretation: If it does not make any difference to the produce of the field whether the *ma'náh* be greater or less, but in connection with the former the ploughing oxen are exhausted even after half a day's work, whereas in connection with the latter they remain fit for work the whole day, it is more profitable to the peasant to make his *ma'náh* as short as practicable.

The word מענה only occurs besides in 1 Sam. xiv. 14, where it is said that Jonathan with his armour-bearer, in connection with an attack upon one of the posts of the enemy, slew twenty men, and that within the short space of about half a מענה, *i.e.* not during a long pursuit and by degrees, but in a brief hot battle on an arena of about a hundred paces. In the passage in the Psalm the back is conceived of as a field which is divided into several long מענות. To our taste the plural is certainly disturbing; the comparison of the back to one long-extended מענה, which may indeed have a hundred furrows, is simpler, and the impression produced by it more forcible; hence the *Keri* supposes the singular מַעֲנִית, which must be regarded as an Aramaizing collateral form of the singular מענה, for the difference in forms like مصنفاة, مصنفاية, مصنفية, مصنفيّة, and مصنّيت in connection with *Lamed He* stems is for the most part only idiomatic.

According to its derivation, מענה (with local *Mem*) is perhaps the portion of a field taken in hand by the ploughman, from עָנָה, to work; or with reference to the two ends, within the limit of which the ploughing is done, the furrow-turning, στροφή, from עָנָה, to turn; or a tract or space of a certain length, from ענה, to strive after, to seek to attain, whence the well-known Arabic word معنى (masculine of מַעֲנָה), that which is striven after, the desired object, then specially that which is aimed at by the language, the drift (the meaning and sense).

The Arabic معناة, together with the greater part of the agrarian terminology, is not found in the original lexicons, because it was not regarded as purely Arabic, but as belonging to the Nabatæan and Syrian dialects. The terms must therefore still be collected among the peasants. I found a good many in the *Merg'*-country, where I had my country estate; but the most interesting were in the *Ḥaurân*, where, too, معناة still belongs to the living language.

www.ingramcontent.com/pod-product-compliance
Lightning Source LLC
Chambersburg PA
CBHW020542300426

44111CB00008B/762